The Definit' GILLINGHAM F.

A complete record

Tony Brown

Volume 20 in a series of club historie.
A *SoccerData* publication

Published in Great Britain by Tony Brown,
4 Adrian Close, Beeston, Nottingham NG9 6FL.
Telephone 0115 973 6086. E-mail soccer@innotts.co.uk
www.soccerdata.com

First published 2003

Illustrations in the book are from the author's collection. The copyright of individual items is acknowledged in the text as appropriate. In some cases, the ownership of the copyright is unknown. If we have unknowingly used your items without permission please contact the publisher.

The cover photograph is © Stuart Clarke and was taken after the final whistle of the 2000 play-off final at Wembley Stadium. Gillingham players are in yellow. To buy a copy of the original photograph, please visit Stuart's web site at homesoffootball.co.uk.

Printed by the Book Factory

Other volumes in this series are:

Rochdale
Northampton Town
Chesterfield
Portsmouth
Barnsley
Queen's Park Rangers
Scunthorpe United
Aldershot
Torquay United
Luton Town
Reading
Hartlepool United
Hull City
Barrow
Darlington
Newton Heath
Cardiff City
Bournemouth
West Ham United

Please write to the publisher for news of future volumes.

ISBN 1 899468 20 X

GILLINGHAM RECORDS PAGE

PLAYERS:

Most Appearances	Ron Hillyard 655 (563 League, 34 FA Cup, 44 League Cup, 14 other) John Simpson 616 (571 League, 26 FA Cup, 19 League Cup)
Most Goals	Brian Yeo 149 (136 League, 4 FA Cup, 9 League Cup)
Most League Goals in a Season	31: Ernie Morgan 1954/55, Brian Yeo 1973/74
Most International caps	Tony Cascarino 3, Republic of Ireland

THE CLUB:

Honours	Southern League Champions 1946/47, 1948/49 FL Division Four Champions 1963/64 FL Division Two play-off winners 1999/2000
Best League performance	11th in Division One 2002/03
Best F.A. Cup performance	Round 6, 1999/2000
Best League Cup performance	Round 4, 1963/64 and 1996/97
Most League points	85 1999/2000 (3 points for a win) 62 1973/74 (2 points for a win)
Most League goals	90 1973/74
Most League wins in a season	25 1973/74, 1984/85, 1999/2000
Best League win	10-0 v Chesterfield, Div. 3, 5 September 1987
Best League away win	5-0 v Burnley, Div. 2, 27 February 1999
Best F.A. Cup win	10-1 v Gorleston, R1, 16 November 1957
Best League run undefeated	20, from 13 October 1973
Undefeated League games, home	48, from 12 April 1963
Undefeated League games, away	10, from 20 October 1973
Best run of League wins	7, from 18 December 1954
Best run of home League wins	10, from 18 September 1963
Longest run of League draws	5, from 28 August 1993

Most appearances; Ron Hillyard

Most goals, Brian Yeo

CONTENTS

INTRODUCTION

This is the first complete record of the club to be published since 'Home of the Shouting Men' in 1994. For those unsure of the connection, Gillingham is thought to have derived its name from the Gilingas, a warrior tribe known as the shouting men! The 1994 book, by Alan Bradley and Roger Triggs, was produced to high standards of presentation and completeness, and has since become a collector's item. This book aims to provide an alternative and up-to-date source of facts and figures on the club.

Gillingham fans are well-served with other books on the club. Roger Triggs' book in the 'Images of England' series from Tempus Press provides a complete illustrated history of the club. The same author has written 'The Men who Made Gillingham Football Club', a "who's who" of every player from the League years. For these reasons, the 'definitive' history in your hands concentrates on the statistical record.

I'm indebted to many fellow statisticians for their help in compiling this volume, in particular Roger Triggs without whose help the book would not have been possible. Michael Joyce allowed me the use of his player database and Brian Tabner provided the official Football League attendances from 1925/26 to 2000/01. Thanks also to Bob Budd for his artwork for the cover.

Tony Brown
October 2003

The Priestfield Ground in 1905

GILLINGHAM FC – A SHORT HISTORY

At some time in the early 1890s, the members of a junior club, playing its matches on a public ground, decided to aim for the big time. Entry to senior competitions meant the club needed to have a ground of its own, fully enclosed, so that gate money could be taken. It meant raising money by the issue of shares, in order to pay for the ground, the administration of the club and (maybe) the players. Chatham Excelsior had gone about as far as they could go in local football in 1893, winning three trophies. It was their players and committee men that were instrumental in forming the New Brompton Football Club Company Limited in 1893.

An area of land "off Gillingham Road" was selected for the ground. There was no Priestfield Road and terraced housing in those days, just open spaces. A pavilion was built and the ground laid out ready for the first match of the 1893/94 season, a friendly with Woolwich Arsenal's reserve team on 2 September. Arsenal won 1-5; their first team played its first ever Football League game on the same day. The new status of the New Brompton club meant their entries to the F.A. Cup and the Amateur Cup were accepted by the Football Association; they lost in the first round of the F.A. Cup to Ilford but, in the Amateur Cup, had victories over Maidstone United and the Royal Scots Fusiliers before losing to Royal Ordnance. The season was filled with friendly matches, with visits from Long Eaton Rangers, Burton Swifts, Swindon Town and Tottenham Hotspur amongst others. The Chatham Charity Cup was won, so there was one item of silverware to show for their efforts.

1894: New Brompton with the Chatham Charity Cup

New Brompton were keen to join the new Southern League when it was formed in January 1894. The guaranteed fixtures against the leading clubs in the south meant that turning professional was essential. In the event, New Brompton's relatively new status as a senior club was perhaps the reason they found themselves in Division Two of the new League. Eleven wins in twelve matches gave them the championship at the first attempt in 1895. Promotion to the First Division followed after a test match against the bottom club, Swindon Town. They were to remain in the First Division until joining the Football League.

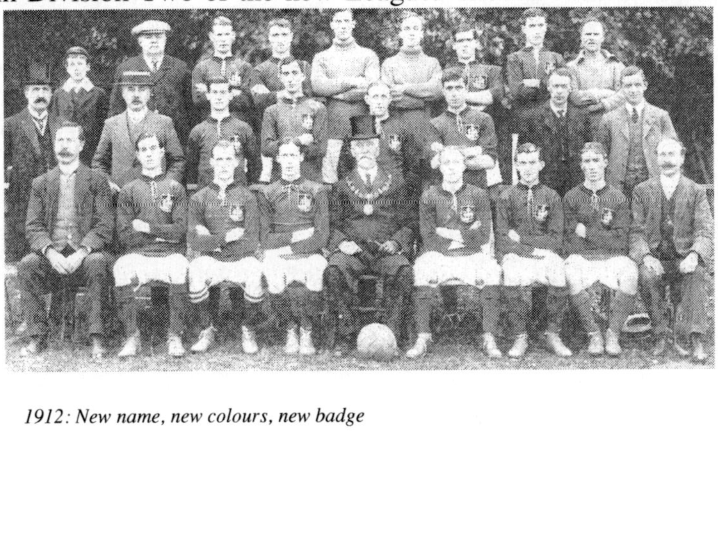

1912: New name, new colours, new badge

New Brompton (and Gillingham) finished bottom of the First Division of the Southern League on three occasions, yet always avoided relegation – something of a record perhaps! When they were bottom in 1907/08, the Division was increased in size. The club changed its name in 1912/13 to reflect the growth of the Borough of Gillingham. Bottom again in 1914/15, the Great War caused the League to be inactive for four seasons and the club remained in the top flight. After the war, the club was bottom again in 1919/20. However, Gillingham F.C. was elected to the new Football League Division Three in 1920, along with the other Southern League clubs.

Ernie Miller; a record 31 League goals in 1954/55

Success remained elusive in the Football League. Bottom in their first season, there were four occasions in all when they successfully applied for re-election. They were finally voted out of the League in 1938, Ipswich Town taking their place. Gillingham joined the Southern League for the 1938/39 season. World War Two led to the suspension of normal League football and Gillingham did not play in competition after 1940 until they joined the Kent Senior League in 1944. They were champions in both 1944/45 and 1945/46.

Gillingham spent five seasons back in the Southern League, winning the championship on two occasions, 1947 and 1949. A run to the third round proper of the F.A. Cup in 1948 saw 23,002 spectators at the game against Queen's Park Rangers, the record for the Priestfield Stadium. The club were elected back into the Football League in 1950 when the third divisions were increased to 24 clubs. Re-organisation of the old regional Third Divisions in 1958 found them in Division Four; the only way now for the club was up! Their first and only League divisional championship to date came in 1963/64 when they were promoted to Division Three, also reaching the fourth round of the League Cup that season. There they remained until 1971, when it was back to Division Four. A season's best 90 League goals saw them promoted in second place in 1973/74; Brian Yeo scored 31 goals that season to equal Ernie Miller's record. Then followed fifteen seasons in Division Three before dropping back to the basement in 1989/90. Consequent financial problems led to the club calling in the receiver in 1995. Since those difficulties, new management has overseen unparalleled success for the club; promotion from Division Three in second place in 1995/96, consistently better season-by-season finishes in Division Two, promotion via the play-offs in 2000 and best-ever progress to the sixth round of the F.A. Cup. More than 50,000 people were at Wembley in May 2000 to see Gillingham win a tense play-off final in extra-time. With 2003/04 representing their fourth successive season in the First Division, Gills' fans have ample grounds for optimism for the future!

Goalie John Simpson, a record 571 League games for the club

New Brompton, 15 September 1894. Back; A Ashdown, S Carr (referee), A Jenner, D Pellatt, A James, A Meager, H Auld, W Murray (trainer). Front; F Manning, H Buckland, D Hutcheson, A Rule, J Dickenson.

1908/09: Back; Crumbie, Negus (directors), W Henderson, Bateup, Hales, Craddock (trainer). Centre; Simmons (mayor), Arthurs, Maven, WP Henderson, Fullarton, Barnes (chairman). Front; Groombridge (secretary), Reynolds, Wood, Whyman, Powell, Reid, Pickett, Swain (treasurer).

28 August 1920, at the first Football League game. Players only – Back; JW Robertson, W Battiste, T Baxter, C Wigmore, T Sisson. Front; A Holt, T Hall, J Branfield, TE Gilbey, A Roe, SP Gore.

1937/38. A Ure (manager), J O'Neill, S Hartley, DL Whitelaw, GE Tweed, GA Holland, Oxberry (trainer). Front; WJB Watson, TH Wilson, FW Herbert, RG Neal, LB Fishlock, WG Ballsom.

1950/51, at one of the public trial matches before the start of the season. Back; Skivington, Boswell, Henson, Marks, Ayres, Burke, Gage, Kingsnorth, Armstrong, Williams. Next to back; Edmed (trainer), O'Donnell (trainer), Collins, Russell, W Burtenshaw, Veck, Lewin, Jenkins, Wright, Briggs, Piper, Day. Seated; McGuire, Fletcher (secretary), Martin, Weller, Cox, Wood (directors), Clark (manager), Swan (assistant secretary), Dorling, Griffiths (trainer). Front; Nobbs, Hales, Carr, Poulton, C Burtenshaw, Warsap, Trumper, Humphreys.

27 February 1954. Back; CWA Marks, J Boswell, H Ayres, T Rigg, F McKee, DR Lewin, O'Donnell (trainer). Front; JW Scarth, WE Evans, E Morgan, PT Sowden, TG Long.

1963/64. Back; Campbell, White, Moss, Ridley, Godfrey, Ballagher, Stacey. Centre; Taylor, Challis, Hudson, Burgess, Simpson, Hunt, Huddart, Yeo, Smith. Front; Newman, Arnott, Gibbs, Francis, Stringfellow, Farrell, Pulley.

1976/77. Back; Williams, Hilton, Armstrong, Fogarty. Centre; Hodgkinson (assistant manager), Shipperley, Knight, Hill, Hillyard, Weatherley, Jolley, Galvin, Collins (trainer). Front; Muskett, Overton, Tydeman, Summers (manager), Richardson, Westwood, Durrell.

INTRODUCTION TO THE STATISTICS PAGES

The season-by-season grids show the results of games in all major competitions, including the Southern League, Football League, F.A. Cup, Football League Cup, Third Division (South) Cup and the Associate Members' Cup. The latter competition has been played under a number of sponsor's names and is currently the LDV Vans Trophy.

Home games are identified by the opponent's name in upper case, away games by the use of lower case. Gillingham's score is always given first. Attendances for League games are taken from the official Football League records for seasons 1925/26 to 2000/01; for other seasons attendances based on newspaper reports have been used.

Substitutes, from season 1965/66 onwards, have the numbers 12, 13 and 14. Number 12 is used if only one substitute was used (no matter what number was on the player's shirt).

A full player list is provided for every player who has made a Football League appearance. Date and place of birth are shown, where known, and the year of death. Players with the same name are given a (1) or (2) after their name to avoid confusion. The next two columns, "seasons played", act as an index to the season-by-season grids. The years shown are the "first year" of the season; for example, 1971 is season 1971/72. The two columns show the season in which the player made his first team debut; and the final season that he played. However, if he only played in one season, the second column is blank. An entry of "2002" in the second column does not imply that the player has left the club, but means that he appeared in the "final season" (2002/03) of the book.

Note that some players also made F.A. Cup appearances in Southern League seasons. If a player also made a League appearance, his F.A. Cup appearances from these non-League seasons are also included in the list. Previous and next clubs show where he was transferred from, and the club he moved to. Non-league club information is included when known.

The appearance columns have separate totals for the League, F.A. Cup, Football League Cup and the other minor tournaments. "Goals scored" are also shown under the four headings. If a player has had more than one spell at the club playing first team football, a consolidated set of appearance and goals are shown on the first line. Subsequent lines show the seasons involved on his return to the club, and his new pair of previous and next clubs.

Summary appearance and goals totals for players in the Southern League are shown in a separate table. An asterisk indicates those players that also appeared in the Football League.

A full record of meetings against all other League clubs (in the Football League) is included. Some clubs have played under different names, but the totals are consolidated under the present day name in this table. Final League tables are also included.

1893/94

Friendly matches and Cup ties

Sep	2	WOOLWICH ARSENAL	1-5
	9	ROYAL ENGINEERS	3-3
	16	WOODSIDE	5-0
	30	Woolwich Arsenal	2-4
Oct	7	SHEPPEY UNITED	3-3
	21	MAIDSTONE UNITED	7-0
	28	FOLKESTONE	1-2
Nov	4	Sittingbourne	2-1
	11	ROYAL SCOTS FUS'RS	2-0
	18	DARTFORD	1-3
	25	SHEPPEY UNITED	3-1
Dec	2	ROYAL ORDNANCE	1-2
	9	AHSFORD UNITED	4-2
	16	ROYAL W KENT REG.	2-2
	23	WOOLWICH ARSENAL	2-2
	26	LONG EATON RANGERS	1-1
	30	ROYAL ORDNANCE	1-0
Jan	13	Ashford United	3-1
	27	HIGHLAND LIGHT INF.	4-1
Feb	3	BURTON SWIFTS	1-7
	10	SWINDON TOWN	2-1
	17	DARTFORD	4-0
	24	SITTINGBOURNE	10-2
Mar	3	Dartford	0-4
	23	LIVERPOOL VICTORIA	2-1
	24	CRAY WANDERERS	1-1
	26	TOTTENHAM HOTSPUR	3-3
	31	SwindonTown	0-2
Apr	7	ROCHESTER	8-1
	14	Sheppey United	3-1
	19	WOOLWICH ARSENAL	2-4
	21	ASHFORD UNITED	1-0
	28	ROYAL ENGINEERS	5-1

Oct 21, Nov 11, Dec 2: F.A. Amateur Cup
Nov 4, Dec 9, Mar 3: Kent Senior Cup
Feb 17, 28, Apr 7, 14: Chatham Charity Cup (winners)
Two games on Feb 17; a reserve side lost 4-5 at Dartford

FA Cup

							Ashdown AH	Auld H	Buckland H	Hutcheson DS	Jenner A	Manning F
Q1	Oct 14	Ilford	3-6	Jenner 2, Hutcheson	500		2	4	11	9	8	7

Also played: Welch (1), Colling (3), Swan (5), Tyler (6), Clark (10)

1894/95

Champions of Southern League Division Two

Promoted after Test Match

						Ashdown AH	Auld H	Buckland H	Dickenson J	Gladwell AP	Hutcheson DS	James A	Jenner A	Keefe D	Manning F	Meager AE	Pellatt D	Read R	Rule R	Russell AE	Thomas WE	Watson JT	Webb A
1	Sep 15	Sheppey United	6-0	Hutcheson 3, Manning, Rule, Button (og)	3000	3	2	7	10		9	5	1		8	6	4		11				
2	22	UXBRIDGE	4-0	Hutcheson, Rule, Manning, Buckland		3	2	7	10		9	5			8	6	4		11	1			
3	Dec 1	OLD ST STEPHENS	5-2	Manning 2, Rule 2, Jenner	300	3	2	10	11		9	5	7		8	6	4			1			
4	29	Chesham	7-2	Webb 3, Hutcheson, Manning, Dickenson, Spratley (og)	300	3	2	10	11		8	5				6	4	7		1			9
5	Jan 19	MAIDENHEAD	6-0	Rule 2, Thomas, Buckland, Hutcheson, Dickenson	2000	3	2	10	11		8					6	5		9	1	7	4	
6	26	SHEPPEY UNITED	3-1	Rule 2, Hutcheson	3000	3	2	10	11		8					6	5		9	1	7	4	
7	Feb 23	Maidenhead	5-0	Hutcheson 2, Buckland, Rule, Dickenson			2	10	11		8				6	3	5		9	1	7	4	
8	Mar 2	Uxbridge	2-0	Jenner 2	400	3	2	10	11				9		8	6	5			1	7	4	
9	9	BROMLEY	1-3	Hutcheson		3	2	10		11	8					6	5		9	1	7	4	
10	23	Bromley	3-2	Buckland 2, Rule	2000	3	2	10	11		8					6	5		9	1	7	4	
11	Apr 12	Old St Stephens	6-0	Rule 3, Hutcheson 2, Pellatt	2500	3		10	11		8		7	2	4	6	5		9	1			
12	13	CHESHAM	9-0	Rule 5, Dickenson 2, Hutcheson, Gladwell		3		10	11	7	8			2	4	5			9	1		6	
					Apps	11	10	12	11	2	11	4	4	2	7	12	11	1	9	11	6	7	1
					Goals			5	5	1	13		3		5		1		18		1		3

Two own goals

Test Match

					Ashdown AH	Auld H	Buckland H	Dickenson J	Gladwell AP	Hutcheson DS	James A	Jenner A	Keefe D	Manning F	Meager AE	Pellatt D	Read R	Rule R	Russell AE	Thomas WE	Watson JT	Webb A
Apr 27	Swindon Town	5-1	Rule 4, Buckland	1000	3		10	11		8			2		6	5		9	1	7	4	

Played at Caversham. Promoted to Diivision One

F.A. Cup

						Ashdown AH	Auld H	Buckland H	Dickenson J	Gladwell AP	Hutcheson DS	James A	Jenner A	Keefe D	Manning F	Meager AE	Pellatt D	Read R	Rule R	Russell AE	Thomas WE	Watson JT	Webb A
Q2	Nov 3	CHATHAM	3-0	Dickenson 3	8000	3	2	10	11		9	5			8	6	4		7	1			
Q3	24	MILLWALL ATHLETIC	0-2		4000	3	2	10	11		9	5			8	6	4		7	1			

		P	W	D	L	F	A	Pts
1	NEW BROMPTON	12	11	0	1	57	10	22
2	Sheppey United	12	6	1	5	25	23	13
3	Old St Stephens	12	6	0	6	26	26	12
4	Uxbridge	12	4	3	5	14	20	11
5	Bromley	12	4	1	7	23	30	9
6	Chesham	12	3	3	6	20	42	9
7	Maidenhead	12	2	4	6	19	33	8

1895/96

6th in Southern League Division One

							Ashdown AH	Bruce D	Bryan T	Buckland H	Cochrane P	Cockrill J	Drew WH	Garside E	Gascoigne JW	Gladwell AP	Guthrie J	Hutcheson DS	Keefe D	Lister A	Manning F	McNamee	Meager AE	Pellatt D	Scott P	Spooner J	Strachan J	Thomas WE	Walker J	Watson JT	Welch C	Wilson J
1	Sep	14	CHATHAM	2-2	Lister 2	6000	3		11	10			6		1			8	2	9	4		5					7				
2		21	READING	3-0	Thomas, Lister, Buckland	1200	3		11	10			6		1			8	2	9	4		5					7				
3	Oct	5	Millwall Athletic	0-8		1000			11	10					1			3	2	9	4		5					7		6		
4		19	ROYAL ORDNANCE	0-0		2000	3		9	10	8				1					11	4		6	5				7				2
5		26	Ilford	2-0	Pellatt, Bryan	1500	3		9	10					1			8			4		6	5				7				2
6	Nov	23	Clapton	1-0	Strachan	1500				10		3			1			8			4	11	6	5			9	7				2
7		30	SOUTHAMPTON	1-0	Strachan	1800				10		3			1		6	8			4	11	2	5			9	7				
8	Dec	7	Reading	0-3		2000				10		3			1		8				4	11	2	5	6		9	7				
9		21	Swindon Town	0-4		1500				10		3			1			8			4		6	5		11	9	7				2
10		28	Chatham	1-1	McNamee	5500						3			1		6	8			4	10	2	5		11	9	7				
11	Jan	14	MILLWALL ATHLETIC	1-2	Hutcheson	2000				10		3		6	1			8				11	4	5			9	7				2
12	Feb	1	Royal Ordnance	2-1	Hutcheson 2	800					11	3			1			8			4	10	6	5			9	7				2
13		8	LUTON TOWN	0-1		3000				10	11	3			1			8			4		6	5			9	7				2
14		29	CLAPTON	6-0	Strachan 2, Gladwell 2, Hutcheson 2	1000				6	11	3			1	7		8			4	10		5			9					2
15	Mar	7	ILFORD	9-1	Hutcheson 3, Strachan 3, Buckland 3	500				10	11	3			1	7		8			4		6	5			9					2
16		28	Southampton	0-5		2000		6		8		3				7		9			4	10	2	5					11		1	
17	Apr	4	Luton Town	1-8	Gladwell	2000		6		11		3			1	7		9			4	10	5									
18		6	SWINDON TOWN	1-1	Gladwell	3000		6		8		3			1	7		9			4	10	2	5					11			
						Apps	4	3	5	16	5	13	2	1	17	5	3	16	3	4	17	10	17	14	1	2	10	13	2	1	1	9
						Goals			1	4						4		8		3		1		1			7	1				

Played in one game: W Barlow (5, at 11), Colling (17, 2), CE Hibbard (17, 8), A Jenner (3, 8)

F.A. Cup

						Ashdown AH	Bruce D	Bryan T	Buckland H	Cochrane P	Cockrill J	Drew WH	Garside E	Gascoigne JW	Gladwell AP	Guthrie J	Hutcheson DS	Keefe D	Lister A	Manning F	McNamee	Meager AE	Pellatt D	Scott P	Spooner J	Strachan J	Thomas WE	Walker J	Watson JT	Welch C	Wilson J
Q1	Oct	12	MILLWALL ATHLETIC	0-1	2000			11	10			6		1			8	2	9	4		5					7				

Slade played at 3

		P	W	D	L	F	A	W	D	L	F	A	Pts
1	Millwall	18	9	0	0	52	6	7	1	1	23	10	33
2	Luton Town	18	8	0	1	49	8	5	1	3	19	6	27
3	Southampton	18	9	0	0	33	3	3	0	6	11	20	24
4	Reading	18	7	0	2	27	16	4	1	4	18	22	23
5	Chatham	18	5	1	3	23	16	4	1	4	20	29	20
6	NEW BROMPTON	18	4	3	2	23	7	3	1	5	7	30	18
7	Swindon Town	18	3	2	4	15	16	3	2	4	23	25	16
8	Clapton	18	3	2	4	17	23	1	0	8	13	44	10
9	Royal Ordnance	18	2	1	6	16	20	1	2	6	7	24	9
10	Ilford	18	0	0	9	2	34	0	0	9	8	47	0

1896/97

8th in Southern League Division One

No.	Date	Opponent	Score	Scorers	Att	Bruce D	Cockrill J	Frettingham JA	Garside E	Gascoigne JW	Gentle A	Gladwell AP	Harrison	Hutcheson DS	Jenner A	Lawrie	Meager AE	Pellatt D	Peters J	Roadley T	Shaves W	Skea DF	Thomas WE	Walker J	Watson J	Wynn
1	Oct 3	SWINDON TOWN	3-1	Hutcheson, Frettingham, Pellatt	2000	6	3	10			2	8		9	1			5	11		4		7			
2	17	Chatham	3-3	Peters 2, Hutcheson	7000	6	3	8		1	2	10		9				5	11		4		7			
3	24	GRAVESEND UNITED	1-3	Hutcheson (p)	1800		3	10		1	4			9		8		5	11	2	6		7			
4	Nov 7	Southampton	3-8	Hutcheson, Walker, Frettingham	4000		3	9		1	4	6		8				5	11	2			7	10		
5	14	SHEPPEY UNITED	0-2		2000			8		1	4			9			3	5	11	2			7	10		6
6	Dec 5	CHATHAM	0-2		4000			9		1	4			8			6	5	11	2		10	7		3	
7	19	Reading	2-3	Skea, Walker					7	1	4			8			6	5	11	2		9		10	3	
8	26	WOLVERTON LNWR	5-0	Skea 2, Hutcheson, Peters, Walker	1000	6		10					1	8			4	5	11	2		9		7	3	
9	Jan 16	Wolverton LNWR	0-1			6		10		1	4			8				5	11	2		9		7	3	
10	30	Northfleet	4-2	Frettingham 3, Skea	500	6		10		1	4			8				5	11	2		9		7	3	
11	Feb 6	SOUTHAMPTON	1-3	McMillan (og)	4000	6		10		1	4			8				5	11	2		9		7	3	
12	13	Swindon Town	1-2	Hutcheson		6		10		1	4			8				5	11	2		9		7	3	
13	20	TOTTENHAM HOTSPUR	2-1	Skea, Peters	2500	6		10		1	4			8				5	11	2		9		7	3	
14	27	READING	1-0	Skea	2000	6		10		1	4			8				5	11	2		9		7	3	
15	Mar 13	Gravesend United	0-4		1200	6		10		1	4	7		8				5	11	2		9			3	
16	20	NORTHFLEET	2-0	Cockrill, Hutcheson	1000		6			1	4	7		8				5	11	2		9		10	3	
17	27	Tottenham Hotspur	0-2		3000		2	8		1	4			7			6	5	11			9		10	3	
18	29	Millwall Athletic	2-2	Hutcheson, Skea	1200	6	2	8			4		1	7				5	11			9		10	3	
19	Apr 10	MILLWALL ATHLETIC	0-2		1800	6	2	10		1	4	7		8			5					9		11	3	
20	19	Sheppey United	2-1	Hutcheson, Frettingham	2000		2	10			4		1	8			5	6	11			9		7	3	

	Bruce D	Cockrill J	Frettingham JA	Garside E	Gascoigne JW	Gentle A	Gladwell AP	Harrison	Hutcheson DS	Jenner A	Lawrie	Meager AE	Pellatt D	Peters J	Roadley T	Shaves W	Skea DF	Thomas WE	Walker J	Watson J	Wynn
Apps	12	9	18	1	16	19	6	3	20	1	1	7	19	19	14	3	15	6	15	15	1
Goals		1	6						9				1	4			7		3		

One own goal

F.A. Cup

Rd	Date	Opponent	Score	Scorers	Att	Bruce D	Cockrill J	Frettingham JA	Garside E	Gascoigne JW	Gentle A	Gladwell AP	Harrison	Hutcheson DS	Jenner A	Lawrie	Meager AE	Pellatt D	Peters J	Roadley T	Shaves W	Skea DF	Thomas WE	Walker J	Watson J	Wynn
Q1	Oct 31	FAVERSHAM	6-1	Peters 2, Frettingham 2, Walker, Pellett	1000	6	3	9		1	4	8						5	11	2			7	10		
Q2	Nov 21	Gravesend United	4-1	Frettingham 2, Walker, Hutcheson	1800		3	9		1	4			8			6	5	11	2			7	10		
Q3	Dec 12	Northfleet	1-3	Thomas	500		3			1	4			8			6	5	11	2			7	10		

Carter played at 9 in Q3

		P	W	D	L	F	A	W	D	L	F	A	Pts
1	Southampton	20	8	2	0	44	11	7	3	0	19	7	35
2	Millwall	20	6	3	1	32	9	7	2	1	31	15	31
3	Chatham	20	7	1	2	35	15	6	0	4	19	14	27
4	Tottenham Hotspur	20	7	2	1	28	13	2	2	6	15	16	22
5	Gravesend United	20	6	1	3	22	13	3	3	4	13	21	22
6	Swindon Town	20	6	1	3	22	16	2	2	6	11	21	19
7	Reading	20	7	1	2	19	16	1	2	7	12	33	19
8	NEW BROMPTON	20	5	0	5	15	14	2	2	6	17	28	16
9	Northfleet	20	3	4	3	17	17	2	0	8	7	29	14
10	Sheppey United	20	3	1	6	22	16	2	0	8	12	31	11
11	Wolverton	20	2	0	8	11	22	0	0	10	6	52	4

1897/98

6th in Southern League Division One

							Bailey	Buckland H	Docherty	Fairclough WO	Ferguson	Ford GF	Frettingham JA	Gallacher H	Gentle A	Gladwell AP	Graham J	Hodgkinson J	Hutcheson DS	Janes JT	Jones S	King ES	Meager AE	Remnant	Roadley T	Skea DF	Stuart J	Watson J	Whittingham
1	Sep	11	CHATHAM	2-1	Ford, Skea	6000						9	8	11	4			6	7		1	2	5			10		3	
2		18	Swindon Town	3-0	Ford 2, Skea	4000						9	8	11			4	6	7		1	2	5			10		3	
3	Oct	2	TOTTENHAM HOTSPUR	1-0	Ford	4000						9	8	11	4			6	7		1	2	5			10		3	
4		9	BRISTOL CITY	1-2	Hutcheson	5000						9	8	11	4		6		7		1	2	5			10		3	
5		23	Chatham	2-2	Ford, Humphrey (og)	7000			7			9		11	4		6		8		1	2	5			10		3	
6	Nov	6	Gravesend United	1-1	Frettingham	2000						9	7	11	4		6		8		1	2	5			10		3	
7		13	SOUTHAMPTON	0-1		3000						9	7	11			6		4	8	1	2	5			10		3	
8	Dec	4	Wolverton LNWR	3-1	Frettingham, Ford, Gladwell	600						9	7	11		8	6		4	2	1	3	5			10			
9		24	GRAVESEND UNITED	0-2		1500		10				9	7	11			6		8	4	1	2	5					3	
10		27	Northfleet	2-3	Frettingham, Bagnall (og)	2000					10	9	7	11			6		8	4	1	3	5		2				
11	Jan	1	SHEPPEY UNITED	3-0	Frettingham 2, Meager	2000						9	7	11			6		8	4		2	5		1	10		3	
12		22	Southampton	1-4	Hutcheson	4000				1		10	7	11			6		8	4		2	5				9	3	
13		29	WOLVERTON LNWR	2-0	Ford, Stuart	1000				1	10	9	7	11			6		4			2	5				8	3	
14	Feb	5	Reading	1-4	Hutcheson	4000				1		9	7	11			6		8	4			5		2		10	3	
15		12	SWINDON TOWN	1-2	Frettingham	1000						9	7	11			6		8	4		2	5		1	10		3	
16		26	MILLWALL ATHLETIC	3-1	Gladwell 2, Hutcheson	1500						9	10	11	1	7	6		8	4		2	5					3	
17	Mar	5	Sheppey United	1-3	Ferguson	2000		7			10	9		11	1	8	6			4		2	5					3	
18		26	Millwall Athletic	3-2	Frettingham, Gallacher, Davis (og)	500	1					10	9	11		8	6		4	2			5	7				3	
19	Apr	2	Tottenham Hotspur	1-3	Ford	5000	1					10	9	11		8	6		5	4		2		7				3	
20		8	NORTHFLEET	1-1	Gladwell	2500	1					10	9	11		7	6		8	4		2	5					3	
21		9	READING	4-3	Gladwell, Remnant, Hutcheson (p), Frettingham	1500						10	9	11		8	6		4	2			5	7				3	1
22		16	Bristol City	1-1	Frettingham	4500						10	9	11	1	7	6		8	4		2	5					3	
						Apps	3	2	1	3	3	22	20	22	8	8	20	3	21	15	10	19	21	3	4	10	3	20	1
						Goals					1	8	9	1		5			5				1	1		2	1		

Three own goals

F.A. Cup

							Bailey	Buckland H	Docherty	Fairclough WO	Ferguson	Ford GF	Frettingham JA	Gallacher H	Gentle A	Gladwell AP	Graham J	Hodgkinson J	Hutcheson DS	Janes JT	Jones S	King ES	Meager AE	Remnant	Roadley T	Skea DF	Stuart J	Watson J	Whittingham
Q1	Sep	25	Northfleet	3-1	Skea 2, Hutcheson	2100						9	8	11	4			6	7		1	2	5			10		3	
Q2	Oct	16	EASTBOURNE SWIFTS	2-0	Hutcheson, Gallacher	2000						9	8	11	4		6		7		1	2	5			10		3	
Q3		30	GRAYS UNITED	6-2	Ford 2, Frettingham 2, Skea, Hutcheson	1200						9	7	11	4		6		8		1	2	5			10		3	
Q4	Nov	20	CHATHAM	1-0	Frettingham	7500						9	7	11			6		8	4	1	2	5			10		3	
Q5	Dec	11	Woolwich Arsenal	2-4	Hutcheson, Frettingham	5000						9	10	11		7	6		8	4	1	2	5					3	

		P	*W*	*D*	*L*	*F*	*A*	*W*	*D*	*L*	*F*	*A*	*Pts*
1	Southampton	22	10	0	1	34	7	8	1	2	19	11	37
2	Bristol City	22	9	2	0	44	15	4	5	2	23	18	33
3	Tottenham Hotspur	22	9	2	0	36	6	3	2	6	16	25	28
4	Chatham	22	7	4	0	37	14	5	0	6	13	20	28
5	Reading	22	7	3	1	26	11	1	4	6	13	20	23
6	NEW BROMPTON	22	6	1	4	18	13	3	3	5	19	24	22
7	Sheppey United	22	9	1	1	30	9	1	0	10	10	40	21
8	Gravesend United	22	4	5	2	15	12	3	1	7	13	27	20
9	Millwall	22	5	1	5	33	20	3	1	7	15	25	18
10	Swindon Town	22	5	1	5	24	20	2	1	8	12	28	16
11	Northfleet	22	4	1	6	19	22	0	2	9	10	38	11
12	Wolverton	22	3	0	8	17	25	0	1	10	11	57	7

1898/99

6th in Southern League Division One

No.	Date	Opponent	Score	Scorers	Att.	Atherton J	Bunyan C	Campbell L	Cooper	Frettingham JA	Gallacher H	Gladwell AP	Graham J	Grieve T	Hutcheson DS	Innes RA	King ES	Lennox M	Leonard P	McDonald J	Robertson JS	Robertson W	Watson J	White W
1	Sep 3	GRAVESEND UNITED	4-0	Campbell. MacDonald, Innes, Lennox	2500	5	1	11		9			6	7		4	2	10		8			3	
2	10	BRIGHTON UNITED	3-0	Grieve 2, Lennox	3000	5	1	11		9			6	7		4	2	10		8			3	
3	17	Southampton	2-0	Frettingham, Lennox	8000	5	1	11		9				7	6	4	2	10		8			3	
4	Oct 1	Chatham	1-1	Frettingham	8500	5	1	11		9				7	6	4	2	10		8			3	
5	8	SWINDON TOWN	5-1	Frettingham 3. MacDonald 2	3000	5	1	11		9				7	6	4	2	10		8			3	
6	15	SHEPPEY UNITED	2-0	Frettingham 2	1000	5	1	11		9				7	6	4	2	10		8			3	
7	22	BEDMINSTER	5-2	Frettingham 2, Watson 2 (2p), Campbell	2000	5	1	11		9			6	7		4	2	10		8			3	
8	Nov 5	CHATHAM	1-0	Campbell	7000	5	1	11		9				7	6	4	2	10		8			3	
9	12	Bedminster	1-4	Frettingham	3000	5	1	11		9			6	7	4		2	10		8			3	
10	Dec 3	ROYAL ARTILLERY	2-1	MacDonald, Freetingham	1500	5	1	7		9	11		6			4	2	10		8			3	
11	24	READING	0-0		3000	5	1			9		7			6	4	2	10	11	8			3	
12	Jan 7	BRISTOL CITY	0-1		4500	5	1			9	11		6	7		4	2	10		8			3	
13	14	Royal Artillery	2-0	Grieve. MacDonald	6000	5	1	11		9			6	7		4	2	10		8			3	
14	Feb 4	Brighton United	1-2	Lennox	3000	5	1	11		9		7	6			4	2	10		8			3	
15	11	Reading	0-2		4000	5	1	11				7	6		9	4	2	10		8			3	
16	Mar 11	Sheppey United	1-3	Frettingham	1000	5	1	11		9			6	7		4		10		8	2		3	
17	13	TOTTENHAM HOTSPUR	1-1	Grieve	3500	5	1	11	7	10			6	9		4				8	2		3	
18	18	Tottenham Hotspur	0-3		5000	5	1	10		9	11		6	7		4				8	2		3	
19	25	Millwall Athletic	4-1	Gallacher, Grieve, MacDonald, Atherton	4000	5	1		7	9	11		6	10		4				8	2		3	
20	Apr 3	Gravesend United	2-2	Campbell, Grieve	3000	5	1	11		9			6	7		4	3			8	2			10
21	8	Swindon Town	0-1		2500	5	1			9			6	10		4				8	2	7	3	11
22	17	MILLWALL ATHLETIC	0-2		1000	5	1	11		9			6			4	3			8	2	7		10
23	22	Bristol City	0-2		6500	5	1	11	7	9	10		6			4	3			8	2			
24	24	SOUTHAMPTON	1-1	Gladwell	1000	5	1	11	7	9		8	10		6	4	3				2			

Game 22 played at Woolwich Arsenal

	Atherton J	Bunyan C	Campbell L	Cooper	Frettingham JA	Gallacher H	Gladwell AP	Graham J	Grieve T	Hutcheson DS	Innes RA	King ES	Lennox M	Leonard P	McDonald J	Robertson JS	Robertson W	Watson J	White W
Apps	24	24	20	4	23	5	4	18	17	9	23	19	16	1	23	9	2	20	3
Goals	1		4		12	1	1		6		1		4		6			2	

F.A. Cup

Rd	Date	Opponent	Score	Scorers	Att.	Atherton J	Bunyan C	Campbell L	Cooper	Frettingham JA	Gallacher H	Gladwell AP	Graham J	Grieve T	Hutcheson DS	Innes RA	King ES	Lennox M	Leonard P	McDonald J	Robertson JS	Robertson W	Watson J	White W
Q3	Oct 29	GRAYS UNITED	3-0	Frettingham 2, MacDonald	1000	5	1	11		9				7	6	4	2	10		8			3	
Q4	Nov 19	SHEPPEY UNITED	2-1	Grieve 2	2000	5	1	11		9		7	6	8		4	2	10					3	
Q5	Dec 10	Gravesend United	1-1	Lennox	500	5	1	11		9				7	6	4	2	10		8			3	
rep	14	GRAVESEND UNITED	2-0	MacDonald, Lennox	2500	5	1			9	11		6	7		4	2	10		8			3	
R1	Jan 28	SOUTHAMPTON	0-1		9000	5	1	11		9			6	7		4	2	10		8			3	

		P	W	D	L	F	A	W	D	L	F	A	Pts
1	Southampton	24	9	2	1	34	9	6	3	3	20	15	35
2	Bristol City	24	11	0	1	39	16	4	3	5	16	17	33
3	Millwall	24	7	2	3	34	17	5	4	3	25	18	30
4	Chatham	24	6	4	2	19	8	4	4	4	13	15	28
5	Reading	24	9	2	1	24	4	0	6	6	7	20	26
6	NEW BROMPTON	24	7	3	2	24	9	3	2	7	14	21	25
7	Tottenham Hotspur	24	8	2	2	24	11	2	2	8	16	25	24
8	Bedminster	24	7	1	4	19	13	3	3	6	16	26	24
9	Swindon Town	24	7	4	1	33	21	2	1	9	10	28	23
10	Brighton United	24	6	2	4	23	13	3	0	9	14	35	20
11	Gravesend United	24	6	3	3	31	20	1	2	9	11	32	19
12	Sheppey United	24	5	2	5	16	18	0	1	11	7	35	13
13	Royal Artillery	24	3	4	5	11	16	1	0	11	6	44	12

1899/1900

11th in Southern League Division One

						Atherton J	Carter J	Frettingham JA	Gladwell AP	Glover J	Graham J	Gray E	Gray T	Hutcheson DS	Innes RA	Jones	Lockie J	MacDonald J	Miller	Nobbs	Pangbourne T	Pinnell A	Robertson JS	Seeley G	Shinner J	Swan A
1	Sep 2	Southampton	2-6	Frettingham, MacDonald	3000	5		9		3			7	6	4			8				1	2	11		10
2	9	MILLWALL ATHLETIC	1-1	MacDonald	4000	5		9	7	3	6				4			8				1	2	11		10
3	16	Queen's Park Rangers	0-2		6000	5		9		3				6	4		2	8		7			1	11		10
4	23	CHATHAM	1-1	Seeley	5000	5		9		3				6	4		2			7	8		1	11		10
5	30	Reading	1-3	Pangbourne	2500	5	1	9		3	6					4	2			7	8			11		10
6	Oct 7	SHEPPEY UNITED	2-2	Graham, Innes	3000	5	1			3	6				4		9	8		7			2	11		10
7	14	Bristol Rovers	1-0	Seeley	3000	5	1			3	6				4		2	8		7	9			11		10
8	Nov 4	PORTSMOUTH	1-0	Frettingham	1500	5	1	11		3	6				4			8	7		9		2			10
9	11	Thames Ironworks	0-0		3000	5	1	7		3	6				4			8			9		2	11		10
10	Dec 2	Gravesend United	0-2		2000	5	1	9		3	6				4			8		7			2	11	10	
11	9	SWINDON TOWN	4-2	MacDonald 2, Swan, Pangbourne		5	1	9	7	3	6				4			8			10		2			11
12	16	Bristol City	1-2	Frettingham	3500	5	1	9		3	6		7		4			8			10		2			11
13	18	BEDMINSTER	5-0	Swan 2, MacDonald, Frettingham, T Gray	1500	5	1	9		3	6		7		4			8			10		2			11
14	30	SOUTHAMPTON	1-2	Swan	2500	5	1	9			6	3	7		4			8			10		2			11
15	Jan 6	Millwall Athletic	1-4	MacDonald	3000	5	1	9			6	3	7		4			8			10		2			11
16	13	QUEEN'S PARK RANGERS	0-3		2000	5	1	9			6	3	7		4			8			10		2			11
17	20	Chatham	2-1	T Gray, Hutcheson	3500	5	1	9			6		7	4			3	8			10		2			11
18	Feb 3	READING	4-2	Frettingham 2, Pangbourne 2	500	5	1	9		3	6		7		4						10		2	11		10
19	10	Sheppey United	2-2	Pangbourne, MacFarlane (og)		5	1	9		3	6		7		4						8		2	11		10
20	24	Bedminster	1-3	Swan		5	1	9		3	6		7		4						8		2	11		10
21	Mar 3	BRISTOL ROVERS	2-0	Innes (p), Frettingham	1800	5	1	9		3	6		7		4						8		2	11		10
22	10	Portsmouth	1-5	Frettingham	5000	5	1	9		3	6		7		4						8		2	11		10
23	17	THAMES IRONWORKS	3-1	Frettingham 2, Pangbourne	1000	5	1	9	7	3				6	4						8		2	11		10
24	24	Tottenham Hotspur	0-1		5000	5	1	9	7	3	6				4						8		2	11		10
25	Apr 7	GRAVESEND UNITED	0-1		1500	5	1	9		3	6		7		4						8		2	11		10
26	14	Swindon Town	1-1	Frettingham	2000	5	1	9		3	6		7		4						8		2	11		10
27	21	BRISTOL CITY	1-0	Swan	1200		1	9	7	3	6		8	5	4								2	11		10
28	28	TOTTENHAM HOTSPUR	1-2	Gladwell	3000	5	1	9	7	3	6		8		4								2	11		10
					Apps	27	24	26	6	24	24	3	16	6	26	1	6	15	1	6	21	2	26	20	1	27
					Goals			11	1		1		2	1	2			6			6			2		6

One own goal

F.A. Cup

						Atherton J	Carter J	Frettingham JA	Gladwell AP	Glover J	Graham J	Gray E	Gray T	Hutcheson DS	Innes RA	Jones	Lockie J	MacDonald J	Miller	Nobbs	Pangbourne T	Pinnell A	Robertson JS	Seeley G	Shinner J	Swan A
Q3	Oct 28	Woolwich Arsenal	1-1	Swan	5500	5	1	9		3				6	4			8		7	10		2	11		
rep	Nov 1	WOOLWICH ARSENAL	0-0		2500	5	1	9		3				6	4			8		7			2	11		10
rep2	6	Woolwich Arsenal	2-2	(aet) Pangbourne 2	3000	5	1	11		3	6				4			8		7	9		2			10
rep3	8	Woolwich Arsenal	1-1	MacDonald	2000	5	1	11		3				6	4			8		7	9		2			10
rep4	14	Woolwich Arsenal	1-0	Atherton		5	1	7		3	6				4			8			9		2	11		10
Q4	18	THAMES IRONWORKS	0-0		3000	5	1	7		3	6				4			8			9		2	11		10
Q4	23	Thames Ironworks	0-2		2000	5	1	7		3	6				4			8			9		2	11		10

Q3 replay 2 at Millwall, replay 3 at Tottenham, replay 4 at Gravesend

		P	W	D	L	F	A	W	D	L	F	A	Pts
1	Tottenham Hotspur	28	13	1	0	42	8	7	3	4	25	18	44
2	Portsmouth	28	14	0	0	39	5	6	1	7	20	24	41
3	Southampton	28	11	0	3	52	14	6	1	7	18	19	35
4	Reading	28	10	2	2	25	6	5	0	9	16	22	32
5	Swindon Town	28	12	1	1	30	11	3	1	10	20	31	32
6	Bedminster	28	9	1	4	27	18	4	1	9	17	27	28
7	Millwall	28	9	0	5	25	17	3	3	8	11	20	27
8	Queen's Park Rangers	28	8	2	4	29	20	4	0	10	21	38	26
9	Bristol City	28	9	0	5	33	23	0	7	7	11	24	25
10	Bristol Rovers	28	9	2	3	31	16	2	1	11	15	39	25
11	NEW BROMPTON	28	7	3	4	26	17	2	3	9	13	32	24
12	Gravesend United	28	7	4	3	28	25	3	0	11	10	33	24
13	Chatham	28	9	1	4	26	16	1	2	11	12	42	23
14	Thames Ironworks	28	6	4	4	19	13	2	1	11	11	32	21
15	Sheppey United	28	1	5	8	10	25	2	2	10	14	41	13

1900/01

12th in Southern League Division One

	Date	Opponent	Result	Scorers	Att	Ambler CJ	Atherton J	Bailey T	Crane AE	Frettingham JA	Gladwell AP	Graham J	Harvey	Haywood A	Hulmes T	Humphrey W	Innes RA	Lissenden AJ	MacDonald J	May G	Neame SR	Neyland M	Robertson JS	Seeley G
1	Sep 1	READING	1-2	Lissendon	2500		5	2		9	8	6			3		4	10		7			1	11
2	8	Kettering	1-2	Lissendon	3000		5		1	9		6	8		3		4	10		7			2	11
3	15	GRAVESEND UNITED	1-1	Seeley	2000	1	5			9		6	8		3		4	10		7			2	11
4	22	Millwall Athletic	1-3	Seeley	4000	1	5			9	7	6			3		4	10	8				2	11
5	29	SOUTHAMPTON	0-1		3000	1	5			9	7	6			3		4	10	8				2	11
6	Oct 13	BRISTOL CITY	1-1	Innes (p)	2000	1	5			7		6		9	3		4	10	8				2	11
7	20	Swindon Town	3-2	Seeley, MacDonald, Frettingham	2000	1	5			7		6		9	3		4	10	8				2	11
8	27	WATFORD	2-1	Frettingham, MacDonald	2000	1	5			7		6		9	3		4	10	8				2	11
9	Nov 10	TOTTENHAM HOTSPUR	1-2	MacDonald	3000	1	5			7		6		9	3		4	10	8				2	11
10	24	PORTSMOUTH	2-0	Frettingham, Seeley	2000		5		1	9	7			8	3		4	10			6		2	11
11	Dec 1	QUEEN'S PARK RANGERS	2-1	Innes (p), Frettingham	1800		5		1	9	7			8	3		4	10			6		2	11
12	15	Reading	1-2	Frettingham	2200		5		1	9	7			8	3		4	10			6		2	11
13	22	KETTERING	2-2	Haywood, Innes (p)	2000		5		1	9	7			8	3		4	10			6		2	11
14	29	Gravesend United	1-1	Frettingham	1000		5		1	9	7			10	3		4	8			6		2	11
15	Jan 5	MILLWALL ATHLETIC	1-3	Seeley	3000		5		1	9	7			8	3		4	10			6		2	11
16	15	Southampton	0-5		1000		5		1	9	7			8	3		4	10			6		2	11
17	26	Queen's Park Rangers	0-2		3000				1	9				8		3	4	6	7		5	10	2	11
18	Feb 9	SWINDON TOWN	1-0	Innes (p)	2000		5		1	9				8		3	4		7		6	10	2	11
19	16	Watford	1-2	Neyland	2000		5		1	9				8		3	4	7			6	10	2	11
20	23	LUTON TOWN	3-1	Frettingham 3	1500		5		1	9		6		8		3	4	7				10	2	11
21	27	Bristol City	0-2		1500		5		1	9				8		3	4		7		6	10	2	11
22	Mar 2	Tottenham Hotspur	1-2	Neyland	4000	1	5			9				8		3	4		7		6	10	2	11
23	9	WEST HAM UNITED	1-1	Neyland	1500	1	5			9				8		3	4		7		6	10	2	11
24	16	Portsmouth	1-3	Neyland	4000	1	5			9				8		3	4		7		6	10	2	11
25	Apr 10	Bristol Rovers	2-0	Frettingham 2	2500	1	5			9				10	7	3	4		8		6		2	11
26	13	Luton Town	2-4	Frettingham, Hulmes	1000	1	5			9				10	7	3	4		8		6		2	11
27	17	BRISTOL ROVERS	2-3	Frettingham, MacDonald	1000	1	5			9				10	7	3	4	6	8				2	11
28	20	West Ham United	0-2		1500	1	5				7			9	11	3	4	6	8		10		2	
					Apps	14	27	1	13	27	11	10	2	23	20	12	28	21	16	3	17	8	28	27
					Goals					13				1	1		4	2	4			4		5

F.A. Cup

	Date	Opponent	Result	Scorers	Att	Ambler CJ	Atherton J	Bailey T	Crane AE	Frettingham JA	Gladwell AP	Graham J	Harvey	Haywood A	Hulmes T	Humphrey W	Innes RA	Lissenden AJ	MacDonald J	May G	Neame SR	Neyland M	Robertson JS	Seeley G
Q3	Nov 3	Grays United	2-0	Frettingham, MacDonald	1000	1	5			7		6		9	3		4	10	8				2	11
Q4	17	WEST HAM UNITED	1-1	Seeley	1000		5		1	7		6		9	3		4	10	8				2	11
rep	21	West Ham United	1-4	Innes ((p)	1500		5		1	7		6		9	3		4	10	8				2	11

		P	W	D	L	F	A	W	D	L	F	A	Pts
1	Southampton	28	13	1	0	44	12	5	4	5	14	14	41
2	Bristol City	28	12	2	0	40	6	5	3	6	14	21	39
3	Portsmouth	28	12	2	0	33	6	5	2	7	23	26	38
4	Millwall	28	11	1	2	36	10	6	1	7	19	22	36
5	Tottenham Hotspur	28	12	1	1	35	8	4	3	7	20	25	36
6	West Ham United	28	10	2	2	28	10	4	3	7	12	18	33
7	Bristol Rovers	28	10	3	1	29	8	4	1	9	17	27	32
8	Queen's Park Rangers	28	9	1	4	28	17	2	3	9	15	31	26
9	Reading	28	7	2	5	16	10	1	6	7	8	15	24
10	Luton Town	28	9	1	4	32	20	2	1	11	11	29	24
11	Kettering	28	7	4	3	21	12	0	5	9	12	34	23
12	NEW BROMPTON	28	5	4	5	20	19	2	1	11	14	32	19
13	Gravesend United	28	5	5	4	23	27	1	2	11	9	58	19
14	Watford	28	6	3	5	17	16	0	1	13	7	36	16
15	Swindon Town	28	3	6	5	15	18	0	2	12	4	29	14

1901/02

10th in Southern League Division One

	Date	Opponent	Score	Scorers	Att	Atherton J	Blair J	Crane AE	Dunkley AE	Evans	French J	Frettingham JA	Gosnell AA	Harris W	Humphrey W	Killean E	Knowlden	Leigh W	Lissenden AJ	Lockie J	Milward A	Neame SR	Otty WJ	Scott F	Wright R	Youngs WW
1	Sep 7	Southampton	1-1	Milward	5000	5	6				4	7		1	3			9		2	10		11	8		
2	14	BRISTOL ROVERS	3-0	Scott, Atherton, Milward	4000	5					4	7		1	3			9	6	2	10		11	8		
3	21	WEST HAM UNITED	0-0		4000	5			11		4	7		1	3			9	6	2	10			8		
4	28	Northampton Town	2-3	Frettingham 2	1000	5	6		11		4	7	9	1	3		2				10			8		
5	Oct 5	WATFORD	2-1	Blair, Scott	3000	5	6		11		4	7	9	1	3					2	10			8		
6	12	Tottenham Hotspur	1-3	Leigh	7000	5	6		11		4	7		1	3			9		2	10			8		
7	26	Portsmouth	0-3		7000	5	6		11		4	7		1	3			9		2	10			8		
8	Nov 9	BRENTFORD	2-0	Milward, Dunkley	1500	5	6		11		4	7		1	3			9		2	10			8		
9	23	Luton Town	1-3	Frettingham		5	6		11		4	8		1	3	2		9			10			7		
10	Dec 7	Queen's Park Rangers	1-1	Leigh	2500	5	6		11			7		1	3	2		9			10	4		8		
11	21	SOUTHAMPTON	3-0	Leigh, Frettingham, Milward	3000	5	6		11			8		1		2		9		3	10	4		7		
12	28	Bristol Rovers	1-2	Milward (p)	4000	5	6					7		1		2		9		3	10	4	11	8		
13	Jan 4	West Ham United	0-0		2000	5	6					7		1		2			10	3	9	4	11	8		
14	11	NORTHAMPTON T	0-1		2000	5	6					7		1		2		9		3	10	4	11	8		
15	18	Watford	0-3		3000	5	6					7		1	2			9		3	10	4	11	8		
16	25	WELLINGBOROUGH	3-2	Frettingham, Milward (p), Dunkley	1800	5	6		11	7		9		1		2		8		3	10	4				
17	Feb 1	Wellingborough	0-0			5	6	1	11		4	9			3	2		8	7		10					
18	8	KETTERING	1-2	Milward	2000	5	6	1	11		4	9			3	2		8	7		10					
19	15	Swindon Town	1-1	Frettingham	1000	5	6		11		4	9		1	3			8	7	2	10					
20	22	Brentford	2-3	Leigh, Frettingham	2000	5	6		11	7	4	9		1		2		8		3	10					
21	Mar 1	Kettering	0-1		2000	5	6		11	7		9		1		2		8	4	3	10					
22	8	LUTON TOWN	3-0	Leigh, Milward, Frettingham	2000	5	6		11	7		9		1		2		8		3	10	4				
23	15	MILLWALL ATHLETIC	2-1	Dunkley, Frettingham	3000	5	6		11	7		9		1		2		8		3	10	4				
24	22	QUEEN'S PARK RANGERS	0-1		3000		6		11	7	5			1		2		9	8	3	10	4				
25	28	Millwall Athletic	1-3	Gosnell	7000		5		11	7			9	1	6	2		8		3	10	4				
26	29	Reading	1-3	Leigh	2000		5	1	11	7			9		6	2		8		3	10	4				
27	Apr 5	TOTTENHAM HOTSPUR	0-0		3000	5	6			7		9		1		2		8		3	10	4				11
28	12	SWINDON TOWN	5-0	Frettingham 2, Leigh 2, Milward		5	6			7		9		1		2		8		3	10	4				11
29	16	PORTSMOUTH	2-0	Leigh 2	3000	5	6					9		1		2		8	11	3	10	4			7	
30	26	READING	1-0	Milward	2000	5	6		11			9		1		2		8		3	10	4			7	
					Apps	27	28	3	21	10	14	27	4	27	16	20	1	27	9	25	30	16	6	15	2	2
					Goals	1	1		3			11	1					10			10			2		

F.A. Cup

	Date	Opponent	Score	Scorers	Att	Atherton J	Blair J	Crane AE	Dunkley AE	Evans	French J	Frettingham JA	Gosnell AA	Harris W	Humphrey W	Killean E	Knowlden	Leigh W	Lissenden AJ	Lockie J	Milward A	Neame SR	Otty WJ	Scott F	Wright R	Youngs WW
Q3	Nov 2	ILFORD	6-1	*see below	2000	5	6		11		4	7		1	3			9		2	10			8		
Q4	16	Clapton	2-2	Leigh, Milward (p)	3000	5	6		11		4	8		1	3	2		9			10		7			
rep	20	CLAPTON	2-0	Scott, Leigh	1500	5	6		11		4	8		1	3	2		9			10			7		
Q5	30	GRAYS UNITED	1-0	Leigh, Milward (p)	3000	5	6		11			7		1	3	2		9			10	4		8		
IR	Dec 14	Walsall	0-2		3000	5	6		11			7		1	3	2		9			10	4		8		

Scorers in Q3: Milward 2 (1p), Dunkley 2, Frettingham, Leigh

		P	W	D	L	F	A	W	D	L	F	A	Pts
1	Portsmouth	30	11	4	0	35	5	9	3	3	32	19	47
2	Tottenham Hotspur	30	11	2	2	42	11	7	4	4	19	11	42
3	Southampton	30	12	2	1	54	10	6	4	5	17	18	42
4	West Ham United	30	10	2	3	27	13	7	4	4	18	15	40
5	Reading	30	10	4	1	38	9	6	3	6	19	15	39
6	Millwall	30	9	3	3	33	13	4	3	8	13	18	32
7	Luton Town	30	8	5	2	16	10	3	5	7	15	26	32
8	Kettering	30	9	4	2	31	12	3	1	11	13	27	29
9	Bristol Rovers	30	11	1	3	37	10	1	4	10	6	29	29
10	NEW BROMPTON	30	10	2	3	27	8	0	5	10	12	30	27
11	Northampton Town	30	7	4	4	40	28	4	1	10	13	37	27
12	Queen's Park Rangers	30	7	4	4	22	16	2	2	11	12	39	24
13	Watford	30	7	2	6	21	19	2	2	11	15	39	22
14	Wellingborough	30	8	2	5	23	18	1	1	13	11	54	21
15	Brentford	30	7	2	6	23	21	0	4	11	11	40	20
16	Swindon Town	30	2	3	10	13	27	0	0	15	4	65	7

1902/03

6th in Southern League Division One

						Archer A	Atherton J	Bradbury JJL	Daw EC	Dunkley AE	Elliott J	Frettingham JA	Goldie H	Harris W	Killean E	Leigh W	McCurdy W	Milward A	Neame SR	Raisbeck W	Satterthwaite C	Smith G	Wright R
1	Sep 6	KETTERING	1-0	Smith	4000	3	5	7	1	11			6		2			10	4		8	9	
2	13	Luton Town	1-1	Leigh	2000	3			1	11	6		5			9	2	7		4	10	8	
3	20	READING	0-4		3000	2		7	1	11	6		5			9	3			4	10	8	
4	27	Queen's Park Rangers	2-1	Smith 2	6000	3		7	1	11	6		5		2			9		4	10	8	
5	Oct 4	SOUTHAMPTON	1-2	Satterthwaite (p)	5000	3		7	1	11	6		5		2			9		4	10	8	
6	11	Wellingborough	1-2	Satterthwaite		3		7		11	6		5	1			2	9		4	10	8	
7	18	BRISTOL ROVERS	0-0		4000	3		7		11	6		5	1			2	9		4	10	8	
8	25	Northampton Town	2-2	Milward, Goldie	3000	2		7	1		6		5			8	3	11		4	10	9	
9	Nov 8	Brentford	2-1	Satterthwaite, Leigh	1500	3		7	1		6		5			8	2	11		4	10	9	
10	Dec 6	MILLWALL ATHLETIC	2-0	Satterthwaite, Smith	2000	3		7	1		6		5			8	2	11		4	10	9	
11	20	Kettering	0-0			3		7	1		6		5			8	2	11		4	10	9	
12	26	SWINDON TOWN	2-1	Satterthwaite(p), Bradbury	5000	2		7			6		5	1		8	3	11		4	10	9	
13	27	LUTON TOWN	1-1	Smith	5000	3		7			6		5	1			2	11		4	10	9	8
14	Jan 3	Reading	0-5					7			6		5	1	2	8	3	11		4	10	9	
15	5	Tottenham Hotspur	1-3	Satterthwaite	3000		5	7	1		6		4		2		3	11			10	8	9
16	10	QUEEN'S PARK RANGERS	0-0		3000		5	7	1		6		4		2		3	11			10	8	9
17	17	Southampton	0-1			3		7	1		6	9	5				2	11		4	10	8	
18	24	WELLINGBOROUGH	5-0	Frettingham 2, Raisbeck, Satterthwaite, Smith	2000	3		7	1		6	9	5				2	11		4	10	8	
19	31	Bristol Rovers	0-2		7000	3		7	1	11	6		5				2	10		4	9	8	
20	Feb 7	NORTHAMPTON T	0-0		3000	3		7	1	11	6		5				2	10		4	9	8	
21	14	Watford	2-2	Milward, Satterthwaite	2500			7	1		6	9	5		2		3	11		4	10	8	
22	21	BRENTFORD	4-0	Smith, Milward, Raisbeck, Satterthwaite	2000			7	1		6	9	5		2		3	11		4	10	8	
23	Mar 7	WEST HAM UNITED	2-0	Smith, Satterthwaite	2000	3	5	7	1	11	6	9	4				2				10	8	
24	14	Portsmouth	0-4		9000	3		7	1		6	9	5		2			11		4	10	8	
25	23	West Ham United	1-1	Dunkley	1000	3		7	1	11	6	9	5				2			4	10	8	
26	28	Swindon Town	1-1	Smith		3		7	1	11	6	9	5				2			4	10	8	
27	Apr 4	PORTSMOUTH	1-0	Satterthwaite	3000	3		7	1	11	6	9	5				2			4	10	8	
28	11	TOTTENHAM HOTSPUR	3-0	Satterthwaite (p), Bradbury, Dunkley	4500	3		7	1	11	6	9	5				2			4	10	8	
29	23	Millwall Athletic	0-0			3		7	1	11	6	9	5				2			4	10	8	
30	25	WATFORD	2-1	Smith, Dunkley	2000	3		7	1	11	6	9	5				2			4	10	8	
					Apps	25	4	29	25	16	29	12	30	5	9	8	26	22	1	26	30	30	3
					Goals			2		3		2	1			2		3		2	12	10	

F.A. Cup

						Archer A	Atherton J	Bradbury JJL	Daw EC	Dunkley AE	Elliott J	Frettingham JA	Goldie H	Harris W	Killean E	Leigh W	McCurdy W	Milward A	Neame SR	Raisbeck W	Satterthwaite C	Smith G	Wright R
Q3	Nov 1	CLAPTON	2-0	Leigh 2	4000	3		7	1		6		5			8	2	11		4	10	9	
Q4	15	Maidstone United	3-0	Milward 3	4000	3		7	1		6		5			8	2	11		4	10	9	
Q5	29	ILFORD	4-1	Satterthwaite 2, Raisbeck, Leigh	2000	3		7	1		6		5			8	2	11		4	10	9	
IR	Dec 13	Glossop	1-2	Smith	1800	3		7	1	8	6		5				2	11		4	10	9	

		P	W	D	L	F	A	W	D	L	F	A	Pts
1	Southampton	30	12	2	1	53	7	8	6	1	30	13	48
2	Reading	30	12	2	1	47	14	7	5	3	25	16	45
3	Portsmouth	30	11	2	2	36	13	6	5	4	33	19	41
4	Tottenham Hotspur	30	10	5	0	34	9	4	2	9	13	22	35
5	Bristol Rovers	30	9	5	1	33	12	4	3	8	13	22	34
6	NEW BROMPTON	30	9	4	2	24	9	2	7	6	13	26	33
7	Millwall	30	9	2	4	33	16	5	1	9	19	21	31
8	Northampton Town	30	7	3	5	23	19	5	3	7	16	29	30
9	Queen's Park Rangers	30	8	3	4	25	16	3	3	9	9	26	28
10	West Ham United	30	8	5	2	25	14	1	5	9	10	35	28
11	Luton Town	30	8	3	4	28	14	2	4	9	15	30	27
12	Swindon Town	30	8	5	2	24	13	2	2	11	14	33	27
13	Kettering	30	5	8	2	19	12	3	3	9	14	28	27
14	Wellingborough	30	9	2	4	27	15	2	1	12	9	41	25
15	Watford	30	5	1	9	22	33	1	3	11	13	54	16
16	Brentford	30	2	1	12	10	36	0	0	15	6	48	5

1903/04

16th in Southern League Division One

							Atherton J	Boucher T	Bradbury JJL	Clutterbuck HJ	Connor MJ	Davidson A	Dickenson J	Elliott J	Evans C	Goldie H	Lagar F	Leigh W	Lissenden AJ	Lloyd GH	McCurdy W	Metherell HS	Raisbeck W	Roberson J	Sears AE	Singleton HB	Smith L	Stevenson J	White JW
1	Sep	5	Kettering	0-2		3000		9	7	1	8			6		5					2		4			11		10	3
2		12	SOUTHAMPTON	0-3		3000		9		1				6		5					2		4	7		11	10	8	3
3		19	Fulham	0-1		6000		10	7	1	9			6		5					2		4	8		11			3
4		26	MILLWALL ATHLETIC	1-1	Boucher	4000	5	10	7	1	9			6			3				2		4	8		11			
5	Oct	3	Queen's Park Rangers	0-3		6500	5	10	7	1	9			6			3				2		4	8		11			
6		10	PLYMOUTH ARGYLE	0-0		5000	5	8	7	1				6			4				2		9	11			10		3
7		17	Reading	0-3		4000	5	8	7	1		10	11	6			4				2		9						3
8		24	WELLINGBOROUGH	0-0		4000			7	1		9	11			5				6	2		4	8				10	3
9		31	Bristol Rovers	0-2		2000		8	7	1		9		6		5					2		4			11		10	3
10	Nov	7	BRIGHTON & HOVE ALB.	2-1	Boucher, Robertson	3000		9	7	1				6		5					2		4	8		11		10	3
11		14	Portsmouth	0-2		6000		9	7	1				6		5					2		4	8		11		10	3
12		21	NORTHAMPTON T	2-2	Stevenson, Goldie	3000		9	7	1				6		5					2		4	8		11		10	3
13	Dec	5	WEST HAM UNITED	0-0		3000		9		1				6		5				4	2		8	7		11		10	3
14		19	LUTON TOWN	2-2	Robertson, White (p)	2000			7					6		5			10	4	2	1		8		11		9	3
15		26	Swindon Town	0-3		5000		9	7	1				6		5				4	2			8		11		10	3
16		28	SWINDON TOWN	3-1	Stevenson 3	3000	5	9	7	1				6						4	2			8		11		10	3
17	Jan	2	KETTERING	1-1	Robertson	3000		9		1				6	7					4	2		5	8		11		10	3
18		9	Southampton	0-4		4000	5	8		1				6	7					4	2		9			11		10	3
19		16	FULHAM	0-0		3000	5	8	7	1				6			2	9					4			11		10	3
20		23	Millwall Athletic	2-0	Leigh, Boucher	4000		8	7	1				6			2	9		5			4			11		10	3
21		30	QUEEN'S PARK RANGERS	2-0	Leigh 2	1000		8	7	1				6			2	9		5			4			11		10	3
22	Feb	1	Brentford	1-1	Leigh	8000		8	7	1				6			2	9		5			4			11		10	3
23		13	READING	0-0		3000		8	7	1				6			2	9		5			4			11		10	3
24		20	Wellingborough	0-1		2000		8	7	1				6			2	9		5			4			11		10	3
25		27	BRISTOL ROVERS	1-1	White	3000		8		1				6	7		2	9		5			4			11		10	3
26	Mar	5	Brighton & Hove Albion	3-1	Singleton, Boucher, Stevenson	4000		8		1				6	7		2	9		5			4			11		10	3
27		12	PORTSMOUTH	1-2	Leigh	6000		8		1				6	7			9		5	2		4			11		10	3
28		16	Plymouth Argyle	0-1		1500		8		1				6	7			9		5	2		4			11		10	3
29		19	Northampton Town	2-2	Durber (og), Boucher	2000	4	8		1				6	7			9		5	2					11		10	3
30		26	BRENTFORD	3-0	Boucher, Stevenson, Robertson(p)	3000		8		1				6	7					5	2		4	9		11		10	3
31	Apr	2	West Ham United	0-0		5000		8		1				6	7			9		5	2		4			11		10	3
32		5	Tottenham Hotspur	0-1		5000	5	8		1				6	7						2		4	9	10	11			3
33		9	TOTTENHAM HOTSPUR	0-1		4000				1				6	7			9		5	2		4	8		11		10	3
34		16	Luton Town	0-1		3000	5			1				6				9		4	2		8	7		11		10	3
						Apps	10	30	20	33	4	3	2	33	11	11	12	14	1	21	26	1	30	18	1	31	2	28	32
						Goals		6								1		5						4		1		6	2

One own goal

F.A. Cup

							Atherton J	Boucher T	Bradbury JJL	Clutterbuck HJ	Connor MJ	Davidson A	Dickenson J	Elliott J	Evans C	Goldie H	Lagar F	Leigh W	Lissenden AJ	Lloyd GH	McCurdy W	Metherell HS	Raisbeck W	Roberson J	Sears AE	Singleton HB	Smith L	Stevenson J	White JW
IR	Dec	12	BRISTOL CITY	1-1	Chambers (og)	6000				1				6		5				4	2		8	7		11	9	10	3
rep		16	Bristol City	2-5	Goldie, Stevenson				7	1				6		5				4	2		9	8		11		10	3

		P	W	D	L	F	A	W	D	L	F	A	Pts
1	Southampton	34	12	3	2	43	15	10	3	4	32	15	50
2	Tottenham Hotspur	34	10	5	2	34	19	6	6	5	20	18	43
3	Bristol Rovers	34	11	4	2	38	12	6	4	7	26	30	42
4	Portsmouth	34	11	4	2	24	11	6	4	7	17	27	42
5	Queen's Park Rangers	34	13	3	1	34	12	2	8	7	19	25	41
6	Reading	34	8	6	3	27	15	6	7	4	21	20	41
7	Millwall	34	10	2	5	41	20	6	6	5	23	22	40
8	Luton Town	34	12	4	1	23	9	2	8	7	15	24	40
9	Plymouth Argyle	34	8	5	4	27	16	5	5	7	17	18	36
10	Swindon Town	34	7	7	3	18	14	3	4	10	12	28	31
11	Fulham	34	7	6	4	23	15	2	6	9	11	21	30
12	West Ham United	34	8	4	5	26	14	2	3	12	13	30	27
13	Brentford	34	8	4	5	25	18	1	5	11	9	30	27
14	Wellingborough	34	7	4	6	34	25	4	1	12	10	38	27
15	Northampton Town	34	8	4	5	22	20	2	3	12	14	40	27
16	NEW BROMPTON	34	4	10	3	18	15	2	3	12	8	28	25
17	Brighton & Hove Alb.	34	5	6	6	27	29	1	6	10	19	40	24
18	Kettering	34	6	4	7	23	23	0	3	14	16	53	19

1904/05

9th in Southern League Division One

No	Month	Day	Opponent	Score	Scorers	Att	Barnfather P	Boucher T	Bull A	Elliott J	Evans C	Felton FJ	Griffiths FJ	Lagar F	Leigh W	Lloyd GH	McKie J	Morris JJ	Taylorson	Travers P	Turner J	Walton J	Watts EA	White JW
1	Sep	3	BRIGHTON & HOVE ALB.	2-2	Barnfather, Morris	4000	7			6			1	2	8	4	9	10			11		5	3
2		10	Wellingborough	3-1	Turner 2 (1p), Leigh	3000	7	8		6			1		9	4		10			11	2	5	3
3		17	SOUTHAMPTON	1-1	Leigh	7000	7	8		6			1		9	4		10			11	2	5	3
4		24	Fulham	1-1	Barnfather	12000	7	8		6			1		9	4		10			11	2	5	3
5	Oct	1	WATFORD	1-0	Turner (p)	5000	7	8		6			1		9	4		10			11	2	5	3
6		8	Plymouth Argyle	2-3	Morris, Elliott	10000	7			6			1		9	4	8	10			11	2	5	3
7		15	WEST HAM UNITED	3-0	Leigh 2, Morris	6000	7			6			1		9	4	8	10			11	2	5	3
8		22	Reading	1-3	Turner	8000	7			6			1		9	4	8	10			11	2	5	3
9		24	BRISTOL ROVERS	1-1	Leigh	3500	7			6			1		9	4	8	10			11	2	5	3
10	Nov	5	Northampton Town	0-2		4000	7	8		6			1		9	4		10			11	2	5	3
11		19	Brentford	2-0	Leigh, Barnfather	5000	7			6			1		9	4	8	10			11	2	5	3
12		26	QUEEN'S PARK RANGERS	4-0	Turner 3 (2p), Leigh	5000				6		7	1		9	4	8	10			11	2	5	3
13	Dec	3	Millwall	1-1	McKie	3000	7			6			1		9	4	8			10	11	2	5	3
14		10	TOTTENHAM HOTSPUR	1-1	Leigh	5000	7			6			1		9	4		10		8	11	2	5	3
15		17	Luton Town	0-1		4000			4	6		7	1	11	9		8	10				2	5	3
16		24	SWINDON TOWN	0-0				11		6			1		9	4	8	10		7		2	5	3
17		26	Swindon Town	2-1	Morris, Leigh	5000		7		6			1		9	4	8	10		11		2	5	3
18		31	Brighton & Hove Albion	1-3	Boucher	4000		7	11	6			1		9	4	8	10				2	5	3
19	Jan	7	WELLINGBOROUGH	3-1	McKie, Morris, Turner	3500			5	6	7		1		9	4	8	10			11	2		3
20		14	Southampton	1-2	McKie	5000				6	7		1		9	4	8	10			11	2	5	3
21		21	FULHAM	3-0	Leigh, Morris, Travers	4500				6			1		9	4	8	10		7	11	2	5	3
22		28	Watford	0-2		3000				6			1		9	4	8	10		7	11	2	5	3
23	Feb	11	West Ham United	0-2		8000				6	7		1			4	9	10		8	11	2	5	3
24		18	READING	1-0	McKie	6000			9	6	7		1			4	8	10			11	2	5	3
25		25	Bristol Rovers	0-0		5000			9	6	7		1			4	8	10			11	2	5	3
26	Mar	4	NORTHAMPTON T	1-1	Morris	6000			9	6	7		1			4	8	10			11	2	5	3
27		11	Portsmouth	1-1	McKie	4000				6	7		1		9	4	8	10			11	2	5	3
28		18	BRENTFORD	0-1			7			6			1		9	4	8	10			11	2	5	3
29		25	Queen's Park Rangers	0-2			7	9		6			1	2		4	8	10			11		5	3
30		27	PLYMOUTH ARGYLE	1-1	Turner	4000				6	7		1	2	9	4	8	10			11		5	3
31	Apr	1	MILLWALL	1-0	McKie	5000			5	6	7		1	2		4	9	10		8	11			3
32		8	Tottenham Hotspur	0-2		7000			5	6	7		1			4	9	10		8	11	2		3
33		15	LUTON TOWN	2-1	Travers, Barnfather	7000	7		9	6			1			4		10		8	11	2	5	3
34		29	PORTSMOUTH	0-3		4000	7		5	6			1	2		4	9	10	11	8				3
						Apps	17	9	10	34	10	2	34	6	25	33	27	33	1	11	29	29	30	34
						Goals	4	1		1					10		6	7		2	9			

F.A. Cup

Rd	Month	Day	Opponent	Score	Scorers	Att	Barnfather P	Boucher T	Bull A	Elliott J	Evans C	Felton FJ	Griffiths FJ	Lagar F	Leigh W	Lloyd GH	McKie J	Morris JJ	Taylorson	Travers P	Turner J	Walton J	Watts EA	White JW
Q3	Oct	29	Clapton	6-2	Morris 2, Turner, McKie, Leigh, White(p)	4000	7			6			1		9	4	8	10			11	2	5	3
Q4	Nov	12	BRIGHTON & HOVE ALB.	0-1		7000	7		4	6			1		9	5	8	10			11	2		3

		P	*W*	*D*	*L*	*F*	*A*	*W*	*D*	*L*	*F*	*A*	*Pts*
1	Bristol Rovers	34	13	4	0	51	11	7	4	6	23	25	48
2	Reading	34	13	3	1	36	12	5	4	8	21	26	43
3	Southampton	34	9	4	4	29	21	9	3	5	25	19	43
4	Plymouth Argyle	34	14	3	0	38	11	4	2	11	19	28	41
5	Tottenham Hotspur	34	10	3	4	34	15	5	5	7	19	19	38
6	Fulham	34	10	5	2	32	9	4	5	8	14	25	38
7	Queen's Park Rangers	34	10	2	5	36	19	4	6	7	15	27	36
8	Portsmouth	34	12	1	4	39	19	4	3	10	22	37	36
9	NEW BROMPTON	34	8	7	2	25	13	3	4	10	15	27	33
10	Watford	34	12	0	5	30	19	3	3	11	14	26	33
11	West Ham United	34	9	3	5	30	15	3	5	9	18	27	32
12	Brighton & Hove Alb.	34	9	2	6	25	15	4	4	9	19	30	32
13	Northampton Town	34	8	4	5	26	17	4	4	9	17	37	32
14	Brentford	34	5	7	5	17	14	5	2	10	16	24	29
15	Millwall	34	7	6	4	26	17	4	1	12	12	30	29
16	Swindon Town	34	11	2	4	30	17	1	3	13	11	42	29
17	Luton Town	34	11	1	5	35	18	1	2	14	10	36	27
18	Wellingborough	34	4	3	10	16	37	1	0	16	9	70	13

1905/06

17th in Southern League Division One

							Barnfather P	Beadsworth A	Bull A	Burns AJ	Campbell J	Elliott J	Evans C	Floyd WB	Griffiths FJ	Lloyd GH	Marriott W	Martin J	Maven FJ	McKie J	Metherell HS	Orr J	Page	Phillips H	Sheridan J	Snelgrove GW	Travers P	Walton J	Webb A
1	Sep	2	Queen's Park Rangers	0-4		10000	7		5			6		3	1	4	11			8				9	10			2	
2		9	BRISTOL ROVERS	0-3		4000	7		5			6		3	1	4	11			8						9	10	2	
3		16	NORTHAMPTON T	2-0	Phillips, Elliott	4000	7		3			6			1	4	11	5		8				9			10	2	
4		23	Portsmouth	0-4		8000	7		3			6			1	4	11		5	8				9			10	2	
5		30	SWINDON TOWN	0-0		4000	7			10		6		3	1		11		5	4				9			8	2	
6	Oct	7	Millwall	0-5		8000				10		6			1	4	11		5	8				7		9		2	3
7		14	LUTON TOWN	1-1	Marriott	5000		10		7		6		3	1		11	5	4						8	9		2	
8		21	Tottenham Hotspur	0-6		14000			3	7		6			1		11	5	4						8	9	10	2	
9		28	BRENTFORD	2-1	Burns, Marriott	4000				7		6			1	4	11		5	9		3			8		10	2	
10	Nov	4	Norwich City	1-4	Burns	6000				7		6			1	4	11		5	9		3			8		10	2	
11		11	PLYMOUTH ARGYLE	1-1	Marriott	3000				7		6			1	4	11	5		9		3			8		10	2	
12		18	Southampton	1-1	McKie	4000						6	7		1	4	11	5		9		3		8			10	2	
13		25	READING	0-3		4000					9	6	7		1	4	11	5		8		3					10	2	
14	Dec	2	Watford	2-2	Marriott, Sheridan	3000	7	10			9	6		3	1	4	11		5						8			2	
15		16	West Ham United	0-1		6000	7	10			9	6		3	1	4	11		5						8			2	
16		23	FULHAM	0-3		4000		10		7	8	6		3	1		11	4	5	9								2	
17		25	BRIGHTON & HOVE ALB.	1-0	Campbell (p)	4000	7	10	4		8	6		3	1		11		5	9								2	
18		30	QUEEN'S PARK RANGERS	0-2		3000	7	10	4		9	6		3			11	1	5								8	2	
19	Jan	6	Bristol Rovers	2-1	Beadsworth, Campbell (p)	5000		10	4		7	6		3			11	1	5			2		9			8		
20		20	Northampton Town	1-0	Burns	3000		10	4	7	9	6		3			11	1	5								8	2	
21		27	PORTSMOUTH	0-1		5500		10	4		7	6		3			11	1	5					9			8	2	
22	Feb	10	MILLWALL	0-1		1500	7	10	4	11		6						1	5	9		3					8	2	
23		17	Luton Town	1-2	White (og)		7	10	4		11	6		3				1	5					9			8	2	
24	Mar	3	Brentford	2-3	Beadsworth, Riley (og)	4000	7	9	4			6		3				1	5	10				11			8	2	
25		5	TOTTENHAM HOTSPUR	1-0	Travers	2500	7	9	4			6		3				1	5	10				11			8	2	
26		10	NORWICH CITY	0-0		3500	7	9	4			6		3				1	5	10				11			8	2	
27		17	Plymouth Argyle	0-5		6000	7	9	4					3				1	5	10		6		11			8	2	
28		19	Swindon Town	0-2			7	9	4					3		6		1	5	10				11			8	2	
29		24	SOUTHAMPTON	0-4		2000	7	9	4	10		6		3	1		11		5								8	2	
30		31	Reading	0-1			7	10	4		9	6		3		5	11				1						8	2	
31	Apr	7	WATFORD	2-0	Campbell, Beadsworth	3000	7	10	4		9	6		3		5	11				1						8	2	
32		14	Brighton & Hove Albion	0-0		4000	7	10	4		9	6		3			11		5		1						8	2	
33		21	WEST HAM UNITED	0-0		3000	7	10	4		9	6		3		5	11				1						8	2	
34		25	Fulham	0-1		3000	7		4		9	6		3		5	11				1		10				8	2	
						Apps	22	21	23	11	15	32	2	24	18	17	27	18	24	19	5	8	1	14	8	4	27	33	1
						Goals		3		3	3	1					4			1				1	1		1		

Two own goals

F.A. Cup

							Barnfather P	Beadsworth A	Bull A	Burns AJ	Campbell J	Elliott J	Evans C	Floyd WB	Griffiths FJ	Lloyd GH	Marriott W	Martin J	Maven FJ	McKie J	Metherell HS	Orr J	Page	Phillips H	Sheridan J	Snelgrove GW	Travers P	Walton J	Webb A
R1	Jan	13	NORTHAMPTON T	2-1	Beadsworth, Marriott	5000		10	4		7	6		3			11	1	5					9			8	2	
R2	Feb	3	SOUTHAMPTON	0-0		4287	7	10	4		11	6		3				1	5					9			8	2	
rep		7	Southampton	0-1		7500	7	10	4		11	6		3				1	5					9			8	2	

		P	W	D	L	F	A	W	D	L	F	A	Pts
1	Fulham	34	10	7	0	22	6	9	5	3	22	9	50
2	Southampton	34	13	2	2	32	11	6	5	6	26	28	45
3	Portsmouth	34	13	3	1	39	11	4	6	7	22	24	43
4	Luton Town	34	13	2	2	45	13	4	5	8	19	27	41
5	Tottenham Hotspur	34	13	2	2	36	11	3	5	9	10	18	39
6	Plymouth Argyle	34	11	3	3	32	13	5	4	8	20	20	39
7	Norwich City	34	8	8	1	30	12	5	2	10	16	26	36
8	Bristol Rovers	34	11	1	5	37	23	4	4	9	19	33	35
9	Brentford	34	11	3	3	28	19	3	4	10	15	33	35
10	Reading	34	9	7	1	34	15	3	2	12	19	31	33
11	West Ham United	34	12	2	3	30	9	2	3	12	12	30	33
12	Millwall	34	9	4	4	26	16	2	7	8	12	25	33
13	Queen's Park Rangers	34	9	3	5	39	14	3	4	10	19	30	31
14	Watford	34	7	6	4	28	20	1	4	12	10	37	26
15	Swindon Town	34	6	4	7	21	23	2	5	10	10	29	25
16	Brighton & Hove Alb.	34	8	5	4	24	24	1	2	14	6	31	25
17	NEW BROMPTON	34	5	5	7	10	20	2	3	12	10	42	22
18	Northampton Town	34	5	4	8	17	22	3	1	13	15	57	21

1906/07

16th in Southern League Division One

							Brisley J	Cunliffe D	Daws	Elliott J	Floyd WB	Godley J	Hartley J	Harvey EA	Lee W	Lissenden G	Lloyd GH	Lunn	Marriott W	Martin J	Maven FJ	McKinnell	Morgan W	Smith S	Walker G	Warrington J	Webb A
1	Sep	1	BRISTOL ROVERS	0-1		5000		8		6	3				9				10	1	5		4	11	2	7	
2		8	Plymouth Argyle	1-2	Cunliffe	8000		8		6	3				9		4			1	5		10	11	2	7	
3		15	BRIGHTON & HOVE ALB.	4-3	Cunliffe 2, Smith, Marriott	5000		8		6	3					4			10	1	5		9	11	2	7	
4		22	Reading	0-3		5000		8			3					6	4		10	1	5		9	11	2	7	
5		29	WATFORD	2-0	Cunliffe (p), Hitch (og)	5000		8			3			2	9		4	10	7	1	5		6	11			
6	Oct	6	Northampton Town	2-1	Lee, Cunliffe	4000		8			3			2	9		4	10	7	1	5		6	11			
7		13	QUEEN'S PARK RANGERS	2-1	Marriott, Cunliffe	6000		8			3		7	2	9		4	10		1	5			11	6		
8		20	Fulham	1-2	Lee	14000		8			3			2	9			10		1	5		4	11	6	7	
9		27	SOUTHAMPTON	0-2		6000		8			3		7	2	9		4	10		1	5			11	6		
10	Nov	3	West Ham United	1-1	Lunn	7000		8			3			2	9		4	10		1	5		6	11		7	
11		10	TOTTENHAM HOTSPUR	0-1		6500		8			3		10	2	9		4			1	5		6	11		7	
12		17	Swindon Town	0-2		3000		8			3			2	9		4		10	1	5		6	11		7	
13		24	NORWICH CITY	0-1		4000		8		6	3		10	2	9					1	5		4	11		7	
14	Dec	1	Luton Town	2-0	Cunliffe 2	3500		8			3			2	9		4		10	1	5		6	11		7	
15		8	WEST HAM UNITED	2-2	Cunliffe, Warrington	4000		8		6	3			2	9		5		10	1			4	11		7	
16		15	Brentford	0-3		6000		8			3			2	9		5	10		1			4	11	6	7	
17		22	MILLWALL	2-1	Cunliffe 2	3500		8			3		9	2			4		10	1	5			11	6	7	
18		25	Portsmouth	1-3	Lee	15000		8			3			2	9		4		10	1	5			11	6	7	
19		29	Bristol Rovers	0-4		5000		8			3			2	9		4		10	1	5			11	6	7	
20	Jan	5	PLYMOUTH ARGYLE	0-2		4800					3		8	2	9		4		7	1	5		10	11	6		
21		19	Brighton & Hove Albion	1-4	Daws	5000		8	7		3		10	2	9					1	5		4	11	6		
22		26	READING	0-0		3000		8	7		3		9	2			4		10	1	5			11	6		
23	Feb	9	NORTHAMPTON T	3-1	Hartley, Godley, Smith					6	3	8	9	2			4	10	7	1	5			11			
24		13	LEYTON	1-2	Maven (p)	1000		8					9	2		6	4	10	7	1	5			11			3
25		16	Queen's Park Rangers	0-3		8000		8					9	2		6	4	10	7	1	5			11	3		
26		23	FULHAM	1-1	Marriott	5500		8				10		2	9		4	6	7	1	5			11	3		
27	Mar	2	Southampton	1-1	Marriott	4000		8				10		2	9	4	5	6	7	1				11	3		
28		16	Tottenham Hotspur	0-2		6000		8				10		2	9		4	6	7	1	5			11	3		
29		20	Watford	2-2	Lee, Cunliffe	2000		8						2	9		4	10	7	1	5	3		11	6		
30		23	SWINDON TOWN	2-1	Hartley, Smith	5000		8					9	2			4	10	7	1	5	3		11	6		
31		29	Leyton	0-0		5000		8			3		9	2			4	10	7	1	5			11	6		
32		30	Norwich City	2-2	Cunliffe, Thompson (og)	4500	3	8					9	2			4	10	7	1	5			11	6		
33	Apr	1	PORTSMOUTH	2-0	Hartley, Marriott	7000		8			3		9	2			4	10	7	1	5			11	6		
34		6	LUTON TOWN	0-0		4000		8			3		9	2			4	10	7	1	5			11	6		
35		13	Crystal Palace	3-1	Hartley 3	5000		8			3		9	2			4	10	7	1	5			11	6		
36		20	BRENTFORD	5-0	Hartley 2, Marriott 2, Cunliffe	4000		8			3		9	2			4	10	7	1	5			11	6		
37		27	Millwall	0-2		4000		8			3	9		2			4	10	7	1	5			11	6		
38		29	CRYSTAL PALACE	4-2	Hartley 2, Cunliffe, Smith	3000		8			3		9	2			4	10	7	1	5			11	6		

	Brisley J	Cunliffe D	Daws	Elliott J	Floyd WB	Godley J	Hartley J	Harvey EA	Lee W	Lissenden G	Lloyd GH	Lunn	Marriott W	Martin J	Maven FJ	McKinnell	Morgan W	Smith S	Walker G	Warrington J	Webb A
Apps	1	36	2	6	30	5	19	34	22	5	33	23	29	38	35	2	16	38	28	15	1
Goals		15	1			1	10		4				7	1				4		1	

Two own goals

F.A. Cup

							Brisley J	Cunliffe D	Daws	Elliott J	Floyd WB	Godley J	Hartley J	Harvey EA	Lee W	Lissenden G	Lloyd GH	Lunn	Marriott W	Martin J	Maven FJ	McKinnell	Morgan W	Smith S	Walker G	Warrington J	Webb A
R1	Jan	12	Burton United	0-0		3000		8			3			2	9		4		7	1	5		10	11	6		
rep		16	BURTON UNITED	0-0	(aet)	5000		8			3			2	9		4		7	1	5		10	11	6		
rep2		21	Burton United	2-0	Wood (og), Hartley			8			3		10	2			4		7	1	5		9	11	6		
R2	Feb	2	Bury	0-1		10019		8		6	3		9	2			4	10	7	1	5			11			

R1 replay 2 at Fulham

		P	*W*	*D*	*L*	*F*	*A*	*W*	*D*	*L*	*F*	*A*	*Pts*
1	Fulham	38	13	5	1	34	12	7	8	4	24	20	53
2	Portsmouth	38	15	3	1	45	11	7	4	8	19	25	51
3	Brighton & Hove Alb.	38	12	4	3	33	16	6	5	8	20	27	45
4	Luton Town	38	12	4	3	37	22	6	5	8	15	30	45
5	West Ham United	38	12	5	2	39	12	3	9	7	21	29	44
6	Tottenham Hotspur	38	13	4	2	46	12	4	5	10	17	33	43
7	Millwall	38	14	3	2	53	12	4	3	12	18	38	42
8	Norwich City	38	9	6	4	34	21	6	6	7	23	27	42
9	Watford	38	9	7	3	31	18	4	9	6	15	25	42
10	Brentford	38	14	3	2	39	16	3	5	11	18	40	42
11	Southampton	38	9	6	4	31	18	4	3	12	18	38	35
12	Reading	38	12	3	4	42	11	2	3	14	15	36	34
13	Leyton	38	9	6	4	26	23	2	6	11	12	37	34
14	Bristol Rovers	38	10	4	5	41	21	2	5	12	14	33	33
15	Plymouth Argyle	38	7	9	3	26	14	3	4	12	17	36	33
16	NEW BROMPTON	38	9	4	6	30	21	3	5	11	17	38	33
17	Swindon Town	38	11	7	1	28	8	0	4	15	15	46	33
18	Queen's Park Rangers	38	9	5	5	32	16	2	5	12	15	39	32
19	Crystal Palace	38	7	4	8	29	28	1	5	13	17	38	25
20	Northampton Town	38	5	8	6	22	25	0	1	18	7	63	19

1907/08

Bottom of Southern League Division One

							Barker	Floyd WB	Fullarton J	Hartley J	Harvey EA	Hopkins J	Lloyd GH	Marriott W	Martin J	Maven FJ	McGibbon CE	McKinnell	McLachlan	Metherell HS	Pass JE	Pickering J	Robotham H	Salter HJ	Smith S	Spriggs F	Walker RH
1	Sep	4	Bristol Rovers	1-9	McGibbon	4000		3	5	8		7			1		9	2				10	6	4	11		
2		7	Queen's Park Rangers	2-2	Pickering 2	7000		3	5	8	2		4	7	1		9					10	6		11		
3		9	SOUTHAMPTON	2-1	Pickering 2	4000		3	5	8	2		4	7	1		9					10	6		11		
4		14	BRISTOL ROVERS	1-0	McGibbon	7000		3	5		2		4	7	1		9					10	6	8	11		
5		21	Tottenham Hotspur	1-2	Pickering	16000		3	5		2		4	7	1		9					10	6	8	11		
6		28	LEYTON	2-2	Salter, Harvey (p)	6000		3	5		2		4	7	1		9					10	6	8	11		
7	Oct	5	Swindon Town	0-1		5000	8	3	6		2		4	7	1	5	9							10	11		
8		12	READING	1-2	Salter	5000	9	3	5		2	7		10	1				4				6	8	11		
9		19	Crystal Palace	3-3	Marriott 3	8000			3	8	2		5	7	1		9					10	6	4	11		
10		26	WATFORD	3-1	McGibbon 3	5000			3	8	2		4	7	1	5	9					10	6		11		
11	Nov	2	Luton Town	2-1	McGibbon, Pickering	5000			3	8	2		4		1	5	9					10	6	7	11		
12		9	NORWICH CITY	2-1	Hartley, McGibbon	7000		3	2	8			4		1	5	9					10	6	7	11		
13		16	Brighton & Hove Albion	0-3		5500		3	2	8			4		1	5	9					10	6	7	11		
14		23	NORTHAMPTON T	0-1		6000		3	4		2			7	1	5	9					10	6	8	11		
15		30	Portsmouth	2-5	Hartley 2	9000		3	6	8	2	7	4			5	9			1				10	11		
16	Dec	14	Bradford Park Avenue	5-5	McGibbon 2, Hopkins, Pickering, Maven			3	2			7	4		1	5	9					10	6	8	11		
17		21	Plymouth Argyle	0-1		7500		3	2			7	4		1	5	9					10	6	8	11		
18		25	West Ham United	2-1	Spriggs, Salter	10000		3	2			7	4		1	5						10	6	8	11	9	
19		26	BRENTFORD	2-1	Hopkins, McGibbon	6000		3	2			7	4		1	5	9					10	6	8	11		
20		28	MILLWALL	0-0		4000		3	2			7	4		1	5	9					10	6	8	11		
21	Jan	4	QUEEN'S PARK RANGERS	0-4		5000		3	6		2	7	4		1	5	9					10		8	11		
22		18	TOTTENHAM HOTSPUR	1-2	Smith	5000		3		10	2		4	7		5	9			1			6	8	11		
23		25	Leyton	0-1		2500		3			2		4	7	1	5	9						6	10	11	8	
24	Feb	8	Reading	0-2				3	6		2		4	7	1	5						10		8	11	9	
25		15	CRYSTAL PALACE	2-2	Hartley, Spriggs	2000		3	6	10	2		4	7	1	5	9								11	8	
26		22	Watford	1-1	Salter	3000		3	6	9	2				1	5						10	4	7	11	8	
27		29	LUTON TOWN	0-1		3000	7	3	6	8	2		4		1	5	9					10			11		
28	Mar	7	Norwich City	1-2	McGibbon	3000		3	2		8	7	4		1	5	9						6	10	11		
29		14	BRIGHTON & HOVE ALB.	2-1	McGibbon (p), Salter	2500		3			2		4	7	1	5	9						6	10	11	8	
30		21	Northampton Town	0-2		4000		3	5		2		4	7	1		9					10	6		11	8	
31		28	PORTSMOUTH	1-3	McGibbon	4000		3	5		2		4	7	1		9				10		6		11		8
32	Apr	1	SWINDON TOWN	0-1		2000		3	5		2	7	4		1		9				10		6		11		8
33		4	Southampton	0-2		3000	7		3		2		4		1	5					9		6	10	11		8
34		11	BRADFORD PARK AVE.	2-3	Marriott, Salter	3000		3	6		2		4	11	1	5	9				10			7			8
35		17	WEST HAM UNITED	3-0	Pass, Salter, McGibbon	5000		3	6		2			11	1	5	9				10		4	7			8
36		18	PLYMOUTH ARGYLE	0-3		5000		3	6		2			11	1	5	9				10		4	7			8
37		20	Brentford	0-1		5000		3	6		2		4	11	1	5	9				10			7			8
38		25	Millwall	0-2		5000		3	5	9	2		4		1						8		6	7		10	11
						Apps	4	34	35	14	30	11	32	21	36	26	32	1	1	2	8	22	30	30	33	8	8
						Goals				4	1	2		4		1	14				1	7		7	1	2	

F.A. Cup

							Barker	Floyd WB	Fullarton J	Hartley J	Harvey EA	Hopkins J	Lloyd GH	Marriott W	Martin J	Maven FJ	McGibbon CE	McKinnell	McLachlan	Metherell HS	Pass JE	Pickering J	Robotham H	Salter HJ	Smith S	Spriggs F	Walker RH
Q5	Dec	7	SHEPHERDS BUSH	6-0	McGibbon 3, Hopkins, Salter, Marriott	5000		3	6		2	7	4	10	1	5	9							8	11		
R1	Jan	11	SUNDERLAND	3-1	McGibbon 3	10620		3		10	2	7	4		1	5	9						6	8	11		
R2	Feb	1	Manchester City	1-1	McGibbon	16000		3			2	7	4		1	5	9					10	6	8	11		
rep		5	MANCHESTER CITY	1-2	McGibbon (p)	12000		3			2	7	4		1	5	9					10	6	8	11		

		P	*W*	*D*	*L*	*F*	*A*	*W*	*D*	*L*	*F*	*A*	*Pts*
1	Queen's Park Rangers	38	12	4	3	46	26	9	5	5	36	31	51
2	Plymouth Argyle	38	13	5	1	33	13	6	6	7	17	18	49
3	Millwall	38	11	5	3	25	9	8	3	8	24	23	46
4	Crystal Palace	38	10	4	5	35	28	7	6	6	19	23	44
5	Swindon Town	38	12	6	1	41	12	4	4	11	14	28	42
6	Bristol Rovers	38	11	5	3	36	19	5	5	9	23	37	42
7	Tottenham Hotspur	38	11	2	6	33	18	6	5	8	26	30	41
8	Northampton Town	38	9	5	5	30	17	6	6	7	20	24	41
9	Portsmouth	38	14	1	4	43	19	3	5	11	21	33	40
10	West Ham United	38	9	6	4	27	16	6	4	9	20	32	40
11	Southampton	38	11	5	3	32	21	5	1	13	19	39	38
12	Reading	38	12	1	6	38	18	3	5	11	17	32	36
13	Bradford PA	38	6	7	6	30	27	6	5	8	23	27	36
14	Watford	38	9	4	6	31	22	3	6	10	16	37	34
15	Norwich City	38	10	4	5	31	16	2	5	12	15	33	33
16	Brentford	38	13	3	3	38	15	1	2	16	11	38	33
17	Brighton & Hove Alb.	38	9	6	4	29	19	3	2	14	17	40	32
18	Luton Town	38	9	4	6	21	17	3	2	14	12	39	30
19	Leyton	38	6	6	7	30	31	2	5	12	22	43	27
20	NEW BROMPTON	38	7	3	9	24	29	2	4	13	20	46	25

1908/09

7th in Southern League Division One

							Arthurs CH	Bateup E	Boyle P	Brown J	Court AC	Eames W	Fullarton D	Hales WH	Henderson W	Henderson WP	Maven FJ	Nobbs AH	Pickett AE	Powell H	Reid J	Reynolds J	Shepherd HC	Whyman A	Wood H
1	Sep	2	NORTHAMPTON T	0-2		3000	6	1	3					2		4	5		11	7	10			9	8
2		5	SOUTHEND UNITED	1-0	Reynolds	6000	6	1	3					2		4	5		11		10	7		9	8
3		9	Swindon Town	1-6	Pickett	3000	6	1	3				4		2		5		11	9	10	7		8	
4		12	Coventry City	4-3	Arthurs 2, Reid, Hales	6000	6	1	3				2	4			5		11	9	10	7		8	
5		19	BRISTOL ROVERS	2-0	Powell, Reid	8000	6	1	3				2	4			5		11	9	10	7		8	
6		26	Watford	1-2	Reid (p)	4000	6	1	3				2	4			5		11		10	7	9	8	
7	Oct	3	NORWICH CITY	2-0	Powell, Whyman	5000	6	1	3				2	4		5			11	9		7	10	8	
8		10	Reading	1-0	Pickett	5000	6	1	3					4	2	5			11	9	10	7		8	
9		17	SOUTHAMPTON	1-1	Eastham (og)	9000	6	1	3					4	2	5			11	9	10	7		8	
10		24	Leyton	0-3		4000	6	1	3				5	4	2				11	9	10	7		8	
11		26	Queen's Park Rangers	1-2	Reynolds	2000	6	1					2	4				3	11	9	8	7	10	5	
12		31	WEST HAM UNITED	2-1	Taylor (og), Pickett	6000	6	1	3				2	4		5			11	9	10	7		8	
13	Nov	7	Brighton & Hove Albion	1-1	Pickett	5000	6	1	3					2		4	5		11		10	7		8	9
14		14	CRYSTAL PALACE	2-1	Reid, Pickett	7000	6	1	3						2	4	5		11	9	10	7		8	
15		21	Brentford	1-1	Maven (p)	4000	6	1	3						2	4	5		11	9	10	7		8	
16		28	LUTON TOWN	1-0	Powell	6000	6	1	3						2	4	5		11	9		7	10	8	
17	Dec	12	PORTSMOUTH	2-3	Eames 2	6000	6	1	3			8		4	2	5			11			7		10	9
18		19	Exeter City	3-1	Whyman 2, Pickett	5000	6	1	3		9		4			5		2	11			7		10	8
19		25	PLYMOUTH ARGYLE	1-2	Court	6000	6	1	3		9		4	2		5			11			7		10	8
20		26	Millwall	0-1		7000	6	1	3			9	4	2		5				8		7		11	10
21		28	Northampton Town	0-7			6	1	3		9	8	2			5						7	11	4	10
22	Jan	2	Southend United	0-1			6	1	3			8	2			4	5		11	9		7		10	
23		9	COVENTRY CITY	0-1		4500	6	1	3			8	2			4	5		11		9	7		10	
24		23	Bristol Rovers	0-1		5000	6	1	3			8	4				5	2	11	9		7		10	
25		30	WATFORD	5-1	Wood 2, Arthurs 2 (2p), Maven	4000	10	1	3				6			4	5	2	11			7		8	9
26	Feb	13	READING	0-3			10	1	3				6			4	5	2	11			7		8	9
27		20	Southampton	0-2			6		3					1		4	5	2	11	8		7	10	9	
28	Mar	6	West Ham United	1-0	Whyman	3000	6	1	3			8	4				5	2	11	7			10	9	
29		10	QUEEN'S PARK RANGERS	1-0	Pickett	2000	6	1	3			8	4				5	2	11			7	10	9	
30		13	BRIGHTON & HOVE ALB.	2-0	Whyman, Eames	5000	6	1	3			8	4				5	2	11	7			10	9	
31		20	Crystal Palace	2-1	Whyman 2	4000	6	1	3			8				4	5	2	11	10		7		9	
32		27	BRENTFORD	1-1	Reynolds	5000	6	1	3			8				4	5	2	11	10		7		9	
33		29	LEYTON	0-4		2000	6	1	3	4		8					5	2	11	10		7		9	
34	Apr	3	Luton Town	0-3			6	1	3			8				4	5	2	11	7			10	9	
35		9	Plymouth Argyle	1-1	Whyman	10000	6	1	3							4	5	2	11		10	7		9	8
36		10	SWINDON TOWN	3-1	Reynolds 2, Eames	7000	6	1	3			8				4	5	2	11		10	7		9	
37		12	MILLWALL	1-0	Reynolds	5000	6	1	3			8				4	5	2	11		10	7		9	
38		17	Portsmouth	1-1	Pickett	10000	6	1	3			8				4	5	2	11		10	7		9	
39		24	EXETER CITY	3-1	Reynolds, Eames, Reid	4000	6	1	3			8	4				5	2	11		10	7		9	
40		26	Norwich City	0-0		2500	6	1	3			8	4				5	2	11		10	7		9	
						Apps	40	39	39	1	3	18	22	16	8	27	29	19	38	23	21	36	10	40	11
						Goals	4				1	5		1			2		8	3	5	7		8	2

Two own goals

F.A. Cup

Q5	Dec	5	Hastings & St Leonards U	2-2	Shpherd, Pickett	3000	6	1	3						2	4	5		11	9		7	10	8	
rep		9	HASTINGS & ST LEN. U	1-2	Shepherd	3249	6	1	3						2	4	5		11	8		7	10	9	

		P	W	D	L	F	A	W	D	L	F	A	Pts
1	Northampton Town	40	15	3	2	55	14	10	2	8	35	31	55
2	Swindon Town	40	18	0	2	68	15	4	5	11	28	40	49
3	Southampton	40	13	4	3	44	26	6	6	8	23	32	48
4	Portsmouth	40	13	5	2	42	17	5	5	10	26	43	46
5	Bristol Rovers	40	13	5	2	39	20	4	4	12	21	43	43
6	Exeter City	40	13	2	5	37	28	5	4	11	19	37	42
7	NEW BROMPTON	40	12	2	6	30	22	5	5	10	18	37	41
8	Reading	40	7	9	4	33	19	4	9	7	27	38	40
9	Luton Town	40	16	1	3	45	15	1	5	14	14	45	40
10	Plymouth Argyle	40	9	6	5	28	16	6	4	10	18	31	40
11	Millwall	40	14	3	3	38	17	2	3	15	21	44	38
12	Southend United	40	12	6	2	33	14	2	4	14	19	40	38
13	Leyton	40	13	3	4	35	12	2	5	13	17	43	38
14	Watford	40	12	7	1	37	16	2	2	16	14	48	37
15	Queen's Park Rangers	40	10	6	4	41	24	2	6	12	11	26	36
16	Crystal Palace	40	10	4	6	42	23	2	8	10	20	39	36
17	West Ham United	40	16	1	3	43	13	0	3	17	13	47	36
18	Brighton & Hove Alb.	40	11	4	5	46	20	3	3	14	14	41	35
19	Norwich City	40	11	8	1	44	18	1	3	16	15	57	35
20	Coventry City	40	10	4	6	44	37	5	0	15	20	54	34
21	Brentford	40	10	5	5	40	26	3	2	15	19	48	33

1909/10

12th in Southern League Division One

	Month	Day	Opponent	Score	Scorers	Att	Bailey AV	Bateup E	Beale PE	Court AC	Fullarton D	Hawkes JM	Higgins M	Hobson J	Johnson AJ	Luff JT	Mahon J	Massey GH	McArthur J	Nobbs AH	Pickett AE	Reid J	Reynolds J	Satterthwaite JN	Strang T	Sutherland A	Taylor J
1	Sep	1	READING	7-0	Taylor 3, Satterthwaite 2, Court 2	3000		1		9			6				4			3	11		7	10	5	2	8
2		4	Plymouth Argyle	0-1		5000		1		9			6				4			3	11		7	10	5	2	8
3		11	SOUTHAMPTON	2-0	Taylor, Glover (og)	8000		1	11	9			6				4			3			7	10	5	2	8
4		15	Reading	1-0	Satterthwaite	2000		1	11	9			6				4		2	3			7	10	5		8
5		18	Croydon Common	2-0	Court, Reynolds	10000		1		9			6				4			3	11		7	10	5	2	8
6		25	MILLWALL	3-2	Pickett, Sattherthwaite, Taylor	6000		1		9			6				4			3	11		7	10	5	2	8
7		29	SOUTHEND UNITED	5-0	Satterthwaite 3, Court, Taylor	3000		1		9			6				4			3	11		7	10	5	2	8
8	Oct	2	EXETER CITY	3-2	Pickett, Reybolds, Case	8000		1		9			6				4			3	11		7	10	5	2	8
9		4	Leyton	2-1	Court, Taylor	6000		1		9			6				4			3	11	10	7		5	2	8
10		9	Northampton Town	1-7	Reynolds (p)	8000		1		9			6				4			3	11	10	7		5	2	8
11		13	Southend United	0-3		3500		1		9			6				4			3	11		7	10	5	2	8
12		16	QUEEN'S PARK RANGERS	1-1	Court	7000		1		9			6				4		2	3	11		7	10	5		8
13		20	LEYTON	1-3	Taylor	2000		1		9			6				4		2	3	11		7	10	5		8
14		23	Luton Town	0-1		4000		1		9			6				4			3	11		7	10	5	2	8
15		30	SWINDON TOWN	3-2	Reid (p), Pickett, Court	8000		1		9			6				4			3	11	10	7		5	2	8
16	Nov	6	Crystal Palace	2-6	Taylor, Court	12000		1		9			6	7			4			3	11			10	5	2	8
17		13	BRIGHTON & HOVE ALB.	1-0	Taylor	8000		1		9			6				4			3	11	10	7		5	2	8
18		27	PORTSMOUTH	2-0	Taylor, Court	6000		1		9			6				4			3	11	10	7		5	2	8
19	Dec	11	NORWICH CITY	5-2	Reid 2 (1p), Court 2, Taylor	5000		1		9	2		6				4			3	11	10	7		5		8
20		18	Brentford	1-4	Taylor	5000		1		9			6				4			3	11	10	7		5	2	8
21		25	WATFORD	2-0	Court, Taylor	6000		1		9					6		4			3	11	10	7		5	2	8
22		27	Coventry City	1-2	Court	9000		1		9					6		4			3	11	10	7		5	2	8
23	Jan	1	West Ham United	2-2	Taylor 2	10000		1		9					6		4			3	11	10	7		5	2	8
24		8	PLYMOUTH ARGYLE	1-1	Reid	7000		1		9			6				4			3	11	10	7		5	2	8
25		22	Southampton	1-1	Taylor			1		9	2	3	6				4				11		7	10	5		8
26		29	CROYDON COMMON	1-3	Court	4000		1		9	2		5	7	6		4			3	11			10			8
27	Feb	5	Millwall	1-2	Pickett								6	7	3	1	4				11	10		9	5	2	8
28		12	Exeter City	2-3	Court, Taylor	6000				9			6	7	3	1	4				11			10	5	2	8
29		19	NORTHAMPTON T	2-1	Hobson, Satterthwaite	3000		1		9			6	7	3		4				11	10		8	5	2	
30		26	Queen's Park Rangers	0-1		8000		1		9		3	6	7			4	10			11			8	5	2	
31	Mar	5	LUTON TOWN	4-0	Reid 2, Pickett, Court	5000		1		9		3		7	6		4				11	10		8	5	2	
32		12	Swindon Town	1-4	Mahon			1		9			6	7			4			3	11	10		8	5	2	
33		19	CRYSTAL PALACE	3-1	Reid 2, Massey	5000		1					6	7			4	10		3	11	9		8	5	2	
34		25	Watford	2-2	Reid, Satterthwaite	6000		1		9			6	7			4			3	11	10		8	5	2	
35		26	Brighton & Hove Albion	1-5	Massey	6000		1	9				6	7			4	10		3	11			8	5	2	
36		28	COVENTRY CITY	0-1		5000		1			6		9	7			4	10		3	11			8	5	2	
37	Apr	2	WEST HAM UNITED	1-0	Satterthwaite			1		9			6	7			4			3	11			10	5	2	8
38		9	Portsmouth	3-4	Court 2, Taylor	6000		1		9			6	7			4			3	11	10			5	2	8
39		16	BRISTOL ROVERS	2-0	Hobson, Reid	4000		1		9			6	7			4			3	11	10			5	2	8
40		23	Norwich City	0-1		4000		1		9			6	7			4			3	11	10			5	2	8
41		27	Bristol Rovers	1-3	Satterthwaite	1000		1		9			6	7			4			3	11			10	5	2	8
42		30	BRENTFORD	3-2	Court 3	3000	1			9			6	7			4			3	11			10	5	2	8

	Bailey AV	Bateup E	Beale PE	Court AC	Fullarton D	Hawkes JM	Higgins M	Hobson J	Johnson AJ	Luff JT	Mahon J	Massey GH	McArthur J	Nobbs AH	Pickett AE	Reid J	Reynolds J	Satterthwaite JN	Strang T	Sutherland A	Taylor J
Apps	1	39	3	38	4	3	38	18	8	2	42	4	3	36	40	20	24	28	41	36	34
Goals				22				2			1	2			5	10	3	11			19

One own goal

F.A. Cup

	Month	Day	Opponent	Score	Scorers	Att	Bailey AV	Bateup E	Beale PE	Court AC	Fullarton D	Hawkes JM	Higgins M	Hobson J	Johnson AJ	Luff JT	Mahon J	Massey GH	McArthur J	Nobbs AH	Pickett AE	Reid J	Reynolds J	Satterthwaite JN	Strang T	Sutherland A	Taylor J
Q4	Nov	20	OXFORD CITY	9-1	* see below	5000		1		9			6				4			3	11	10	7		5	2	8
Q5	Dec	4	Rotherham Town	1-0	Court	6000		1		9			6				4			3	11	10	7		5	2	8
R1	Jan	15	Leyton	0-0				1		9			6				4			3	11	10	7		5	2	8
rep		19	LEYTON	2-2	Court, Pickett	6000		1		9			6				4			3	11	10	7		5	2	8
rep2		24	Leyton	0-1		5268		1		9	2		5		6		4			3	11		7	10			8

Scorers in Q4: Pickett 3, Reid 2, Taylor, Court, Higgins, Harrison (og)

Replay 2 at Tottenham

		P	*W*	*D*	*L*	*F*	*A*	*W*	*D*	*L*	*F*	*A*	*Pts*
1	Brighton & Hove Alb.	42	18	2	1	50	11	5	11	5	19	17	59
2	Swindon Town	42	15	3	3	63	20	7	7	7	29	26	54
3	Queen's Park Rangers	42	12	5	4	41	28	7	8	6	15	19	51
4	Northampton Town	42	16	3	2	66	11	6	1	14	24	33	48
5	Southampton	42	11	7	3	39	25	5	9	7	25	30	48
6	Portsmouth	42	13	5	3	43	17	7	2	12	27	46	47
7	Crystal Palace	42	13	3	5	48	20	7	3	11	21	30	46
8	Coventry City	42	11	6	4	50	24	8	2	11	21	36	46
9	West Ham United	42	10	7	4	43	23	5	8	8	26	33	45
10	Leyton	42	11	4	6	45	22	5	7	9	15	24	43
11	Plymouth Argyle	42	14	5	2	40	8	2	6	13	21	46	43
12	NEW BROMPTON	42	16	2	3	52	21	3	3	15	24	53	43
13	Bristol Rovers	42	13	5	3	25	8	3	5	13	12	40	42
14	Brentford	42	13	5	3	33	13	3	4	14	17	45	41
15	Luton Town	42	10	7	4	45	34	5	4	12	27	58	41
16	Millwall	42	9	6	6	24	17	6	1	14	21	42	37
17	Norwich City	42	11	5	5	42	26	2	4	15	17	52	35
18	Exeter City	42	12	4	5	45	22	2	2	17	15	47	34
19	Watford	42	8	8	5	32	24	2	5	14	19	52	33
20	Southend United	42	10	4	7	26	17	2	5	14	25	73	33
21	Croydon Common	42	8	2	11	29	38	5	3	13	23	58	31
22	Reading	42	7	6	8	27	25	0	4	17	11	48	24

1910/11

18th in Southern League Division One

	Date	Opponent	Score	Scorers	Att	Arthurs CH	Bailey AV	Cannon F	Court AC	Hawkes JM	Higgins M	Holmes T	Johns CW	Johnson AJ	Mahon J	Massey GH	Mosley A	Nobbs AH	Pickett AE	Reynolds J	Satterthwaite JN	Strang T	Sutherland A	Taylor J	Westwood E
1	Sep 3	Millwall	0-1						9		6	1			4			3	11	7	10	5	2	8	
2	10	QUEEN'S PARK RANGERS	1-0	Court	6000				9		6	1			4			3	11	7	10	5	2	8	
3	17	West Ham United	0-2		11000				9		6	1			4			3	11	7	10	5	2	8	
4	24	LUTON TOWN	2-1	Pickett, Taylor	7000			10	9		6	1			4			3	11	7		5	2	8	
5	28	BRENTFORD	2-1	Reynolds, Higgins	4000			10	9		6	1			4			3	11	7		5	2	8	
6	Oct 1	Portsmouth	0-2		7000			10	9		6	1			4			3	11			5	2	8	7
7	8	NORTHAMPTON T	0-0		6000			10	9		6	1			4			3	11	7		5	2	8	
8	15	Brighton & Hove Albion	0-2		7000	11		10	9	2	6	1			4			3		7		5		8	
9	22	EXETER CITY	1-0	Cannon	6000			10	9	2	6	1			4			3	11	7		5		8	
10	29	Swindon Town	0-5					10	9		6	1			4			3		7	11	5	2	8	
11	Nov 5	BRISTOL ROVERS	1-0	Taylor	5000			10	9		6	1	11		4			3		7		5	2	8	
12	12	Crystal Palace	2-3	Taylor, Satterthwaite	7000				9		6	1	11		4			3		7	10	5	2	8	
13	26	Leyton	1-2	Taylor				9		2	6	1	11		4			3		7	10	5		8	
14	Dec 10	Plymouth Argyle	0-3		4500	4		9			6	1	11				2	3		7	10	5		8	
15	17	SOUTHAMPTON	0-3		5000			9			6	1			4		2	3	11	7	10	5		8	
16	24	Southend United	2-2	Westwood, Court				8	9		6	1		5	4		2	3		7				10	11
17	26	COVENTRY CITY	2-1	Taylor, Court	7000	3		8	9		6	1		5	4		2			7				10	11
18	27	Coventry City	2-5	Reynolds, Taylor	7000	3	1	8	9		6			5	4		2			7				10	11
19	31	MILLWALL	0-2		4000			8	9	3	6	1		5	4		2			7				10	11
20	Jan 7	Queen's Park Rangers	0-5		4000				9		6	1			4		2	3		7	8	5		10	11
21	21	WEST HAM UNITED	1-1	Taylor	5000			10	9		6	1			4		2	3		7		5		8	11
22	28	Luton Town	0-3		5000			10			6	1			4		2	3		7	9	5		8	11
23	Feb 3	PORTSMOUTH	1-0	Court	5000			10	9		6	1			4		2	3		7		5		8	11
24	11	Northampton Town	1-2	Satterthwaite	4000			9			6	1			4	11	2	3		7	10	5		8	
25	18	BRIGHTON & HOVE ALB.	1-0	Reynolds	5000				9		6	1			4	11	2	3		7	10	5		8	
26	25	Exeter City	2-2	Reynolds, Arthurs (p)	4000	6			9			1			4	11	2	3		7	10	5		8	
27	Mar 4	SWINDON TOWN	1-0	Reynolds	6000				9		6	1			4	11	2	3		7	10	5		8	
28	11	Bristol Rovers	2-6	Court (p), Satterthwaite	5000				9		6	1			4	11	2	3		7	10	5		8	
29	18	CRYSTAL PALACE	2-0	Strang, Court	5000				9		6	1			4	11	2	3		7	10	5		8	
30	22	WATFORD	1-1	Satterthwaite	2500	5			9		6	1			4	11	2	3		7	10			8	
31	25	Brentford	2-0	Satterthwaite, Taylor		6		9				1			4	11	2	3		7	10	5		8	
32	Apr 1	LEYTON	0-1		4000	6		9				1			4	11	2	3		7	10	5		8	
33	8	Watford	0-3		3000				9		6	1			4	11	2	3		7	10	5		8	
34	14	NORWICH CITY	1-1	Taylor	7000				9		6	1			4	11	2	3		7	10	5		8	
35	15	PLYMOUTH ARGYLE	1-1	Satterthwaite (p)	5000				9		6	1			4	11	2	3		7	10	5		8	
36	17	Norwich City	1-2	Satterthwaite	11000			9		2	6	1	11		4	10		3		7	8	5			
37	22	Southampton	0-0							2	6	1	11		4	10		3		7	9	5		8	
38	29	SOUTHEND UNITED	1-2	Pickett				9		2	6	1		5	4			3	11	7	10			8	
					Apps	8	1	23	28	7	35	37	6	5	37	14	22	35	10	37	25	32	10	37	9
					Goals	1		1	6		1								2	5	7	1		9	1

F.A. Cup

	Date	Opponent	Score	Scorers	Att	Arthurs CH	Bailey AV	Cannon F	Court AC	Hawkes JM	Higgins M	Holmes T	Johns CW	Johnson AJ	Mahon J	Massey GH	Mosley A	Nobbs AH	Pickett AE	Reynolds J	Satterthwaite JN	Strang T	Sutherland A	Taylor J	Westwood E
Q4	Nov 19	Royal Engs. Aldershot	2-2	Taylor, Satterthwaite	2000				9		6	1	11		4			3		7	10	5	2	8	
rep	23	ROYAL ENGINEERS	7-0	Taylor 5, Cannon 2	3000			9		2	6	1			4			3	11	7	10	5		8	
Q5	Dec 3	CATFORD SOUTHEND	4-1	Cannon 3, Reynolds	3000			9		2	6	1	11		4			3		7	10	5		8	
R1	Jan 14	BRADFORD CITY	0-1		8600			10	9		6	1			4		2	3		7		5		8	11

		P	W	D	L	F	A	W	D	L	F	A	Pts
1	Swindon Town	38	16	2	1	54	9	8	3	8	26	22	53
2	Northampton Town	38	14	3	2	39	7	4	9	6	15	20	48
3	Brighton & Hove Alb.	38	15	2	2	41	12	5	6	8	17	24	48
4	Crystal Palace	38	11	5	3	35	23	6	8	5	20	25	47
5	West Ham United	38	12	6	1	44	17	5	5	9	19	29	45
6	Queen's Park Rangers	38	11	6	2	37	16	2	8	9	15	25	40
7	Leyton	38	13	3	3	37	15	3	5	11	20	37	40
8	Plymouth Argyle	38	10	6	3	37	14	5	3	11	17	41	39
9	Luton Town	38	13	4	2	42	18	2	4	13	25	45	38
10	Norwich City	38	12	5	2	31	13	3	3	13	15	35	38
11	Coventry City	38	12	4	3	47	21	4	2	13	18	47	38
12	Brentford	38	12	5	2	32	13	2	4	13	9	29	37
13	Exeter City	38	8	5	6	31	28	6	4	9	20	25	37
14	Watford	38	10	5	4	32	23	3	4	12	17	42	35
15	Millwall	38	8	3	8	21	20	3	6	10	21	34	31
16	Bristol Rovers	38	6	6	7	24	23	4	4	11	18	32	30
17	Southampton	38	8	3	8	25	28	3	5	11	17	39	30
18	NEW BROMPTON	38	10	5	4	19	15	1	3	15	15	50	30
19	Southend United	38	7	4	8	28	26	3	5	11	19	38	29
20	Portsmouth	38	6	10	3	21	15	2	1	16	13	38	27

1911/12

18th in Southern League Division One

	Date	Opponent	Score	Scorers	Att	Bailey AV	Bell A	Church AG	Corbett F	Court AC	Diddams E	Frost CJ	Goffin RFA	Gudgeon CW	Hawkes JM	Johns CW	Johnson AJ	Kelly T	Lee A	Mahon J	Massey GH	Mosley A	Nobbs AH	Strang T	Taylor J	Weavers SD	Westwood E	Whiteside E
1	Sep 2	LUTON TOWN	0-0		5000	1				9			8					6		4	11	2	3	5			7	10
2	9	Exeter City	1-8	Whiteside	7000	1				9									6	4	11	2	3	5		8	7	10
3	16	BRENTFORD	2-1	Lee (p), Goffin	5000	1							9			11		6	5	4		2	3		7	8		10
4	23	Queen's Park Rangers	0-3		12000	1							9			11		6	5	4		2	3		7	8		10
5	30	MILLWALL	1-3	Whiteside	4000	1				10			9					6	5	4		2	3		7	8		11
6	Oct 7	West Ham United	0-0		6000	1				9			8					6	5	4	11	2	3		10	7		
7	14	BRISTOL ROVERS	0-0		4000	1				9			8					6	5	4	11	2	3		10	7		
8	21	Swindon Town	0-5			1							8					6	5	4	11	2	3		10	9	7	
9	28	NORTHAMPTON T	1-3	Taylor	5000	1							8					6	5	4	11	2	3		10	9	7	
10	Nov 4	Brighton & Hove Albion	0-7		6000	1		7				11		9				6	5	4		2	3		8			10
11	11	STOKE	1-1	Court	5000	1		7	9	10									6	4	11	2	3	5	8			
12	25	LEYTON	0-2		3000	1		7	9				10					6	2	4	11		3	5	8			
13	Dec 2	Norwich City	0-1		5000	1			9	10			8		3				6	4		2		5	7			11
14	9	CRYSTAL PALACE	1-1	Corbett	5000	1			9	10			8					6		4	11	2	3	5	7			
15	16	Southampton	0-3			1			9	10			8						6	4	11	2	3	5	7			
16	23	PLYMOUTH ARGYLE	0-1		4000	1			9	10			8			11			6	4		2	3	5	7			
17	25	READING	1-0	Lee	5000	1				9			8			11		6	5	4		2	3		7			10
18	26	Reading	0-2		3000	1			9							11		6	5	4		2	3		7	8		10
19	20	Luton Town	0-3			1			9							11		6	5	4		2	3		7	8		10
20	Jan 6	EXETER CITY	4-1	Court 2, Johns, Taylor	1500	1		7		10	9					11		6	5	4		2	3		8			
21	20	Brentford	1-7	Goffin	3000		1	7			9		10			11		6	5	4		2	3		8			
22	27	QUEEN'S PARK RANGERS	1-2	Lee (p)	4000		1	7		10	9				3	11	6		5	4		2			8			
23	Feb 3	Millwall	1-1	Taylor	10000	1				10	9		7		3	11	6		5	4		2			8			
24	10	WEST HAM UNITED	0-3		5000	1				10	9		7		3	11	6		5	4		2			8			
25	17	Bristol Rovers	1-0	Lee	3000	1			9	10			7		3	11	6		5	4		2			8			
26	24	Coventry City	2-3	Goffin, Jones	5000	1			9	10			7		3	11	6		5	4		2			8			
27	Mar 2	Northampton Town	2-1	Taylor, Johns	4000	1			9	10			7		3	11	6		5	4		2			8			
28	9	BRIGHTON & HOVE ALB.	0-0		5000	1			9				7			11	6		5	4	10	2	3		8			
29	16	Stoke	0-2		5000	1			9	10			7		3	11	6		5	4		2			8			
30	23	COVENTRY CITY	3-3	Goffin, Lee, Mahon	2000	1			9	10			7		3		6		5	4		2			8			11
31	30	Leyton	2-0	Johnson, Corbett	3000	1			9	10			7		3		6		5	4		2			8			11
32	Apr 5	WATFORD	1-0	Corbett	5000	1			9	10			7		3		6		5	4		2			8			11
33	6	NORWICH CITY	3-1	Corbett 2, Taylor	7000	1			9	10			7		3		6		5	4		2			8			11
34	8	Watford	1-0	Corbett	7000	1			9	10			7		3		6		5	4		2			8			11
36	13	Crystal Palace	1-1	Whiteside	7000	1			9	10			7		3		6		5	4		2			8			11
35	17	SWINDON TOWN	3-1	Whiteside, Taylor, Goffin		1			9	10			7		3		6		5	4		2			8			11
37	20	SOUTHAMPTON	1-0	Lee	6000	1			9	10			7		3		6		5	4		2			8			11
38	27	Plymouth Argyle	0-2		9000	1			9	10			7		3		6		5	4		2			8			11
					Apps	36	2	6	22	28	5	1	31	1	17	16	17	16	36	38	11	37	21	8	36	10	4	19
					Goals				6	3			5			3	1		6	1					6			4

F.A. Cup

	Date	Opponent	Score	Scorers	Att	Bailey AV	Bell A	Church AG	Corbett F	Court AC	Diddams E	Frost CJ	Goffin RFA	Gudgeon CW	Hawkes JM	Johns CW	Johnson AJ	Kelly T	Lee A	Mahon J	Massey GH	Mosley A	Nobbs AH	Strang T	Taylor J	Weavers SD	Westwood E	Whiteside E
Q4	Nov 22	CROYDON COMMON	1-2	Church		1		9		10									6	4	11	2	3	5	8		7	

		P	W	D	L	F	A	W	D	L	F	A	Pts
1	Queen's Park Rangers	38	12	5	2	36	14	9	6	4	23	21	53
2	Plymouth Argyle	38	16	2	1	42	7	7	4	8	21	24	52
3	Northampton Town	38	16	2	1	57	15	6	5	8	25	26	51
4	Swindon Town	38	14	3	2	52	19	7	3	9	30	31	48
5	Brighton & Hove Alb.	38	15	2	2	54	12	4	7	8	19	23	47
6	Coventry City	38	14	3	2	46	15	3	5	11	20	39	42
7	Crystal Palace	38	11	5	3	43	14	4	5	10	27	32	40
8	Millwall	38	11	6	2	43	19	4	4	11	17	38	40
9	Watford	38	10	5	4	35	20	3	5	11	21	48	36
10	Stoke	38	11	4	4	35	25	2	6	11	16	38	36
11	Reading	38	10	7	2	35	14	1	7	11	8	45	36
12	Norwich City	38	8	10	1	27	17	2	4	13	13	43	34
13	West Ham United	38	10	3	6	40	27	3	4	12	24	42	33
14	Brentford	38	10	5	4	43	18	2	4	13	17	47	33
15	Exeter City	38	8	6	5	30	22	3	5	11	18	40	33
16	Southampton	38	9	3	7	29	27	1	8	10	17	36	31
17	Bristol Rovers	38	7	8	4	24	18	2	5	12	17	44	31
18	NEW BROMPTON	38	7	6	6	23	23	4	3	12	12	49	31
19	Luton Town	38	7	5	7	33	28	2	5	12	16	33	28
20	Leyton	38	6	8	5	15	19	1	3	15	12	43	25

1912/13

15th in Southern League Division One

							Bailey AV	Bell MD	Boden J	Caldwell T	Church AG	Court AC	Crane HE	Frost CJ	Glen P	Goffin RFA	Hafekost CH	Johns CW	Johnson AJ	Lagan TH	Lee A	Leslie T	Mahon J	Mosley A	Taylor J	Wolstenholme A
1	Sep	7	Northampton Town	1-2	Wolstenholme	8000	1	5		11		9				7	8		6	3			4	2		10
2		14	QUEEN'S PARK RANGERS	0-0		8000	1	5		11		9				7	8		6	3			4	2		10
3		21	Brentford	1-0	Court	6000	1	5		11		9				7	8		6	3			4	2		10
4		28	MILLWALL	0-0		8000	1	5		11				7		8	9		6	3			4	2		10
5	Oct	2	Reading	1-2	Frost		1	5		11				7		8	9		6	3			4	2		10
6		5	Bristol Rovers	2-0	Wolstenholme, Goffin	5000	1	5						11		7			6	3		9	4	2	8	10
7		12	SWINDON TOWN	0-0			1	5		11						7			6	3		9	4	2	8	10
8		16	READING	0-4		3000	1	5				10		11		7			6	3		9	4	2	8	
9		19	Portsmouth	1-2	Hafekost	12000	1	5						11		7	9		6	3		10	4	2	8	
10		26	EXETER CITY	0-4		3000	1	5	9					11		7	8		6	3			4	2		10
11	Nov	2	West Ham United	0-4		10000		5	9	11			1	7		8			6	3			4	2		10
12		9	BRIGHTON & HOVE ALB.	0-0		6000		8	9			10	1			7		11	6		5	3	4	2		
13		16	Coventry City	2-1	Boden, Goffin	7000		8	9				1	11		7			6		5	3	4	2		10
14		23	WATFORD	2-0	Boden, Taylor			4	9				1			7	11		6		5	3		2	8	10
15		30	MERTHYR TOWN	1-1	Boden	5000		4	9				1			7	11		6		5	3		2	8	10
16	Dec	7	CRYSTAL PALACE	1-2	Boden	5000		4	9	11			1			7			6		5	3		2	8	10
17		21	SOUTHAMPTON	0-1		5000		4	9	11			1				7		6		5	3		2	8	10
18		25	NORWICH CITY	1-0	Goffin	4000		4	9	11			1			7				6	5	3		2	8	10
19		26	Norwich City	0-4		6000		4	9	11			1				7			6	5	3		2	8	10
20		28	NORTHAMPTON T	2-1	Caldwell, Johnson (p)	5000		5	9	11			1			7			6	4		3		2	8	10
21	Jan	4	Queen's Park Rangers	0-2		8000		5	9	11			1			7			6			3	4	2	8	10
22		18	BRENTFORD	0-4		5000		4	9	11			1			7			6		5	3		2	8	10
23		25	Millwall	1-2	Wolstenholme		1	8		11					9	7			6		5	3	4	2		10
24	Feb	8	BRISTOL ROVERS	1-0	Wolstenholme	5000	1	8		11					9	7			6		5	3	4	2		10
25		15	Swindon Town	1-2	Boden		1		9	11						8			6		5	3	4	2	7	10
26		22	PORTSMOUTH	2-0	Taylor 2		1	4	9	11						7			6		5	3		2	8	10
27	Mar	1	Exeter City	0-2		5000	1		9	11						7			6		5	3	4	2	8	10
28		8	WEST HAM UNITED	2-2	Hafekost, Caldwell	4000	1	5		11	7					8	9	10	6			3	4	2		
29		15	Brighton & Hove Albion	0-1		3500	1	5		11	7					8	9	10	6			3	4	2		
30		21	STOKE	0-0		5000	1	5		11	7					8	9	10	6			3	4	2		
31		22	COVENTRY CITY	3-0	Goffin 2, Hafekost	6000	1			11	7					8	9	10	6		5	3	4	2		
32		24	Stoke	2-0	Lee 2		1			11	7					8	9	10	6		5	3	4	2		
33		29	Watford	1-1	Hafekost		1			11	7					8	9	10	6		5	3	4	2		
34	Apr	5	Merthyr Town	0-0			1			11	7					8	9	10	6		5	3	4	2		
35		12	Crystal Palace	1-0	Church	10000	1			11	7					8	9	10	6		5	3	4	2		
36		19	Plymouth Argyle	0-4		9000	1			11	7					8	9	10	6		5	3	4	2		
37		26	Southampton	3-3	Hafekost, Johns, Frost		1			11				7		8	9	10	6		5	3	4	2		
38		30	PLYMOUTH ARGYLE	4-2	Johnson 2 (2p), Johns, Lee	1500	1			11				7		8	9	10	6		5	3	4	2		
						Apps	26	28	16	30	9	5	12	10	2	36	22	12	36	14	22	31	29	38	16	24
						Goals			5	2	1	1		2		5	5	2	3		3				3	4

F.A. Cup

							Bailey AV	Bell MD	Boden J	Caldwell T	Church AG	Court AC	Crane HE	Frost CJ	Glen P	Goffin RFA	Hafekost CH	Johns CW	Johnson AJ	Lagan TH	Lee A	Leslie T	Mahon J	Mosley A	Taylor J	Wolstenholme A
Q5	Dec	14	Spennymoor United	1-1	Wolstenholme	5000		4	9	11			1				7		6		5	3		2	8	10
rep		18	SPENNYMOOR UTD.	3-0	Wolstenholme 2 (1p), Taylor	1600		4	9	11			1				7		6		5	3		2	8	10
R1	Jan	11	BARNSLEY	0-0		11321		4	9	11			1			7			6		5	3		2	8	10
rep		16	Barnsley	1-3	Goffin	9561		4	9	11			1			7			6		5	3		2	8	10

Walkover in Q4 when drawn against Leyton

		P	*W*	*D*	*L*	*F*	*A*	*W*	*D*	*L*	*F*	*A*	*Pts*
1	Plymouth Argyle	38	15	2	2	47	9	7	4	8	30	27	50
2	Swindon Town	38	13	5	1	44	16	7	3	9	22	25	48
3	West Ham United	38	11	6	2	39	15	7	6	6	27	31	48
4	Queen's Park Rangers	38	14	4	1	33	10	4	6	9	13	26	46
5	Crystal Palace	38	13	3	3	38	13	4	8	7	17	23	45
6	Millwall	38	14	0	5	36	17	5	7	7	26	26	45
7	Exeter City	38	13	3	3	29	16	5	5	9	19	28	44
8	Reading	38	12	3	4	34	20	5	5	9	25	35	42
9	Brighton & Hove Alb.	38	12	5	2	39	19	1	7	11	9	28	38
10	Northampton Town	38	11	4	4	42	17	1	8	10	19	31	36
11	Portsmouth	38	11	5	3	28	15	3	3	13	13	34	36
12	Merthyr Town	38	9	8	2	27	17	3	4	12	16	43	36
13	Coventry City	38	9	4	6	42	27	4	4	11	11	32	34
14	Watford	38	8	5	6	28	24	4	5	10	15	26	34
15	GILLINGHAM	38	7	7	5	19	21	5	3	11	17	32	34
16	Bristol Rovers	38	9	6	4	37	23	3	3	13	18	41	33
17	Southampton	38	7	7	5	28	25	3	4	12	12	47	31
18	Norwich City	38	8	7	4	26	17	2	2	15	13	33	29
19	Brentford	38	10	3	6	27	17	1	2	16	15	38	27
20	Stoke	38	8	3	8	21	17	2	1	16	18	58	24

1913/14

13th in Southern League Division One

							Bailey AV	Caldwell T	Court AC	Diddams E	Fotheringham CD	Frost CJ	Frost WG	Gilligan SA	Glen P	Goffin RFA	Hafekost CH	Hulses S	Johns CW	Johnson AJ	Lee A	Leslie T	Mahon J	Mosley A	Pepper W	Pinkney E	Tatton JH	Weavers SD	Whiteside T
1	Sep	3	COVENTRY CITY	0-2		5000	1	11						8			9		10	6	5	3	4	2		7			
2		6	QUEEN'S PARK RANGERS	1-0	Gilligan	6000	1	11						8			9		10	6	5	3	4	2		7			
3		11	Coventry City	3-2	Caldwell, Pinkney, Gilligan	5000	1	11						8			9		10	6	5	3	4	2		7			
4		13	Northampton Town	1-3	Hafekost		1	11						8			9		10	6	5	3	4	2		7			
5		20	SOUTHEND UNITED	4-2	Lee 2, Glen, Johnson (p)	6000		11						8	9		10			6	5	3	4	2	1	7			
6		24	PLYMOUTH ARGYLE	4-0	Caldwell, Gilligan, Hafekost, Pinkney	5000	1	11						8	9		10			6	5	3	4	2		7			
7		27	Brighton & Hove Albion	0-2		6000	1	11						8	9		10			6	5	3	4	2		7			
8	Oct	4	PORTSMOUTH	0-1		8000	1	11						8	9		10			6	5	3	4	2		7			
9		11	Millwall	0-0			1	11						8	9		10			6	5	3	4	2		7			
10		18	EXETER CITY	2-0	Gilligan, Glen	7000	1	11						8	9		10			6	5	3	4	2		7			
11		25	Cardiff City	0-2		11000	1	11						8	9		10			6	5	3	4	2		7			
12	Nov	1	SWINDON TOWN	2-3	Glen 2	12000	1	11						8	9		10			6	5	3	4	2		7			
13		8	Bristol Rovers	1-3	Hafekost		1	11						8	9		10			6	5	3	4	2		7			
14		15	MERTHYR TOWN	2-1	Pinkney, Glen	6000	1	11	10					8	9					6	5	3	4	2		7			
15		22	West Ham United	1-3	Caldwell	10000	1	11						8	9	7	10				5	3	4	2					6
16	Dec	6	Southampton	1-3	Glen		1							8	9		10	5	11	6		3	4	2		7			
17		20	Crystal Palace	0-1		6000	1					11		8	9		10			6	5	3	4	2			7		
18		25	Watford	2-0	Hafekost 2		1							9		8	10			6	5	3	4	2		7	11		
19		26	WATFORD	3-0	Hafekost, Goffin, Glen	6000	1								9	8	10			6	5	3	4	2		7	11		
20		27	Queen's Park Rangers	0-0		8000	1								9	8	10			6	5	3	4	2		7	11		
21	Jan	3	NORTHAMPTON T	1-1	Pinkney	6000	1						2	9		8	10			6	5	3	4			7	11		
22		17	Southend United	3-2	Pinkney, Gilligan, Glen		1							8	9		10			6	5	3	4	2		7	11		
23		24	BRIGHTON & HOVE ALB.	4-0	Hafekost 2, Mahon, Leslie (p)	6000	1							8	9		10			6	5	3	4	2		7	11		
24	Feb	7	Portsmouth	0-0		7000	1				11			8	9				10	6	5	3	4	2		7			
25		14	MILLWALL	2-2	Weavers, Hafekost	6000	1							8			10			6	5	3	4	2		7	11	9	
26		21	Exeter City	0-2		2500	1							8			10			6	5	3	4	2		7	11	9	
27		28	CARDIFF CITY	0-0		6000	1							8	9		10			6	5	3	4	2		7	11		
28	Mar	7	Swindon Town	1-5	Hafekost		1							8	9	7	10			6	5	3	4	2			11		
29		14	BRISTOL ROVERS	3-0	Leslie (p), Pinkney, Goffin	5000	1								9	7	10			6	5	3	4	2		8	11		
30		21	Merthyr Town	0-2		5000	1								9	7	10			6	5	3	4	2		8	11		
31		28	WEST HAM UNITED	3-1	Gilligan 2, Pinkney	7000	1	11						10	9					6	5	3	4	2		8	7		
32	Apr	1	READING	0-0		5000	1	11						10	9					6	5	3	4	2		8	7		
33		4	Plymouth Argyle	0-1		6000	1	11	9				2	10						6	5	3	4			8	7		
34		10	NORWICH CITY	0-0		7000	1	11							9		10			6	5	3	4	2		8	7		
35		11	SOUTHAMPTON	3-1	Pinkney 2, McAlphine (og)	7000	1	11		5				10	9	7				6		3	4	2		8			
36		13	Norwich City	0-2		12000	1	11		5				10	9	7				6		3	4	2		8			
37		18	Reading	0-1			1			5	11			10	9					6		3	4	2		8	7		
38		25	CRYSTAL PALACE	1-1	Fotheringham	8000	1				11			10	9					6	5	3	4	2		8	7		
						Apps	37	21	2	3	3	1	2	33	29	10	29	1	6	37	34	38	38	36	1	35	19	2	1
						Goals		3			1			7	8	2	10			1	2	2	1			9		1	

One own goal

F.A. Cup

							Bailey AV	Caldwell T	Court AC	Diddams E	Fotheringham CD	Frost CJ	Frost WG	Gilligan SA	Glen P	Goffin RFA	Hafekost CH	Hulses S	Johns CW	Johnson AJ	Lee A	Leslie T	Mahon J	Mosley A	Pepper W	Pinkney E	Tatton JH	Weavers SD	Whiteside T
Q4	Nov	29	NUNHEAD	2-0	Glen, Gilligan	5000	1	11						8	9	7	10			6	5	3	4	2					
Q5	Dec	13	WATFORD	1-0	Lee	6000	1								9		10		11	6	5	3	4	2		7		8	
R1	Jan	10	BLACKPOOL	1-0	Leslie (p)	10581	1							8	9		10			6	5	3	4	2		7	11		
R2		31	Liverpool	0-2		42045	1							8	9		10			6	5	3	4	2		7	11		

		P	W	D	L	F	A	W	D	L	F	A	Pts
1	Swindon Town	38	14	3	2	57	11	7	5	7	24	30	50
2	Crystal Palace	38	12	5	2	41	13	5	11	3	19	19	50
3	Northampton Town	38	11	8	0	31	11	3	11	5	19	26	47
4	Reading	38	14	4	1	32	12	3	6	10	11	24	44
5	Plymouth Argyle	38	11	6	2	25	12	4	7	8	21	30	43
6	West Ham United	38	9	7	3	39	22	6	5	8	22	38	42
7	Brighton & Hove Alb.	38	12	5	2	30	16	3	7	9	13	29	42
8	Queen's Park Rangers	38	10	6	3	28	14	6	3	10	17	29	41
9	Portsmouth	38	10	7	2	31	13	4	5	10	26	35	40
10	Cardiff City	38	10	6	3	27	11	3	6	10	19	31	38
11	Southampton	38	11	2	6	36	23	4	5	10	19	31	37
12	Exeter City	38	7	8	4	21	11	3	8	8	18	27	36
13	GILLINGHAM	38	10	6	3	35	15	3	3	13	13	34	35
14	Norwich City	38	7	10	2	34	19	2	7	10	15	32	35
15	Millwall	38	10	6	3	34	20	1	6	12	17	36	34
16	Southend United	38	7	7	5	29	28	3	5	11	12	38	32
17	Bristol Rovers	38	10	5	4	32	25	0	6	13	14	42	31
18	Watford	38	9	4	6	37	20	1	5	13	13	36	29
19	Merthyr Town	38	7	7	5	23	18	2	3	14	15	43	28
20	Coventry City	38	4	8	7	28	28	2	6	11	15	40	26

1914/15

Bottom of Southern League Division One

No	Month	Day	Opponent	Score	Scorers	Att	Bailey AV	Branfield J	Burgess GF	Fotheringham CD	Frost WG	Gilligan SA	Glen P	Gray GR	Hall FJ	Hooper W	Johnson AJ	Lee A	Leslie T	Lovett M	Mahon J	Mosley A	Pinkney E	Tatton JH	Thomas WSL	Weavers SD	Weightman D	Wimsett WJ
1	Sep	1	West Ham United	1-2	Glen	5000	1						9			7	6	5	3	10	4	2	8	11				
2		5	Brighton & Hove Albion	1-2	Pinkney	3000	1					10	9			7	6	5	3		4	2	8	11				
3		9	WEST HAM UNITED	4-0	Glen, Leslie (p), Lee, Hooper	2500	1					10	9			7	6	5	3		4	2	8	11				
4		12	CARDIFF CITY	1-1	Lee	2500	1					10	9			7	6	5	3		4	2	8	11				
5		19	Exeter City	0-2		4000	1					10	9			7	6	5	3		4	2	8	11				
6		26	LUTON TOWN	2-4	Leslie (p), Lee	5000	1					10	9			7	6	5	3		4	2	8	11				
7	Oct	3	Portsmouth	0-1		8000	1				11	9	8	4			6	5	3			2	10	7				
8		10	SWINDON TOWN	4-0	Gilligan 2, Leslie (p), Pinkney	8000	1					9	10			7	6	5	3		4	2	8	11				
9		17	Southend United	1-1	Thomas		1					9		8		7	6	5	3		4	2		11	10			
10		24	QUEEN'S PARK RANGERS	0-1		7000	1						9			7	6	5	3		4	2	8	11	10			
11		31	Millwall	0-3			1			11		9	8				6	5	3		4	2	7		10			
12	Nov	7	BRISTOL ROVERS	0-1		7000	1					9	8			7	6	4	3		4	2		11	10			
13		14	Croydon Common	1-8	Pinkney	4000			2			9			1	7	6	5	3		4		8	11	10			
14		21	READING	0-5		3000	1		2				10	6		7		5	3		4		8		11	9		
15		28	Southampton	1-2	Mahon	2000	1					8		6		7		5	3		4	2		11	10	9		
16	Dec	5	NORTHAMPTON T	2-2	Weavers, Leslie (p)	2000	1					8		6		7		5	3		4	2		11	10	9		
17		12	Watford	0-4		2500	1					10		6		7			3		4	2	8	11	9		5	
18		19	PLYMOUTH ARGYLE	0-0		6500	1					10		6		7		5	3		4	2	8	11			9	
19		25	NORWICH CITY	3-3	Gilligan, Weightman, Glen	2000	1					10	9			7			3		4	2	8	11		6	5	
20		26	Norwich City	0-4		3000	1		2			10	9			7			3		4		8	11		6	5	
21	Jan	2	BRIGHTON & HOVE ALB.	1-3	Glen	2500	1		2			9	10	6		7			3		4		8	11			5	
22		16	Cardiff City	1-3	Thomas	4000	1					8		6				5	3		4	2	7	11	10		9	
23		23	EXETER CITY	0-0		2000	1							4			6	5	3			2	8	7	10		9	11
24		30	Luton Town	1-3	Weightman		1					8		5			6		3		4	2	7		10		9	11
25	Feb	6	PORTSMOUTH	3-1	Weightman, Thomas, Gilligan	2000	1					8		5			6		3		4	2	7		10		9	11
26		13	Swindon Town	1-5	Weightman		1					8		5			6		3		4	2	7		10		9	11
27		20	SOUTHEND UNITED	1-0	Gilligan	3000	1					8		5		11	6		3		4	2	7		10		9	
28		20	Queen's Park Rangers	0-3		3000	1						8	5			6		3		4	2	7		10		9	11
29	Mar	6	MILLWALL	0-0			1					8					6	5	3		4	2	7		10		9	11
30		13	Bristol Rovers	1-2	Gilligan	3000	1					8	9				6	5	3		4	2	7	11			10	
31		20	CROYDON COMMON	2-2	Glen, Pinkney	3000	1					8	9				6	5	3		4	2	7	11			10	
32		27	Reading	0-1			1					8	9				6	5	3		4	2	7	11			10	
33	Apr	2	CRYSTAL PALACE	3-0	Tatton 2, Weightman	6000	1					8	9			7	6	5	3		4	2		11			10	
34		3	SOUTHAMPTON	4-3	Glen 2, Gilligan 2	3000		1				8	9			7	6	5	3		4	2		11			10	
35		5	Crystal Palace	0-1				1				8	9			7	6	5	3		4	2		11			10	
36		10	Northampton Town	0-4			1					8	9			7	6	5	3		4	2		11			10	
37		17	WATFORD	2-3	Leslie (p), Glen	3000	1					10	9				6	5	3		4	2		11	7		8	
38		24	Plymouth Argyle	2-3	Weightman 2	5000	1						9	5		7	6		3	8	4	2		11			10	
						Apps	35	2	4	1	1	32	25	16	1	25	29	28	38	2	36	34	28	30	18	5	22	6
						Goals						8	8			1		3	5		1		4	2	3	1	7	

F.A. Cup

Rd	Month	Day	Opponent	Score	Scorers	Att	Bailey AV	Branfield J	Burgess GF	Fotheringham CD	Frost WG	Gilligan SA	Glen P	Gray GR	Hall FJ	Hooper W	Johnson AJ	Lee A	Leslie T	Lovett M	Mahon J	Mosley A	Pinkney E	Tatton JH	Thomas WSL	Weavers SD	Weightman D	Wimsett WJ
R1	Jan	9	Rochdale	0-2		6000	1					9	10				6	5	3		4	2	7	11			8	

		P	W	D	L	F	A	W	D	L	F	A	Pts
1	Watford	38	12	4	3	37	15	10	4	5	31	31	52
2	Reading	38	12	4	3	37	16	9	3	7	31	27	49
3	Cardiff City	38	16	1	2	51	12	6	3	10	21	26	48
4	West Ham United	38	14	4	1	42	18	4	5	10	16	29	45
5	Northampton Town	38	11	5	3	37	22	5	6	8	19	29	43
6	Southampton	38	14	3	2	56	28	5	2	12	22	46	43
7	Portsmouth	38	10	5	4	26	14	6	5	8	28	28	42
8	Millwall	38	9	4	6	28	23	7	6	6	22	28	42
9	Swindon Town	38	11	5	3	55	21	4	6	9	22	38	41
10	Brighton & Hove Alb.	38	11	5	3	29	16	5	2	12	17	31	39
11	Exeter City	38	10	3	6	32	16	5	5	9	18	25	38
12	Queen's Park Rangers	38	8	4	7	30	28	5	8	6	25	28	38
13	Norwich City	38	10	6	3	33	16	1	8	10	20	40	36
14	Luton Town	38	6	3	10	27	34	7	5	7	34	39	34
15	Crystal Palace	38	8	4	7	24	25	5	4	10	23	36	34
16	Bristol Rovers	38	12	2	5	42	28	2	1	16	11	47	31
17	Plymouth Argyle	38	8	7	4	34	25	0	7	12	17	36	30
18	Southend United	38	8	5	6	27	20	2	3	14	17	44	28
19	Croydon Common	38	7	6	6	28	18	2	3	14	19	45	27
20	GILLINGHAM	38	6	7	6	32	29	0	1	18	11	54	20

1915/16 to 1918/19

No League games played due to the Great War.

1919/20

Bottom of Southern League Division One

No	Month	Day	Opponent	Result	Scorers	Att	Beale RH	Branfield J	Buchanan R	Cartwright W	Cavanna R	Chalmers D	Elliott CJ	Frost WG	Griffiths JA	Hibden WJ	Johns CW	Kelly H	Kennedy JJ	Lee A	Lee H	Leslie TH	Mahon J	McCormick D	Nash HE	Neill J	Ramsell LT	Read B	Redpath A	Savage W	Steel A	Steel RL	Wood AB
1	Aug	30	WATFORD	0-0		7000	1		2		6	10										3	4			7				11			9
2	Sep	1	Luton Town	0-2		4000	1		2		6	10		8								3	4			7				11			9
3		6	Swansea Town	1-0	Savage	2304	1		2		6	10		8						5		3	4			7				11			9
4		10	LUTON TOWN	2-0	Wood 2 (1p)		1		2		6	10		8						5		3	4			7				11			9
5		13	EXETER CITY	0-0		7808	1					10				6				5		3	4			7		8		11			9
6		17	SOUTHEND UNITED	0-1		6000	1		2			10		8		6				5		3	4			7				11			9
7		20	Cardiff City	0-5		10000	1		2		6	8		7		10				5		3	4							11			9
8		27	QUEEN'S PARK RANGERS	0-1		7432	1									6	10			5	8	3	4		7					11			9
9	Oct	4	Swindon Town	2-5	Chalmers, Wood (p)	5000	1			2		10				6	11			5	8	3	4		7								9
10		6	PLYMOUTH ARGYLE	0-2		2500				2				8		6	10			5		3	4		7					11			9
11		11	MILLWALL	2-0	Wood 2	7000	1			2		8				6	11			5		3	4		7					10			9
12		18	Brighton & Hove Albion	0-3		8000	1			2		8				6				5		3	4		7			10		11			9
13		25	NEWPORT COUNTY	1-3	Johns	8000	1			2		8				6	11			5		3	4		7				10				9
14	Nov	1	Portsmouth	0-4		10000				2		8				6				5		3	4		7				10	11			9
15		8	NORTHAMPTON T	0-0		7000			3	2						6					7		4						10				8
16		15	Crystal Palace	1-4	Redpath				3	2						6					7		4					9	10				8
17		29	Norwich City	0-5		6000				2						10		11	5		7	3	4				9				6		8
18	Dec	6	BRENTFORD	0-2		7000				2								11	5	4		3	8		7			9	10		6		
19		13	Merthyr Town	0-4						2								11	5	4		3			7			9	8		6	10	
20		25	READING	1-2	B Read	8000			2							4		11		5	8	3					7	9			6	10	
21		26	Reading	0-3				1	2				4					11	5			3		8			7	9			6	10	
22		27	Bristol Rovers	1-1	R Steel	14000		1	2				4					11	9	5		3		8			7				6	10	
23	Jan	3	Watford	1-2	McCormick	4000		1	2				11							5		3	4	8			7	9			6	10	
24		24	Exeter City	1-2	Savage	6000		1	2									11				3	4				7	9		10	6	5	8
25	Feb	7	Queen's Park Rangers	0-0				1		2								11			9	3	4					7	10		6	5	8
26		14	SWINDON TOWN	3-1	H Lee 2, R Steel	10000		1		2								11	6		9	3	4					7	10			5	8
27		21	Millwall	0-1		12000		1		2									5		9	3	4					7	10	11	6		8
28		28	BRIGHTON & HOVE ALB.	2-3	Wood 2	10000		1		2			7					11	5		9	3	4								6	10	8
29	Mar	6	Newport County	0-4				1		2								11			9	3	4		7				10		5	6	8
30		13	PORTSMOUTH	0-0		7783		1		2								11		4	9	3			7					10	6	5	8
31		17	CARDIFF CITY	3-0	H Lee, B Read, Savage	6000		1		2								11		4	8	3			7			9		10	6	5	
32		20	Northampton Town	0-1				1		2								11		4	8	3			7			9		10	6	5	
33		27	CRYSTAL PALACE	2-4	B Read, Wood (p)	7000		1		2				7				11		4	8	3						9			6	5	10
34	Apr	2	SOUTHAMPTON	2-0	Wood, Kelly	8794		1		2				7				11		5	9	3	4								6	10	8
35		3	Southend United	1-0	Wood	7000		1	3					7			11			5	9		4								6	10	8
36		5	Southampton	0-2		12000		1	3					7			11			5			4					9			6	10	8
37		10	NORWICH CITY	1-0	Wood	6000		1	3									11		5			4	9		7				10	6		8
38		17	Brentford	2-1	H Lee, Wood			1	3									11		5	9		4			7					6	10	8
39		19	SWANSEA TOWN	0-1		2000		1										11	6	5	9	3	4			7			10				8
40		24	MERTHYR TOWN	3-1	R Steel, A Lee (p), Griffiths	7000		1	3						7	6		11		5	9		4				8					10	
41		26	Plymouth Argyle	0-2		9000		1	3						7			11		5	9	2	4				8		10		6		
42	May	1	BRISTOL ROVERS	2-2	B Read, Mahon (p)	6000									7					5	8	3	4				10	9			6		
						Apps	12	21	19	21	5	12	4	10	3	15	7	21	9	30	22	35	34	4	13	9	9	17	12	18	23	19	31
						Goals						1			1		1	1		1	4		1	1				4	1	3	1	2	12

Played in one game: C Denny (15, at 9), W Hunter (5, at 2),
TF Turner (1, at 8), SP Gore (42, 11)
TW Read played at 1 in games 10 and 14
JH Meath played at 1 in games 17 and 42
Played in games 15 and 16 only: AH Harris (5), H Dawson (11), JW Joyce (1)
AW Bluer played at 5 in games 1 and 2, and at 2 in game 8. W Bower played ay 1 in games 18, 19 and 20
JW Robertson played in seven games at 2; 35 to 40 inclusive, and 42

F.A. Cup

Rd	Month	Day	Opponent	Result	Scorers	Att	Beale RH	Branfield J	Buchanan R	Cartwright W	Cavanna R	Chalmers D	Elliott CJ	Frost WG	Griffiths JA	Hibden WJ	Johns CW	Kelly H	Kennedy JJ	Lee A	Lee H	Leslie TH	Mahon J	McCormick D	Nash HE	Neill J	Ramsell LT	Read B	Redpath A	Savage W	Steel A	Steel RL	Wood AB
Q6	Dec	20	SWANSEA TOWN	1-1	Leslie (p)	10000			2							4		11		5	7	3						9			6	10	8
rep		24	Swansea Town	1-1	Ramsell	10000			2			10				4		11		5	8	3					7	9			6		
rep2		29	Swansea Town	0-0		6000		1	2				4					11		5	8	3					7	9			6	10	
rep3		30	Swansea Town	3-1	Wood 2, R Steel	15000		1	2									11		5		3	4				7	9			6	10	8
R1	Jan	17	West Stanley	1-3	B Read			1	2									11		5		3	4				7	9			6	10	8

Replay 2 at Cardiff, Replay 3 at Stamford Bridge

W Bower played at 1 in Q6 and Q6 replay

		P	*W*	*D*	*L*	*F*	*A*	*W*	*D*	*L*	*F*	*A*	*Pts*
1	Portsmouth	42	13	6	2	48	14	10	6	5	25	13	58
2	Watford	42	15	3	3	39	12	11	3	7	30	30	58
3	Crystal Palace	42	15	5	1	44	15	7	7	7	25	28	56
4	Cardiff City	42	15	3	3	44	14	3	14	4	26	29	53
5	Plymouth Argyle	42	13	5	3	35	8	7	5	9	21	21	50
6	Queen's Park Rangers	42	12	7	2	39	13	6	3	12	23	37	46
7	Reading	42	11	5	5	30	14	5	8	8	21	29	45
8	Southampton	42	13	4	4	51	22	5	4	12	21	41	44
9	Swansea Town	42	11	4	6	28	14	5	7	9	25	31	43
10	Exeter City	42	14	3	4	44	22	3	6	12	13	30	43
11	Southend United	42	10	8	3	32	18	3	9	9	14	30	43
12	Norwich City	42	12	7	2	46	17	3	4	14	18	40	41
13	Swindon Town	42	13	4	4	45	25	4	3	14	20	42	41
14	Millwall	42	10	7	4	32	20	4	5	12	20	35	40
15	Brentford	42	11	5	5	35	21	4	5	12	18	38	40
16	Brighton & Hove Alb.	42	11	5	5	43	28	3	3	15	17	44	36
17	Bristol Rovers	42	10	7	4	43	29	1	6	14	19	49	35
18	Newport County	42	11	5	5	32	18	2	2	17	13	52	33
19	Northampton Town	42	8	4	9	35	40	4	5	12	29	63	33
20	Luton Town	42	7	7	7	29	28	3	3	15	22	48	30
21	Merthyr Town	42	7	6	8	30	32	2	5	14	17	47	29
22	GILLINGHAM	42	7	5	9	24	23	3	2	16	10	51	27

1920/21

Bottom of Football League Division Three

No	Month	Day	Opponent	Score	Scorers	Att	Battiste W	Baxter TJC	Branfield J	Carter AJ	Gilbey TE	Gore SP	Griffiths JA	Hall T	Holt A	Howard JF	McCormick D	McMillan ST	Milton A	Needham GW	Ollerenshaw E	Robertson JW	Robinson TJD	Roe A	Russell GT	Shaw GE	Sisson T	Thompson TN	Waugh J	Wigmore C	Wood AB	Wright H
1	Aug	28	SOUTHAMPTON	1-1	Gilbey	12000	4	5	1		9	11		8	7							2		10			3			6		
2	Sep	1	Reading	2-1	Roe, Gilbey	7000	4	5	1		9	11		8	7							2		10			3			6		
3		4	Southampton	0-3		14000	4	5	1		9	11		8	7							2		10			3			6		
4		8	READING	1-0	Gilbey	7000	4	5	1		9	11		8	7				3			2		10						6		
5		11	MERTHYR TOWN	0-0		9500	4		1		9	11		8	7							2		10		3		5		6		
6		15	PORTSMOUTH	1-1	Battiste	5000	7	4	1		9	11		8								2		10			3	5		6		
7		18	Merthyr Town	1-6	Thompson	14000	7	4	1	11				9		8				6		2		10			3	5				
8		25	Plymouth Argyle	1-3	Hall	16000	7	4	1	11	9			8						6		2	10				3	5				
9	Oct	2	PLYMOUTH ARGYLE	0-1		10000	7	4	1			11		8						6		2		10			3	5			9	
10		9	Exeter City	1-2	Wood	10000	7		1		9			8						6		2					3	5		4	10	11
11		16	EXETER CITY	2-1	Battiste 2	10000	7		1					8						6		2		9			3	5		4	10	11
12		23	Millwall	0-4		20000	7		1			11		8						6		2		9			3	5		4	10	
13		30	MILLWALL	0-0		12000	7		1				4	8						6		2		9			3	5			10	11
14	Nov	6	Newport County	0-1		8000	8		1				4	9	7					6		2					3	5			10	11
15		13	NEWPORT COUNTY	1-4	Needham	8000	7	4	1					8			10			6		2					3	5			9	11
16		27	Portsmouth	2-2	Gilbey, Robinson	15000	7	4	1		9									6		2	10				3	5			8	11
17	Dec	11	Swindon Town	1-1	Gilbey	9000	7	4	1		9			10						6		2					3	5			8	11
18		25	NORTHAMPTON T	2-5	Gilbey, Hall	8000	7	4	1		9			10						6		2					3	5	8			11
19		27	Northampton Town	0-2		10000	7	4	1					10						6		2					3	5	8		9	11
20		28	Luton Town	0-5		11000		4	1					10		8				9		2					3	6	5		7	11
21	Jan	1	Watford	1-3	Roe	6000		4	1				7	10		8				6		2		9			3	5				11
22		15	BRENTFORD	1-3	Hall	8000	7	4						10						9	1					2	3	6	5		8	11
23		22	Brentford	3-3	Needham 2, Wood	9000	7	4	1					10						9		2					3	6	5		8	11
24		29	BRISTOL ROVERS	1-0	Needham	8000	4		1					10						9		2			7		3	6	5		8	11
25	Feb	5	Bristol Rovers	0-2		9000	4		1					10						9		2			7		3	6	5		8	11
26		12	NORWICH CITY	0-0		7000	4		1					10						9		2			7		3	6	5		8	11
27		19	Norwich City	1-2	Hall	8000	7		1				4	10						9		2					3	6	5		8	11
28		26	CRYSTAL PALACE	0-1		8000	7	9	1					10						6		2					3	4	5		8	11
29	Mar	5	Crystal Palace	1-4	Hall	10000		9	1				7	10						6		2					3	4	5		8	11
30		12	BRIGHTON & HOVE ALB	1-0	Waugh	7000		9	1					10		7				6		2					3	4	5		8	11
31		16	WATFORD	1-1	Hall	6000			1					10				7		6		2		9			3	4	5		8	11
32		19	Brighton & Hove Albion	0-1		9000			1					10				7		6		2		9			3	4	5		8	11
33		25	SOUTHEND UNITED	1-1	Hall	11000			1					10				7		6		2		9			3	4	5		8	11
34		26	Grimsby Town	0-2		11000	8		1					10				7		6		2		9			3	4	5			11
35		28	Southend United	0-1		10000			1					10		4		7		6		2				9	3		5		8	11
36	Apr	2	GRIMSBY TOWN	2-1	Waugh, Wood	7000	9		1					10				7		6		2					3	4	5		8	11
37		9	Queen's Park Rangers	1-0	Wood	10000	9		1					10				7		6		2					3	4	5		8	11
38		13	SWINDON TOWN	1-1	Wood	8000	8		1					10				7		6		2					3	4	5		8	11
39		16	QUEEN'S PARK RANGERS	1-2	Hall	8000	8		1					10				7		6		2					3	4	5		9	11
40		23	Swansea Town	0-2		13000	8	9	1					10				7		6		2					3	4	5			11
41		30	SWANSEA TOWN	2-1	Hall, Wood	8000			1					10		8		7		6		2					3	4	5		9	11
42	May	7	LUTON TOWN	0-0		6000	7		1					10		8				6		2					3	4	5		9	11
						Apps	33	21	41	2	11	8	5	41	6	7	1	11	1	36	1	41	2	16	3	3	40	37	24	9	30	32
						Goals	3				6			9						4			1	2				1	2		6	

F.A. Cup

Rd	Month	Day	Opponent	Score	Scorers	Att	Battiste W	Baxter TJC	Branfield J	Carter AJ	Gilbey TE	Gore SP	Griffiths JA	Hall T	Holt A	Howard JF	McCormick D	McMillan ST	Milton A	Needham GW	Ollerenshaw E	Robertson JW	Robinson TJD	Roe A	Russell GT	Shaw GE	Sisson T	Thompson TN	Waugh J	Wigmore C	Wood AB	Wright H
Q4	Nov	20	MAIDSTONE UNITED	1-0	Gilbey	6725	4		1		9			8						6		2	11	10			3	5			7	
Q5	Dec	4	DULWICH HAMLET	2-1	Hall, Gilbey	8000	7	4	1		9			10						6		2					3	5			8	11
Q6		18	Northampton Town	1-3	Hall	10000	7	4	1		9			10						6		2					3	5			8	11

		P	W	D	L	F	A	W	D	L	F	A	Pts
1	Crystal Palace	42	15	4	2	45	17	9	7	5	25	17	59
2	Southampton	42	14	5	2	46	10	5	11	5	18	18	54
3	Queen's Park Rangers	42	14	4	3	38	11	8	5	8	23	21	53
4	Swindon Town	42	14	5	2	51	17	7	5	9	22	32	52
5	Swansea Town	42	9	10	2	32	19	9	5	7	24	26	51
6	Watford	42	14	4	3	40	15	6	4	11	19	29	48
7	Millwall	42	11	5	5	25	8	7	6	8	17	22	47
8	Merthyr Town	42	13	5	3	46	20	2	10	9	14	29	45
9	Luton Town	42	14	6	1	51	15	2	6	13	10	41	44
10	Bristol Rovers	42	15	3	3	51	22	3	4	14	17	35	43
11	Plymouth Argyle	42	10	7	4	25	13	1	14	6	10	21	43
12	Portsmouth	42	10	8	3	28	14	2	7	12	18	34	39
13	Grimsby Town	42	12	5	4	32	16	3	4	14	17	43	39
14	Northampton Town	42	11	4	6	32	23	4	4	13	27	52	38
15	Newport County	42	8	5	8	20	23	6	4	11	23	41	37
16	Norwich City	42	9	10	2	31	14	1	6	14	13	39	36
17	Southend United	42	13	2	6	32	20	1	6	14	12	41	36
18	Brighton & Hove Albion	42	11	6	4	28	20	3	2	16	14	41	36
19	Exeter City	42	9	7	5	27	15	1	8	12	12	39	35
20	Reading	42	8	4	9	26	22	4	3	14	16	37	31
21	Brentford	42	7	9	5	27	23	2	3	16	15	44	30
22	GILLINGHAM	42	6	9	6	19	24	2	3	16	15	50	28

1921/22

18th in Division Three (South)

						Battiste W	Branfield J	Cassell L	Freeman CR	Hall T	Howard JF	McAlpine JW	McMillan ST	Marshall OT	Martin HJ	Needham GW	Robertson JW	Rowden HL	Simms S	Sisson T	Thompson TN	Thomson J	Travers JEG	Wakefield GE	Waterall T	Waugh J	Wood AB	Wright H
1	Aug 27	Southampton	0-2		10000				8	10		6	7	2					4	3		1			11	5	9	
2	31	CHARLTON ATHLETIC	2-0	Battiste, Freeman	8000	7	1		8	10		6		2					4	3					11	5	9	
3	Sep 3	SOUTHAMPTON	2-0	Freeman, Waterall	11000	7	1		8	10		6		2					4	3					11	5	9	
4	5	Charlton Athletic	0-0		8000	7	1		8	10		6		2					4	3					11	5	9	
5	10	PLYMOUTH ARGYLE	1-2	Simms (p)	12000	7	1		8	10		6		2					4	3					11	5	9	
6	14	MILLWALL	0-1		8000	7	1		8	10		6		2					4	3			9		11	5		
7	17	Plymouth Argyle	0-3		9000	7	1		8	10		6		2						3			9	4	11	5		
8	24	MERTHYR TOWN	5-0	* See below	12000	7			8	10				2		6				3		1	9	4	11	5		
9	Oct 1	Merthyr Town	0-2		12000	7			8	10				2		6				3		1	9	4	11	5		
10	8	PORTSMOUTH	1-2	Waugh (p)	17000	7			8	10		4		2		6				3		1	9		11	5		
11	15	Portsmouth	1-4	Wood	18000	7			8	10		4		2		6				3		1			11	5	9	
12	22	SOUTHEND UNITED	1-0	Freeman	10000	7	1		10	9		4	8	2		6				3					11	5		
13	29	Southend United	0-2		6000	7	1		10	9		4	8			6	2			3				5	11			
14	Nov 5	Swansea Town	0-2		12000	7	1			10		4				6	2			3			8	5	11		9	
15	12	SWANSEA TOWN	0-0		8000	7	1			10		4		2		6			9	3					11	5	8	
16	19	Exeter City	1-1	Wood	6000	7	1		10			4	8	2		6				3						5	9	11
17	Dec 10	Millwall	0-1		12000	7	1		10		9	6	8	2		11				3				4		5		
18	24	SWINDON TOWN	2-2	McMillan 2	6000	7	1		10		9	6	8			11	2			3				4		5		
19	26	NORTHAMPTON T	3-2	Needham, Freeman 2	10000	7	1		10		9	6	8			11	2	4		3	5							
20	27	Northampton Town	1-3	Howard	12000	7	1		10		9	6	8			11	2	5		3				4				
21	31	Luton Town	0-7		8000	7	1		10		9	6	8			11	2	5		3					4			
22	Jan 14	LUTON TOWN	0-1		7000	7			10		9	4	8	3		6	2					1			11	5		
23	21	Queen's Park Rangers	0-1		5000	7			10		9	4	8	3		6	2					1			11	5		
24	28	QUEEN'S PARK RANGERS	1-2	Freeman	10000	7		9	10			6	8	3		11	2					1	4			5		
25	Feb 4	Norwich City	0-2		4000	7		9	10			6	8	3		11	2					1	4			5		
26	11	NORWICH CITY	5-2	Freeman, Hall 3, Cassell	7000			9	8	10		6	7	3		11	2					1	4			5		
27	18	Reading	1-2	Hall	8000			9	8	10		6	7	3		11	2					1	4			5		
28	25	READING	2-0	Hall, Needham	7000	4		9	8	10		6	7	3		11	2					1				5		
29	Mar 6	EXETER CITY	3-0	Howard, Hall, Freeman	6000	4			8	10	9	6	7	3		11	2					1				5		
30	11	BRISTOL ROVERS	3-2	Waugh (p), Needham, Howard	8000	7			8	10	9	6		3		11	2				4	1				5		
31	18	BRENTFORD	0-0		7000	4			8	10	9	6	7	3		11	2					1				5		
32	20	Swindon Town	0-0		2000	7			8	10	9	6		3		11	2				4	1				5		
33	25	Brentford	1-0	Needham	8000	7			8	10		6		3		11	2				4	1				5	9	
34	Apr 1	ABERDARE ATHLETIC	3-1	Wood, Needham, Hall	7000	7			8	10		6		3		11	2				4	1				5	9	
35	8	Aberdare Athletic	1-6	Freeman (p)	8000	7			8	10		6		3		11	2				4	1				5	9	
36	10	Bristol Rovers	3-0	Hall 2, Wood	4000	7			8	10		6		3		11	2				4	1				5	9	
37	14	NEWPORT COUNTY	0-2		11000	7			8	10		6		3		11	2				4	1				5	9	
38	15	BRIGHTON & HOVE ALB	1-0	Freeman	7000	7			8			6		3	10	11	2				4	1				5	9	
39	17	Newport County	1-1	Martin	1000	7			8			6		3	10	11	2				4	1				5	9	
40	22	Brighton & Hove Albion	1-0	Needham	6000	7			8			6		3	10	11	2					1		4		5	9	
41	29	Watford	0-1		5000	7			8	10		6		3		11	2				4	1				5	9	
42	May 6	WATFORD	1-1	Wood	6000	7			8			6	10	3		11	2				5	1		4			9	
					Apps	39	16	5	40	28	11	40	19	36	3	35	27	3	7	21	12	26	10	10	18	36	19	1
					Goals	2		1	11	10	3		2		1	7			1				1		1	2	5	

Scorers in game 8: Freeman, Travers, Hall, Battiste, Needham

F.A. Cup

Q5	Dec 3	Northfleet United	0-0		11000	7	1		10			4	8	2		6				3						5	9	11
rep	7	NORTHFLEET UNITED	3-1	Freeman 2, Needham	8000	7	1		10	11		4	8	2		9			6	3						5		
Q6	17	ST ALBANS CITY	3-1	Needham, Freeman, Howard	8500	7	1		10		9	6	8			11	2			3				4		5		
R1	Jan 7	OLDHAM ATHLETIC	1-3	Howard	11000	7	1		10		9	4	8	3		6	2								11	5		

		P	W	D	L	F	A	W	D	L	F	A	Pts
1	Southampton	42	14	7	0	50	8	9	8	4	18	13	61
2	Plymouth Argyle	42	17	4	0	43	4	8	7	6	20	20	61
3	Portsmouth	42	13	5	3	38	18	5	12	4	24	21	53
4	Luton Town	42	16	2	3	47	9	6	6	9	17	26	52
5	Queen's Park Rangers	42	13	7	1	36	12	5	6	10	17	32	49
6	Swindon Town	42	10	7	4	40	21	6	6	9	32	39	45
7	Watford	42	9	9	3	34	21	4	9	8	20	27	44
8	Aberdare Athletic	42	11	6	4	38	18	6	4	11	19	33	44
9	Brentford	42	15	2	4	41	17	1	9	11	11	26	43
10	Swansea Town	42	11	8	2	40	19	2	7	12	10	28	41
11	Merthyr Town	42	14	2	5	33	15	3	4	14	12	41	40
12	Millwall	42	6	13	2	22	10	4	5	12	16	32	38
13	Reading	42	10	5	6	28	15	4	5	12	12	32	38
14	Bristol Rovers	42	8	8	5	32	24	6	2	13	20	43	38
15	Norwich City	42	8	10	3	29	17	4	3	14	21	45	37
16	Charlton Athletic	42	10	6	5	28	19	3	5	13	15	37	37
17	Northampton Town	42	13	3	5	30	17	0	8	13	17	54	37
18	GILLINGHAM	42	11	4	6	36	20	3	4	14	11	40	36
19	Brighton & Hove Albion	42	9	6	6	33	19	4	3	14	12	32	35
20	Newport County	42	8	7	6	22	18	3	5	13	22	43	34
21	Exeter City	42	7	5	9	22	29	4	7	10	16	30	34
22	Southend United	42	7	5	9	23	23	1	6	14	11	51	27

1922/23

16th in Division 3 (South)

No	Date	Opponent	Score	Scorers	Att	Arnold WJ	Batchelor JW	Battiste W	Bettridge W	Fox FS	Freeman CR	Hall T	Henderson J	Marshall OT	Martin HJ	McAlpine JW	Needham GW	Oswald W	Palmer W	Ramsay R	Read AH	Reay AF	Robertson JW	Rowden HL	Sisson T	Thompson TN	Thomson J	Williams HF
1	Aug 26	BRENTFORD	2-0	Palmer, Williams	9000			7			8	10	5	2		4	6		11						3		1	9
2	28	Northampton Town	0-1		10000						8	10	5	2		4	6	7	11						3		1	9
3	Sep 2	Brentford	0-2		10000						8	10	5	2			6	7	11					4	3		1	9
4	6	NORTHAMPTON T	0-3		6000						8	10	5			4	6		11				2		3	7	1	9
5	9	Queen's Park Rangers	1-2	Hall	10000			7			8	10	5				6		11			3	2			4	1	9
6	16	QUEEN'S PARK RANGERS	0-1		8000			7			8	10	5				6		11			3	2			4	1	9
7	23	Swansea Town	0-1		15000			7			8	10	5				6		11			3	2			4	1	9
8	30	SWANSEA TOWN	2-2	Arnold, Thompson	7000	10		7			8	9	5				6		11			3	2			4	1	
9	Oct 7	Brighton & Hove Albion	0-3		9000	10		7		1	8		5				6	9	11				2		3	4		
10	14	BRIGHTON & HOVE ALB	2-0	Williams 2	7000		11	7		1	8	10	5				6						2		3	4		9
11	21	WATFORD	1-4	Hall	7000		11	7		1	8	10	5				6						2		3	4		9
12	28	Watford	2-5	Freeman, Williams	7000			7		1	8	10				4	6		11				2		3	5		9
13	Nov 4	SWINDON TOWN	0-0		6000			7		1	10	9	5				6		11	8	4		2		3			
14	11	Swindon Town	1-0	Hall	6000					1	8	10	5				6		11	7	4		2		3			9
15	18	ABERDARE ATHLETIC	4-0	Hall 2, Williams 2	7000					1	8	10	5				6		11	7	4		2		3			9
16	25	Aberdare Athletic	0-2		6000			7		1	8	10	5				6		11		4		2		3			9
17	Dec 9	Newport County	1-2	Freeman	8000			7	3	1	8	10	5				6		11		4		2					9
18	23	Norwich City	1-1	Hall	6429			7		1	8	10	5				6	9	11		4	3	2					
19	25	MILLWALL	3-0	Hall, Freeman, Palmer	8000			7		1	8	10	5				6	9	11		4	3	2					
20	26	Millwall	1-3	Oswald	20000			7	2	1	8	10	5				6	9	11		4	3						
21	30	BRISTOL CITY	1-1	Henderson	5000			7		1	8	10	5				6	9	11		4	3	2					
22	Jan 6	Bristol City	1-2	Freeman	15000			7		1	8	10	5				6	9	11		4	3	2					
23	13	NEWPORT COUNTY	3-0	Freeman, Batiste, Henderson	6000			7			8	10	5			6		9	11		4	3	2				1	
24	20	PORTSMOUTH	4-2	Henderson 3, Freeman	7000			7			8	10	5			6		9	11		4	3	2				1	
25	27	Portsmouth	1-6	Oswald	7000			7			8	10	5			6		9	11		4	3	2				1	
26	Feb 10	Charlton Athletic	1-3	Oswald	7000			7	2		8	10	5				6	9	11		4	3					1	
27	14	CHARLTON ATHLETIC	2-2	Hall, Freeman	3000		11	7	2		8	10	5								4	3				6	1	9
28	17	PLYMOUTH ARGYLE	1-0	Williams	7000			7	2	1	8	10	5		11		6				4	3						9
29	Mar 3	BRISTOL ROVERS	0-1		7000			7	3	1	8	10	5				6		11		4		2					9
30	10	Bristol Rovers	0-1		8000			7	3	1	8		5		10		6	9			4		2					11
31	17	Reading	1-1	Martin	8000			7	3	1	8		5		10		6		11		4		2					9
32	24	READING	2-1	Williams, Henderson	6000			7	3	1	8		5		10		6		11		4		2					9
33	30	LUTON TOWN	1-0	Williams	8000			7	3	1	8	10	5				6		11				2			4		9
34	31	Southend United	1-1	Freeman	9000			7	3	1	8	10	5				6		11				2			4		9
35	Apr 2	Luton Town	0-2		5000			7	3	1	8	10	5				6		11				2			4		9
36	7	SOUTHEND UNITED	1-0	Williams	6000			7	3	1	8	10	5				6		11		4		2					9
37	14	Merthyr Town	0-1		3000			7	3	1	8	10	5				6		11				2			4		9
38	18	Plymouth Argyle	0-2		11508			7	3	1	8	10	5				11				4		2			6		9
39	21	MERTHYR TOWN	2-0	Freeman, Henderson	5000			7	3	1	8	10	5				9		11		4		2			6		
40	25	NORWICH CITY	5-0	* See below	2000			7	3	1	8	10	5				9		11		4		2			6		
41	28	Exeter City	1-0	Palmer	5000			7	3	1	8	10	5				9		11		4		2			6		
42	May 5	EXETER CITY	2-1	Henderson, Palmer	5000			7	3	1	8	10	5				9		11		4		2			6		
					Apps	2	3	37	19	29	42	38	41	3	4	7	38	13	36	3	26	15	35	1	12	19	13	26
					Goals	1		1			10	9	9		1		1	3	5							1		10

Scorers in game 40: Palmer. Needham, Henderson, Hall, Freeman

F.A. Cup

Rd	Date	Opponent	Score	Scorers	Att	Arnold WJ	Batchelor JW	Battiste W	Bettridge W	Fox FS	Freeman CR	Hall T	Henderson J	Marshall OT	Martin HJ	McAlpine JW	Needham GW	Oswald W	Palmer W	Ramsay R	Read AH	Reay AF	Robertson JW	Rowden HL	Sisson T	Thompson TN	Thomson J	Williams HF
Q5	Dec 2	London Caledonians	2-1	Hall 2	6000			7		1	8	10	5				6		11		4	3	2					9
Q6	16	BLYTH SPARTANS	1-4	Williams	7160			7		1	8	10	5				6		11		4	3	2					9

		P	W	D	L	F	A	W	D	L	F	A	Pts
1	Bristol City	42	16	4	1	43	13	8	7	6	23	27	59
2	Plymouth Argyle	42	18	3	0	47	6	5	4	12	14	23	53
3	Swansea Town	42	13	6	2	46	14	9	3	9	32	31	53
4	Brighton & Hove Albion	42	15	3	3	39	13	5	8	8	13	21	51
5	Luton Town	42	14	4	3	47	18	7	3	11	21	31	49
6	Millwall	42	9	10	2	27	13	5	8	8	18	27	46
7	Portsmouth	42	10	5	6	34	20	9	3	9	24	32	46
8	Northampton Town	42	13	6	2	40	17	4	5	12	14	27	45
9	Swindon Town	42	14	4	3	41	17	3	7	11	21	39	45
10	Watford	42	10	6	5	35	23	7	4	10	22	31	44
11	Queen's Park Rangers	42	10	4	7	34	24	6	6	9	20	25	42
12	Charlton Athletic	42	11	6	4	33	14	3	8	10	22	37	42
13	Bristol Rovers	42	7	9	5	25	19	6	7	8	10	17	42
14	Brentford	42	9	4	8	27	23	4	8	9	14	28	38
15	Southend United	42	10	6	5	35	18	2	7	12	14	36	37
16	GILLINGHAM	42	13	4	4	38	18	2	3	16	13	41	37
17	Merthyr Town	42	10	4	7	27	17	1	10	10	12	31	36
18	Norwich City	42	8	7	6	29	26	5	3	13	22	45	36
19	Reading	42	9	8	4	24	15	1	6	14	12	40	34
20	Exeter City	42	10	4	7	27	18	3	3	15	20	66	33
21	Aberdare Athletic	42	6	8	7	25	23	3	3	15	17	47	29
22	Newport County	42	8	6	7	28	21	0	5	16	12	49	27

1923/24

15th in Division Three (South)

No	Month	Day	Opponent	Score	Scorers	Att	Allen HA	Barnard WE	Battiste W	Berry WG	Butler CJW	Cartmell JR	Cosgrove WH	Edmed RA	Fox FS	Hall T	Henderson J	Hendrie R	Jones NE	Needham GW	North EJ	Read AH	Read TW	Robertson JW	Rowden HL	Savage WHM	Sinning AE	Smith G (1)	Thompson TN	Tredwell JW	Williams TH
1	Aug	25	BRISTOL ROVERS	1-0	North	8000			7		3				1	10	5		8	6	9	4		2			11				
2		29	Brighton & Hove Albion	2-2	Sinning, Hall	5000			7		3				1	10	5		8	6	9	4		2			11				
3	Sep	1	Bristol Rovers	0-2		11000			7						1	10		3	8	6	9	4		2	5		11				
4		5	BRIGHTON & HOVE ALB	1-1	Sinning	5000			7						1	10	5	3	8	6	9	4		2			11				
5		8	Watford	1-1	North	8000			7						1	10	5	3	4	6	9			2			11	8			
6		15	WATFORD	0-0		7000			7						1		5	3	4	6	9			2		10	11	8			
7		22	Swansea City	1-3	North	15000			7						1	10	5	3	4	6	8			2		9	11				
8		29	SWANSEA CITY	0-1		8000			7				8		1	10	5	3			9	4		2			11		6		
9	Oct	6	NORTHAMPTON T	1-1	Hall	7000			7				8		1	10		3		6	9	4		2			11		5		
10		13	Northampton Town	0-2		10000			7			11	8		1	10	5	3	4	6				2		9					
11		20	NEWPORT COUNTY	2-1	Cosgrove, Hall	7000			7			11	8		1	10	5	3	4	6				2		9					
12		27	Newport County	1-2	Needham	8000			7			11	8		1	10	5	3	4	6	9			2							
13	Nov	3	QUEEN'S PARK RANGERS	0-0		6000			7			11	8		1	10	5	3	4	9		6		2							
14		10	Queen's Park Rangers	1-1	Cosgrove	9000			7				8		1	10	5	3	4		9	6		2			11				
15		17	PLYMOUTH ARGYLE	1-0	North	6000			7				8		1	10	5	3	4		9	6		2			11				
16		24	Plymouth Argyle	0-3		7000	11		7				8		1	10	5	3	4		9	6		2							
17	Dec	8	Merthyr Town	2-0	North 2	1500			7				8		1	10		3	4		9	5		2			11		6		
18		22	Brentford	2-3	North, Battiste (p)	6000	11		7				8		1			3	4		9	5		2				10	6		
19		25	NORWICH CITY	3-1	North 2, Cosgrove	8000	11	2	7				8		1			3	4		9	6			5			10			
20		26	Norwich City	0-1		9000	11	2	7				8		1			3	4		9	6			5			10			
21		29	CHARLTON ATHLETIC	0-1		6000	11	2	7				8		1			3	4		9	6			5			10			
22	Jan	5	Charlton Athletic	0-0		8000	11		7		2				1	10	5	3	4		9							8	6		
23		19	LUTON TOWN	0-0		5000			7						1	10	5	3	4	11	9	6		2				8			
24		26	Luton Town	1-1	Hall				7						1	8	5	3	4		10	6		2				9		11	
25	Feb	2	READING	1-0	Smith	5000			7						1	8	5	3	4		10	6		2				9		11	
26		9	Reading	0-4					7				8		1	11	5	3	4		9	6		2				10			
27		16	BOURNEMOUTH	1-0	Williams	5000			7	11					1	8	5	3	4		10	6		2							9
28		23	Bournemouth	0-0					7	11					1	8	5	3	4		10	6		2							9
29	Mar	1	MILLWALL	0-2		6000			7	11					1	8	5	3	4		10	6		2							9
30		8	Millwall	0-5		20000			7	11						8	5	3	4		10	6	1	2							9
31		12	MERTHYR TOWN	2-1	Williams, Read (p)	3000			7	11	2				1		5	3	8		9	4			6						10
32		15	Aberdare Athletic	1-1	Hall				7	11	2				1	8	5	3	4		9	6									10
33		19	BRENTFORD	6-0	* see below	3000			7	11	2				1	10	5	3	4		9	6									8
34		22	ABERDARE ATHLETIC	3-1	Hall 2, Read (p)				7	11	2				1	10	5	3	4		9	6									8
35		29	Southend United	2-3	Battiste, North	4000			7	11	2				1	10	5	3	4		9	6									8
36	Apr	5	SOUTHEND UNITED	3-2	Hall 2, North	6000			7	11					1	10	5	3	4		9	6		2							8
37		12	Exeter City	1-2	Hall	4000				11	2			7	1	10	5	3	4		9	6									8
38		18	SWINDON TOWN	1-0	Williams	9000			7	11	2				1	10	5	3	4		9	6									8
39		19	EXETER CITY	1-1	Jones	5000				11	2			7	1	10	5	3	4		9	6									8
40		21	Swindon Town	1-4	Williams				7	11					1	10	5	3	4		9	6		2							8
41		26	Portsmouth	0-3		13850			7	11	2				1	10	5	3	4		9	6									8
42	May	3	PORTSMOUTH	0-2		7000			7	11	2				1	10	5	3	4		9	6									8
						Apps	6	3	40	16	13	4	15	2	41	36	35	40	40	13	39	35	1	28	5	4	12	11	5	2	16
						Goals			2	1			3			11			1	1	11	3					2	1			6

Scorers in game 33: Williams 2, Hall, Read, Berry, Pearson (og)

One own goal

F.A. Cup

Rd	Month	Day	Opponent	Score	Scorers	Att	Allen HA	Barnard WE	Battiste W	Berry WG	Butler CJW	Cartmell JR	Cosgrove WH	Edmed RA	Fox FS	Hall T	Henderson J	Hendrie R	Jones NE	Needham GW	North EJ	Read AH	Read TW	Robertson JW	Rowden HL	Savage WHM	Sinning AE	Smith G (1)	Thompson TN	Tredwell JW	Williams TH
Q5	Dec	1	Nunhead	6-0	North 5, Hall	3500			7			11	8		1	10	5	3	4		9	6		2							
Q6		15	TRANMERE ROVERS	1-0	North	9128			7				8		1	10	5	3	4		9	6		2			11				
R1	Jan	12	Cardiff City	0-0		20000	11		7						1	10	5	3	4		9	6		2				8			
rep		16	CARDIFF CITY	0-2		19472	11		7						1	10	5	3	4		9	6		2				8			

		P	W	D	L	F	A	W	D	L	F	A	Pts
1	Portsmouth	42	15	3	3	57	11	9	8	4	30	19	59
2	Plymouth Argyle	42	13	6	2	46	15	10	3	8	24	19	55
3	Millwall	42	17	3	1	45	11	5	7	9	19	27	54
4	Swansea Town	42	18	2	1	39	10	4	6	11	21	38	52
5	Brighton & Hove Albion	42	16	4	1	56	12	5	5	11	12	25	51
6	Swindon Town	42	14	5	2	38	11	3	8	10	20	33	47
7	Luton Town	42	11	7	3	35	19	5	7	9	15	25	46
8	Northampton Town	42	14	3	4	40	15	3	8	10	24	32	45
9	Bristol Rovers	42	11	7	3	34	15	4	6	11	18	31	43
10	Newport County	42	15	4	2	39	15	2	5	14	17	49	43
11	Norwich City	42	13	5	3	45	18	3	3	15	15	41	40
12	Aberdare Athletic	42	9	9	3	35	18	3	5	13	10	40	38
13	Merthyr Town	42	11	8	2	33	19	0	8	13	12	46	38
14	Charlton Athletic	42	8	7	6	26	20	3	8	10	12	25	37
15	GILLINGHAM	42	11	6	4	27	15	1	7	13	16	43	37
16	Exeter City	42	14	3	4	33	17	1	4	16	4	35	37
17	Brentford	42	9	8	4	33	21	5	0	16	21	50	36
18	Reading	42	12	2	7	35	20	1	7	13	16	37	35
19	Southend United	42	11	7	3	35	19	1	3	17	18	65	34
20	Watford	42	8	8	5	35	18	1	7	13	10	36	33
21	Bournemouth	42	6	8	7	19	19	5	3	13	21	46	33
22	Queen's Park Rangers	42	9	6	6	28	26	2	3	16	9	51	31

1924/25

13th in Division Three (South)

	Date	Opponent	Score	Scorers	Att	Berry WG	Brown F	Butler CJW	Chance GH	Cook G	Craddock CW	Crockford H	Davis CH	Edmed RA	Fox FS	Hall T	Hendrie R	Hook AE	Jones NE	Keegan JE	Marshall F	Orford CH	Ramsell LT	Robertson JW	Rutherford J	Smith SJ	Sykes AV	Vango AJ	Wilkinson T
1	Aug 30	Luton Town	0-0		8000	11	8	3	7				5		1	10		6			4			2					9
2	Sep 3	BRENTFORD	1-0	Hall	5500		8	3	7				5		1	10		6		11	4			2		9			
3	6	WATFORD	0-0		6000		8	3	7						1	10		6	4	11	5			2		9			
4	8	Brentford	1-2	Hall	6000		9	3	11					7	1	10		6	4					2		8		5	
5	13	BOURNEMOUTH	0-0		5500		8	2	7				6		1		3		9	11	4		10					5	
6	20	Brighton & Hove Albion	0-2		11000		8	3	7						1	10		6		11	4			2				5	9
7	27	PLYMOUTH ARGYLE	0-3		8000	11	8	3	7						1	10		5	6		4			2					9
8	Oct 4	Bristol City	1-2	Marshall	9000	11		3	7						1	9		6	4		8		10	2				5	
9	11	SWINDON TOWN	1-1	Hall	7000	11		3	7						1	9		6	4		8		10	2				5	
10	18	Aberdare Athletic	1-2	Brown	3000	11	9	3	7						1	6		5	4		8		10	2					
11	22	MILLWALL	1-0	Hall	3000	11	9	3	7				5		1	10		6	4		8			2					
12	25	Northampton Town	0-1		7000	11	9	3	7				5		1	10		6	4		8			2					
13	Nov 1	CHARLTON ATHLETIC	2-0	Brown 2	2000	11	9	3	7						1	10		6	4		8			2	5				
14	8	Queen's Park Rangers	1-1	Hall	9000	11	9	3	7						1	10		6	4		8			2	5				
15	15	MERTHYR TOWN	2-1	Brown, Marshall	6000	11	9	3	7						1	10		6	4		8			2	5				
16	22	Reading	1-0	Hall	6000	11	9	3	7						1	10		6	4		8			2	5				
17	Dec 6	Exeter City	3-3	Brown, Berry, Hall	6000	11	9	3	7						1	10		6	4		8			2	5				
18	20	Newport County	0-2		8000	11	9	3	7						1	10		6	4		8			2	5				
19	25	SOUTHEND UNITED	3-1	Hook, Marshall 2	8000	11	9		7						1		3	6	4		8		10	2	5				
20	26	Southend United	0-4		9000	11	9		7						1		3	6	4		8		10	2	5				
21	27	LUTON TOWN	4-1	Marshall, Ramsell 2, Chance	1000	11	9		7	6					1		3		4		8		10	2	5				
22	Jan 3	Watford	2-1	Berry, Brown	5000	11	9		7						1	10	3	6	4		8			2	5				
23	17	Bournemouth	0-3		6000	11	9		7	6					1	10	3		4		8			2	5				
24	24	BRIGHTON & HOVE ALB	2-0	Chance 2	6000	11	9	2	7	6					1	10	3		4		8				5				
25	31	Plymouth Argyle	0-2		10401	11	9		7	6					1	10	3		4		8			2	5				
26	Feb 7	BRISTOL CITY	1-1	Chance	5000	11	8		7	6					1	10	3		4		5			2					9
27	11	BRISTOL ROVERS	0-0		4000	11	9		7	6					1	10	3		4		8			2	5				
28	14	Swindon Town	0-2		5000	11	9		7						1	6	3		4		8		10	2	5				
29	21	ABERDARE ATHLETIC	2-0	Marshall, Brown	5000	11	9		7	6					1		3		4		8		10	2	5				
30	28	NORTHAMPTON T	0-1		6000	11	8		7						1	10	3		4		6			2	5				9
31	Mar 7	Charlton Athletic	0-2		7000	11	10		7			9			1	6	3		4		8			2	5				
32	14	QUEEN'S PARK RANGERS	1-0	Crockford	5000	11			7			9				10	3		4		8	6		2	5		1		
33	18	SWANSEA TOWN	0-0		3800	11	10	2	7			9				6	3		4		8				5		1		
34	21	Merthyr Town	0-0			11	10	2	7			9				6	3		4		8				5		1		
35	28	READING	0-0		5000	11	10		7			9				6	3		8		4			2	5		1		
36	Apr 4	Swansea Town	0-2		11300	11	9		7			10			1	6	3		8		4			2	5				
37	10	NORWICH CITY	3-1	Marshall, Berry 2	6000	11	10		7		9				1	6	3		8		4			2	5				
38	11	EXETER CITY	1-1	Marshall	6500	11	9		7			10			1	6	3		4		8			2	5				
39	13	Norwich City	0-0		12000	11	10		7						1	6	3		4		8			2	5	9			
40	18	Bristol Rovers	0-0		6000	11	9		7						1	6	3		4		8		10	2	5				
41	25	NEWPORT COUNTY	1-0	Craddock	5000	11	10				9			7		6	3		4		8			2	5		1		
42	May 2	Millwall	0-2		10000	11	10				9			7		6	3		4		8			2	5		1		
					Apps	37	39	21	40	7	3	7	5	3	36	37	25	20	39	4	41	1	10	38	29	4	6	5	5
					Goals	4	7		4		1	1				7		1			8		2						

F.A. Cup

	Date	Opponent	Score	Scorers	Att	Berry WG	Brown F	Butler CJW	Chance GH	Cook G	Craddock CW	Crockford H	Davis CH	Edmed RA	Fox FS	Hall T	Hendrie R	Hook AE	Jones NE	Keegan JE	Marshall F	Orford CH	Ramsell LT	Robertson JW	Rutherford J	Smith SJ	Sykes AV	Vango AJ	Wilkinson T
Q5	Nov 29	Kettering Town	1-1	Brown	8986	11	9	3	7				5		1	10		6	4		8			2					
rep	Dec 3	KETTERING TOWN	6-2	Brown 2, Hall 2, Marshall, Berry	8202	11	9	3	7				5		1	10		6	4		8			2					
Q6	13	Barrow	0-0		9000	11	9	3	7						1	10		6	4		5		8	2					
rep	18	BARROW	1-1	(aet) Jones	3600	11	9	3	7						1	10		6	4		5			2		8			
rep2	22	Barrow	1-1	(aet) Smith	2342	11	9		7						1	10	3	6	4		5			2		8			
rep3	30	Barrow	1-1	(aet) Hall	2325	11	9		7	6					1	10	3	5	4		8			2					
rep4	31	Barrow	1-2	Marshall (p)	4242		9		7					11	1	10	3	6	4		5			2		8			

Q6 replay 2 at Molineux, replay 3 at Highbury, replay 4 at Millwall

		P	W	D	L	F	A	W	D	L	F	A	Pts
1	Swansea Town	42	17	4	0	51	12	6	7	8	17	23	57
2	Plymouth Argyle	42	17	3	1	55	12	6	7	8	22	26	56
3	Bristol City	42	14	5	2	40	10	8	4	9	20	31	53
4	Swindon Town	42	17	2	2	51	13	3	9	9	15	25	51
5	Millwall	42	12	5	4	35	14	6	8	7	23	24	49
6	Newport County	42	13	6	2	35	12	7	3	11	27	30	49
7	Exeter City	42	13	4	4	37	19	6	5	10	22	29	47
8	Brighton & Hove Albion	42	14	3	4	43	17	5	5	11	16	28	46
9	Northampton Town	42	12	3	6	34	18	8	3	10	17	26	46
10	Southend United	42	14	1	6	34	18	5	4	12	17	43	43
11	Watford	42	12	3	6	22	20	5	6	10	16	27	43
12	Norwich City	42	10	8	3	39	18	4	5	12	14	33	41
13	GILLINGHAM	42	11	8	2	25	11	2	6	13	10	33	40
14	Reading	42	9	6	6	28	15	5	4	12	9	23	38
15	Charlton Athletic	42	12	6	3	31	13	1	6	14	15	35	38
16	Luton Town	42	9	10	2	34	15	1	7	13	15	42	37
17	Bristol Rovers	42	10	5	6	26	13	2	8	11	16	36	37
18	Aberdare Athletic	42	13	4	4	40	21	1	5	15	14	46	37
19	Queen's Park Rangers	42	10	6	5	28	19	4	2	15	14	44	36
20	Bournemouth	42	8	6	7	20	17	5	2	14	20	41	34
21	Brentford	42	8	7	6	28	26	1	0	20	10	65	25
22	Merthyr Town	42	8	3	10	24	27	0	2	19	11	50	21

1925/26

10th in Division Three (South)

							Berry WG	Brown F	Butler CIW	Craddock CW	Edmed RA	Ellis FC	Ferguson ASB	Gear F	Goodman AA	Hall T	Hendrie R	Jones NE	Marshall F	McKee R	McWhirr J	Nichol JB	Record CR	Reddock C	Richards AC	Robertson JW	Rutherford J	Sykes AV	Taylor TC	Ward J
1	Aug	29	QUEEN'S PARK RANGERS	3-0	Berry 2, McKee	7612	11						1		4	10	3		8	9				6	7	2	5			
2	Sep	3	Merthyr Town	0-0		6327	11						1		4	10	3		8	9	7			6		2	5			
3		5	Bristol Rovers	0-2		4783	11						1		4	10	3		8	9	7			6		2	5			
4		9	MERTHYR TOWN	3-1	Edmed, McKee, Marshall (p)	3793	11				7		1		4	10	3		8	9				6		2	5			
5		12	SWINDON TOWN	0-1		7312	11				7		1		4	10	3		8	9				6		2	5			
6		19	Exeter City	1-2	McKee	3854	11				7				4	10	3		8	9				6		2	5	1		
7		26	READING	4-1	Brown, Berry, McKee 2	6211	11	8	3		7		1			10			4	9				6		2	5			
8		30	NORTHAMPTON T	1-1	Hall	4347	11	8	3		7		1			10			4	9				6		2	5			
9	Oct	3	Bournemouth	2-1	Edmed 2	5794	11	8	3		7		1			10			4	9				6		2	5			
10		10	CHARLTON ATHLETIC	0-0		7544	11	8	3	7			1			10			4	9				6		2	5			
11		17	MILLWALL	0-0		10065	11	7	3			10	1	9					4	8				6		2	5			
12		24	Norwich City	0-1		6942	11	10	3				1						8	9		4		6	7	2	5			
13		31	BRIGHTON & HOVE ALB	3-1	Brown 2, McKee	6814	11	10	3		7		1						8	9		4		6		2	5			
14	Nov	7	Aberdare Athletic	1-0	Marshall	3260	11	10	3		7		1					4	8	9		5		6		2				
15		14	BRISTOL CITY	0-1		6779	11	10	3	8	7		1						4	9		6				2	5			
16		21	Crystal Palace	2-0	McKee, Edmed	11879	11	10	3		7		1					4	8	9		6				2	5			
17	Dec	5	Watford	1-3	Brown	4540	11	10	3		7		1					4	8	9		6				2	5			
18		19	Plymouth Argyle	1-2	Brown	6590	11	9	3		7		1					4	8			5		6	10	2				
19		25	LUTON TOWN	2-1	Brown 2	6350	11	9	3		7		1					4	8			5		6	10	2				
20		26	Luton Town	3-5	Berry, Nichol (p), Brown	9898	11	9	3		7		1					4		8		5		6	10	2				
21		28	Northampton Town	2-1	Richards, Berry	7075	11	9	3		7		1					4		8		6			10	2	5			
22	Jan	2	Queen's Park Rangers	1-0	Edmed	7287		9	3	10	7		1					4		8		6			11	2	5			
23		9	BRENTFORD	1-3	Marshall	6093		10	3		7		1					4	8	9		6			11	2	5			
24		16	BRISTOL ROVERS	6-3	Record, Edmed, Brown 3, Richards	3319		9	3		7		1					4	8			6	10		11	2	5			
25		20	SOUTHEND UNITED	3-1	Brown, Richards, Edmed	3493		9	3		7		1					4	8			6	10		11	2	5			
26		23	Swindon Town	0-1		3368		9	3				1	4					8		7	6	10		11	2	5			
27		30	EXETER CITY	2-0	Craddock, Brown	5556		9	3	10			1					4	8		7	6			11	2	5			
28	Feb	6	Reading	0-1		12307		9	3	10			1					4	8	7		6			11	2	5			
29		13	BOURNEMOUTH	1-2	Craddock	6075		9	3	10			1					4	8	7		6			11	2	5			
30		20	Charlton Athletic	0-1		6658	11	9	3	10			1					4	8	7		6				2	5			
31		27	Millwall	0-0		12169	11	10	3				1						8			4		6	7	2	5			9
32	Mar	6	NORWICH CITY	2-0	Brown, Richards	5962	11	10	3				1						8			4		6	7	2	5			9
33		13	Brighton & Hove Albion	2-1	McKee 2	9612	11	10	3				1						8	9		4		6	7	2	5			
34		20	ABERDARE ATHLETIC	0-1		4689	11	10	3				1						8	9		4		6	7	2	5			
35		27	Bristol City	0-4		10569		10	3	7			1	4					8	9	11			6		2	5			
36	Apr	2	NEWPORT COUNTY	2-0	McKee 2	7138		10	3	7			1						8	9		4		6	11	2	5			
37		3	CRYSTAL PALACE	1-1	Brown	7371		10	3	7			1						8	9		4		6	11	2	5			
38		5	Newport County	0-4		5500		10	3	7			1						8	9		4		6	11	2	5			
39		10	Brentford	0-0		7942		10	3	7			1						8	9		4		6	11	2	5			
40		17	WATFORD	0-1		4979		10	3	7			1						8	9		4		6	11	2	5			
41		24	Southend United	1-1	Marshall	6083		10	3				1						8	9		4		6	11	2	5		7	
42	May	1	PLYMOUTH ARGYLE	2-0	McKee, Marshall	10651		10	3				1						8	9	7	4		6	11	2	5			
						Apps	26	36	36	13	19	1	41	3	6	10	6	15	39	34	6	30	3	29	25	42	38	1	1	2
						Goals	5	15		2	7					1			5	12		1	1		4					

F.A. Cup

R1	Nov	28	SOUTHALL	6-0	* see below	4500	11	10	3		7		1					4	8	9		6				2	5			
R2	Dec	12	Southend	0-1		10000	11	10	3		7		1						8	9		4		6		2	5			

Scorers in R1: McKee, Adams (og), Marshall, Brown, Berry, Rutherford

		P	W	D	L	F	A	W	D	L	F	A	Pts
1	Reading	42	16	5	0	49	16	7	6	8	28	36	57
2	Plymouth Argyle	42	16	2	3	71	33	8	6	7	36	34	56
3	Millwall	42	14	6	1	52	12	7	5	9	21	27	53
4	Bristol City	42	14	3	4	42	15	7	6	8	30	36	51
5	Brighton & Hove Albion	42	12	4	5	47	33	7	5	9	37	40	47
6	Swindon Town	42	16	2	3	48	22	4	4	13	21	42	46
7	Luton Town	42	16	4	1	60	25	2	3	16	20	50	43
8	Bournemouth	42	10	5	6	44	30	7	4	10	31	61	43
9	Aberdare Athletic	42	11	6	4	50	24	6	2	13	24	42	42
10	GILLINGHAM	42	11	4	6	36	19	6	4	11	17	30	42
11	Southend United	42	13	2	6	50	20	6	2	13	28	53	42
12	Northampton Town	42	13	3	5	47	26	4	4	13	35	54	41
13	Crystal Palace	42	16	1	4	50	21	3	2	16	25	58	41
14	Merthyr Town	42	13	3	5	51	25	1	8	12	18	50	39
15	Watford	42	12	5	4	47	26	3	4	14	26	63	39
16	Norwich City	42	11	5	5	35	26	4	4	13	23	47	39
17	Newport County	42	11	5	5	39	27	3	5	13	25	47	38
18	Brentford	42	12	4	5	44	32	4	2	15	25	62	38
19	Bristol Rovers	42	9	4	8	44	28	6	2	13	22	41	36
20	Exeter City	42	13	2	6	54	25	2	3	16	18	45	35
21	Charlton Athletic	42	9	7	5	32	23	2	6	13	16	45	35
22	Queen's Park Rangers	42	5	7	9	23	32	1	2	18	14	52	21

1926/27

20th in Division Three (South)

	Date		Opponent	Score	Scorers	Att	Amos ST	Arblaster WJ	Bartley JWE	Bradley PJ	Brown F	Butler CJW	Ellis FC	Fairclough A	Ferguson ASB	Foster J	Hillier S	Jones NE	Kelly J	Marshall F	Mason SM	McKee R	Meston SW	Nichol JB	Pickering WH	Robertson JW	Rogers D	Rutherford J
1	Aug	28	BRISTOL CITY	1-1	Marshall (p)	9118	9	10				3			1	11				8			7	4		2	6	5
2	Sep	1	QUEEN'S PARK RANGERS	2-2	Arblaster, Amos	6208	9	10							1	11				8			7	4	3	2	6	5
3		4	Bournemouth	2-4	Amos, Foster	6791	9	10				3			1	11				8			7	4		2	6	5
4		6	Coventry City	2-0	Arblaster, Amos	8496	9	10				3	6		1	11				8			7	4		2		5
5		11	PLYMOUTH ARGYLE	4-1	Arblaster, Marshall, Amos 2	9274	9	10				3	6		1	11				8			7	4		2		5
6		15	COVENTRY CITY	2-0	Meston, Arblaster	5084	9	10				3	6		1	11				8			7	4		2		5
7		18	Newport County	0-1		7141	9	10				3	6		1	11				8			7	4		2		5
8		25	ABERDARE ATHLETIC	2-1	Amos, Foster	7395	9	10	3				6		1	11				8			7	4		2		5
9	Oct	2	Luton Town	1-2	Rutherford	9138	9	10	3				6		1	11				8			7	4		2		5
10		9	Watford	0-4		6010	9	10	3				6		1	11				8			7	4		2		5
11		16	BRIGHTON & HOVE ALB	2-3	Arblaster, Marshall	6385	9	10	3						1	11				8	4		7	6		2		5
12		23	Norwich City	0-0		7796	9	10					6		1	11				8	4		7		3	2		5
13		30	SOUTHEND UNITED	2-3	Arblaster, Foster	4809		10							1	11				8	4	9	7	6	3	2		5
14	Nov	6	Merthyr Town	0-2		2704	9	10							1	11				8	4		7	6	3	2		5
15		13	EXETER CITY	3-2	Amos 3	1029	9	10			8				1	11				4			7	6	3	2	5	
16		20	Swindon Town	0-1		5493	9	10			8				1	11				4			7	6	3	2	5	
17	Dec	4	Millwall	0-2		12021	9			11	10				1			4		8			7	6	3	2		5
18		18	Northampton Town	1-2	McKee	4979		10		11	8		6		1							9	7	4	3	2		5
19		25	Charlton Athletic	0-3		8514		10		11			6		1					8		9	7	5	3	2	4	
20		27	CHARLTON ATHLETIC	1-1	McKee	8575				11	10				1					8		9	7	6	3	2	4	5
21	Jan	1	Queen's Park Rangers	1-1	Meston	7714	9			11					1		10			8	5		7	6	3	2	4	
22		8	NEWPORT COUNTY	0-1		4611	9			11					1		10			8	5		7	6	3	2	4	
23		15	Bristol City	4-9	Amos 2, Arblaster 2	11081	9	8		11					1		10				5		7	6	3	2	4	
24		22	BOURNEMOUTH	1-0	Hillier	1740	9	8		11					1		10				5		7	6	3	2	4	
25		29	Plymouth Argyle	0-0		8141	9	8		11					1		10				5		7	6	3	2	4	
26	Feb	12	Aberdare Athletic	1-2	Amos	2038	9	8		11					1		10				5		7	6	3	2	4	
27		19	LUTON TOWN	0-0		3979		8		11				9			10		1		5		7	6	3	2	4	
28		26	WATFORD	3-0	Arblaster, Mason, Bradley	3909		10		11	8			9					1		5		7	6	3	2	4	
29	Mar	5	Brighton & Hove Albion	2-3	Meston, Arblaster	9447		10		11	8			9					1		5		7	6	3	2	4	
30		12	NORWICH CITY	1-0	Arblaster	4448		10		11	8			9					1		5		7	6	3	2	4	
31		19	Southend United	0-1		6605		10		11	8			9					1		5		7	6	3	2	4	
32		23	BRISTOL ROVERS	2-0	Arblaster 2	1777		10		11	8			9		7			1		5			6	3	2	4	
33		26	MERTHYR TOWN	0-1		3213		10		11	8			9		7			1		5			6	3	2	4	
34		30	BRENTFORD	1-2	Arblaster	2947		10		11	8			9				7	1		5			6	3	2	4	
35	Apr	2	Exeter City	1-5	Jones	3088		10	2	11	8			9				7	1		5			6	3		4	
36		9	SWINDON TOWN	4-4	Bradley 2, Fairclough, Arblaster	3724		10	2	11	8			9			6		1				7	5	3		4	
37		15	CRYSTAL PALACE	2-1	Fairclough 2	7584		10	2	11	8			9			6		1				7	5	3		4	
38		16	Bristol Rovers	1-2	Brown (p)	8322	9	10	2	11	8						6		1				7	5	3		4	
39		18	Crystal Palace	2-2	Foster, Arblaster	10386	9	10	2		8					11	6	7	1					5	3		4	
40		23	MILLWALL	2-1	Arblaster, Brown	4523	9	10	2	7	8					11	6		1					5	3		4	
41		30	Brentford	0-0		5793	9	10			8					11	6		1				7	5	3	2	4	
42	May	7	NORTHAMPTON T	1-2	Brown	4128	9	10		11	8						6		1				7	5	3	2	4	

	Amos ST	Arblaster WJ	Bartley JWE	Bradley PJ	Brown F	Butler CJW	Ellis FC	Fairclough A	Ferguson ASB	Foster J	Hillier S	Jones NE	Kelly J	Marshall F	Mason SM	McKee R	Meston SW	Nichol JB	Pickering WH	Robertson JW	Rogers D	Rutherford J
Apps	27	38	10	24	20	6	10	11	26	21	14	4	16	21	19	4	36	41	32	36	29	17
Goals	12	17		3	3			3		4	1	1		3	1	2	3					1

F.A. Cup

	Date		Opponent	Score	Scorers	Att	Amos ST	Arblaster WJ	Bartley JWE	Bradley PJ	Brown F	Butler CJW	Ellis FC	Fairclough A	Ferguson ASB	Foster J	Hillier S	Jones NE	Kelly J	Marshall F	Mason SM	McKee R	Meston SW	Nichol JB	Pickering WH	Robertson JW	Rogers D	Rutherford J
R1	Nov	27	Barking	0-0		5000	9	10			8				1	11				4			7	6	3	2	5	
rep	Dec	1	BARKING	2-0	Marshall, Brown	4000	9			11	10				1			4		8			7	6	3	2		5
R2		11	BRENTFORD	1-1	Arblaster	10076	9	10		11	8				1					4			7	6	3	2		5
rep		15	Brentford	0-1		6965	9	10		11	8				1					4			7	6	3	2		5

		P	W	D	L	F	A	W	D	L	F	A	Pts
1	Bristol City	42	19	1	1	71	24	8	7	6	33	30	62
2	Plymouth Argyle	42	17	4	0	52	14	8	6	7	43	47	60
3	Millwall	42	16	2	3	55	19	7	8	6	34	32	56
4	Brighton & Hove Albion	42	15	4	2	61	24	6	7	8	18	26	53
5	Swindon Town	42	16	3	2	64	31	5	6	10	36	54	51
6	Crystal Palace	42	12	6	3	57	33	6	3	12	27	48	45
7	Bournemouth	42	13	2	6	49	24	5	6	10	29	42	44
8	Luton Town	42	12	9	0	48	19	3	5	13	20	47	44
9	Newport County	42	15	4	2	40	20	4	2	15	17	51	44
10	Bristol Rovers	42	12	4	5	46	28	4	5	12	32	52	41
11	Brentford	42	10	9	2	46	20	3	5	13	24	41	40
12	Exeter City	42	14	4	3	46	18	1	6	14	30	55	40
13	Charlton Athletic	42	13	5	3	44	22	3	3	15	16	39	40
14	Queen's Park Rangers	42	9	8	4	41	27	6	1	14	24	44	39
15	Coventry City	42	11	4	6	44	33	4	3	14	27	53	37
16	Norwich City	42	10	5	6	41	25	2	6	13	18	46	35
17	Merthyr Town	42	11	5	5	42	25	2	4	15	21	55	35
18	Northampton Town	42	13	4	4	36	23	2	1	18	23	64	35
19	Southend United	42	12	3	6	44	25	2	3	16	20	52	34
20	GILLINGHAM	42	10	5	6	36	26	1	5	15	18	46	32
21	Watford	42	9	6	6	36	27	3	2	16	21	60	32
22	Aberdare Athletic	42	8	2	11	38	48	1	5	15	24	53	25

1927/28

16th in Division Three (South)

							Amos ST	Arblaster WJ	Bartley JWE	Boswell W	Bradley PJ	Bromage E	Brown JT	Brown S	Crawford GW	Dee A	Dominy AA	Donaghy E	Dowell L	Ellis FC	Hebden GHR	Hillier S	Hodnett JE	Meston SW	Millington T	Nichol JB	Pickering WH	Poxton JH	Robertson JW	Rogers D	Sly H	Tyler S	Wilcox JC
1	Aug	27	Charlton Athletic	0-1		11752		10				11						6			1	8	5	7		4	3		2				9
2	Sep	1	Queen's Park Rangers	3-3	Wilcox, Hillier 2	9241		10				11									1	8	5	7		4	3		2	6			9
3		3	BRISTOL ROVERS	3-1	Wilcox, Arblaster, Hillier	6818		10				11									1	8	5	7		6	3			4		2	9
4		7	QUEEN'S PARK RANGERS	1-2	Hodnott	5499		10				11						6			1	8	5	7			3			4		2	9
5		10	Plymouth Argyle	2-2	Arblaster 2	10282		10				11									1	6	5	7			3			4	8	2	9
6		17	MERTHYR TOWN	1-1	Arblaster	5642		10				11									1	6	5	7		4	3				8	2	9
7		24	Walsall	4-7	Sly, Bromage, Wilcox 2	6923		10				11	7								1	6	5			4	3				8	2	9
8	Oct	1	NORTHAMPTON T	1-3	Arblaster	4226		10				11	7								1	6	5			4	3				8	2	9
9		8	COVENTRY CITY	1-2	Wilcox	4667	5	10			11										1	6		7		4	3				8	2	9
10		15	Newport County	1-1	Nichol	6589	4				11			1				10				6		7		5	3				8	2	9
11		22	Bournemouth	0-3		4119	4				11			1				10				6		7		5	3				8	2	9
12		29	BRIGHTON & HOVE ALB	0-1		4681					11	10		1						6			5	7		4	3				8	2	9
13	Nov	5	Southend United	2-1	Meston, Arblaster	6756	8	10	2		11			1	5					6				7		4	3						9
14		12	BRENTFORD	2-1	Wilcox 2	3293		10		8	11			1	5					6				7		4			2			3	9
15		19	Luton Town	1-6	Meston	4527		10		8	11			1	5					6			4	7					2			3	9
16	Dec	3	Crystal Palace	2-2	Wilcox, Arblaster	9299		10		8	11				5					6	1		4	7					2			3	9
17		17	Torquay United	1-1	Boswell	2992		10		8	11				5					6	1			7					2	4		3	9
18		24	NORWICH CITY	3-0	Boswell, Meston, Wilcox	4078		10		8		11			5					6	1			7					2	4		3	9
19		27	WATFORD	0-3		3310		10		8		11			5					6	1			7					2	4		3	9
20		31	CHARLTON ATHLETIC	1-1	Bromage	4134				8		11			5				10	6	1			7					2	4		3	9
21	Jan	7	Bristol Rovers	4-2	Wilcox 2, Meston, Boswell	5572				8		11			5				10	6	1			7					2	4		3	9
22		21	PLYMOUTH ARGYLE	3-1	Wilcox 2, Bromage	4473				8		11			5				10	6	1			7					2	4		3	9
23	Feb	4	WALSALL	2-0	Wilcox 2	4296						11			5				10	6	1	8		7					2	4		3	9
24		11	Northampton Town	0-1		9538				8		11			5				10	6	1			7					2	4		3	9
25		18	Coventry City	2-1	Boswell, Meston	8500				8		11			5				10	6	1			7					2	4		3	9
26		25	NEWPORT COUNTY	4-0	Bromage 2, Wilcox 2	5932				8		11			5				10	6	1			7					2	4		3	9
27	Mar	3	BOURNEMOUTH	2-1	Bromage, Wilcox	6817				8		11			5				10	6	1			7					2	4		3	9
28		10	Brighton & Hove Albion	0-0		7860						11			5		8		10	6	1				7				2	4		3	9
29		12	Merthyr Town	1-3	Robertson (p)	683						11			5		8		10	6	1				7				2	4		3	9
30		17	SOUTHEND UNITED	1-0	Wilcox	6240									5		8		10	6	1				7			11	2	4		3	9
31		24	Brentford	0-2		6107				8					5		10			6	1				7			11	2	4		3	9
32		28	EXETER CITY	1-1	Millington	3138				8					5		10			6	1				7			11	2	4		3	9
33		31	LUTON TOWN	0-4		4045									5	8	10			6	1				7			11	2	4		3	9
34	Apr	6	SWINDON TOWN	0-1		7930									5	6	8		10		1				7			11	2	4		3	9
35		7	Exeter City	2-2	Poxton, Pool (og)	6001				4							8		10	6	1		5		7			11	2			3	9
36		9	Swindon Town	1-6	Poxton	7901				4							8		10		1		5		7			11	2	6		3	9
37		14	CRYSTAL PALACE	3-1	Poxton 2, Wilcox	3623									5		8		10	6	1				7			11	2	4		3	9
38		21	Millwall	0-6		20744								1	5		8		10	6					7			11	2	4		3	9
39		25	MILLWALL	0-1		5794								1	5		8		10	6					7			11	2	4		3	9
40		28	TORQUAY UNITED	4-1	Wilcox 3, Dominy	3868			3								8		10	6	1		5		7			11	2	4			9
41	May	2	Watford	3-5	Wilcox, Dominy 2	3645			3							6	10				1		5		7			11	2	4	8		9
42		5	Norwich City	0-0		6556			2							6			10	3	1		5		7			11		4	8		9
																	14		19														
						Apps	4	16	4	17	9	21	2	8	25	4	14	4	19	28	34	12	16	25	15	12	13	13	30	29	10	36	42
						Goals		6		4		6					3					3	1	5	1	1		4	1		1		25

One own goal

F.A. Cup

							Amos ST	Arblaster WJ	Bartley JWE	Boswell W	Bradley PJ	Bromage E	Brown JT	Brown S	Crawford GW	Dee A	Dominy AA	Donaghy E	Dowell L	Ellis FC	Hebden GHR	Hillier S	Hodnett JE	Meston SW	Millington T	Nichol JB	Pickering WH	Poxton JH	Robertson JW	Rogers D	Sly H	Tyler S	Wilcox JC
R1	Nov	26	PLYMOUTH ARGYLE	2-1	Boswell, Meston	7900		10		8	11				5					6	1		4	7					2			3	9
R2	Dec	10	SOUTHEND UNITED	2-0	Wilcox 2	10215		10		8	11				5					6	1			7					2	4		3	9
R3	Jan	14	Stoke City	1-6	Wilcox	14855				8		11			5				10	6	1			7					2	4		3	9

		P	*W*	*D*	*L*	*F*	*A*	*W*	*D*	*L*	*F*	*A*	*Pts*
1	Millwall	42	19	2	0	87	15	11	3	7	40	35	65
2	Northampton Town	42	17	3	1	67	23	6	6	9	35	41	55
3	Plymouth Argyle	42	17	2	2	60	19	6	5	10	25	35	53
4	Brighton & Hove Albion	42	14	4	3	51	24	5	6	10	30	45	48
5	Crystal Palace	42	15	3	3	46	23	3	9	9	33	49	48
6	Swindon Town	42	12	6	3	60	26	7	3	11	30	43	47
7	Southend United	42	14	2	5	48	19	6	4	11	32	45	46
8	Exeter City	42	11	6	4	49	27	6	6	9	21	33	46
9	Newport County	42	12	5	4	52	38	6	4	11	29	46	45
10	Queen's Park Rangers	42	8	5	8	37	35	9	4	8	35	36	43
11	Charlton Athletic	42	12	5	4	34	27	3	8	10	26	43	43
12	Brentford	42	12	4	5	49	30	4	4	13	27	44	40
13	Luton Town	42	13	5	3	56	27	3	2	16	38	60	39
14	Bournemouth	42	12	6	3	44	24	1	6	14	28	55	38
15	Watford	42	10	5	6	42	34	4	5	12	26	44	38
16	GILLINGHAM	42	10	3	8	33	26	3	8	10	29	55	37
17	Norwich City	42	9	8	4	41	26	1	8	12	25	44	36
18	Walsall	42	9	6	6	52	35	3	3	15	23	66	33
19	Bristol Rovers	42	11	3	7	41	36	3	1	17	26	57	32
20	Coventry City	42	5	8	8	40	36	6	1	14	27	60	31
21	Merthyr Town	42	7	6	8	38	40	2	7	12	15	51	31
22	Torquay United	42	4	10	7	27	36	4	4	13	26	67	30

1928/29

Bottom of Division Three (South)

No	Date	Opponent	Score	Scorers	Att	Bartley JWE	Bruce H	Crawford GW	Dominy AA	Dowell L	Ellis FC	Forsyth J	Hanney WPE	Hebden GHR	Legge AE	Millington T	Pearce H	Picken AH	Poxton JH	Rivers W	Robertson JW	Rutherford J(2)	Sly H	Taylor FE	Tyler S	Wilcox JC	Williams WJ	Wilson J	Young A
1	Aug 25	FULHAM	2-2	Dominy, Poxton	9457		4	5	8	10				1	7				11		2				3	9			6
2	29	TORQUAY UNITED	1-1	Poxton	4501		4	5	8	10				1	7				11		2				3	9			6
3	Sep 1	Queen's Park Rangers	0-1		12969		4	5	8				9	1	7				11		2				3	10			6
4	5	Torquay United	1-2	Wilcox	5006		4		8					1	7		10		11		2				3	9	5		6
5	8	BRISTOL ROVERS	1-0	Pearce	5632	2	4		8					1		7	10		11						3	9	5		6
6	15	Watford	0-1		9881		4		8					1		7			11		2			10	3	9	5		6
7	22	WALSALL	1-4	Poxton	5314		4		10		6			1	7				11		2			8	3	9	5		
8	29	Newport County	0-5		4354		4		8	10	6			1	7				11		2			9	3		5		
9	Oct 6	CRYSTAL PALACE	0-1		5923				7		6	4		1					11	8	2			10	3	9	5		
10	13	Swindon Town	1-2	Wilcox	6751				7		6	4		1					11	8	2			10	3	9	5		
11	20	EXETER CITY	1-3	Rivers	3741				7		6	4		1					11	8	2			10	3	9	5		
12	27	Brighton & Hove Albion	1-3	Legge	6558				7			6		1	9		10	11		8	2		4		3		5		
13	Nov 3	NORWICH CITY	4-0	Legge, Dominy 3	4356		5		10			6		1	9	7		11		8	2		4		3				
14	10	Charlton Athletic	1-1	Taylor	8488		5		10			6		1		7		11			2		4	8	3	9			
15	17	NORTHAMPTON T	2-1	Taylor, Picken	5312		5		10			6		1	9	7		11			2		4	8	3				
16	Dec 1	LUTON TOWN	1-0	Dominy	4661		5		10			6		1	9		8	7	11		2				3				4
17	8	Coventry City	0-2		13444		5		10			6		1	8	7			11		2			9	3				4
18	15	BOURNEMOUTH	2-2	Dominy 2	3202		4	5	10			6		1	9	7			11		2			8	3				
19	22	Merthyr Town	3-2	Dominy, Taylor 2	1669		5		10			6		1		7			11		2			8	3	9			4
20	25	Plymouth Argyle	0-3		15608		5		10			6		1	11	7					2			8	3	9			4
21	26	PLYMOUTH ARGYLE	2-0	Hanney 2	4346		5		10			6	9	1	11	7					2			8	3				4
22	29	Fulham	2-4	Taylor, Dominy	16816		5		10			6	9	1	11	7					2			8				3	4
23	Jan 5	QUEEN'S PARK RANGERS	0-0		4493		5		10			6	9	1	11	7								8	3			2	4
24	12	Brentford	1-4	Taylor	5042			5	10			6	9	1	11	7								8	3			2	4
25	19	Bristol Rovers	4-2	Hanney, Dominy 2, Poxton	4913			5	10			6	9	1	7				11		2			8	3				4
26	26	BRENTFORD	1-2	Dominy	3756			5	10			6		1	7				11		2			8	3	9			4
27	Feb 2	Walsall	0-4		3777		5		10			6	9		7				11		2	1		8	3				4
28	9	NEWPORT COUNTY	0-4		3223		5		10			6	9		7			11			2	1		8	3				4
29	23	SWINDON TOWN	0-0		3618		5		8	10	6	4		1		7		11			2			9	3				
30	Mar 2	Exeter City	2-4	Taylor 2	3787		5		8	10	6	4		1		7		11			2			9	3				
31	9	BRIGHTON & HOVE ALB	1-1	Hanney	3961		5		8			6	9	1		7	10		11		2		4		3				
32	16	Norwich City	2-1	Legge, Dominy	5385		4	5	8			6		1	9	7	10		11						3			2	
33	23	CHARLTON ATHLETIC	1-0	Legge	5070		4	5	8			6		1	9	7	10		11						3			2	
34	29	SOUTHEND UNITED	0-2		7693		4	5	8			6		1	9	7	10		11						3			2	
35	30	Northampton Town	0-1		10058		4	5	7	10		6		1	9				11					8	3			2	
36	Apr 1	Southend United	0-2		7773		4	5	7	10		6		1	9				11					8	3			2	
37	6	COVENTRY CITY	1-1	Crawford	4042			5	8	10	6	4		1	9	7			11						3			2	
38	13	Luton Town	0-8		7278		4	5		10		6	9	1	7				11					8	3			2	
39	24	WATFORD	0-0		2217			5	8	10	6	4			7				11		2	1		9	3				
40	27	Bournemouth	3-4	Dominy, Millington, Legge	4370				8	10	6	4			9	7			11		2	1		5	3				
41	May 1	Crystal Palace	0-3		15679				8	10	6	4	9			7			11		2	1		5	3				
42	4	MERTHYR TOWN	1-0	Pearce	2300	3			10		6	4			9	7	8		11		2	1		5					
					Apps	2	30	15	41	12	12	34	11	36	31	23	9	8	30	5	32	6	5	29	40	14	9	10	18
					Goals			1	14				4		5	1	2	1	4	1				8		2			

F.A. Cup

Rd	Date	Opponent	Score	Scorers	Att	Bartley JWE	Bruce H	Crawford GW	Dominy AA	Dowell L	Ellis FC	Forsyth J	Hanney WPE	Hebden GHR	Legge AE	Millington T	Pearce H	Picken AH	Poxton JH	Rivers W	Robertson JW	Rutherford J(2)	Sly H	Taylor FE	Tyler S	Wilcox JC	Williams WJ	Wilson J	Young A
R1	Nov 24	TORQUAY UNITED	0-0		5869		5		10			6		1		7		11			2		4	8	3	9			
rep	28	Torquay United	1-5	Poxton (p)	7000		5		10			6		1	9	7			11		2			8	3				4

		P	W	D	L	F	A	W	D	L	F	A	Pts
1	Charlton Athletic	42	14	5	2	51	22	9	3	9	35	38	54
2	Crystal Palace	42	14	2	5	40	25	9	6	6	41	42	54
3	Northampton Town	42	14	6	1	68	23	6	6	9	28	34	52
4	Plymouth Argyle	42	14	6	1	51	13	6	6	9	32	38	52
5	Fulham	42	14	3	4	60	31	7	7	7	41	40	52
6	Queen's Park Rangers	42	13	7	1	50	22	6	7	8	32	39	52
7	Luton Town	42	16	3	2	64	28	3	8	10	25	45	49
8	Watford	42	15	3	3	55	31	4	7	10	24	43	48
9	Bournemouth	42	14	4	3	54	31	5	5	11	30	46	47
10	Swindon Town	42	12	5	4	48	27	3	8	10	27	45	43
11	Coventry City	42	9	6	6	35	23	5	8	8	27	34	42
12	Southend United	42	10	7	4	44	27	5	4	12	36	48	41
13	Brentford	42	11	4	6	34	21	3	6	12	22	39	38
14	Walsall	42	11	7	3	47	25	2	5	14	26	54	38
15	Brighton & Hove Albion	42	14	2	5	39	28	2	4	15	19	48	38
16	Newport County	42	8	6	7	37	28	5	3	13	32	58	35
17	Norwich City	42	12	3	6	49	29	2	3	16	20	52	34
18	Torquay United	42	10	3	8	46	36	4	3	14	20	48	34
19	Bristol Rovers	42	9	6	6	39	28	4	1	16	21	51	33
20	Merthyr Town	42	11	6	4	42	28	0	2	19	13	75	30
21	Exeter City	42	7	6	8	49	40	2	5	14	18	48	29
22	GILLINGHAM	42	7	8	6	22	24	3	1	17	21	59	29

1929/30

21st in Division Three (South)

No.	Date	Opponents	Score	Scorers	Att	Bartley JWE	Beacham AJ	Beby JV	Bethell R	Bishop GA	Brennan TJ	Castle FR	Cheesmur FH	Collins AJ	Dowell L	Durnion AJ	Ellis FC	Geddes J	Gore SP	Jones WG	Martin SH	McCafferty J	Pateman GE	Robertson JW	Robinson RJC	Rutherford J(2)	Smith DL	Speed JG	Whyte C	Wilson J	Woolven LE
1	Aug 31	WALSALL	2-1	Castle, Cheesmur	8160		4		10	6		9	8	5					11			7		2			1			3	
2	Sep 4	Exeter City	0-3		5297				10	6		9	8	5			4		11			7		2			1			3	
3	7	Queen's Park Rangers	1-2	Cheesmur	11875	2	4		10	6		9	8	5				3	11			7					1				
4	11	EXETER CITY	2-0	Castle 2	4574	2			10	6		9	8	5			4	3	11								1		7		
5	14	FULHAM	0-1		7901	2			10	6		9	8	5			4	3	11								1		7		
6	16	Luton Town	0-2		7168	2	5			6		9	8		10		4		11								1		7	3	
7	21	Norwich City	0-2		9981	2	4			6		9	8	5	10				11								1		7	3	
8	28	CRYSTAL PALACE	1-1	Dowell	6818	2	4			6		9	8	5	10				11								1		7	3	
9	Oct 5	Plymouth Argyle	0-3		5777	2	4			6		9	8	5	10				11			7					1			3	
10	12	Northampton Town	1-3	Pateman	10663		4			6		9	10	5				2	11			7	8				1			3	
11	19	SWINDON TOWN	0-0		5597		4			6		9	10	5				2	11			7	8				1			3	
12	26	Brighton & Hove Albion	0-2		7504		4						9	5		10	6		11			7	8	2			1			3	
13	Nov 2	BRISTOL ROVERS	3-3	Cheesmur, Collins, Pateman	4794		4						9	5		10	6		11			7	8	2			1			3	
14	9	Brentford	1-2	Cheesmur	9603		4			6			9	5		10			11			7	8	2			1			3	
15	16	CLAPTON ORIENT	2-0	Cheesmur 2	1889		4			6			9	5		10			11		8	7		2			1			3	
16	23	Coventry City	0-5		8755		5			6			9			10	4		11		8	7		2			1			3	
17	Dec 7	Newport County	1-5	Geddes	1991		4			6		10	8					7						2	5		1		9	3	11
18	14	TORQUAY UNITED	0-2		3310	2	4			6		10	9						11				8		5		1		7	3	
19	21	Merthyr Town	1-1	Dowell	1352	2	4			6		9	8	5	10				11								1		7	3	
20	25	BOURNEMOUTH	1-5	Castle	3954		4			6		9	8	5	10				11					2			1		7	3	
21	26	Bournemouth	2-1	Durnion 2	11481		4	1		6			8		10	9	3		11	5				2					7		
22	28	Walsall	2-1	Durnion, Dowell	3568		5	1		6			8		10	9	3		11	4				2					7		
23	Jan 4	QUEEN'S PARK RANGERS	3-1	Durnion, Whyte, Cheesmur	5961			1		6			8	5	10	9	3		11	4				2					7		
24	11	WATFORD	1-2	Whyte	5562			1		6			8	5	10	9	3		11	4				2					7		
25	18	Fulham	1-2	Dowell	15196			1		6			8	5	10	9	3		11	4				2					7		
26	25	NORWICH CITY	1-2	Dowell	3249		4	1		6			8	5	10	9	3		11					2					7		
27	Feb 1	Crystal Palace	1-5	Whyte	8783		4	1		6			8	5	10		3	9	11					2					7		
28	8	PLYMOUTH ARGYLE	0-0		4905		4	1		6			8	5	10	9		3				11		2					7		
29	15	NORTHAMPTON T	5-2	Durnion 4, Cheesmur	4665		4	1		6			8	5	10	9		3				11		2					7		
30	22	Swindon Town	0-3		3070		4	1		6			8	5	10	9		3	11					2					7		
31	Mar 1	BRIGHTON & HOVE ALB	2-2	Durnion, Dowell	5035		4	1		6			8	5	10	9		3	11					2					7		
32	8	Bristol Rovers	0-3		5011		4	1		6			8	5	10	9			11					2					7	3	
33	15	BRENTFORD	1-3	Dowell	6749		4	1		6				5	10	9			11				8	2					7	3	
34	22	Clapton Orient	0-2		9348		4	1	8	6		9		5	10				11					2					7	3	
35	29	COVENTRY CITY	0-3		3865		4	1		6			8	5	10	9			11										7	3	
36	Apr 5	Watford	1-4	Brennan	4787		4	1		3	10		9	5	6	8				7				2							11
37	12	NEWPORT COUNTY	5-0	Ellis, Bethell, Cheesmur 2, Jones	2743		4	1	10	3	8		9	5			6			7				2				11			
38	18	SOUTHEND UNITED	1-0	Jones	7964		4	1	10	3	8		9	5			6			7				2				11			
39	19	Torquay United	1-1	Bethell	3472		4	1	10	3	8		9	5			6			7				2				11			
40	21	Southend United	0-0		9036		4	1	10	3	8		9	5			6			7				2				11			
41	26	MERTHYR TOWN	6-0	Cheesmur 6	3513				10	3	8		9	5			6			4		7		2		1		11			
42	May 3	LUTON TOWN	2-0	Cheesmur, Speed	4831		4		10	3	8		9	5			6			7				2		1		11			
					Apps	9	35	20	12	40	7	16	40	36	22	19	20	11	32	12	2	14	7	30	2	2	20	6	24	21	2
					Goals				2		1	4	17	1	7	9	1	1		2			2					1	3		

RA Baird played at 2 in game 35

F.A. Cup

Rd	Date	Opponents	Score	Scorers	Att	Bartley JWE	Beacham AJ	Beby JV	Bethell R	Bishop GA	Brennan TJ	Castle FR	Cheesmur FH	Collins AJ	Dowell L	Durnion AJ	Ellis FC	Geddes J	Gore SP	Jones WG	Martin SH	McCafferty J	Pateman GE	Robertson JW	Robinson RJC	Rutherford J(2)	Smith DL	Speed JG	Whyte C	Wilson J	Woolven LE
R1	Nov 30	MARGATE	0-2		4150		5			6			9			10		4	11		8	7		2			1			3	

		P	W	D	L	F	A	W	D	L	F	A	Pts
1	Plymouth Argyle	42	18	3	0	63	12	12	5	4	35	26	68
2	Brentford	42	21	0	0	66	12	7	5	9	28	32	61
3	Queen's Park Rangers	42	13	5	3	46	26	8	4	9	34	42	51
4	Northampton Town	42	14	6	1	53	20	7	2	12	29	38	50
5	Brighton & Hove Albion	42	16	2	3	54	20	5	6	10	33	43	50
6	Coventry City	42	14	3	4	54	25	5	6	10	34	48	47
7	Fulham	42	12	6	3	54	33	6	5	10	33	50	47
8	Norwich City	42	14	4	3	55	28	4	6	11	33	49	46
9	Crystal Palace	42	14	5	2	56	26	3	7	11	25	48	46
10	Bournemouth	42	11	6	4	47	24	4	7	10	25	37	43
11	Southend United	42	11	6	4	41	19	4	7	10	28	40	43
12	Clapton Orient	42	10	8	3	38	21	4	5	12	17	41	41
13	Luton Town	42	13	4	4	42	25	1	8	12	22	53	40
14	Swindon Town	42	10	7	4	42	25	3	5	13	31	58	38
15	Watford	42	10	4	7	37	30	5	4	12	23	43	38
16	Exeter City	42	10	6	5	45	29	2	5	14	22	44	35
17	Walsall	42	10	4	7	45	24	3	4	14	26	54	34
18	Newport County	42	9	9	3	48	29	3	1	17	26	56	34
19	Torquay United	42	9	6	6	50	38	1	5	15	14	56	31
20	Bristol Rovers	42	11	3	7	45	31	0	5	16	22	62	30
21	GILLINGHAM	42	9	5	7	38	28	2	3	16	13	52	30
22	Merthyr Town	42	5	6	10	39	49	1	3	17	21	86	21

1930/31

16th in Division Three (South)

							Battiste W	Beacham AJ	Bethell R	Bishop GA	Boylen RH	Brennan TJ	Cheesmur FH	Collins AJ	Death WG	Dowell L	Ellis FC	French JB	Harbot JW	Jamieson HJ	Jones WG	Lester FC	Loasby H	McGregor J	Pateman GE	Robertson JW	Rutherford J(2)	Scott G	Smeaton AR	Smith DL	White WW	Woods A
1	Aug	30	BRIGHTON & HOVE ALB	0-0		5325	7	4		3		10		5	11			8					9			2	1		6			
2	Sep	3	BRISTOL ROVERS	1-1	Loasby	5230	7		10	3				5	11			8			4		9			2	1		6			
3		6	Torquay United	0-3		5728		4		3		8	10	5	11		6				7		9			2	1					
4		10	NEWPORT COUNTY	4-1	Loasby 2, Cheesmur 2	3181	7	4	11	3		8	10	5			6						9			2	1					
5		13	NORTHAMPTON T	0-2		4821		4	11	3	7	8	10	5			6						9	2			1					
6		15	Newport County	3-1	Death, Loasby 2	2291		4	7				10	5	11		6	8					9	3		2	1					
7		20	Brentford	1-1	Bethell	9407		4	7				10	5	11		6	8					9	3		2	1					
8		27	CRYSTAL PALACE	6-2	Loasby 4, Bethell 2	7123		4	7				10	5	11		6	8					9	3		2	1					
9	Oct	4	Southend United	2-3	French, Death	7476		4	7				10	5	11		6	8					9	3		2	1					
10		11	LUTON TOWN	4-0	Death, Loasby 2 (1p), Bethell	7491		4	7	6			10	5	11			8					9	3		2	1					
11		18	CLAPTON ORIENT	0-0		8445		4	7	6			10	5	11			8					9	3		2	1					
12		25	Notts County	1-2	Bethell	11740		4	7	3			10	5	11		6						9	2	8		1					
13	Nov	1	WATFORD	4-2	Brennan, Bethell, Loasby 2	3717		4	7	3		8	10	5	11		6						9	2			1					
14		8	Bournemouth	1-2	Bethell	5490		4	7	3	11	8	10	5			6						9	2			1					
15		15	SWINDON TOWN	0-1		5909		4	7	3	11	8	10	5			6						9	2			1					
16		22	Fulham	1-1	Bethell	9067		4	7	3		8	10	5	11		6						9	2			1					
17	Dec	6	Walsall	2-2	McGregor (p), Loasby	4692		4	7	3		8	10	5	11		6						9	2			1					
18		17	QUEEN'S PARK RANGERS	2-2	Death, Loasby	2204		5	7	3					11		6	8					9	2			1		4		10	
19		20	Norwich City	0-4		6061		4	7					5	11		6	8					9	3		2	1				10	
20		25	THAMES	3-1	White, Bethell, Jamieson	6325		5	7	3					11		6			8	4		9			2	1				10	
21		26	Thames	2-2	White, Bethell	1477		5	7	3						11	6			8	4		9			2	1				10	
22		27	Brighton & Hove Albion	0-5		7610		5	7							11	3			8	4		9		10	2	1				6	
23	Jan	3	TORQUAY UNITED	2-3	Death, Loasby	3381			7					5	11		6			8	4		9	3		2	1				10	
24		10	COVENTRY CITY	2-0	Death, Bethell	3478		4	7	3				5	11		6			8			9	2			1				10	
25		17	Northampton Town	1-0	Loasby	6452		4	7	3				5			6	11		8			9	2			1				10	
26		28	BRENTFORD	1-1	Bethell	2547		4	7	3				5	11		6			8			9	2			1				10	
27		31	Crystal Palace	0-5		15052		4	7	3				5	11		6			8				2	9		1				10	
28	Feb	7	SOUTHEND UNITED	1-0	White	4223		4	7	3				5	11		6	8						2	9		1				10	
29		14	Luton Town	1-4	Fraser (og)	5837		4	7	3				5			6	8						2	9		1	11			10	
30		21	Clapton Orient	2-0	White, Pateman	5193		4	7	3				5			6	8						2	9		1	11			10	
31		28	NOTTS COUNTY	0-5		8264		4	7	3				5			6	8					9	2			1	11			10	
32	Mar	7	Watford	0-1		3665		4	7	3				5	11		6	10		8			9	2			1					
33		14	BOURNEMOUTH	0-0		5023		4	10	6				5	11							3	9	2			1	7			8	
34		21	Swindon Town	2-5	White, Loasby	4112			10	6				5	11		4					3	9	2			1	7			8	
35		28	FULHAM	3-2	Bethell, Loasby, White	4898			7	6				5			4	10				3	9	2			1	11			8	
36	Apr	3	EXETER CITY	3-5	Collins, Bethell, Harbot	6408			7	6				5			4	10	9			3		2				11		1	8	
37		4	Coventry City	2-1	White, Pateman	7031		5	7	6							4					3	9	2	10		1	11			8	
38		6	Exeter City	0-3		7146		5	7	6							4						9	3	10	2		11		1	8	
39		11	WALSALL	2-0	Scott, White	4946		5	7	6							4					3	9	2	10			11		1	8	
40		18	Queen's Park Rangers	0-1		6890		5	7	6					10		4					3	9	2				11		1	8	
41		25	NORWICH CITY	2-1	White, Pateman	2693		5	7						10		4					3		2	9			11		1	8	6
42	May	2	Bristol Rovers	0-1		4657			7					5	10		4		9			3		2				11		1	8	6
						Apps	3	36	40	33	3	9	15	33	27	2	37	18	2	9	6	9	35	35	10	16	36	13	3	6	24	2
						Goals			14			1	2	1	6			1	1	1			19	1	3			1			9	

One own goal

F.A. Cup

							Battiste W	Beacham AJ	Bethell R	Bishop GA	Boylen RH	Brennan TJ	Cheesmur FH	Collins AJ	Death WG	Dowell L	Ellis FC	French JB	Harbot JW	Jamieson HJ	Jones WG	Lester FC	Loasby H	McGregor J	Pateman GE	Robertson JW	Rutherford J(2)	Scott G	Smeaton AR	Smith DL	White WW	Woods A
R1	Nov	29	GUILDFORD	7-2	Loasby 3,Death 2,Cheesmur,Beacham	7000		4		3			10	5	11		6	8			7		9	2			1					
R2	Dec	13	Aldershot	1-3	Death	8392		4	7	3				5	11	10	6	8					9	2			1					

		P	W	D	L	F	A	W	D	L	F	A	Pts
1	Notts County	42	16	4	1	58	13	8	7	6	39	33	59
2	Crystal Palace	42	17	2	2	71	20	5	5	11	36	51	51
3	Brentford	42	14	3	4	62	30	8	3	10	28	34	50
4	Brighton & Hove Albion	42	13	5	3	45	20	4	10	7	23	33	49
5	Southend United	42	16	0	5	53	26	6	5	10	23	34	49
6	Northampton Town	42	10	6	5	37	20	8	6	7	40	39	48
7	Luton Town	42	15	3	3	61	17	4	5	12	15	34	46
8	Queen's Park Rangers	42	15	0	6	57	23	5	3	13	25	52	43
9	Fulham	42	15	3	3	49	21	3	4	14	28	54	43
10	Bournemouth	42	11	7	3	39	22	4	6	11	33	51	43
11	Torquay United	42	13	5	3	56	26	4	4	13	24	58	43
12	Swindon Town	42	15	5	1	68	29	3	1	17	21	65	42
13	Exeter City	42	12	6	3	55	35	5	2	14	29	55	42
14	Coventry City	42	11	4	6	55	28	5	5	11	20	37	41
15	Bristol Rovers	42	12	3	6	49	36	4	5	12	26	56	40
16	GILLINGHAM	42	10	6	5	40	29	4	4	13	21	47	38
17	Walsall	42	9	5	7	44	38	5	4	12	34	57	37
18	Watford	42	9	4	8	41	29	5	3	13	31	46	35
19	Clapton Orient	42	12	3	6	47	33	2	4	15	16	58	35
20	Thames	42	12	5	4	34	20	1	3	17	20	73	34
21	Newport County	42	10	5	6	45	31	1	1	19	24	80	28
22	Norwich City	42	10	7	4	37	20	0	1	20	10	56	28

1931/32

21st in Division Three (South)

							Ames LEG	Beacham AJ	Bethell R	Bishop GA	Buckle GF	Burnett N	Collins AJ	Cronin WJ	Gellatly CT	Jamieson HJ	Jones WJ	Kidd GI	Lester FC	Lewis D	McGregor J	Renwick J	Robertson JW	Rotherham AE	Scott G	Shaw J	Shipley T	Smith AA	Vallance H	Watkins ET	White WW	Williams AL	Woolven LE
1	Aug	29	Southend United	0-2		10665		4		6			5						3	1	2	9			11	10					8	7	
2	Sep	2	READING	1-1	Renwick	5553				6		1	5						3		2	9		4	11	10					8	7	
3		5	FULHAM	2-1	Renwick, White	7368		4	10	6		1	5						3		2	9			11						8	7	
4		9	LUTON TOWN	1-3	Renwick	5950		4	10	6		1	5						3		2	9			11						8	7	
5		12	Thames	0-3		1991		4		6		1	5						3		2	9			11	10					8	7	
6		14	Luton Town	0-2		6333	11	4		6		1	5		9				3		2					8					10	7	
7		19	BRENTFORD	0-2		7225				6			5		3					1				4	11	8	2			9	10	7	
8		26	Exeter City	0-4		5353							5		3	6				1				4	11	10	2			9	8	7	
9	Oct	3	COVENTRY CITY	1-3	Williams	5199			8	6			5						3	1	2			4						10	9	7	11
10		10	Watford	0-2		10079		4	10	6			5		3					1	2				11					9	8	7	
11		17	CRYSTAL PALACE	0-0		4856		4	9				5		3	10	6			1	2				11						8	7	
12		24	Bournemouth	2-0	White, Scott	5365		4	9		1		5		3	10	6				2				11						8	7	
13		31	QUEEN'S PARK RANGERS	1-0	White	5457		4	9		1		5		3	10	6				2				11						8	7	
14	Nov	7	Bristol Rovers	2-5	Ames, Bethell	6414	11	4	9		1		5		3	10	6						2								8	7	
15		14	TORQUAY UNITED	1-1	Bethell	3919	11	4	9		1		5		3	10	6						2								8	7	
16		21	Clapton Orient	1-3	Williams	5405	10	4	9	6	1		5	8	3										11		2					7	
17	Dec	5	Norwich City	1-1	Vallance	7721		4	10	6	1		5		3						2				11				9		8	7	
18		19	Mansfield Town	1-3	Scott	5400		4	10	6	1		5		3						2				11				9		8	7	
19		25	NORTHAMPTON T	3-2	White, Scott (p), Williams	6823		4	10		1		5		3		6				2				11				9		8	7	
20		26	Northampton Town	0-1		12491		4	10		1		5		3		6				2				11				9		8	7	
21	Jan	2	SOUTHEND UNITED	4-0	Scott, Vallance 3	5353		4	10		1		5		3		6				2				11				9		8	7	
22		9	SWINDON TOWN	2-1	Scott, Vallance	6287		4	10		1		5		3		6				2				11				9		8	7	
23		16	Fulham	2-0	White, Bethell	11953		4	10		1		5		3		6				2				11				9		8	7	
24		23	THAMES	2-0	White, Vallance	6224		4	10		1		5		3		6				2				11				9		8	7	
25		30	Brentford	1-1	Bethell	11361		4	10		1		5		3	7	6				2				11				9		8		
26	Feb	6	EXETER CITY	0-1		8233		4	10		1		5		3		6				2				11				9		8	7	
27		13	Coventry City	4-6	White, Vallence, Bethell 2	11181		4	10		1		5		3		6								11		2		9		8	7	
28		20	WATFORD	0-1		5712		4	10	2	1		5		3		6								11				9		8	7	
29		27	Crystal Palace	0-1		11596		4	10	2	1		5		3		6								11				9		8	7	
30	Mar	5	BOURNEMOUTH	1-4	Scott (p)	5087		4	10	2	1		5		3	8	6								11						9	7	
31		10	Queen's Park Rangers	0-7		3881		4	10	6	1		5		3			9			2										8	7	11
32		19	BRISTOL ROVERS	1-0	McGregor (p)	3965		4	10	6	1		5		3		7	9			2										8		
33		25	CARDIFF CITY	1-1	Smith	8015		4	11	6	1		5		3		7				2					10		9			8		
34		26	Torquay United	0-1		3038		4	10	6	1		5		3		11				2							9			8	7	
35		28	Cardiff City	0-1		10455		4	10	6	1		5		3		11				2					8					9	7	
36	Apr	2	CLAPTON ORIENT	0-2		4105		4	11		1		5		3		6	9			2					10					8	7	
37		9	Swindon Town	0-4		2775		4	11		1		5	10	3		8	9			2											7	
38		13	BRIGHTON & HOVE ALB	0-0		2174		4	11		1		5		3		8	9			2										10	7	
39		16	NORWICH CITY	3-3	Williams 2, White	2049		4	10		1		5		3		6	9			2										8	7	11
40		23	Brighton & Hove Albion	0-7		4583		4	10		1		5		3		8	6			2										9	7	11
41		30	MANSFIELD TOWN	2-0	Collins, Williams	2936	11	4	10			1	5		3		8	6			2										9	7	
42	May	7	Reading	0-2		6292		4	10	11		1	5		3		8	6			2										9	7	
						Apps	5	38	36	21	29	7	42	2	36	8	28	9	7	6	33	5	2	4	26	9	4	2	13	4	40	39	4
						Goals	1		6				1								1	3			6			1	7		9	5	

WS Parker played in game 32 at 11

J Graham played at 6 in games 37 and 38

F.A. Cup

							Ames LEG	Beacham AJ	Bethell R	Bishop GA	Buckle GF	Burnett N	Collins AJ	Cronin WJ	Gellatly CT	Jamieson HJ	Jones WJ	Kidd GI	Lester FC	Lewis D	McGregor J	Renwick J	Robertson JW	Rotherham AE	Scott G	Shaw J	Shipley T	Smith AA	Vallance H	Watkins ET	White WW	Williams AL	Woolven LE
R1	Nov	28	Bristol Rovers	1-5	Bethell	8000		4	9	6	1		5		3	10										11	2				8	7	

		P	W	D	L	F	A	W	D	L	F	A	Pts
1	Fulham	42	15	3	3	72	27	9	6	6	39	35	57
2	Reading	42	19	1	1	65	21	4	8	9	32	46	55
3	Southend United	42	12	5	4	41	18	9	6	6	36	35	53
4	Crystal Palace	42	14	7	0	48	12	6	4	11	26	51	51
5	Brentford	42	11	6	4	40	22	8	4	9	28	30	48
6	Luton Town	42	16	1	4	62	25	4	6	11	33	45	47
7	Exeter City	42	16	3	2	53	16	4	4	13	24	46	47
8	Brighton & Hove Albion	42	12	4	5	42	21	5	8	8	31	37	46
9	Cardiff City	42	14	2	5	62	29	5	6	10	25	44	46
10	Norwich City	42	12	7	2	51	22	5	5	11	25	45	46
11	Watford	42	14	4	3	49	27	5	4	12	32	52	46
12	Coventry City	42	17	2	2	74	28	1	6	14	34	69	44
13	Queen's Park Rangers	42	11	6	4	50	30	4	6	11	29	43	42
14	Northampton Town	42	12	3	6	48	26	4	4	13	21	43	39
15	Bournemouth	42	8	8	5	42	32	5	4	12	28	46	38
16	Clapton Orient	42	7	8	6	41	35	5	3	13	36	55	35
17	Swindon Town	42	12	2	7	47	31	2	4	15	23	53	34
18	Bristol Rovers	42	11	6	4	46	30	2	2	17	19	62	34
19	Torquay United	42	9	6	6	49	39	3	3	15	23	67	33
20	Mansfield Town	42	11	5	5	54	45	0	5	16	21	63	32
21	GILLINGHAM	42	8	6	7	26	26	2	2	17	14	56	28
22	Thames	42	6	7	8	35	35	1	2	18	18	74	23

1932/33

7th in Division Three (South)

							Armfield WC	Bethell R	Collins AJ	Cropper A	Darling HL	Forbes AS	Gellatly CT	High S	Holland T	Jackson R	Kidd GI	Lester FC	Liddle JF	Nicol G	Purcell GW	Raleigh S	Robertson IW	Shipley T	Torr F
1	Aug	27	Brighton & Hove Albion	0-1		9517	7		5	10	4		3		1	2	6		11		8	9			
2		31	NORWICH CITY	0-2		6824	7	10	5		4		3		1	2	6		11		8	9			
3	Sep	3	BRISTOL ROVERS	2-0	Purcell, Collins	3270	7		5	10	4				1		6	3	11		8	9		2	
4		5	Norwich City	0-2		8583	7		5	10	4				1		6	3	11		8	9		2	
5		10	Aldershot Town	0-3		5966	7		5	10	4				1		6	3	11		8	9		2	
6		17	QUEEN'S PARK RANGERS	4-1	Armfield, Liddle, Nicol, Cropper	7375	7		5	10	4				1	2	6		11	9	8			3	
7		24	Southend United	2-2	Liddle, Shipley (p)	5278	7		5	10	4				1	2	6		11	9	8			3	
8	Oct	1	CRYSTAL PALACE	2-0	Nicol 2	9827	7		5	10	4				1	2	6		11	9	8			3	
9		8	Luton Town	1-2	Nicol	6244	7		5	10	4				1	2	6		11	9	8			3	
10		15	Watford	0-2		8128	7	10	5	8	4				1		6	3	11	9			2		
11		22	EXETER CITY	1-2	Nicol	5885	7	6	5	10	4				1	2		3	11	9	8				
12		29	Torquay United	2-1	Nicol, Raleigh	3118		7			4	5		6	1	2			11	9	8	10		3	
13	Nov	5	BRENTFORD	1-3	Raleigh	12880		7			4	5		6	1	2			11	9	8	10		3	
14		12	Coventry City	2-4	Nicol, Liddle	11691		7			4	5		6	1	2			11	9	8	10		3	
15		19	BRISTOL CITY	4-2	Nicol 2, Bethell, Purcell	4553		7				5		4	1	2	6		11	9	8	10		3	
16	Dec	3	CLAPTON ORIENT	3-1	Liddle, Purcell 2 (1p)	5638		7	5	10		4	3	6	1	2			11	9	8				
17		17	BOURNEMOUTH	4-0	Bethell 2, Nicol 2	4843		7	5			4	3	6	1	2			11	9	8	10			
18		24	Newport County	2-0	Purcell, Bethell	4113		7	5			4	3	6	1	2			11	9	8	10			
19		26	Cardiff City	0-1		11178		7	5	10		4	3	6	1	2			11	9	8				
20		27	CARDIFF CITY	1-1	Cropper	10449		7	5	10		4	3	6	1	2			11	9		8			
21		31	BRIGHTON & HOVE ALB	2-0	Purcell, Nicol	5818	7	10	5			4			1	2	6	3	11	9	8				
22	Jan	7	Bristol Rovers	0-1		7903	7	10	5			4			1	2	6	3	11	9	8				
23		14	Northampton Town	0-1		3289	7	3	5			4			1	2	6			9	8	10			11
24		21	ALDERSHOT TOWN	5-2	Liddle, Purcell, Raleigh, Nicol, Kidd	4924		10	5			4			1	2	6	3	11	9	8	7			
25		28	Queen's Park Rangers	1-1	Raleigh	4169		10	5			4			1		6	3	11	9	8	7		2	
26	Feb	4	SOUTHEND UNITED	3-2	Raleigh 2 (1p), Liddle	5816		10	5	8		4			1	2	6	3	11	9		7			
27		11	Crystal Palace	1-5	Raleigh	8280	7	8	5			4			1	2	6	3	11	9		10			
28		22	LUTON TOWN	1-1	Nicol	2152	7		5	10		4			1	2	6	3	11	9		8			
29		25	WATFORD	3-3	Liddle, Armfield, Nicol (p)	4208	7	10	5			4			1	2	6	3	11	9	8				
30	Mar	4	Exeter City	1-2	Armfield	7309	7					5		4	1	2	6	3	11	9	8	10			
31		11	TORQUAY UNITED	1-1	Liddle	5786	7			10		5		4	1	2	6	3	11	9		8			
32		18	Brentford	2-1	Armfield, Nicol	11445	7	10	5			4			1	2	6	3	11	9		8			
33		25	COVENTRY CITY	3-0	Bethell 2, Nicol	6691	7	10	5			4			1	2	6	3	11	9		8			
34	Apr	1	Bristol City	1-1	Armfield	7309	7	10	5			4			1	2	6	3	11	9		8			
35		8	NORTHAMPTON T	5-1	Armfield, Raleigh 2, Nicol 2 (1p)	7352	7	10	5			4			1	2	6	3	11	9		8			
36		14	READING	4-1	Liddle 2, Nicol, Armfield	12246	7	10	5			4			1	2	6	3	11	9		8			
37		15	Clapton Orient	2-1	Nicol 2	5152	7	10	5			4			1	2	6	3	11	9	8				
38		17	Reading	0-4		9756	7	10	5			4			1	2	6	3	11	9	8				
39		22	SWINDON TOWN	3-1	Liddle, Nicol 2	6272	7	10	5			4			1	2	6	3	11	9		8			
40		26	Swindon Town	1-1	Purcell	2754	7		5			4	3		1	2	6		11	9	8	10			
41		29	Bournemouth	0-1		2710	7		5			4	3		1	2	6		11	9	8	10			
42	May	6	NEWPORT COUNTY	2-0	Nicol (p), Raleigh	5737	7		5			4	3		1	2	6		11	9	8	10			
						Apps	30	28	36	16	14	31	10	11	42	37	33	23	41	37	30	29	1	12	1
						Goals	7	6	1	2							1		11	25	8	10		1	

F.A. Cup

							Armfield WC	Bethell R	Collins AJ	Cropper A	Darling HL	Forbes AS	Gellatly CT	High S	Holland T	Jackson R	Kidd GI	Lester FC	Liddle JF	Nicol G	Purcell GW	Raleigh S	Robertson IW	Shipley T	Torr F
R1	Nov	26	WYCOMBE WANDERERS	1-1	Bethell			7			4	5		6	1	2			11	9	8	10		3	
rep		30	Wycombe Wanderers	4-2	Nicol 2, Cox (og), Cropper			7	5	10		4	3	6	1	2			11	9	8				
R2	Dec	10	Bristol Rovers	1-1	Nicol	11000		7	5	6		4	3		1	2			11	9	8	10			
rep		14	BRISTOL ROVERS	1-3	Purcell (p)	6511		7	5	6		4	3		1	2			11	9	8	10			

		P	W	D	L	F	A	W	D	L	F	A	Pts
1	Brentford	42	15	4	2	45	19	11	6	4	45	30	62
2	Exeter City	42	17	2	2	57	13	7	8	6	31	35	58
3	Norwich City	42	16	3	2	49	17	6	10	5	39	38	57
4	Reading	42	14	5	2	68	30	5	8	8	35	41	51
5	Crystal Palace	42	14	4	3	51	21	5	4	12	27	43	46
6	Coventry City	42	16	1	4	75	24	3	5	13	31	53	44
7	GILLINGHAM	42	14	4	3	54	24	4	4	13	18	37	44
8	Northampton Town	42	16	5	0	54	11	2	3	16	22	55	44
9	Bristol Rovers	42	13	5	3	38	22	2	9	10	23	34	44
10	Torquay United	42	12	7	2	51	26	4	5	12	21	41	44
11	Watford	42	11	8	2	37	22	5	4	12	29	41	44
12	Brighton & Hove Albion	42	13	3	5	42	20	4	5	12	24	45	42
13	Southend United	42	11	5	5	39	27	4	6	11	26	55	41
14	Luton Town	42	12	8	1	60	32	1	5	15	18	46	39
15	Bristol City	42	11	5	5	59	37	1	8	12	24	53	37
16	Queen's Park Rangers	42	9	8	4	48	32	4	3	14	24	55	37
17	Aldershot	42	11	6	4	37	21	2	4	15	24	51	36
18	Bournemouth	42	10	7	4	44	27	2	5	14	16	54	36
19	Cardiff City	42	12	4	5	48	30	0	3	18	21	69	31
20	Clapton Orient	42	7	8	6	39	35	1	5	15	20	58	29
21	Newport County	42	9	4	8	42	42	2	3	16	19	63	29
22	Swindon Town	42	7	9	5	36	29	2	2	17	24	76	29

1933/34

17th in Division Three (South)

	Date	Opponent	Result	Scorers	Att	Barrie G	Bethell R	Clark JF	Collins AJ	Forbes AS	Gellatly CT	Griffiths S	Holland T	Hopkins TE	Jackson R	Kidd GI	Lester FC	Liddle JF	Mills AS	Mooney H	Nicol G	Purcell GW	Raleigh S	Robinson CA	Scott A	Stanbury GH	Syred TG	Williams AL
1	Aug 26	Coventry City	1-7	Purcell	17520		10		5	4	3		1		2	6		11			9	8	7					
2	30	SOUTHEND UNITED	0-0		8416		7		5	4			1		2	6	3	11			9	8	10					
3	Sep 2	READING	5-1	Purcell 2, Nicol, Scott, Raleigh	7757				5	4			1		2	6	3	11			9	8	7		10			
4	6	Southend United	2-1	Kidd, Scott	7208				5	4			1		2	6	3	11			9	8	7		10			
5	9	Watford	1-2	Purcell	8267				5	4			1			6	3	11				8	7	2	10		9	
6	16	CHARLTON ATHLETIC	1-1	Raleigh	10086				5	4			1		2	6	3	11			9	8	7		10			
7	23	Bournemouth	1-1	Mills	4874				5	4			1		2	6	3	11	7		9	8	10					
8	30	CARDIFF CITY	6-2	* see below	8907				5	4			1		2	6	3	11	7		9	8	10					
9	Oct 7	Exeter City	0-2		6985				5	4			1		2	6	3		7	11	9	8	10					
10	14	NEWPORT COUNTY	1-0	Purcell (p)	4630				5	4			1		2	6	3	11	7		9	8	10					
11	21	Norwich City	1-4	Purcell (p)	9384		10		5	4			1		2	6	3	11	7		9	8						
12	28	BRISTOL CITY	2-1	Nicol, Purcell (p)	6238		10		5	4			1		2	6	3	11	7		9	8						
13	Nov 4	Clapton Orient	1-2	Scott	7242			5		4			1		2	6	3	11				8	7		9			10
14	11	SWINDON TOWN	3-3	Nicol, Scott, Liddle	6068		3			5			1		2	6		11			9	10	7	4	8			
15	18	Brighton & Hove Albion	2-5	Nicol, Purcell (p)	5186		3		5	4			1		2	6		11	7		9	10	8					
16	Dec 2	Luton Town	2-4	Mills (p), Raleigh	5447		10		5	4			1		2	6	3	11	7				9		8			
17	16	Torquay United	1-2	Raleigh	2294		8		5	4		10	1			6	3	11	7				9	2				
18	23	QUEEN'S PARK RANGERS	1-4	Raleigh	6979				5	4		10	1		2	6		11				8	9	3	7			
19	25	Bristol Rovers	2-4	Raleigh, Nicol	17582		10	5		4	3		1		2	6		11	7		9		8					
20	26	BRISTOL ROVERS	3-2	Mills (p), Nicol 2	4516		10		5	4	3		1			6		11	7		9		8	2				
21	30	COVENTRY CITY	3-7	Mills 3 (1p)	5169		10		5	4	3		1			6		11	7		9		8	2				
22	Jan 6	Reading	0-2		7528		10	5		2	3					4		11	7	6	9		8			1		
23	17	ALDERSHOT TOWN	1-2	Raleigh	2272		10	5		2	3		1			4		11	7	6	9		8					
24	20	WATFORD	3-3	Mills, Raleigh 2	4614		10	5		4			1		2	6	3	11	7				9		8			
25	29	Charlton Athletic	2-2	Purcell, Mills	3954		10		5	2	3	11	1			6			7			8	9	4				
26	Feb 3	BOURNEMOUTH	5-1	Liddle, Scott 2, Raleigh, Mills	2633		10		5	2	3		1			6		11	7				9	4	8			
27	10	Cardiff City	3-1	Liddle, Raleigh 2	5194		10		5	2	3		1			6		11	7				9	4	8			
28	17	EXETER CITY	1-1	Liddle	5898		4		5	2	3		1			6		11	7	10			9		8			
29	24	Newport County	1-3	Scott	3589		10		5				1		2	6	3	11	7				9	4	8			
30	Mar 3	NORWICH CITY	1-2	Nicol	7480								1	4	2	6	3	11	7		9		10	5	8			
31	10	Bristol City	1-1	Roberts (og)	6890								1	4	2	6	3	11	7				9	5	8			10
32	17	CLAPTON ORIENT	1-1	Nicol	5423	5						11	1		2	6	3	10	7		9		8	4				
33	24	Swindon Town	1-3	Liddle	6168	5	10						1		2	6	3	11	7				9	4	8			
34	30	Crystal Palace	2-3	Scott, Raleigh	12836	5	10						1		2	6	3	11	7				9	4	8			
35	31	BRIGHTON & HOVE ALB	3-0	Scott, Raleigh, Mills	6690	5	10						1		2	6	3	11	7				9	4	8			
36	Apr 2	CRYSTAL PALACE	0-5		9089	5	10						1		2	6	3	11	7				9	4	8			
37	7	Aldershot Town	2-0	Raleigh, Mills	2832	5				2			1			6	3	11	7		9		10	4	8			
38	11	NORTHAMPTON T	5-1	Liddle, Raleigh 3, Scott	3398	5				2			1			6	3	11	7		9		10	4	8			
39	14	LUTON TOWN	1-1	Nicol	4729	5				2			1			6	3	11	7		9		10	4	8			
40	21	Northampton Town	0-1		3702	5				2			1			6	3	11	7		9		10	4	8			
41	28	TORQUAY UNITED	3-3	Nicol 2, Scott	2821	5				2			1			6	3	11	7		9		10	4	8			
42	May 5	Queen's Park Rangers	0-5		5129	5				2			1			6	3	11	7		9			4	8			10
					Apps	11	23	5	23	34	10	4	41	2	26	42	29	40	33	4	26	17	39	23	25	1	1	3
					Goals					1						1		7	12		13	10	18		11			

Scorers in game 8: Liddle, Forbes, Nicol, Purcell, Russell(og), Mills

Two own goals

F.A. Cup

	Date	Opponent	Result	Scorers	Att	Barrie G	Bethell R	Clark JF	Collins AJ	Forbes AS	Gellatly CT	Griffiths S	Holland T	Hopkins TE	Jackson R	Kidd GI	Lester FC	Liddle JF	Mills AS	Mooney H	Nicol G	Purcell GW	Raleigh S	Robinson CA	Scott A	Stanbury GH	Syred TG	Williams AL
R1	Nov 25	Oxford City	5-1	Scott, Mills, Liddle, Purcell(p), Nicol	7533				5	4			1		2	6	3	11	7		9	10			8			
R2	Dec 9	Charlton Athletic	0-1						5	4			1		2	6	3	11	7			10	9		8			

Division Three (South) Cup

	Date	Opponent	Result	Scorers	Att	Barrie G	Bethell R	Clark JF	Collins AJ	Forbes AS	Gellatly CT	Griffiths S	Holland T	Hopkins TE	Jackson R	Kidd GI	Lester FC	Liddle JF	Mills AS	Mooney H	Nicol G	Purcell GW	Raleigh S	Robinson CA	Scott A	Stanbury GH	Syred TG	Williams AL
R1	Jan 25	Norwich City	0-4		2763		10	5		4	3		1		2	6		11	7		9				8			

		P	W	D	L	F	A	W	D	L	F	A	Pts
1	Norwich City	42	16	4	1	55	19	9	7	5	33	30	61
2	Coventry City	42	16	3	2	70	22	5	9	7	30	32	54
3	Reading	42	17	4	0	60	13	4	8	9	22	37	54
4	Queen's Park Rangers	42	17	2	2	42	12	7	4	10	28	39	54
5	Charlton Athletic	42	14	5	2	53	27	8	3	10	30	29	52
6	Luton Town	42	14	3	4	55	28	7	7	7	28	33	52
7	Bristol Rovers	42	14	4	3	49	21	6	7	8	28	26	51
8	Swindon Town	42	13	5	3	42	25	4	6	11	22	43	45
9	Exeter City	42	12	5	4	43	19	4	6	11	25	38	43
10	Brighton & Hove Albion	42	12	7	2	47	18	3	6	12	21	42	43
11	Clapton Orient	42	14	4	3	60	25	2	6	13	15	44	42
12	Crystal Palace	42	11	6	4	40	25	5	3	13	31	42	41
13	Northampton Town	42	10	6	5	45	32	4	6	11	26	46	40
14	Aldershot	42	8	6	7	28	27	5	6	10	24	44	38
15	Watford	42	12	4	5	43	16	3	3	15	28	47	37
16	Southend United	42	9	6	6	32	27	3	4	14	19	47	34
17	GILLINGHAM	42	8	8	5	49	41	3	3	15	26	55	33
18	Newport County	42	6	9	6	25	23	2	8	11	24	47	33
19	Bristol City	42	7	8	6	33	22	3	5	13	25	63	33
20	Torquay United	42	10	4	7	32	28	3	3	15	21	65	33
21	Bournemouth	42	7	7	7	41	37	2	2	17	19	65	27
22	Cardiff City	42	6	4	11	32	43	3	2	16	25	62	24

1934/35

20th in Division Three (South)

							Anstiss HA	Balcombe SL	Baldwin W	Barrie G	Bethell R	Crompton W	Doncaster AR	Forbes AS	Harvey JD	Holland T	Hopkins TE	Kidd GI	Lester FC	Marsden H	Nicol G	Orr A	Raleigh S	Randle HC	Robinson CA	Syred TG	Vallance H	Varty WC	Wiggins JA	Williams AL
1	Aug	25	TORQUAY UNITED	3-0	Raleigh 3	8128			8	5		7	11	4		1		6	3			10	9						2	
2		29	MILLWALL	1-3	Forsyth (og)	8669			8	5		7	11			1		6	3			10	9	4					2	
3	Sep	1	Reading	0-3		9681			8	5		7	11	4		1		6	3			10	9						2	
4		8	NORTHAMPTON T	3-1	Raleigh, Crompton 2	6938	8			5		7	11	4		1		6	3			10	9						2	
5		15	Bournemouth	1-1	Crompton	6208	8			5		7	11	4		1		6	3	2		10	9							
6		17	Millwall	2-3	Crompton, Anstiss	8877	8			5		7	11			1		6	3	2		10	9							
7		22	WATFORD	1-2	Doncaster (p)	4404	8			5		7	11			1		6	3	2		10	9	4						
8		29	Newport County	2-2	Crompton, Williams	5460				5		7			1			6	3		9	10	8	4					2	11
9	Oct	6	EXETER CITY	2-1	Barrie, Raleigh	6064				5		7			1			6	3		9	10	8	4					2	11
10		13	Bristol City	1-3	Crompton	9862						7			1			6	3			10	9	4	5	8			2	11
11		20	QUEEN'S PARK RANGERS	0-0		5898						7				1		6	3			10	9	4	5	8		11	2	
12		27	Crystal Palace	0-2		12942			8		6	7				1		10	3	2			9	4	5			11		
13	Nov	3	ALDERSHOT	1-1	Raleigh	4863					8	7				1		6	3	2	9		10	4	5			11		
14		10	Swindon Town	0-3		5289	8				10	7				1		6	3	2			9	4	5			11		
15		17	SOUTHEND UNITED	2-2	Doncaster, Baldwin	4168	8		9		7		10			1		6	3					4	5			11	2	
16	Dec	1	BRIGHTON & HOVE ALB	0-0		4115	8		10		7				1			6	3	2			9	4	5			11		
17		8	Cardiff City	2-0	Varty, Syred	8463	8		10		7				1			6	3	2				4	5	9		11		
18		15	CHARLTON ATHLETIC	3-6	Varty, Randle (p), Baldwin	5101	8		10		7				1			6	3	2				4	5	9		11		
19		22	Bristol Rovers	3-4	Baldwin 2, Randle (p)	7270	8		9	5	7		10		1			6	3	2				4				11		
20		25	Coventry City	0-4		24226	8		9	5	7		11		1			6	3	2		10		4						
21		26	COVENTRY CITY	2-5	Bethell 2	9233	8		9	5	7		10		1		4	6	3	2										11
22		29	Torquay United	0-5		3408	8		9	5	7		10		1		4	6	3	2								11		
23	Jan	5	READING	1-1	Baldwin	5094	8		9		7		10		1		4	6	3	2					5					11
24		19	Northampton Town	1-2	Anstiss	3783	8		9		7		10		1		4	6	3	2					5					11
25		26	BOURNEMOUTH	3-1	Vallance, Bethell, Doncaster	2672	8		10	5	7		11		1		4	6	3	2							9			
26	Feb	2	Watford	1-3	Baldwin	9622	8		10	5	7		11		1		4	6	3	2							9			
27		9	NEWPORT COUNTY	5-0	Doncaster,Baldwin 2,Vallance,Anstiss	3689	8		10	5			11			1		6	3	2				4		7	9			
28		16	Exeter City	0-2		4220	8		10	5			11			1		6	3	2				4		7	9			
29		23	BRISTOL CITY	1-0	Anstiss	4713	8		9	5	10		11			1		6	3	2				4		7				
30	Mar	2	Queen's Park Rangers	0-2		8157	8	7	9	5	10		11			1		6	3	2				4						
31		9	CRYSTAL PALACE	2-0	Doncaster, Baldwin	2712	8	7	9	5	10		11			1		6	3	2				4						
32		16	Aldershot	1-4	Baldwin	3515	8	7	9	5	10		11		1			6	3	2				4						
33		23	SWINDON TOWN	2-0	Baldwin, Vallance	3796	8	7	10	5			11			1		6	3	2				4			9			
34		30	Southend United	0-0		5936	8	7	10	5			11			1		6	3	2				4					9	
35	Apr	6	LUTON TOWN	1-1	Baldwin	4139	8	7	9	5			10			1		6	3	2				4						11
36		13	Brighton & Hove Albion	1-1	Doncaster	5227	8	7	9	5	10		11			1	6		3	2				4						
37		19	Clapton Orient	2-2	Doncaster, Baldwin	8131	8	7	9	5	10		11			1	6		3	2				4						
38		20	CARDIFF CITY	1-0	Anstiss	5820	8	7	9	5	10		11			1	6		3	2				4						
39		22	CLAPTON ORIENT	1-0	Doncaster	7034	8	7	9	5	10		11			1	6		3	2				4						
40		27	Charlton Athletic	0-2		13782	8	7	9	5	6		11			1			3	2				4						10
41	May	1	Luton Town	2-2	Bethell, Baldwin	3996	8		9	5	10		11			1	6		3					4		7			2	
42		4	BRISTOL ROVERS	1-1	Anstiss	3815	8	7	9	5	10		11			1	6		3					4					2	
						Apps	33	12	32	31	26	14	32	4	15	27	12	35	42	31	3	12	15	32	11	8	5	10	12	8
						Goals	6		14	1	4	6	8										6	2		1	3	2		1

One own goal

F.A. Cup

							Anstiss HA	Balcombe SL	Baldwin W	Barrie G	Bethell R	Crompton W	Doncaster AR	Forbes AS	Harvey JD	Holland T	Hopkins TE	Kidd GI	Lester FC	Marsden H	Nicol G	Orr A	Raleigh S	Randle HC	Robinson CA	Syred TG	Vallance H	Varty WC	Wiggins JA	Williams AL
R1	Nov	24	Bristol City	0-2		10055	8		10		7				1			6	3	2			9	4	5			11		

Division Three (South) Cup

							Anstiss HA	Balcombe SL	Baldwin W	Barrie G	Bethell R	Crompton W	Doncaster AR	Forbes AS	Harvey JD	Holland T	Hopkins TE	Kidd GI	Lester FC	Marsden H	Nicol G	Orr A	Raleigh S	Randle HC	Robinson CA	Syred TG	Vallance H	Varty WC	Wiggins JA	Williams AL
R1	Sep	26	LUTON TOWN	1-3	Williams				10	5		7			1			6	3	2			9	4		8				11

		P	*W*	*D*	*L*	*F*	*A*	*W*	*D*	*L*	*F*	*A*	*Pts*
1	Charlton Athletic	42	17	2	2	62	20	10	5	6	41	32	61
2	Reading	42	16	5	0	59	23	5	6	10	30	42	53
3	Coventry City	42	14	5	2	56	14	7	4	10	30	36	51
4	Luton Town	42	12	7	2	60	23	7	5	9	32	37	50
5	Crystal Palace	42	15	3	3	51	14	4	7	10	35	50	48
6	Watford	42	14	2	5	53	19	5	7	9	23	30	47
7	Northampton Town	42	14	4	3	40	21	5	4	12	25	46	46
8	Bristol Rovers	42	14	6	1	54	27	3	4	14	19	50	44
9	Brighton & Hove Albion	42	15	4	2	51	16	2	5	14	18	46	43
10	Torquay United	42	15	2	4	60	22	3	4	14	21	53	42
11	Exeter City	42	11	5	5	48	29	5	4	12	22	46	41
12	Millwall	42	11	4	6	33	26	6	3	12	24	36	41
13	Queen's Park Rangers	42	14	6	1	49	22	2	3	16	14	50	41
14	Clapton Orient	42	13	3	5	47	21	2	7	12	18	44	40
15	Bristol City	42	14	3	4	37	18	1	6	14	15	50	39
16	Swindon Town	42	11	7	3	45	22	2	5	14	22	56	38
17	Bournemouth	42	10	5	6	36	26	5	2	14	18	45	37
18	Aldershot	42	12	6	3	35	20	1	4	16	15	55	36
19	Cardiff City	42	11	6	4	42	27	2	3	16	20	55	35
20	GILLINGHAM	42	10	7	4	36	25	1	6	14	19	50	35
21	Southend United	42	10	4	7	40	29	1	5	15	25	49	31
22	Newport County	42	7	4	10	36	40	3	1	17	18	72	25

1935/36

16th in Division Three (South)

#	Month	Day	Opponent	Score	Scorers	Att.	Balcombe SL	Baldwin W	Barrie G	Ballsom WG	Bond GA	Dann RW	Doncaster AR	Duncan WMcK	Fisher F	Fowler AJ	Holland T	Hopkins TE	Lester FC	Loftus JL	Pybus G	Randle HC	Rossiter A	Scott EJ	Tadman GH	Turton GF	Watson WJB	Whitelaw DL
1	Aug	31	Northampton Town	0-0		15826		9	5				11	10			1	6	3			4	2		7		8	
2	Sep	4	Notts County	3-3	Doncaster, Bond, Tadman	9863			5		9		11	10			1	6	3			4	2		7		8	
3		7	CRYSTAL PALACE	0-2		8914			5		9		11	10			1	6	3			4	2		7		8	
4		11	NOTTS COUNTY	0-0		5162			5		9		11	10			1	6	3	8		4	2		7			
5		14	Reading	0-1		11008			5		9		11	10				6	3	8		4			7	2		1
6		18	Bristol Rovers	3-4	Baldwin, Duncan 2	5471		9	5				11	10				6	3		8	4			7	2		1
7		21	CARDIFF CITY	3-0	Duncan, Baldwin, Fisher	5663		9	5				11	10	8			6	3			4			7	2		1
8		28	Exeter City	5-2	Duncan 2, Doncaster 2, Tadman	5583		9	5				11	10	8			6	3			4			7	2		1
9	Oct	5	Bournemouth	2-1	Watson, Balcombe	9186	7	9	5			6	11		8				3			4	2				10	1
10		12	LUTON TOWN	0-1		8252	7	9	5				11		8			6	3			4	2				10	1
11		19	NEWPORT COUNTY	3-0	Tadman, Doncaster, Watson	5025		9	5				11	10				6	3			4	2		7		8	1
12		26	Coventry City	0-4		14811		9	5				11	10				6	3			4	2		7		8	1
13	Nov	2	SWINDON TOWN	3-1	Watson, Tadman, Bond	5058			5		9		11	10				6	3			4	2		7		8	1
14		9	Brighton & Hove Albion	1-1	Duncan	6220			5		9		11	10				6	3			4	2		7		8	1
15		16	TORQUAY UNITED	1-0	Tadman	4953			5		9		11	10				6	3			4	2		7		8	1
16		23	Millwall	1-4	Tadman	10693			5		9		11	10				6	3			4	2		7		8	1
17	Dec	7	Watford	2-1	Watson, Tadman	3914		9	5				11	10				6	3			4	2		7		8	1
18		21	Aldershot Town	2-0	Watson, Doncaster	3324		9	5				11	10				6	3			4	2		7		8	1
19		25	Clapton Orient	1-3	Tadman	9480		9	5	2			11			10		6	3			4			7		8	1
20		26	CLAPTON ORIENT	3-0	Tadman 2, Doncaster	10679		9	5	2			11	10				6	3			4			7		8	1
21		28	NORTHAMPTON T	2-3	Watson, Hopkins	6763		9	5	2			11	10				6	3			4			7		8	1
22	Jan	4	Crystal Palace	1-1	Baldwin	11726		9	5				11	10				6	3			4			7	2	8	1
23		11	BRISTOL CITY	2-1	Tadman, Baldwin (p)	7587		9	5				11	10				6	3			4			7	2	8	1
24		18	READING	2-0	Baldwin, Gregory (og)	7454		9	5				11	10				6	3			4			7	2	8	1
25		25	Cardiff City	0-4		5998		9	5				11	10				6	3			4			7	2	8	1
26	Feb	1	EXETER CITY	2-2	Baldwin, Tadman	6333		9	5				11	10				6	3			4			7	2	8	1
27		8	BOURNEMOUTH	1-2	Pybus	6342		9	5					11				6	3		8	4			7	2	10	1
28		15	Luton Town	2-1	Fisher, Doncaster	12276			5				11	10	9		1	6	3			4			7	2	8	
29		29	BRIGHTON & HOVE ALB	1-2	Fisher	4931			5				11	10	9		1	6	3			4	2		7		8	
30	Mar	7	Queen's Park Rangers	2-5	Fisher, Tadman	11119			5	3			11	10	9		1	6				4	2		7		8	
31		14	COVENTRY CITY	1-1	Baldwin	5990		9	5	2			11	10				6	3			4			7		8	1
32		19	Newport County	2-4	Baldwin 2	2515		9	5	2			11		10		1	6	3		8	4			7			
33		21	Torquay United	2-4	Tadman, Doncaster	2875		9	5				11		10		1	6	3		8	4	2		7			
34		28	MILLWALL	1-3	Wallbanks (og)	5634			5					10	9			6	3			4	2	11	7		8	1
35	Apr	4	Bristol City	1-2	Watson	6065		9	5	2			11	10				6	3			4			7		8	1
36		10	SOUTHEND UNITED	2-1	Fisher 2	7763		10	5	2		6	11		9				3			4			7		8	1
37		11	WATFORD	0-0		4920		9	5	2		6	11		10				3			4			7		8	1
38		13	Southend United	2-4	Duncan, Tadman (p)	10568			5	2		6	11	10	9				3			4			7		8	1
39		18	Swindon Town	0-3		5502		9	5	2		6			10							4	3	11	7		8	1
40		22	QUEEN'S PARK RANGERS	2-2	Tadman 2 (1p)	2405			5	2	9	6			10				3			4		11	7		8	1
41		25	ALDERSHOT TOWN	4-2	Tadman, Watson 3	2719		9	5	2		6			10				3		4			11	7		8	1
42	May	2	BRISTOL ROVERS	1-2	Watson	3640		9	5	2		6			10				3		4			11	7		8	1
						Apps	2	28	42	14	9	8	36	31	17	1	9	34	40	2	6	40	19	5	40	11	35	33
						Goals	1	9			2		10	5	6			1			1				18		11	

Two own goals

F.A. Cup

Round	Month	Day	Opponent	Score	Scorers	Att.	Balcombe SL	Baldwin W	Barrie G	Ballsom WG	Bond GA	Dann RW	Doncaster AR	Duncan WMcK	Fisher F	Fowler AJ	Holland T	Hopkins TE	Lester FC	Loftus JL	Pybus G	Randle HC	Rossiter A	Scott EJ	Tadman GH	Turton GF	Watson WJB	Whitelaw DL
R1	Nov	30	Exeter City	4-0	Baldwin 3, Tadman	8000		9	5				11	10				6	3			4	2		7		8	1
R2	Dec	14	Crewe Alexandra	1-2	Baldwin	8800		9	5				11	10				6	3			4	2		7		8	1

Division Three (South) Cup

Round	Month	Day	Opponent	Score	Scorers	Att.	Balcombe SL	Baldwin W	Barrie G	Ballsom WG	Bond GA	Dann RW	Doncaster AR	Duncan WMcK	Fisher F	Fowler AJ	Holland T	Hopkins TE	Lester FC	Loftus JL	Pybus G	Randle HC	Rossiter A	Scott EJ	Tadman GH	Turton GF	Watson WJB	Whitelaw DL
R1	Oct	2	EXETER CITY	0-0		2000		9	5				11	10	8			6	3			4			7	2		1
rep		16	Exeter City	2-4	Baldwin, Hopkins	2500		9	5	3			11					6			4	8	2		7		10	1

		P	W	D	L	F	A	W	D	L	F	A	Pts
1	Coventry City	42	19	1	1	75	12	5	8	8	27	33	57
2	Luton Town	42	13	6	2	56	20	9	6	6	25	25	56
3	Reading	42	18	0	3	52	20	8	2	11	35	42	54
4	Queen's Park Rangers	42	14	4	3	55	19	8	5	8	29	34	53
5	Watford	42	12	3	6	47	29	8	6	7	33	25	49
6	Crystal Palace	42	15	4	2	64	20	7	1	13	32	54	49
7	Brighton & Hove Albion	42	13	4	4	48	25	5	4	12	22	38	44
8	Bournemouth	42	9	6	6	36	26	7	5	9	24	30	43
9	Notts County	42	10	5	6	40	25	5	7	9	20	32	42
10	Torquay United	42	14	4	3	41	27	2	5	14	21	35	41
11	Aldershot	42	9	6	6	29	21	5	6	10	24	40	40
12	Millwall	42	9	8	4	33	21	5	4	12	25	50	40
13	Bristol City	42	11	5	5	32	21	4	5	12	16	38	40
14	Clapton Orient	42	13	2	6	34	15	3	4	14	21	46	38
15	Northampton Town	42	12	5	4	38	24	3	3	15	24	66	38
16	GILLINGHAM	42	9	5	7	34	25	5	4	12	32	52	37
17	Bristol Rovers	42	11	6	4	48	31	3	3	15	21	64	37
18	Southend United	42	8	7	6	38	21	5	3	13	23	41	36
19	Swindon Town	42	10	5	6	43	33	4	3	14	21	40	36
20	Cardiff City	42	11	5	5	37	23	2	5	14	23	50	36
21	Newport County	42	8	4	9	36	44	3	5	13	24	67	31
22	Exeter City	42	7	5	9	38	41	1	6	14	21	52	27

1936/37

11th in Division Three (South)

	Date	Opponent	Result	Scorers	Att	Armstrong W	Ballsom WG	Barrie G	Dodds JA	Duncan WMcK	Fowler AJ	Hartley S	Hopkins TE	Lester FC	McAleer J	Randle HC	Robinson TE	Scott EJ	Smethurst CFV	Watson WJB	Wheeler AJ	Whitelaw DL	Wilson TH	Wilson WR
1	Aug 29	BRIGHTON & HOVE ALB	1-0	McAleer	7338	5	2		9	10	7			3	11				4	8		1		6
2	Sep 2	Bournemouth	0-1		7034	5	2		9		7			3	11		10		4	8		1		6
3	5	Watford	1-6	Watson	9055	5	2			10				3	11	6	9	7	4	8		1		
4	9	BOURNEMOUTH	1-0	Dodds	4421	5			9			2	6	3	7	4	10	11		8		1		
5	12	SOUTHEND UNITED	1-0	Dodds	7873	5			9			2	6	3	7	4	10	11		8		1		
6	19	Newport County	0-0		8436	5			9			2	6	3	7	4	10	11		8		1		
7	21	Millwall	0-3		6580	5			9		7	2	6	3		4	10	11		8		1		
8	26	CRYSTAL PALACE	2-0	Watson, Scott	6441	5				10	7	2	6	3		4	9	11		8		1		
9	Oct 3	ALDERSHOT TOWN	1-2	Robinson	7260	5				10	7	2	6	3		4	9	11		8		1		
10	10	Swindon Town	0-3		8748	5				10	7	2	6	3		4	9	11		8		1		
11	17	Exeter City	1-1	Watson	5634	5						2	6	3		4	10	11		8	7	1	9	
12	24	READING	2-1	Robinson, Watson	7474	5					7	2	6	3		4	10	11		9		1	8	
13	31	Queen's Park Rangers	1-0	Robinson	5687	5					7	2	6	3		4	10	11		9		1	8	
14	Nov 7	BRISTOL CITY	5-3	Watson 3, Robinson 2	4023	5					7	2	6	3		4	10	11		9		1	8	
15	14	Torquay United	2-0	Watson, Scott	3612	5					7	2	6	3		4	10	11		9		1	8	
16	21	NOTTS COUNTY	3-0	Watson 3	12215	5					7	2	6	3		4	10	11		9		1	8	
17	Dec 5	WALSALL	2-2	Fowler, Watson (p)	7713	5					7	2	6	3		4	10	11		9		1	8	
18	19	CARDIFF CITY	0-0		8361	5					7	2	6	3		4	10	11		9		1	8	
19	25	BRISTOL ROVERS	1-0	Robinson	9440	5					7	2	6	3		4	10	11		9		1	8	
20	26	Brighton & Hove Albion	0-4		13977	5					7	2	6	3		4	10	11		9		1	8	
21	28	Bristol Rovers	3-0	Watson, Dodds, Robinson	7064	5	3		7	10		2	6			4	9			8	11	1		
22	Jan 2	WATFORD	2-1	Dodds, Wheeler	8320	5			7	10		2	6	3		4	9			8	11	1		
23	9	Southend United	2-0	Wheeler, Robinson	6456		5		7	10		2	6	3		4	9			8	11	1		
24	16	Clapton Orient	0-2		8305		5		7	10		2	6	3		4	9			8	11	1		
25	23	NEWPORT COUNTY	4-4	McAleer 2, Robinson (p), Watson	6125			5	7			2	6	3	11	4	10			9		1	8	
26	30	Crystal Palace	1-1	T Wilson	6566			5	7			2	6	3	11	4	10			9		1	8	
27	Feb 6	Aldershot Town	0-3		3797			5	7			2	6	3		4	10	11		9		1	8	
28	13	SWINDON TOWN	4-1	Dodds, Watson 3	6442		5		7			2	6	3	11	4	10			9		1	8	
29	24	EXETER CITY	2-2	Wheeler, Duncan	3464	5			7	10		2	6	3		4				9	11	1	8	
30	27	Reading	2-6	Robinson, Duncan	6775	5			7	10		2	6	3		4	9				11	1	8	
31	Mar 6	QUEEN'S PARK RANGERS	0-0		6965		5		7			2	6	3		4	10			9	11	1	8	
32	13	Bristol City	0-2		7803		5		7	10		2	6	3			8	11		9		1		4
33	20	TORQUAY UNITED	1-0	Robinson	5723	5			10		7	2	6	3		4	9	11				1	8	
34	26	NORTHAMPTON T	2-0	Watson, Robinson (p)	9426	5					7	2	6	3		4	10	11		9		1	8	
35	27	Notts County	0-2		20821	5					7	2	6	3		4	10	11		9		1	8	
36	29	Northampton Town	0-5		10164	5			7	11		2	10	3		4	8			9		1		6
37	Apr 3	CLAPTON ORIENT	0-2		6277	5					7	2	6	3		4	10	11		9		1	8	
38	7	Luton Town	2-5	Watson, Hartley	13386	5	2		7	10		9	6	3		4				11		1	8	
39	10	Walsall	1-2	Morgan (og)	4417	5	2		7	10		9	6	3		4				11		1	8	
40	17	LUTON TOWN	1-0	Dodds	7327	5			7	10		2	6	3		4		11		9		1	8	
41	24	Cardiff City	0-2		8358	5			7	10		2	6	3		4		11		9		1	8	
42	May 1	MILLWALL	1-0	Duncan	4453	5			7	10		2	6	3				11		9		1	8	4
					Apps	34	11	3	25	18	19	39	39	41	9	38	35	27	3	40	8	42	26	5
					Goals				6	3	1	1			3		12	2		19	3		1	

One own goal

F.A. Cup

	Date	Opponent	Result	Scorers	Att	Armstrong W	Ballsom WG	Barrie G	Dodds JA	Duncan WMcK	Fowler AJ	Hartley S	Hopkins TE	Lester FC	McAleer J	Randle HC	Robinson TE	Scott EJ	Smethurst CFV	Watson WJB	Wheeler AJ	Whitelaw DL	Wilson TH	Wilson WR
R1	Nov 28	Ryde Sports	5-1	Watson 2, Wilson, Fowler, Scott	3000	5					7	2	6	3		4	10	11		9		1	8	
R2	Dec 12	Wrexham	0-2		8184	5					7	2	6	3		4	10	11		9		1	8	

Division Three (South) Cup

	Date	Opponent	Result	Scorers	Att	Armstrong W	Ballsom WG	Barrie G	Dodds JA	Duncan WMcK	Fowler AJ	Hartley S	Hopkins TE	Lester FC	McAleer J	Randle HC	Robinson TE	Scott EJ	Smethurst CFV	Watson WJB	Wheeler AJ	Whitelaw DL	Wilson TH	Wilson WR
R1	Sep 30	Bristol City	2-0	Wheeler, Robinson	1150	5	3			10		2	6		7	4	9			8	11	1		
R2	Oct 28	Watford	2-3	Wheeler, Dodds	2000	5	3		7	10		2					8		4	9	11	1		6

		P	*W*	*D*	*L*	*F*	*A*	*W*	*D*	*L*	*F*	*A*	*Pts*
1	Luton Town	42	19	1	1	69	16	8	3	10	34	37	58
2	Notts County	42	15	3	3	44	23	8	7	6	30	29	56
3	Brighton & Hove Albion	42	15	5	1	49	16	9	0	12	25	27	53
4	Watford	42	14	4	3	53	21	5	7	9	32	39	49
5	Reading	42	14	5	2	53	23	5	6	10	23	37	49
6	Bournemouth	42	17	3	1	45	20	3	6	12	20	39	49
7	Northampton Town	42	15	4	2	56	22	5	2	14	29	46	46
8	Millwall	42	12	4	5	43	24	6	6	9	21	30	46
9	Queen's Park Rangers	42	12	2	7	51	24	6	7	8	22	28	45
10	Southend United	42	10	8	3	49	23	7	3	11	29	44	45
11	GILLINGHAM	42	14	5	2	36	18	4	3	14	16	48	44
12	Clapton Orient	42	10	8	3	29	17	4	7	10	23	35	43
13	Swindon Town	42	12	4	5	52	24	2	7	12	23	49	39
14	Crystal Palace	42	11	7	3	45	20	2	5	14	17	41	38
15	Bristol Rovers	42	14	3	4	49	20	2	1	18	22	60	36
16	Bristol City	42	13	3	5	42	20	2	3	16	16	50	36
17	Walsall	42	11	3	7	38	34	2	7	12	25	51	36
18	Cardiff City	42	10	5	6	35	24	4	2	15	19	63	35
19	Newport County	42	7	7	7	37	28	5	3	13	30	70	34
20	Torquay United	42	9	5	7	42	32	2	5	14	15	48	32
21	Exeter City	42	9	5	7	36	37	1	7	13	23	51	32
22	Aldershot	42	5	6	10	29	29	2	3	16	21	60	23

1937/38

Bottom of Division Three (South): Not re-elected

		Date	Opponent	Score	Scorers	Att	Armstrong W	Ballsom WG	Brallisford A	Brickenden NR	Campbell CWG	Dalton BL	Duncan WMcK	Emmerson GAH	Fishlock LB	Fowler AJ	Hartley S	Herbert FW	Holland GA	Jones EJ	Lester FC	Neal RG	Nichol JB	O'Neill J	Scott EJ	Smith F	Smith J	Taylor A	Tweed GE	Walker CJ	Watson WJB	Whitelaw DL	Wilson TH	Young AW
2	Sep	1	NEWPORT COUNTY	1-0	Walker	6295	5					11					2		6		3		4			7				8	9	1	10	
3		4	WATFORD	0-0		8408	5					11					2		6		3			4		7				8	9	1	10	
4		9	Newport County	0-2		5662	5					11					2		6		3			4		7		9		8	10	1		
5		11	Mansfield Town	1-3	Watson	7921	5					11					2				3		4	6		7				8	9	1	10	
6		15	READING	1-2	Watson	4160	5					11					2				3		4	6		7				8	9	1	10	
7		18	Exeter City	5-3	Wilson, Smith 2, Walker 2	5846	5										2				3		4		11	7				8	9	1	10	6
8		25	SWINDON TOWN	0-0		5792	5										2				3		4		11	7				9	8	1	10	6
9	Oct	2	Aldershot	0-2		5238	5	2													3		4		11	7				9	8	1	10	6
10		9	MILLWALL	2-3	Watson, Wilson	9831	5	2									4				3				11	7				9	8	1	10	6
11		16	BRISTOL ROVERS	0-1		6628	5	3					10				2								11	7					9	1	8	6
12		23	Northampton Town	1-4	Taylor	7618	5	3											6				4		11	7		9	2		8	1	10	
13		30	WALSALL	3-0	Watson 2, Scott	4328	5		9								2		6						11	7			3		8	1	10	4
14	Nov	6	Cardiff City	0-4		14818	5										2		6						11	7		9	3		8	1	10	4
15		13	BOURNEMOUTH	0-2		4648	5									7	2								11			9	3		8	1	10	6
16		20	Brighton & Hove Albion	0-1		7701	5	2	9							7			6						11				3		8	1	10	4
17	Dec	4	Southend United	0-2		6700	5		9				10				2								11	7	4		3		8	1		6
18		18	Torquay United	0-1		2317	5		9							7	2								11		4		3		8	1	10	6
19		27	Notts County	0-1		23337	5		9							7	2										4	11	3		8	1	10	6
20	Jan	1	BRISTOL CITY	1-0	Brallisford	5126	5		9							7	2			6							4	11	3		8	1	10	
21		8	QUEEN'S PARK RANGERS	1-5	Fowler	7699	5									7	2			6		10					4	11	3		9	1	8	
22		15	Watford	1-1	Watson	7843	5		9						11	7	2			6							4		3		8	1	10	
23		22	MANSFIELD TOWN	0-0		5590	5		9						11	7	2			6							4		3		8	1	10	
24		29	EXETER CITY	2-1	Fishlock, Herbert	3844	5				6				11		2	9							7		4		3		8	1	10	
25	Feb	5	Swindon Town	0-3		8543	5				6				11		2	9							7		4		3		8	1	10	
26		12	ALDERSHOT	2-0	Herbert, Watson	3138	5				6				11		2	9							7		4		3		8	1	10	
27		19	Millwall	0-5		17358					6				11		2	9				8		4	7				3			1	10	
28		23	CLAPTON ORIENT	1-2	Herbert	1789		5	7		6				11		2	9		4									3		8	1	10	
29		26	Bristol Rovers	1-2	Taylor	4289		5							11		2		6			10		4	7			9	3			1	8	
30	Mar	5	NORTHAMPTON T	2-1	Herbert 2	4582		5							11		2	9	6			10		4					3		7	1	8	
31		12	Walsall	1-3	Neal	3665		5							11		2	9	6			10		4					3		7	1	8	
32		16	NOTTS COUNTY	2-1	Watson, Hartley	3949		5						7	11		2	9				4							3		8	1	10	6
33		19	CARDIFF CITY	1-0	Herbert	6710		5						7	11		2	9				4							3		8	1	10	6
34		26	Bournemouth	0-2		6559		5						7	11		2	9				4							3		8	1	10	6
35	Apr	2	BRIGHTON & HOVE ALB	1-1	Wilson	6450		5						7	11		2	9				4					6		3		8	1	10	
36		9	Queen's Park Rangers	0-2		10356		5	10						11		2	9				6					4		3		7	1	8	
37		15	Crystal Palace	0-3		15390		5	9	1				7	11		2					6					4		3		8		10	
38		16	SOUTHEND UNITED	2-1	Brallisford, Neal	6822		5	10	1				7	11		2	9				6							3				8	4
39		18	CRYSTAL PALACE	2-4	Herbert, Brallisford (p)	6602		5	10	1				7	11		2	9				6							3				8	4
40		23	Clapton Orient	0-3		5970		5						7	11		2	9				10					4		3			1	8	6
41		30	TORQUAY UNITED	1-1	Fishlock	2364		5			4			7	11		2	9											3		10	1	8	6
42	May	7	Reading	0-2		3958	5	2	10		4			7				9							11				3			1	8	6
						Apps	26	20	14	3	7	5	2	10	20	8	37	17	10	5	9	14	7	8	18	14	14	8	31	9	35	38	39	20
						Goals			3						2	1	1	7				2			1	2		3		3	8		3	

Played in one game: F Donoghue (27, 5), LT Williams (11, at 4), WL Williams (15, 4)

F.A. Cup

		Date	Opponent	Score	Scorers	Att	Armstrong W	Ballsom WG	Brallisford A	Brickenden NR	Campbell CWG	Dalton BL	Duncan WMcK	Emmerson GAH	Fishlock LB	Fowler AJ	Hartley S	Herbert FW	Holland GA	Jones EJ	Lester FC	Neal RG	Nichol JB	O'Neill J	Scott EJ	Smith F	Smith J	Taylor A	Tweed GE	Walker CJ	Watson WJB	Whitelaw DL	Wilson TH	Young AW
R1	Nov	27	SWINDON TOWN	3-4	Watson 3 (2p)		5	2	9										6						11	7			3		8	1	10	4

Division Three (South) Cup

		Date	Opponent	Score	Scorers	Att	Armstrong W	Ballsom WG	Brallisford A	Brickenden NR	Campbell CWG	Dalton BL	Duncan WMcK	Emmerson GAH	Fishlock LB	Fowler AJ	Hartley S	Herbert FW	Holland GA	Jones EJ	Lester FC	Neal RG	Nichol JB	O'Neill J	Scott EJ	Smith F	Smith J	Taylor A	Tweed GE	Walker CJ	Watson WJB	Whitelaw DL	Wilson TH	Young AW
R1	Sep	28	BRIGHTON & HOVE ALB.	3-1	Watson 2, Walker	2000	5										2				3		4		11		7			9	8	1	10	6
R2	Nov	8	Millwall	0-4		2000	5				6	11				7	2	9										4	3		8	1		

Played at 10 in R2: R Maudsley

		P	W	D	L	F	A	W	D	L	F	A	Pts
1	Millwall	42	15	3	3	53	15	8	7	6	30	22	56
2	Bristol City	42	14	6	1	37	13	7	7	7	31	27	55
3	Queen's Park Rangers	42	15	3	3	44	17	7	6	8	36	30	53
4	Watford	42	14	4	3	50	15	7	7	7	23	28	53
5	Brighton & Hove Albion	42	15	3	3	40	16	6	6	9	24	28	51
6	Reading	42	17	2	2	44	21	3	9	9	27	42	51
7	Crystal Palace	42	14	4	3	45	17	4	8	9	22	30	48
8	Swindon Town	42	12	4	5	33	19	5	6	10	16	30	44
9	Northampton Town	42	12	4	5	30	19	5	5	11	21	38	43
10	Cardiff City	42	13	7	1	57	22	2	5	14	10	32	42
11	Notts County	42	10	6	5	29	17	6	3	12	21	33	41
12	Southend United	42	12	5	4	43	23	3	5	13	27	45	40
13	Bournemouth	42	8	10	3	36	20	6	2	13	20	37	40
14	Mansfield Town	42	12	5	4	46	26	3	4	14	16	41	39
15	Bristol Rovers	42	10	7	4	28	20	3	6	12	18	41	39
16	Newport County	42	9	10	2	31	15	2	6	13	12	37	38
17	Exeter City	42	10	4	7	37	32	3	8	10	20	38	38
18	Aldershot	42	11	4	6	23	14	4	1	16	16	45	35
19	Clapton Orient	42	10	7	4	27	19	3	0	18	15	42	33
20	Torquay United	42	7	5	9	22	28	2	7	12	16	45	30
21	Walsall	42	10	4	7	34	37	1	3	17	18	51	29
22	GILLINGHAM	42	9	5	7	25	25	1	1	19	11	52	26

1938/39

3rd in Southern League Division One

	Date	Opponent	Score	Scorers	Att	Armstrong W	Bradbury T	Brallisford A	Bryant HA	Campbell CWG	Costello R	Day R	Donoghue F	Foreman E	Herbert FW	Johnson W	Jones EJ	Langmaid A	McAdams TE	McGee T	Neal RG	Ross J	Rowley HB	Scott EJ	Smith A	Smith J	Strong GJ	Tweed GE	Whitelaw DL	Williams LT	Wilson TH
1	Aug 27	Colchester United	0-2		8142	5		8			3	7				9					6	11	10			4	1	2			
2	29	TUNBRIDGE WELLS RGS	2-0	Wilson, Ross	2500	5					3	7				9					6	11	10			4	1	2			8
3	Sep 1	Newport County Res	3-3	Johnson 2, Wilson	2000	5					3	7				9					6	11	10			4	1	2			8
4	3	WORCESTER CITY	3-1	Rowley (p), Day, Ross	4000	5					3	7				9					6	11	10			4	1	2			8
5	8	Yeovil Town	1-4	Herbert		5		8			3				9	11					6	7	10			4	1	2			
6	10	Arsenal Res	1-0	Scott		5					3			2		9				7	6		10	11		4	1				8
7	17	NEWPORT COUNTY RES	3-0	Scott, Johnson, McGee		5					3			2		9				7	6		10	11		4	1				8
8	24	Ipswich Town Res	0-3		6000			9			3	7	5	2							6		10	11		4	1				8
9	28	BRISTOL ROVERS RES	1-1	Braillisford				9			3	7	5	2						11	6		10			4	1				8
10	Oct 1	Torquay United Res	1-3	Day							3	7	5	2			9			11	6		10			4	1				8
11	12	Dartford	1-1	Wilson			2				3	7	5				9				6	11	10			4	1				8
12	15	IPSWICH TOWN RES	3-0	Wilson 2, Ross		5	2		7		3										6	9	10	11		4	1				8
13	19	Aldershot Res	1-0	Wilson		5	2		7							9		3			6		10	11		4	1				8
14	22	Plymouth Argyle Res	0-4			5	2		7							9		3			6		10	11		4	1				8
15	29	EXETER CITY RES	3-1	Johnson 2, Wilson (p)	3000	5	2						4			9		3	11		6			7		10	1				8
16	Nov 5	TORQUAY UTD RES	2-0	Wilson 2		5	2						6			9		3	7		10			11	4		1				8
17	19	Norwich City Res	2-6	Wilson, Neal		5	2		7	6	3				9						10			11		4	1				8
18	26	CARDIFF CITY RES	3-1	Rowley, Johnson, Wilson		5	2				3					9				7	6		10	11		4			1		8
19	Dec 3	Tunbridge Wells Rangers	3-3	Rowley 2, Johnson		5	2				3					9				7	6		10	11		4			1		8
20	17	Barry Town	3-1	Wilson, Johnson, Rowley		5	2				3					10				7	6		9	11		4			1		8
21	26	Guildford City	1-0	Wilson		5	2				3					10				7	6		9	11		4			1		8
22	27	FOLKESTONE	2-1	Wilson, Rowley		5	2				3					10				7	6		9	11		4			1		8
23	Jan 4	Cardiff City Res	2-1	Neal, Johnson		5	2				3	11				10				7	6	8	9			4			1		
24	7	Folkestone	1-1	Scott		5	2				3					10				7	6		9	11		4			1		8
25	14	COLCHESTER UNITED	1-3	Rowley	3900	5	2				3					10				7	6		9	11		4			1		8
26	28	CHELTENHAM TOWN	6-1	Wilson 2, Rowley 2, McGee 2		5	2				3					10				7	6		9	11		4			1		8
27	Feb 18	Worcester City	4-1	McGee 2, Rowley, Wilson		5	2				3					10				7	6		9	11		4			1		8
28	22	Bristol Rovers Res	4-1	Rowley, McGee, Day, Johnson		5	2				3	11				10				7	6		9			4			1		8
29	25	ARSENAL RES	2-1	Rowley 2 (1p)	2665	5	2				3					10				7	6		9	11		4			1		8
30	Mar 4	Exeter City Res	3-1	Rowley, Scott, Wilson		5	2				3					10				7	6		9	11		4			1		8
31	11	NORWICH CITY RES	6-0	Rowley 3, McGee, Johnson, Wilson		5	2				3					10				7	6		9	11		4			1		8
32	15	GUILDFORD CITY	3-1	Rowley 2 (1p), Johnson		5	2				3					10				7	6		9	11		4	1				8
33	18	Cheltenham Town	0-1					10	7	6		11		2	8							9			4		1	3		5	
34	25	BARRY TOWN	6-0	Rowley 4 (1p), Wilson, Johnson		5	2				3					10				7	6		9	11		4			1		8
35	29	DARTFORD	3-0	Rowley 3 (1p)		5	2				3					10				7	6		9	11		4			1		8
36	Apr 1	CHELMSFORD CITY	2-1	Rowley 2 (1p)		5	2				3					10				7	6		9	11		4			1		8
37	7	Bath City	1-2	Rowley		5	2				3					10				7	6		9	11		4			1		8
38	8	BATH CITY	5-1	McGee 2, Scott 2, Wilson		5	2				3					10				7	6		9	11		4			1		8
39	15	SWINDON TOWN RES	3-1	Rowley, Wilson, Johnson		5	2			6	3					10				7			9	11		4			1		8
40	19	ALDERSHOT RES	3-1	Rowley 2 (1p), Wilson		5	2			6	3					10				7			9	11		4			1		8
41	24	PLYMOUTH ARG. RES	1-0	McGee		5	2			6	3				10					7			9	11		4			1		8
42	29	Swindon Town Res	2-2	Wilson, Rowley		5	2			6						10		3		7			9	11		4			1		8
43	May 3	Chelmsford City	5-3	Rowley 3, Wilson, McGee	4000	5	2			6		11				10		3		7			9			4			1		8
44	6	YEOVIL TOWN	2-0	Rowley 2 (1p)	2000	5	2			6						10		3		7			9	11		4			1		8
					Apps	39	33	5	5	8	36	12	6	6	4	36	2	7	2	30	37	9	40	32	2	42	19	6	25	1	40
					Goals			1				3			1	14				11	2	3	38	6							25

F.A. Cup

	Date	Opponent	Score	Scorers	Armstrong W	Bradbury T	Brallisford A	Bryant HA	Campbell CWG	Costello R	Day R	Donoghue F	Foreman E	Herbert FW	Johnson W	Jones EJ	Langmaid A	McAdams TE	McGee T	Neal RG	Ross J	Rowley HB	Scott EJ	Smith A	Smith J	Strong GJ	Tweed GE	Whitelaw DL	Williams LT	Wilson TH
Q4	Nov 12	TUNBRIDGE WELLS RGS	2-4	Scott, Wilson	5	2		7							9		3			6		10	11		4	1				8

Southern League Cup

	Date	Opponent	Score	Scorers	Armstrong W	Bradbury T	Brallisford A	Bryant HA	Campbell CWG	Costello R	Day R	Donoghue F	Foreman E	Herbert FW	Johnson W	Jones EJ	Langmaid A	McAdams TE	McGee T	Neal RG	Ross J	Rowley HB	Scott EJ	Smith A	Smith J	Strong GJ	Tweed GE	Whitelaw DL	Williams LT	Wilson TH
R1	Dec 14	DARTFORD	5-2	Rowley 3, Wilson 2	5	2				3					10				7	6		9	11		4			1		8
R2	Feb 15	Folkestone	0-0		5	2				3	11				10				8	6	7	9			4			1		
rep	Mar 8	FOLKESTONE	1-2	Wilson	5	2				3	11				10				7	6		9			4			1		8

		P	W	D	L	F	A	Pts
1	Colchester United	44	31	5	8	110	37	67
2	Guildford City	44	30	6	8	126	52	66
3	GILLINGHAM	44	29	6	9	104	57	64
4	Plymouth Arg. Res	44	26	5	13	128	63	57
5	Yeovil & Petters U	44	22	10	12	85	70	54
6	Arsenal Res	44	21	9	14	92	57	51
7	Cardiff City Res	44	24	3	17	105	73	51
8	Tunbridge Wells Rgs	44	22	6	16	93	76	50
9	Norwich City Res	44	23	4	17	86	76	50
10	Chelmsford City	44	18	8	18	74	73	44
11	Bath City	44	16	12	16	58	74	44
12	Barry	44	18	7	19	76	90	43
13	Cheltenham Town	44	16	9	19	76	105	41
14	Ipswich Town Res	44	14	12	18	64	76	40
15	Worcester City	44	13	14	17	72	90	40
16	Folkestone	44	16	6	22	74	85	38
17	Newport County Res	44	13	10	21	74	108	36
18	Exeter City Res	44	12	9	23	51	107	33
19	Torquay Utd. Res	44	12	8	24	53	89	32
20	Swindon Town Res	44	11	9	24	66	101	31
21	Aldershot Res	44	12	6	26	69	92	30
22	Bristol Rovers Res	44	9	11	24	66	85	29
23	Dartford	44	8	5	31	53	119	21

1939/40

Southern League Division One

					Whitelaw DL	Foreman	Costello	Campbell CWG	Clark	Browning	Fowler AJ	Wilson TH	Rowley	Cowe	Scott EJ	Cusworth	O'Connor
1	Aug	26 Tunbridge Wells Rangers	2-0	Wilson, Rowley	1	2	3	4	5	6	7	8	9	10	11		
2		30 NEWPORT CO. RES	4-3	Rowley 3, Scott	1	2	3	4	5	6	7	8	9	10	11		
3	Sep	2 Worcester City	0-1		1		3	8	5	6	7		9	10	11	2	4

War declared on September 3 and the competition was cancelled.
After a few weeks, organised football resumed; Gillingham joined the Kent Regional League

Kent Regional League (Eastern Group)

1	Nov	2 Margate	1-1	Hickson
2		16 LLOYDS	4-0	Day 2, Campbell, Herbert
3		23 Canterbury Waverley	7-4	Scott 2, Walsh 2, Hickson, Lee, Piper
4		30 DOVER	5-2	Walsh 3, Fowler, Lee
5	Dec	7 Sittingbourne	5-1	Hickson 2, Walsh 2, Herbert
6		13 MARGATE	10-0	Hickson 5, Herbert 2, Campbell, Lee, Walsh (p)
7		26 MAIDSTONE UNITED	5-1	Herbert 2, Lee 2, Golding
8	Jan	6 CANTAB WAVERLEY	3-0	Wilson (p), Lee, Hickson
9	Feb	17 SHORTS SPORTS	4-3	Jackson 2, Lee, Hickson
10		24 AYLESFORD PAPER M.	7-2	Lee 3, Keenan 2, Wilson, Herbert (p)
11	Mar	9 Dover	5-3	Wilson 2, Herbert, Hickson, Lee
12		16 RAMSGATE GRENVILLE	3-3	Herbert 2, Lee
13		22 Ashford Town	3-4	Hickson 2, Herbert
14		23 ASHFORD TOWN	6-3	Herbert 3 (2p), Lee, Golding, Hickson
15	Apr	6 Aylesford Paper Mills	3-1	Hickson 2, Lee
16		10 Shorts Sports	0-2	
17		20 Lloyds	7-2	Hickson 4, Batchelor 2, Herbert
18		27 SITTINGBOURNE	6-0	Wilson 3, Bryant 2, Batchelor
19	May	1 Maidstone United	7-0	Hickson 3, Lee 3, Wood

The away game with Ramsgate Grenville was not played

		P	W	D	L	F	A	Pts
1	Shorts Sports	20	18	1	1	115	29	37
2	GILLINGHAM	19	15	2	2	91	32	32
3	Aylesford PM	19	9	1	9	65	60	19
4	Margate	20	7	5	8	47	44	19
5	Dover	18	9	1	8	56	58	19
6	Lloyds	19	6	4	9	58	69	16
7	Sittingbourne	19	4	8	7	48	66	16
8	Cantab Waverley	16	6	3	7	37	57	15
9	Ramsgate Gren.	15	5	3	7	40	62	13
10	Ashford Town	19	4	4	11	44	59	12
11	Maidstone U	18	1	2	15	23	88	4

Tunbridge Wells Rangers withdrew and their record was expunged.
Competition abandoned in May 1940

Kent Senior Cup

R1	Jan	13 Dover	3-5	Hickson 3

Southern League Cup

R1	Feb	10 Chelmsford City	1-4	Keenan

Kent Senior Shield

R1	May	11 Dover	6-1	Hickson 2, Herbert 2, Wood, Lee
R2		18 SITTINGBOURNE	4-0	Hickson 3, Herbert

SF v. Margate was not played as the competition was abandoned

1940/41 to 1943/44

The club withdrew from competitive fixtures during this period

1944/45

Kent Senior League (Champions)

1	Aug	26	GRAVESEND UNITED	4-2	Tadman 2, Hole, Busbridge		Beby	Marks	Nobbs	Williams	Duhig	Martin	Mills	Wilson T	Hole	Tadman	Busbridge
2	Sep	2	RN Depot	6-4	Wilson 3, Hole, Tadman, Olver	750	Beby	Marks	Nobbs	Williams	Price	Dougall	Mills	Wilson T	Hole	Tadman	Olver
3		9	Gravesend United	2-4	Hughes, Jarman		Beby	Marks	Cleaves	Williams	Price	Hughes	Mills	Wilson T	Hole	Tadman	Jarman
4		16	DARTFORD AMS	5-0	Trumper 2, Wilson 2, Hole		Dowling	Marks	Cleaves	Boswell	Nobbs	Martin	Mills	Wilson T	Hole	Trumper	Olver
5		30	Snowdown CW	4-2	Tadman 2, Wilson, Trumper	1400	Dowling	Marks	Cleaves	Harris	Price	Martin	Olver	Wilson T	Hole	Trumper	Tadman
6	Oct	21	Ford Sports	1-4	Trumper		Dowling	Marks	Cleaves	Harris	Price	Martin	Olver	Wilson T	Hole	Trumper	Tadman
7		28	FORD SPORTS	1-3	Hole	1500	Rennie	Marks	Gladdish	Harris	Chapman H	Martin	Olver	Wilson T	Jarman	Trumper	Hole
8	Nov	11	TB ROYAL ENGINEERS	4-2	Olver 2, Hole, Trumper		Rennie	Marks	Cleaves	Harris	Price	Martin	Hole	Wilson T	Jarman	Trumper	Olver
9		18	Dartford Amateurs	4-1	Hole 3, Wilson		Rennie	Marks	Cleaves	Harris	Price	Martin	Olver	Wilson T	Hole	Trumper	Jarman
10	Dec	2	Lloyds Paper Mills	6-1	Wilson 2, Hole 2, Jones, Harris (og)		Rennie	Marks	Lukehurst	Harris	Henson	Martin	Olver	Wilson T	Hole	Trumper	Jones
11		9	ROYAL MARINES	6-2	E Chapman 3, Wilson, Olver, Trumper	1500	Rennie	Marks	Cleaves	Harris	Price	Martin	Olver	Wilson T	Hole	Chapman E	Trumper
12		23	SNOWDOWN CW	11-3	Bond 3, Wilson 2, Hole 2, Olver 2, Trumper 2		Rennie	Marks	Cleaves	Martin	Price	Lillis	Olver	Wilson T	Hole	Trumper	Bond
13		30	Royal Marines	3-3	Wilson 2, Walker		Gledhill	Marks	Cleaves	Lillis	Price	Martin	Olver	Wilson T	Walker	Trumper	Bond
14	Feb	3	RN Depot	3-2	Hole, Wilson, Wlaker		Rennie	Marks	Cleaves	Martin	Price	Lillis	Olver	Wilson T	Hole	Trumper	Walker
15		10	LLOYDS PM	6-1	Hole 2, Wilson 2, Trumper 2	1200	Rennie	Marks	Cleaves	Martin	Price	Lillis	Olver	Wilson T	Hole	Trumper	Walker
16	Ap	18	TB Royal Engineers	5-2	Jackson 3, Jones 2		Brown	Marks	Cleaves	Martin	Price	Lillis	Olver	Wilson T	Jackson	Trumper	Jones
17	May	5	Shorts Sports	3-1	Wrigglesworth, E Chapman, Jackson		Brown	Marks	Chapman H	Wilson	Price	Lillis	Chapman E	Wrigglesworth	Jackson	Thomas	Bain
18		19	SHORTS SPORTS	3-1	Hole 2, Jackson	5300	Brown	Dudley	Fisher	Wilson	Price	Lillis	Wrigglesworth	Thomas	Hole	Jackson	Jones

Kent League Cup

QR	Mar	3	Gravesend United	2-2	Jones, Wilson		Beby	Marks	Cleaves	Martin	Price	Lillis	Olver	Wilson T	Jones	Trumper	Dartnell
QR		24	RN DEPOT	2-3	Tudman, Lillis (p)	2000	Rowe	Luckhurst	Cleaves	Henson	Price	Chapman H	Olver	Wilson T	Newman	Trumper	Lillis
QR	Apr	14	GRAVESEND UNITED	1-2	Olver		Rowe	Henson	Sarson	Martin	Price	Lillis	Wilson T	Jones	Roberts	Trumper	Olver

The Kent Senior League fixture with RN Depot on 3 February also counted towards this competition. Gillingham did not qualify for the competition proper.

Kent Senior Cup

R2	Dec	16	RN DEPOT	3-1	Hole 2, Trumper	1700	Rennie	Marks	Cleaves	Lillis	Price	Martin	Olver	Wilson T	Hole	Trumper	Bond
R3	Jan	20	ERITH & BELVEDERE	2-1	Hole, Jones	`1700	Rennie	Marks	Cleaves	Martin	Price	Lillis	Olver	Wilson T	Hole	Trumper	Jones
R4	Feb	17	Bromley	3-1	Wilson 2, Jones	1700	Rowe	Marks	Cleaves	Martin	Price	Lillis	Olver	Wilson T	Jones	Trumper	Walker
SF	Mar	17	LLOYDS PM	1-2	Tadman	4140	Rowe	Marks	Cleaves	Martin	Price	Lillis	Olver	Wilson T	Jones	Trumper	Tadman

Guest players included:

Eddie Chapman (West Ham)
GH Jones (Sheffield United)

1945/46

Kent League (Champions)

1	Aug	25 SHEPPEY UNITED	9-1	Hole 5, Martin, Trumper, Price, Lillis	2513	Brown	Marks	Chapman H	Price	Armstrong	Lillis	Martin	Wilson T	Hole	Trumper	Ling
2	Sep	1 Ramsgate Athletic	2-2	Lillis (p), T Wilson		Brown	Marks	Chapman H	Wright	Price	Lillis	Oliver	Wilson T	Hole	Trumper	Wells
3		8 DARTFORD AMS	6-3	Hole 3, Harrison 3	2000	Berwick	Jackson	Cleaves	Wright	Daniels	Weight	Ravenscroft	Martin	Hole	Harrison	Ling
4		15 Dartford Amateurs	0-4			Berwick	Marks	Poole	Martin	Daniels	Harris	Ravenscroft	Hilton	Iverson	Trumper	Wells
5		29 FOLKESTONE	4-1	T Wilson 2, Hole, Ling	3090	Berwick	Marks	Cleaves	Henson	Price	Lillis	Wilson I	Wilson T	Hole	Trumper	Ling
6	Oct	27 Snowdown CW	5-2	T Wilson 3, Trumper 2		Berwick	Timmins	Chapman H	Henson	Wheller	Temlett	Wilson I	Thomas	Martin	Trumper	Ling
7	Nov	10 Royal Marines	5-3	Trumper 3, T Wilson 2		Brown	Timmins	Chapman H	Henson	Price	Hales	Wilson I	Wilson T	Hole	Trumper	Ling
8		24 Sheppey United	4-0	T Wilson 2, Hole, I Wilson	2000	Brown	Marks	Chapman H	Henson	Williams	Hales	Wilson I	Wilson T	Hole	Trumper	Warsap
9	Dec	1 RAMSGATE ATH.	4-2	Hole 2, Price, Clark	2600	Brown	Foreman	Chapman H	Price	Williams	Hales	Wilson I	Wilson T	Hole	Trumper	Clark
10		20 SHORTS SPORTS	2-0	Clark, Ravenscroft	3500	Brown	Marks	Chapman H	Henson	Price	Hales	Ravenscroft	Wilson T	Wilson I	Clark	Warsap
11		24 Folkestone	8-1	Hole 4, Warsap 2, Trumper, I Wilson		Brown	Marks	Cleaves	Henson	Price	Hales	Wilson I	Wilson T	Hole	Trumper	Warsap
12		27 GRAVESEND UNITED	8-1	T Wilson 2 (1p), Warsap 2, Hole 2, Trumper 2	4000	Brown	Marks	Cleaves	Henson	Price	Hales	Wilson T	Thomas	Hole	Trumper	Warsap
13	Nov	7 Lloyds PM	4-3	Hole 2, T Wilson 2		Collins	Marks	Cleaves	Henson	Price	Hales	Wilson I	Wilson T	Hole	Trumper	Herbert
14	Jan	19 SNOWDOWN CW	11-1	Thomas 3, Hole 3, Warsap 2, T Wilson 2, Trumper	2000	Collins	Marks	Chapman H	Henson	Price	Hales	Wilson T	Thomas	Hole	Trumper	Warsap
15		26 12th ITC (Canterbury)	9-2	Hole 4, Trumper 4, I Wilson		Collins	Marks	Chapman H	Henson	Price	Hales	Wilson I	Wilson T	Hole	Trumper	Warsap
16	Feb	2 ROYAL MARINES	6-1	Thomas 5, Hales		Collins	Marks	Chapman H	Henson	Price	Hales	Wilson I	Wilson T	Thomas	Trumper	Warsap
17		9 12th ITC (CANTERBURY)	10-1	E Chapman 3, Thomas 2, Trumper 2, T Wilson, Boswell, Lee		Collins	Marks	Chapman H	Boswell	Price	Hales	Chapman E	Wilson T	Thomas	Trumper	Lee
18	Mar	9 LLOYDS P.M.	8-3	E Chapman 4, Thomas 2, T Wilson, Warsap		Kain	Marks	Chapman H	Boswell	Price	Hales	Hole	Wilson T	Chapman E	Thomas	Warsap
19		30 Gravesend United	3-0	Piper, Warsap, E Chapman		Collins	Marks	Chapman H	Henson	Price	Piper	Ravenscroft	Wilson T	Chapman E	Thomas	Warsap
20	May	1 Shorts Sports	3-2	T Parker, Armstrong (og), Piper		Day	Cleaves	Poole	Piper	Donaldson	Allerton	Allbut	Parker J	Wrigglesworth	Parker T	Scott

Match 4 played by the reserves whilst the first team drew 3-3 in a friendly with Norwich City

F.A. Cup

Q4	Nov	3 SUTTON UNITED	3-9	Martin, Hole, T Wilson	6258	Berwick	Marks	Cleaves	Henson	Price	Chapman H	Martin	Wilson T	Hole	Trumper	Ling

Kent League Cup (Winners)

QR	Mar	2 SHORTS SPORTS	2-1	T Wilson 2	2500	Collins	Marks	Chapman H	Boswell	Price	Hales	Hole	Wilson T	Thomas	Trumper	Warsap
QR	Apr	6 Shorts Sports	1-2	Thomas	2200	Day	Marks	Chapman H	Henson	Price	Hales	Boswell	Wilson T	Hole	Thomas	Scott
QR		13 ROYAL MARINES	3-0	Thomas, E Chapman, T Wilson		Collins	Marks	Chapman H	Piper	Price	Henson	Chapman E	Wilson T	Hole	Thomas	Warsap
QR		20 Royal Marines	4-0	Warsap 2, Thomas, Hole		Collins	Marks	Chapman H	Boswell	Price	Henson	Chapman E	Wilson T	Hole	Thomas	Warsap
SF		27 GRAVESEND UNITED	4-1	Warsap 2, Thomas, E Chapman		Collins	Marks	Chapman H	Piper	Price	Hales	Chapman E	Wilson T	Hole	Thomas	Warsap
F	May	4 Lloyds P.M.	2-1	T Wilson, E Chapman	3500	Collins	Marks	Chapman H	Henson	Price	Hales	Hole	Wilson T	Chapman E	Thomas	Warsap

Kent Senior Cup (Winners)

R1	Jan	12 HMS ROBERTSON	6-0	Hole 3, T Wilson 2, Warsap		Brown	Marks	Chapman H	Boswell	Price	Hales	Ravenscroft	Wilson T	Hole	Trumper	Warsap
R2	Feb	16 RAMSGATE ATHLETIC	4-1	T Wilson 2, Thomas, Trumper	4000	Collins	Marks	Chapman H	Boswell	Price	Hales	Wilson I	Wilson T	Thomas	Trumper	Warsap
SF	Mar	16 Gravesend United	2-0	Thomas, T Wilson	5000	Collins	Marks	Chapman H	Boswell	Price	Hales	Chapman E	Wilson T	Thomas	Trumper	Warsap
F	Apr	22 12th ITC (Canterbury)	5-1	Thomas 2, E Chapman 2, Warsap	10000	Collins	Marks	Chapman H	Boswell	Price	Hales	Chapman E	Wilson T	Hole	Thomas	Warsap

Final played at Maidstone. 12th ITC were the 12th Infantry Training Corps (Canterbury).

Kent Senior Shield (Winners)

R1	Feb	23 GRAVESEND UNITED	6-0	Thomas 3, Marks, Warsap, T Wilson		Collins	Marks	Chapman H	Henson	Price	Hales	Wilson T	Wilson T	Hole	Trumper	Warsap
SF	Mar	23 SHORTS SPORTS	5-1	T Wilson 3, Ravenscroft, Thomas	4500	Collins	Marks	Chapman H	Henson	Price	Henson	Ravenscroft	Wilson T	Chapman E	Thomas	Warsap
F	May	11 Folkestone	3-0	E Chapman, T Wilson, Hole	3429	Collins	Marks	Chapman H	Henson	Price	Hales	Hole	Wilson T	Chapman E	Thomas	Warsap

Kent Challenge Cup (Winners on toss of coin)

F	Apr	19 MILLWALL	2-2	(aet) T Wilson, Hole	3000	Day	Marks	Southam	Rawcliffe	Henson	Hales	Olver	Wilson T	Hole	Thomas	Dicker

1946/47

Champions of Southern League Division One

							Akers W	Berwick C	Boswell J	Briggs J	Chapman H	Collins L	Dorling GC	Edwards F	Henson L	Hole V	Hopper T	Kingsnorth TH	Marks CWA	Nobbs J	Piper GH	Poole CJ	Price R	Russell HW	Sylvester D	Trumper S	Warsap WJB	Wilson TH
1	Aug	31	Bath City	4-3	Boswell, Wilson, Hole, Trumper	5000			4		3	1				9			2		6	11	5	10		7		8
2	Sep	7	BARRY TOWN	4-1	Hole 2, Warsap, Wilson	6539	7		4		3	1				9			2		6		5	10			11	8
3		14	CHELMSFORD CITY	1-2	Wilson	6171	7		4		3	1				9			2		6		5	10			11	8
4		21	Worcester City	6-1	Trumper 3, Russell 3		7	1	4		3				5				2		6	11		9		10		8
5		28	Merthyr Tydfil	0-1			7	1	4		3								2		6		5	9		10	11	8
6	Oct	19	YEOVIL TOWN	4-0	Hole 2, Akers, Warsap	7016	7		4		3	1				9		5	2		6	11					10	8
7		26	Cheltenham Town	5-3	Russell 2, Kingsnorth (p), Wilson, Warsap	3000	7				3	1				10		5	2		6		4	9			11	8
8	Nov	9	GLOUCESTER CITY	12-1	Russell 9 (1p), Akers, Wilson, Briggs	5083	7		4	11	3	1							2		6		5	9		10		8
9		23	Gloucester City	5-2	Russell 2, Akers 2, Kingsnorth (p)	500	7		4	10								5	2			3		9	1	6	11	8
10	Dec	7	Gravesend & Northfleet	1-5	Wilson	3077	7		4	10		1						5	2		6	3		9			11	8
11		21	Chelmsford City	0-0		3278	7		4	10		1						5	2		6	3		9			11	8
12		25	Colchester United	1-0	Briggs		7		4	10		1						5	2	3	6			9			11	8
13		26	COLCHESTER UNITED	4-2	Akers 2, Kingsnorth (p), Wilson	11242	7		4	10		1						5	2	3	6			9			11	8
14		28	DARTFORD	4-0	Akers 2, Warsap, Kingsnorth (p)	7623	7		4			1				10		5	2	3	6			9			11	8
15	Jan	18	Hereford United	3-3	Akers, Wilson, Boswell		7		4	10								5	2	6		3		9	1		11	8
16	Feb	1	MERTHYR TYDFIL	3-2	Wilson, Russell, Akers	4869	7		4	10		1						5	2		6	3		9			11	8
17		19	MILLWALL RES	4-1	Russell 3, Hole	2500			4	10	1					7		5	2		6	3		9			11	8
18		22	Exeter City Res	6-0	Wilson 2, Briggs 2, Russell 2	3570			4	10		1				7		5	2		6	3		9			11	8
19	Mar	1	HEREFORD UNITED	2-0	Russell, Wilson	6830	7		4	10		1						5	2		6	3		9			11	8
20		8	CHELTENHAM TOWN	4-1	Briggs 3, Russell	5930	7		4	10		1						5	2		6	3		9			11	8
21		15	Barry Town	6-6	Russell 4, Briggs, Wilson	400			4	10				1		7		5	2		6	3		9			11	8
22		29	EXETER CITY RES	4-0	Briggs 2, Russell, Hopper	6000	7		4	10		1					8	5	2		6	3		9			11	
23	Apr	4	GUILDFORD CITY	0-0		10572	10		4			1					7	5	2		6	3		9			11	8
24		5	BATH CITY	1-1	Warsap	8061	7		4	10		1						5	2		6	3		9			11	8
25		7	Guildford City	1-2	Hopper	8000	7		4	10		1					8	5	2		6	3		9			11	
26		19	Yeovil Town	1-4	Russell	7000	4			10		1					7	5	2		6	3		9			11	8
27	May	3	WORCESTER CITY	3-1	Akers, Harris (og), Russell	6017	7		4	10	3	1						5	2		6			9			11	8
28		10	Bedford Town	4-1	Wilson 3, Hole	1000	7		4	10	3	1				9			2	5	6						11	8
29		26	GRAVESEND & N'FLEET	4-2	Akers 2, Wilson 2	6859	7		4	10	3	1				9		5	2		6						11	8
30		31	Dartford	0-0		4500	7		4	10		1	3					5	2		6			9			11	8
31	Jun	14	BEDFORD TOWN	6-0	Akers 2, Wilson 2, Russell 2	6982	7		4	10		1	3					5	2		6			9			11	8
						Apps	27	2	29	22	12	25	2	1	1	11	4	24	31	5	29	18	6	28	2	5	28	29
						Goals	15		2	10						7	2	4						33		4	5	20

Away fixture with Millwall not played

One own goal

F.A. Cup

							Akers W	Berwick C	Boswell J	Briggs J	Chapman H	Collins L	Dorling GC	Edwards F	Henson L	Hole V	Hopper T	Kingsnorth TH	Marks CWA	Nobbs J	Piper GH	Poole CJ	Price R	Russell HW	Sylvester D	Trumper S	Warsap WJB	Wilson TH
Q4	Nov	16	Guildford City	2-1	Akers, Russell	6313	7		4			1						5	2		6	3		9		10	11	8
R1		30	GRAVESEND & N'FLEET	4-1	Russell 2, Briggs, Warsap	10784	7		4	10		1						5	2		6	3		9			11	8
R2	Dec	14	Bristol City	2-1	Wilson, Russell	21684	7		4	10		1						5	2		6	3		9			11	8
R3	Jan	11	Swansea Town	1-4	Wilson	30000	7		4	10		1						5	2		6	3		9			11	8

Southern League Cup

							Akers W	Berwick C	Boswell J	Briggs J	Chapman H	Collins L	Dorling GC	Edwards F	Henson L	Hole V	Hopper T	Kingsnorth TH	Marks CWA	Nobbs J	Piper GH	Poole CJ	Price R	Russell HW	Sylvester D	Trumper S	Warsap WJB	Wilson TH
QR	Sep	18	Guildford City	1-2	Hales		7		4		3	1							2		6	11	5	10				8
QR		25	GUILDFORD CITY	7-1	Russell 3, Boswell, Marks, Wilson, Trumper	5498			4		3	1				7			2		6		5	9		10	11	8
QR	Oct	2	DARTFORD	2-1	Wilson, Warsap	4577		1	4		3					7			2		6		5	9		10	11	8
QR		16	GRAVESEND & N'FLEET	2-1	Hales 2	3500			4		3	1				7			2		6		5			10	11	8
QR	Nov	6	Dartford	0-2		2207			4		3	1				7					6		5	9		10		8
QR		20	Gravesend & Northfleet	3-1	Wilson, Briggs, Russell				4	10		1						5	2		6	3		9			11	8
SF	Jun	7	COLCHESTER UNITED	3-2	Piper, Briggs, Russell		7		4	10		1	3					5	2		6			9			11	8
F1	Aug	23	YEOVIL TOWN	4-1	Briggs 2, Akers, Wilson	7780	7		4	10		1						5	2		6	3		9			11	8
F2		30	Yeovil Town	0-1			7		4	10		1						5	2		6	3		9			11	8

Final legs played at start of 1947/48 season

T Cudahay played at 11 on Nov 6
WH Hales played at 9 on Sep 18 and Oct 16
GVW Lukehurst played at 2 on Nov 6
D Morris played at 7 on Nov 20

		P	*W*	*D*	*L*	*F*	*A*	*Pts*
1	GILLINGHAM	31	20	6	5	103	45	47
2	Guildford City	32	21	4	7	86	39	46
3	Merthyr Tydfil	31	21	2	8	104	37	45
4	Yeovil Town	32	19	6	7	100	49	44
5	Chelsmford City	31	17	3	11	90	60	38
6	Gravesend & N'fleet	32	17	4	11	82	58	38
7	Barry Town	30	14	6	10	89	61	36
8	Colchester United	31	15	4	12	65	60	35
9	Cheltenham Town	31	14	3	14	68	75	32
10	Millwall Res	24	8	5	11	59	57	29
11	Dartford	32	10	5	17	71	100	25
12	Bedford Town	32	8	8	16	63	98	24
13	Hereford United	32	8	7	17	37	85	23
14	Worcester City	31	8	5	18	55	90	22
15	Exeter City Res	32	10	2	20	69	126	22
16	Bath City	32	7	7	18	52	93	21
17	Gloucester City	32	8	1	23	57	120	17

Millwall Reserves unable to fulfill their fixtures.
One point awarded to each club for the missing games.

1947/48

Second in Southern League Division One

	Date	Opponent	Score	Scorers	Att	Akers W	Boswell J	Briggs J	Burgess C	Burke JJ	Chapman H	Collins L	Day JN	Diggins B	Dimmock E	Dorling GC	Forrester GL	Kingsnorth TH	Marks CWA	Milton G	Morris R	Nobbs J	Piper GH	Poole CJ	Russell HW	Skinner GEH	Trumper S	Walker D	Warsap WJB	Wilson TH
1	Aug 27	GUILDFORD CITY	4-1	Warsap 2, Briggs, Russell	6710		4	11				1				3		5	2				6		9	10			7	8
2	Sep 6	Chelmsford City	1-4	Warsap	6000	7		10				1			4	2		5					6	3	9	8			11	
3	13	BATH CITY	4-1	Warsap 2, Wilson, Briggs	7225		4	11				1				2	10	5					6	3	9				7	8
4	27	BEDFORD TOWN	2-0	Russell, Wilson	7275	7	4	10		1						3		5	2				6		9				11	8
5	Oct 4	Cheltenham Town	1-0	Forrester	4000	4		11		1						3	10	5	2				6		9				7	8
6	11	DARTFORD	3-0	Russell, Wilson, Piper	7288	4		11		1						3	10	5					6	2	9				7	8
7	25	Gloucester City	1-2	Wilson	2000	4	9	11		1						3	10	5					6	2					7	8
8	Nov 8	Torquay United Res	2-1	Russell, Wilson			4	10		1							11	5	2				6	3	9				7	8
9	22	HEREFORD UNITED	3-2	Akers 2, Russell	6270	7	4	10		1						2		5					6	3	9				11	8
10	Dec 6	Worcester City	2-0	Russell 2	4500	7	4	10		1						2	8	5					6	3	9				11	
11	25	Colchester United	0-3		7207	7	4	10		1						2		5		8			6	3	9				11	
12	26	COLCHESTER UNITED	2-2	Boswell, Wright (og)	12548		4	10		1						2	11	5					6	3	9				7	8
13	27	GRAVESEND & N'FLEET	4-1	Russell, Forrester, Warsap, Wilson	6900		4	10					1			2	11	5					6	3	9				7	8
14	Jan 24	CHELMSFORD CITY	0-0		6877		4	10		1							8	5	2				6	3	9				11	7
15	31	Bath City	2-2	Diggins, Akers	3000	7	4	10		1				9			11	5	2				6	3						8
16	Feb 14	Bedford Town	2-0	Russell, Wilson	3000	7	4	10		1						2	11	5					6	3	9					8
17	26	Lovell's Athletic	1-4	Trumper			4			1				9		2	11	5					6	3	8		10			7
18	28	Dartford	1-2	Briggs			4	10				1					11	5	2				6	3	9		7			8
19	Mar 10	BARRY TOWN	2-1	Nobbs 2	3000		4			1						2	11	5		7		9	6	3			10			8
20	13	GLOUCESTER CITY	4-0	Russell, Wilson, Akers, Briggs	6701	7	4	10				1				2	11	5					6	3	9					8
21	17	EXETER CITY RES	0-0		3000		4	10		1						2		5			7			3	9		6		11	8
22	20	Hereford United	2-4	Russell, Briggs	4600	7	4	10				1				2	11	5					6	3	9					8
23	26	Barry Town	2-2	Wilson, Briggs	2500		4	10	7			1				2	11	5					6	3	9					8
24	27	LOVELL'S ATHLETIC	4-1	Wilson 2, Akers, Russell	8175	7	4	10				1				2	11	5					6	3	9					8
25	31	CHELTENHAM TOWN	5-1	Warsap 3, Briggs, Russell	2711		4	10		1						2	11	5						3	9		6		7	8
26	Apr 3	Yeovil Town	1-0	Warsap			4					1				2	11	5					6	3	9			10	7	8
27	7	Gravesend & Northfleet	2-0	Russell 2			4			1						2	11	5					6	3	9			10	7	8
28	10	TORQUAY UTD RES	2-2	Kingsnorth (p), Wilson	7618		4	10	7			1				2	11	5					6	3	9					8
29	14	MERTHYR TYDFIL	4-2	Wilson, Russell, Kingsnorth (p), Forrester			4	10		1						3	7	5	2				6	11	9					8
30	17	Exeter City Res	6-0	Poole 2, Wilson 2, Russell, Forrester	6616		4	10		1						3	7	5	2				6	11	9					8
31	21	Guildford City	1-0	Briggs			4	10	7	1						3		5	2				6	11				9		8
32	24	WORCESTER CITY	5-0	Poole 3, Wilson, Briggs	7800		4	10		1						3	7	5	2				6	9					11	8
33	28	YEOVIL TOWN	5-0	Poole 2, Forrester 2, Walker	8294		4			1						3	8		2				5	9			6	7	11	10
34	May 1	Merthyr Tydfil	1-4	Walker			4	10		1	3						7		2			6	5	11				9		8
					Apps	13	31	29	3	23	1	10	1	2	1	29	27	32	13	2	1	2	32	31	27	2	6	5	20	31
					Goals	5	1	9						1			6	2				2	1	7	17		1	2	10	16

One own goal

F.A. Cup

	Date	Opponent	Score	Scorers	Att	Akers W	Boswell J	Briggs J	Burgess C	Burke JJ	Chapman H	Collins L	Day JN	Diggins B	Dimmock E	Dorling GC	Forrester GL	Kingsnorth TH	Marks CWA	Milton G	Morris R	Nobbs J	Piper GH	Poole CJ	Russell HW	Skinner GEH	Trumper S	Walker D	Warsap WJB	Wilson TH
Q4	Nov 15	BARNET	3-1	(aet) Russell 3			4	10		1						2	11	5					6	3	9				7	8
R1	29	LEYTON ORIENT	1-0	Akers	15561	7	4			1						2	10	5					6	3	9				11	8
R2	Dec 13	Rochdale	1-1	(aet) Russell	11110		4	10		1						2	11	5					6	3	9				7	8
rep	20	ROCHDALE	3-0	Forrester, Wilson, Briggs	17078		4	10		1						2	11	5					6	3	9				7	8
R3	Jan 10	QUEEN'S PARK RANGERS	1-1	(aet) Russell	23002	7	4	10		1						2	11	5					6	3	9					8
rep	17	Queen's Park Rangers	1-3	Warsap	27557		4	10		1						2	8	5					6	3	9				11	7

Southern League Cup

	Date	Opponent	Score	Scorers	Att	Akers W	Boswell J	Briggs J	Burgess C	Burke JJ	Chapman H	Collins L	Day JN	Diggins B	Dimmock E	Dorling GC	Forrester GL	Kingsnorth TH	Marks CWA	Milton G	Morris R	Nobbs J	Piper GH	Poole CJ	Russell HW	Skinner GEH	Trumper S	Walker D	Warsap WJB	Wilson TH
QR	Sep 3	GRAVESEND & N'FLEET	0-0		6462			11				1						5	2				6	3	9	10			7	8
QR	10	Guildford City	2-0	Forrester, Russell								1			4	3	10	5	2				6	11	9	8			7	
QR	17	Gravesend & N'fleet	3-6	Wilson 2, Forrester											4	3	10	5	2				6	11		9			7	8
QR	24	GUILDFORD CITY	2-2	Briggs, Warsap	4318			11		1							10	5	2				6	3		8			7	4
QR	Oct 1	DARTFORD	2-1	Wilson, Skinner	3571		4			1						3	10	5	2				6	11		9			7	8
QR	15	Dartford	1-2	Kingsnorth (p)						1						3	11	5	9			6	4	2		10			7	8

L Henson played at 4 on Sep 3
V Hole played at 9 on Sep 24
Thompson played at 1 on Sep 17
Both Exeter games shown as away

		P	W	D	L	F	A	Pts
1	Merthyr Tydfil	34	23	7	4	84	38	53
2	GILLINGHAM	34	21	5	8	81	43	47
3	Worcester City	34	21	3	10	74	45	45
4	Colchester United	34	17	10	7	88	41	44
5	Hereford United	34	16	10	8	77	53	42
6	Lovells Athletic	34	17	6	11	74	50	40
7	Exter City Res	34	15	7	12	65	57	37
8	Yeovil Town	34	12	11	11	56	50	35
9	Chelmsford City	34	14	7	13	62	58	35
10	Cheltenham Town	34	13	9	12	71	71	35
11	Bath City	34	12	8	14	55	62	32
12	Barry Town	34	10	9	15	60	70	29
13	Gravesend & N'fleet	34	11	6	17	52	81	28
14	Guildford City	34	11	4	19	69	74	26
15	Dartford	34	10	6	18	35	62	26
16	Gloucester City	34	8	6	20	45	78	22
17	Torquay U Res	34	6	9	19	43	95	21
18	Bedford Town	34	6	3	25	41	104	15

1948/49

Champions of Southern League Division One

							Boswell J	Briggs J	Burke JJ	Carr J	Dorling GC	Forrester GL	Gore LF	Granville NY	Henson L	Kingsnorth TH	Lambourne JC	Marks CWA	Nobbs J	O'Sullivan CJ	Piper GH	Poole CJ	Russell HW	Vigor DRJ	Warsap WJB	Wilson TH
1	Aug	21	GRAVESEND & N'FLEET	2-1	Forrester, Dorling	8128	4	10	1		2	11	7		3	5					6		9			8
2		28	Guildford City	4-4	Russell 2, Boswell, Briggs	5789	4	10	1		2	11	7		3	5					6		9			8
3	Sep	1	Dartford	5-0	Russell 2, Forrester, Wilson, Dorling		4		1	10	2	11	7		3	5					6		9			8
4		4	LOVELL'S ATHLETIC	0-0		9278	4	10	1		2	11	7		3	5					6		9			8
5		18	YEOVIL TOWN	2-0	Kingsnorth (p), Russell	8514	4	10	1		2	11	7	6	3	5							9			8
6		22	Torquay United Res	2-1	Wilson, Briggs		4	10	1		2	11	7		3	5					6		9			8
7	Oct	9	Worcester City	1-2	Briggs	5968	4	10	1		2	11				5					6	3	9		7	8
8		16	WORCESTER CITY	3-0	Russell 2, Wilson	9112		10	1		2	11		4		5					6	3	9		7	8
9		23	Hereford United	1-3	Carr, Russell	5433				10	2	9		7		5				1	6	3		4	11	8
10		30	Bath City	0-1					1	10	2	11	7		3	5					6		9	4		8
11	Nov	6	CHINGFORD	3-2	Russell 2, Cook (og)	8002	4	10	1		2	11	7		5						6	3	9			8
12		20	CHELTENHAM TOWN	5-1	Wilson 2, Briggs, Russell, Forrester	7887	4	10	1			7			3	5		2				11	9	6		8
13		27	Bedford Town	2-0	Briggs, Forrester	2300	4	10	1		2	7			3	5						11	9	6		8
14	Dec	4	BARRY TOWN	6-0	Russell 4, Poole, Forrester	7336	4	10	1		2	7			3	5						11	9	6		8
15		11	Kidderminster Harriers	3-2	Briggs, Forrester, Poole	1500	4	10	1		3	7				5		2				11	9	6		8
16		18	BATH CITY	3-0	Wilson, Poole, Briggs	7300	4	10	1		3	7				5		2				11	9	6		8
17		25	Chelmsford City	3-3	Forrester 3		4	10	1		3	7				5		2				11	9	6		8
18		27	CHELMSFORD CITY	0-1		9562	4	10	1		3	7				5		2				11	9	6		8
19	Jan	1	COLCHESTER UNITED	1-1	Russell	7953	4	10	1		3	7				5		2			6	11	9			8
20		15	EXETER CITY RES	7-1	Carr 3, Russell 3 (1p), Warsap	6698	4		1	10	3	11				5		2			6		9		7	8
21		22	Gravesend & Northfleet	1-0	Carr	5871	4		1	10	3	11				5		2			6		9		7	8
22		29	GUILDFORD CITY	3-1	Russell, Warsap, Forrester	9171	4		1	10		11				5		2			6	3	9		7	8
23	Feb	12	TORQUAY UTD RES	6-0	Russell 5 (1p), Warsap	6845	4		1	10	3	11				5		2			6		9		7	8
24		19	Yeovil Town	1-3	Carr	4000	4		1	10	3	11				5		2			6		9		7	8
25		24	Lovell's Athletic	1-1	Piper		4		1	10	3					5		2			6	11	9		7	8
26		26	HASTINGS UNITED	2-2	Poole, Boswell	8733	4	10	1	8	3					5		2			6	11	9		7	
27	Mar	5	Hastings United	4-1	Russell, Briggs, Piper	6400	4	11	1	8	3	10				5		2			6		9		7	
28		10	Chingford	3-0	Forrester, Dorling, Warsap	1500	4	11	1	8	3	10				5		2			6		9		7	
29		19	Merthyr Tydfil	2-2	Gore, Forrester	7000		11	1	8	2	10	7			5					6	3	9			4
30		23	Exeter City Res	2-2	Wilson, Russell				1	10	2	11	7			5		4			6	3	9			8
31		26	HEREFORD UNITED	3-1	Russell 3	7959	4	11	1	8	2	10	7			5					6	3	9			
32		28	GLOUCESTER CITY	4-1	Carr, Gore, Forrester, Russell	5047	4	11	1	8	2	10	7			5					6	3	9			
33	Apr	2	Gloucester City	0-0		3000	4	11	1	10	2	8	7			5					6	3	9			
34		9	DARTFORD	1-3	Wilson	7747	4	11	1	10		7			5			2			6	3	9			8
35		13	MERTHYR TYDFIL	2-1	Warsap, Tabram (og)	9287	4	10	1	8	3			6		5		2				11	9		7	
36		15	TONBRIDGE	2-1	Carr 2	9421	4	10	1	8	3			6		5		2				11	9		7	
37		16	BEDFORD TOWN	3-1	Russell, Carr, Forrester	8019		10	1	8	2	11		4		5					6	3	9		7	
38		20	Colchester United	1-0	Whitney (og)		4		1	10	3	11					5	2			6	9	8		7	
39		23	KIDDERMINSTER H.	3-0	Briggs, Carr, Russell	8522	4	10	1	8		11				5		2			6	3	9		7	
40		25	Tonbridge	2-2	Poole, Warsap		4		1	8	3	10				5		2	9		6	11			7	
41	May	2	Barry Town	2-0	Carr, Warsap		4	10	1	8	3		7			5		2			6	9			11	
42		7	Cheltenham Town	3-2	Russell 2 (1p), Briggs	9340	4	10	1	8	3		7			5		2			6		9		11	
						Apps	36	30	41	26	38	36	15	6	12	39	1	24	1	1	32	28	39	9	20	28
						Goals	2	10		12	3	14	2			1					2	5	35		7	8

Three own goals

F.A. Cup

							Boswell J	Briggs J	Burke JJ	Carr J	Dorling GC	Forrester GL	Gore LF	Granville NY	Henson L	Kingsnorth TH	Lambourne JC	Marks CWA	Nobbs J	O'Sullivan CJ	Piper GH	Poole CJ	Russell HW	Vigor DRJ	Warsap WJB	Wilson TH
Q4	Nov	13	Romford	1-2	(aet) Briggs	14154	4	10	1		2	11	7			5					6	3	9			8

Southern League Cup

							Boswell J	Briggs J	Burke JJ	Carr J	Dorling GC	Forrester GL	Gore LF	Granville NY	Henson L	Kingsnorth TH	Lambourne JC	Marks CWA	Nobbs J	O'Sullivan CJ	Piper GH	Poole CJ	Russell HW	Vigor DRJ	Warsap WJB	Wilson TH
R1	Sep	8	KIDDERMINSTER HARR.	2-0	Wilson 2	5516	4		1	10	2	11	7		3	5					6		9			8
R2		29	GUILDFORD CITY	2-0	Gore, Wilson	5545			1	10	2	11	7	4	3	5					6		9			8
SF	Apr	6	COLCHESTER UNITED	2-4	Carr, Russell	11042	4	11	1	8	2	10	7			5					6	3	9			

		P	W	D	L	F	A	Pts
1	GILLINGHAM	42	26	10	6	104	48	62
2	Chelmsford City	42	27	7	8	115	64	61
3	Merthyr Tydfil	42	26	8	8	133	54	60
4	Colchester U	42	21	10	11	94	61	52
5	Worcester City	42	22	7	13	87	56	51
6	Dartford	42	21	9	12	73	53	51
7	Gravesend & N'fleet	42	20	9	13	60	46	49
8	Yeovil Town	42	19	9	14	90	53	47
9	Cheltenham Town	42	19	9	14	71	64	47
10	Kidderminster H.	42	19	6	17	77	94	44
11	Exeter City Res	42	18	7	17	83	73	43
12	Hereford United	42	17	6	19	83	84	40
13	Bath City	42	15	8	19	72	87	38
14	Hastings United	42	14	10	18	69	93	38
15	Torquay U Res	42	15	7	20	73	93	37
16	Lovell's Athletic	42	14	8	20	73	74	36
17	Guildford City	42	12	12	18	58	85	36
18	Gloucester City	42	12	10	20	78	100	34
19	Barry Town	42	12	10	20	55	95	34
20	Tonbridge	42	9	7	26	54	105	25
21	Chungford Town	42	6	9	27	43	94	21
22	Bedford Town	42	5	8	29	32	101	18

1949/50

5th in Southern League Division One

No	Month	Date	Opponent	Score	Scorers	Att	Armstrong G	Bates WH	Boswell J	Briggs J	Burke JJ	Burtenshaw CE	Burtenshaw WF	Carr J	Collier F	Collins WH	Cook V	Day JN	Dorling GC	Forrester GL	Hales WH	Kingsnorth TH	Marks CWA	McGuire LGR	Millbank JH	Piper GH	Poulton GH	Russell HW	Trumper S	Warsap WJB	Williams HS
1	Aug	20	Gravesend & Northfleet	0-3		4915		7	4	10					3		1		2	11		5				6		8			9
2		24	HASTINGS UNITED	8-0	Williams 6, Carr, Forrester	7568			4	10				8				1	2	11		5	3			6				7	9
3		27	GLOUCESTER CITY	6-1	Williams 2, Warsap 2, Carr, Russell(p)	9164			4	11				8			1		2			5	3			6		10		7	9
4	Sep[	3	Hereford United	1-1	Carr	5548		7	4	11	1			8					2				3		5	6		10			9
5		7	Hastings United	1-2	Carr	1995			4	11	1			8					2	10			3		5	6		9		7	
6		14	CHELMSFORD CITY	2-2	Carr, Briggs	7772		11	4	10	1			8					2	9		5	3			6				7	
7		17	CHELTENHAM TOWN	3-1	Briggs 2, Kingsnorth (p)	8580		11	4	10	1			8					2	9		5	3						6	7	
8		21	Chelmsford City	1-1	Warsap	6500			4		1			8					2	10		5	3			6		7		11	9
9		24	Colchester United	1-2	Williams	10918		7	4		1			8					2	10		5	3			6				11	9
10	Oct	1	Cheltenham Town	2-1	Carr, Russell	3213		7	4		1			10					2	11		5	3			6		9			8
11		8	TORQUAY UTD RES	1-1	Williams	9312			4		1			10					2	11		5	3			6		9		7	8
12		15	Worcester City	1-2	W Burtenshaw	4464			4	10	1	7	8			6			2	11		5	3					9			
13		29	Dartford	1-2	Forrester	5883	2		4	10	1	7	8			6				11		5	3					9			
14	Nov	5	KIDDERMINSTER H.	4-2	W Burtenshaw 2, Forrester, Russell	5937			4	10	1	7	8			6			2	11		5	3					9			
15		19	WORCESTER CITY	2-0	Russell 2	9479			4	10		7	8			6		1	2	11		5	3					9			
16	Dec	3	BEDFORD TOWN	1-0	Potter (og)	7945			4	11		7	8			6		1	2			5	3					9			10
17		24	Gloucester City	1-3	Williams	3253			4	11		7		10		6		1	2			5	3					9			8
18		26	TONBRIDGE	3-0	C Burtenshaw, Russell, Briggs	10381			4	11		7		10		6		1	2	8		5	3					9			
19		27	Tonbridge	1-2	Briggs	6756			4	11		7		10		6		1	2	8		5	3					9			
20		31	YEOVIL TOWN	0-1		11577			4	11		7		10		6		1	2	8	9	5	3								
21	Jan	7	LOVELL'S ATHLETIC	2-0	Carr, W Burtenshaw	7571			4			7	8	10		6		1	2	11	9	5	3								
22		14	Bedford Town	1-1	W Burtenshaw	3954			4			7	8	10		6		1	2	11		5	3								9
23		28	Torquay United Res	2-1	Williams 2	1962			4			7	8	10		6		1	2	11		5	3								9
24	Feb	4	GRAVESEND & N'FLEET	4-2	Williams,Russell, W Burtenshaw,Forrester	11158			4				8	10		6		1	2	11		5	3					7			9
25		11	EXETER CITY RES	4-1	Russell, W Burtenshaw, Carr, Williams	7609			4				8	10		6		1	2	11		5	3					7			9
26		25	Lovell's Athletic	2-2	W Burtenshaw, Williams	500			4				8	10		6		1	2	11		5	3					7			9
27	Mar	4	Barry Town	3-0	W Burenshaw 2, Williams	171			4		1	11	8	10		6			2			5	3					7			9
28		9	Chingford	2-1	W Burtenshaw, Russell	307					1	11	8	10		6			2			5	3			4		7			9
29		11	BATH CITY	1-1	Carr	7749			4		1	11	8	10		6			2			5	3					7			9
30		15	HEREFORD UNITED	4-0	McGuire,Carr, C Burtenshaw(p),Williams	6000			4		1	11		8		6			2			5	3	10				7			9
31		25	Yeovil Town	1-2	Russell				4	11	1			8		6			2	10			3			5		9		7	
32	Apr	1	GUILDFORD CITY	0-0		7973				10	1	7				4			2	8		5	3			6		9		11	
33		5	HEADINGTON	2-0	Forrester 2	4086					1	7		8		6			2	10		5	3			4		9		11	
34		7	WEYMOUTH	1-1	Briggs	9233				11	1			8		6			2	10		5	3			4		9		7	
35		8	CHINGFORD	4-1	Hales 2, Kingsnorth, Warsap	6277				11	1			8		6			2	10	9	5	3			4				7	
36		12	Kidderminster Harriers	2-0	Hales, C Burtenshaw						1	7		8		6			2	10	9	5	3						4	11	
37		15	Exeter City Res	1-5	Briggs					11	1	7		8		6			2	10	9	5	3						4		
38		17	Merthyr Tydfil	0-4			2					8				6		1			9	5	3	10		4	11			7	
39		22	Headington	3-1	Briggs 2, Forrester	5500	2			10	1	7		8		6				9		5	3			4				11	
40		24	Weymouth	0-2							1	7	8	10		6			2	9		5	3	11		4					
41		26	DARTFORD	2-0	Russell, Kingsnorth (p)	4000	2					7	8			6		1		10		5	3			4		9		11	
42		28	BARRY TOWN	1-0	Carr	3423	2					7	8	10		6		1				5				3		9	4	11	
43		29	COLCHESTER UNITED	6-1	Hales 3, Warsap, Russell, Briggs	4875	2			10	1			8		6				6	9	5	3					7		11	
44	May	1	Bath City	1-3	W Burtenshaw		2				1	9	8			6							3	10	5	4		7		11	
45		3	MERTHYR TYDFIL	3-1	Russell, Warsap, Carr	8126	2			10	1			8		4				6	9	5	3					7		11	
46		6	Guildford City	1-4	Piper		2			10	1			8		4				11	9	5	3			6		7			
						Apps	9	6	30	25	28	26	18	36	1	35	2	16	37	35	9	42	44	4	3	23	1	32	4	21	19
						Goals				10		3	12	12						7	6	3		1		1		13		6	18

One own goal

F.A. Cup

Rd	Month	Date	Opponent	Score	Scorers	Att	Armstrong G	Bates WH	Boswell J	Briggs J	Burke JJ	Burtenshaw CE	Burtenshaw WF	Carr J	Collier F	Collins WH	Cook V	Day JN	Dorling GC	Forrester GL	Hales WH	Kingsnorth TH	Marks CWA	McGuire LGR	Millbank JH	Piper GH	Poulton GH	Russell HW	Trumper S	Warsap WJB	Williams HS
Q4	Nov	12	Guildford City	3-2	C Burtenshaw, Russell, Briggs	7227			4	10	1	7	8			6			2	11		5	3					9			
R1		26	Hastings United	3-1	Collins (p), Russell, C Burtenshaw	9150			4	10		7	8			6		1	2	11		5	3					9			
R2	Dec	10	Yeovil Town	1-3	Russell (p)	12041			4	10		7	8			6		1	2	11		5	3					9			

Southern League Cup

Rd	Month	Date	Opponent	Score	Scorers	Att	Armstrong G	Bates WH	Boswell J	Briggs J	Burke JJ	Burtenshaw CE	Burtenshaw WF	Carr J	Collier F	Collins WH	Cook V	Day JN	Dorling GC	Forrester GL	Hales WH	Kingsnorth TH	Marks CWA	McGuire LGR	Millbank JH	Piper GH	Poulton GH	Russell HW	Trumper S	Warsap WJB	Williams HS
R1	Sep	10	BARRY TOWN	3-1	Forrester, Briggs, Carr	7690		7	4	11	1			8					2	10		5	3					9	6		
R2	Oct	12	COLCHESTER UNITED	0-1		6639		11	4									1	2	6		5	3					10			9

Played in R2: J Kay (7), TH Wilson (8)

	Team	P	W	D	L	F	A	Pts
1	Merthyr Tydfil	46	34	3	9	143	62	71
2	Colchester United	46	31	9	6	109	51	71
3	Yeovil Town	46	29	7	10	104	45	65
4	Chelmsford City	46	26	9	11	121	64	61
5	GILLINGHAM	46	23	9	14	93	61	55
6	Dartford	46	20	9	17	70	65	49
7	Worcester City	46	21	7	18	85	80	49
8	Guildford City	46	18	11	17	79	73	47
9	Weymouth	46	19	9	18	80	81	47
10	Barry Town	46	18	10	18	78	72	46
11	Exeter City Res	46	16	14	16	73	83	46
12	Lovell's Athletic	46	17	10	19	86	78	44
13	Tonbridge	46	16	12	18	65	76	44
14	Hastings United	46	17	8	21	92	140	42
15	Gravesned & N'fleet	46	16	9	21	88	81	41
16	Torquay U Res	46	14	12	20	80	89	40
17	Bath City	46	16	7	23	61	78	39
18	Gloucester City	46	14	11	21	72	101	39
19	Hereford United	46	15	8	23	74	76	38
20	Cheltenham Town	46	13	11	22	75	96	37
21	Headington Utd.	46	15	7	24	72	97	37
22	Bedford Town	46	12	11	23	63	79	35
23	Kidderminster H.	46	12	11	23	64	108	35
24	Chingford Town	46	10	6	30	63	151	26

1950/51

22nd in Football League Division Three (South)

	Date	Opponent	Res	Scorers	Att	Ayres H	Boswell J	Briggs J	Burke JJ	Burtenshaw CE	Burtenshaw WF	Campbell J	Carr J	Collins WH	Dorling GJ	Forrester GL	Gage LA	Hales WH	Henson L	Jenkins RI	Kingsnorth TH	Lewin DR	Lewis DIE	Maguire LGR	Marks CWA	Piper GH	Russell HW	Skivington MN	Thomas DWJ	Veck R	Warsap WJB
1	Aug 19	COLCHESTER UNITED	0-0		19525	10	4			7	8			6			1				5	3			2		9			11	
2	23	Bournemouth	1-3	Veck	16070	10	4			7	8			6			1				5	3			2		9			11	
3	26	Bristol City	0-2		21531		4	10		7	8			6			1					3			2		9	5		11	
4	30	BOURNEMOUTH	2-2	Veck (p), Russell	15397		4	10		7				6			1			8		3			2		9	5		11	
5	Sep 2	MILLWALL	4-3	Russell, Veck, Briggs, C Burtenshaw	20126		4	10		7		8		6			1					3			2		9	5		11	
6	4	Bristol Rovers	0-3		14414		4	10		7	9	8		6			1					3			2			5		11	
7	9	Watford	0-5		10529		4	10		7		8		6			1				5	3			2		9			11	
8	13	BRISTOL ROVERS	1-0	Veck (p)	12293	6	4	10				8					1				5	3	9		2		7			11	
9	16	WALSALL	4-1	Lewis 3, Campbell	14718	6	4	10				8					1				5	3	9		2		7			11	
10	23	Leyton Orient	0-4		16005	6	4	10				8					1				5	3	9		2					11	7
11	30	IPSWICH TOWN	0-1		12853	6	4	10			5	8					1					2	9		3					11	7
12	Oct 7	Crystal Palace	3-4	Veck, Briggs (og), Marks	18896	6	5	11		7	8			4			1					2			3		9			10	
13	14	BRIGHTON & HOVE ALB	1-1	Forrester	15060	6	5			7				4		11	1					2			3		10		9	8	
14	21	Newport County	0-1		9828	6	5			7		8		4	2	11	1								3				9	10	
15	28	NORWICH CITY	2-2	Thomas, Veck (p)	14348	6							8	4	2	11	1								3	5	7		9	10	
16	Nov 4	Northampton Town	1-4	Carr	10785	6	4						8		2	11	1								3	5	7		9	10	
17	11	PORT VALE	1-1	Thomas, Veck (p)	12103	6	5	10		7				4	2	8	1								3				9	11	
18	18	Nottingham Forest	2-9	Veck, Thomas	20639	6	5	10		7				4	2	11	1								3				9	8	
19	Dec 2	Aldershot	4-2	Thomas 3, Carr	7253	6	4			7	8		11		2		1			10		3						5	9		
20	16	Colchester United	2-4	Briggs, Thomas	6941		4	10		7	8		11		2	6	1					3						5	9		
21	23	BRISTOL CITY	1-2	W Burtenshaw	8579	6	4			7	8		11				1					3	10		2			5	9		
22	25	READING	0-3		9539		4	10		7	8		11		2	6	1								3			5	9		
23	26	Reading	1-1	W Burtenshaw	17464	6	4			7	8					10	1				5	3			2				9	11	
24	30	Millwall	3-4	Thomas, C Burtenshaw, Lewis	20630	6	4			7	8						1				5	3	10		2				9	11	
25	Jan 13	WATFORD	3-1	Thomas, Eggleston (og), Veck	10036	6	4			7	8						1				5	3	10		2				9	11	
26	17	EXETER CITY	9-4	* see below	4701	6	4			7							1				5	3	8	10	2				9	11	
27	20	Walsall	1-2	Lewis	8817	6	4			7							1				5	3	8	10	2				9	11	
28	Feb 3	LEYTON ORIENT	1-0	Veck	8352	6	4			7		10					1				5	3	8		2				9	11	
29	7	Exeter City	2-1	Campbell, Thomas	5188	6	4			7		8				10	1				5	3			2				9	11	
30	10	TORQUAY UNITED	2-0	Veck (p), C Burtenshaw	12995	6	4			7		8				10	1				5	3			2				9	11	
31	17	Ipswich Town	1-5	C Burtenshaw	9676	6				7	8						1				5	3			2	4	10		9	11	
32	24	CRYSTAL PALACE	0-0		11478	6				7	8						1				5	3			2	4	10		9	11	
33	Mar 3	Brighton & Hove Albion	2-2	Thomas 2	10903	6	4				8					11	1				5	3			2		10		9	7	
34	10	NEWPORT COUNTY	0-1		9040	6	4				8						1				5	3	10		2		7		9	11	
35	17	Norwich City	0-2		19010	6	4						7			11	1				5	3	8		2		10		9		
36	23	SOUTHEND UNITED	0-0		15356	6	4						7				1				5	3	8		2		10		9	11	
37	24	NORTHAMPTON T	3-1	Veck, Lewis, Thomas	10657	6	4						7				1				5	3	8		2		10		9	11	
38	26	Southend United	0-4		10544	6	4						7				1				5	3	8		2		10		9	11	
39	31	Port Vale	3-4	Hales 3	5947		4				7					6	1	9			5	3			2		10		8	11	
40	Apr 7	NOTTM. FOREST	1-4	Thomas	13845	6	4						7				1	9			5	3		10	2				8	11	
41	14	Torquay United	2-1		6666		4		1		7							9	6		5	3	8	11	2				10		
42	18	Plymouth Argyle	0-2		11340		4		1		7					11		9	6		5	3	8		2				10		
43	21	ALDERSHOT	3-0	W Burtenshaw, Hales, Thomas	10492		4				7					11		9	6		5	3	8		2				10		
44	28	Swindon Town	0-2		3915				1		7					11		9	6		5	3	8		2				10	4	
45	May 2	SWINDON TOWN	2-1	Hales 2 (1p)	8295	6	4		1		7				3	11		9	5				8		2				10		
46	5	PLYMOUTH ARGYLE	1-2	W Burtenshaw	12096	6	4		1		7	8			3			9	5					11	2				10		
					Apps	34	42	14	5	26	24	12	11	13	10	18	40	8	6	2	28	38	20	5	44	4	21	8	34	36	2
					Goals			2		4	4	2	2			1		6					9	2	1		2		19	12	

Played in one game: JN Day (43, at 1)

Scorers in game 26: Lewis 3, Thomas 2, McGuire 2, Veck, Doyle (og)

Three own goals

F.A. Cup

	Date	Opponent	Res	Scorers	Att	Ayres H	Boswell J	Briggs J	Burke JJ	Burtenshaw CE	Burtenshaw WF	Campbell J	Carr J	Collins WH	Dorling GJ	Forrester GL	Gage LA	Hales WH	Henson L	Jenkins RI	Kingsnorth TH	Lewin DR	Lewis DIE	Maguire LGR	Marks CWA	Piper GH	Russell HW	Skivington MN	Thomas DWJ	Veck R	Warsap WJB
R1	Nov 25	Linby Colliery	4-1	* see below	4635	6	4			7	8		11		2		1			10		3						5	9		
R2	Dec 9	Bristol Rovers	2-2	Thomas, Carr	15479	6	4			7	8		11		2		1			10		3						5	9		
rep	Dec 13	BRISTOL ROVERS	1-1	(aet) Carr	10642	6	4			7	8		11		2		1			10		3						5	9		
rep2	Dec 18	Bristol Rovers	1-2	Lewis	3927	6	4			7	8				2		1					3	10					5	9	11	

R2 replay 2 at White Hart Lane

Scorers in R1: Thomas, C Burtenshaw, W Burtenshaw, Jenkins

		P	W	D	L	F	A	W	D	L	F	A	Pts
1	Nottingham Forest	46	16	6	1	57	17	14	4	5	53	23	70
2	Norwich City	46	16	6	1	42	14	9	8	6	40	31	64
3	Reading	46	15	6	2	57	17	6	9	8	31	36	57
4	Plymouth Argyle	46	16	5	2	54	19	8	4	11	31	36	57
5	Millwall	46	15	6	2	52	23	8	4	11	28	34	56
6	Bristol Rovers	46	15	7	1	46	18	5	8	10	18	24	55
7	Southend United	46	15	4	4	64	27	6	6	11	28	42	52
8	Ipswich Town	46	15	4	4	48	24	8	2	13	21	34	52
9	Bournemouth	46	17	5	1	49	16	5	2	16	16	41	51
10	Bristol City	46	15	4	4	41	25	5	7	11	23	34	51
11	Newport County	46	13	4	6	48	25	6	5	12	29	45	47
12	Port Vale	46	13	6	4	35	24	3	7	13	25	41	45
13	Brighton & Hove Albion	46	11	8	4	51	31	2	9	12	20	48	43
14	Exeter City	46	11	4	8	33	30	7	2	14	29	55	42
15	Walsall	46	12	4	7	32	20	3	6	14	20	42	40
16	Colchester United	46	12	5	6	43	25	2	7	14	20	51	40
17	Swindon Town	46	15	4	4	38	17	3	0	20	17	50	40
18	Aldershot	46	11	8	4	37	20	4	2	17	19	68	40
19	Leyton Orient	46	13	2	8	36	28	2	6	15	17	47	38
20	Torquay United	46	13	2	8	47	39	1	7	15	17	42	37
21	Northampton Town	46	8	9	6	39	30	2	7	14	16	37	36
22	GILLINGHAM	46	10	7	6	41	30	3	2	18	28	71	35
23	Watford	46	8	5	10	29	28	1	6	16	25	60	29
24	Crystal Palace	46	6	5	12	18	39	2	6	15	15	45	27

1951/52

22nd in Division Three (South)

						Ayres H	Baldwin JG	Bean RE	Boswell J	Briggs J	Burtenshaw CE	Burtenshaw WF	Forrester GL	Hales RJ	Hales WH	Henson L	Hillman DV	Kelly JL	Lewin DR	Lewis DIE	Maguire LGR	Marks CWA	Murray JG	Niblett V	Poulton GH	Rigg T	Russell HW	Scarth JW	Thomas DWJ	Warsap WJB
1	Aug 18	MILLWALL	1-1	Thomas (p)	17214	6			4	11							7		3	8		2		5		1	10		9	
2	22	Exeter City	2-4	Thomas 2	7883	6			4	11							7		3	8		2		5		1	10		9	
3	25	Bournemouth	3-3	Lewis 2, Thomas	12573	6			4	11							7		3	8		2		5		1	10		9	
4	29	EXETER CITY	2-1	Russell, Thomas	12329	6			4	11							7		3	8		2		5		1	10		9	
5	Sep 1	SOUTHEND UNITED	2-0	Lewis 2	14381	6			4	11							7		3	8		2		5		1	10		9	
6	5	Torquay United	1-2	Briggs	8014	6			4	11							7		3	8		2		5		1	10		9	
7	8	Newport County	1-1	Lewis	10725	6			4	11							7		3	8		2		5		1	10		9	
8	12	TORQUAY UNITED	3-0	Lewis 2, Thomas	12229	6			4	11							7		3	8		2		5		1	10		9	
9	15	READING	1-1	Lewis	11760	6			4	11							7		3	8		2		5		1	10		9	
10	22	Northampton Town	1-2	Briggs	12853				4	11			6				7		3	8		2		5		1	10		9	
11	29	PORT VALE	4-2	Lewis 2, Briggs, Thomas	14354	6			4	11							7		3	8		2		5		1	10		9	
12	Oct 6	Crystal Palace	2-0	Lewis 2	20380	6			4	11							7		3	8		2		5		1	10		9	
13	13	SWINDON TOWN	4-0	Lewis 2, Briggs, Thomas	15704	6			4	11							7		3	8		2		5		1	10		9	
14	20	Leyton Orient	0-1		13839	6	4			11							7		3	8		2		5		1	10		9	
15	27	WALSALL	4-1	Thomas 2 (1p), Briggs, Lewis	14490	6				11			4				7		3	8		2		5		1	10		9	
16	Nov 3	Shrewsbury Town	2-2	Lewis, Thomas	8267	6				11			4				7		3	8		2		5		1	10		9	
17	10	ALDERSHOT	3-3	Briggs 2, Thomas	14759	6				11			4				7		3	8		2		5		1	10		9	
18	17	Watford	2-2	Lewis, Thomas	10771	6			4	11		7							3	8		2		5		1	10		9	
19	Dec 1	Plymouth Argyle	2-4	Thomas 2	18409	6			4	11		7							3	8		2		5		1	10		9	
20	8	NORWICH CITY	1-2	Russell	10499	6			4	11		7							3	8		2		5		1	10		9	
21	22	BOURNEMOUTH	0-2		10296	6			4	11			10	2			7		3					5		1	8		9	
22	25	COLCHESTER UNITED	1-2	Briggs	9774	6		1	4	11		8		2			7		3					5			10		9	
23	26	Colchester United	0-1		11127	6		1	4	11		8		2			7		3					5			10		9	
24	29	Southend United	1-3	Lewis	8563	6		1	4				11	2				7	3	8				5			10		9	
25	Jan 5	NEWPORT COUNTY	2-3	Briggs, Lewis	10410	6			4	11				2				7	3	8				5		1	10		9	
26	12	Bristol City	2-3	Thomas, Russell	13567	6			4	11		8							3	10		2		5		1	7		9	
27	19	Reading	1-2	Thomas	13670	6			4			8	11						3	10		2		5		1	7		9	
28	26	NORTHAMPTON T	2-1	Lewis, W Burtenshaw	9625				4	11		8	6							10		2	3	5		1	7		9	
29	Feb 2	BRIGHTON & HOVE ALB	2-3	W Burtenshaw, Thomas	15538				4	11		8	6							10		2	3	5		1	7		9	
30	9	Port Vale	0-1		12768	6			4				10						11	8		2	3	5		1	7		9	
31	16	CRYSTAL PALACE	4-4	Lewis 2, W Hales 2	11991	6			4	11			10		9					8		2	3	5		1	7			
32	23	Brighton & Hove Albion	0-0		21669	6			4			8	10		9		11		3			2		5		1		7		
33	Mar 1	Swindon Town	1-2	W Hales	9769	6			4				10		9				3			2		5	11	1	8	7		
34	8	LEYTON ORIENT	1-1	Russell	13191				4		7		11			6			3			2		5		1	10	8	9	
35	15	Walsall	0-1		6942				4				11		9	6			3			2		5		1	10	7	8	
36	22	SHREWSBURY TOWN	0-0		10577	6			4				10						3			2		5		1	9	7	8	11
37	31	Millwall	1-3	Forrester	6350	6			4				10						3			2		5		1	9	7	8	11
38	Apr 5	WATFORD	1-0	Russell	9578	6			4			7	10						3			2		5		1	9	8		11
39	11	IPSWICH TOWN	1-1	Russell	14084	6			4			8	10						3			2		5		1	9	7		11
40	12	Bristol Rovers	0-5		12877	6			4			8	11						3		10	2		5		1	9	7		
41	14	Ipswich Town	1-1	Scarth	12538	6			4	10					11				3			2		5		1	8	7	9	
42	16	Aldershot	1-2	Poulton	5115	6			4	10					9			8	3			2		5	11	1		7		
43	19	PLYMOUTH ARGYLE	1-2	Briggs	14639	6			4	10					9				3			2		5	11	1		7	8	
44	23	BRISTOL ROVERS	2-1	Thomas, Ayres	9812	6			4		8		10						3			2		5	11	1		7	9	
45	26	Norwich City	0-5		14370	6			4			8	10						3			2		5	11	1		7	9	
46	May 3	BRISTOL CITY	5-0	W Burtenshaw 2, Thomas 2, Forrester	12017	6			4	11		8	10						3			2		5		1		7	9	
					Apps	41	1	3	42	32	2	15	23	5	7	2	21	3	43	28	1	41	4	46	5	43	40	15	39	4
					Goals	1				10		4	2		3					22					1		6	1	21	

F.A. Cup

						Ayres H	Baldwin JG	Bean RE	Boswell J	Briggs J	Burtenshaw CE	Burtenshaw WF	Forrester GL	Hales RJ	Hales WH	Henson L	Hillman DV	Kelly JL	Lewin DR	Lewis DIE	Maguire LGR	Marks CWA	Murray JG	Niblett V	Poulton GH	Rigg T	Russell HW	Scarth JW	Thomas DWJ	Warsap WJB
R1	Nov 24	Crystal Palace	1-0	Thomas	21868	6			4	11		7							3	8		2		5		1	10		9	
R2	Dec 15	ROCHDALE	0-3		15651	6			4	11		7							3	8		2		5		1	10		9	

		P	W	D	L	F	A	W	D	L	F	A	Pts
1	Plymouth Argyle	46	19	3	1	70	19	10	5	8	37	34	66
2	Reading	46	19	2	2	73	23	10	1	12	39	37	61
3	Norwich City	46	18	1	4	55	15	8	8	7	34	35	61
4	Millwall	46	16	5	2	46	21	7	7	9	28	32	58
5	Brighton & Hove Albion	46	15	4	4	57	24	9	6	8	30	39	58
6	Newport County	46	13	7	3	45	26	8	5	10	32	50	54
7	Bristol Rovers	46	14	5	4	60	20	6	7	10	29	33	52
8	Northampton Town	46	17	1	5	65	31	5	4	14	28	43	49
9	Southend United	46	16	6	1	56	17	3	4	16	19	49	48
10	Colchester United	46	12	7	4	32	22	5	5	13	24	55	46
11	Torquay United	46	10	3	10	53	42	7	7	9	33	56	44
12	Aldershot	46	11	4	8	40	27	7	4	12	38	62	44
13	Port Vale	46	11	11	1	33	16	3	4	16	17	50	43
14	Bournemouth	46	11	4	8	42	30	5	6	12	27	45	42
15	Bristol City	46	13	6	4	44	26	2	6	15	14	43	42
16	Swindon Town	46	9	9	5	29	22	5	5	13	22	46	42
17	Ipswich Town	46	12	4	7	45	31	4	5	14	18	43	41
18	Leyton Orient	46	12	5	6	39	26	4	4	15	16	42	41
19	Crystal Palace	46	9	7	7	32	28	6	2	15	29	52	39
20	Shrewsbury Town	46	11	3	9	35	29	2	7	14	27	57	36
21	Watford	46	7	7	9	34	37	6	3	14	23	44	36
22	GILLINGHAM	46	10	7	6	47	31	1	6	16	24	50	35
23	Exeter City	46	10	4	9	40	36	3	5	15	25	50	35
24	Walsall	46	11	3	9	38	31	2	2	19	17	63	31

1952/53

21st in Division Three (South)

							Ayres H	Blake AJ	Boswell J	Briggs J	Cherry RA	Forrester GL	Hall W	King G	Lambert K	Lewin DR	Lewis T	Long TG	Marks CWA	McKee F	Moorcroft M	Niblett V	Rigg T	Scarth JW	Sowden PT	Thomas DWJ	Warsap WJB
1	Aug	23	Newport County	2-1	Scarth, Lambert	11711	6		4						10	3		11	2			5	1	7	8	9	
2		27	Crystal Palace	0-0		15754	6		4						10	3		11	2			5	1	7	8	9	
3		30	MILLWALL	0-1		18774	6		4						10	3		11	2			5	1	7	8	9	
4	Sep	3	CRYSTAL PALACE	1-0	Blake	13023	6	9	4						10	3		11	2			5	1	7	8		
5		6	Bristol Rovers	1-3	Scarth	20254	6		4				9		10	3		11	2			5	1	7	8		
6		10	Swindon Town	0-0		8291		2	4				9		10	3		11		6		5	1	7	8		
7		13	EXETER CITY	1-0	Scarth	13773		2	4				9		10	3		11		6		5	1	7	8		
8		17	SWINDON TOWN	0-0		10788		2	4			11	9		10	3				6		5	1	7	8		
9		20	Coventry City	1-2	Sowden	12258	6	2	4			10	9			3				11		5	1	7	8		
10		24	Bournemouth	2-4	Lewin, Long	8062		2	4			10	9			3		11		6		5	1	7	8		
11		27	NORWICH CITY	0-3		14384		2	4				9		10	3		11		6		5	1	7	8		
12	Oct	1	ALDERSHOT	2-0	Thomas 2	6670		2	4			10				3		11		6		5	1	7	8	9	
13		4	Colchester United	1-1	Long	8529		2	4						10	3		11		6		5	1	7	8	9	
14		11	Bristol City	0-4		19755		2	4						10	3		11		6		5	1	7	8	9	
15		18	TORQUAY UNITED	2-1	Long, Lambert	12623			4					9	10	3		11	2	6		5	1	7	8		
16		25	Northampton Town	1-3	Boswell	13689			4			11			10	3		7	2	6		5	1	9	8		
17	Nov	1	LEYTON ORIENT	3-2	Scarth 3	11562			4			11		9		3		7	2	6		5	1	8	10		
18		8	Ipswich Town	1-1	Lambert	9440			4					9	11	3		7	2	6		5	1	8	10		
19		15	READING	2-1	Long, King	12383			4					9	11	3		7	2	6		5	1	8	10		
20		29	SOUTHEND UNITED	1-1	Scarth	11537			4			11			10	3		7	2	6		5	1	9	8		
21	Dec	13	BRIGHTON & HOVE ALB	1-2	Sowden	10269			4						10	3		11	2	6		5	1	7	8	9	
22		20	NEWPORT COUNTY	1-1	Lambert	7179			4				9		10	3		11	2	6		5	1	7	8		
23		26	WALSALL	3-1	Lambert, King, Long	9326			4					9	10	3		11	2	6		5	1	7	8		
24		27	Walsall	3-1	King, Long, Lambert	6898			4					9	10	3		11	2	6		5	1	7	8		
25	Jan	3	Millwall	1-3	Lambert	20200			4					9	10	3		11	2	6		5	1	7	8		
26		10	QUEEN'S PARK RANGERS	3-0	King, Lambert, Long	11907			4					9	10	3		11	2	6		5	1	7	8		
27		17	BRISTOL ROVERS	0-4		15237			4					9	10	3		11	2	6		5	1	7	8		
28		24	Exeter City	0-0		9305			4			6	7	9	10	3		11	2			5	1		8		
29		31	Queen's Park Rangers	1-1	Long	10565			4			6		9	10	3	7	11	2			5	1		8		
30	Feb	7	COVENTRY CITY	0-0		10383			4	11		6		9	10	3	7		2			5	1		8		
31		14	Norwich City	2-3	Scarth, Lambert	12221			4			6		9	10	3	7	11	2			5	1	8			
32		21	COLCHESTER UNITED	1-1	Long	11299			4			6		9	10	3	7	11	2			5	1	8			
33		28	BRISTOL CITY	0-1		12571			4			6		9	10	3	7	11	2			5	1	8			
34	Mar	7	Torquay United	2-3	Marks, Cherry	6278			4		9	6		8		3	7	11	2			5	1		10		
35		14	NORTHAMPTON T	1-1	King	10250			4			6		9		3	7	11	2			5	1	8	10		
36		21	Leyton Orient	1-1	Long	11418			4			6			9	3	7	11	2			5	1	10	8		
37		28	IPSWICH TOWN	1-1	Murchison (og)	8868			4			6			9	3	7	11	2			5	1	8	10		
38	Apr	3	SHREWSBURY TOWN	4-2	Sowden 2 (1p), Cherry, Lambert	12082			4	11	9	6			10	3	7		2			5	1		8		
39		4	Reading	2-3	Cherry, Sowden	12267			4	11	9	6			10	3	7		2		1	5			8		
40		6	Shrewsbury Town	1-3	Boswell	8324			4		9	6		8		3	11		2		1	5		7	10		
41		11	BOURNEMOUTH	1-2	Warsap	10448	5		4		9	6		8		3	7		2		1				10		11
42		16	Watford	0-0		8322	5		4			6			10	3	7		2		1			9	8		11
43		18	Southend United	1-3	Ayres	7390	5		4			6			10	3	7		2		1			9	8		11
44		22	Aldershot	2-3	Sowden, Cherry	4789	5		4	11	9	6			10	3			2		1			7	8		
45		25	WATFORD	2-1	Briggs 2	10507	5		4	11		6			10	3	7		2		1			9	8		
46	May	2	Brighton & Hove Albion	0-5		10092	5		4	11	9	6				3	7		2		1			8	10		
						Apps	12	10	46	6	7	26	9	19	37	46	17	34	37	22	8	40	38	39	43	7	3
						Goals	1	1	2	2	4			5	10	1		10	1					8	6	2	1

One own goal

F.A. Cup

							Ayres H	Blake AJ	Boswell J	Briggs J	Cherry RA	Forrester GL	Hall W	King G	Lambert K	Lewin DR	Lewis T	Long TG	Marks CWA	McKee F	Moorcroft M	Niblett V	Rigg T	Scarth JW	Sowden PT	Thomas DWJ	Warsap WJB
R1	Nov	22	Wellington Town	1-1	Forrester	5942			4			11		9		3		7	2	6		5	1	8	10		
rep	Nov	26	WELLINGTON TOWN	3-0	Scarth, Forrester, Long	7383			4			11		9		3		7	2	6		5	1	8	10		
R2	Dec	6	Stockport County	1-3	Thomas	12500			4			11				3		7	2	6		5	1	8	10	9	

		P	W	D	L	F	A	W	D	L	F	A	Pts
1	Bristol Rovers	46	17	4	2	55	19	9	8	6	37	27	64
2	Millwall	46	14	7	2	46	16	10	7	6	36	28	62
3	Northampton Town	46	18	4	1	75	30	8	6	9	34	40	62
4	Norwich City	46	16	6	1	56	17	9	4	10	43	38	60
5	Bristol City	46	13	8	2	62	28	9	7	7	33	33	59
6	Coventry City	46	15	5	3	52	22	4	7	12	25	40	50
7	Brighton & Hove Albion	46	12	6	5	48	30	7	6	10	33	45	50
8	Southend United	46	15	5	3	41	21	3	8	12	28	53	49
9	Bournemouth	46	15	3	5	49	23	4	6	13	25	46	47
10	Watford	46	12	8	3	39	21	3	9	11	23	42	47
11	Reading	46	17	3	3	53	18	2	5	16	16	46	46
12	Torquay United	46	15	4	4	61	28	3	5	15	26	60	45
13	Crystal Palace	46	12	7	4	40	26	3	6	14	26	56	43
14	Leyton Orient	46	12	7	4	52	28	4	3	16	16	45	42
15	Newport County	46	12	4	7	43	34	4	6	13	27	48	42
16	Ipswich Town	46	10	7	6	34	28	3	8	12	26	41	41
17	Exeter City	46	11	8	4	40	24	2	6	15	21	47	40
18	Swindon Town	46	9	5	9	38	33	5	7	11	26	46	40
19	Aldershot	46	8	8	7	36	29	4	7	12	25	48	39
20	Queen's Park Rangers	46	9	9	5	37	34	3	6	14	24	48	39
21	GILLINGHAM	46	10	7	6	30	26	2	8	13	25	48	39
22	Colchester United	46	9	9	5	40	29	3	5	15	19	47	38
23	Shrewsbury Town	46	11	5	7	38	35	1	7	15	30	56	36
24	Walsall	46	5	9	9	35	46	2	1	20	21	72	24

1953/54

10th in Division Three (South)

	Date	Opponent	Score	Scorers	Att.	Ayres H	Boswell J	Cherry RA	Durkin J	Evans A	Evans WE	Forrester GL	Kirman H	Lewin DR	Lewis T	Long TG	Marks CWA	McKee F	Millar W	Morgan E	Nekrews TJ	Niblett V	Rigg T	Riggs LJ	Scarth JW	Sowden PT
1	Aug 19	Bristol City	1-1	Miller	19506		4				8	6		3		11	2		10	9		5	1		7	
2	22	READING	3-0	Durkin 2, Long	13672		4		9		10	6		3		11	2			8		5	1		7	
3	26	COVENTRY CITY	2-0	Long, Morgan	14407		4		9		10	6		3		11	2			8		5	1		7	
4	29	Southend United	1-1	Long	10905		4		9		10	6		3	7	11	2			8		5	1			
5	31	Coventry City	1-2	Morgan	11410		4		9		10	6		3	7	11	2			8		5	1			
6	Sep 5	BRIGHTON & HOVE ALB	0-0		16203		4	9			10	6		3		11	2			8		5	1		7	
7	9	Ipswich Town	1-6	Scarth	12459		4		9		10	6		3		11	2			8		5	1		7	
8	12	Watford	1-6	Morgan	12929		4		9		8	6		3		11	2			10		5	1		7	
9	16	IPSWICH TOWN	1-1	Evans	9634	5	4		9		8	6		3		11	2			10			1		7	
10	19	TORQUAY UNITED	0-4		11824	5	4		9		8	6		3		11	2			10			1			7
11	24	Leyton Orient	1-3	Scarth	8407		4		7		8	6		3		11	2			10		5	1		9	
12	26	Northampton Town	1-1	Morgan	12096		4		7		8	6		3		11	2			10		5	1		9	
13	30	LEYTON ORIENT	1-2	Scarth	6371	5	4		7		8	6		3		11	2						1		9	10
14	Oct 3	NORWICH CITY	3-1	Evans, Morgan, Scarth	11092	5	4		7		8	6		3		11	2			10			1		9	
15	10	Southampton	0-1		17801	5	4		7		8	6		3			2		11	10			1		9	
16	17	COLCHESTER UNITED	2-0	Morgan 2 (1p)	8296	5	4		7		8	6		3			2		11	10			1		9	
17	24	Crystal Palace	2-1	Millar, Scarth	15856	5	4		7		8	6		3			2		11	10			1		9	
18	31	BRISTOL CITY	2-2	Evans, Morgan	10968	5	4		7		8	6		3			2		11	10			1		9	
19	Nov 7	Aldershot	2-1	Millar, Durkin	5024	5	4		7		8	6		3			2		11	10			1		9	
20	14	SWINDON TOWN	1-0	Morgan	11682	5	4		7		8	6		3			2		11	10			1		9	
21	28	SHREWSBURY TOWN	2-0	Scarth, Millar	10307	5	4		7	1	8			3			2	6	11	10					9	
22	Dec 5	Exeter City	2-1	Morgan 2	7946	5	4		7	1	8			3			2	6	11	10					9	
23	12	NEWPORT COUNTY	0-1		10204	5	4		7	1	8			3			2	6	11	10					9	
24	19	Reading	1-0	Millar	8380	5	4		7	1	8			3			2	6	11	10					9	
25	25	MILLWALL	2-0	Morgan, Scarth	10058	5	4		7	1	8			3			2	6	11	10					9	
26	26	Millwall	1-3	Morgan	13843	5	4		7	1	8			3		11	2	6		10					9	
27	Jan 2	SOUTHEND UNITED	3-1	Morgan 2, Scarth	7557	5	4		7	1	8			3			2	6	11	10					9	
28	9	Bournemouth	1-4	Durkin	9215	5	4		7	1	8			3		11	2	6		10					9	
29	16	Brighton & Hove Albion	1-3	Morgan	16019	5	4		7	1	8	11		3			2	6		10					9	
30	23	WATFORD	2-3	Millar, Morgan	9547	5	4				8	6		3	7		2		11	10			1		9	
31	30	BOURNEMOUTH	1-0	Evans	4207	5	4				8	6		3	7		2		11				1		9	10
32	Feb 6	Torquay United	3-3	Millar, Sowden, Lewis	6017	5	4				8	6		3	7		2		11				1		9	10
33	13	NORTHAMPTON T	2-1	Sowden, Morgan	9558	5	4				8	6		3			2		11	9			1		7	10
34	24	Norwich City	0-0		6697	5	4				8			3		11	2	6		9			1		7	10
35	27	SOUTHAMPTON	2-0	Long, Sowden	13024	5	4				8			3		11	2	6		9			1		7	10
36	Mar 6	Colchester United	1-0	Morgan	8651	5	4				8			3		11	2	6		9			1		7	10
37	13	WALSALL	3-0	Boswell, Morgan, Evans	9483	5	4				8		2	3		11		6		9			1		7	10
38	20	Shrewsbury Town	0-0		7137	5	4				8		2	3		11		6		9			1		7	10
39	27	ALDERSHOT	1-3	Sowden	10627	5	4				8			3		11		6		9		2	1		7	10
40	Apr 3	Swindon Town	1-2	Sowden	7180	5	4							3	7			6	11	10		2	1		9	8
41	10	EXETER CITY	0-1		9440	5	4				7		2	3				6	11	10			1		9	8
42	16	QUEEN'S PARK RANGERS	1-0	Sowden	10769			9			8		2	3		11		6			5		1	4	7	10
43	17	Newport County	0-1		9409	5		9			8		2	3		11		6					1	4	7	10
44	19	Queen's Park Rangers	1-3	Evans	9576	5				1	8	11	2	3	7			6		10				4	9	
45	24	CRYSTAL PALACE	3-2	Sowden 2, Morgan	8729	5				1	8	6	2	3		11				9				4	7	10
46	29	Walsall	1-1	Sowden	6683	5	4				8	6	2	3		11				9			1		7	10
					Apps	35	42	3	27	11	45	28	8	46	7	26	36	20	19	41	1	12	35	4	43	17
					Goals		1		4		6				1	4			7	21					8	9

F.A. Cup

	Date	Opponent	Score	Scorers	Att.	Ayres H	Boswell J	Cherry RA	Durkin J	Evans A	Evans WE	Forrester GL	Kirman H	Lewin DR	Lewis T	Long TG	Marks CWA	McKee F	Millar W	Morgan E	Nekrews TJ	Niblett V	Rigg T	Riggs LJ	Scarth JW	Sowden PT
R1	Nov 21	Walthamstow Avenue	0-1		9000	5	4		7		8	6		3			2		11	10			1		9	

		P	W	D	L	F	A	W	D	L	F	A	Pts
1	Ipswich Town	46	15	5	3	47	19	12	5	6	35	32	64
2	Brighton & Hove Albion	46	17	3	3	57	31	9	6	8	29	30	61
3	Bristol City	46	18	3	2	59	18	7	3	13	29	48	56
4	Watford	46	16	3	4	52	23	5	7	11	33	46	52
5	Northampton Town	46	18	4	1	63	18	2	7	14	19	37	51
6	Southampton	46	17	5	1	51	22	5	2	16	25	41	51
7	Norwich City	46	13	5	5	43	28	7	6	10	30	38	51
8	Reading	46	14	3	6	57	33	6	6	11	29	40	49
9	Exeter City	46	12	2	9	39	22	8	6	9	29	36	48
10	GILLINGHAM	46	14	3	6	37	22	5	7	11	24	44	48
11	Leyton Orient	46	14	5	4	48	26	4	6	13	31	47	47
12	Millwall	46	15	3	5	44	24	4	6	13	30	53	47
13	Torquay United	46	10	10	3	48	33	7	2	14	33	55	46
14	Coventry City	46	14	5	4	36	15	4	4	15	25	41	45
15	Newport County	46	14	4	5	42	28	5	2	16	19	53	44
16	Southend United	46	15	2	6	46	22	3	5	15	23	49	43
17	Aldershot	46	11	5	7	45	31	6	4	13	29	55	43
18	Queen's Park Rangers	46	10	5	8	32	25	6	5	12	28	43	42
19	Bournemouth	46	12	5	6	47	27	4	3	16	20	43	40
19	Swindon Town	46	13	5	5	48	21	2	5	16	19	49	40
21	Shrewsbury Town	46	12	8	3	48	34	2	4	17	17	42	40
22	Crystal Palace	46	11	7	5	41	30	3	5	15	19	56	40
23	Colchester United	46	7	7	9	35	29	3	3	17	15	49	30
24	Walsall	46	8	5	10	22	27	1	3	19	18	60	26

1954/55

4th in Division Three (South)

No	Date		Opponent	Score	Scorers	Att	Adey AL	Ayres H	Boswell J	Durkin J	Evans A	Evans WE	Forrester GL	Lewin DR	Lewis T	Long TG	Marks CWA	McKee F	Millar W	Morgan E	Nekrews TJ	Niblett V	Phoenix WE	Rigg T	Riggs LJ	Scarth JW	Smith PJ(1)	Sowden PT	West E
1	Aug	21	BRISTOL CITY	1-1	Morgan	14404	9	5	4			8		3			2	6	11	10				1		7			
2		25	SOUTHAMPTON	1-0	W Evans (p)	12034	9	5	4			8		3			2	6	11	10				1		7			
3		28	Walsall	1-0	Adey	15484	9	5	4			8		3			2	6	11	10				1		7			
4	Sep	1	Southampton	1-3	Morgan	16678	9	5	4			8		3			2	6	11	10				1		7			
5		4	SHREWSBURY TOWN	3-3	Morgan 2, Millar	11166	9	5	4			8		3			2	6	11	10				1		7			
6		6	Coventry City	1-4	Millar	18249	9	5	4			8		3			2	6	11	10				1		7			
7		11	Reading	2-2	Scarth, Morgan	8376		5	4		1	8		3		11	2	6		10						7		9	
8		15	COVENTRY CITY	2-1	Marks, Morgan	10425		5	4		1	8		3		11	2	6		10						7		9	
9		18	SWINDON TOWN	2-1	Long, W Evans	12125			4		1	8		3		11	2	6		10		5				7		9	
10		23	Brentford	0-3		9241		5	4			8		3		11	2	6		10				1		7		9	
11		25	LEYTON ORIENT	0-0		11636	9	5					6			7	2		11	10				1	4			8	3
12		29	BRENTFORD	2-1	Millar, Scarth	8202		5	4			8	6				2		11	10				1		7		9	3
13	Oct	2	Millwall	2-3	Millar, W Evans	18037		5	4			8	6			11	2		7	10				1				9	3
14		9	Northampton Town	1-4	Morgan	7827		5	4			8	6				2		11	10				1		7		9	3
15		16	WATFORD	0-1		10232		5	4			8	6	3			2		11	10				1		7		9	
16		23	Bournemouth	2-1	Millar, W Evans	10047			4			7		3			2		11	8		5		1	6	9		10	
17		30	ALDERSHOT	0-2		10004			4			7		3			2		11	8		5		1	6	9		10	
18	Nov	6	Newport County	3-1	Millar 2, Durkin	9181			4	9		10		3	7		2		11			5		1	6	8			
19		13	EXETER CITY	1-1	Lewis	9276			4	9		10		3	7		2		11			5		1	6	8			
20		27	NORWICH CITY	2-1	Morgan, Millar	8484			4	9		8		3			2		11	10		5		1	6	7			
21	Dec	4	Southend United	1-3	Morgan	6797			4			8		3		9	2		11	10		5		1	6	7			
22		18	Bristol City	4-1	Morgan 3, Sowden	17880			4			8					2		11	10		5		1	6	9		7	3
23		25	Torquay United	3-1	Sowden 2, Riggs	5761			4			8					2		11	10		5		1	6	9		7	3
24		27	TORQUAY UNITED	3-1	Morgan 2, Sowden	14712			4			8					2		11	10		5		1	6	9		7	3
25	Jan	1	WALSALL	3-2	Sowden, Millar, Morgan	9741			4			8					2		11	10		5		1	6	9		7	3
26		8	Crystal Palace	2-0	Scarth, Morgan	8379			4			8					2		11	10		5		1	6	9		7	3
27		22	READING	5-1	Millar 2, Scarth 2, W Evans	6160			4			8					2		11	10		5		1	6	9		7	3
28		29	CRYSTAL PALACE	2-1	Morgan, W Evans	11338			4			8					2	6	11	10		5		1		7		9	3
29	Feb	5	Swindon Town	1-2	Scarth	6477			4			8					2		11	10		5		1	6	7		9	3
30		12	Leyton Orient	2-2	Morgan 2	19836			4			8					2		11	10		5		1	6	7		9	3
31		19	MILLWALL	1-1	Millar	10838			4			8					2		11	10		5		1	6	7		9	3
32		26	NORTHAMPTON T	2-2	Morgan, Marks (p)	8523			4			8					2		11	10		5		1	6	7		9	3
33	Mar	5	Watford	1-1	Morgan	9298			4			8					2		11	10		5		1	6	7		9	3
34		12	BOURNEMOUTH	0-2		8236			4			8					2		11	10		5		1	6	7		9	3
35		19	Aldershot	2-0	Sowden, Morgan	5201			4			8					2		11	10		5		1	6	7		9	3
36		26	NEWPORT COUNTY	4-2	Morgan 2, Scarth, Millar	7784			4			8		3			2		11	10		5		1	6	7		9	
37	Apr	2	Exeter City	1-1	Davey (og)	5179			4			8					2		11	10		5		1	6	7		9	3
38		8	BRIGHTON & HOVE ALB	1-1	Morgan	13867			4			8					2		11	10		5		1	6	7		9	3
39		9	COLCHESTER UNITED	2-1	Millar, Morgan	10306			4			7					2		11	10		5	8	1	6			9	3
40		11	Brighton & Hove Albion	0-1		11083			4			7					2		11	10		5	8	1	6			9	3
41		16	Norwich City	2-1	Millar 2	11006			4			10					2		11			5	8	1	6	7		9	3
42		20	QUEEN'S PARK RANGERS	3-1	Morgan 2, Millar	9528			4			8					2		11	10		5		1	6	7		9	3
43		23	SOUTHEND UNITED	1-1	Marks (p)	9830			4								2		11	10		5	8	1	6	7		9	3
44		28	Colchester United	2-2	Miller, Morgan	5070			4			7					2		11	10		5		1	6		9	8	3
45		30	Queen's Park Rangers	1-1	Morgan	9104			4			8					2		11	10	5			1	6	7		9	3
46	May	2	Shrewsbury Town	1-1	Morgan	7237			4			8					2		11	10		5		1	6	7		9	3
						Apps	7	14	45	3	3	44	5	18	2	7	46	11	42	43	1	31	4	43	31	41	1	36	28
						Goals	1			1		6			1	1	3		18	31					1	7		6	

One own goal

F.A. Cup

Rd	Date		Opponent	Score	Scorers	Att	Adey AL	Ayres H	Boswell J	Durkin J	Evans A	Evans WE	Forrester GL	Lewin DR	Lewis T	Long TG	Marks CWA	McKee F	Millar W	Morgan E	Nekrews TJ	Niblett V	Phoenix WE	Rigg T	Riggs LJ	Scarth JW	Smith PJ(1)	Sowden PT	West E
R1	Nov	20	NEWPORT COUNTY	2-0	Morgan, Millar	10287			4	9		8		3			2		11	10		5		1	6	7			
R2	Dec	11	READING	1-1	Durkin	12298			4	9		8		3			2		11	10		5		1	6	7			
rep		13	Reading	3-5	Sowden, Morgan, Marks	5000			4	9				3			2	6	11	10		5		1		7		8	

		P	W	D	L	F	A	W	D	L	F	A	Pts
1	Bristol City	46	17	4	2	62	22	13	6	4	39	25	70
2	Leyton Orient	46	16	2	5	48	20	10	7	6	41	27	61
3	Southampton	46	16	6	1	49	19	8	5	10	26	32	59
4	GILLINGHAM	46	12	8	3	41	28	8	7	8	36	38	55
5	Millwall	46	14	6	3	44	25	6	5	12	28	43	51
6	Brighton & Hove Albion	46	14	4	5	47	27	6	6	11	29	36	50
7	Watford	46	11	9	3	45	26	7	5	11	26	36	50
8	Torquay United	46	12	6	5	51	39	6	6	11	31	43	48
9	Coventry City	46	15	5	3	50	26	3	6	14	17	33	47
10	Southend United	46	13	5	5	48	28	4	7	12	35	52	46
11	Brentford	46	11	6	6	44	36	5	8	10	38	46	46
11	Norwich City	46	13	5	5	40	23	5	5	13	20	37	46
13	Northampton Town	46	13	5	5	47	27	6	3	14	26	54	46
14	Aldershot	46	12	6	5	44	23	4	7	12	31	48	45
15	Queen's Park Rangers	46	13	7	3	46	25	2	7	14	23	50	44
16	Shrewsbury Town	46	14	5	4	49	24	2	5	16	21	54	42
17	Bournemouth	46	7	8	8	32	29	5	10	8	25	36	42
18	Reading	46	7	10	6	32	26	6	5	12	33	47	41
19	Newport County	46	8	8	7	32	29	3	8	12	28	44	38
20	Crystal Palace	46	9	11	3	32	24	2	5	16	20	56	38
21	Swindon Town	46	10	8	5	30	19	1	7	15	16	45	37
22	Exeter City	46	9	7	7	30	31	2	8	13	17	42	37
23	Walsall	46	9	6	8	49	36	1	8	14	26	50	34
24	Colchester United	46	7	6	10	33	40	2	7	14	20	51	31

1955/56

10th in Division Three (South)

#	Date	Opponent	Res	Scorers	Att	Baxter LR	Boswell J	Cousans WE	Crombie TR	Crossan EG	Hawkins DJ	Hughes A	Kingshott FJ	Maher J	Marks CWA	Millar W	Morgan E	Nekrews TJ	Niblett V	Parry W	Phoenix WE	Rigg T	Riggs LJ	Smith PJ(1)	Sowden PT	Sperring GB	West E
1	Aug 20	Brentford	4-1	Morgan,Maher,Bragg(og),Crossan	12247		4			7				8	2	11	10		5			1	6		9		3
2	24	LEYTON ORIENT	0-1		13526		4			7				8	2	11	10		5			1	6		9		3
3	27	WATFORD	3-0	Sowden, Phoenix, Morgan	11227		4			7					2	11	10		5		8	1	6		9		3
4	Sep 1	Leyton Orient	0-2		13341		4			7					2	11	10		5		8	1	6		9		3
5	3	Reading	2-1	Millar, Crossan	9276		4			7						11	10		5	2	8	1	6		9		3
6	7	COVENTRY CITY	1-1	Kirk (og)	10709		4			7						11	10		5	2	8	1	6		9		3
7	10	MILLWALL	4-3	Sowden, Boswell, Millar, Riggs	11815		4			7						11	10		5	2	8	1	6		9		3
8	12	Coventry City	0-2		18386		4			7						11	10		5	2	8	1	6		9		3
9	17	BRIGHTON & HOVE ALB	1-0	Millar	12228		4			7						11	10		5	2	8	1	6		9		3
10	21	EXETER CITY	2-1	Millar, Morgan	8266		4		5	7						11	10			2	8	1	6		9		3
11	24	Bournemouth	2-1	Millar 2	8350		4		5	7						11	10			2	8	1	6		9		3
12	29	Colchester United	1-1	Sowden	5208		4		5	7						11	10			2	8	1	6		9		3
13	Oct 1	NORWICH CITY	3-1	Poenix, Morgan, Sowden	13022					7					2	11	10		5	4	8	1	6		9		3
14	8	Shrewsbury Town	1-3	Sowden	9724		4			7					2	11	10		5		8	1	6		9		3
15	15	IPSWICH TOWN	0-0		12193		4			7						11	10		5	2	8	1	6		9		3
16	22	Walsall	1-2	Morgan	11469	8	4			7						11	10		5	2		1	6		9		3
17	29	TORQUAY UNITED	1-3	Morgan	10228	8	4			7						11	10		5	2		1	6		9		3
18	Nov 5	Newport County	2-3	Millar, Crossan	6745	8	4			7						11	10		5	2		1	6		9		3
19	12	SWINDON TOWN	4-0	Morgan 2, Crossan, Millar	9412	8	4		3	7			1			11	10		5	2			6		9		
20	26	NORTHAMPTON T	0-2		8429	8	4			7						11	10		5	2		1	6		9		3
21	Dec 3	Aldershot	2-2	Crossan, Morgan	5770	8	5			7						11	10			2		1	6	4		9	3
22	17	BRENTFORD	1-2	Morgan	5867	8	6			7		9				11	10		5	2		1		4			3
23	24	Watford	1-0	Baxter	5091	11	4			7					2		10		5	9		1	6		8		3
24	26	Southend United	2-2	Boswell, Parry	9643	11	4			7					2		10		5	9		1	6		8		3
25	27	SOUTHEND UNITED	2-3	Marks (p), Morgan	10563	11	4			7					2		10		5	9		1	6		8		3
26	31	READING	2-0	Parry, Morgan	7088		4			7					2	11	10		5	9		1	6		8		3
27	Jan 7	Queen's Park Rangers	2-2	Crossan, Petchey (og)	7345	11	4			7					2		10		5	9		1	6		8		3
28	14	Millwall	0-5		9458	11	4			7					2		10		5	9		1	6		8		3
29	21	Brighton & Hove Albion	0-5		17192		4		2	7						11	10		5	9		1	6		8		3
30	28	CRYSTAL PALACE	1-1	Hawkins	4281	10	5	11	2	7	9									4		1	6		8		3
31	Feb 11	Norwich City	1-5	Millar	7586		5		2	7	9					11	10			4		1	6		8		3
32	18	SHREWSBURY TOWN	3-1	Hawkins, Millar, Sowden	4071		5			7	9		1		2	11	10			4			6		8		3
33	25	Ipswich Town	1-1	Hawkins	12957		5			7	9		1		2	11	10			4			6		8		3
34	Mar 3	WALSALL	0-1		5190		5			7	9		1		2	11	10			4			6		8		3
35	10	Torquay United	1-1	Hawkins	5644	10	5	11		7	9		1		2					4			6		8		3
36	17	NEWPORT COUNTY	3-2	Crossan, Parry, Baxter	6203	11	5			7	9		1		2		10			4			6		8		3
37	24	Swindon Town	1-0	Marks	7035	11	5			7	9				2		10			4		1	6		8		3
38	30	SOUTHAMPTON	1-2	Hawkins	9764	11	5			7	9				2		10			4		1	6		8		3
39	31	QUEEN'S PARK RANGERS	0-2		5462	8	5			7					2	11	10			4		1	6		9		3
40	Apr 2	Southampton	1-1	Morgan	11233	11	4			7	9	10	1				8	5		2			6				3
41	7	Northampton Town	2-0	Baxter, Hawkins	6553	11	4			7	9	10	1				8	5		2			6				3
42	14	ALDERSHOT	2-0	Morgan, Hawkins	3369	11				7	9	10	1		2		8	5		4			6				3
43	21	Crystal Palace	3-1	Hughes, Crossan, Hawkins	10495	11	4			7	9	10	1				8	5		2			6				3
44	25	COLCHESTER UNITED	2-1	Crossan 2	5526	11	4			7			1		9	10	8	5		2			6				3
45	28	Exeter City	1-2	Parry	6887	11	4			7	10		1		9		8	5		2			6				3
46	May 2	BOURNEMOUTH	2-1	Morgan 2	5214	11	4			7			1		9		8	5		2			6		10		3
					Apps	25	44	2	7	46	14	5	13	2	24	30	44	7	25	41	13	33	45	2	38	1	45
					Goals	3	2			10	8	1		1	2	10	16			4	2		1		6		

Three own goals

F.A. Cup

#	Date	Opponent	Res	Scorers	Att	Baxter LR	Boswell J	Cousans WE	Crombie TR	Crossan EG	Hawkins DJ	Hughes A	Kingshott FJ	Maher J	Marks CWA	Millar W	Morgan E	Nekrews TJ	Niblett V	Parry W	Phoenix WE	Rigg T	Riggs LJ	Smith PJ(1)	Sowden PT	Sperring GB	West E
R1	Nov 19	SHREWSBURY TOWN	1-1	Millar	11347	8	4		3	7			1			10			5	2			6		9		
rep	24	Shrewsbury Town	1-4	Millar	8878	8	4			7			1			11	10		5	2			6		9		3

Played at 11 on Nov. 19: D Jones

		P	W	D	L	F	A	W	D	L	F	A	Pts
1	Leyton Orient	46	18	3	2	76	20	11	5	7	30	29	66
2	Brighton & Hove Albion	46	20	2	1	73	16	9	5	9	39	34	65
3	Ipswich Town	46	16	6	1	59	28	9	8	6	47	32	64
4	Southend United	46	16	4	3	58	25	5	7	11	30	55	53
5	Torquay United	46	11	10	2	48	21	9	2	12	38	42	52
6	Brentford	46	11	8	4	40	30	8	6	9	29	36	52
7	Norwich City	46	15	4	4	56	31	4	9	10	30	51	51
8	Coventry City	46	16	4	3	54	20	4	5	14	19	40	49
9	Bournemouth	46	13	6	4	39	14	6	4	13	24	37	48
10	GILLINGHAM	46	12	3	8	38	28	7	7	9	31	43	48
11	Northampton Town	46	14	3	6	44	27	6	4	13	23	44	47
12	Colchester United	46	14	4	5	56	37	4	7	12	20	44	47
13	Shrewsbury Town	46	12	9	2	47	21	5	3	15	22	45	46
14	Southampton	46	13	6	4	60	30	5	2	16	31	51	44
15	Aldershot	46	9	9	5	36	33	3	7	13	34	57	40
16	Exeter City	46	10	6	7	39	30	5	4	14	19	47	40
17	Reading	46	10	2	11	40	37	5	7	11	30	42	39
18	Queen's Park Rangers	46	10	7	6	44	32	4	4	15	20	54	39
19	Newport County	46	12	2	9	32	26	3	7	13	26	53	39
20	Walsall	46	13	5	5	43	28	2	3	18	25	56	38
21	Watford	46	8	5	10	31	39	5	6	12	21	46	37
22	Millwall	46	13	4	6	56	31	2	2	19	27	69	36
23	Crystal Palace	46	7	3	13	27	32	5	7	11	27	51	34
24	Swindon Town	46	4	10	9	18	22	4	4	15	16	56	30

1956/57

22nd in Division Three (South)

							Ackland ME	Baxter LR	Boswell J	Brasted GA	Chiswick PJH	Clark R	Crombie TR	Crossan EG	Grant WF	Gray IW	Greenhalgh JR	Kingshott FJ	Lucas P	Marks CWA	McDonald J	Morgan E	Nekrews TJ	Parry W	Pollock S	Riggs LJ	Simpson GL	Smith PJ(1)	Taylor J	Taylor RJ	Watts JA	West E
1	Aug	18	WATFORD	0-3		9934			4	9	1	11		7								8		2	10	6						3
2		22	Aldershot	0-0		6335		9	4		1	11		7								8	5	2	10	6						3
3		25	Shrewsbury Town	0-1		8357		9	4		1	11		7								8	5	2	10	6						3
4		29	ALDERSHOT	6-2	Brasted 3,Clarke,Reddie(og),Simpson	4363		7	4	9	1	11										8	5	2		6	10					3
5	Sep	1	WALSALL	2-1	Morgan 2	7860		7	4	9	1	11										8	5	2		6	10					3
6		5	SWINDON TOWN	3-0	J Taylor, Brasted, Baxter	6783		7	4	9		11	3					1		2		10	5				6		8			
7		8	Ipswich Town	1-1	J Taylor	11659		7	4			11	3				9	1		2		10	5				6		8			
8		12	Swindon Town	3-2	J Taylor 3	6082		7	4				3			11	9	1		2		10	5				6		8			
9		15	BOURNEMOUTH	1-0	J Taylor	9646		7	4				3			11	9	1		2		10	5				6		8			
10		18	Brentford	2-3	J Taylor 2	15603		9	4					7		11		1		2		10	5			6			8			3
11		22	Torquay United	3-3	Marks (p), Smith (og), J Taylor	7123		7	4							11	10	1	9	2			5			6			8			3
12		26	BRENTFORD	2-1	J Taylor 2	7903		7	4								9	1	11	2		10	5			6			8			3
13		29	MILLWALL	1-3	Baxter	11758		9	4							11	10	1	7	2			5			6			8			3
14	Oct	6	CRYSTAL PALACE	4-1	J Taylor 2, Barwell, Morgan	8567		7	4			11	3				6	1	9	2		10	5						8			
15		13	Exeter City	0-4		6524		7	5	9			3		6			1	11	2		10		4					8			
16		20	SOUTHAMPTON	0-0		10365		7	5									1	11	2		10		4	9	6			8			3
17		27	Coventry City	1-4	J Taylor	16993		7	5									1	11	2				4	9	6	10		8			3
18	Nov	3	NORWICH CITY	1-1	Lucas	8253		7	5									1	11	2				4	9	6	10		8			3
19		10	Colchester United	0-0		8891			5									1	11	2	7	10		4	9	6			8			3
20		24	Reading	0-4		6909			5				3	7				1	11	2		10		4	9	6			8			
21	Dec	1	PLYMOUTH ARGYLE	0-3		6879			4			11	3	7				1	9	2		10		5		6			8			
22		15	Watford	3-2	Crossan 2, Lucas	3684			5		1		3	7			9		11	2		10		4		6			8			
23		22	SHREWSBURY TOWN	1-1	Morgan	5051			5		1		3	7			9		11	2		10		4		6			8			
24		25	BRIGHTON & HOVE ALB	0-0		5237			5		1			7					11	3		9		4	10	6		2	8			
25		26	Brighton & Hove Albion	1-3	J Taylor	7362			5		1			7					11	3		9		4	10	6		2	8			
26		29	Walsall	2-2	Baxter, Crossan	12510		10	5		1			7			6		11			9		2		4			8			3
27	Jan	5	Northampton Town	1-4	J Taylor	6601		10	5		1			7			6		11			9		2		4			8			3
28		12	IPSWICH TOWN	1-1	Crossan	6191					1			7		11	4		10			8	5	2		6			9			3
29		19	Bournemouth	1-3	Morgan	10002					1			7		11	4		9			10	5	2		6			8			3
30		26	NORTHAMPTON T	1-2	Lucas	5724		11	5		1			7			4		10	2		9				6			8			3
31	Feb	2	TORQUAY UNITED	1-1	Clark	4710		8	4			10		7				1	11	2		9	5			6						3
32		9	Millwall	1-2	Lucas	15730		8	4			10		7				1	11	2			5			6					9	3
33		16	Crystal Palace	2-1	Clark, Watts	11410		8	4			10		7				1	11	3			5	2		6					9	
34		23	EXETER CITY	2-1	Crossan, Clark	3268		8	4			10		7				1	11	3			5	2		6					9	
35	Mar	2	Southampton	1-0	Lucas	16559		8	4			10		7				1	11	3			5	2		6					9	
36		9	QUEEN'S PARK RANGERS	0-1		7581		8	4			10		7				1	11	3			5	2		6					9	
37		16	Norwich City	3-1	Baxter, Crossan, Clark	13764		8				10		7				1	11	3			5	2		6				4	9	
38		23	COLCHESTER UNITED	1-2	Lucas	9983		8				10		7				1	11	3			5	2		6				4	9	
39		30	Newport County	0-4		7017		10										1	11	3			5	2		6		7	8	4	9	
40	Apr	6	READING	0-0		5402		10	4			6		7		11		1		2			5						8		9	3
41		13	Plymouth Argyle	0-2		10633		8	4			11		7				1		2			5			6			10		9	3
42		19	SOUTHEND UNITED	0-2		7089	9	8	4			10		7		11		1		2			5			6						3
43		20	COVENTRY CITY	1-2	Lucas	5076		10	4					7				1	11	2			5	9		6			8			3
44		22	Southend United	0-5		9318	9	8	4					7				1	11	3			5	2		6				10		
45		27	NEWPORT COUNTY	1-1	Greenhalgh	4237		8	4					7			10	1	11	3			5	2		6					9	
46		29	Queen's Park Rangers	0-5		6237		11	4					7			8	1	10	2			5			6					9	3
						Apps	2	36	41	5	14	20	10	30	1	9	16	32	33	37	1	27	31	30	10	39	8	3	29	4	12	25
						Goals		4	1	4		5		6			1		7	1		5					1		16		1	

R Carberry played at 5 in game 1

Two own goals

F.A. Cup

							Ackland ME	Baxter LR	Boswell J	Brasted GA	Chiswick PJH	Clark R	Crombie TR	Crossan EG	Grant WF	Gray IW	Greenhalgh JR	Kingshott FJ	Lucas P	Marks CWA	McDonald J	Morgan E	Nekrews TJ	Parry W	Pollock S	Riggs LJ	Simpson GL	Smith PJ(1)	Taylor J	Taylor RJ	Watts JA	West E
R1	Nov	17	Yiewsley	2-2	Riggs, Morgan	5400		9	5					7				1	11	2		10		4		6			8			3
rep		21	YIEWSLEY	2-0	Morgan, Pollock	7038		7	5				3					1	11	2		10		4	9	6			8			
R2	Dec	8	NEWPORT COUNTY	1-2	Crossan	8700			5				3	7			9	1	11	2		10		4		6			8			

		P	W	D	L	F	A	W	D	L	F	A	Pts
1	Ipswich Town	46	18	3	2	72	20	7	6	10	29	34	59
2	Torquay United	46	19	4	0	71	18	5	7	11	18	46	59
3	Colchester United	46	15	8	0	49	19	7	6	10	35	37	58
4	Southampton	46	15	4	4	48	20	7	6	10	28	32	54
5	Bournemouth	46	15	7	1	57	20	4	7	12	31	42	52
6	Brighton & Hove Albion	46	15	6	2	59	26	4	8	11	27	39	52
7	Southend United	46	14	3	6	42	20	4	9	10	31	45	48
8	Brentford	46	12	9	2	55	29	4	7	12	23	47	48
9	Shrewsbury Town	46	11	9	3	45	24	4	9	10	27	55	48
10	Queen's Park Rangers	46	12	7	4	42	21	6	4	13	19	39	47
11	Watford	46	11	6	6	44	32	7	4	12	28	43	46
12	Newport County	46	15	6	2	51	18	1	7	15	14	44	45
13	Reading	46	13	4	6	44	30	5	5	13	36	51	45
14	Northampton Town	46	15	5	3	49	22	3	4	16	17	51	45
15	Walsall	46	11	7	5	49	25	5	5	13	31	49	44
16	Coventry City	46	12	5	6	52	36	4	7	12	22	48	44
17	Millwall	46	13	7	3	46	29	3	5	15	18	55	44
18	Plymouth Argyle	46	10	8	5	38	31	6	3	14	30	42	43
19	Aldershot	46	11	5	7	43	35	4	7	12	36	57	42
20	Crystal Palace	46	7	10	6	31	28	4	8	11	31	47	40
21	Exeter City	46	8	8	7	37	29	4	5	14	24	50	37
22	GILLINGHAM	46	7	8	8	29	29	5	5	13	25	56	37
23	Swindon Town	46	12	3	8	43	33	3	3	17	23	63	36
24	Norwich City	46	7	5	11	33	37	1	10	12	28	57	31

1957/58

22nd in Division Three (South)

No	Date	Opponent	Score	Scorers	Att	Baxter LR	Boswell J	Brodie CTG	Clark R	Darvell RD	Dibden WK	Evans JL	Fletcher JA	Hannaway J	Hazel C	Hutton J	Laing D	Lucas P	McCorkindale J	Morgan W	Nekrews TJ	Parry W	Payne B	Proverbs RJ	Riggs LJ	Rossiter DP	Saunders R	Simpson JL	Taylor DG	Taylor J	Taylor RI
1	Aug 24	BRIGHTON & HOVE ALB	0-1		11249	7			11	5			8	3			6					2			4	10	9	1			
2	28	Torquay United	2-3	Fletcher 2	9443	7			11	5			8	3		10	6					2			4		9	1			
3	31	Southampton	1-5	Saunders	18057	7				5			8	3		10	6					2	11		4		9	1			
4	Sep 4	TORQUAY UNITED	1-0	Saunders	7287		5						8	3		10	6	11				2	7				9	1			4
5	7	NEWPORT COUNTY	0-1		8705		5						8	3		10	6	11				2	7				9	1			4
6	11	Crystal Palace	0-3		7343		5							3		8	6	11		10		2	7				9	1			4
7	14	Port Vale	0-2		14717		5	1	11			4		3		10	6			8		2	7				9				
8	18	CRYSTAL PALACE	3-0	Hutton, Noakes (og), Payne	6324		5	1	11			4		3		10	6			8		2	7				9				
9	21	PLYMOUTH ARGYLE	1-0	Hutton	9560		5	1	11			4		3		10	6			8		2	7				9				
10	25	Exeter City	3-1	Morgan, Payne, Clarke	5968		5	1	11			4		3		10	6			8		2	7				9				
11	28	Aldershot	0-2		5349		5		10			4		3			6	11		8		2	7				9	1			
12	Oct 2	EXETER CITY	1-1	Hutton	5457		5	1	11			4		3		10	6			8		2	7				9				
13	5	SWINDON TOWN	2-1	Payne, Saundes	8544		5	1				4		3		10	6	11		8		2	7				9				
14	12	Brentford	0-1		12488		5	1						3		10	6		11	8		2	7		4		9				
15	19	COLCHESTER UNITED	2-3	Saunders 2	8535		5	1						3		10	6		11	8		2	7		4		9				
16	26	Norwich City	0-2		17999		5	1						3		10	6		11	8		2	7		4		9				
17	Nov 9	Walsall	1-1	Fletcher	6452		5	1					8	3		10		11		4		2	7		6		9				
18	23	Shrewsbury Town	1-2	Fletcher	6125		5	1	11				8	3			6			10		2	7		4		9				
19	30	READING	2-1	Fletcher 2	7696		5	1					8	3		10	6			11		2	7		4		9				
20	Dec 14	WATFORD	1-1	Saunders	7996		5	1					8	3		10	6			11		2	7		4		9				
21	21	Brighton & Hove Albion	2-5	Saunders 2	10459		5	1					8	3		10	6	11		7		2			4		9				
22	25	QUEEN'S PARK RANGERS	1-1	Morgan	7233		5	1					8	3		10	6	11		7		2			4		9				
23	26	Queen's Park Rangers	1-1	Saunders	8658		5	1					8	3			6		10	11		2	7				9				4
24	28	SOUTHAMPTON	2-1	Saunders, Morgan	10884		5	1			10		8	3			6		11	7		2					9				4
25	Jan 11	Newport County	0-5		6206		5	1					8	3			6		11	10		2	7		4		9				
26	18	PORT VALE	0-2		7407		5						8	3		10	6			11		2	7		4		9	1			
27	Feb 1	Plymouth Argyle	1-2	Saunders	17566		5						9	3			6		11			2	7		4		10	1	8		
28	8	ALDERSHOT	1-1	Fletcher	5893		5						9	3			6		11			2	7		4		10	1	8		
29	15	Swindon Town	1-1	Hutton	13141		5						10	3		8				11		2			6		9	1	7		4
30	22	BRENTFORD	3-2	Saunders 3	6626		5						10	3		8				11		2			6		9	1	7		4
31	Mar 1	Colchester United	2-3	Saunders, R Taylor	8150		5						10	3		8				11		2			6		9	1	7		4
32	8	NORWICH CITY	1-0	Saunders	6591		5							3		8				11		2	7		6		9	1	10		4
33	15	Bournemouth	1-2	Saunders	11451		5							3	7	8				11		2			6		9	1	10		4
34	17	Millwall	1-3	D Taylor	6449		5							3		8		11		7		2			6		9	1	10		4
35	22	SHREWSBURY TOWN	1-3	Laing	5437		5							3	7	8	10			11		2			6		9	1			4
36	27	Northampton Town	1-3	Riggs	2412								9	3			10	11			5	2	7	4	6			1	8		
37	29	Watford	0-3		6375								8	3			10	11			5	2	7	4	6		9	1			
38	Apr 4	SOUTHEND UNITED	2-0	R Taylor, Fletcher	7450		5						10	3		8	4			11		2			6		9	1			7
39	5	WALSALL	3-0	Gutteridge(og), Saunders, R Taylor	5081		5							3		8	4			11		2			6		9	1	10		7
40	7	Southend United	0-2		12244		5							3		8	4			11		2			6		9	1	10		7
41	12	Reading	0-4		8441		5							3		7				11		2			6		9	1	8	10	4
42	16	BOURNEMOUTH	1-1	R Taylor	3469		5							3		10	4			11		2			6		9	1	8		7
43	19	NORTHAMPTON T	1-2	R Taylor	5721		5		11					3		8	4			10		2			6		9	1			7
44	23	MILLWALL	1-0	D Taylor	4406		5		11					3		10	4					2	7				9	1	8		6
45	26	Coventry City	1-1	Hutton	6939		5		11					3		8	6					2			4		9	1	10		7
46	30	COVENTRY CITY	3-2	Hutton, D Taylor (p), Laing	4146				11					3		10	6					2			4		9	1	8		7

BJ Judges played at 5 in game 46

	Baxter LR	Boswell J	Brodie CTG	Clark R	Darvell RD	Dibden WK	Evans JL	Fletcher JA	Hannaway J	Hazel C	Hutton J	Laing D	Lucas P	McCorkindale J	Morgan W	Nekrews TJ	Parry W	Payne B	Proverbs RJ	Riggs LJ	Rossiter DP	Saunders R	Simpson JL	Taylor DG	Taylor J	Taylor RI
Apps	3	40	18	13	3	1	7	23	46	2	36	38	11	8	34	2	46	27	2	33	1	45	28	16	1	21
Goals				1				8			6	2			3			3		1		18		3		5

Two own goals

F.A. Cup

Rd	Date	Opponent	Score	Scorers	Att	Baxter LR	Boswell J	Brodie CTG	Clark R	Darvell RD	Dibden WK	Evans JL	Fletcher JA	Hannaway J	Hazel C	Hutton J	Laing D	Lucas P	McCorkindale J	Morgan W	Nekrews TJ	Parry W	Payne B	Proverbs RJ	Riggs LJ	Rossiter DP	Saunders R	Simpson JL	Taylor DG	Taylor J	Taylor RI
R1	Nov 16	GORLESON	10-1	* see below	8123		5	1	11				8	3			6			10		2	7		4		9				
R2	Dec 7	Millwall	1-1	Fletcher	13415		5	1					8	3		10	6			11		2	7		4		9				
rep	11	MILLWALL	6-1	Payne 2, Fletcher 2, Saunders, Hutton	8320		5	1					8	3		10	6			11		2	7		4		9				
R3	Jan 4	Nottingham Forest	0-2		24546		5	1			10		8	3			6			11		2	7		4		9				

Scorers in R1: Saunders 5, Fletcher 2, Clark 2, Morgan

		P	W	D	L	F	A	W	D	L	F	A	Pts
1	Brighton & Hove Albion	46	13	6	4	52	30	11	6	6	36	34	60
2	Brentford	46	15	5	3	52	24	9	5	9	30	32	58
3	Plymouth Argyle	46	17	4	2	43	17	8	4	11	24	31	58
4	Swindon Town	46	14	7	2	47	16	7	8	8	32	34	57
5	Reading	46	14	5	4	52	23	7	8	8	27	28	55
6	Southampton	46	16	3	4	78	31	6	7	10	34	41	54
7	Southend United	46	14	5	4	56	26	7	7	9	34	32	54
8	Norwich City	46	11	9	3	41	28	8	6	9	34	42	53
9	Bournemouth	46	16	5	2	54	24	5	4	14	27	50	51
10	Queen's Park Rangers	46	15	6	2	40	14	3	8	12	24	51	50
11	Newport County	46	12	6	5	40	24	5	8	10	33	43	48
12	Colchester United	46	13	5	5	45	27	4	8	11	32	52	47
13	Northampton Town	46	13	1	9	60	33	6	5	12	27	46	44
14	Crystal Palace	46	12	5	6	46	30	3	8	12	24	42	43
15	Port Vale	46	12	6	5	49	24	4	4	15	18	34	42
16	Watford	46	9	8	6	34	27	4	8	11	25	50	42
17	Shrewsbury Town	46	10	6	7	29	25	5	4	14	20	46	40
18	Aldershot	46	7	9	7	31	34	5	7	11	28	55	40
19	Coventry City	46	10	9	4	41	24	3	4	16	20	57	39
20	Walsall	46	10	7	6	37	24	4	2	17	24	51	37
21	Torquay United	46	9	7	7	33	34	2	6	15	16	40	35
22	GILLINGHAM	46	12	5	6	33	24	1	4	18	19	57	35
23	Millwall	46	6	6	11	37	36	5	3	15	26	55	31
24	Exeter City	46	10	4	9	37	35	1	5	17	20	64	31

1958/59

11th in Division Four

No.	Date	Opponent	Score	Scorers	Att.	Bacon RAS	Bentley A	Edgar J	Hannaway J	Hughes HJ	Hunt DP	Judges BJ	Laing D	Moore SC	Parry W	Patrick WCG	Payne B	Payton CC	Proverbs RJ	Pulley GA	Saunders R	Simpson JL	Smith PJ	Taylor DG	Taylor RI	Terry PA	Tudor TE
1	Aug 23	MILLWALL	1-2	Laing	9147	7		10	3	5			6		2	8			4	11	9	1					
2	26	Carlisle United	2-1	Saunders 2	10759	7		10	3	5			6		2	8			4	11	9	1					
3	30	Walsall	2-1	Patrick, Pulley	10131	7		10	3	5			6		2	8			4	11	9	1					
4	Sep 1	CARLISLE UNITED	1-1	Hughes	8106	7		10	3	5			6		2	8			4	11	9	1					
5	6	DARLINGTON	0-0		7997	7		8	3	5			6		2	9				11		1		10	4		
6	10	BARROW	4-2	Edgar 4 (1p)	6656	7		8	3	5			6		2	9				11		1		10	4		
7	13	Shrewsbury Town	2-3	Patrick, Edgar	8782			8	3	5			6	7	2	9				11		1		10	4		
8	15	Barrow	2-2	Edgar, Patrick	5249			8	3			5	6	7	2	9			4	11		1		10			
9	20	COVENTRY CITY	2-0	Patrick, Edgar	8859	7		8	3	5			6		2	9			4	11		1		10			
10	22	Oldham Athletic	1-3	Edgar	2732	7		8	3	5			6		2	9			4	11		1					10
11	27	Exeter City	0-3		8524	7		8	3			5	6	10	2	9			4	11		1					
12	Oct 1	OLDHAM ATHLETIC	3-2	Edgar 2 (1p), Pulley	4705	7		8	2		3		6	10	5	9			4	11		1					
13	4	CREWE ALEXANDRA	3-0	Patrick, Bacon, Edgar	7481	7		8	2		3		6	10	5	9			4	11		1					
14	8	GATESHEAD	3-0	Edgar 2, Patrick	4335	7		8	2		3		6	10	5	9			4	11		1					
15	11	Workington	1-0	Terry	5867	7		8	3	5			6		2	10			4	11		1				9	
16	18	YORK CITY	2-2	Patrick, Pulley	12023	7		8	3	5			6		2	10			4	11		1				9	
17	25	Bradford Park Avenue	0-2		7459	7		8	3	5			6		2	10			4	11		1				9	
18	Nov 1	PORT VALE	0-2		9940	7		8	3	5			6	10	2				4	11		1				9	
19	8	Crystal Palace	1-4	Terry	13640	7		8	3	5			6		2		10		4	11		1				9	
20	22	Watford	2-2	Edgar, Terry	10369	7		8	3				6		5	9			2	11		1			4	10	
21	29	HARTLEPOOLS UNITED	4-1	Edgar 3, Patrick	6121	7		8	3				6		5	9			2	11		1			4	10	
22	Dec 20	Millwall	0-2		11176	7		8	3				6		5	9			2	11		1			4	10	
23	26	NORTHAMPTON T	4-1	Terry 2, Edgar, Bacon	6947	7		8	4		3		6		5	10			2	11		1				9	
24	27	Northampton Town	2-4	Smith, Claypole (og)	9538	7		8	2		3		6		5	10				11		1	4			9	
25	Jan 3	WALSALL	4-2	Pulley 2, Terry, Patrick	6007	7		8	2		3		6		5	10				11		1	4			9	
26	17	CHESTER	3-3	Patrick, Terry, Bacon	5331	7		8	2		3		6		5	10				11		1	4			9	
27	24	Southport	1-2	Terry	3763	7			6		3		8		5	10			2	11		1	4			9	
28	31	SHREWSBURY TOWN	2-1	Terry, Edgar	5819	7		8	4		3		6		5	10	11		2			1				9	
29	Feb 7	Coventry City	1-1	Moore	13452	7		8			3		4	10	5	6	11		2			1				9	
30	14	EXETER CITY	0-2		6474	7		8			3		4	10	5	6	11		2			1				9	
31	21	Crewe Alexandra	2-0	Patrick, Edgar (p)	5255	7		9	4	5	3		6	8	2	10				11		1					
32	28	WORKINGTON	5-1	Terry 2, Moore, Edgar, Laing	6787	7		8	4	5			6	10	2	3				11		1				9	
33	Mar 7	York City	1-3	Bacon	5246	7		8	4	5			6	10	2	3				11		1				9	
34	14	BRADFORD PARK AVE.	1-1	Laing	6371	7		8	4	5	3		6		2	10				11		1				9	
35	21	Port Vale	1-3	Payton	11119	7		8	4	5	3		6			2		10		11		1				9	
36	27	ALDERSHOT	3-0	Edgar, Bacon, Terry	7470	7		8	4	5	3		6	11	2			10				1				9	
37	28	CRYSTAL PALACE	1-1	Payton	8714	7		8	4	5	3		6	11				10	2			1				9	
38	30	Aldershot	2-4	Payton, Terry	3033	7		8	4	5	3		6	11				10	2			1				9	
39	Apr 4	Chester	2-1	Patrick, Terry	5513	7		8	6	5	3		11			4		10	2			1				9	
40	8	TORQUAY UNITED	3-2	Terry 2, Patrick	4031	7		8	6	5	3		11			4		10	2			1				9	
41	11	WATFORD	2-1	Terry 2	6205	7	1	8	6	5	3		11			4		10	2							9	
42	16	Darlington	2-1	Terry, Payton	1944	7	1	8	6	5	3		11			4		10	2							9	
43	18	Hartlepools United	1-3	Terry	3169	7	1	8	6	5	3		11			4		10	2							9	
44	20	Gateshead	0-2		3094	7	1	8	6	5	3		11			4		10	2							9	
45	25	SOUTHPORT	2-0	Edgar, Terry	3817	7	1	8	6	5	3					4	11	10	2							9	
46	29	Torquay United	1-3	Bacon	4227	7	1	8	6	5	3					4	11	10	2							9	
										30		2															
					Apps	44	6	45	44	30	25	2	44	15	35	41	6	12	34	32	4	40	4	5	6	31	1
					Goals	6		23		1			3	2		13		4		5	2		1			21	

One own goal

F.A. Cup

Rd	Date	Opponent	Score	Scorers	Att.	Bacon RAS	Bentley A	Edgar J	Hannaway J	Hughes HJ	Hunt DP	Judges BJ	Laing D	Moore SC	Parry W	Patrick WCG	Payne B	Payton CC	Proverbs RJ	Pulley GA	Saunders R	Simpson JL	Smith PJ	Taylor DG	Taylor RI	Terry PA	Tudor TE
R1	Nov 15	Plymouth Argyle	2-2	Patrick, Edgar	21759	7		8	4	5	3		6		2	9				11		1				10	
rep	19	PLYMOUTH ARGYLE	1-4	Terry	10150	7		8	4	5	3		6		2	9				11		1				10	

		P	W	D	L	F	A	W	D	L	F	A	Pts
1	Port Vale	46	14	6	3	62	30	12	6	5	48	28	64
2	Coventry City	46	18	4	1	50	11	6	8	9	34	36	60
3	York City	46	12	10	1	37	17	9	8	6	36	35	60
4	Shrewsbury Town	46	15	5	3	59	24	9	5	9	42	39	58
5	Exeter City	46	16	4	3	55	24	7	7	9	32	37	57
6	Walsall	46	13	5	5	56	25	8	5	10	39	39	52
7	Crystal Palace	46	12	8	3	54	27	8	4	11	36	44	52
8	Northampton Town	46	14	5	4	48	25	7	4	12	37	53	51
9	Millwall	46	13	6	4	46	23	7	4	12	30	46	50
10	Carlisle United	46	11	6	6	37	30	8	6	9	25	35	50
11	GILLINGHAM	46	14	6	3	53	27	6	3	14	29	50	49
12	Torquay United	46	11	5	7	45	32	5	7	11	33	45	44
13	Chester	46	10	5	8	39	33	6	7	10	33	51	44
14	Bradford Park Avenue	46	15	1	7	51	29	3	6	14	24	48	43
15	Watford	46	10	6	7	46	36	6	4	13	35	43	42
16	Darlington	46	7	8	8	37	36	6	8	9	29	32	42
17	Workington	46	9	10	4	40	32	3	7	13	23	46	41
18	Crewe Alexandra	46	11	5	7	52	32	4	5	14	18	50	40
19	Hartlepools United	46	11	4	8	50	41	4	6	13	24	47	40
20	Gateshead	46	11	3	9	33	30	5	5	13	23	55	40
21	Oldham Athletic	46	15	0	8	39	29	1	4	18	20	55	36
22	Aldershot	46	8	4	11	37	45	6	3	14	26	52	35
23	Barrow	46	6	6	11	34	45	3	4	16	17	59	28
24	Southport	46	7	8	8	26	25	0	4	19	15	61	26

1959/60

7th in Division Four

							Albury WF	Bacon RAS	Brown G	Hannaway J	Hughes HJ	Hunt DP	Moore SC	Parry W	Patrick WCG	Payne B	Payton CC	Proverbs RJ	Pulley GA	Shepherd JHE	Simpson C	Simpson JL	Smith PJ	Stinson HMJ	Terry PA
1	Aug	22	GATESHEAD	5-4	Terry 3, Patrick, Albury	7352	6	7	11		5	3			10		8	2				1	4		9
2		27	Rochdale	0-1		6382	6	7	11		5	3			10		8	2				1	4		9
3		29	Darlington	1-2	Payton	7800	6	7	11		5	3			10		8	2				1	4		9
4	Sep	3	ROCHDALE	2-0	Moore, Bacon	5649	6	7	11		5	3	8	2			10					1	4		9
5		5	ALDERSHOT	3-1	Moore, Terry, Albury (p)	7036	6	7	11		5	3	8	2			10					1	4		9
6		10	Northampton Town	1-2	Terry	9622	8		11	6	5	3		2		7	10					1	4		9
7		12	Barrow	1-0	Albury (p)	6871	8		11		5		9	2	6	7	10	3				1	4		
8		16	NORTHAMPTON T	2-1	Albury, Terry	5970	8		11		5	3		2		7	10	6				1	4		9
9		19	CHESTER	3-1	Albury 2 (1p), Brown	7551	8	7	11		5	3	9	2			10	6				1	4		
10		24	Workington	1-1	Moore	4720	8	7	11		5	3	9	2			10	6				1	4		
11		26	SOUTHPORT	4-1	Albury 2 (1p), Moore 2	7265	8	7	11		5	3	9	2			10	6				1	4		
12		30	WORKINGTON	2-2	Terry 2	5821		7	11	6	5	3	10		8			2				1	4		9
13	Oct	3	Millwall	3-3	Brown 2, P Brady (og)	20652	8	7	11	6	5	3	10					2				1	4		9
14		7	TORQUAY UNITED	1-0	Moore	5806	8	7	11	6	5	3	10					2				1	4		9
15		10	Bradford Park Avenue	0-3		6104	8	7	11	6	5	3	10					2				1	4		9
16		17	STOCKPORT COUNTY	0-2		7850	8	7	11	6	5	3	9					2				1	4	10	
17		24	Exeter City	0-2		7119	6	7		3	5	8	10	2	9				11			1	4		
18		31	WATFORD	2-0	Brown, Terry	7107		7	10	6	5	3	8	2					11			1	4		9
19	Nov	7	Oldham Athletic	1-3	Bacon	3011		7	10	6	5	3	8	2					11			1	4		9
20		21	Notts County	1-3	Moore	13856	8	7		6	5		10	3				2	11			1	4		9
21		28	WALSALL	2-0	Terry, Brown	5853	8	7	11	6	5			3			10	2				1	4		9
22	Dec	12	CREWE ALEXANDRA	1-1	Hannaway	4589	8	7	11	10	5	3		2				4				1	6		9
23		19	Gateshead	2-2	Brown, Terry	1884	8	7	11	10	5	3		2				4				1	6		9
24		28	Crystal Palace	3-3	Hannaway 2, Poverbs	18248	8	7	11	10	5	3		2				4				1	6		9
25	Jan	2	DARLINGTON	2-0	Terry 2	5747	8	7	11	10	5	3		2				4				1	6		9
26		16	Aldershot	1-3	Terry	3401	8	7	11	10	5	3		2				4				1	6		9
27		23	BARROW	1-0	Albury	3671	8	7	11	10	5	3	9	2				4				1	6		
28		30	Hartlepools United	1-3	Albury	2659	8	7	11	10	5	3	9	2				4				1	6		
29	Feb	6	Chester	2-4	Albury, Hannaway	5022	8	7	11	10	5	3		2				4				1	6		9
30		13	Southport	1-1	Shepherd	2551	4	7	11	6	5	3		2					10	8		1			9
31		20	MILLWALL	3-1	Shepherd 2, Brown	7606	4	7	11	6	5	3						2	10	8		1			9
32		27	BRADFORD PARK AVE.	2-0	Terry, Shepherd	7281	4	7	11	6	5	3						2	10	8		1			9
33	Mar	5	Stockport County	1-1	Brown	6077	4	7	11	6	5	3						2	10	8		1			9
34		12	EXETER CITY	2-1	Shepherd, Foley (og)	7419	4	7	11	6	5	3						2	10	8		1			9
35		19	Watford	1-3	Albury (p)	12550	4	7	11	6	3			5				2	10	8		1			9
36		26	OLDHAM ATHLETIC	2-2	Terry, Pulley	5216	4	7		6	5	3	10					2	11	8		1			9
37	Apr	2	Carlisle United	1-0	Brown	2538	4	7	10	6	5	3		9				2	11	8		1			
38		9	NOTTS COUNTY	0-1		7655	4	7	10	6	5	3		9				2	11	8		1			
39		15	Doncaster Rovers	0-3		7048	4	7	10	6	5	3						2	11	8		1			9
40		16	Walsall	3-2	Shepherd 2, Terry	10527		7	11	6	5	3						2	10	8		1	4		9
41		18	DONCASTER ROVERS	2-1	Brown, Pulley (p)	6966		7	11	6	5	3						2	10	8		1	4		9
42		23	HARTLEPOOLS UNITED	3-1	Brown, Terry, Smith (p)	5373		7	11	6	5	3						2	8		10	1	4		9
43		27	Torquay United	0-2		8749	8	7	11	6	5	3						2	10			1	4		9
44		30	Crewe Alexandra	2-1	Terry, Shepherd	6517		7	11	6	5	3						2	10	8		1	4		9
45	May	4	CRYSTAL PALACE	0-0		5077		7	11	6	5	3						2	10	8		1	4		9
46		6	CARLISLE UNITED	3-1	Shepherd, Pulley, Brown	3469	4	7	11	6	5	3						2	10	8		1			9
						Apps	38	43	43	36	46	42	18	25	6	3	12	39	21	15	1	46	35	1	36
						Goals	12	2	12	4			7		1		1	1	3	9			1		19

Two own goals

F.A. Cup

							Albury WF	Bacon RAS	Brown G	Hannaway J	Hughes HJ	Hunt DP	Moore SC	Parry W	Patrick WCG	Payne B	Payton CC	Proverbs RJ	Pulley GA	Shepherd JHE	Simpson C	Simpson JL	Smith PJ	Stinson HMJ	Terry PA
R1	Nov	14	Bedford Town	4-0	Terry 2, Albury, Pulley	8000	8	7			5	3		2	10			6	11			1	4		9
R2	Dec	5	TORQUAY UNITED	2-2	Albury 2 (1p)	10142	8	7	11	6	5			3			10	2				1	4		9
rep		9	Torquay United	2-1	Terry, Hannaway	5981	8	7	11	10	5	3		2				4				1	6		9
R3	Jan	9	SWANSEA TOWN	1-4	Griffiths (og)	15301	8	7	11	10	5	3		2				4				1	6		9

		P	W	D	L	F	A	W	D	L	F	A	Pts
1	Walsall	46	14	5	4	57	33	14	4	5	45	27	65
2	Notts County	46	19	1	3	66	27	7	7	9	41	42	60
3	Torquay United	46	17	3	3	56	27	9	5	9	28	31	60
4	Watford	46	17	2	4	62	28	7	7	9	30	39	57
5	Millwall	46	12	8	3	54	28	6	9	8	30	33	53
6	Northampton Town	46	13	6	4	50	22	9	3	11	35	41	53
7	GILLINGHAM	46	17	4	2	47	21	4	6	13	27	48	52
8	Crystal Palace	46	12	6	5	61	27	7	6	10	23	37	50
9	Exeter City	46	13	7	3	50	30	6	4	13	30	40	49
10	Stockport County	46	15	6	2	35	10	4	5	14	23	44	49
11	Bradford Park Avenue	46	12	10	1	48	25	5	5	13	22	43	49
12	Rochdale	46	15	4	4	46	19	3	6	14	19	41	46
13	Aldershot	46	14	5	4	50	22	4	4	15	27	52	45
14	Crewe Alexandra	46	14	3	6	51	31	4	6	13	28	57	45
15	Darlington	46	11	6	6	40	30	6	3	14	23	43	43
16	Workington	46	10	8	5	41	20	4	6	13	27	40	42
17	Doncaster Rovers	46	13	3	7	40	23	3	7	13	29	53	42
18	Barrow	46	11	8	4	52	29	4	3	16	25	58	41
19	Carlisle United	46	9	6	8	28	28	6	5	12	23	38	41
20	Chester	46	10	8	5	37	26	4	4	15	22	51	40
21	Southport	46	9	7	7	30	32	1	7	15	18	60	34
22	Gateshead	46	12	3	8	37	27	0	6	17	21	59	33
23	Oldham Athletic	46	5	7	11	20	30	3	5	15	21	53	28
24	Hartlepools United	46	9	2	12	40	41	1	5	17	19	68	27

1960/61

15th in Division Four

	Date	Opponent	Score	Scorers	Att.	Bacon RAS	Brown G	Challis RLA	Cockburn WR	Farrall A	Friday TJ	Griffiths EG	Hughes HJ	Hunt DP	McIntyre PF	McManus EJ	Morris FW	Parry W	Proverbs RJ	Pulley GA	Shepherd JHE	Simpson C	Simpson JL	Terry PA	Wilson RSW
1	Aug 20	Chester	2-2	Shepherd, Hunt	7097	7			6	10			5	3		9			2	11	8		1		4
2	24	CREWE ALEXANDRA	0-0		8452				6	10			5	3		7			2	11	8		1	9	4
3	27	WORKINGTON	4-2	Terry 2, Farrall, Shepherd	6747	7	11			10			4	3				5	2		8		1	9	6
4	31	Crewe Alexandra	1-2	Bacon	8972	7	11		6	10			5	3					2		8		1	9	4
5	Sep 3	Oldham Athletic	1-1	Farrall	6412	7	11		6	10			5	3					2		8		1	9	4
6	7	ACCRINGTON STANLEY	2-1	Farrall, Bacon	6209	7	11		6	10			5	3					2		8		1	9	4
7	10	ALDERSHOT	5-2	Terry 3, Shepherd, Bacon	7122	7	11		6	10			5	3					2		8		1	9	4
8	12	Accrington Stanley	0-3		4941	7	11		6	10			5	3					2		8		1	9	4
9	17	Northampton Town	1-3	Terry	9575	7	11		6	10			5	3					2		8		1	9	4
10	21	YORK CITY	3-2	Shepherd, Terry, Brown	5081	7	11		6	10			5	3					2		8		1	9	4
11	24	BRADFORD PARK AVE.	3-4	Terry 2, Shepherd	6998	7	11		6	10			5	3					2		8		1	9	4
12	26	York City	0-0		8577	7		3	6				5	4		8			2	11	10		1	9	
13	Oct 1	PETERBOROUGH UTD.	4-4	Raynor (og), Pulley, Farrall, Terry	11840	7		3	4	8			5	6					2	11	10		1	9	
14	8	Darlington	2-2	Shepherd 2	6708	7				8			5	3				2	6	11	10		1	9	4
15	15	CRYSTAL PALACE	1-2	Shepherd	10999	7				10			5	3				2	6	11	8		1	9	4
16	22	Doncaster Rovers	3-2	Terry 3	5029	7	11			10			5	3				2	6		9		1	8	4
17	29	HARTLEPOOLS UNITED	5-1	Pulley 2, Bacon, Shepherd, Terry	3816	7				10			5	3				2	6	11	9		1	8	4
18	Nov 12	CARLISLE UNITED	1-1	Terry	5604	7				10			5	3				2	6	11	9		1	8	4
19	19	Rochdale	0-2		3044	7				10			5	3				2	6	11	9		1	8	4
20	Dec 10	EXETER CITY	4-2	Pulley 2, Bacon 2	4795	7	11						5	3				2	6	11	8		1	8	4
21	17	CHESTER	3-0	Pulley 2, Shepherd	4902	7	11						5	3				2	6	10	8		1	9	4
22	26	Millwall	2-1	Pulley, Shepherd	11219	7	11			9			5	3				2	6	10	8		1	9	4
23	27	MILLWALL	1-2	Hughes (p)	12048	7	11			9			5	3				2	6	10	8		1		4
24	31	Workington	0-2		2975	7	11						5	3				2	6	10	8	9	1		4
25	Jan 2	Carlisle United	3-1	Shepherd, Terry, Pulley	3364	7	11		6				5					2	3	10	8		1	9	4
26	14	OLDHAM ATHLETIC	2-3	Terry 2	5524					11			5	3			7	2	6	10	8		1	9	4
27	21	Aldershot	1-0	Morris	6310	10			6	7			5	3			8	2		11			1	9	4
28	Feb 11	Bradford Park Avenue	0-0		7483	7	11		6	4			5	3			8	2		10			1	9	
29	18	Peterborough United	0-2		12652	8	11		6	4			5	3			7	2		10			1	9	
30	25	DARLINGTON	0-1		4537	8	11		6	4			5	3			7	2		10			1	9	
31	Mar 4	Crystal Palace	0-2		22559	7			6	4			5	3			10	2		11	9	8	1		
32	6	Stockport County	0-2		4759				6	4			5	3			7	2		11	8	10	1	9	
33	8	Wrexham	0-0		4913	7			6	8			5	3			9	2	4	11			1	10	
34	11	DONCASTER ROVERS	2-0	Terry, Hughes (p)	4871	7			6	8			5	3			11	2	4		10		1	9	
35	18	Hartlepools United	0-1		2332	7			6	4	1		5	3			10		2	11	8			9	
36	25	WREXHAM	0-3		3934	7			6	8	1		5	3				2	4	11	9			10	
37	31	Southport	2-1	Pulley, Shepherd	5695				6	8		7	5	3					2	11	9		1	10	4
38	Apr 3	SOUTHPORT	2-0	Farrall, Shepherd	4128	7			6	8			5	3					2	11	9		1	10	4
39	8	ROCHDALE	0-0		4807	7			6	8			5	3					2	11	9		1	10	4
40	12	NORTHAMPTON T	0-1		4831	7	11			6			5	3					2	10		8	1	9	4
41	15	Mansfield Town	0-1		4070	7	11			6			5	3					2		10	8	1	9	4
42	17	Barrow	1-0	Terry	3232	7	11	2		6			5	3							10	8	1	9	4
43	22	STOCKPORT COUNTY	1-1	Farrall	4287	7	11	2		6			5	3							10	8	1	9	4
44	27	BARROW	2-2	Bacon, Hughes (p)	3423	7	11	2		6			5	3						10		8	1	9	4
45	29	Exeter City	0-2		3792	7				6			5	3	2					11	10	8	1	9	4
46	May 3	MANSFIELD TOWN	0-0		3154					6			5	3	2		7			11	10	8	1	9	4
					Apps	41	24	5	26	41	2	1	46	45	2	3	11	23	35	32	39	10	44	41	35
					Goals	7	1			6			3	1			1			10	14			20	

Game 36 played at Stonebridge Road, following crowd trouble at game 26

One own goal

F.A. Cup

	Date	Opponent	Score	Scorers	Att.	Bacon RAS	Brown G	Challis RLA	Cockburn WR	Farrall A	Friday TJ	Griffiths EG	Hughes HJ	Hunt DP	McIntyre PF	McManus EJ	Morris FW	Parry W	Proverbs RJ	Pulley GA	Shepherd JHE	Simpson C	Simpson JL	Terry PA	Wilson RSW
R1	Nov 5	Ashford Town	2-1	Hughes, Shepherd	5500	7				10			5	3				2	6	11	9		1	8	4
R2	26	SOUTHEND UNITED	3-2	Shepherd 2, Terry	10220	7	11						5	3				2	6	10	8		1	9	4
R3	Jan 7	LEYTON ORIENT	2-6	Terry, Hughes (p)	13164	7	11						5	3				2	6	10	8		1	9	4

F.L. Cup

	Date	Opponent	Score	Scorers	Att.	Bacon RAS	Brown G	Challis RLA	Cockburn WR	Farrall A	Friday TJ	Griffiths EG	Hughes HJ	Hunt DP	McIntyre PF	McManus EJ	Morris FW	Parry W	Proverbs RJ	Pulley GA	Shepherd JHE	Simpson C	Simpson JL	Terry PA	Wilson RSW
R2	Oct 19	PRESTON NORTH END	1-1	Cunningham (og)	5735	7				10			5	3				2	6	11	9		1	8	4
rep	25	Preston North End	0-3		9218	7	11			10			5	3				2	6		8		1	9	4

Bye in R1

		P	W	D	L	F	A	W	D	L	F	A	Pts
1	Peterborough United	46	18	3	2	85	30	10	7	6	49	35	66
2	Crystal Palace	46	16	4	3	64	28	13	2	8	46	41	64
3	Northampton Town	46	16	4	3	53	25	9	6	8	37	37	60
4	Bradford Park Avenue	46	16	5	2	49	22	10	3	10	35	52	60
5	York City	46	17	3	3	50	14	4	6	13	30	46	51
6	Millwall	46	13	3	7	56	33	8	5	10	41	53	50
7	Darlington	46	11	7	5	41	24	7	6	10	37	46	49
8	Workington	46	14	3	6	38	28	7	4	12	36	48	49
9	Crewe Alexandra	46	11	4	8	40	29	9	5	9	21	38	49
10	Aldershot	46	16	4	3	55	19	2	5	16	24	50	45
11	Doncaster Rovers	46	15	0	8	52	33	4	7	12	24	45	45
12	Oldham Athletic	46	13	4	6	57	38	6	3	14	22	50	45
13	Stockport County	46	14	4	5	31	21	4	5	14	26	45	45
14	Southport	46	12	6	5	47	27	7	0	16	22	40	44
15	GILLINGHAM	46	9	7	7	45	34	6	6	11	19	32	43
16	Wrexham	46	12	4	7	38	22	5	4	14	24	34	42
17	Rochdale	46	13	7	3	43	19	4	1	18	17	47	42
18	Accrington Stanley	46	12	4	7	44	32	4	4	15	30	56	40
19	Carlisle United	46	10	7	6	43	37	3	6	14	18	42	39
20	Mansfield Town	46	10	3	10	39	34	6	3	14	32	44	38
21	Exeter City	46	12	3	8	39	32	2	7	14	27	62	38
22	Barrow	46	10	6	7	33	28	3	5	15	19	51	37
23	Hartlepools United	46	10	4	9	46	40	2	4	17	25	63	32
24	Chester	46	9	7	7	38	35	2	2	19	23	69	31

1961/62

20th in Division Four

							Bentley A	Challis RLA	Cockburn WR	Farrall A	Godfrey PR	Hughes HJ	Hunt DP	Jervis WJ	Johnston TB	Livesey CE	McIntyre PF	Proverbs RI	Pulley GA	Ridley RM	Sanders PCW	Simpson C	Simpson JL	Vaessen LH	Waldock R	Wilson K
1	Aug	19	DONCASTER ROVERS	2-2	Wilson, Godfrey	6516				6	7	5	3			9		2	11			10	1	4		8
2		23	Crewe Alexandra	2-5	Pulley, Godfrey	6637	1			6	7	5	3			9		2	11			10		4		8
3		26	Workington	1-5	Livesey	4540	1			10	7	5	3			9		2	11			8		6		4
4		30	CREWE ALEXANDRA	0-1		4966			4		7	5	3			9		2	11	8			1	6		10
5	Sep	2	YORK CITY	1-2	Wilson	5222			4		7	5	3			9		2	11	8			1	6		10
6		6	Rochdale	1-3	Proverbs	5239			4		7	5	3			9		2	11	8		10	1	6		
7		9	Chesterfield	2-3	Hunt, Godfrey	3993			6		7	5	8			9	2	3	10	11			1	4		
8		16	Stockport County	1-3	Livesey	4365		3	5		7	9	2			10		4	11	8		6	1			
9		20	ALDERSHOT	0-1		4251			6	8		5	3			10		2	11	7		4	1	9		
10		23	MILLWALL	3-1	Johnson, R Brady (og), Livesey	8205	1		4	8		5	3		9	10		2	11	7				6		
11		27	Aldershot	0-4		7307			4	8		5	3		9	10		2	11	7			1	6		
12		30	Mansfield Town	1-3	Livesey	10597			4	6		5	3		9	8		2	11	7		10	1			
13	Oct	4	BARROW	3-2	Livesey 2, Johnston	3706			3	6	7	5	2		9	8			11	10			1	4		
14		7	BRADFORD CITY	3-1	Ridley 2, Pulley	7264			3	6	7	5	2		9				11	8			1	4	10	
15		9	Barrow	0-7		2900			3	6		5	2	7	9	8			11	10			1	4		
16		14	Carlisle United	2-1	Waldock, Ridley	7713			3	6		5	2		9	8			11	7			1	4	10	
17		21	COLCHESTER UNITED	2-1	Hughes, Johnston	8962			3	6		5	2		9	8			11	7			1	4	10	
18		28	Chester	1-1	Farrall	4439			3	6		5	2		9	8			11	7			1	4	10	
19	Nov	11	Southport	1-1	Johnston	4259			3	6		5	2		9	8		4	11	7			1		10	
20		18	HARTLEPOOLS UNITED	4-0	Pulley, Farrall 2, Livesey	6562			3	6		5	2		9	8		4	11	7			1		10	
21	Dec	9	Oldham Athletic	1-1	Livesey	9631			3	6		5	2		9	8		4	11	7			1		10	
22		16	Doncaster Rovers	1-2	Waldock	3710			3	6		5	2		9	8		4	11	7			1		10	
23		23	WORKINGTON	4-2	Pulley, Ridley, Copeland (og), Johnston	5183			3	4		5	2		9	8		6	11	7			1		10	
24		26	Exeter City	3-1	Waldock 2, Cockburn	4324			3	4		5	2		9	8		6	11	7			1		10	
25		30	EXETER CITY	2-2	Hughes (p), Pulley	6786			3	4		5	2		9	8		6	11	7			1		10	
26	Jan	6	TRANMERE ROVERS	0-1		6785			3	4		5	2		9	8		6	11	7			1		10	
27		13	York City	0-4		5456			3	4	7	5	2		9	8		6	11				1		10	
28		20	CHESTERFIELD	5-1	Hughes (p), Livesey 2, Waldock 2	5289			2	6	7	5	3		9	10			11				1	4	8	
29		27	Darlington	1-1	Livesey	4706			2	6	7	5			9	10		3	11				1	4	8	
30	Feb	3	STOCKPORT COUNTY	1-1	Livesey	5991				6	7	5	3		9	10		2	11				1	4	8	
31		10	Millwall	0-0		14987	1			6	7	5	3		9	10		2	11					4	8	
32		17	MANSFIELD TOWN	2-2	Waldock. Farrall	5928	1			6		5	3		10			2	11	7	9			4	8	
33		24	Bradford City	2-5	Pulley, Waldock	4501	1			6		5	3		10			2	11	7	9			4	8	
34	Mar	3	CARLISLE UNITED	4-1	Johnston 2, Waldock, Pulley	5483	1			6		5	3		9	10		2	11	7				4	8	
35		10	Colchester United	0-6		4503			6			5	3		9	10		2	11	7			1	4	8	
36		17	CHESTER	0-0		5187			2			5	3		9	10		4	11	7			1	6	8	
37		24	Tranmere Rovers	2-4	Johnston, Livesey	5850		3	2	6	7	5	4		9	10			11				1		8	
38		31	SOUTHPORT	4-0	Waldock, Livesey, Johnston, Pulley	3921			2	6	7	5	3		9	10			11				1	4	8	
39	Apr	7	Hartlepools United	3-1	Pulley 2, Farrall	2434			2	6	7	5	3		9	10			11				1	4	8	
40		14	DARLINGTON	2-2	Pulley, Johnston	4391			2	6	7	5	3		9	10			11				1	4	8	
41		20	Wrexham	0-3		13575			2	6	7	5	3		9	10		4	11				1		8	
42		23	WREXHAM	2-3	Pulley 2	6590			2	8	7	5	3		9	10		6	11				1		4	
43		28	OLDHAM ATHLETIC	0-2		3953			2	8	7	5	3		9	10		6	11				1		4	
44	May	3	ROCHDALE	4-2	Hughes (p), Waldock, Pulley, Livesey	2964			2	6		5	3		9	10		4	11	7			1		8	
						Apps	7	2	36	37	22	44	43	1	35	41	1	33	44	29	2	7	37	28	30	5
						Goals			1	5	3	4	1		10	15		1	14	4					11	2

Two own goals

F.A. Cup

							Bentley A	Challis RLA	Cockburn WR	Farrall A	Godfrey PR	Hughes HJ	Hunt DP	Jervis WJ	Johnston TB	Livesey CE	McIntyre PF	Proverbs RI	Pulley GA	Ridley RM	Sanders PCW	Simpson C	Simpson JL	Vaessen LH	Waldock R	Wilson K
R1	Nov	4	Coventry City	0-2		10628			3	6		5	2		9	8			11	7			1	4	10	

F.L. Cup

							Bentley A	Challis RLA	Cockburn WR	Farrall A	Godfrey PR	Hughes HJ	Hunt DP	Jervis WJ	Johnston TB	Livesey CE	McIntyre PF	Proverbs RI	Pulley GA	Ridley RM	Sanders PCW	Simpson C	Simpson JL	Vaessen LH	Waldock R	Wilson K
R1	Sep	13	Nottingham Forest	1-4	Ridley	11336		3	5		7	9	10					2	11	8		6	1			

Played at 4: EG Griffiths

		P	W	D	L	F	A	W	D	L	F	A	Pts
1	Millwall	44	16	3	3	47	18	7	7	8	40	44	56
2	Colchester United	44	17	4	1	78	24	6	5	11	26	47	55
3	Wrexham	44	12	6	4	56	23	10	3	9	40	33	53
4	Carlisle United	44	15	3	4	35	22	7	5	10	29	41	52
5	Bradford City	44	14	5	3	58	32	7	4	11	36	54	51
6	York City	44	17	2	3	62	19	3	8	11	22	34	50
7	Aldershot	44	16	4	2	56	20	6	1	15	25	40	49
8	Workington	44	12	6	4	40	23	7	5	10	29	47	49
9	Barrow	44	12	7	3	49	20	5	7	10	25	38	48
10	Crewe Alexandra	44	16	3	3	53	24	4	3	15	26	46	46
11	Oldham Athletic	44	12	7	3	47	26	5	5	12	30	44	46
12	Rochdale	44	14	3	5	47	28	5	4	13	24	43	45
13	Darlington	44	13	5	4	37	24	5	4	13	24	49	45
14	Mansfield Town	44	14	3	5	51	19	5	3	14	26	47	44
15	Tranmere Rovers	44	15	2	5	53	37	5	2	15	17	44	44
16	Stockport County	44	13	3	6	42	27	4	6	12	28	42	43
17	Southport	44	13	5	4	36	25	4	4	14	25	46	43
18	Exeter City	44	11	5	6	43	32	2	6	14	19	45	37
19	Chesterfield	44	11	3	8	43	38	3	6	13	27	49	37
20	GILLINGHAM	44	10	6	6	48	30	3	5	14	25	64	37
21	Doncaster Rovers	44	8	5	9	34	29	3	2	17	26	56	29
22	Hartlepools United	44	6	5	11	27	35	2	6	14	25	66	27
23	Chester	44	5	9	8	36	37	2	3	17	18	59	26

1962/63

5th in Division Four

	Date		Opponent	Result	Scorers	Att	Arnott JH	Ballagher J	Burgess MR	Campbell D	Challis RLA	Farrall A	Francis GE	Gibbs BR	Godfrey PR	Huddart DJ	Hughes HJ	Hunt DP	Livesey CE	Matthews GT	McIntyre PF	Moss RG	Pulley GA	Ridley RM	Simpson JL	Smith RGJ	Stringfellow P	Towers EJ	Vaessen LH	Waldock R	Wright GW
1	Aug	18	CHESTER	2-1	Livesey, Farrall	6911	4				3	6	9				5		10				11	7	1					8	2
2		21	Brentford	2-1	Hughes (p), Waldock	11914	4					6	10				5	3		9			11	7	1					8	2
3		25	Crewe Alexandra	2-2	Matthews, Francis	6416	4					6	10				5	3		9			11	7	1					8	2
4		29	BRENTFORD	1-4	Hughes (p)	8822	4					6	10				5	3	8	9			11	7	1						2
5	Sep	1	ALDERSHOT	1-0	Francis	7119		8				6	10				5	3		9	2		11	7	1	4					
6		8	STOCKPORT COUNTY	1-0	Francis	6605		9				6	10		7		5	3			2		11		1	4				8	
7		12	ROCHDALE	2-1	Francis, Waldock	5851		9				6	10		7		5	3			2		11		1	4				8	
8		15	Doncaster Rovers	0-1		4709	4	9				6	10				5	3			2		11	7	1					8	
9		17	York City	3-0	Francis 2, Godfrey	5417	6			3		9	10		7		5				2			11	1	4				8	
10		22	MANSFIELD TOWN	0-1		11503	4			3		9	10		7		5				2			11	1	6				8	
11		26	YORK CITY	0-0		6240	4	8		3		11	10				5		9		2			7	1	6					
12		29	Workington	2-5	Johnston (og), Godfrey	4523	4	8		2	3		10		7		5			9				11	1	6					
13	Oct	6	Oxford United	3-2	Livesey, Pulley, Hughes	8477	4	7		3	2	6	9				5		8				11	10	1						
14		10	Oldham Athletic	1-2	Farrall	17175	4	7		3		6	9				5	2	8				11		1					10	
15		13	BRADFORD CITY	2-1	Waldock, Ballagher	7706	2	7		3		6	9				5		8	4				11	1					10	
16		20	Tranmere Rovers	1-2	Ballagher	9520	2	7		3		6	10				5			4		9		11	1					8	
17		27	TORQUAY UNITED	4-2	Pulley 3, Moss	7650	2			3		6	10	9	7	1	5					8	11							4	
18	Nov	10	OLDHAM ATHLETIC	4-3	Pulley, Arnott, Hughes, Gibbs	8426	2			3		6	9	10	7	1	5					8	11							4	
19		17	Barrow	1-1	Hughes (p)	2493	2			3			9	10	7		5			6		8	11		1					4	
20	Dec	1	Darlington	0-2		2904	2			3		6	9	10	7		5					8	11		1					4	
21		8	SOUTHPORT	3-1	Gibbs, Pulley, Francis	6332	2			3		6	9	10	7		5					8	11		1					4	
22		15	Chester	0-1		3663	2			3		6	9	8			5			10			11		1				7	4	
23		22	CREWE ALEXANDRA	4-0	Francis 2, Moss, Pulley	7154	4			2			10	9	7		5	3				8	11		1					6	
24		26	CHESTERFIELD	2-1	Moss, Godfrey	7911	4			2			10	9	7		5	3				8	11		1					6	
25	Feb	16	WORKINGTON	2-2	Francis, Towers	6519	4			3			8	9	7		5	2					11		1			10		6	
26	Mar	5	Rochdale	1-1	Godfrey	2442	9		5	3		6	11	10	7	1		2										8		4	
27		9	TRANMERE ROVERS	0-0		4300	8		5	3		6	11	9	7	1		2										10		4	
28		16	Torquay United	0-0		4369	2		5	3		6	11	9	7	1				8								10		4	
29		23	LINCOLN CITY	3-0	Towers 3 (1p)	6135	4		5	3		6	8	9	7	1		2					11					10			
30		30	HARTLEPOOLS UNITED	5-1	Francis, Arnott, Towers, Gibbs, Francis	5330	4		5	3		6	8	9	7	1		2					11					10			
31	Apr	1	Hartlepools United	1-1	Ballagher	2629	4	11	5	3		6	8	9	7	1	2													10	
32		6	BARROW	2-3	Ridley, Towers	6607	4		5	3		6	8	9	7	1		2						11				10			
33		12	EXETER CITY	4-0	Ridley, Ballagher, Gibbs 2	9272	4	10	5			6	8	9			2	3					11	7	1						
34		13	Newport County	0-2		2821	4	9	5	3		6	8	10			2	11						7	1						
35		15	Exeter City	0-0		7004	4	9	5			6		10			2	3				8	11	7	1						
36		20	DARLINGTON	1-0	Hughes (p)	4683	4	9	5			6		10			2	3				8	11	7	1						
37		24	NEWPORT COUNTY	3-1	Gibbs 3	5867	4	9	5			6		8			2	3					11	7	1		10				
38		27	Southport	0-0		2920	4	9	5			6		8	7		2	3					11		1		10				
39		29	Chesterfield	2-0	Gibbs, Ballagher	6722	4	9	5			6		8	7		2	3					11		1		10				
40	May	1	DONCASTER ROVERS	1-0	Pulley	5359	4	9	5			6		8	7		2	3					11		1		10				
41		4	Mansfield Town	0-0		9431		9	5			6		8	7		2	3					11		1		10			4	
42		8	Bradford City	1-1	Stringfellow	1738		9	5			6		8	7		2	3				11			1		10			4	
43		11	Aldershot	1-0	Devereux (og)	4685		9	5			6		8			2	3				7		11	1		10			4	
44		15	Lincoln City	1-2	Francis	1993	7		5	3		6	9				2							11	1		10	8		4	
45		18	Stockport County	0-0		2206	4	9	5	3		6		8	7									11	1		10			2	
46		20	OXFORD UNITED	2-1	Ballagher, Stringfellow	9051	4	9	5	3		6		8	7									11	1		10			2	
						Apps	40	24	21	28	3	41	35	29	27	9	38	27	6	10	7	12	29	23	37	7	10	8	1	30	4
						Goals	2	6				3	12	9	4		6		2	1		3	8	2			2	6		3	

Two own goals

F.A. Cup

	Date		Opponent	Result	Scorers	Att	Arnott JH	Ballagher J	Burgess MR	Campbell D	Challis RLA	Farrall A	Francis GE	Gibbs BR	Godfrey PR	Huddart DJ	Hughes HJ	Hunt DP	Livesey CE	Matthews GT	McIntyre PF	Moss RG	Pulley GA	Ridley RM	Simpson JL	Smith RGJ	Stringfellow P	Towers EJ	Vaessen LH	Waldock R	Wright GW
R1	Nov	3	Andover Town	1-0	Godfrey	3484	2			3		6	9		7	1	5			10		8	11							4	
R2		24	BEDFORD TOWN	3-0	Farrall 2, Gibbs	21097	2			3		6	9	10	7		5					8	11		1					4	
R3	Feb	27	PORT VALE	2-4	Gibbs, Francis	6713	4	10		3		6	9	8	7		5	2							1					11	

F.L. Cup

	Date		Opponent	Result	Scorers	Att	Arnott JH	Ballagher J	Burgess MR	Campbell D	Challis RLA	Farrall A	Francis GE	Gibbs BR	Godfrey PR	Huddart DJ	Hughes HJ	Hunt DP	Livesey CE	Matthews GT	McIntyre PF	Moss RG	Pulley GA	Ridley RM	Simpson JL	Smith RGJ	Stringfellow P	Towers EJ	Vaessen LH	Waldock R	Wright GW
R1	Sep	5	Newport County	1-2	Ballagher	3864		8			3	6	10			1	5			9	2		11	7		4					

		P	W	D	L	F	A	W	D	L	F	A	Pts
1	Brentford	46	18	2	3	59	31	9	6	8	39	33	62
2	Oldham Athletic	46	18	4	1	65	23	6	7	10	30	37	59
3	Crewe Alexandra	46	15	4	4	50	21	9	7	7	36	37	59
4	Mansfield Town	46	16	4	3	61	20	8	5	10	47	49	57
5	GILLINGHAM	46	17	3	3	49	23	5	10	8	22	26	57
6	Torquay United	46	14	8	1	45	20	6	8	9	30	36	56
7	Rochdale	46	16	6	1	48	21	4	5	14	19	38	51
8	Tranmere Rovers	46	15	3	5	57	25	5	7	11	24	42	50
9	Barrow	46	14	7	2	52	26	5	5	13	30	54	50
10	Workington	46	13	4	6	42	20	4	9	10	34	48	47
11	Aldershot	46	9	9	5	42	32	6	8	9	31	37	47
12	Darlington	46	13	3	7	44	33	6	3	14	28	54	44
13	Southport	46	11	9	3	47	35	4	5	14	25	71	44
14	York City	46	12	6	5	42	25	4	5	14	25	37	43
15	Chesterfield	46	7	10	6	43	29	6	6	11	27	35	42
16	Doncaster Rovers	46	9	10	4	36	26	5	4	14	28	51	42
17	Exeter City	46	9	6	8	27	32	7	4	12	30	45	42
18	Oxford United	46	10	10	3	44	27	3	5	15	26	44	41
19	Stockport County	46	9	7	7	34	29	6	4	13	22	41	41
20	Newport County	46	11	6	6	44	29	3	5	15	32	61	39
21	Chester	46	11	5	7	31	23	4	4	15	20	43	39
22	Lincoln City	46	11	1	11	48	46	2	8	13	20	43	35
23	Bradford City	46	8	5	10	37	40	3	5	15	27	53	32
24	Hartlepools United	46	5	7	11	33	39	2	4	17	23	65	25

1963/64

Champions of Division Four: Promoted

							Arnott JH	Ballagher J	Burgess MR	Campbell D	Farrall A	Francis GE	Gibbs BR	Godfrey PR	Hudson GA	Hunt DP	Meredith JF	Moss RG	Newman RV	Pulley GA	Ridley RM	Simpson JL	Stacey TJ	Stringfellow P	Taylor RV	Waldock R	White J	Yeo BG
1	Aug	24	BRADFORD PARK AVE.	2-0	Pulley, Gibbs	8562	4		5		6		8	7	2	3		9		11		1		10				
2		28	BRADFORD CITY	0-0		7923	4	9	5		6		8	7	2	3				11		1		10				
3		31	Southport	1-1	Farrall	4123	4		5		6		8	7	2	3				11		1		10		9		
4	Sep	7	EXETER CITY	0-0		8381	4		5		6		10		2	3				11	7	1		8		9		
5		11	Bradford City	2-0	Gibbs, Godfrey	2399	4		5		6		8	7	2	3				11		1		10			9	
6		14	Hartlepools United	0-0		3022	4		5		6		8	7	2	3				11		1		10			9	
7		18	LINCOLN CITY	1-0	Hudson	6949	4		5		6	9	8	7	2	3				11		1		10				
8		21	DARLINGTON	2-1	Gibbs, Newman	8269	4		5		6	9	8		2	3			7	11		1		10				
9		27	Tranmere Rovers	0-0		10277	4		5		6	9	8		2	3			7	11		1		10				
10	Oct	2	Lincoln City	3-0	Francis 2, Gibbs	8968	4		5		6	9	8		2	3			7	11		1		10				
11		5	HALIFAX TOWN	2-1	Francis 2	10745	4		5		6	9	8		2	3			7	11		1		10				
12		9	CARLISLE UNITED	2-0	Marsden (og), Francis	17421	4		5		6	9	10		2	3			7	11		1		8				
13		12	Doncaster Rovers	2-1	Gibbs 2	6670	4		5		6	9	10		2	3			7	11		1		8				
14		15	Carlisle United	1-3	Gibbs	11900	4		5		6	9	10		2	3			7	11		1		8				
15		19	BRIGHTON & HOVE ALB	1-0	White	13451	4		5		6		10		2	3			7	11		1		8			9	
16		23	TORQUAY UNITED	2-0	Yeo, Gibbs	15338	4		5		6		10		2	3			7	11		1					9	8
17		26	Chester	0-1		8395	4		5		6		10	7	2	3				11		1					9	8
18		30	Torquay United	0-1		4892	4	9	5		6		10		2	3			11			1		8				7
19	Nov	2	YORK CITY	1-0	Ballagher	9548	4	10	5		6		8		2	3			7	11		1		9				
20		9	Barrow	3-0	Gibbs 2, Pulley	3606	4	10	5		6		8		2	3			7	11		1					9	
21		23	Oxford United	1-3	Gibbs	8567		9	5		6		8		2	3			7	11		1		10	4			
22		30	WORKINGTON	3-1	Gibbs 2, Hunt	9852	4		5	2	6		10	7		3			8	11		1					9	
23	Dec	14	Bradford Park Avenue	0-1		4930	4		5		6		10	7	2	3			8	11		1					9	
24		21	SOUTHPORT	5-1	Newman 3, Yeo, Pulley	5529	4		5		6		9		2	3			7	11		1		10				8
25		26	Chesterfield	3-0	Pulley 2 (2p), Newman	6590	4		5		6		9		2	3			7	11		1		10				8
26		28	CHESTERFIELD	1-0	Gibbs	10792	4		5		6		9		2	3			7	11		1		10				8
27	Jan	4	ROCHDALE	0-0		8099			5		6		9		2	3			7	11		1		10		4		8
28		11	Exeter City	0-0		10915	4	7	5		6		10		2	3			11			1					9	8
29		18	HARTLEPOOLS UNITED	2-0	Newman 2	7536	4	9	5		6		10		2	3			7	11		1						8
30	Feb	1	Darlington	1-1	Pulley	2814			5		6	9	10		2	3			7	11		1				4		8
31		8	TRANMERE ROVERS	2-2	Newman, Francis	8166	4		5		6	10	8		3				7	11		1	2			9		
32		15	Halifax Town	0-0		2080	4		5		6	9	10		3			8	7	11		1	2					
33		22	DONCASTER ROVERS	1-1	Gibbs	7681	4		5		6	9	8		2	3			7	11		1						10
34		29	Brighton & Hove Albion	1-2	Ballagher	15349	4	10	5		6	9	8	7		3					11	1	2					
35	Mar	7	CHESTER	2-1	Ridley, Ballagher	5274	4	10	5		6		9	7		3			8		11	1	2					
36		27	ALDERSHOT	2-0	Newman, Hunt (p)	12171	4	9	5		6		10			3	11		7		8	1	2					
37		28	Stockport County	0-2		2649	4	9	5				10	7	2	3	11		8			1				6		
38		30	Aldershot	1-1	Newman	7183	4	9	5		6		10			3	11		7		8	1	2					
39	Apr	8	BARROW	3-1	Hunt (p), Burgess, Ridley	11583	4	9	5		6		10			3	11		7		8	1	2					
40		11	Workington	0-1		6536	4	10	5		6		9			3	11		8		7	1	2					
41		15	OXFORD UNITED	2-0	Gibbs, Ballagher	12051	4	9	5		6		8			3	11		7			1	2	10				
42		18	NEWPORT COUNTY	1-1	Gibbs	9584	4	9	5		6		8			3	11		7			1	2	10				
43		22	STOCKPORT COUNTY	0-0		12846	4	9	5		6		8		2	3	11		7			1		10				
44		25	Rochdale	1-2	Godfrey	2737	4		5		6	9	8	7	2	3	11		10			1						
45		27	York City	1-0	Newman	3317	4		5		6	10	8			3	11		7			1	2				9	
46		30	Newport County	1-0	Francis	3229	4		5		6	9	10		3		11		7			1	2				8	
						Apps	43	17	46	1	45	16	46	13	36	43	11	2	37	31	7	46	12	25	1	6	11	11
						Goals		4	1		1	7	17	2	1	3			11	6	2						1	2

One own goal

F.A. Cup

							Arnott JH	Ballagher J	Burgess MR	Campbell D	Farrall A	Francis GE	Gibbs BR	Godfrey PR	Hudson GA	Hunt DP	Meredith JF	Moss RG	Newman RV	Pulley GA	Ridley RM	Simpson JL	Stacey TJ	Stringfellow P	Taylor RV	Waldock R	White J	Yeo BG
R1	Nov	16	Queen's Park Rangers	1-4	Arnott	12141	4	10	5		6			8		2	3			7	11		1				9	

F.L. Cup

							Arnott JH	Ballagher J	Burgess MR	Campbell D	Farrall A	Francis GE	Gibbs BR	Godfrey PR	Hudson GA	Hunt DP	Meredith JF	Moss RG	Newman RV	Pulley GA	Ridley RM	Simpson JL	Stacey TJ	Stringfellow P	Taylor RV	Waldock R	White J	Yeo BG
R1	Sep	4	BRISTOL CITY	4-2	Stringfellow 2, Waldock, Gibbs	5940	4		5		6		10		2	3				11	7	1		8		9		
R2		25	BURY	3-0	Pulley 2, Eastham (og)	14979	4		5		6	9	8		2	3			7	11		1		10				
R3	Nov	4	Bristol Rovers	1-1	Ballagher	10149	4	9	5		6		10		2	3			7	11		1		8				
rep		6	BRISTOL ROVERS	3-1	Newman 2, Pulley (p)	10771	4		5		6	10			2	3			8	11	7	1					9	
R4		27	Leicester City	1-3	Francis	10356	4		5	2	6	10	8			3			7	11		1					9	

		P	*W*	*D*	*L*	*F*	*A*	*W*	*D*	*L*	*F*	*A*	*Pts*
1	GILLINGHAM	46	16	7	0	37	10	7	7	9	22	20	60
2	Carlisle United	46	17	3	3	70	20	8	7	8	43	38	60
3	Workington	46	15	6	2	46	19	9	5	9	30	33	59
4	Exeter City	46	12	9	2	39	14	8	9	6	23	23	58
5	Bradford City	46	15	3	5	45	24	10	3	10	31	38	56
6	Torquay United	46	16	6	1	60	20	4	5	14	20	34	51
7	Tranmere Rovers	46	12	4	7	46	30	8	7	8	39	43	51
8	Brighton & Hove Albion	46	13	3	7	45	22	6	9	8	26	30	50
9	Aldershot	46	15	3	5	58	28	4	7	12	25	50	48
10	Halifax Town	46	14	4	5	47	28	3	10	10	30	49	48
11	Lincoln City	46	15	2	6	49	31	4	7	12	18	44	47
12	Chester	46	17	3	3	47	18	2	5	16	18	42	46
13	Bradford Park Avenue	46	13	5	5	50	34	5	4	14	25	47	45
14	Doncaster Rovers	46	11	8	4	46	23	4	4	15	24	52	42
15	Newport County	46	12	3	8	35	24	5	5	13	29	49	42
16	Chesterfield	46	8	9	6	29	27	7	3	13	28	44	42
17	Stockport County	46	12	7	4	32	19	3	5	15	18	49	42
18	Oxford United	46	10	7	6	37	27	4	6	13	22	36	41
19	Darlington	46	8	9	6	40	37	6	3	14	26	56	40
20	Rochdale	46	9	8	6	36	24	3	7	13	20	35	39
21	Southport	46	12	6	5	42	29	3	3	17	21	59	39
22	York City	46	9	3	11	29	26	5	4	14	23	40	35
23	Hartlepools United	46	8	7	8	30	36	4	2	17	24	57	33
24	Barrow	46	4	10	9	30	36	2	8	13	21	57	30

1964/65

7th in Division Three

No.	Date	Opponent	Score	Scorers	Att.	Arnott JH	Burgess MR	Farrall A	Gibbs BR	Godfrey PR	Green HR	Huddart DJ	Hudson GA	Hunt DP	Meredith JF	Newman RV	Pulley GA	Rackstraw C	Ridley RM	Riggs LJ	Ryder R	Simpson JL	Stacey TJ	Taylor RV	Weston AD	White J	Yeo BG
1	Aug 22	Walsall	1-0	Rackstraw (p)	6825	4	5	6	8		9		2	3	11	7		10				1					
2	26	SCUNTHORPE UNITED	0-0		14167	4	5	6	8		9		2	3	11	7		10				1					
3	29	WATFORD	5-2	Green 2,Farrall,Welbourne (og),Gibbs	11408	4	5	6	8		9		2	3	11	7		10				1					
4	Sep 5	Workington	1-1	Gibbs	5311	4	5	6	8		9		2	3	11	7		10				1					
5	9	BARNSLEY	1-0	Meredith	13677	4	5	6	8		9		2	3	11	7		10				1					
6	12	HULL CITY	1-0	Gibbs	11144	4	5	6	8		9		2	3	11	7		10				1					
7	15	Barnsley	0-1		5025	4	5	6	8		9		2	3	11	7		10				1					
8	19	Brentford	0-2		13075	4	5	6	8		9		2	3	11	7		10				1					
9	26	Bristol City	2-1	Gibbs, Farrall	11556	2	5	6	8	7	9		3		11					4		1				10	
10	30	SOUTHEND UNITED	1-0	Rackstraw	13109	2	5	6	9				3		11	7		8		4		1				10	
11	Oct 3	QUEEN'S PARK RANGERS	2-2	Rackstraw (p), Gibbs	12581	2	5	6	9				3		11	7		8		4		1				10	
12	5	Southend United	1-3	Yeo	9001	2	5	6	9	7			3		11			8		4		1					10
13	10	PORT VALE	2-0	Gibbs 2	8839	2	5	6	8				3		7		11			4		1				10	9
14	13	Shrewsbury Town	0-2		8005	4	5		10				3		11			7		6		1	2			8	9
15	17	Carlisle United	1-3	Gibbs	7342	4	5	6	8		9		3		11							1	2			10	7
16	21	SHREWSBURY TOWN	5-0	Yeo 2 (1p), Gibbs, Newman, Meredith	7770	4	5	6	10		9		3		11	7						1	2				8
17	24	LUTON TOWN	5-0	Green 2, Yeo 3	9424	4	5	6	10		9		3		11	7						1	2				8
18	27	Bristol Rovers	0-3		12383	4	5	6	10		9		3		11	7						1	2				8
19	31	Mansfield Town	1-3	Riggs	7073	4	5				9		2	3	11	7				6		1				10	8
20	Nov 3	Scunthorpe United	3-2	Green 2, Gibbs	4290	4	5		8	7	9		3	2	11			10		6		1					
21	7	GRIMSBY TOWN	0-0		11087	4	5		8		9		3		11			10	7			1			2		6
22	21	BOURNEMOUTH	1-1	Gibbs	9652	4	5	6	10		9		2	3	7		11					1					8
23	28	Exeter City	1-1	Rackstraw	5088	4	5	6		7	9		2	3	11			10		8		1					
24	Dec 12	WALSALL	4-0	Rackstraw 2, Gibbs 2	6077	4	5	6	8		9		2	3	11	7		10				1					
25	19	Watford	2-1	Rackstraw, Green	6412	4	5	6	8		9		3		11	7		10				1			2		
26	26	COLCHESTER UNITED	2-1	Green 2	10692	4	5	6	8		9		2	3	11	7		10				1					
27	28	Colchester United	1-2	Green	3966	4	5	6	8		9		2	3	11	7		10				1					
28	Jan 2	WORKINGTON	5-1	Green 3, Gibbs, Rackstraw	9089	4	5	6	8		9		2	3	11	7		10				1					
29	16	Hull City	1-1	Green	24426	4	5	6	10		9		3		11	7		8				1			2		
30	23	BRENTFORD	1-0	Weston	14475	4	5	6	10		9		3		11	7		8				1			2		
31	30	OLDHAM ATHLETIC	2-1	Gibbs 2	8549	4	5	6	10		9		3		11	7		8				1			2		
32	Feb 6	BRISTOL CITY	2-0	Newman 2	10867	4	5	6	10		9		3		11	7		8				1			2		
33	13	Queen's Park Rangers	1-3	Gibbs	6633		5	6	10		9		3		11	7		8		4		1			2		
34	20	Port Vale	4-0	Gibbs 2, Green 2	4203	4	5		8		9		3		11		7	10		6		1			2		
35	27	CARLISLE UNITED	1-0	Green	14384	4			8		9		3		11		7	10		6		1			2	5	
36	Mar 6	Oldham Athletic	0-2		6366	4	5		10		9		3		11		7	8		6		1			2		
37	13	MANSFIELD TOWN	0-0		11849	4	5	6	8		9		3		11	7		10				1			2		
38	20	Grimsby Town	1-1	Rackstraw	4191	4	5	6	10		9		3		11	7		8				1			2		
39	26	PETERBOROUGH UTD.	2-0	Burgess, Newman	15552	4	5	6	8				3		11	9	7	10				1			2		
40	Apr 3	Bournemouth	2-1	Gibbs, Newman	7508	4	5	6	8				3		11	9	7	10				1			2		
41	10	EXETER CITY	0-1		10567	4	5	6	8				3		11	9	7	10				1			2		
42	16	READING	2-1	Farrall 2	14323	4	5	6	10				3		11	9	7	8				1			2		
43	17	Luton Town	2-0	Rackstraw 2 (1p)	6102	4		6	10				3		11	9	7	8				1			2	5	
44	19	Reading	0-3		8282	4	5	6	10				3		11	9	7	8				1			2		
45	24	BRISTOL ROVERS	1-3	Gibbs	11157	4		6	10				3		11	9	7	8				1			2	5	
46	28	Peterborough United	0-1		6405				8			1			11	9		10	7	6	3			4	2	5	
					Apps	44	42	38	44	4	33	1	45	16	46	34	12	38	2	14	1	45	5	1	20	11	10
					Goals		1	4	21		17				2	5		11		1					1		6

One own goal

F.A. Cup

Rd	Date	Opponent	Score	Scorers	Att.	Arnott JH	Burgess MR	Farrall A	Gibbs BR	Godfrey PR	Green HR	Huddart DJ	Hudson GA	Hunt DP	Meredith JF	Newman RV	Pulley GA	Rackstraw C	Ridley RM	Riggs LJ	Ryder R	Simpson JL	Stacey TJ	Taylor RV	Weston AD	White J	Yeo BG
R1	Nov 14	GUILDFORD CITY	2-2	Riggs, Gibbs	7500	4	5	6	8		9		2	3	11	7				10		1					
rep	18	Guildford City	1-0	Gibbs	10959	4	5	6	10		9		2	3	11	7		8				1					
R2	Dec 5	Luton Town	0-1		5968	4	5	6	8		9		2	3	11	7		10				1					

F.L. Cup

Rd	Date	Opponent	Score	Scorers	Att.	Arnott JH	Burgess MR	Farrall A	Gibbs BR	Godfrey PR	Green HR	Huddart DJ	Hudson GA	Hunt DP	Meredith JF	Newman RV	Pulley GA	Rackstraw C	Ridley RM	Riggs LJ	Ryder R	Simpson JL	Stacey TJ	Taylor RV	Weston AD	White J	Yeo BG
R1	Sep 2	Exeter City	0-2		7788	4	5	6	8		9		2	3	11	7		10				1					

		P	W	D	L	F	A	W	D	L	F	A	Pts
1	Carlisle United	46	14	5	4	46	24	11	5	7	30	29	60
2	Bristol City	46	14	6	3	53	18	10	5	8	39	37	59
3	Mansfield Town	46	17	4	2	61	23	7	7	9	34	38	59
4	Hull City	46	14	6	3	51	25	9	6	8	40	32	58
5	Brentford	46	18	4	1	55	18	6	5	12	28	37	57
6	Bristol Rovers	46	14	7	2	52	21	6	8	9	30	37	55
7	GILLINGHAM	46	16	5	2	45	13	7	4	12	25	37	55
8	Peterborough United	46	16	3	4	61	33	6	4	13	24	41	51
9	Watford	46	13	8	2	45	21	4	8	11	26	43	50
10	Grimsby Town	46	11	10	2	37	21	5	7	11	31	46	49
11	Bournemouth	46	12	4	7	40	24	6	7	10	32	39	47
12	Southend United	46	14	4	5	48	24	5	4	14	30	47	46
13	Reading	46	12	8	3	45	26	4	6	13	25	44	46
14	Queen's Park Rangers	46	15	5	3	48	23	2	7	14	24	57	46
15	Workington	46	11	7	5	30	22	6	5	12	28	47	46
16	Shrewsbury Town	46	10	6	7	42	38	5	6	12	34	46	42
17	Exeter City	46	8	7	8	33	27	4	10	9	18	25	41
18	Scunthorpe United	46	9	8	6	42	27	5	4	14	23	45	40
19	Walsall	46	9	4	10	34	36	6	3	14	21	44	37
20	Oldham Athletic	46	10	3	10	40	39	3	7	13	21	44	36
21	Luton Town	46	6	8	9	32	36	5	3	15	19	58	33
22	Port Vale	46	7	6	10	27	33	2	8	13	14	43	32
23	Colchester United	46	7	6	10	30	34	3	4	16	20	55	30
24	Barnsley	46	8	5	10	33	31	1	6	16	21	59	29

1965/66

6th in Division Three

	Date		Opponent	Score	Scorers	Att	Arnott JH	Brown WFT	Burgess MR	Gibbs BR	Grace DG	Hunt DP	Meredith JF	Miller RE	Moffatt RW	Newman RV	Pulley GA	Rackstraw C	Ridley RM	Riggs LJ	Simpson JL	Stocks DH	Taylor RV	Taylor TWJ	Weston AD	White J	Williamson M	Yeo BG
1	Aug	21	Peterborough United	0-1		9670	4			10		5	11	2		12	7	8			1	3				6		9
2		25	EXETER CITY	1-1	Gibbs	10540	6			10		5	11	2				9	7	12	1	3				4		8
3		28	MILLWALL	1-0	Rackstraw	11711	6			10		5	11	2				9	7		1	3				4		8
4	Sep	4	BOURNEMOUTH	2-0	Rackstraw (p), Gibbs	7996	6		12	10		5	11	2				9	7		1	3				4		8
5		11	Oldham Athletic	3-5	Gibbs 3	5293	6			10		12	11	2				9	7	5	1	3				4		8
6		15	Reading	2-2	Gibbs 2	8583	4			10	7		11	2				9		6	1	3				5		8
7		18	WATFORD	2-2	Rackstraw (p), Gibbs	7908	4			10	7		11	2				9		6	1	3				5		8
8		25	Scunthorpe United	1-0	Rackstraw	4252				10	9		11	2	4		7	8			1	3	6			5		
9	Oct	2	BRIGHTON & HOVE ALB	3-1	Yeo, Gibbs, Newman	10078				10			11	2	4	8		9			1	3	6			5		7
10		9	Swindon Town	1-0	Butler (og)	13325				10			11	2	4	8		9			1	3	6			5		7
11		16	SHREWSBURY TOWN	0-1		9235				10			11	2	4	8		9			1	3	6			5		7
12		23	Grimsby Town	1-3	Yeo	8176				10			11	2	4	8		9			1	3	6			5		7
13		30	BRENTFORD	1-0	Newman	8235	4			9			11			8		10			1	3	6		2	5		7
14	Nov	6	Bristol Rovers	0-0		8422	4			8			11			9		7			1	3	6		2	5	10	
15		20	Oxford United	4-0	Gibbs 2, Yeo, Beavon (og)	7204	6			8			11	4				7			1	3	12	10	2	5		9
16		27	SWANSEA TOWN	2-0	Gibbs, Yeo	5435	6			8			11	4		12		7			1	3		10	2	5		9
17	Dec	4	Exeter City	1-3	Miller	5141	6			9	7		11	4		8					1	3		10	2	5		
18		11	WORKINGTON	1-0	Miller	6046	6			8			11	4				7			1	3		10	2	5		9
19	Jan	1	SWINDON TOWN	1-0	Miller	7705	6			8			11	4				7			1	3		10	2	5		9
20		8	York City	2-1	Yeo, Gibbs	4006	6			8			11	4				7			1	3		10	2	5		9
21		29	PETERBOROUGH UTD.	1-1	Gibbs	8727	6			8			11	4		12		7			1	3		10	2	5		9
22	Feb	5	Millwall	0-2		16726	6						11	4		8		7			1	3	12	10	2	5		9
23		19	Bournemouth	1-1	Brown	6565	6	10		8			11	4				7			1	3			2	5		9
24		23	HULL CITY	0-3		10527	6	10		8			11	4				7			1	3		12	2	5		9
25	Mar	5	GRIMSBY TOWN	3-2	Rackstraw 2, Gibbs	7915	4	9		10			11	6				8	7		1	3			2	5		
26		9	Hull City	0-1		30122	6	9		10			11	4				8	7		1	3			2	5		
27		12	Watford	0-1		5141	6	9		10			11	4				8	7		1	3			2	5		
28		14	Mansfield Town	0-0		5251		9		8			11	4				7			1	3		6	2	5		10
29		19	SCUNTHORPE UNITED	0-1		6110		9		10			11	4				7			1	3		6	2	5		8
30		23	READING	2-4	Rackstraw, Brown	5339	6	9		8			11	4				7			1	3		10	2	5		
31		26	Brighton & Hove Albion	1-0	Brown	7875	6	9		8			11	4				7			1	3		10	2	5		
32		30	Shrewsbury Town	1-2	Brown	4203	6	9		8			11	4				7			1	3			2	5		10
33	Apr	2	BRISTOL ROVERS	2-0	Gibbs, Brown	5344		9		10			11	4				8			1	3		6	2	5		7
34		8	Southend United	2-5	Rackstraw (p), Brown	8888		9		8			11	4				7			1	3		6	2	5		10
35		9	Walsall	1-6	Rackstraw (p)	6632	6	9		8			11	4				7			1	3			2	5		10
36		11	SOUTHEND UNITED	1-0	Weston	6613		9		8			11	4	6	7		10			1	3			2	5		
37		16	OXFORD UNITED	1-2	Brown	5017		9		8			11	4	6	10		7			1	3			2	5		
38		23	Swansea Town	3-0	Gibbs 2, Newman	7736		9		8			11	6	4	10		7			1	3			2	5		
39		25	Queen's Park Rangers	3-1	Gibbs 2, Newman	7582		9		8			11	4		10		7			1	3		6	2	5		
40		27	OLDHAM ATHLETIC	3-0	Brown, Gibbs, Miller	6231		9		8			11	4		10		7			1	3		6	2	5		
41		30	WALSALL	1-0	Brown	6528		9		8			11	4		10		7			1	3		6	2	5		
42	May	3	MANSFIELD TOWN	2-0	Rackstraw 2 (1p)	6127		9		8			11	4		7		10			1	3		6	2	5		
43		7	Workington	0-1		2375		9		8			11	4		10		7			1	3		6	2	5		
44		18	QUEEN'S PARK RANGERS	3-1	Gibbs 2, Newman	7147	5	9		8			11	4	6	10		7			1	3			2			
45		21	YORK CITY	0-0		5812	5	9		8			11	4	6	7		10			1	3			2			
46		28	Brentford	2-0	Weston, Rackstraw	4457	5	9		8		3	11	4	6	10		7			1				2			
						Apps	29	24	1	45	4	6	46	44	11	22	2	45	7	4	46	45	9	20	34	43	1	27
						Goals		10		23				4		4		12							2			5

Two own goals

F.A. Cup

	Date		Opponent	Score	Scorers	Att	Arnott JH	Brown WFT	Burgess MR	Gibbs BR	Grace DG	Hunt DP	Meredith JF	Miller RE	Moffatt RW	Newman RV	Pulley GA	Rackstraw C	Ridley RM	Riggs LJ	Simpson JL	Stocks DH	Taylor RV	Taylor TWJ	Weston AD	White J	Williamson M	Yeo BG
R1	Nov	13	FOLKESTONE TOWN	1-2	R Taylor	9311	4			10			11					9			1	3	6		2	5	8	7

F.L. Cup

	Date		Opponent	Score	Scorers	Att	Arnott JH	Brown WFT	Burgess MR	Gibbs BR	Grace DG	Hunt DP	Meredith JF	Miller RE	Moffatt RW	Newman RV	Pulley GA	Rackstraw C	Ridley RM	Riggs LJ	Simpson JL	Stocks DH	Taylor RV	Taylor TWJ	Weston AD	White J	Williamson M	Yeo BG
R2	Sep	22	Blackpool	2-5	Gibbs, Pulley	6717	4			8	9		11	2			7	10			1	3	6			5		

Bye in R1

		P	W	D	L	F	A	W	D	L	F	A	Pts
1	Hull City	46	19	2	2	64	24	12	5	6	45	38	69
2	Millwall	46	19	4	0	47	13	8	7	8	29	30	65
3	Queen's Park Rangers	46	16	3	4	62	29	8	6	9	33	36	57
4	Scunthorpe United	46	9	8	6	44	34	12	3	8	36	33	53
5	Workington	46	13	6	4	38	18	6	8	9	29	39	52
6	GILLINGHAM	46	14	4	5	33	19	8	4	11	29	35	52
7	Swindon Town	46	11	8	4	43	18	8	5	10	31	30	51
8	Reading	46	13	5	5	36	19	6	8	9	34	44	51
9	Walsall	46	13	7	3	48	21	7	3	13	29	43	50
10	Shrewsbury Town	46	13	7	3	48	22	6	4	13	25	42	49
11	Grimsby Town	46	15	6	2	47	25	2	7	14	21	37	47
12	Watford	46	12	4	7	33	19	5	9	9	22	32	47
13	Peterborough United	46	13	6	4	50	26	4	6	13	30	40	46
14	Oxford United	46	11	3	9	38	33	8	5	10	32	41	46
15	Brighton & Hove Albion	46	13	4	6	48	28	3	7	13	19	37	43
16	Bristol Rovers	46	11	10	2	38	15	3	4	16	26	49	42
17	Swansea Town	46	14	4	5	61	37	1	7	15	20	59	41
18	Bournemouth	46	9	8	6	24	19	4	4	15	14	37	38
19	Mansfield Town	46	10	5	8	31	36	5	3	15	28	53	38
20	Oldham Athletic	46	8	7	8	34	33	4	6	13	21	48	37
21	Southend United	46	15	1	7	43	28	1	3	19	11	55	36
22	Exeter City	46	9	6	8	36	28	3	5	15	17	51	35
23	Brentford	46	9	4	10	34	30	1	8	14	14	39	32
24	York City	46	5	7	11	30	44	4	2	17	23	62	27

1966/67

11th in Division Three

No	Date		Opponent	Score	Scorers	Att	Arnott JH	Bailey RR	Bellotti DC	Brown WFT	Crickmore CA	Gibbs BR	Harrison R	Hunt DP	Machin M	Meredith JF	Miller RE	Rackstraw C	Riddick GG	Ridley RM	Ryder R	Simpson JL	Thear AC	Weston AD	Yeo BG
1	Aug	20	Scunthorpe United	2-1	Crickmore, Gibbs	5171	5	6		9	10	8		3	7	11	4					1		2	
2		27	WORKINGTON	1-1	Meredith	8408	5	6		9	10	8		3	7	11	4					1		2	
3	Sep	3	WALSALL	0-0		6343	5	6	1	9	10	8		3	7	11	4	12						2	
4		5	Peterborough United	0-2		7292	5	9	1		10	8		3	6	11	4	7						2	
5		9	Orient	1-0	Rackstraw	5999	5	9	1		10	8		3	6	11	4	7						2	
6		17	BOURNEMOUTH	0-0		7247		6	1	9	10	8		3	4	11	5	7						2	
7		24	Swansea Town	1-1	Crickmore	6081		5	1	9	10	8		2	4	11	6	7						3	
8	Oct	1	MIDDLESBROUGH	5-1	Machin 2, Smith (og), Gibbs, Brown	5789	5	6	1	9	10	8		3	7	11	4			12				2	
9		5	PETERBOROUGH UTD.	2-2	Bailey, Machin	7829	5	6	1	9	10	8		3	7	11	4			12				2	
10		8	Torquay United	1-4	Crickmore	5771	5	6	1	9	10	8		3	7	11	4							2	
11		11	Walsall	0-3		10236		5		9	10	8		3	6	11	4			7		1		2	
12		15	BRIGHTON & HOVE ALB	2-0	Machin, Yeo	7758		5		10	7	8		3	6	11	4					1		2	9
13		18	Bristol Rovers	1-4	Yeo	9113		5		10	7	8		3	6	11	4					1		2	9
14		22	Darlington	1-1	Gibbs	5819		5		10	7	8		3	6	11	4					1		2	9
15		29	QUEEN'S PARK RANGERS	2-2	Yeo 2	11951		5		10		8		3	6	11	4	7				1		2	9
16	Nov	5	Watford	1-1	Brown	5874	6	5		10		8		3	4	11		7				1		2	9
17		12	SWINDON TOWN	1-0	Rackstraw	7286		5		10		8		3	6	11	4	7				1		2	9
18		16	BRISTOL ROVERS	1-0	Yeo	6707		5		10		8		3	6	11	4	7				1		2	9
19		19	Reading	1-2	Gibbs	5994		5		10		8		3	6	11	4	7				1		2	9
20	Dec	3	Mansfield Town	1-4	Meredith	6158		5		10		8		3	6	11	4	7				1		2	9
21		10	GRIMSBY TOWN	2-0	Crickmore, Gibbs	5327		5		10	7	8		3	6	11	4					1		2	9
22		17	SCUNTHORPE UNITED	0-1		5468		5		10	7	8		3	6	11	4					1		2	9
23		26	Oxford United	1-1	Crickmore	7405		5		10	7	8		3	6	11	4					1		2	9
24		27	OXFORD UNITED	3-1	Yeo 2, Gibbs	7591		5		9	7	8		3	6	11	4					1		2	10
25		31	Workington	3-1	Brown 2, Gibbs	1857		5		10	7	8		3	6	11	4					1		2	9
26	Jan	14	ORIENT	0-0		7011		5		9		8		3	6	11	4			7		1		2	10
27		21	Bournemouth	0-1		4937	5	9				8		3	6	11	4			7		1		2	10
28	Feb	4	SWANSEA TOWN	0-0		6593	5	6			7	9		3	8	11	4					1		2	10
29		11	Middlesbrough	1-1	Brown	18945	5	6		9	7	8			4	11					3	1		2	10
30		18	COLCHESTER UNITED	2-1	Gibbs, Yeo	6147	4	5		9	7	8			6	11					3	1		2	10
31		25	TORQUAY UNITED	0-0		6370	5	6		9	7	8			4	11					3	1		2	10
32	Mar	4	Brighton & Hove Albion	2-2	Yeo, Gibbs	11112	5	6		9	7	8			4	11	2				3	1			10
33		11	Colchester United	0-0		4915	5	6		9	7	8			4	11					3	1		2	10
34		18	DARLINGTON	1-2	Crickmore	5652		5		9	7	8			6	11			4		3	1		2	10
35		25	Queen's Park Rangers	0-2		14612	12	5		9	7	8			6	11	3		4			1		2	10
36		27	OLDHAM ATHLETIC	1-0	Yeo	5940	5	6			7	8		3	10	11			4			1		2	9
37		29	Oldham Athletic	1-2	Yeo	5167		6		8	7			3	10	11	5		4			1		2	9
38	Apr	1	WATFORD	4-1	Riddick, Brown, Gibbs, Crickmore	6016		5		9	7	8		3		11	6		4			1		2	10
39		8	Swindon Town	0-2		10543		6		10	7	8		3		11	5		4			1		2	9
40		12	Shrewsbury Town	1-3	Meredith	3632		6		10	7	8		3		11	5		4			1		2	9
41		15	READING	0-2		5418		5		9	7	8	10	3	6	11			4			1		2	
42		21	Doncaster Rovers	3-2	Gibbs, Riddick, Crickmore	3364		5		10	7	8		3	6	11			4			1		2	9
43		26	SHREWSBURY TOWN	1-1	Gibbs	4683		5		10	7	8		3	6	11			4			1		2	9
44		29	MANSFIELD TOWN	5-2	Gibbs 3, Brown 2	4880		5		9	7	8		3	6	11			4			1		2	10
45	May	6	Grimsby Town	0-4		3658	5	6	1	10	7			3		11			4				8	2	9
46		13	DONCASTER ROVERS	3-1	Yeo, Brown, Riddick	4179	5			10	7	8		3	6	11			4			1		2	9
						Apps	20	45	9	41	38	44	1	39	42	46	33	11	13	5	6	37	1	45	34
						Goals		1		9	8	15			4	3		2	3						12

One own goal

F.A. Cup

Rd	Date		Opponent	Score	Scorers	Att	Arnott JH	Bailey RR	Bellotti DC	Brown WFT	Crickmore CA	Gibbs BR	Harrison R	Hunt DP	Machin M	Meredith JF	Miller RE	Rackstraw C	Riddick GG	Ridley RM	Ryder R	Simpson JL	Thear AC	Weston AD	Yeo BG
R1	Nov	26	TAMWORTH	4-1	Yeo 2, Rackstraw (p), Gibbs	8248		5		10	12	8		3	6	11	4	7				1		2	9
R2	Jan	7	Walsall	1-3	Gibbs	10418		5		9	7	8		3	6	11	4	12				1		2	10

F.L. Cup

Rd	Date		Opponent	Score	Scorers	Att	Arnott JH	Bailey RR	Bellotti DC	Brown WFT	Crickmore CA	Gibbs BR	Harrison R	Hunt DP	Machin M	Meredith JF	Miller RE	Rackstraw C	Riddick GG	Ridley RM	Ryder R	Simpson JL	Thear AC	Weston AD	Yeo BG
R1	Aug	24	Southend United	0-0		5661	5	6		9	10	8		3	7	11	4					1		2	
rep		31	SOUTHEND UNITED	2-0	Brown, Crickmore	7010	5	6	1	9	10	8		3	7	11	4							2	
R2	Sep	13	Arsenal	1-1	Crickmore	13029		5	1	9	10	8		3	6	11	4	7						2	
rep		21	ARSENAL	1-1	Rackstraw (p)	20566		5	1	9	10	8		3	6	11	4	7						2	
rep2		28	Arsenal	0-5		18409		5	1	9	10	8		3	6	11	4	7						2	

R1 replay and R2 replay a.e.t.

		P	W	D	L	F	A	W	D	L	F	A	Pts
1	Queen's Park Rangers	46	18	4	1	66	15	8	11	4	37	23	67
2	Middlesbrough	46	16	3	4	51	20	7	6	10	36	44	55
3	Watford	46	15	5	3	39	17	5	9	9	22	29	54
4	Reading	46	13	7	3	45	20	9	2	12	31	37	53
5	Bristol Rovers	46	13	8	2	47	28	7	5	11	29	39	53
6	Shrewsbury Town	46	15	5	3	48	24	5	7	11	29	38	52
7	Torquay United	46	17	3	3	57	20	4	6	13	16	34	51
8	Swindon Town	46	14	5	4	53	21	6	5	12	28	38	50
9	Mansfield Town	46	12	4	7	48	37	8	5	10	36	42	49
10	Oldham Athletic	46	15	4	4	51	16	4	6	13	29	47	48
11	GILLINGHAM	46	11	9	3	36	18	4	7	12	22	44	46
12	Walsall	46	12	8	3	37	16	6	2	15	28	56	46
13	Colchester United	46	14	3	6	52	30	3	7	13	24	43	44
14	Orient	46	10	9	4	36	27	3	9	11	22	41	44
15	Peterborough United	46	12	4	7	40	31	2	11	10	26	40	43
16	Oxford United	46	10	8	5	41	29	5	5	13	20	37	43
17	Grimsby Town	46	13	5	5	46	23	4	4	15	15	45	43
18	Scunthorpe United	46	13	4	6	39	26	4	4	15	19	47	42
19	Brighton & Hove Albion	46	10	8	5	37	27	3	7	13	24	44	41
20	Bournemouth	46	8	10	5	24	24	4	7	12	15	33	41
21	Swansea Town	46	9	9	5	50	30	3	6	14	35	59	39
22	Darlington	46	8	7	8	26	28	5	4	14	21	53	37
23	Doncaster Rovers	46	11	6	6	40	40	1	2	20	18	77	32
24	Workington	46	9	3	11	35	35	3	4	16	20	54	31

1967/68

12th in Division Three

							Arnott JH	Bailey RR	Brown WFT	Crickmore CA	Furie JPC	Gibbs BR	Gilbert CG	Hall P	Hunt DP	Machin M	Meredith JF	Miller RE	Moffatt RW	Moore H	Quirke DJ	Riddick GG	Ryder R	Simpson JL	Thear AC	Weston AD	Williams WT	Woodley DG	Yeo BG
1	Aug	19	NORTHAMPTON T	2-0	Yeo, Brown	7890	5	6	10	7		8			3		11					4		1		2			9
2		26	Walsall	0-3		8288	5	6	10	7		8			3		11					4		1		2			9
3	Sep	2	SOUTHPORT	1-4	Crickmore	5211	5	6	10	7		8			12	9	11	3				4		1		2			
4		4	Tranmere Rovers	1-2	Crickmore (p)	5604		5	10	9	7	8					11	6				4	3	1		2			
5		9	GRIMSBY TOWN	1-0	Crickmore (p)	4568	5		9	11		8			3		10	6		7		4		1		2			
6		16	Torquay United	1-2	Brown	8581			9	11		8			3		10	6		7		4		1		2	5		12
7		23	READING	3-0	Brown, Crickmore, Meredith	5790		5	9	11		8			3		10	6		7		4		1		2			
8		27	TRANMERE ROVERS	1-1	Meredith	6711		5	9	11		8			3		10	6		7		4		1		2			
9		30	Swindon Town	2-2	Brown 2	12983		6	9	11		8					10	3		7		4		1		2	5		
10	Oct	4	STOCKPORT COUNTY	3-1	Riddick 2, Brown	6292		6	9	11		8					10	3		7		4		1		2	5		
11		7	Oldham Athletic	1-0	Gibbs	4604		6	9	11		8					10	3		7		4		1		2	5		
12		14	BRISTOL ROVERS	0-0		6118		6	9	11		8					10	3		7		4		1		2	5		
13		21	Barrow	1-0	Gibbs	6479		6	9	11		8					10	3		7		4		1		2	5		
14		23	Stockport County	1-1	Crickmore (p)	6059		6	9	11		8					10	3		7		4		1		2	5		
15		28	OXFORD UNITED	2-1	Gibbs, Brown	5802		6	9	11		8					10	3		7		4		1		2	5		12
16	Nov	4	Bury	2-3	Hall, Machin (p)	6004		6	9			8		11		2	10	3		7		4		1			5		
17		11	BOURNEMOUTH	0-0		7419		6	9			8		11		2	10	3		7		4		1			5		
18		13	Southport	1-4	Brown	5808		6	9			8		11		2	10	3		7		4		1			5		
19		18	Colchester United	2-2	Gibbs 2	4190		6	9		2	8		7	3	4	11							1			5		10
20		25	PETERBOROUGH UTD.	3-2	Gibbs 2, Brown	5957		6	10		2	8		7	3	4	11					9		1			5		
21	Dec	2	Mansfield Town	1-0	Brown	5403		6	10		2	8		7	3	4	11					9		1			5		12
22		16	Northampton Town	1-1	Gibbs	7411		6	10		2	8		7	3	4	11					9		1			5		
23		23	WALSALL	0-1		8092		6	10		2	8		7	3	4	11					9		1			5		
24		26	Brighton & Hove Albion	0-3		12896		6	10		2	8		7	3	12	9			11		4		1			5		
25		30	BRIGHTON & HOVE ALB	1-1	Hunt	6174		6	10		2	8			3	4	11			7		9		1			5		
26	Jan	20	TORQUAY UNITED	1-1	Machin (p)	5863		6	10		2	8			3	4	11			7		9		1			5		
27		26	Scunthorpe United	1-2	Gibbs	3484		6	10		2	8			3	4						9		1	11		5	7	12
28	Feb	3	Reading	1-3	Gibbs	6679			10			8			3	6	11	2			12	4		1			5	7	9
29		10	SWINDON TOWN	3-1	Riddick, Machin (p), Thear	5116	5					8			3	6		2	11			4		1	10			7	9
30		17	Shrewsbury Town	2-1	Yeo, Gibbs	7032	5		12			8			3	6		2	11			4		1	10			7	9
31		24	OLDHAM ATHLETIC	1-0	Machin	4186	5		10			8			3	6		2	11			4		1				7	9
32	Mar	2	Bristol Rovers	1-1	Brown	5478			10			8			3	6		2	11			4		1			5	7	9
33		9	ORIENT	2-3	Riddick, Moffat	5991	5		10			8			3	6		2	11			4		1				7	9
34		13	Grimsby Town	1-1	Riddick	3504			10		2	8			3	6			11			4		1			5	7	9
35		16	BARROW	3-0	Yeo, Brown 2	4987			10		2	8			3	6			11			4		1			5	7	9
36		23	Oxford United	0-3		5596	12		10		2	8			3	6			11			4		1			5	7	9
37		30	BURY	2-0	Brown, Gibbs	6201			10		2	8			3	6			11			4		1	7		5		9
38	Apr	6	Bournemouth	0-4		4915			10		2	8			3	6	12		11			4		1			5	7	9
39		13	COLCHESTER UNITED	1-0	Gibbs	5334			10			8			3	6	11	2				4		1			5	7	9
40		15	SCUNTHORPE UNITED	3-1	Gibbs, Machin (p), Yeo	5031			10			8			3	6	11	2	12			4		1			5	7	9
41		20	Peterborough United	0-3		5430	4					8			3	6	10	2	11					1	9		5	7	12
42		24	WATFORD	0-0		4890			10			8			3	6	11	2				4		1			5	7	9
43		27	MANSFIELD TOWN	2-1	Riddick, Gilbert	3928					2	8	9		3	6	11		10			4		1			5	7	
44	May	4	Watford	0-3		7973					2	8	10		3	6	11					4		1			5	7	9
45		7	Orient	4-0	Riddick 2, Woodley, Gibbs	4618						8	10		3	6	11				4	9		1		2	5	7	
46		11	SHREWSBURY TOWN	0-1		5157						8	10		3	6	11				4	9		1		2	5	7	
						Apps	10	25	40	15	17	46	4	9	35	32	36	26	13	17	3	44	1	46	5	17	35	19	23
						Goals			14	5		15	1	1	1	5	2		1			8			1			1	4

F.A. Cup

							Arnott JH	Bailey RR	Brown WFT	Crickmore CA	Furie JPC	Gibbs BR	Gilbert CG	Hall P	Hunt DP	Machin M	Meredith JF	Miller RE	Moffatt RW	Moore H	Quirke DJ	Riddick GG	Ryder R	Simpson JL	Thear AC	Weston AD	Williams WT	Woodley DG	Yeo BG
R1	Dec	18	Newport County	0-3		2452		6	10		2	8			3	4	11					9		1			5		7

F.L. Cup

							Arnott JH	Bailey RR	Brown WFT	Crickmore CA	Furie JPC	Gibbs BR	Gilbert CG	Hall P	Hunt DP	Machin M	Meredith JF	Miller RE	Moffatt RW	Moore H	Quirke DJ	Riddick GG	Ryder R	Simpson JL	Thear AC	Weston AD	Williams WT	Woodley DG	Yeo BG
R1	Aug	22	Orient	3-1	Yeo, Gibbs, Crickmore	4830	5	6	10	7		8			3		11					4		1		2			9
R2	Sep	13	TORQUAY UNITED	2-2	Crickmore (p), Riddick	5823	5		9	11		8			3		10	6		7		4		1		2			
rep		20	Torquay United	0-2		6281	12	5	9	11		8			3		10	6		7		4		1		2			

		P	W	D	L	F	A	W	D	L	F	A	Pts
1	Oxford United	46	18	3	2	49	20	4	10	9	20	27	57
2	Bury	46	19	3	1	64	24	5	5	13	27	42	56
3	Shrewsbury Town	46	14	6	3	42	17	6	9	8	19	32	55
4	Torquay United	46	15	6	2	40	17	6	5	12	20	39	53
5	Reading	46	15	5	3	43	17	6	4	13	27	43	51
6	Watford	46	15	3	5	59	20	6	5	12	15	30	50
7	Walsall	46	12	7	4	47	22	7	5	11	27	39	50
8	Barrow	46	14	6	3	43	13	7	2	14	22	41	50
9	Peterborough United	46	14	4	5	46	23	6	6	11	33	44	50
10	Swindon Town	46	13	8	2	51	16	3	9	11	23	35	49
11	Brighton & Hove Albion	46	11	8	4	31	14	5	8	10	26	41	48
12	GILLINGHAM	46	13	6	4	35	19	5	6	12	24	44	48
13	Bournemouth	46	13	7	3	39	17	3	8	12	17	34	47
14	Stockport County	46	16	5	2	49	22	3	4	16	21	53	47
15	Southport	46	13	6	4	35	22	4	6	13	30	43	46
16	Bristol Rovers	46	14	3	6	42	25	3	6	14	30	53	43
17	Oldham Athletic	46	11	3	9	37	32	7	4	12	23	33	43
18	Northampton Town	46	10	8	5	40	25	4	5	14	18	47	41
19	Orient	46	10	6	7	27	24	2	11	10	19	38	41
20	Tranmere Rovers	46	10	7	6	39	28	4	5	14	23	46	40
21	Mansfield Town	46	8	7	8	32	31	4	6	13	19	36	37
22	Grimsby Town	46	10	7	6	33	21	4	2	17	19	48	37
23	Colchester United	46	6	8	9	29	40	3	7	13	21	47	33
24	Scunthorpe United	46	8	9	6	36	34	2	3	18	20	53	32

1968/69

20th in Division Three

No	Date	Opponent	Score	Scorers	Att	Bailey RR	Bellotti DC	Folds RJ	Gibbs BR	Gilbert CG	Green MC	Machin M	Meredith JF	Osborn KG	Quirke DJ	Riddick GG	Simpson JL	Simpson TJN	Smillie AT	Thear AC	Weston AD	Williams WT	Woodley DG	Yeo BG
1	Aug 10	Tranmere Rovers	0-2		6926	6			8	10	3	2	11		4	9	1	12				5	7	
2	17	ORIENT	2-2	Woodley, Simpson	5524	6			8		3	2	10		4		1	11		9		5	7	
3	24	Barnsley	1-0	Gibbs	8646	6	1	12	8			3	11		4	9		2				5	7	10
4	27	Rotherham United	0-1		10762	6	1		8		3		11		4	9		2				5	7	10
5	31	LUTON TOWN	1-3	Williams	8227	6	1		8		3	4	11			9		2				5	7	10
6	Sep 7	Torquay United	0-2		8334		1			10	3	6	11		4	8		2				5	7	9
7	14	BRIGHTON & HOVE ALB	5-0	Yeo 2, Gilbert 2, Woodley	4465	6	1			10	3	4	11			9		2				5	7	8
8	16	Barrow	1-2	Yeo	5513	6	1			10	3	4	11			9		2				5	7	8
9	20	Southport	2-4	Yeo, Woodley	2592	6	1			10	3	4	11		12	9		2				5	7	8
10	28	MANSFIELD TOWN	1-1	Woodley	4650	6	1			10	3	4	11			8		2				5	7	9
11	Oct 4	Reading	2-3	Yeo 2	10399	6	1	10			3	4	11		12	9		2				5	7	8
12	9	ROTHERHAM UNITED	2-0	Gilbert, Yeo	5533		1			10	3	4	11		6	9		2				5	7	8
13	12	STOCKPORT COUNTY	0-0		5314		1			10	3	4	11		6	8		2				5	7	9
14	19	Bristol Rovers	1-5	Riddick	5551		1			10	3	4	11		6	8		2				5	7	9
15	26	PLYMOUTH ARGYLE	1-0	Riddick	5170		1				3	4	11		6	8		10			2	5	7	9
16	Nov 2	Watford	1-2	Simpson	11625		1				3	4	11			9		6	10		2	5	7	8
17	5	Northampton Town	1-0	Yeo	5545	9	1				3	6	11					4	10		2	5	7	8
18	9	WALSALL	4-0	Smillie, Yeo 2, Riddick	4857		1				3	6	11			9		4	10		2	5	7	8
19	23	SHREWSBURY TOWN	4-1	Simpson, Riddick, Yeo, Machin (p)	5270		1				3	6	11			9		4	10		2	5	7	8
20	30	Bournemouth	0-2		7655	12	1				3	6	11			9		4	10		2	5	7	8
21	Dec 13	Stockport County	0-5		7698	6	1					3	11		12	9		4	10		2	5	7	8
22	21	BRISTOL ROVERS	0-2		4289	6	1					3	11		12	9		4	10		2	5	7	8
23	26	READING	2-2	Yeo 2	4692	5		11			3	6				9	1	4	10		2		7	8
24	28	Plymouth Argyle	1-1	Riddick	7627	5		11			3	6				9	1	4	10		2		7	8
25	Jan 11	WATFORD	0-5		6523			11			3	4				9	1	6	10		2	5	7	8
26	25	NORTHAMPTON T	2-0	Yeo, Woodley	4532						3	6	11			9	1	4	10		2	5	7	8
27	28	Walsall	1-2	Yeo (p)	6536						3	6	11			9	1	4	10		2	5	7	8
28	Feb 1	HARTLEPOOL	2-2	Simpson, Woodley	4885						3	6	11			9	1	4	10		2	5	7	8
29	25	Swindon Town	0-1		17690	9					3	6	11		12		1	4	10		2	5	7	8
30	Mar 1	TRANMERE ROVERS	1-1	Gilbert	3860	4				9	3		11		12		1	6	10		2	5	7	8
31	5	SWINDON TOWN	2-0	Riddick, Gilbert	6084					9	3		11		6	8	1	4	10		2	5	7	
32	8	Orient	1-1	Gilbert	4988					9	3		11		6	8	1	4	10		2	5	7	
33	10	Hartlepool	1-1	Riddick	2401	12				9	3		11		6	8	1	4	10		2	5	7	
34	14	BARNSLEY	1-1	Riddick	5961					9	3		11		6	8	1	4	10		2	5	7	
35	22	Luton Town	1-1	Yeo	14562	7					3		11		6	8	1	4	10		2	5		9
36	26	CREWE ALEXANDRA	1-0	Yeo	4872	12					3		11		6	8	1	4	10		2	5	7	9
37	29	TORQUAY UNITED	0-0		6306	6					3		11		4	9	1		10		2	5	7	8
38	Apr 4	Oldham Athletic	0-1		5507	4				12	3	7	11		6	8	1		10		2	5		9
39	5	Mansfield Town	0-2		4959	4				9	3		11	7	6		1		10		2	5		8
40	7	BARROW	2-0	Gilbert 2	6037					9	3		11		6	4	1		10		2	5	7	8
41	12	SOUTHPORT	0-0		4511					9	3		11		6	4	1		10		2	5	7	8
42	16	OLDHAM ATHLETIC	2-0	Williams 2	5735					9	3		11		6	4	1		10		2	5	7	8
43	19	Brighton & Hove Albion	2-0	Gilbert, Smillie	11959					9	3		11		6	4	1		10		2	5	7	8
44	22	BOURNEMOUTH	0-0		6615					9	3		11		6	4	1		10		2	5	7	8
45	30	Crewe Alexandra	2-4	Woodley, Riddick	2636					9	3	12	11		6	4	1		10		2	5	7	8
46	May 5	Shrewsbury Town	1-1	Riddick	7847						3	9	11		6	4	1		10		2	5	7	8
					Apps	24	20	5	5	22	43	31	43	1	31	41	26	36	31	1	32	44	43	40
					Goals				1	9		1				10		4	2			3	7	17

F.A. Cup

Rd	Date	Opponent	Score	Scorers	Att	Bailey RR	Bellotti DC	Folds RJ	Gibbs BR	Gilbert CG	Green MC	Machin M	Meredith JF	Osborn KG	Quirke DJ	Riddick GG	Simpson JL	Simpson TJN	Smillie AT	Thear AC	Weston AD	Williams WT	Woodley DG	Yeo BG
R1	Nov 16	Orient	1-1	Smillie	4903		1				3	6	11			9		4	10		2	5	7	8
rep	20	ORIENT	2-1	Riddick 2	9563		1				3	6	11			9		4	10		2	5	7	8
R2	Dec 7	Luton Town	1-3	Yeo (p)	12035	10	1				3		11		6	9		4			2	5	7	8

F.L. Cup

Rd	Date	Opponent	Score	Scorers	Att	Bailey RR	Bellotti DC	Folds RJ	Gibbs BR	Gilbert CG	Green MC	Machin M	Meredith JF	Osborn KG	Quirke DJ	Riddick GG	Simpson JL	Simpson TJN	Smillie AT	Thear AC	Weston AD	Williams WT	Woodley DG	Yeo BG
R1	Aug 14	ORIENT	2-2	Quirke 2	5998	6			8		3	2	11		4	9	1	12		10		5	7	
rep	20	Orient	0-3		7289	6			8		3	2	11		4	12	1	9		10		5	7	

		P	W	D	L	F	A	W	D	L	F	A	Pts
1	Watford	46	16	5	2	35	7	11	5	7	39	27	64
2	Swindon Town	46	18	4	1	38	7	9	6	8	33	28	64
3	Luton Town	46	20	3	0	57	14	5	8	10	17	24	61
4	Bournemouth	46	16	2	5	41	17	5	7	11	19	28	51
5	Plymouth Argyle	46	10	8	5	34	25	7	7	9	19	24	49
6	Torquay United	46	13	4	6	35	18	5	8	10	19	28	48
7	Tranmere Rovers	46	12	3	8	36	31	7	7	9	34	37	48
8	Southport	46	14	8	1	52	20	3	5	15	19	44	47
9	Stockport County	46	14	5	4	49	25	2	9	12	18	43	46
10	Barnsley	46	13	6	4	37	21	3	8	12	21	42	46
11	Rotherham United	46	12	6	5	40	21	4	7	12	16	29	45
12	Brighton & Hove Albion	46	12	7	4	49	21	4	6	13	23	44	45
13	Walsall	46	10	9	4	34	18	4	7	12	16	31	44
14	Reading	46	13	3	7	41	25	2	10	11	26	41	43
15	Mansfield Town	46	14	5	4	37	18	2	6	15	21	44	43
16	Bristol Rovers	46	12	6	5	41	27	4	5	14	22	44	43
17	Shrewsbury Town	46	11	8	4	28	17	5	3	15	23	50	43
18	Orient	46	10	8	5	31	19	4	6	13	20	39	42
19	Barrow	46	11	6	6	30	23	6	2	15	26	52	42
20	GILLINGHAM	46	10	10	3	35	20	3	5	15	19	43	41
21	Northampton Town	46	9	8	6	37	30	5	4	14	17	31	40
22	Hartlepool	46	6	12	5	25	29	4	7	12	15	41	39
23	Crewe Alexandra	46	11	4	8	40	31	2	5	16	12	45	35
24	Oldham Athletic	46	9	6	8	33	27	4	3	16	17	56	35

1969/70

20th in Division Three

							Bailey RR	Bellotti DC	Folds RJ	Galvin D	Gilbert CG	Green MC	Machin M	Osborn KG	Peach DS	Pound JHK	Quirke DJ	Riddick GG	Ronaldson K	Simpson JL	Smillie AT	Tydeman R	Weston AD	Williams WT	Woodley DG	Yeo BG
1	Aug	9	Mansfield Town	0-1		6034	12		11			3				8	6	4		1	10		2	5	7	9
2		16	READING	1-3	Bailey	5795	12		11			3				8	6	4		1	10		2	5	7	9
3		23	Fulham	1-2	Machin	8648			11			3	4			8	6	9		1	10		2	5	7	12
4		25	Stockport County	0-1		3880					8	3	4			11	6	9		1	10		2	5	7	
5		30	LUTON TOWN	0-2		7792						3	4			11	6	9		1	10		2	5	7	8
6	Sep	6	Brighton & Hove Albion	1-3	Folds	13836		1	12			3	4	7		11	6	9			10		2	5		8
7		13	ROCHDALE	2-2	Yeo, Pound	4364		1				3	4			11	6	9			10		2	5	7	8
8		17	BRISTOL ROVERS	1-0	Gilbert	5397		1	4		12	3	2			11	6	9			10			5	7	8
9		20	Rotherham United	1-0	Riddick	7042		1	4			3	2		12	11	6	9			10			5	7	8
10		27	BARNSLEY	1-3	Peach	5446		1	4		9	5	2		3	11	6				10				7	8
11	Oct	1	SOUTHPORT	2-4	Yeo, Riddick	4876		1	11				2		3	8	6	9			10			5	7	4
12		4	Torquay United	2-3	Riddick, Green	6998	5		4			12	2		3	7	6	9		1	10	11				8
13		8	Reading	0-1		6128	5		11		9	4	2		3	10	6	8		1		12			7	
14		11	TRANMERE ROVERS	0-0		4319	10		11			9	4		3		6	8		1		12	2	5	7	
15		18	Barrow	1-1	Green	2877	5		11			9	2		3		6	8		1	10	4			7	
16		25	ORIENT	0-1		5452	5		11				4		3	8	6	9		1	10		2		7	
17	Nov	1	Bradford City	0-1		8883	4		11	5			2		3	7	6	9		1	10					8
18		8	WALSALL	1-3	Peach (p)	4259			11	5		9	2		3	8	6			1		4			7	10
19		22	Bournemouth	1-2	Peach	4772	9		11	5		4	2		3	8	6			1		10			7	
20		26	PLYMOUTH ARGYLE	4-0	Green, Bailey, Pound, Smillie	4127	4			5		9	2		11	3	6		10	1	12	8			7	
21	Dec	13	Rochdale	0-0		5439	4		11	5		9	2		3	7	6			1	10	8				
22		20	BRIGHTON & HOVE ALB	0-1		3930	4			5		9	2		3	11	6			1	10	8		12	7	
23		26	FULHAM	2-0	Bailey, Pound	8510	4			5		9	2		3	11	6			1	10	8			7	
24		27	Luton Town	2-1	Green 2	17402	4			5		9	2		3	11	6			1	10	8			7	
25	Jan	10	ROTHERHAM UNITED	1-1	Yeo	4802	4			5		9	2		3	11	6		10	1					7	8
26		17	Barnsley	1-5	Green	9092	4			5		9	2		3	11	6		10	1					7	8
27		31	TORQUAY UNITED	2-4	Peach (p), Tydeman	6263	4			5		9	2		3	7	6		11	1		10				8
28	Feb	18	DONCASTER ROVERS	2-1	Pound 2	4621	4			5		9	2		3	11				1	12	8		6	7	10
29		25	Plymouth Argyle	2-2	Green, Yeo	8185	4			5		9	2		3	11				1		10		6	7	8
30		28	BARROW	0-1		5018	4			5		9	2		3	11				1	12	10		6	7	8
31	Mar	3	Bury	3-1	Green 2, Peach (p)	3129	4			5		9	2		3	10	6			1	11	7				8
32		11	SHREWSBURY TOWN	2-1	Smillie 2	4524	4			5		9	2		3	10	6			1	11	7				8
33		14	Doncaster Rovers	0-1		4282	4			5		9	2		3	10	6			1	11	7				8
34		17	Halifax Town	1-1	Bailey	3173	4			5		9	2		3	11	6			1	10	7				8
35		21	BURY	1-0	Green	4599	4			5		9	2		3	11	6			1	10	7				8
36		27	BRADFORD CITY	1-1	Yeo	7347	4			5		9	2		3	11	6			1	10	7				8
37		28	Shrewsbury Town	2-2	Smillie, Green	3542	4			5		9	2		3	11	6			1	10	7				8
38		31	Walsall	1-0	Yeo	4295	4		10	5		9	2		3	11	6			1		7				8
39	Apr	4	STOCKPORT COUNTY	0-2		5614	4			5		9	2		3	11	6		10	1		7				8
40		10	MANSFIELD TOWN	3-3	Yeo 2, Pound	3993	8			5		9	2		3	11	6			1		7		4	12	10
41		14	Bristol Rovers	2-1	Pound 2	18978	8			5		9	2		3	11	6			1		7		4		10
42		17	Southport	1-1	Peach (p)	3436	8			5		9	4		3	11	6			1	12	7	2			10
43		20	Tranmere Rovers	0-0		5604	8		12			9	4		3	11	6			1	7		2	5		10
44		22	HALIFAX TOWN	2-0	Pound, Green	4539	8					9	4		3	11	6			1		7	2	5		10
45		25	BOURNEMOUTH	0-0		8638				4		9	8		3	11	6			1	12	7	2	5		10
46		27	Orient	2-1	Green, Yeo	16334				5		9	4		3	11	6			1		8	2		7	10
						Apps	34	6	19	28	4	43	44	1	38	44	43	16	5	40	32	30	14	20	27	35
						Goals	4		1		1	13	1		6	9		3			4	1				9

F.A. Cup

							Bailey RR	Bellotti DC	Folds RJ	Galvin D	Gilbert CG	Green MC	Machin M	Osborn KG	Peach DS	Pound JHK	Quirke DJ	Riddick GG	Ronaldson K	Simpson JL	Smillie AT	Tydeman R	Weston AD	Williams WT	Woodley DG	Yeo BG
R1	Nov	15	Southend United	0-0		8114			11	4		12	2		3	8	6			1		10		5	7	9
rep		19	SOUTHEND UNITED	2-1	Yeo 2	6919	12		11	5		4	2		3	8	6			1		10			7	9
R2	Dec	6	TAMWORTH	6-0	Bailey 3, Pound, Green, Smillie	6798	4			5		9	2		3	11	6			1	10	8			7	
R3	Jan	3	NEWPORT COUNTY	1-0	Machin	9522	4			5		9	2		3	11	6			1	10	8			7	
R4	Jan	24	PETERBOROUGH U	5-1	Green 2, Yeo 2, Ronaldson	13746	4			5		9	2		3	12	6		11	1		10			7	8
R5	Feb	7	Watford	1-2	Yeo	25868	4			5		9	3			11				1	7	8	2	6	12	10

F.L. Cup

							Bailey RR	Bellotti DC	Folds RJ	Galvin D	Gilbert CG	Green MC	Machin M	Osborn KG	Peach DS	Pound JHK	Quirke DJ	Riddick GG	Ronaldson K	Simpson JL	Smillie AT	Tydeman R	Weston AD	Williams WT	Woodley DG	Yeo BG
R1	Aug	13	Aldershot	1-0	Folds	5179			11			3				8	6	10		1	4		2	5	7	9
R2	Sep	3	Blackpool	1-3	Yeo	10767		1	12			3	4			11	6	9			10		2	5	7	8

		P	W	D	L	F	A	W	D	L	F	A	Pts
1	Orient	46	16	5	2	43	15	9	7	7	24	21	62
2	Luton Town	46	13	8	2	46	15	10	6	7	31	28	60
3	Bristol Rovers	46	15	5	3	51	26	5	11	7	29	33	56
4	Fulham	46	12	9	2	43	26	8	6	9	38	29	55
5	Brighton & Hove Albion	46	16	4	3	37	16	7	5	11	20	27	55
6	Mansfield Town	46	14	4	5	46	22	7	7	9	24	27	53
7	Barnsley	46	14	6	3	43	24	5	9	9	25	35	53
8	Reading	46	16	3	4	52	29	5	8	10	35	48	53
9	Rochdale	46	11	6	6	39	24	7	4	12	30	36	46
10	Bradford City	46	11	6	6	37	22	6	6	11	20	28	46
11	Doncaster Rovers	46	13	4	6	31	19	4	8	11	21	35	46
12	Walsall	46	11	4	8	33	31	6	8	9	21	36	46
13	Torquay United	46	9	9	5	36	22	5	8	10	26	37	45
14	Rotherham United	46	10	8	5	36	19	5	6	12	26	35	44
15	Shrewsbury Town	46	10	12	1	35	17	3	6	14	27	46	44
16	Tranmere Rovers	46	10	8	5	38	29	4	8	11	18	43	44
17	Plymouth Argyle	46	10	7	6	32	23	6	4	13	24	41	43
18	Halifax Town	46	10	9	4	31	25	4	6	13	16	38	43
19	Bury	46	13	4	6	47	29	2	7	14	28	51	41
20	GILLINGHAM	46	7	6	10	28	33	6	7	10	24	31	39
21	Bournemouth	46	8	9	6	28	27	4	6	13	20	44	39
22	Southport	46	11	5	7	31	22	3	5	15	17	44	38
23	Barrow	46	7	9	7	28	27	1	5	17	18	54	30
24	Stockport County	46	4	7	12	17	30	2	4	17	10	41	23

1970/71

Bottom of Division Three: Relegated

	Date		Opponent	Score	Scorers	Att	Bailey RR	Darrell MA	Folds RJ	Galvin D	Green MC	Kent MJ	Knight GJ	Machin M	McVeigh J	Peach DS	Pound JHK	Quirke DJ	Ronaldson K	Simpson JL	Smillie AT	Tydeman R	Watson T	Williams WT	Woodley DG	Yeo BG
1	Aug	15	READING	0-0		6368	2				9					3	11	6		1	10	8	12	5	7	4
2		22	Bury	1-2	Williams	3770	2				9					3	11	6		1	10	8	7	5		4
3		29	HALIFAX TOWN	2-1	Smillie, Green	5240	2				9					3	11	6		1	10	8	7	5		4
4	Sep	2	Chesterfield	0-2		8442	2		8		9					3	11	6		1	10		7	5		4
5		5	Rotherham United	0-0		7631	2		8		9					3	11	6		1	10		7	5		4
6		12	TORQUAY UNITED	1-2	Green	4349	2		8		9					3	11	6		1	10		7	5		4
7		19	Port Vale	1-1	Green	5178	2				9			10		3	11	6		1		8		5	7	4
8		23	Aston Villa	1-2	Peach	29416	4		2		9					3	12	6		1		8	11	5	7	10
9		26	MANSFIELD TOWN	2-2	Yeo, Green	4706	2		10		9					3	11	6		1	12	8	7	5		4
10		29	Barnsley	1-3	Bailey	7585	2		10	12	9					3	11	6		1	8		7	5		4
11	Oct	2	Tranmere Rovers	0-1		3056	2		10	3	9						11	6		1	8		7	5		4
12		10	BRISTOL ROVERS	1-4	Pound	4748			3	2	9						10	6	8	1	4		11	5	7	
13		17	Reading	2-3	Green, Watson	6352	2		3	12	9						11	6		1	10	8	7	5		4
14		21	WALSALL	2-1	Green 2 (1p)	2965	8		3		9			2			11	6		1	4			5	7	10
15		24	Swansea City	0-1		8117	4		3		9			2		7	11	6		1	10			5		8
16		31	SHREWSBURY TOWN	0-2		3938	4		12		9			2	3	10	11	6		1	8		7	5		
17	Nov	7	Plymouth Argyle	1-2	Watson	7440	10		11	5	9			4	2	3		6		1		8	7			
18		10	Rochdale	1-0	Watson	3291	10		11	5	9			4	2	3	8	6		1			7			
19		14	BRIGHTON & HOVE ALB	1-1	Peach (p)	3008			10	5	9			4	2	3	11	6		1		8	7			
20		28	WREXHAM	1-2	Yeo	3191			11	5	9			4	2	3		6		1		8			7	10
21	Dec	5	Preston North End	0-1		10274			12	2	9				4	3	11	6		1		10		5	7	8
22		19	BURY	1-2	Yeo	3246		10	12		9				2	3		6		1		8	11	5	7	4
23		28	Fulham	0-1		7071		10	11		9				2	3	12	6		1	7	8		5		4
24	Jan	9	BARNSLEY	2-1	Green, Tydeman	3169		10	11		9				2	3		6		1	7	4		5		8
25		12	BRADFORD CITY	2-1	Yeo, Peach	3978	2	10			9				3	11	12	6		1	7	4		5		8
26		16	Walsall	0-3		3752	2				9				3	11	12	6		1	7	4	10	5		8
27		23	DONCASTER ROVERS	0-1		3209	2	10			9				3	11	12	6		1	7	4		5		8
28	Feb	6	PRESTON NORTH END	2-1	Yeo, Pound	4798	2	10			9				3	11	12	6		1	7	4		5		8
29		13	Doncaster Rovers	2-2	Yeo, McVeigh	2735	2	10			9				3	11	12	6		1	7	4		5		8
30		20	ROCHDALE	0-0		3979	2	10		5	9				3	11	12	6		1	7	4				8
31		26	Shrewsbury Town	0-0		3428	2	10		5	9				3	11	12	6		1	7	4				8
32	Mar	1	Wrexham	4-3	Yeo 2, Green, Galvin	3524	7	10		5	9				2	3	12	6		1	11	4				8
33		6	SWANSEA CITY	0-0		2492	7	10		5	9				2	3		6		1	11	4				8
34		10	ASTON VILLA	0-0		10812	7	10		5	9				2	3		6		1	11	4				8
35		13	Brighton & Hove Albion	1-3	Darrell	10794	11	10		5	9	7			2	3		6		1		4				8
36		17	Bradford City	1-0	Yeo	3830		10		5	9	7			2	3		6		1	11	4				8
37		20	PLYMOUTH ARGYLE	0-2		4162		10		5	9	7			2	3	12	6		1	11	4				8
38		27	ROTHERHAM UNITED	2-1	Watson, Yeo	2955		12			9	7			2	3		6		1	11	4	10	5		8
39	Apr	3	Halifax Town	1-2	Green	4026	12	10			9	7			2	3		6		1		4	11	5		8
40		10	FULHAM	1-3	Green	9481		10			9	7			2	3		6		1		4	11	5		8
41		12	TRANMERE ROVERS	0-0		2664	10				9	7			2	3		6		1		4	11	5		8
42		13	Torquay United	3-2	Bailey, Watson 2	4404	10	12			9	7			2	3		6		1	8	4	11	5		
43		17	Bristol Rovers	0-2		5252	7	10			9		12		2	3		6		1	8	4	11	5		
44		24	PORT VALE	1-1	Williams	2207		10			9	7	12		2	3		6		1		4	11	5	8	
45		28	CHESTERFIELD	1-1	Woodley	1887					9	10	8		2	3		6		1		4	11	5	7	
46	May	1	Mansfield Town	0-2		4251		12			9	10	8		2	3		6		1		4	11	5	7	
						Apps	32	22	20	17	46	11	4	8	31	42	29	46	1	46	31	36	27	34	11	36
						Goals	2	1		1	11				1	3	2				1	1	6	2	1	10

F.A. Cup

	Date		Opponent	Score	Scorers	Att	Bailey RR	Darrell MA	Folds RJ	Galvin D	Green MC	Kent MJ	Knight GJ	Machin M	McVeigh J	Peach DS	Pound JHK	Quirke DJ	Ronaldson K	Simpson JL	Smillie AT	Tydeman R	Watson T	Williams WT	Woodley DG	Yeo BG
R1	Nov	21	Brentford	1-2	Green	8000	4		11	5	9			2	3		12	6		1		8	7			10

F.L. Cup

	Date		Opponent	Score	Scorers	Att	Bailey RR	Darrell MA	Folds RJ	Galvin D	Green MC	Kent MJ	Knight GJ	Machin M	McVeigh J	Peach DS	Pound JHK	Quirke DJ	Ronaldson K	Simpson JL	Smillie AT	Tydeman R	Watson T	Williams WT	Woodley DG	Yeo BG
R1	Aug	19	LUTON TOWN	0-1		7328	2				9					3	11	6	10	1		8	12	5	7	4

		P	W	D	L	F	A	W	D	L	F	A	Pts
1	Preston North End	46	15	8	0	42	16	7	9	7	21	23	61
2	Fulham	46	15	6	2	39	12	9	6	8	29	29	60
3	Halifax Town	46	16	2	5	46	22	6	10	7	28	33	56
4	Aston Villa	46	13	7	3	27	13	6	8	9	27	33	53
5	Chesterfield	46	13	8	2	45	12	4	9	10	21	26	51
6	Bristol Rovers	46	11	5	7	38	24	8	8	7	31	26	51
7	Mansfield Town	46	13	7	3	44	28	5	8	10	20	34	51
8	Rotherham United	46	12	10	1	38	19	5	6	12	26	41	50
9	Wrexham	46	12	8	3	43	25	6	5	12	29	40	49
10	Torquay United	46	12	6	5	37	26	7	5	11	17	31	49
11	Swansea City	46	11	5	7	41	25	4	11	8	18	31	46
12	Barnsley	46	12	6	5	30	19	5	5	13	19	33	45
13	Shrewsbury Town	46	11	6	6	37	28	5	7	11	21	34	45
14	Brighton & Hove Albion	46	8	10	5	28	20	6	6	11	22	27	44
15	Plymouth Argyle	46	6	12	5	39	33	6	7	10	24	30	43
16	Rochdale	46	8	8	7	29	26	6	7	10	32	42	43
17	Port Vale	46	11	6	6	29	18	4	6	13	23	41	42
18	Tranmere Rovers	46	8	11	4	27	18	2	11	10	18	37	42
19	Bradford City	46	7	6	10	23	25	6	8	9	26	37	40
20	Walsall	46	10	1	12	30	27	4	10	9	21	30	39
21	Reading	46	10	7	6	32	33	4	4	15	16	52	39
22	Bury	46	7	9	7	30	23	5	4	14	22	37	37
23	Doncaster Rovers	46	8	5	10	28	27	5	4	14	17	39	35
24	GILLINGHAM	46	6	9	8	22	29	4	4	15	20	38	33

1971/72

13th in Division Four

						Bickle MJ	Galvin D	Hill HA	Hill KG	Housden D	Knight GJ	McVeigh J	Parmenter TL	Peach DS	Quirke DJ	Shearing PF	Simpson JL	Tooze RW	Tydeman R	Watson T	Wilks A	Williams WT	Woolcott RA	Yeo BG
1	Aug 21	SOUTHPORT	2-1	Yeo 2	6421		4		5		8	2		3	6		1		10	7	9			11
2	28	Chester	1-5	Yeo	3302		4		5		8	2		3	6		1		7	9	10	12		11
3	Sep 1	CAMBRIDGE UNITED	2-0	Williams, Yeo	6424		4				8		2	3	6	1			7	10	9	5		11
4	4	ALDERSHOT	0-1		5406		4				8		2	3	6	1			7	10	9	5		11
5	11	Crewe Alexandra	1-0	Watson	2575		4				8		2	3	6	1			7	10	9	5		11
6	18	HARTLEPOOL	1-0	Yeo	5477		4				8		2	3	6	1			7	10	9	5		11
7	25	Peterborough United	1-2	Yeo	5492		4	12			8		2	3	6	1			7	10	9	5		11
8	29	WORKINGTON	0-0		5856		4				8		2	3	6	1			7	10	9	5		11
9	Oct 2	DONCASTER ROVERS	2-0	Yeo, Peach	4899		4				8	2		3	6	1			7	10	9	5		11
10	9	Grimsby Town	1-2	Yeo	10539		4	4			8			3	6	1			7	10	9	5		11
11	16	DARLINGTON	4-2	Peach (p), Yeo 2, Wilks	4625		4				8		2	3	6	1			7	10	9	5		11
12	20	Exeter City	1-1	Yeo	3656		4		12		8		2	3	6	1			7	10	9	5		11
13	23	NEWPORT COUNTY	1-2	Tydeman	5887		4			10	8		2	3	6	1			7	12	9	5		11
14	29	Colchester United	2-2	Peach (p), Yeo	6622		4				8		2	3	6	1			7	10	9	5		11
15	Nov 6	STOCKPORT COUNTY	3-2	Knight, Wilks, Yeo	4896	9	4				8		2	3	6	1			7		10	5		11
16	13	Reading	2-1	Knight, Tydeman	4491	9	4				8		2	3	6	1			7		10	5		11
17	27	Brentford	3-1	Peach, Bickle, Yeo	10945	9	4				8		2	3	6	1			7		10	5		11
18	Dec 4	SCUNTHORPE UNITED	0-1		6488	9	4				8		2	3	6	1			7		10	5		11
19	18	Aldershot	2-0	Bickle, Peach	3746	9	4				8		2	3	6		1		7		10	5		11
20	27	NORTHAMPTON T	4-1	Yeo 2, Wilks, Peach	11795	9	4				8		2	3	6		1		7		10	5		11
21	Jan 1	Hartlepool	1-3	Galvin	2932	9	4				8		2	3	6		1		7		10	5		11
22	8	CHESTER	1-0	Bickle	5614	9	4				8		2	3	6		1		7		10	5		11
23	22	Workington	1-1	Williams	2405	9	4		3		8		2		6	1			7		10	5		11
24	29	EXETER CITY	0-2		3755	9	4		5			8	2	3	6	1			7		10			11
25	Feb 5	BARROW	1-1	Wilks	4331	9					4	8	2	3	6	1			7		10	5		11
26	12	Newport County	2-1	Galvin, Yeo	3148	9	4		5		7	8	2	3	6	1					10			11
27	19	COLCHESTER UNITED	0-2		5313	9	4		5		8	7	2	3	6		1				10			11
28	26	Stockport County	1-2	Bickle	1596	9			5		7		2	3	4	1			6		8		10	11
29	Mar 4	READING	4-2	Woolcott, Yeo, Wilks, K Hill	4351	9			5		8		2	3	6	1			4	12	7		10	11
30	9	Lincoln City	1-1	Bickle	8621	9			5		8	3	2		4	1			7		11	6	10	
31	11	GRIMSBY TOWN	0-1		4279	9			6		8	2	3		4			1	7	12	11	5	10	
32	15	BURY	2-0	Yeo, Bickle	5244	7			5		8	3	2		4			1			11	6	10	9
33	18	Southport	0-1		2561	7			5		8	3	2		4			1			11	6	10	9
34	21	Bury	0-5		3276	7			5		8	3	2		4			1			11	6	10	9
35	25	CREWE ALEXANDRA	2-1	Woolcott 2	3733	7			5		8	3	2		4			1	6		11		10	9
36	Apr 1	Northampton Town	1-6	Woolcott	2625					12	8	3	2		4			1	6	10	7	5	9	11
37	3	PETERBOROUGH UTD.	1-1	Williams	4228				5		8	2		3	6			1	7	12	9	4	10	11
38	4	Doncaster Rovers	1-1	Wilks	2769				5		8	3	2	10	4	1				7	11	6		9
39	8	Barrow	0-1		1986				5		8	7	2	3	4	1				9	11	6		10
40	15	BRENTFORD	0-1		5819	10			5		8		3	2	4	1			7	12	9	6		11
41	19	LINCOLN CITY	3-3	Peach, Bickle, Yeo	3538	10			5		8		2	3	6	1			7		9	4		11
42	22	Scunthorpe United	3-3	Yeo 2, Knight	5752	10			5		8		2	3	6	1			7		9	4		11
43	26	Cambridge United	1-2	Wilks	3260				5		8		2	3	6	1			7		9	4	10	11
44	29	SOUTHEND UNITED	0-0		6092				5		8		2	3	6	1			7		9	4	10	11
45	May 1	Darlington	0-0		2339	10			5	12	8		2	3	6	1			7		9	4		11
46	3	Southend United	2-2	Wilks, Woolcott	16098	11			5	4	8		2	3	6	1			7	12	9		10	
					Apps	26	26	2	25	4	45	17	41	38	46	32	7	7	39	22	46	38	13	43
					Goals	7	2		1		3			7					2	1	8	3	5	22

F.A. Cup

						Bickle MJ	Galvin D	Hill HA	Hill KG	Housden D	Knight GJ	McVeigh J	Parmenter TL	Peach DS	Quirke DJ	Shearing PF	Simpson JL	Tooze RW	Tydeman R	Watson T	Wilks A	Williams WT	Woolcott RA	Yeo BG
R1	Nov 20	PLYMOUTH ARGYLE	3-2	Galvin, Wilks, Yeo	7842	9	4				8		2	3	6	1			7		10	5		11
R2	Dec 11	Romford	1-0	Wilks	8359	9	4				8		2	3	6	1			7		10	5		11
R3	Jan 15	Swansea City	0-1		5099	9	4				8		2	3	6	1			7		10	5		11

F.L. Cup

						Bickle MJ	Galvin D	Hill HA	Hill KG	Housden D	Knight GJ	McVeigh J	Parmenter TL	Peach DS	Quirke DJ	Shearing PF	Simpson JL	Tooze RW	Tydeman R	Watson T	Wilks A	Williams WT	Woolcott RA	Yeo BG
R1	Aug 18	READING	4-0	K Hill, Wilks, Watson, Tydeman	6578		4		5		8	2		3	6		1		7	10	9			11
R2	Sep 8	Notts County	2-1	Wilks, Watson	12650		4				8		2	3	6	1			7	10	9	5		11
R3	Oct 6	GRIMSBY TOWN	1-1	Yeo	9038		4	12			8	2		3	6	1			7	10	9	5		11
rep	12	Grimsby Town	0-1		15804		4	2	12		8			3	6	1			7	10	9	5		11

		P	W	D	L	F	A	W	D	L	F	A	Pts
1	Grimsby Town	46	18	3	2	61	26	10	4	9	27	30	63
2	Southend United	46	18	2	3	56	26	6	10	7	25	29	60
3	Brentford	46	16	2	5	52	21	8	9	6	24	23	59
4	Scunthorpe United	46	13	8	2	34	15	9	5	9	22	22	57
5	Lincoln City	46	17	5	1	46	15	4	9	10	31	44	56
6	Workington	46	12	9	2	34	7	4	10	9	16	27	51
7	Southport	46	15	5	3	48	21	3	9	11	18	25	50
8	Peterborough United	46	14	6	3	51	24	3	10	10	31	40	50
9	Bury	46	16	4	3	55	22	3	8	12	18	37	50
10	Cambridge United	46	11	8	4	38	22	6	6	11	24	38	48
11	Colchester United	46	13	6	4	38	23	6	4	13	32	46	48
12	Doncaster Rovers	46	11	8	4	35	24	5	6	12	21	39	46
13	GILLINGHAM	46	11	5	7	33	24	5	8	10	28	43	45
14	Newport County	46	13	5	5	34	20	5	3	15	26	52	44
15	Exeter City	46	11	5	7	40	30	5	6	12	21	38	43
16	Reading	46	14	3	6	37	26	3	5	15	19	50	42
17	Aldershot	46	5	13	5	27	20	4	9	10	21	34	40
18	Hartlepool	46	14	2	7	39	25	3	4	16	19	44	40
19	Darlington	46	9	9	5	37	24	5	2	16	27	58	39
20	Chester	46	10	11	2	34	16	0	7	16	13	40	38
21	Northampton Town	46	8	9	6	43	27	4	4	15	23	52	37
22	Barrow	46	8	8	7	23	26	5	3	15	17	45	37
23	Stockport County	46	7	10	6	33	32	2	4	17	22	55	32
24	Crewe Alexandra	46	9	4	10	27	25	1	5	17	16	44	29

1972/73

9th in Division Four

No	Date	Opponents	Score	Scorers	Att	Aitken GL	Bickle MJ	Galvin D	Gibson MJ	Hill KG	Housden D	Jacks GC	Jacques J	Knight GJ	Lindsey K	Parmenter TL	Peach DS	Quirke DJ	Richardson DJ	Rogers KJ	Shearing PF	Tydeman R	Wilks A	Yeo BG
1	Aug 12	NEWPORT COUNTY	0-0		3719		9		1	5		8		7		2	3	6				4	10	11
2	19	Bury	1-2	Hill	3072		9	2	1	5	11	8		7			3	6				4	10	
3	25	NORTHAMPTON T	1-3	Knight	3544		9	2	1	5	11	8		7			3	6				4	10	
4	Sep 2	Barnsley	1-1	Galvin	3113		10	2	1	5	11	4		8			3	6				7	9	
5	8	DONCASTER ROVERS	3-0	Jacks, Wilks, Peach (p)	1575		10	5	1	3		7		8			2	4				6	9	11
6	11	Stockport County	3-2	Wilks 2, Housden	5074		9	2	1	5	11	8		7			3	6				4	10	12
7	16	Hereford United	0-0		6796			2	1	5	9	8		7		12	3	6				4	10	11
8	18	Mansfield Town	0-2		5399			2	1	5	9			7		8	3	6				4	10	11
9	23	ALDERSHOT	1-2	Jacks	3055			2	1	5	9	7		12		3	8	6				4	10	11
10	26	CAMBRIDGE UNITED	1-2	Jacks	2173			5	1		9	8				2	3	6		10		4	7	11
11	30	Crewe Alexandra	1-1	Yeo	1699			12	1	5		8		7		2	3	6		10		4	9	11
12	Oct 7	Torquay United	0-0		2762				1	5	8	7		2			3	6		11		4	10	9
13	10	DARLINGTON	4-0	Wilks, Jacks, Yeo 2	1932			7	1	5	12	8		2			3	6		11		4	10	9
14	14	READING	1-0	Galvin	3438			7	1	5		8		2			3	6		11		4	10	9
15	21	Lincoln City	0-1		5215			7	1	5		8		2			3	6		11		4	10	9
16	23	Hartlepool	0-2		3462			7	1	5		8		2			3	6		11		4	10	9
17	28	WORKINGTON	0-2		2860			5	1	9	12	7		2			3	6		11		4	8	10
18	Nov 4	Cambridge United	1-3	Galvin	4656			4	1	5	8	11		2		3		6	9			7	10	
19	11	MANSFIELD TOWN	2-1	Richardson, Wilks	2766	11		4	1	5		8		2		3		6	9			7	10	
20	25	BRADFORD CITY	4-2	Richardson 2 (1p), Rogers, Jacks	2249	3		12	1	5		8	4	2				6	9	11		7	10	
21	Dec 9	CHESTER	1-0	Yeo	2727	3			1	5		8	6	4	2				9			7	10	11
22	16	Exeter City	2-3	Stacey (og), Richardson	3823	4			1	5		8	6	12	2		3		9			7	10	11
23	23	PETERBOROUGH UTD.	2-0	Yeo, Wilks	2472			5	1			8	6		2		3	4	9			7	10	11
24	26	Aldershot	0-0		5016			5	1			8	4		2		3	6	9			7	10	11
25	30	BURY	2-2	Yeo, Peach	3718			5	1			8	4		2		3	6	9			7	10	11
26	Jan 6	Northampton Town	1-2	Yeo	2452			5	1			8	4		2		3	6	9			7	10	11
27	13	HARTLEPOOL	2-0	Galvin, Richardson	2772			5	1	12		8	6	11	2		3	4	9			7	10	
28	20	BARNSLEY	5-1	Tydeman 2, Jacks, Richardson, Knight	2550			5	1	10		8	6	11	2		3	4	9			7		
29	26	Doncaster Rovers	1-0	Knight	3059	12		5		11		8	6	10	2		3	4	9		1	7		
30	Feb 3	Darlington	3-2	Jacks, Richardson, Peach	1805			5		11		8	6	10	2		3	7	9		1	4		
31	10	HEREFORD UNITED	2-0	Richardson, Peach (p)	6115			5		11		8	4	10	2		3	6	9		1	7		12
32	17	Newport County	1-5	Richardson	4235			5	1	7		8		10	2		3	6	9			4	11	
33	24	EXETER CITY	1-0	Peach (p)	4695			5		7		8		11	2		3	6	9		1	4	10	
34	Mar 2	TORQUAY UNITED	1-1	Peach (p)	5073			5		10		8	4		2		3	6	9		1	7	12	11
35	6	Southport	0-0		4078			5		8		11	6		2		3	4	9		1	7		10
36	10	Reading	1-3	Richardson	5369			5		8		11	6	12	2		3	4	9		1	7		10
37	17	LINCOLN CITY	1-1	Yeo	3479				1	5		4	6	8	2		3		9			7	10	11
38	24	Workington	1-1	Yeo	918			4	1	6			5	8	2		3		9	12		7	10	11
39	31	Bradford City	1-3	Hill	2703			5	1	4		8	6		2		3		9	10		7		11
40	Apr 6	COLCHESTER UNITED	2-1	Yeo, Jaques	2672				1	5		8	6		2		3	4	9	11		7		10
41	14	Chester	0-1		1435			6	1	5		8		10	2		3	4	9			7		11
42	21	SOUTHPORT	2-0	Yeo, Dunleavy (og)	3895				1	5		8		10	2		3	4	9			7	6	11
43	23	CREWE ALEXANDRA	3-2	Peach (p), Richardson 2	2676				1	5		8	6	10	2		3	4	9			7	11	
44	24	Peterborough United	1-0	Richardson	4378	10			1	5		8	6	2			3	4	9			7	11	
45	28	STOCKPORT COUNTY	3-0	Wilks, Yeo, Richardson	3130				1	5		8	6	10	2		3	4	9				7	11
46	30	Colchester United	0-4		2590	8			1	5		10	6	7	2		3	4	9					11
					Apps	7	6	35	39	41	12	44	23	37	25	8	42	41	29	12	7	44	36	32
					Goals			4		2	1	7	1	3			7		14	1		2	7	12

Two own goals

F.A. Cup

Rd	Date	Opponents	Score	Scorers	Att	Aitken GL	Bickle MJ	Galvin D	Gibson MJ	Hill KG	Housden D	Jacks GC	Jacques J	Knight GJ	Lindsey K	Parmenter TL	Peach DS	Quirke DJ	Richardson DJ	Rogers KJ	Shearing PF	Tydeman R	Wilks A	Yeo BG
R1	Nov 18	READING	1-2	Tydeman	4432	12	7	4	1	5		11		3		2		6	9			8	10	

F.L. Cup

Rd	Date	Opponents	Score	Scorers	Att	Aitken GL	Bickle MJ	Galvin D	Gibson MJ	Hill KG	Housden D	Jacks GC	Jacques J	Knight GJ	Lindsey K	Parmenter TL	Peach DS	Quirke DJ	Richardson DJ	Rogers KJ	Shearing PF	Tydeman R	Wilks A	Yeo BG
R1	Aug 16	COLCHESTER UNITED	1-0	Noble (og)	3966		9	2	1	5	12	8		7			3	6				4	10	11
R2	Sep 5	MILLWALL	0-2		6044		9	2	1	5		8		7			3	6				4	10	11

		P	W	D	L	F	A	W	D	L	F	A	Pts
1	Southport	46	17	4	2	40	19	9	6	8	31	29	62
2	Hereford United	46	18	4	1	39	12	5	8	10	17	26	58
3	Cambridge United	46	15	6	2	40	23	5	11	7	27	34	57
4	Aldershot	46	14	6	3	33	14	8	6	9	27	24	56
5	Newport County	46	14	6	3	37	18	8	6	9	27	26	56
6	Mansfield Town	46	15	7	1	52	17	5	7	11	26	34	54
7	Reading	46	14	7	2	33	7	3	11	9	18	31	52
8	Exeter City	46	13	8	2	40	18	5	6	12	17	33	50
9	GILLINGHAM	46	15	4	4	44	20	4	7	12	19	38	49
10	Lincoln City	46	12	7	4	38	27	4	9	10	26	30	48
11	Stockport County	46	14	7	2	38	18	4	5	14	15	35	48
12	Bury	46	11	7	5	37	19	3	11	9	21	32	46
13	Workington	46	15	7	1	44	20	2	5	16	15	41	46
14	Barnsley	46	9	8	6	32	24	5	8	10	26	36	44
15	Chester	46	11	6	6	40	19	3	9	11	21	33	43
16	Bradford City	46	12	6	5	42	25	4	5	14	19	40	43
17	Doncaster Rovers	46	10	8	5	28	19	5	4	14	21	39	42
18	Torquay United	46	8	10	5	23	17	4	7	12	21	30	41
19	Peterborough United	46	10	8	5	42	29	4	5	14	29	47	41
20	Hartlepool	46	8	10	5	17	15	4	7	12	17	34	41
21	Crewe Alexandra	46	7	8	8	18	23	2	10	11	20	38	36
22	Colchester United	46	8	8	7	36	28	2	3	18	12	48	31
23	Northampton Town	46	7	6	10	24	30	3	5	15	16	43	31
24	Darlington	46	5	9	9	28	41	2	6	15	14	44	29

1973/74

Second in Division Four: Promoted

	Month	Day	Opponent	Score	Scorers	Att	Aitken GL	Coxhill D	Galvin D	Gibson MJ	Hill KG	Jacks GC	Jacques J	Johnson KP	Knight GJ	Lindsey K	Peach DS	Quirke DJ	Richardson DJ	Rogers KJ	Thorpe IR	Tydeman R	Wilks A	Wiltshire DJ	Yeo BG
1	Aug	25	Crewe Alexandra	0-1		2091			10	1	5	8	6		2		3	4	9	12		7			11
2	Sep	1	NEWPORT COUNTY	1-1	Yeo	3971				1	5	8	6			2	3	4	9			7	10		11
3		8	Swansea City	3-0	Lindsey, Yeo, Tydeman	2144				1	5	8	6			2	3	4	9			7	10		11
4		12	SCUNTHORPE UNITED	7-2	Yeo 3, Wilks, Richardson 2, Tydeman	4610				1	5	8	6			2	3	4	9			7	10		11
5		15	DARLINGTON	0-1		5446				1	5	8	6			2	3	4	9			7	10		11
6		18	Rotherham United	1-1	Yeo	3757				1	5	8	6		12	2	3	4	9			7	10		11
7		22	Hartlepool	1-2	Jacks	1399		12		1	5	8	6		2		3	4	9			7	10		11
8		29	DONCASTER ROVERS	5-1	Yeo, Wilks, Richardson 2, Peach (p)	3864					5	8	6			2	3	4	9		1	7	10		11
9	Oct	3	ROTHERHAM UNITED	1-1	Yeo	5330					5	8	6			2	3	4	9		1	7	10		11
10		6	Exeter City	1-2	Peach	4744			10		5	8	6			2	3	4	9		1	7	12		11
11		13	BURY	3-0	Hill, Yeo 2	4531		12		1	5	8	6			2	3	4	9			7	10		11
12		20	Chester	4-2	Peach, Yeo 2, Richardson	2187	2		4	1	5	8	6				3		9			7	10		11
13		23	Scunthorpe United	1-1	Jacks	2544	2	4	5	1		8	6				3		9			7	10		11
14		27	STOCKPORT COUNTY	2-1	Peach (p), Wilks	5777		4	5	1		8	6		2		3	12	9			7	10		11
15		31	Bradford City	0-0		2567		6	5	1	4	8				2	3		9			7	10		11
16	Nov	3	Reading	1-0	Yeo	8248		4	5	1		8	6			2	3		9			7	10		11
17		10	TORQUAY UNITED	2-1	Yeo 2	6201		4	5	1		8	6			2	3		9			7	10		11
18		14	WORKINGTON	4-0	Wilks 3, Yeo	6804	12	4	5	1		8	6			2	3		9			7	10		11
19		17	Mansfield Town	2-2	Yeo, Peach (p)	2908		4	5		12	8	6			2	3		9		1	7	10		11
20	Dec	1	Brentford	3-0	Richardson 2, Galvin	5748		4	5	1		8	6		2		3		9			7	10		11
21		8	COLCHESTER UNITED	4-1	Richardson, Wilks 2, Jacks	8411		4	5	1		8	6		2		3		9			7	10		11
22		22	Doncaster Rovers	2-1	Tydeman, Jacks	1878		4	5	1		8	6		12	2	3		9			7	10		11
23		26	NORTHAMPTON T	3-1	Yeo 3	11313		4	5	1		8	6		12	2	3		9			7	10		11
24		29	SWANSEA CITY	1-1	Jacks	9960			5	1		8	6			2	3	4	9			7	10		11
25	Jan	1	Newport County	3-3	Jacks, Wilks, Peach	5888			5	1		8	6			2	3	4	9			7	10		11
26		5	BARNSLEY	1-1	Richardson	6825			4	1	5	8	6			2	3		9			7	10		11
27		12	Darlington	3-1	Richardson, Peach, Yeo	2204	12		4		5	8			2		3	6	9		1	7	10		11
28		20	CREWE ALEXANDRA	3-0	Yeo, Richardson (p), Jacks	11478	3	4	5	1	6	8			2				9			7	10		11
29	Feb	3	Lincoln City	3-2	Wilks, Yeo 2	7150	3	4	5	1		8	6			2			9			7	10		11
30		10	HARTLEPOOL	3-0	Potter (og), Wilks, Yeo	8724	3	4	5	1		8	6			2			9			7	10		11
31		17	Bury	2-3	Swan (og), Coxhill	8813	3	4	5	1		8	6			2			9			7	10		11
32		23	EXETER CITY	2-1	Yeo, Wilks	7994	3	4	5	1		8	6		9	2						7	10		11
33	Mar	3	Northampton Town	0-0		8583	3	4	5	1		8	6	9		2						7	10		11
34		10	Stockport County	0-2		1940		4	5	1	6	8			9	2		3				7	10	12	11
35		17	CHESTER	1-0	Richardson	7481		4	5	1		8	6		3	2		12	9			7	10		11
36		23	Torquay United	1-0	Richardson	2887		4	5	1		8	6		3	2		11	9			7	10		
37		26	Barnsley	1-3	Richardson	5132	12	4	5	1		8	6		3	2		11	9			7	10		
38		30	READING	0-1		7140	3		4	1		8	5		12	2		6	9			7	10		11
39	Apr	3	PETERBOROUGH UTD.	1-0	Lindsey (p)	12577	3	4	5	1		8	6		10	2			9			7			11
40		6	Workington	3-3	Richardson 2, Jacks	1181	3	4	5	1	11	8	6		10	2			9			7		12	
41		13	MANSFIELD TOWN	2-2	Lindsey (p), Yeo	7972	3	4	5	1		8	6			2			9			7	10		11
42		15	BRADFORD CITY	2-0	Yeo, Wilks	7720		4	5	1	12	8	6		3	2			9			7	10		11
43		20	Colchester United	2-0	Yeo 2	10007		4		1	5	8	6		3	2			9			7	10		11
44		24	LINCOLN CITY	2-0	Yeo, Tydeman	9094		4		1	5	8	6		3	2			9			7	10		11
45		27	BRENTFORD	1-0	Hill	9319		4		1	5	8	6		3	2			9			7	10		11
46	May	1	Peterborough United	2-4	Lindsey (p), Wilks	17569			4	1	5	8	6		3	2			9			7	10		11

	Aitken GL	Coxhill D	Galvin D	Gibson MJ	Hill KG	Jacks GC	Jacques J	Johnson KP	Knight GJ	Lindsey K	Peach DS	Quirke DJ	Richardson DJ	Rogers KJ	Thorpe IR	Tydeman R	Wilks A	Wiltshire DJ	Yeo BG
Apps	15	30	34	41	24	46	42	1	23	37	27	20	43	1	5	46	43	2	43
Goals		1	1		2	8				4	7		16			4	14		31

Two own goals

F.A. Cup

	Month	Day	Opponent	Score	Scorers	Att	Aitken GL	Coxhill D	Galvin D	Gibson MJ	Hill KG	Jacks GC	Jacques J	Johnson KP	Knight GJ	Lindsey K	Peach DS	Quirke DJ	Richardson DJ	Rogers KJ	Thorpe IR	Tydeman R	Wilks A	Wiltshire DJ	Yeo BG
R1	Nov	24	Cambridge United	2-3	Richardson, Tydeman	4831		4	5	1		8	6		2		3		9			7	10		11

F.L. Cup

	Month	Day	Opponent	Score	Scorers	Att	Aitken GL	Coxhill D	Galvin D	Gibson MJ	Hill KG	Jacks GC	Jacques J	Johnson KP	Knight GJ	Lindsey K	Peach DS	Quirke DJ	Richardson DJ	Rogers KJ	Thorpe IR	Tydeman R	Wilks A	Wiltshire DJ	Yeo BG
R1	Aug	16	COLCHESTER UNITED	4-2	Peach, Quirke, Wilks, Yeo	3991				1	5	8	6			2	3	4	9			7	10		11
R2	Sep	5	CARLISLE UNITED	1-2	Richardson	7871				1	5	8	6			2	3	4	9			7	10		11

		P	W	D	L	F	A	W	D	L	F	A	Pts
1	Peterborough United	46	19	4	0	49	10	8	7	8	26	28	65
2	GILLINGHAM	46	16	5	2	51	16	9	7	7	39	33	62
3	Colchester United	46	16	5	2	46	14	8	7	8	27	22	60
4	Bury	46	18	3	2	51	14	6	8	9	30	35	59
5	Northampton Town	46	14	7	2	39	14	6	6	11	24	34	53
6	Reading	46	11	9	3	37	13	5	10	8	21	24	51
7	Chester	46	13	6	4	31	19	4	9	10	23	36	49
8	Bradford City	46	14	7	2	45	20	3	7	13	13	32	48
9	Newport County	46	13	6	4	39	23	3	8	12	17	42	45
10	Exeter City	45	12	5	6	37	20	6	3	13	21	35	44
11	Hartlepool	46	11	4	8	29	16	5	8	10	19	31	44
12	Lincoln City	46	10	8	5	40	30	6	4	13	23	37	44
13	Barnsley	46	15	5	3	42	16	2	5	16	16	48	44
14	Swansea City	46	11	6	6	28	15	5	5	13	17	31	43
15	Rotherham United	46	10	9	4	33	22	5	4	14	23	36	43
16	Torquay United	46	11	7	5	37	23	2	10	11	15	34	43
17	Mansfield Town	46	13	8	2	47	24	0	9	14	15	45	43
18	Scunthorpe United	45	12	7	3	33	17	2	5	16	14	47	42
19	Brentford	46	9	7	7	31	20	3	9	11	17	30	40
20	Darlington	46	9	8	6	29	24	4	5	14	11	38	39
21	Crewe Alexandra	46	11	5	7	28	30	3	5	15	15	41	38
22	Doncaster Rovers	46	10	7	6	32	22	2	4	17	15	58	35
23	Workington	46	10	8	5	33	26	1	5	17	10	48	35
24	Stockport County	46	4	12	7	22	25	3	8	12	22	44	34

1974/75

10th in Division Three

No.	Month	Day	Opponent	Score	Scorers	Att.	Aitken GL	Chadwick DE	Coxhill D	Feely PJ	Fogarty WF	Galvin D	Gauden A	Gregory BC	Hill KG	Hillyard RW	Jacks GC	Jacques J	Knight GJ	Ley OAG	Lindsey K	O'Donnell N	Richardson DJ	Shipperley DJ	Swaine MA	Tydeman R	Weatherly CM	Wilks A	Wiltshire DJ	Yeo BG
1	Aug	17	WALSALL	2-2	Yeo, Richardson (p)	6141			8			4		12		1	10		3		2	7	9	5		6				11
2		24	Bournemouth	0-2		7252	3		8			4		10	6	1			2			7	9	5			12			11
3		31	CHARLTON ATHLETIC	0-1		9636			7			4				1	8		3			12	9	5		6		10	2	11
4	Sep	7	Port Vale	1-2	Wiltshire	2704			7			4			8	1	10		3			6	9	5					2	11
5		14	ALDERSHOT	0-0		5380						5			4	1	8	6		3	2	7	9					10		11
6		18	BURY	1-0	Hill	4824		7				5			6	1	8	4		3	2		9					10	12	11
7		21	Plymouth Argyle	1-1	Lindsey (p)	5556		7				5			6	1	8	4		3	2		9					10		11
8		25	Watford	0-0		6268		7				5			6	1	8	4		3	2		9		11			10	12	
9		28	PETERBOROUGH UTD.	1-1	Richardson	6636		10				6			5	1		4		3	2	12	9			7		8		11
10	Oct	2	Blackburn Rovers	1-4	Richardson	8587		7				5			6	1	10	4		3	2	11	9			8				
11		5	Colchester United	2-4	Feely 2	4684		7		11					5	1	8	4		3	2		9			6		10		
12		12	HEREFORD UNITED	2-3	Jacks, Feely	5357		7		11		12			5	1	8	4		3	2		9			6		10		
13		19	Grimsby Town	1-2	Richardson	5296		7		10		4			12	1	8			3		11	9	5		6			2	
14		22	Preston North End	0-1		9867		10		11		4				1	8		12	3		7	9	5		6			2	
15		26	BRIGHTON & HOVE ALB	2-1	Feely, Jacks	5985		10		11		4				1	8		7	3			9	5		6		12	2	
16	Nov	1	Southend United	2-2	Feely, Richardson (p)	5563		10		11		4				1	8		7	3	2		9	5		6				
17		6	PRESTON NORTH END	2-1	Feely 2	10494		10		11		4				1	8		7	3	2		9	5		6		12		
18		9	HALIFAX TOWN	4-0	Richardson (p), Feely 3	5809		10		11		4				1	8		7	3			9	5		6			2	
19		16	Swindon Town	0-1		9048		10		11		4				1	8		7	3			9	5		6			2	12
20		30	WREXHAM	2-1	Tydeman, Ley (p)	5203		10		11		4				1	8		7	3				5		6		12	2	9
21	Dec	7	Huddersfield Town	2-0	Feely 2	4761		8		10		4				1			7	3		11		5		6			2	9
22		21	CHESTERFIELD	4-0	Chadwick, Richardson 2, Feely	5425		10		11		4				1			7	3		8	9	5		6		12	2	
23		26	Aldershot	1-2	Richardson (og)	4195		10		11		4				1			7	3		8	9	5		6		12	2	
24		28	CRYSTAL PALACE	3-1	Shipperley, Richardson, Gauden	14565		10		11		4	8			1	6			3		7	9	5					2	
25	Jan	11	HUDDERSFIELD T	3-2	Ley, Feely, Galvin	7916		10		11		4	8			1	7			3			9	5		6		12	2	
26		18	Wrexham	1-0	Richardson	3691		10		11		4	8			1	7		2	3			9	5		6				
27		25	TRANMERE ROVERS	2-3	Richardson 2 (1p)	6941		10		11		4	8			1	7		2	3			9	5		6		12		
28	Feb	1	Halifax Town	1-1	Richardson	1742		10		11		6	8		5	1	7			3			9			4			2	
29		8	SOUTHEND UNITED	2-1	Tydeman, Chadwick	7598		10		11		4	8			1	7		12	3			9	5		6			2	
30		11	Bury	1-0	Galvin	4473		10		11		4	8			1	7			3			9	5		6			2	
31		14	Tranmere Rovers	1-1	Richardson	2914		10		11		4	8			1	7			3			9	5		6			2	
32		22	SWINDON TOWN	3-1	Gauden, Richardson, Chadwick	9172		10				4	8			1	7			3			9	5		6			2	11
33		28	Charlton Athletic	1-2	Feely	18929		10		11		4	8			1	7			3		12	9	5		6			2	
34	Mar	8	WATFORD	2-1	Galvin, Richardson	7281		10		11		4	8			1	7			3			9	5		6			2	
35		15	Peterborough United	0-0		6389		10		11		4	8			1	7			3			9	5		6			2	12
36		18	Walsall	1-1	Feely	6390		10		11		4	8			1	7			3			9	5		6			2	
37		22	PORT VALE	0-0		7524		10		11		4	8			1	7			3		12	9	5		6			2	
38		29	Chesterfield	1-2	Galvin	4166		10		11		4	8			1	7			3			9	5		6			2	12
39		31	PLYMOUTH ARGYLE	2-2	Yeo 2	11211		10				4	8			1	7			3		12	9	5		6			2	11
40	Apr	5	Brighton & Hove Albion	3-4	Richardson (p), Yeo, Shipperley	10497						4	8			1	7			3		10	9	5		6			2	11
41		9	BLACKBURN ROVERS	1-1	Richardson (p)	7567		10					8		4	1	7		12	3			9	5		6			2	11
42		12	COLCHESTER UNITED	2-1	Yeo, Richardson (p)	6464							8		4	1	7			3		10	9	5		6			2	11
43		19	Hereford United	1-1	Richardson (p)	5643							8		2	1	7			3		10	9	5		4	12		6	11
44		23	BOURNEMOUTH	1-0	Tydeman	5725							8		4	1	7			3		10	9	5		6	12		2	11
45		26	GRIMSBY TOWN	2-0	Weatherley, Yeo	5765							8		4	1				3		7	9	5		6	10		2	11
46		29	Crystal Palace	0-4		13950					12		8		4	1				3		7	9	5		6	10		2	11
						Apps	1	35	4	27	1	39	23	2	18	46	39	8	18	42	11	22	44	37	1	39	5	15	34	22
						Goals		3		16		4	2		1		2			2	1		20	2		3	1		1	6

One own goal

F.A. Cup

Rd	Month	Day	Opponent	Score	Scorers	Att.	Aitken GL	Chadwick DE	Coxhill D	Feely PJ	Fogarty WF	Galvin D	Gauden A	Gregory BC	Hill KG	Hillyard RW	Jacks GC	Jacques J	Knight GJ	Ley OAG	Lindsey K	O'Donnell N	Richardson DJ	Shipperley DJ	Swaine MA	Tydeman R	Weatherly CM	Wilks A	Wiltshire DJ	Yeo BG
R1	Nov	26	Hereford United	0-1		7362		10		11		4				1	8		7	3			9	5		6		12	2	

F.L. Cup

Rd	Month	Day	Opponent	Score	Scorers	Att.	Aitken GL	Chadwick DE	Coxhill D	Feely PJ	Fogarty WF	Galvin D	Gauden A	Gregory BC	Hill KG	Hillyard RW	Jacks GC	Jacques J	Knight GJ	Ley OAG	Lindsey K	O'Donnell N	Richardson DJ	Shipperley DJ	Swaine MA	Tydeman R	Weatherly CM	Wilks A	Wiltshire DJ	Yeo BG
R1	Aug	21	BOURNEMOUTH	1-1	Richardson	6469	3		7			4			12	1	8		2			6	9	5				10		11
rep		28	Bournemouth	1-1	(aet) Jacks	5774			8			4			12	1	7		3			6	9	5				10	2	11
rep2	Sep	3	Bournemouth	1-2	(aet) Galvin	1570			8			4			12	1	10		3			7	9	5		6			2	11

Replay 2 at Brentford

		P	W	D	L	F	A	W	D	L	F	A	Pts
1	Blackburn Rovers	46	15	7	1	40	16	7	9	7	28	29	60
2	Plymouth Argyle	46	16	5	2	38	19	8	6	9	41	39	59
3	Charlton Athletic	46	15	5	3	51	29	7	6	10	25	32	55
4	Swindon Town	46	18	3	2	43	17	3	8	12	21	41	53
5	Crystal Palace	46	14	8	1	48	22	4	7	12	18	35	51
6	Port Vale	46	15	6	2	37	19	3	9	11	24	35	51
7	Peterborough United	46	10	9	4	24	17	9	3	11	23	36	50
8	Walsall	46	15	5	3	46	13	3	8	12	21	39	49
9	Preston North End	46	16	5	2	42	19	3	6	14	21	37	49
10	GILLINGHAM	46	14	6	3	43	23	3	8	12	22	37	48
11	Colchester United	46	13	7	3	45	22	4	6	13	25	41	47
12	Hereford United	46	14	6	3	42	21	2	8	13	22	45	46
13	Wrexham	46	10	8	5	41	23	5	7	11	24	32	45
14	Bury	46	13	6	4	38	17	3	6	14	15	33	44
15	Chesterfield	46	11	7	5	37	25	5	5	13	25	41	44
16	Grimsby Town	46	12	8	3	35	19	3	5	15	20	45	43
17	Halifax Town	46	11	10	2	33	20	2	7	14	16	45	43
18	Southend United	46	11	9	3	32	17	2	7	14	14	34	42
19	Brighton & Hove Albion	46	14	7	2	38	21	2	3	18	18	43	42
20	Aldershot	46	13	5	5	40	21	1	6	16	13	42	38
21	Bournemouth	46	9	6	8	27	25	4	6	13	17	33	38
22	Tranmere Rovers	46	12	4	7	39	21	2	5	16	16	36	37
23	Watford	46	9	7	7	30	31	1	10	12	22	44	37
24	Huddersfield Town	46	9	6	8	32	29	2	4	17	15	47	32

1975/76

15th in Division Three

						Armstrong GS	Davis JL	Durrell JT	Emanuel WJM	Feely PJ	Fogarty WF	Galvin D	Gauden A	Hill KG	Hillyard RW	Hilton PJ	Hughes SJ	Jacks GC	Knight GJ	Ley OAG	O'Donnell N	Owers P	Richardson DJ	Shipperley DJ	Tydeman R	Weatherly CM	Westwood DR	Wilks A	Wiltshire DJ
1	Aug	16 Bury	0-2		3932					11		5	8	6	1			7		3			9		4	12		10	2
2		23 GRIMSBY TOWN	3-0	Weatherly 2, Richardson (p)	4811							4	8	5	1			7		3	12		9		6	11		10	2
3		30 Swindon Town	2-2	Galvin, Feely	6970					11		4	8	5	1			7	12	3			9		6			10	2
4	Sep	6 PRESTON NORTH END	1-0	Feely	5886					11	12	4	8	5	1			7	2	3			9		6			10	
5		13 Wrexham	0-2		2654						12	4	8	5	1			7	11	3			9		6			10	2
6		20 MANSFIELD TOWN	3-1	Feely, Jacks, Hilton	5635					11		4	8		1	10		7		3			9	5	6			12	2
7		23 ROTHERHAM UNITED	0-0		5493					11		4	8		1	10		7		3			9	5	6			12	2
8		27 Hereford United	1-1	Shipperley	5512					11		4	8		1	10		7	12	3			9	5	6				2
9	Oct	4 HALIFAX TOWN	1-1	Gauden	5864					11		4	8		1			7	12	3			9	5	6			10	2
10		11 PORT VALE	2-1	Feely, Shipperley	5041					11			8	4	1	10		7	2	3			9	5	6			12	
11		18 Shrewsbury Town	0-1		3242					11			8	4	1	10			2	3	7		9	5	6				12
12		21 CHESTERFIELD	2-2	Hill, Feely	5573					11			8	4	1	10		7	2	3			9	5	6				12
13		25 WALSALL	2-3	Richardson, Feely	5942					11			8	4	1	10		7	6	3			9	5					2
14	Nov	1 Aldershot	0-3		4290					11		4	8		1	12		7	10	3			9	5	6				2
15		5 Sheffield Wednesday	0-1		8390					10	12		8		1	11		7	2	3			9	5	6				4
16		8 CARDIFF CITY	2-2	Richardson (p), Jacks	5762			11		10			8		1	12		7	2	3			9	5	6				4
17		15 Millwall	2-2	Jacks, Richardson	6858			11					8		1			7	2	3			9	5	6	12	10		4
18		29 COLCHESTER UNITED	0-1		5407		2						8		1	11		7	4	3			9	5	6		10	12	
19	Dec	6 Chester	2-2	Westwood, Ley	4684		2					6			1			8	7	3			9	5	4		10	11	
20		20 PETERBOROUGH UTD.	2-2	Richardson, Durrell	4086			11			6	4			1			8	2	3			9	5	7	12	10		
21		27 BRIGHTON & HOVE ALB	1-0	Richardson	9294			11			8	4			1			7	2	3			9	5	6		10		
22		30 Crystal Palace	1-0	Westwood	20841			11			8	4			1			7	2	3			9	5	6		10		
23	Jan	10 SWINDON TOWN	3-2	Durrell, Westwood, Richardson	6459			11			8	4			1			7	2	3			9	5	6		10		
24		17 Mansfield Town	1-1	Westwood	5939			11			8	4			1			7	2	3			9	5	6		10		
25		24 WREXHAM	1-1	Shipperley	5849			11			8	4			1			7	2	3			9	5	6	12	10		
26		31 Chesterfield	1-0	Westwood	2948			11			8	4			1			7	2	3			9	5	6		10		12
27	Feb	7 SHEFFIELD WEDNESDAY	0-0		8090			11	4		8			6	1				2	3			9	5	7		10		
28		14 Cardiff City	1-4	Morgan (og)	10912			11	4		8			6	1				2	3			9	5	7		10		
29		21 MILLWALL	3-1	Wiltshire, Shipperley, Westwood	9111			11	7		8				1				2	3			9	5	6		10		4
30		24 Rotherham United	0-2		4462			11	7		8				1	12			2	3			9	5	6		10		4
31		27 Walsall	0-4		5493			11			8			5	1	12		7	2	3					6	9	10		4
32	Mar	1 Southend United	2-2	Westwood 2	4949						8	4			1	11			7	3			9	5	6		10		2
33		6 ALDERSHOT	1-1	Durrell	5028			11			8	4			1	7			2	3			9	5	6		10		12
34		9 Halifax Town	1-1	Knight	1772			11			8	4			1			7	2	3			9	5	6	12	10		
35		13 Port Vale	1-1	Durrell	3517			11			8	12			1			7	2	3				5	6	9	10		4
36		16 SHREWSBURY TOWN	2-1	Knight, Weatherly	5139						8	4			1				7	3			9	5	6	11	10		2
37		20 Colchester United	2-2	Richardson (p), Durrell	3981			12			8	4			1				7	3			9	5	6	11	10		2
38		27 CHESTER	2-0	Knight, Weatherly	4983			11			8	4			1	12			7	3			9	5	6	10			2
39		31 Peterborough United	1-1	Weatherly	4594			11			8	4			1			7	2	3			9	5	6	10			
40	Apr	3 BURY	2-0	Galvin, Durrell	4732			11			8	4			1				2	3			9	5	6	7	10		
41		6 HEREFORD UNITED	3-4	Durrell 2, Ritchie (og)	8081			11			8	4			1				7	3			9	5	6	12	10		2
42		10 Preston North End	0-4		6349			11			8	4		5	1	12		7	2	3			9		6		10		
43		13 SOUTHEND UNITED	1-2	Shipperley	5776			11				4			1	2	12		8	3			9	5	6	7	10		
44		17 CRYSTAL PALACE	1-2	Richardson (p)	12880			11			8			6	1	2			7	3			9	5	4	12	10		
45		19 Brighton & Hove Albion	1-1	Westwood	19152			11						4		2			7	3		1	9	5	6	8	10		
46		24 Grimsby Town	1-2	Shipperley	4631	3	12	11						4		2			7			1	9	5	6	8	10		
					Apps	1	3	27	4	14	27	30	18	16	44	21	1	30	42	45	2	2	44	39	45	18	28	11	26
					Goals			8		6		2	1	1		1		3	3	1			9	6		5	9		1

Two own goals

F.A. Cup

						Armstrong GS	Davis JL	Durrell JT	Emanuel WJM	Feely PJ	Fogarty WF	Galvin D	Gauden A	Hill KG	Hillyard RW	Hilton PJ	Hughes SJ	Jacks GC	Knight GJ	Ley OAG	O'Donnell N	Owers P	Richardson DJ	Shipperley DJ	Tydeman R	Weatherly CM	Westwood DR	Wilks A	Wiltshire DJ
R1	Nov	22 Weymouth	2-0	Richardson 2	3149		2								1	10		7	8	3			9	5	6			11	4
R2	Dec	13 BRIGHTON & HOVE ALB.	0-1		10579			11			6	4	12		1			7	8	3			9	5		10			2

F.L. Cup

						Armstrong GS	Davis JL	Durrell JT	Emanuel WJM	Feely PJ	Fogarty WF	Galvin D	Gauden A	Hill KG	Hillyard RW	Hilton PJ	Hughes SJ	Jacks GC	Knight GJ	Ley OAG	O'Donnell N	Owers P	Richardson DJ	Shipperley DJ	Tydeman R	Weatherly CM	Westwood DR	Wilks A	Wiltshire DJ
R1/1	Aug	20 Reading	1-0	Alleyne (og)	4846							4	8	5	1			7		3			9		6	11		10	2
R1/2		25 READING	1-1	Richardson	5016					12		4	8	5	1			7		3	6		9			11		10	2
R2	Sep	9 Carlisle United	0-2		5274						11	4	8	5	1			7	2	3			9		6	12		10	

		P	W	D	L	F	A	W	D	L	F	A	Pts
1	Hereford United	46	14	6	3	45	24	12	5	6	41	31	63
2	Cardiff City	46	14	7	2	38	13	8	6	9	31	35	57
3	Millwall	46	16	6	1	35	14	4	10	9	19	29	56
4	Brighton & Hove Albion	46	18	3	2	58	15	4	6	13	20	38	53
5	Crystal Palace	46	7	12	4	30	20	11	5	7	31	26	53
6	Wrexham	46	13	6	4	38	21	7	6	10	28	34	52
7	Walsall	46	11	8	4	43	22	7	6	10	31	39	50
8	Preston North End	46	15	4	4	45	23	4	6	13	17	34	48
9	Shrewsbury Town	46	14	2	7	36	25	5	8	10	25	34	48
10	Peterborough United	46	12	7	4	37	23	3	11	9	26	40	48
11	Mansfield Town	46	8	11	4	31	22	8	4	11	27	30	47
12	Port Vale	46	10	10	3	33	21	5	6	12	22	33	46
13	Bury	46	11	7	5	33	16	3	9	11	18	30	44
14	Chesterfield	46	11	5	7	45	30	6	4	13	24	39	43
15	GILLINGHAM	46	10	8	5	38	27	2	11	10	20	41	43
16	Rotherham United	46	11	6	6	35	22	4	6	13	19	43	42
17	Chester	46	13	7	3	34	19	2	5	16	9	43	42
18	Grimsby Town	46	13	7	3	39	21	2	3	18	23	53	40
19	Swindon Town	46	11	4	8	42	31	5	4	14	20	44	40
20	Sheffield Wednesday	46	12	6	5	34	25	0	10	13	14	34	40
21	Aldershot	46	10	8	5	34	26	3	5	15	25	49	39
22	Colchester United	46	9	6	8	25	27	3	8	12	16	38	38
23	Southend United	46	9	7	7	40	31	3	6	14	25	44	37
24	Halifax Town	46	6	5	12	22	32	5	8	10	19	29	35

1976/77

12th in Division Three

No	Date	Opponent	Score	Scorers	Att	Armstrong GS	Brindley JC	Cawston MW	Crabbe SAJ	Durrell JT	Fogarty WF	Galvin D	Hill KG	Hillyard RW	Hilton PJ	Hughes SJ	Jolley TA	Knight GJ	Nicholl TJ	Overton J	Price KG	Richardson DJ	Shipperley DJ	Spearritt EA	Tydeman R	Weatherly CM	Westwood DR	Wheatley SJ	Williams NJ
1	Aug 21	READING	2-2	Galvin, Brindley	5314		2			11		4	5					7		8		9		3	6	12	10	1	
2	24	Shrewsbury Town	2-4	Richardson 2	3858		2			11		4						7		8		9	5	3	6	10	12	1	
3	28	Walsall	2-1	Richardson, Serella (og)	5787		2	1				4						7		8		9	5	3	6	10			11
4	Sep 4	NORTHAMPTON T	1-1	Westwood	5375		2	1				4			12			7		8		9	5	3	6	11	10		
5	11	Port Vale	2-1	Richardson, Galvin	3015		2	1		11		4						7		8		9	5	3	6		10		12
6	18	PORTSMOUTH	2-1	Richardson (p), Weatherly	6873		2	1		11		4			12					8		9	5	3	6	10			7
7	25	Swindon Town	2-2	Richardson (p), Weatherly	8901		2	1		11		4						12		8		9	5	3	6	10			7
8	Oct 2	CHESTERFIELD	2-1	Williams, Galvin	5907		2	1				4			11					8		9	5	3	6	10			7
9	9	Sheffield Wednesday	0-2		15306		2	1							12			7		8		9	4	3	6	11	10		5
10	16	LINCOLN CITY	0-1		6053	12	2	1		11	7									8		9	5	3	6		10		4
11	23	Wrexham	1-2	Overton	7370		2	1				6							11	8		9	5	3	7	10			4
12	30	PRESTON NORTH END	1-1	Westwood	5070		2	1		11		4							7	8		9	5	3	6		10		
13	Nov 2	GRIMSBY TOWN	1-1	Westwood	4729		2	1		11		4							7	8		9	5	3	6		10		
14	6	Peterborough United	1-0	Durrell	5651		2	1		11		4							7			9	5	3	6		10		8
15	13	MANSFIELD TOWN	3-1	Westwood 3	5457		2	1		11		6						4	7			9	5	3			10		8
16	26	Bury	1-3	Westwood	4626		2	1		11		4			12			8	7				5	3		9	10		6
17	Dec 4	ROTHERHAM UNITED	1-2	Spearritt (p)	4715		2	1		11		4							7		9		5	3	6	12	10		8
18	11	Oxford United	1-3	Price	3724	3		1		11		4						2	7		9		5		6		10		8
19	17	Tranmere Rovers	0-2		2054	3	2	1		12		4						8	7		9		5	6			10		11
20	27	CRYSTAL PALACE	0-3		11237	3	2	1		11								8	7	6	9		5				10		4
21	29	Brighton & Hove Albion	0-2		16896	3		1									11	8	7	6	9		5	2		12	10		4
22	Jan 8	York City	2-2	Richardson (p), Westwood	2153	3						6		1				2	7	8	11	9	5				10		4
23	22	Reading	2-1	Price, Crabbe	6390	3			8			4		1				2	7	6	9	11	5				10		
24	29	OXFORD UNITED	1-1	Price	4919	3			8	12		4		1				2	7	6	9	11	5				10		
25	Feb 5	WALSALL	1-0	Richardson (p)	4717	3			8			4		1		6		2	7		9	11	5				10		
26	12	Northampton Town	2-1	Price, Richardson (p)	4391	3	12		8			4		1		6		2	7		9	11	5				10		
27	15	SHREWSBURY TOWN	2-1	Richardson, Westwood	4798	3			8			4		1		6		2	7		9	11	5				10		
28	19	PORT VALE	1-1	Richardson	5084	3			8			4		1		6		2	7		9	11	5				10		
29	22	Chester	0-1		4293	3			8			4		1		6		2	7		9	11	5				10		
30	26	Portsmouth	2-3	Westwood 2	10102	3			8			4		1		6		2	7			11	5			9	10		12
31	Mar 5	SWINDON TOWN	2-2	Westwood, Hughes	4994	3			8	12		4		1		6		2	7		9	11	5				10		
32	12	Chesterfield	0-1		4400	3			8			4		1		6		2	7	12	9		5			11	10		
33	19	SHEFFIELD WEDNESDAY	1-0	Hughes	6022	3			8			4		1		6		2	7		9		5			11	10		
34	22	PETERBOROUGH UTD.	1-1	Crabbe (p)	4198	3			8	12		4		1		6		2	7		9		5			11	10		
35	26	Lincoln City	0-4		5126	3			8	12		5		1		6		2	7		9	11					10		4
36	Apr 2	WREXHAM	2-0	Price 2	4419	3			8	11		4		1		6		2	7		9	10	5						
37	5	Crystal Palace	1-3	Crabbe	17609	3			8	10		4		1		6		2	7		9	11	5						
38	9	BRIGHTON & HOVE ALB	0-1		11588	3			8					1		6		2	7		9	11	5			12	10		4
39	11	Grimsby Town	1-1	Price	3029	3			8			4		1				6	7		9	11	5				10		2
40	16	CHESTER	1-0	Richardson (p)	3963	3			8	11		4		1		6			7		9	10	5						2
41	23	Mansfield Town	2-2	Richardson (p), Overton	8191	3			8					1				6	7	4	9	11	5				10		2
42	26	Preston North End	0-1		4943	3			8					1		6		12	7	4	9	11	5				10		2
43	30	BURY	1-0	Overton	3418	3			8			4		1					7	6	9	11	5				10		2
44	May 3	YORK CITY	2-0	Richardson 2	3094	3			8			4		1					7	6	9	11	5			12	10		2
45	7	Rotherham United	0-1		3004	3			8					1		4			7	6	9	11	5				10		2
46	14	TRANMERE ROVERS	3-0	Westwood, Price, Richardson	3260	3			8					1		6			7	4	9	11	5				10		2
					Apps	30	20	19	24	22	1	37	1	25	5	18	1	33	36	25	29	37	44	19	16	18	38	2	28
					Goals		1		3	1		3				2				3	8	16		1		2	13		1

One own goal

F.A. Cup

Rd	Date	Opponent	Score	Scorers	Att	Armstrong GS	Brindley JC	Cawston MW	Crabbe SAJ	Durrell JT	Fogarty WF	Galvin D	Hill KG	Hillyard RW	Hilton PJ	Hughes SJ	Jolley TA	Knight GJ	Nicholl TJ	Overton J	Price KG	Richardson DJ	Shipperley DJ	Spearritt EA	Tydeman R	Weatherly CM	Westwood DR	Wheatley SJ	Williams NJ
R1	Nov 20	WATFORD	0-1		6818		2	1		11		4			12			8	7			9	5	3			10		6

F.L. Cup

Rd	Date	Opponent	Score	Scorers	Att	Armstrong GS	Brindley JC	Cawston MW	Crabbe SAJ	Durrell JT	Fogarty WF	Galvin D	Hill KG	Hillyard RW	Hilton PJ	Hughes SJ	Jolley TA	Knight GJ	Nicholl TJ	Overton J	Price KG	Richardson DJ	Shipperley DJ	Spearritt EA	Tydeman R	Weatherly CM	Westwood DR	Wheatley SJ	Williams NJ
R1/1	Aug 14	Aldershot	1-1	Galvin	2641		2			11		4		1				7		8		9	5		6		10		3
R1/2	18	ALDERSHOT	2-0	Richardson 2 (1p)	4862		2			11		4		1				7		8		9	5	3	6		10		
R2	Sep 1	NEWCASTLE UNITED	1-2	Weatherly	11203		2	1		11		4						7		8		9	5	3	6	12	10		

		P	W	D	L	F	A	W	D	L	F	A	Pts
1	Mansfield Town	46	17	6	0	52	13	11	2	10	26	29	64
2	Brighton & Hove Albion	46	19	3	1	63	14	6	8	9	20	26	61
3	Crystal Palace	46	17	5	1	46	15	6	8	9	22	25	59
4	Rotherham United	46	11	9	3	30	15	11	6	6	39	29	59
5	Wrexham	46	15	6	2	47	22	9	4	10	33	32	58
6	Preston North End	46	15	4	4	48	21	6	8	9	16	22	54
7	Bury	46	15	2	6	41	21	8	6	9	23	38	54
8	Sheffield Wednesday	46	15	4	4	39	18	7	5	11	26	37	53
9	Lincoln City	46	12	9	2	50	30	7	5	11	27	40	52
10	Shrewsbury Town	46	13	7	3	40	21	5	4	14	25	38	47
11	Swindon Town	46	12	6	5	48	33	3	9	11	20	42	45
12	GILLINGHAM	46	11	8	4	31	21	5	4	14	24	43	44
13	Chester	46	14	3	6	28	20	4	5	14	20	38	44
14	Tranmere Rovers	46	10	7	6	31	23	3	10	10	20	30	43
15	Walsall	46	8	7	8	39	32	5	8	10	18	33	41
16	Peterborough United	46	11	4	8	33	28	2	11	10	22	37	41
17	Oxford United	46	9	8	6	34	29	3	7	13	21	36	39
18	Chesterfield	46	10	6	7	30	20	4	4	15	26	44	38
19	Port Vale	46	9	7	7	29	28	2	9	12	18	43	38
20	Portsmouth	46	8	9	6	28	26	3	5	15	25	44	36
21	Reading	46	10	5	8	29	24	3	4	16	20	49	35
22	Northampton Town	46	9	4	10	33	29	4	4	15	27	46	34
23	Grimsby Town	46	10	6	7	29	22	2	3	18	16	47	33
24	York City	46	7	8	8	25	34	3	4	16	25	55	32

1977/78

7th in Division Three

	Date		Opponent	Score	Scorers	Att	Armstrong GS	Burrows PA	Buttress MD	Crabbe SAJ	Hillyard RW	Hughes SJ	Hunt PJ	Knight GJ	Nicholl TJ	Overton J	Price KG	Richardson DJ	Shipperley DJ	Walker PJA	Weatherly CM	Westwood DR	Wheatley SJ	Williams NJ	Young CF
1	Aug	20	COLCHESTER UNITED	1-3	Westwood	3450	3				1	12		6	7	4	9	11	5		8	10		2	
2		27	Cambridge United	3-2	Hughes, Westwood 2	3397	3			11	1	6	8		7	4		9	5			10		2	
3	Sep	3	BRADFORD CITY	4-1	Westwood 2, Nicholl, Richardson	3875	3			8	1	4	11		7	6		9	5			10		2	
4		7	Hereford United	0-2		3441	3			11	1	6	8		7	4	12	9	5			10		2	
5		10	OXFORD UNITED	2-1	Richardson (p), Westwood	4381	3				1	6	8	2	7	4	11	9	5			10			
6		13	Bury	2-2	Shipperley, Price	5179	3				1	6	8	2	7	4	9	11	5			10			
7		17	Chester	2-2	Shipperley, Westwood	3594	3				1	6	8	2	7	4	9	11	5			10			
8		24	TRANMERE ROVERS	1-1	Richardson (p)	5007	3				1	6	8	2	7	4	9	11	5			10			
9		27	CHESTERFIELD	3-0	Westwood, Crabbe, Weatherly	5580	3			6	1		8	4	7		9	11	5		12	10		2	
10	Oct	1	Plymouth Argyle	3-1	Richardson 2 (1p), Price	12635	3			6	1		8	4	7		9	11	5		12	10		2	
11		8	ROTHERHAM UNITED	2-1	Price 2	7854				6	1		8	3	7	4	9	11	5			10		2	
12		10	Port Vale	2-2	Price, Crabbe	3418				6	1		8	3	7	4	9	11	5			10		2	
13		15	Preston North End	0-2		7212				6	1	12	8	3	7	4	9	11	5			10		2	
14		22	CARLISLE UNITED	1-1	Westwood	7022		3		6	1		8	2	7	4	9	11	5			10			
15		29	SHREWSBURY TOWN	1-1	Price	7938		3		6	1		8	2	7	4	9	11	5			10			
16	Nov	5	Swindon Town	2-3	Westwood, Overton	7293		3		6	1	12	8	2	7	4	9	11	5			10			
17		12	EXETER CITY	1-0	Price	5714		3		6	1		8	2	7	4	9	11	5		12	10			
18		19	Sheffield Wednesday	0-0		9902		3		6	1		8	2	7	4	9	11	5			10			
19	Dec	3	WALSALL	3-1	Richardson 2 (1p), Westwood	5243				6	1		8	2	7	4	9	11	5			10		3	
20		6	Shrewsbury Town	2-1	Nicholl, Richardson	3149				6	1		8	2	7	4	9	11	5			10		3	
21		10	Lincoln City	2-0	Westwood, Price	3902				6	1		8	3	7	4	9	11	5			10		2	
22		26	PORTSMOUTH	0-0		9723	3			6	1		8	2	7	4	9	11	5		12	10			
23		27	Peterborough United	1-1	Armstrong	10156	3			6	1			2	7	4	9	11	5		8	10			
24		31	SWINDON TOWN	2-2	Westwood, Richardson (p)	7712	3			6	1	12		2	7	4	9	11	5		8	10			
25	Jan	2	Wrexham	3-3	Price 2, Richardson	16281	3			6	1			5	7	4	9	11			8	10		2	
26		7	HEREFORD UNITED	4-0	Price 2, Richardson, Nicholl	6765	3			6	1			5	7	4	9	11			8	10		2	
27		13	Colchester United	1-1	Walker	6447	3			6	1	9	7	5		4		11		12	8	10		2	
28		21	CAMBRIDGE UNITED	3-1	Price 2, Richardson	10541	3			6	1	12		5	7	4	9	11			8	10		2	
29	Feb	4	Oxford United	1-1	Westwood	5002	3			6	1			5	7	4	9	11			8	10		2	
30		21	CHESTER	1-0	Knight	7863	3			6	1	12		5	7	4	9	11			8	10		2	
31		25	PLYMOUTH ARGYLE	1-1	Crabbe	9120	3			6	1	12	8	5	7	4	9	11				10		2	
32	Mar	1	Bradford City	1-2	Westwood	6060	3			6	1	8		5	7	4	9	11		12		10		2	
33		4	Rotherham United	0-2		3731	3			6	1	7		5		4	9	11		12	8	10		2	
34		7	BURY	1-4	Price	8095	3			6	1			5	7	4	9	11			8	10		2	
35		11	PRESTON NORTH END	2-1	Price, Westwood	9568			3	6	1	8		2	7	4	9	11				10			5
36		18	Carlisle United	0-1		5094			3	6	1	8			7	4	9	11			12	10		2	5
37		25	PETERBOROUGH UTD.	0-0		8328	3		2	6	1	8			7	4	9	11				10			5
38		27	Portsmouth	1-1	Weatherly	8108	3			6	1			2	7	4	9	11			8	10			5
39	Apr	1	WREXHAM	0-0		10978	3			6	1			2	7	4	9	11			8	10			5
40		4	PORT VALE	1-1	Price	7627				6	1	3		2	7	4	9	11		12	8	10			5
41		8	Exeter City	1-2	Nicholl	3992			3	6	1	11		2	7	4	9			12	8	10			5
42		11	Tranmere Rovers	1-1	Price	2076			12	6	1	3		5	7	4	9			11	8	10		2	
43		15	SHEFFIELD WEDNESDAY	2-1	Westwood, Young	7238				6	1	3		2	7	4	9	11		8	12	10			5
44		22	Walsall	1-2	Overton	4707	12			6		3		2	8	4	9	11		7		10	1		5
45		26	Chesterfield	2-5	Price, Crabbe	2748			3	6		11		2	8	4	9	10		7	12		1		5
46		29	LINCOLN CITY	0-0		5481	3			6	1	11		2	8	4	9			7	12	10			5

	Armstrong GS	Burrows PA	Buttress MD	Crabbe SAJ	Hillyard RW	Hughes SJ	Hunt PJ	Knight GJ	Nicholl TJ	Overton J	Price KG	Richardson DJ	Shipperley DJ	Walker PJA	Weatherly CM	Westwood DR	Wheatley SJ	Williams NJ	Young CF
Apps	28	5	6	41	44	27	23	41	44	44	43	43	24	10	24	45	2	24	11
Goals	1			4		1		1	4	2	19	12	2	1	2	17			1

F.A. Cup

	Date		Opponent	Score	Scorers	Att	Armstrong GS	Burrows PA	Buttress MD	Crabbe SAJ	Hillyard RW	Hughes SJ	Hunt PJ	Knight GJ	Nicholl TJ	Overton J	Price KG	Richardson DJ	Shipperley DJ	Walker PJA	Weatherly CM	Westwood DR	Wheatley SJ	Williams NJ	Young CF
R1	Nov	26	WEYMOUTH	1-1	Westwood	5834	3			6	1		8	2	7	4	9	11	5		12	10			
rep		30	Weymouth	1-0	Shipperley	2704				6	1		8	2	7	4	9	11	5		12	10		3	
R2	Dec	17	PETERBROUGH UTD.	1-1	Nicholl	10181				6	1		8	2	7	4	9	11	5		12	10		3	
rep		20	Peterborough United	0-2		8542				6	1		8	2	7	4	9	11	5		12	10		3	

F.L. Cup

	Date		Opponent	Score	Scorers	Att	Armstrong GS	Burrows PA	Buttress MD	Crabbe SAJ	Hillyard RW	Hughes SJ	Hunt PJ	Knight GJ	Nicholl TJ	Overton J	Price KG	Richardson DJ	Shipperley DJ	Walker PJA	Weatherly CM	Westwood DR	Wheatley SJ	Williams NJ	Young CF
R1/1	Aug	13	WIMBLEDON	1-1	Westwood	4782	3			8	1	6			7	4	9	11	5			10		2	
R1/2		16	Wimbledon	1-3	Price	3868	3			8	1	6			7	4	9	11	5		12	10		2	

		P	*W*	*D*	*L*	*F*	*A*	*W*	*D*	*L*	*F*	*A*	*Pts*
1	Wrexham	46	14	8	1	48	19	9	7	7	30	26	61
2	Cambridge United	46	19	3	1	49	11	4	9	10	23	40	58
3	Preston North End	46	16	5	2	48	19	4	11	8	15	19	56
4	Peterborough United	46	15	7	1	32	11	5	9	9	15	22	56
5	Chester	46	14	8	1	41	24	2	14	7	18	32	54
6	Walsall	46	12	8	3	35	17	6	9	8	26	33	53
7	GILLINGHAM	46	11	10	2	36	21	4	10	9	31	39	50
8	Colchester United	46	10	11	2	36	16	5	7	11	19	28	48
9	Chesterfield	46	14	6	3	40	16	3	8	12	18	33	48
10	Swindon Town	46	12	7	4	40	22	4	9	10	27	38	48
11	Shrewsbury Town	46	11	7	5	42	23	5	8	10	21	34	47
12	Tranmere Rovers	46	13	7	3	39	19	3	8	12	18	33	47
13	Carlisle United	46	10	9	4	32	26	4	10	9	27	33	47
14	Sheffield Wednesday	46	13	7	3	28	14	2	9	12	22	38	46
15	Bury	46	7	13	3	34	22	6	6	11	28	34	45
16	Lincoln City	46	10	8	5	35	26	5	7	11	18	35	45
17	Exeter City	46	11	8	4	30	18	4	6	13	19	41	44
18	Oxford United	46	11	10	2	38	21	2	4	17	26	46	40
19	Plymouth Argyle	46	7	8	8	33	28	4	9	10	28	40	39
20	Rotherham United	46	11	5	7	26	19	2	8	13	25	49	39
21	Port Vale	46	7	11	5	28	23	1	9	13	18	44	36
22	Bradford City	46	11	6	6	40	29	1	4	18	16	57	34
23	Hereford United	46	9	9	5	28	22	0	5	18	6	38	32
24	Portsmouth	46	4	11	8	31	38	3	6	14	10	37	31

1978/79

4th in Division Three

No	Date	Opponent	Score	Scorers	Att	Armstrong GS	Barker AM	Buttress MD	Crabbe SAJ	Funnell A	Hillyard RW	Hughes SJ	Jolley TA	Knight GI	Nicholl TJ	Overton J	Price KG	Richardson DJ	Sharpe JWH	Walker PJA	Weatherly CM	Westwood DR	White D	Williams NJ	Young CF
1	Aug 19	ROTHERHAM UNITED	0-0		4157	3			6		1			2	7	4	9	11		12	8	10			5
2	21	Mansfield Town	1-1	Price	5802	3			6		1			2	7	4	9	10		11	8	12	5		
3	26	Bury	2-2	Weatherly, Nicholl	3414	3			6		1	2			7	4	9	10		11	8	12	5		
4	Sep 2	WATFORD	2-3	Overton, Westwood	8248	3			6		1				7	4	9	11		12	8	10	5	2	
5	9	Tranmere Rovers	1-1	Price	1589				6		1			3		4	9	11	2	7	8	10	5		
6	12	SHEFFIELD WEDNESDAY	0-0		5835	3			6		1	7				4	9	11	2	12	8	10	5		
7	16	CHESTER	1-0	Richardson	4743			12	6		1	3			7		9	11	2	8	4	10	5		
8	23	Brentford	2-0	Price, Hughes	6977	3			6		1	8			7		9	11	2		4	10	5		
9	26	Blackpool	0-2		5772	3			6		1	8			7		9	11	2	12	4	10	5		
10	30	CHESTERFIELD	2-1	Westwood, Richardson	4596	3			6		1	8			7	4	9	11	2		5	10			
11	Oct 7	Exeter City	0-0		4241	3			6		1	8			7	4	9	11	2		5	10			
12	14	HULL CITY	2-0	Crabbe (p), Jolley	5460	3			6		1	8	12		7	4	9	11	2		5	10			
13	17	LINCOLN CITY	4-2	Westwood 2, Jolley, Hughes	5783				3		1	8	6		7	4	9	11	2		5	10			
14	21	Peterborough United	1-1	Nicholl	5001	3			6		1	8			7	4	9	11	2		5	10			
15	28	Oxford United	1-1	Price	4668	3			6		1	8			7	4	9	11	2		5	10			
16	Nov 4	SWANSEA CITY	2-0	Price, Crabbe (p)	11329	3			6		1	8			7	4	9	11	2		5	10			
17	11	Watford	0-1		13941	3			6		1	8	12		7	4	9	11	2		5	10			
18	18	BURY	3-3	Jolley 2, Richardson	6291				3		1	8	6		7	4	9	11	2		5	10			
19	Dec 2	CARLISLE UNITED	0-0		4325	3			6		1	8			7	4	9	11	2	12	5	10			
20	9	Shrewsbury Town	1-1	Westwood	3924	3			6		1	8			7	4		11	2		5	10	9		
21	26	SOUTHEND UNITED	1-0	Jolley	6644	3			6		1	8	9		7	4		11	2		5	10			
22	30	PLYMOUTH ARGYLE	2-0	Nicholl, Westwood	5951	3			6		1	8	9		7	4		11	2		5	10			
23	Jan 13	TRANMERE ROVERS	3-2	Price, Westwood (p), Nicholl	5480	3			6		1	8	9		7	4	12	11	2		5	10			
24	27	BRENTFORD	0-0		6899		3		6		1	8	11		7	4	9		2	12	5	10			
25	Feb 3	BLACKPOOL	2-0	Westwood 2 (1p)	6146		3		6		1	8	11		7	4	9		2		5	10			
26	21	Chester	1-1	Barker	2617		3		6		1	8			7	4	9	11	2		5	10			
27	24	Hull City	1-0	Price	4345		3		6		1				7	4	9	11	2		5	10	8		
28	Mar 3	PETERBOROUGH UTD.	1-0	Richardson	6890		3		6		1				7	4	9	11	2		5	10	8		
29	6	Sheffield Wednesday	1-2	Westwood	8349		3		6		1	12			7	4	9	11	2		5	10	8		
30	10	OXFORD UNITED	2-1	Overton, Weatherly	6065		3		6		1	8	11		7	4	9		2		5	10			
31	16	Swansea City	1-3	White (p)	10832		3		6		1	8	12		7	4	9		2		5	10	11		
32	20	Walsall	1-0	Westwood	3084		3		6		1	8			7	4	9		2		5	10	11		
33	24	MANSFIELD TOWN	0-0		6935		3		6		1	12	11		7	4	9		2		5	10	8		
34	27	Rotherham United	1-1	Westwood	3239	12	3		6		1	8			7	4	9		2		5	10	11		
35	31	SWINDON TOWN	2-2	White, Westwood	9460		3			11	1	6			7	4	9				5	10	8		2
36	Apr 7	Carlisle United	0-1		5093	11	3			8	1	6	12		7	4	9		2		5		10		
37	10	WALSALL	3-1	White (p), Price 2	7342	3				11	1	6			7	4	9		2		5	10	8		
38	14	Southend United	1-0	Westwood	7579		3			11	1	6			7	4	9		2		5	10	8		
39	16	COLCHESTER UNITED	3-0	Price, Westwood, Funnell	12030		3			11	1	6			7	4	9		2		5	10	8		
40	21	Plymouth Argyle	1-2	Funnell	5868		3			11	1	6			7	4	9		2		5	10	8		
41	25	Lincoln City	4-2	Funnell 2, Westwood, Price	1864		3			11	1	6			7	4	9		2		5	10	8		
42	28	SHREWSBURY TOWN	2-0	Price 2	14902		3			11	1	6			7	4	9				5	10	8		2
43	May 5	Swindon Town	1-3	Funnell	15357	12	3			11	1	6			7	4	9		2		5	10	8		
44	7	Colchester United	2-2	Armstrong, Westwood	6317	7	3			11	1	6				4	9				5	10	8		2
45	14	EXETER CITY	2-0	Price, Funnell	8788	8	3			11	1	6			7	4	9				5	10	12		2
46	19	Chesterfield	2-0	Westwood, Funnell	2802	8	3			11	1	6			7	4		9			5	10			2
					Apps	26	22	1	34	12	46	40	13	3	43	43	42	28	37	10	46	45	27	1	6
					Goals	1	1		2	7		2	5		4	2	14	4			2	18	3		

F.A. Cup

Rd	Date	Opponent	Score	Scorers	Att	Armstrong GS	Barker AM	Buttress MD	Crabbe SAJ	Funnell A	Hillyard RW	Hughes SJ	Jolley TA	Knight GI	Nicholl TJ	Overton J	Price KG	Richardson DJ	Sharpe JWH	Walker PJA	Weatherly CM	Westwood DR	White D	Williams NJ	Young CF
R1	Nov 25	Reading	0-0		6910	3			6		1	8			7	4	9	11	2		5	10			
rep	28	READING	1-2	(aet) Westwood	6441				6		1	3	8		7	4	9	11	2		5	10	12		

F.L. Cup

Rd	Date	Opponent	Score	Scorers	Att	Armstrong GS	Barker AM	Buttress MD	Crabbe SAJ	Funnell A	Hillyard RW	Hughes SJ	Jolley TA	Knight GI	Nicholl TJ	Overton J	Price KG	Richardson DJ	Sharpe JWH	Walker PJA	Weatherly CM	Westwood DR	White D	Williams NJ	Young CF
R1/1	Aug 12	Reading	1-3	Price	3246	3			6		1	12		2		4	9	11			8	10			5
R1/2	15	READING	1-2	Young	5184	3			6		1	12		2	7	4	9	11			8	10			5

Played at 7 in R1: PJ Hunt (subbed)

	Team	P	W	D	L	F	A	W	D	L	F	A	Pts
1	Shrewsbury Town	46	14	9	0	36	11	7	10	6	25	30	61
2	Watford	46	15	5	3	47	22	9	7	7	36	30	60
3	Swansea City	46	16	6	1	57	32	8	6	9	26	29	60
4	GILLINGHAM	46	15	7	1	39	15	6	10	7	26	27	59
5	Swindon Town	46	17	2	4	44	14	8	5	10	30	38	57
6	Carlisle United	46	11	10	2	31	13	4	12	7	22	29	52
7	Colchester United	46	13	9	1	35	19	4	8	11	25	36	51
8	Hull City	46	12	9	2	36	14	7	2	14	30	47	49
9	Exeter City	46	14	6	3	38	18	3	9	11	23	38	49
10	Brentford	46	14	4	5	35	19	5	5	13	18	30	47
11	Oxford United	46	10	8	5	27	20	4	10	9	17	30	46
12	Blackpool	46	12	5	6	38	19	6	4	13	23	40	45
13	Southend United	46	11	6	6	30	17	4	9	10	21	32	45
14	Sheffield Wednesday	46	9	8	6	30	22	4	11	8	23	31	45
15	Plymouth Argyle	46	11	9	3	40	27	4	5	14	27	41	44
16	Chester	46	11	9	3	42	21	3	7	13	15	40	44
17	Rotherham United	46	13	3	7	30	23	4	7	12	19	32	44
18	Mansfield Town	46	7	11	5	30	24	5	8	10	21	28	43
19	Bury	46	6	11	6	35	32	5	9	9	24	33	42
20	Chesterfield	46	10	5	8	35	34	3	9	11	16	31	40
21	Peterborough United	46	8	7	8	26	24	3	7	13	18	39	36
22	Walsall	46	7	6	10	34	32	3	6	14	22	39	32
23	Tranmere Rovers	46	4	12	7	26	31	2	4	17	19	47	28
24	Lincoln City	46	5	7	11	26	38	2	4	17	15	50	25

1979/80

16th in Division Three

	Date		Opponent	Score	Scorers	Att	Adams MR	Armstrong GS	Barker AM	Bottiglieri A	Bruce SR	Crabbe SAJ	Duncan CJ	Ford C	Funnell A	Hillyard RW	Hughes SJ	Jolley TA	Nicholl TJ	Overton J	Price KG	Richardson DJ	Sharpe JWH	Walker PJA	Weatherly CM	Westwood DR	White D	Young CF
1	Aug	18	Blackpool	1-2	Westwood	5253			3		8	6			9	1	12		7	4		11			5	10		2
2		25	MILLWALL	1-1	Price	8769			3		8	6			10	1			7	4	9	11	2		5	12		
3	Sep	1	Reading	3-1	Price 2, Westwood	6406			3		8	6			10	1			7	4	9	11	2		5	12		
4		8	Carlisle United	2-1	Price, Bruce	3412			3		8	6			10	1			7	4	9	11	2		5			
5		15	CHESTER	2-2	Price 2	7397			3		8	6			10	1			7	4	9	11	2		5	12		
6		18	WIMBLEDON	1-0	Crabbe	8074			3		8	6			10	1			7	4	9	11	2		5			
7		22	Hull City	0-0		6142			3		8	6			10	1			7	4	9	11	2		5			
8		29	EXETER CITY	1-0	Funnell	7538			3		8	6			10	1			7	4	9	11	2			12		5
9	Oct	6	BLACKBURN ROVERS	1-2	Funnell	7851			3		8	6			11	1		12	7	4	9		2		5	10		
10		13	Barnsley	0-2		9132			3		8	6			10	1	12		7	4	9	11	2		5			
11		20	GRIMSBY TOWN	0-1		6378			3		8	6			12	1	7			4	9	11	2		5	10		
12		23	OXFORD UNITED	4-0	Westwood 2, Barker (p), Bruce	5094			3		8	6				1			7	4	9	11	2		5	10		
13		27	Mansfield Town	0-2		4598			3		8	6			12	1			7	4	9	11	2		5	10		
14		29	Southend United	3-0	Westwood, Bruce, Crabbe	4704			3		8	6			11	1			7	4		9	2		5	10		
15	Nov	3	BLACKPOOL	1-1	Sharpe	6517			3		8	6				1			7	4	9	11	2		5	10		
16		7	Oxford United	1-1	Nicholl	4430			3		4	6				1	8		7		9	11	2		5	10		
17		10	Sheffield United	0-4		14329			3		8	6				1	12		7	4	9	11	2		5	10		
18		13	SOUTHEND UNITED	1-0	Price	5286		3			8	6			12	1			7	4	9	11			5	10		2
19		17	BURY	2-1	Price, Funnell	5731			3			6			12	1			7	4	9	11			5	10	8	2
20	Dec	1	SWINDON TOWN	0-0		8029			3		8	6			11	1	7			4	9	12			5	10	2	
21		8	Rotherham United	1-2	Price	4648			3		8	6			11	1	7			4	9	12			5	10	2	
22		26	Colchester United	2-2	Overton, Westwood	5145			3		2	6			11	1	8		7	4	9				5	10		
23		29	Millwall	0-2		6913			3		2	6			11	1	8		7	4	9	12			5	10		
24	Jan	5	Brentford	2-0	Price, Westwood	7849			3		4	6				1	8	11	7		9		2		5	10		
25		12	READING	1-1	Weatherly	6238			3			6				1	8		7	4	9		2	11	5	10		
26		19	CARLISLE UNITED	1-1	Westwood	5106			3			6				1	8	11	7	4	9	12	2		5	10		
27		26	Plymouth Argyle	2-2	Hughes, Price	6413			3		10	6		2		1	8		7	4	9	11		12	5			
28	Feb	12	Wimbledon	0-1		3697			3		4	6	10		12	1	8		7		9	11	2		5			
29		16	Exeter City	1-3	Price	3427			3		4	6	10		12	1			7		9	11	2	8	5			
30		23	BARNSLEY	1-1	Walker	5800			3		4	6	8			1		12	7		10	11	2	9	5			
31		26	CHESTERFIELD	0-1		4726					4	6	11			1	8			3	9	12	2	7	5	10		
32	Mar	1	Grimsby Town	0-1		11502			3		8	6	7			1	10			4	9	11	2		5			
33		4	HULL CITY	1-0	Duncan	4161			3		7	6	10			1	8			4	9	11	2		5	12		
34		8	MANSFIELD TOWN	2-0	Overton, Richardson	4572			3	12	7	6	8			1				4	9	11	2		5	10		
35		14	Blackburn Rovers	1-3	Bruce	11636			3		7	6	10			1				4	9	11	2	8	5	12		
36		18	SHEFFIELD WEDNESDAY	1-1	Walker	6717			3		7	6	10			1				4		11	2	8	5	9		
37		22	SHEFFIELD UNITED	3-0	Westwood 2, Bruce	7076			3		7	6	8			1				4	9	11	2		5	10		
38		29	Bury	2-0	White 2	2764			3			6	8			1				4	9	11			5	10	7	2
39	Apr	1	Chesterfield	0-0		8952			3			6	8			1				4	9	11			5	10	7	2
40		5	COLCHESTER UNITED	2-2	Price, Bruce	6561			3		7	6	8			1				4	9	11	2		5	10		
41		7	Sheffield Wednesday	0-1		22920			3		7	6	8			1				4	9	11	2		5	10		
42		12	BRENTFORD	0-1		5889			3		7	6	8			1				4	9	11	2		5	10	12	
43		19	Swindon Town	0-3		9367	12		3		7	6	8			1				4	9	11	2		5	10		
44		26	ROTHERHAM UNITED	0-1		3479	10		3			6	8			1		12		4	9	11	2		5		7	
45		30	Chester	2-0	White, Crabbe	2187	11				4	6	8			1		10		3		9	2		5		7	
46	May	3	PLYMOUTH ARGYLE	0-1		4020	11				4	6	8			1		10		3		9	2	12	5		7	
						Apps	4	1	42	1	40	46	19	1	21	46	17	7	27	41	41	42	36	8	45	34	9	6
						Goals			1		6	3	1		3		1		1	2	13	1	1	2	1	10	3	

F.A. Cup

	Date		Opponent	Score	Scorers	Att	Adams MR	Armstrong GS	Barker AM	Bottiglieri A	Bruce SR	Crabbe SAJ	Duncan CJ	Ford C	Funnell A	Hillyard RW	Hughes SJ	Jolley TA	Nicholl TJ	Overton J	Price KG	Richardson DJ	Sharpe JWH	Walker PJA	Weatherly CM	Westwood DR	White D	Young CF
R1	Nov	24	WIMBLEDON	0-0		7027			3			6			12	1			7	4	9	11			5	10	8	2
rep		27	Wimbledon	2-4	Price 2	4612			3			6			12	1			7	4	9	11			5	10	8	2

F.L. Cup

	Date		Opponent	Score	Scorers	Att	Adams MR	Armstrong GS	Barker AM	Bottiglieri A	Bruce SR	Crabbe SAJ	Duncan CJ	Ford C	Funnell A	Hillyard RW	Hughes SJ	Jolley TA	Nicholl TJ	Overton J	Price KG	Richardson DJ	Sharpe JWH	Walker PJA	Weatherly CM	Westwood DR	White D	Young CF
R1/1	Aug	11	LUTON TOWN	3-0	Price 2, Barker (p)	6222			3		8	6			12	1			7	4	9	11	2		5	10		
R1/2		14	Luton Town	1-1	Crabbe	5509			3		8	6				1			7	4	9	11			5	10		2
R2/1		28	NORWICH CITY	1-1	Overton	10594			3		8	6			10	1			7	4	9	11	2		5			
R2/2	Sep	5	Norwich City	2-4	Bruce 2	10656			3		8	6			10	1			7	4	9	11	2		5	12		

		P	W	D	L	F	A	W	D	L	F	A	Pts
1	Grimsby Town	46	18	2	3	46	16	8	8	7	27	26	62
2	Blackburn Rovers	46	13	5	5	34	17	12	4	7	24	19	59
3	Sheffield Wednesday	46	12	6	5	44	20	9	10	4	37	27	58
4	Chesterfield	46	16	5	2	46	16	7	6	10	25	30	57
5	Colchester United	46	10	10	3	39	20	10	2	11	25	36	52
6	Carlisle United	46	13	6	4	45	26	5	6	12	21	30	48
7	Reading	46	14	6	3	43	19	2	10	11	23	46	48
8	Exeter City	46	14	5	4	38	22	5	5	13	22	46	48
9	Chester	46	14	6	3	29	18	3	7	13	20	39	47
10	Swindon Town	46	15	4	4	50	20	4	4	15	21	43	46
11	Barnsley	46	10	7	6	29	20	6	7	10	24	36	46
12	Sheffield United	46	13	5	5	35	21	5	5	13	25	45	46
13	Rotherham United	46	13	4	6	38	24	5	6	12	20	42	46
14	Millwall	46	14	6	3	49	23	2	7	14	16	36	45
15	Plymouth Argyle	46	13	7	3	39	17	3	5	15	20	38	44
16	GILLINGHAM	46	8	9	6	26	18	6	5	12	23	33	42
17	Oxford United	46	10	4	9	34	24	4	9	10	23	38	41
18	Blackpool	46	10	7	6	39	34	5	4	14	23	40	41
19	Brentford	46	10	6	7	33	26	5	5	13	26	47	41
20	Hull City	46	11	7	5	29	21	1	9	13	22	48	40
21	Bury	46	10	4	9	30	23	6	3	14	15	36	39
22	Southend United	46	11	6	6	33	23	3	4	16	14	35	38
23	Mansfield Town	46	9	9	5	31	24	1	7	15	16	34	36
24	Wimbledon	46	6	8	9	34	38	4	6	13	18	43	34

1980/81

15th in Division Three

No		Date	Opponent	Result	Scorers	Att	Adams MR	Bottiglieri A	Bruce SR	Crabbe SAJ	Donn AN	Duncan CJ	Ford AC	Henderson P	Hillyard RW	Hughes SJ	Lee TC	Lloyd KJJ	Nicholl TJ	Overton J	Price KG	Richardson DJ	Sharpe JWH	Sutton G	Walker PJA	Weatherly CM	Westwood DR	White D	Young CF
1	Aug	16	Exeter City	1-2	Ford	3630			11	6	7	8	3	10	1					4	9		2		12	5			
2		19	READING	2-0	Henderson, Richardson	5193	11		7	6		8	3	10	1					4		9	2			5			
3		23	BARNSLEY	1-1	Henderson	5222	11		7	6		8	3	10	1					4		9	2		12	5			
4		30	Chesterfield	0-2		5535			5	6		8	3	10	1	12				4		11	2				9	7	
5	Sep	6	NEWPORT COUNTY	3-2	Hughes, Price, Richardson	4712	11		7			8	3	10	1	6				4	9		2		12	5			
6		13	Carlisle United	0-0		2961	11		7			8	3	10	1	6				4	9		2			5	12		
7		16	HUDDERSFIELD T	0-0		5092	11		7			8	3	12	1	6				4	9	10	2			5			
8		20	Plymouth Argyle	1-4	Price	6719		12	7		11	8	3		1	6				4	9				2	5	10		
9		27	OXFORD UNITED	1-1	Richardson	4137			7	6		8	3		1	11				4	9	12			2	5	10		
10		30	Huddersfield Town	0-1		7716			7	6		8	3		1	11				4	9	10			2	5			
11	Oct	4	Blackpool	0-4		6588			7	6		8	3		1	11				4		9	2		12	5	10		
12		7	SWINDON TOWN	0-0		4066			7				3		1	10			8	4	9		2		11	5		6	
13		11	FULHAM	1-0	Westwood	4730			4	6			3		1	11			8		9				2	5	10	7	
14		18	Rotherham United	0-2		5903			4	6			3		1	11			8		9		2			5	10	7	
15		20	Brentford	3-3	Price 2, Westwood	6786			4	6			3		1	11			8	5	9		2				10	7	
16		25	HULL CITY	2-0	Bruce, Westwood	4100			4	6			3		1	11			8		9		2			5	10	7	
17		28	SHEFFIELD UNITED	2-2	Bruce, Westwood	4976			4	6			3		1	11			8		9		2			5	10	7	
18	Nov	1	Walsall	3-3	Nicholl, Westwood, Price	4060				6			3		1	11			8	4	9		2			5	10	7	
19		4	Swindon Town	0-0		4965				6			3		1	11			8	4	9		2			5	10	7	
20		8	PORTSMOUTH	0-1		6623				6			3		1	11			8	4	9		2			5	10	7	
21		12	Reading	1-0	Hughes	4876			4	6			3		1	11			8		9		2			5	10	7	
22		15	EXETER CITY	1-5	Westwood	3725			4			6	3		1	11		12	8		9		2			5	10	7	
23		29	Burnley	2-3	White, Nicholl	5797		10		6		8	3		1	12			7	4	9		2			5		11	
24	Dec	6	CHARLTON ATHLETIC	0-1		8775		8		6			3		1				7	4	9		2			5	10	11	
25		20	Chester	2-1	Crabbe, Price	1934			12	6			3		1	8			7	4	9		2			5	10	11	
26		26	MILLWALL	1-2	Weatherly	4603	11	10	8	6			3		1				7	4	9	12	2			5			
27		27	Colchester United	1-2	Price	3879			4	6		8	3						7		9	10	2	1		5		11	
28	Jan	3	ROTHERHAM UNITED	0-0		3748			4	6			3			8			7			9		1	2	5	10	11	
29		17	Sheffield United	1-0	Ford (p)	8778			4	6		8	3				10		7		9		2	1		5		11	
30		24	CHESTERFIELD	1-0	Bruce	5022			4	6		8	3		1		10		7		9	12			2	5		11	
31		31	Barnsley	3-3	White, Lee, Price	13703			4	6		8	3		1		10		7		9				2	5		11	
32	Feb	7	CARLISLE UNITED	0-1		4927	12		4	6		8	3				10		7		9	11		1	2	5			
33		14	Newport County	1-1	Lee	5227			4	6		8	3				11		7		10			1	2	5		9	
34		21	Oxford United	1-1	Lee	3877			4	6		8	3				10		7		9			1	2	5		11	
35		28	PLYMOUTH ARGYLE	0-1		4396	11		4			8	3				10		7		9	12		1	2	5		6	
36	Mar	7	BLACKPOOL	3-1	White 2, Price	3424			4	6		8	3				10		7		9			1	2	5		11	
37		14	Fulham	2-3	Price, Ford	5445	12		4	6		8	3				10		7		9			1	2	5		11	
38		21	BRENTFORD	2-0	Overton, White (p)	3916			4	6		8			1		10		7	3	9				2	5		11	
39		28	Hull City	2-2	Lee 2	3309			4	6		8			1	12	10		7	3	9				2	5		11	
40	Apr	3	WALSALL	1-0	Price	4112			4	6		8	3		1		10		7		9		2			5		11	
41		7	BURNLEY	0-0		4412			4	6		8			1		10		7	3	9					5		11	2
42		11	Portsmouth	0-0		9172			4	6		8	3		1		10		7	5	9							11	2
43		18	COLCHESTER UNITED	0-0		4408	12		4	6		8			1		10		7	3	9					5		11	2
44		20	Millwall	0-0		4214	6		4			8	3		1		10		7		9				2	5		11	
45		25	CHESTER	2-1	Bruce, Raynor (og)	3228	6		4			8	3		1		10		7		9				2	5		11	
46	May	2	Charlton Athletic	1-2	Lee	9367	6		4			8	3		1		10				9		2		7	5		11	
						Apps	13	4	41	36	2	32	42	7	37	23	18	1	34	25	41	13	26	9	23	43	18	34	3
						Goals			4	1			3	3		2	6		2	1	11	2				1	6	5	

One own goal

F.A. Cup

Rd		Date	Opponent	Result	Scorers	Att	Adams MR	Bottiglieri A	Bruce SR	Crabbe SAJ	Donn AN	Duncan CJ	Ford AC	Henderson P	Hillyard RW	Hughes SJ	Lee TC	Lloyd KJJ	Nicholl TJ	Overton J	Price KG	Richardson DJ	Sharpe JWH	Sutton G	Walker PJA	Weatherly CM	Westwood DR	White D	Young CF
R1	Nov	22	DAGENHAM	2-1	Price, Ford	4390		10		6		8	3		1				7	4	9		2		11	5			
R2	Dec	13	MAIDSTONE UNITED	0-0		9009		8		6			3		1	12			7	4	9		2			5	10	11	
rep		16	Maidstone United	0-0	(aet)	7465				6			3		1	8			7	4	9		2			5	10	11	
rep2		22	MAIDSTONE UNITED	0-2		7941			4	6			3		1	8		12	7	5	9		2				10	11	

F.L. Cup

Rd		Date	Opponent	Result	Scorers	Att	Adams MR	Bottiglieri A	Bruce SR	Crabbe SAJ	Donn AN	Duncan CJ	Ford AC	Henderson P	Hillyard RW	Hughes SJ	Lee TC	Lloyd KJJ	Nicholl TJ	Overton J	Price KG	Richardson DJ	Sharpe JWH	Sutton G	Walker PJA	Weatherly CM	Westwood DR	White D	Young CF
R1/1	Aug	9	Colchester United	2-0	Price, Bruce	2514			11		7	8	3	10	1	6				4	9		2			5			
R1/2		12	COLCHESTER UNITED	2-1	Ford, Bruce	5220			11	6	7	8	3	10	1					4	9		2			5			
R2/1		27	Blackburn Rovers	0-0		7316			7	6		8	3	10	1					4		11	2			5	9	12	
R2/2	Sep	2	BLACKBURN ROVERS	1-2	(aet) Bruce	6315	11		7			8	3	10	1	6				4	9		2			5	12		

		P	W	D	L	F	A	W	D	L	F	A	Pts
1	Rotherham United	46	17	6	0	43	8	7	7	9	19	24	61
2	Barnsley	46	15	5	3	46	19	6	12	5	26	26	59
3	Charlton Athletic	46	14	6	3	36	17	11	3	9	27	27	59
4	Huddersfield Town	46	14	6	3	40	11	7	8	8	31	29	56
5	Chesterfield	46	17	4	2	42	16	6	6	11	30	32	56
6	Portsmouth	46	14	5	4	35	19	8	4	11	20	28	53
7	Plymouth Argyle	46	14	5	4	35	18	5	9	9	21	26	52
8	Burnley	46	13	5	5	37	21	5	9	9	23	27	50
9	Brentford	46	7	9	7	30	25	7	10	6	22	24	47
10	Reading	46	13	5	5	39	22	5	5	13	23	40	46
11	Exeter City	46	9	9	5	36	30	7	4	12	26	36	45
12	Newport County	46	11	6	6	38	22	4	7	12	26	39	43
13	Fulham	46	8	7	8	28	29	7	6	10	29	35	43
14	Oxford United	46	7	8	8	20	24	6	9	8	19	23	43
15	GILLINGHAM	46	9	8	6	23	19	3	10	10	25	39	42
16	Millwall	46	10	9	4	30	21	4	5	14	13	39	42
17	Swindon Town	46	10	6	7	35	27	3	9	11	16	29	41
18	Chester	46	11	5	7	25	17	4	6	13	13	31	41
19	Carlisle United	46	8	9	6	32	29	6	4	13	24	41	41
20	Walsall	46	8	9	6	43	43	5	6	12	16	31	41
21	Sheffield United	46	12	6	5	38	20	2	6	15	27	43	40
22	Colchester United	46	12	7	4	35	22	2	4	17	10	43	39
23	Blackpool	46	5	9	9	19	28	4	5	14	26	47	32
24	Hull City	46	7	8	8	23	22	1	8	14	17	49	32

1981/82

6th in Division Three

							Adams MR	Bottiglieri A	Bowman RD	Bruce SR	Cascarino AG	Donn AN	Duncan CJ	Ford AC	Grewcock N	Hillyard RW	Kemp DM	Lee TC	Miller MJ	Ovard FC	Powell CD	Price KG	Sage M	Sharpe JWH	Shaw PK	Sitton JE	Sutton G	Tydeman R	Weatherly CM	Westwood DR	White D	Young CF
1	Aug	29	BURNLEY	3-1	Price, Laws (og), Lee	4663			6	4			8	3				10			7	11		2			1	9	5		12	
2	Sep	5	Reading	2-3	Lee, Price	3731	12		6	4			8	3				10			7	11					1	9	5			2
3		12	CHESTER	0-1		3990			6	4			8	3		1		10			7	11		2				9	5		12	
4		19	Preston North End	1-1	Westwood	4565			6	4			8	3		1					7	11				2		9	5	10		
5		21	Brentford	1-0	Tydeman	5425	12		6	4			8	3		1					7	11				2		9	5	10		
6		26	EXETER CITY	2-3	Bowman, Price	4158			6	4			8	3		1		12			7	11				2		9	5	10		
7		29	BRISTOL CITY	1-1	Price	3887	7		6	4			8	3		1		10				11		12		2		9	5			
8	Oct	3	Wimbledon	2-0	Bowman 2 (1p)	2510			6	4			8	3		1		10				11				2		9	5		7	
9		10	Plymouth Argyle	2-1	Lee, Bowman	3094	9		6	4			8	3		1		10				11				2			5		7	
10		17	HUDDERSFIELD T	3-2	Price, Bruce, Willis	4432			6	4			8	3		1		10			7	11		12		2			5		9	
11		20	PORTSMOUTH	4-2	Bowman (p), White 2, Price	5546			6	4			8	3		1		10			7	11		2					5		9	
12		24	Millwall	2-1	White 2	5765			6	4			8	3		1		10			7	11		2					5		9	
13		31	SWINDON TOWN	1-0	White	8410			6	4			8	3		1		10			7	11		2					5		9	
14	Nov	2	Southend United	0-3		6235			6	4			8	3		1		10		12	7	11		2					5		9	
15		7	Bristol Rovers	0-2		5518			6	4			8	3		1		10			7	11		2				12	5		9	
16		14	DONCASTER ROVERS	3-0	Lee, White 2	8189			6	4				3		1		10			7	11		2				8	5		9	
17		28	Carlisle United	0-2		4196		10	6	4			12	3		1					7	11		2				8	5		9	
18	Dec	5	WALSALL	1-4	White (p)	5845			6	4				3		1		10		12	7	11		2				8	5		9	
19		28	NEWPORT COUNTY	1-1	Kemp	6055				4			8	3		1	10				7	11		2				6	5		9	
20	Jan	16	Lincoln City	0-2		2796	3			4			6			1	10			7		11		2		5		8			9	12
21		30	PRESTON NORTH END	0-2		5379	3			4		12	6			1	10	8			7	11		2		5					9	
22	Feb	2	Burnley	0-1		5848	3	12		4	11		8	6		1	10				7			2		5					9	
23		6	Chester	0-0		1707	3			4	11		6			1	10		7					2		5		8			9	
24		9	BRENTFORD	1-1	White	3931	3			4	12		6			1	10		7			11		2		5		8			9	
25		13	WIMBLEDON	6-1	* see below	4214	3			4	12		6			1	10				7	11		2		5		8			9	
26		20	Exeter City	1-1	Duncan	2888	3			4	12		6			1	10		9		7	11		2	5			8				
27		27	PLYMOUTH ARGYLE	3-2	Bruce, Cascarino, Kemp	4835	3			4	12		6			1	10		9		7	11		2	5			8				
28	Mar	6	Huddersfield Town	0-2		5338	3	6		4	10					1					7	11		2	5	12		8			9	
29		9	Portsmouth	0-1		6711	3	12		4	10					1				7		11		2	5	6		8			9	
30		12	MILLWALL	1-1	Cascarino	5508	3			4	10					1				7		11		2	5	6		8			9	
31		16	SOUTHEND UNITED	2-0	Bruce, Price	3784	3			4	10					1				7		11		2	5	6		8	12		9	
32		20	Swindon Town	1-0	Adams	5149	3			4	10					1						11		2	6	7		8	5		9	
33		27	BRISTOL ROVERS	2-0	White (p), Price	5100	3			4	10					1						11		2	6	7		8	5		9	
34		31	Oxford United	1-1	Adams	5406	3			4	10				12	1						11		2	6	7		8	5		9	
35	Apr	3	Doncaster Rovers	1-1	Sitton	3902	3			4	12				10	1		9			7	11		2		6		8	5			
36		6	CHESTERFIELD	3-2	Sitton, Lee 2	5111	3			4	10				9	1		12			7	11		2		6		8	5			
37		10	FULHAM	2-0	Bruce, Powell	9895	3			4	10				9	1		8			7	11		2		6			5			
38		12	Newport County	2-4	Price 2	4353	3			4	10				9	1		8			7	11		2		6			5		12	
39		17	Walsall	0-1		2684	3				10				9	1		12			7	11		2	4	6			5		8	
40		24	CARLISLE UNITED	0-0		5809	3			4					9	1		10			7	11		2	6			8	5		12	
41	May	1	Bristol City	1-2	Lee	4183	3			4	10				9	1		11			7		12		6			8	5		2	
42		4	LINCOLN CITY	1-0	Cascarino	3245	3			4	10				9	1		8			7	11		2		6			5			
43		8	OXFORD UNITED	2-1	Bruce, Weatherly	4690	3			4	10				11	1		8			7			2	5	6			9		12	
44		11	Fulham	0-0		7176	3			4	10				11	1					7			2	5	6		8	9			
45		15	Chesterfield	3-1	Cascarino, Grewcock, Pollard (og)	2235	3			4	10				11	1		8			7			2	5	6		9				
46		18	READING	2-1	Sharpe, Lee	3870	3			4	10				11	1		9	12		7			2	5	6		8				
						Apps	31	4	18	45	24	1	25	20	13	44	9	27	5	6	34	39	1	39	16	30	2	33	33	3	32	2
						Goals	2		5	6	5		2		1		2	8			1	12		1		2		1	1	1	12	

Scorers in game 25: White (p), Price 2, Bruce, Duncan, Cascarino

Two own goals

F.A. Cup

							Adams MR	Bottiglieri A	Bowman RD	Bruce SR	Cascarino AG	Donn AN	Duncan CJ	Ford AC	Grewcock N	Hillyard RW	Kemp DM	Lee TC	Miller MJ	Ovard FC	Powell CD	Price KG	Sage M	Sharpe JWH	Shaw PK	Sitton JE	Sutton G	Tydeman R	Weatherly CM	Westwood DR	White D	Young CF
R1	Nov	21	Plymouth Argyle	0-0		5471			6	4			8	3		1				10	7	11		2					5		9	
rep		24	PLYMOUTH ARGYLE	1-0	Bowman	7370			6	4			12	3		1		10			7	11		2				8	5		9	
R2	Dec	15	BARKING	1-1	White (p)	4363			2				6	3		1		10		12	7	11				4		8			9	5
rep	Jan	2	BARKING	3-1	(aet) Bruce, Price, Powell	4770	3			4			6			1				10	7	11		2				8	5		9	
R3		5	OLDHAM ATHLETIC	2-1	Kemp, White (p)	9247	3			4			6			1	10				7	11		2		12		8	5		9	
R4	Jan	23	WEST BROMWICH ALB.	0-1		16000	3			4			6			1	10				7	11		2		5		8			9	

F.L. Cup

							Adams MR	Bottiglieri A	Bowman RD	Bruce SR	Cascarino AG	Donn AN	Duncan CJ	Ford AC	Grewcock N	Hillyard RW	Kemp DM	Lee TC	Miller MJ	Ovard FC	Powell CD	Price KG	Sage M	Sharpe JWH	Shaw PK	Sitton JE	Sutton G	Tydeman R	Weatherly CM	Westwood DR	White D	Young CF
R1/1	Sep	1	Colchester United	0-2		2431			6	4			8	3				10			7	11		2			1	9	5			
R1/2		15	COLCHESTER UNITED	1-1	Price	3409			6	4			8	3				10			7	11		2			1	9	5		12	

F.L. Group Cup

							Adams MR	Bottiglieri A	Bowman RD	Bruce SR	Cascarino AG	Donn AN	Duncan CJ	Ford AC	Grewcock N	Hillyard RW	Kemp DM	Lee TC	Miller MJ	Ovard FC	Powell CD	Price KG	Sage M	Sharpe JWH	Shaw PK	Sitton JE	Sutton G	Tydeman R	Weatherly CM	Westwood DR	White D	Young CF
Gp	Aug	15	Wimbledon	0-4		1352	12			4			8	3		1		11			7			2				9	5	10	6	
Gp		19	SOUTHEND UNITED	0-0		1974				4			8	3		1		10			7			2				9	5	11	6	
Gp		22	ORIENT	1-1		2234				4			8	3		1		10			7			2			12	9	5	11	6	

Did not qualify for quarter-finals

Played at 14 on Aug 15: P Henderson

1982/83

13th in Division Three

	Date	Opponent	Score	Scorers	Att	Adams MR	Bowman RD	Bruce SR	Cascarino AG	Duncan CJ	Foley PJ	Grewcock N	Handford PM	Hillyard RW	Hodge MJ	Horrix DV	Johnson JD	Lansdowne W	Mehmet DN	Miller MJ	Powell CD	Price KG	Sage M	Sharpe JWH	Shaw PK	Sitton JE	Stokes WD	Tydeman R	Weatherly CM	White D
1	Aug 28	OXFORD UNITED	0-1		4079			4	10			9		1							7	11		2	6	3		8	5	
2	Sep 4	Exeter City	2-2	Price, Cascarino	2409	12		4	10			9		1							7	11		2	6	3		8	5	
3	7	Bristol Rovers	1-2	Parkin (og)	3798	3		5	10			12		1							8	11		2	7	4		9	6	
4	11	MILLWALL	1-0	Cascarino	4663	3		4	9					1							7	11		2	6	10		8	5	
5	18	Wrexham	0-1		2122	3		4	9			11		1						12				2	6	10		8	5	
6	25	WALSALL	3-0	Sinnott (og), Cascarino, Weatherly	3229	3		4	9			11		1							7			2	5	6		8	10	
7	28	READING	1-0	Cascarino	3621	3		4	9			10		1			12				7			2	5	6		8	11	
8	Oct 2	Sheffield United	2-0	Weatherly, Bruce	12319	3		4	9			10		1			8				7			2	5	6			11	
9	9	PRESTON NORTH END	2-1	Grewcock, Cascarino	4390	3		4	9			10		1			8				7	12		2		6		5	11	
10	16	Cardiff City	0-1		4828	3		4	9			10		1			8				7	12		2	5			6	11	
11	19	ORIENT	4-0	Grewcock 2, Weatherly, Tydeman	3849	3		4	9			10		1			8				7			2	5			6	11	
12	23	Bournemouth	1-0	Bruce (p)	5528	3		4	9			10		1			8				7	12		2	5			6	11	
13	30	HUDDERSFIELD T	1-3	Bruce	5919	3		4				10		1			8				7	9	12	2	5			6	11	
14	Nov 2	Chesterfield	2-1	Weatherly, Henderson (og)	2322	3		4				10		1			8				7	9		2	6			5	11	
15	6	Portsmouth	0-1		12212	3		4	9			10		1			8				7	12		2	5			6	11	
16	13	DONCASTER ROVERS	1-1	Miller	4451	3		4	9			10		1			2			7		11						6	5	12
17	27	WIGAN ATHLETIC	0-2		3952	3		4	9			10		1			8				7			2				6	5	11
18	Dec 4	Newport County	1-2	Weatherly	3727	3		4	9			10		1			8					12		2		5		6	11	7
19	18	Plymouth Argyle	0-2		4179	3			9					1			8			12	7	11			4	2		6	5	10
20	27	SOUTHEND UNITED	1-0	Weatherly	5035	3		4	9					1			8			12		10		2		5		6	11	7
21	28	Brentford	1-1	Bruce	7796	3		4	9					1			8				7	10		2				6	5	11
22	Jan 1	LINCOLN CITY	0-2		5535	3		4	9					1			8				7	11		2	12			6	5	10
23	3	Bradford City	1-1	Weatherly	4294	3		4	9					1			8					11		2	5	12		6	10	7
24	8	EXETER CITY	4-4	Weatherly, White 3 (1p)	2970	3		4	11				8	1							7	12		2	5			6	10	9
25	15	Oxford United	1-1	Weatherly	4936	3		4	11				8		1							7		2	5	12		6	10	9
26	22	WREXHAM	1-1	Adams	3798	3		4	11				8		1			10			12	7		2		5		6		9
27	30	Millwall	1-4	Cascarino	3813	3		4	11			12	8		1		6	10			7				5	2				9
28	Feb 5	Walsall	0-0		2608	3		4	11				8		1		7						10		5	2		6		9
29	15	CHESTERFIELD	3-1	Handford, Bruce, Cascarino	2187	3		4	11				8	1			7						12	2		5		6	10	9
30	19	Preston North End	0-0		3475	3		4					8	1			7	10					9	2		5		6	11	
31	26	CARDIFF CITY	2-3	Johnson, Lansdowne	4587	3		4			9	12	8	1			7	10						2		5		6	11	
32	Mar 1	Orient	0-2		2241	3		4		12	9		8	1			7	11						2		5		6	10	
33	5	BOURNEMOUTH	2-5	Bruce (p), Lansdowne	3485	3		4			9	11		1		8		10						2		7		6	5	
34	12	Huddersfield Town	2-3	Duncan, Mehmet	8264	3		4		11	9			1		7	8		10							2		6	5	
35	15	SHEFFIELD UNITED	0-2		3387	3		4		11	9			1		8	7		10				12			2		6	5	
36	19	PORTSMOUTH	1-0	Duncan	6489	3		4	12	11				1		8	7		10					2	5			6	9	
37	25	Doncaster Rovers	2-0	Bowman, Cascarino	2528	3	8	4	11	6				1		12			10					2	5			7	9	
38	Apr 1	Southend United	1-1	Cascarino	4553	3	8	4	11	6				1		12			10					2	5			7	9	
39	2	BRENTFORD	2-2	Whitehead (og), Cascarino	4168	3	8	4	11					1		12			10				6	2	5			7	9	
40	9	NEWPORT COUNTY	2-0	Weatherly, Bruce (p)	4265	3	8	4	11					1		12	7		10					2	5			6	9	
41	16	Reading	0-0		2816	3	8		11			6		1		12	7		10					2	5	4			9	
42	23	PLYMOUTH ARGYLE	2-1	Cascarino 2	3356	3	8		11					1		12	7		10					2	5	4		6	9	
43	30	Wigan Athletic	2-2	Adams, Mehmet	3610	3	8		11					1		12	7		10					2	5	4		6	9	
44	May 3	BRADFORD CITY	3-0	Mehmet, Cascarino, Johnson	2716	3			11	8			6	1		9	7		10				12	2		4			5	
45	7	BRISTOL ROVERS	1-0	Cascarino	3624	3			11	8			6	1		7			10				12	2		4	5		9	
46	14	Lincoln City	1-3	Cascarino	2241		8		11				6	1		9			10				2			3	4	7	5	
					Apps	44	8	39	38	8	5	21	12	42	4	14	31	6	13	4	21	20	9	39	29	30	2	41	43	14
					Goals	2	1	7	15	2		3	1				2	2	3	1		1						1	10	3

TC Lee played in games 1 (at 12) and 5 (at 7, subbed)
PL Walker played in games 16 (at 8) and 17 (12)

Four own goals

F.A. Cup

	Date	Opponent	Score	Scorers	Att	Adams MR	Bowman RD	Bruce SR	Cascarino AG	Duncan CJ	Foley PJ	Grewcock N	Handford PM	Hillyard RW	Hodge MJ	Horrix DV	Johnson JD	Lansdowne W	Mehmet DN	Miller MJ	Powell CD	Price KG	Sage M	Sharpe JWH	Shaw PK	Sitton JE	Stokes WD	Tydeman R	Weatherly CM	White D
R1	Nov 20	DAGENHAM	1-0	Cascarino	3884	3		4	9			10		1			8			7		11		2				6	5	12
R2	Dec 11	NORTHAMPTON TOWN	1-1	Johnson	4054	3		4	9								8				7	12		2		5		6	11	10
rep	14	Northampton Town	2-3	Weatherly 2	4290	3			12			10					8				7	9		2	4	5		6	11	

Played at 1 in R2 and R2 replay: G Sutton

F.L. Cup (Milk Cup)

	Date	Opponent	Score	Scorers	Att	Adams MR	Bowman RD	Bruce SR	Cascarino AG	Duncan CJ	Foley PJ	Grewcock N	Handford PM	Hillyard RW	Hodge MJ	Horrix DV	Johnson JD	Lansdowne W	Mehmet DN	Miller MJ	Powell CD	Price KG	Sage M	Sharpe JWH	Shaw PK	Sitton JE	Stokes WD	Tydeman R	Weatherly CM	White D
R1/2	Aug 31	LEYTON ORIENT	3-0	Cascarino 2, Bruce	2894			4	10			9									7	11		2	6	3		8	5	
R1/2	Sep 14	Leyton Orient	0-2		2003	3		4	9					1							7	11		2	6	10		8	5	
R2/1	Oct 5	OLDHAM ATHLETIC	2-0	Shaw, Cascarino	4070	3		4	9			10		1			8				7	12		2	5	6			11	
R2/2	26	Oldham Athletic	0-1		3302	3		4	9			10		1			8				12	7		2	5			6	11	
R3	Nov 9	TOTTENHAM HOTSPUR	2-4	Johnson, Price	14446	3		4	9			10		1			8				7	12		2	5			6	11	

Played at 1 in R1/1: G Sutton

1983/84

8th in Division Three

	Date	Opponent	Score	Scorers	Att	Armstrong GS	Bruce SR	Cascarino AG	Cavener P	Clarke CJ	Cochrane GT	Daniel RC	Duncan CJ	Fry DP	Garner P	Handford PM	Hillyard RW	Johnson JD	Leslie JA	Mehmet DN	Musker R	Sage M	Scotting A	Sharpe JWH	Shaw PK	Sitton JE	Sparrow BE	Tydeman R	Weatherly CM	Woodhead A
1	Aug 27	Sheffield United	0-4		10405								3			6	1		9	10		2			5	4		8	11	7
2	Sep 3	HULL CITY	1-2	Leslie	2919							6				12	1	7	9	10		3		2	5	4		8	11	
3	6	BOLTON WANDERERS	2-0	Mehmet, Weatherly	3098			12				7			3	6	1	8	9	10		2			5	4			11	
4	10	Plymouth Argyle	1-1	Sitton	3192			12				7			3	6	1	8	9	10		2			5	4			11	
5	17	OXFORD UNITED	2-3	Johnson, Sitton	3370			11				7			3		1	8	9	10		6		2		4			5	
6	24	Bournemouth	0-2		3045		12	11				7		1	3	6		8	9	10				2		4			5	
7	Oct 1	BRENTFORD	4-2	Leslie 2, Mehmet 2	3268		4	11						1	3			8	9	10		7		2		6			5	
8	8	PRESTON NORTH END	2-0	Cochrane, Weatherly	3725		4	11			7			1				8	9	10		3		2		6			5	12
9	15	Burnley	3-2	Cochrane, Cascarino, Mehmet	5590		4	11			7			1				8	9	10		3		2		6			5	
10	18	EXETER CITY	3-1	Bruce, Weatherly 2	3943		4	11	12		7			1				8	9	10		3		2		6			5	
11	22	Wigan Athletic	2-1	Cochrane, Weatherly	4189		4	11			7			1				8	9	10		3		2		6			5	
12	24	Orient	1-1	Cascarino	4013		4	11			7			1				8	9	10		3		2		6			5	
13	29	MILLWALL	3-3	Leslie, Sage, Mehmet	6226		4	11			7			1				8	9	10		3		2		6			5	
14	Nov 5	LINCOLN CITY	2-0	Johnson, Mehmet (p)	4428		4	11			7			1				8	9	10		3		2		6			5	
15	12	Walsall	1-3	Cascarino	4639		4	11			7			1				8	9	10		3		2		6			5	
16	26	ROTHERHAM UNITED	4-2	Weatherly 2, Mehmet 2	4152		4				7			1				8	9	10	11	3		2		6			5	
17	Dec 3	Port Vale	1-0	Cochrane	3086		4				7			1				8	9	10	11	3		2	12	6			5	
18	17	Scunthorpe United	0-2		2127	3	4		12		7					11	1		9	10	8				2	6			5	
19	26	SOUTHEND UNITED	5-1	Weatherly, Musker, Mehmet 2, Bruce	5511		4				7					12	1	8	9	10	11			2	6	3			5	
20	27	Bristol Rovers	0-3		5996		4				7						1	8	9	10	11			2	6	3			5	
21	31	WIMBLEDON	0-1		5024	3	4	12			7			1				8	9	10	11				6	2			5	
22	Jan 14	SHEFFIELD UNITED	4-2	Bruce 2, Weatherly, Cochrane	5408	3	4	11			7			1				8	9	10	12				6	2			5	
23	Feb 4	Brentford	3-2	Musker, Cascarino, Leslie	4317	12	4	11			7			1				8	9	10	5	3			6	2				
24	11	BOURNEMOUTH	2-1	Mehmet, Leslie	4891	3	4	11			7			1				8	9	10	5	2			6					
25	14	BRADFORD CITY	0-0		4390	3	4	11			7			1				8	9	10	5	2			6	12				
26	19	Millwall	2-2	Cascarino, Cochrane	6344	3	4	11	12		7			1		5			9	10		8			6	2				
27	25	WIGAN ATHLETIC	3-0	Mehmet 2, Cascarino	4013	3	4	11			7			1		5			9	10	8	2			6					
28	Mar 3	Exeter City	0-0		2801		4	11	12		7			1		5			9	10	8	2			6		3			
29	7	Lincoln City	0-4		1575		4	11			7			1		5			9	10	8	2			6	12	3			
30	10	WALSALL	1-3	Cascarino	4544		4	11	12		7			1					9	10	8	2			6	5	3			
31	13	Oxford United	1-0	Cavener	7654		4	11	10		7			1					9		8	2			6	5	3			
32	17	Preston North End	2-2	Musker, Sparrow	3874		4	11	10		7			1					9	12	8	2			6	5	3			
33	24	BURNLEY	0-1		4319		4	11	7	8				1		12			9	10	5	2			6	3				
34	27	Newport County	0-1		1849		4	12		8	7			1		11			9	10	5	3			6	2				
35	31	ORIENT	3-1	Leslie, Cascarino, Mehmet	3090		4	11			7			1		8			9	10	5	3			6	2				
36	Apr 7	Bolton Wanderers	1-0	Cascarino	4815		4	11		8	7			1					9	10	5	3			6	2				
37	11	Bradford City	2-3	Mehmet, Clarke	3523		4	11	7	8				1				6	9	10		3			5	2			12	
38	14	PORT VALE	1-1	Leslie	3323		4	11		8	7			1				5	9	10		3			6	2			12	
39	17	Hull City	0-0		7779			11		8				1		7		5	9	10	12	3			6	2			4	
40	20	Southend United	1-3	Sage	3690		4	11		8	7			1				5		10	12	3			6	2			9	
41	23	BRISTOL ROVERS	1-2	Musker	2973		4			8	7			1				5	12	10	11	2	3		6				9	
42	28	Rotherham United	0-3		3198		4				7			1		6		8	10		11	2	3			5			9	
43	May 1	PLYMOUTH ARGYLE	2-1	Leslie, Shaw	2273		4	11			7			1		5			9	10	8	2			6	3			12	
44	5	NEWPORT COUNTY	4-1	Musker, Cascarino 2, Bruce (p)	2273		4	11			7			1		8		12	9		5	3			6	2			10	
45	7	Wimbledon	3-1	Bruce, Cascarino, Sitton	6043		4	11	12					1		5		8	9	10		3			6	2			7	
46	12	SCUNTHORPE UNITED	1-1	Mehmet	2914		4	11						1		5		8	9	10	12	3			6	2			7	
					Apps	8	40	37	10	8	34	5	1	38	5	20	8	32	45	43	27	40	2	16	33	42	5	2	32	2
					Goals		6	12	1	1	6							2	9	16	5	2			1	3	1		9	

Played in game one only : CJ Duncan (3), WD Stokes (12)

F.A. Cup

	Date	Opponent	Score	Scorers	Att	Armstrong GS	Bruce SR	Cascarino AG	Cavener P	Clarke CJ	Cochrane GT	Daniel RC	Duncan CJ	Fry DP	Garner P	Handford PM	Hillyard RW	Johnson JD	Leslie JA	Mehmet DN	Musker R	Sage M	Scotting A	Sharpe JWH	Shaw PK	Sitton JE	Sparrow BE	Tydeman R	Weatherly CM	Woodhead A
R1	Nov 19	AP Leamington	1-0	Handford	2223		4				7			1		11		8	9	10		3		2		6			5	
R2	Dec 10	CHELMSFORD CITY	6-1	* see below	4812	12	4	11			7			1					9	8	6	3			5	2			10	
R3	Jan 7	BRENTFORD	5-3	* see below	6509	3	4	12			7			1				8	9	10	11				6	2			5	
R4	28	Everton	0-0		22380		4	11			7			1				8	9	10	12				6	2	3		5	
rep	31	EVERTON	0-0	(aet)	15339		4	11			7			1				8	9	10	5	3			6	2				
rep2	Feb 6	EVERTON	0-3		17817		4	11			7			1				8	9	10	5	2			6		3			

Scorers in R2: Shaw, Bruce, Sage, Weatherly, Mehmet, Leslie. Scorers in R3: Cochrane, Weatherly, Musker, Leslie, Cascarino.

F.L. Cup (Milk Cup)

	Date	Opponent	Score	Scorers	Att	Armstrong GS	Bruce SR	Cascarino AG	Cavener P	Clarke CJ	Cochrane GT	Daniel RC	Duncan CJ	Fry DP	Garner P	Handford PM	Hillyard RW	Johnson JD	Leslie JA	Mehmet DN	Musker R	Sage M	Scotting A	Sharpe JWH	Shaw PK	Sitton JE	Sparrow BE	Tydeman R	Weatherly CM	Woodhead A
R1/1	Aug 30	CHELSEA	1-2	Shaw	8633											6	1		9	10		3		2	4	5		7	11	12
R1/2	Sep 13	Chelsea	0-4		9704			8								6	1	7	9	10		3		2	4	5		12	11	

Played at 8 in R1/1: RD Bowman (subbed)

Associate Members' Cup

	Date	Opponent	Score	Scorers	Att	Armstrong GS	Bruce SR	Cascarino AG	Cavener P	Clarke CJ	Cochrane GT	Daniel RC	Duncan CJ	Fry DP	Garner P	Handford PM	Hillyard RW	Johnson JD	Leslie JA	Mehmet DN	Musker R	Sage M	Scotting A	Sharpe JWH	Shaw PK	Sitton JE	Sparrow BE	Tydeman R	Weatherly CM	Woodhead A
R1	Feb 28	Millwall	3-4	Cascarino 2, Sparrow	2364			11	7							12	1		9		8	2	6	4		5	3			14

Played at 10: P Collins

1984/85

4th in Division Three

No	Date	Opponent	Result	Scorers	Att	Cascarino AG	Cochrane GT	Collins P	Fry DP	Hales DD	Hillyard RW	Hinnigan JP	Johnson JD	Leslie JA	Macowat IS	McDonagh JM	Mehmet DN	Micallef C	Musker R	Oakes KB	Robinson MJ	Rushbury DG	Sage M	Sharpe JWH	Shaw PK	Shearer DJ	Shinners P	Sitton JE	Weatherly CM
1	Aug 25	NEWPORT COUNTY	1-1	Cascarino	3422	11	7				1	2	8	12			10		5	4			3		6				9
2	Sep 1	Orient	4-2	Cascarino, Corbett (og), Leslie, Oakes	2750	11	7				1		8	9			10			4			3		6	12		2	5
3	8	CAMBRIDGE UNITED	3-0	Cascarino, Leslie, Mehmet	3352	11	7				1	2	8	9			10			4			3		6				5
4	15	Wigan Athletic	1-0	Cascarino	3198	11					1	2	7	10			8	9		4			3		5				6
5	18	Hull City	0-2		5240	11					1	2	10	9			8	7		4			3		6	12			5
6	22	WALSALL	3-0	Cascarino 2, Leslie	4102	11	7				1	2	8	9			10			4			3		6				5
7	29	Swansea City	1-0	Mehmet	3784	11	7				1	3	8	9			10		12	4			2		6				5
8	Oct 2	PLYMOUTH ARGYLE	3-3	Cascarino, Hinnigan, Oakes	4442	11					1	2	8	9			10		7	4			3		6		12		5
9	6	MILLWALL	1-4	Sage	6881	11					1	3	8	9			10		5	4			2		6	12	7		
10	13	Bristol City	0-2		7088	11					1	2	5	9			10			4	7		3		6	8			12
11	20	Brentford	2-5	Cochrane, Oakes	4053	11	7		1				8	2			10			4	9		3		6				5
12	23	READING	4-1	Cascarino 2, Cochrane, Wood (og)	3568	11	7		1			12	8	2			10			4	9		3		6				5
13	27	BRADFORD CITY	2-2	Weatherly, Cascarino	3896	11	7		1				8	2			10			4	9		3		6				5
14	Nov 3	York City	1-7	Shearer	2921	11			1				8	2			10			4	9		3		6	7			5
15	6	Burnley	1-0	Robinson	3595	11	7		1			2					10		12	4	9		3		6	8			5
16	10	ROTHERHAM UNITED	2-1	Mehmet, Shearer	3568	11	7		1			3		12			10		5	4	9		2		6	8			
17	24	Bolton Wanderers	2-1	Cochrane, Shearer	4381	11	7				1	3					10		5	4	9		2		6	8			
18	Dec 1	PRESTON NORTH END	4-0	Cascarino, Shearer 2, Welsh (og)	4055	11	7				1	3					10		5	4	9		2		6	8			
19	15	Lincoln City	0-2		1920	11	7				1	3					10		5	4	9		2		6	8			
20	22	Doncaster Rovers	1-0	Cochrane	3035	11	7				1	3		9			10		5	4				2	6	8			12
21	26	DERBY COUNTY	3-2	Hinnigan, Shearer 2	7140	11	7				1	3					10		5	4	9		2		6	8			
22	29	BRISTOL ROVERS	4-1	Cochrane, Hinnigan, Robinson, Shearer	6598	11	7				1	3					10		5	4	9		2		6	8			12
23	Jan 1	Bournemouth	0-2		5305		7		1			3					10		5	4	9		2		6	8	12		11
24	12	ORIENT	2-0	Robinson 2	4899		10				1	3	9						5	4	8		2		6	7	12		11
25	Feb 2	SWANSEA CITY	1-1	Robinson	4851	11	7				1	3		8			10			4	9		2		6				5
26	23	YORK CITY	1-0	Robinson	5193	11	7				1	3		12			10		8	4	9		2		6				5
27	26	HULL CITY	1-0	Mehmet	6051	11	7				1	3		12			10		8	4	9		2		6				5
28	Mar 2	Bradford City	1-1	Shearer	8344	11	7		1			3		8			10		5	4	9		2		6	12			
29	9	BRENTFORD	2-0	Hinnigan, Mehmet (p)	5799	11	7		1			3					10		5	4	9		2		6	8			12
30	12	Newport County	3-0	Cascarino, Mehmet, Musker	2129	11	7		1			3					10		5	4	9		2		6	8			
31	16	BRISTOL CITY	1-3	Cascarino	6369	11	7		1			3					10		5	4	9		2		6	8			12
32	19	Plymouth Argyle	1-1	Mehmet (p)	4852	11	7					3				1	10		5	4	9		2		6	8			
33	23	Millwall	1-2	Mehmet	8256	11	7					4				1	10		5		9	3	2		6	8			12
34	29	BURNLEY	1-1	Oakes	5935	11				8		2	12			1	10			4	9	3	7		6				5
35	Apr 2	Cambridge United	2-1	Mehmet, Robinson	1803	11	7			8						1	10		5	4	9	3			6			2	12
36	6	Derby County	0-1		10002		7			8			5			1	10			4	9	3			6			2	11
37	9	BOURNEMOUTH	3-2	Cochrane, Hales, Robinson	5157	11	7			8			5			1	10			4	9	3			6			2	
38	13	Rotherham United	0-1		3022	11	7			8			5			1	10			4	9	3			6			2	12
39	16	Walsall	1-0	Cascarino	3585	11	7			8		2	5			1	10			4	9	3			6				
40	20	BOLTON WANDERERS	2-3	Hinnigan, Cochrane	5132	11	7			8		2	5			1	10			4	9	3			6				12
41	27	Preston North End	0-0		3201	11	7	12		8		2	5			1	10			4	9	3							6
42	May 4	LINCOLN CITY	3-2	Mehmet 2, Robinson	3219	11		7		12	1	2	5				10		8	4	9	3							6
43	7	Bristol Rovers	2-3	Robinson, Shaw	2761	10		6		11	1	5	7				8		12	3	9				2				4
44	11	DONCASTER ROVERS	2-1	Cascarino, Mehmet	2332	11		9		8	1	2	5				10		12	4		3	7						6
45	14	Reading	2-0	Cascarino, Mehmet	2311	11		7			1				3		10		9	4		6	2			8			5
46	17	WIGAN ATHLETIC	5-1	Collins, Oakes, Shearer 3 (1p)	2604	11	12	8			1	2			3		10		6	4			7			9			5
					Apps	43	35	6	11	11	25	37	25	20	2	10	45	2	28	45	33	12	36	1	41	23	4	5	35
					Goals	16	7	1		1		5		3			13		1	5	10		1		1	12			1

Three own goals

F.A. Cup

Rd	Date	Opponent	Result	Scorers	Att	Cascarino AG	Cochrane GT	Collins P	Fry DP	Hales DD	Hillyard RW	Hinnigan JP	Johnson JD	Leslie JA	Macowat IS	McDonagh JM	Mehmet DN	Micallef C	Musker R	Oakes KB	Robinson MJ	Rushbury DG	Sage M	Sharpe JWH	Shaw PK	Shearer DJ	Shinners P	Sitton JE	Weatherly CM
R1	Nov 17	WINDSOR & ETON	2-1	Mehmet, Cascarino	3597	11	7		1			3					10		5	4	9		2		6	8			
R2	Dec 8	Colchester United	5-0	Shearer 3, Robinson, Cascarino	4487	11	7				1	3					10		5	4	9		2		6	8			
R3	Jan 21	CARDIFF CITY	2-1	Robinson, Leslie	5452						1	3	10	7					5	4	9		2		6		8		11
R4	26	Ipswich Town	2-3	Leslie, Sage	16547		7				1	3		10					5	4	9		2	12	6		8		11

F.L. Cup (Milk Cup)

Rd	Date	Opponent	Result	Scorers	Att	Cascarino AG	Cochrane GT	Collins P	Fry DP	Hales DD	Hillyard RW	Hinnigan JP	Johnson JD	Leslie JA	Macowat IS	McDonagh JM	Mehmet DN	Micallef C	Musker R	Oakes KB	Robinson MJ	Rushbury DG	Sage M	Sharpe JWH	Shaw PK	Shearer DJ	Shinners P	Sitton JE	Weatherly CM
R1/1	Aug 28	COLCHESTER UNITED	3-2	Weatherly, Mehmet, Leslie	2689	11	7				1	2	8	9			10			4			3		6				5
R1/2	Sep 4	Colchester United	2-0	Weatherly 2	2162	11	7				1		8	2			10		5	4			3		6	12			9
R2/1	25	LEEDS UNITED	1-2	Cascarino	8881	11	7				1	2	8	9			10			4			3		6				5
R2/2	Oct 10	Leeds United	2-3	Shearer, Cascarino	11109	11					1	3	8	9			10		5	4			2		6	7			12

A.M. Cup (Freight Rover)

Rd	Date	Opponent	Result	Scorers	Att	Cascarino AG	Cochrane GT	Collins P	Fry DP	Hales DD	Hillyard RW	Hinnigan JP	Johnson JD	Leslie JA	Macowat IS	McDonagh JM	Mehmet DN	Micallef C	Musker R	Oakes KB	Robinson MJ	Rushbury DG	Sage M	Sharpe JWH	Shaw PK	Shearer DJ	Shinners P	Sitton JE	Weatherly CM
R1/1	Jan 23	COLCHESTER UNITED	2-2	Oakes, Shinners	963			6	1				10	7	3					4	9			2			8	5	12
R1/2	Feb 5	Colchester United	0-2		1762	11		6	1			4	7		3		10							2			8	5	9

Played in R1/1: I Young (at 11, subbed by P Edwards (14))
P Edwards also played (at 12) in R1/2

1985/86

5th in Division Three

						Byrne DS	Cascarino AG	Cochrane GT	Collins P	Elsey KW	Hales DD	Hillyard RW	Hinnigan JP	Macowat IS	Mehmet DN	Musker R	Oakes KB	Robinson MJ	Sage M	Shaw PK	Shearer DJ	Tempest DM	Tong DJ	Weatherly CM	Westley GN
1	Aug 17	Lincoln City	0-1		2099		10	7		9		1	3		11	5	4		2	6	8			12	
2	24	DARLINGTON	1-1	Sage	2949	12	11	7	9	3		1			10		4		2	6	8			5	
3	26	Bristol City	2-1	Cascarino 2	5883	12	11	7	9	3		1				10	4		2	6	8			5	
4	31	BOLTON WANDERERS	2-1	Hinnigan, Cascarino	2773	7	11		10	9	8	1	3				4		2	6				5	
5	Sep 7	Notts County	1-1	Byrne	3624	7	11	8		9		1	3		10	6	4		2					5	
6	14	CHESTERFIELD	1-1	Cascarino	3201	7	11	8	12	9	10	1	3			6	4		2					5	
7	17	WIGAN ATHLETIC	2-0	Mehmet (p), Elsey	3401	7	11	8	5	9		1	3		10		4		2	6					
8	21	Bury	2-1	Mehmet, Cochrane	2802	7	11	8	5	9		1	3		10		4		2	6				12	
9	28	YORK CITY	1-2	Collins	3509		11	7	5	9	12	1	2	3	10		4		8	6					
10	Oct 1	Plymouth Argyle	0-3		4135		11	7	5	9	12	1	2	3	10		4		8	6					
11	5	Blackpool	2-2	Elsey, Cascarino	4571	7	11	8	10	9	12	1	3				4		2	6				5	
12	12	CARDIFF CITY	2-0	Oakes, Weatherly	3367	8	11	7	10	3	9	1					4	12	2	6				5	
13	19	Bournemouth	3-2	Cascarino 2, Shearer	3561		11	7	10	3		1	5		12		4	9	2	6	8				
14	22	DERBY COUNTY	1-2	Mehmet	4613			7	9	5	12	1	3		10		4	11	2	6	8				
15	26	SWANSEA CITY	5-1	Shearer 3, Hales 2 (1p)	3082	11		7	6	3	9	1	5		10		4	12	2		8				
16	Nov 2	Newport County	1-1	Byrne	1970	9	11	7	6	3		1	5		10		4	12	2		8				
17	6	Rotherham United	1-1	Weatherly	2461	7	11			3	12	1	5		10		4	9	2		8			6	
18	9	WALSALL	5-2	Hales 2, Cascarino, Shearer, Robinson	3339	6	11			3	9	1			10		4	7	2		8			5	
19	23	Wolverhampton Wan.	3-1	Cochrane, Shearer 2	3543		11	7		3	9	1	12		10		4	6	2		8			5	
20	30	DONCASTER ROVERS	4-0	Robinson, Mehmet (p), Cochrane, Shearer	3592		11	7		3	9	1			10		4	6	2		8			5	
21	Dec 14	Bristol Rovers	0-1		4224		11	7		3	9	1	12		10		4	6	2		8			5	
22	20	Darlington	2-3	Shearer, Cascarino	2075	12	11	7		3	9	1	4			10		6	2		8			5	
23	28	BRISTOL CITY	1-1	Cascarino	4672	7	11			3		1	6		10	12	4	9	2		8			5	
24	Jan 1	Reading	2-1	Byrne, Elsey	10885	7	11			3		1	6		10		4	9	2		8			5	
25	11	Bolton Wanderers	1-0	Cochrane	5232		11	7		3		1	6		10	5		9	2	4	8				
26	18	LINCOLN CITY	2-0	Cochrane, Weatherly	3797		11	7		3	12	1	6			10		9	2	4	8			5	
27	25	Chesterfield	1-1	Hinnigan	2521		11	7	10	3	8	1	6					9	2	4				5	
28	Feb 1	NOTTS COUNTY	4-0	Robinson 2, Oakes, Musker	4368		11	7	10	3	8	1	6			12	4	9	2					5	
29	8	BOURNEMOUTH	2-0	Cascarino, Hales	3890	9	11	7	10	3	8	1	6		12		4		2					5	
30	15	Wigan Athletic	3-3	Elsey, Weatherly, Mehmet	5017		11	7	10	3	8	1	6		12		4		2		9			5	
31	22	BURY	1-0	Weatherly	4212		11	7	10	3	8	1	6				4	9	2					5	
32	Mar 1	York City	0-2		4351		11	7		3	8	1	6		10		4	9	2		12			5	
33	4	PLYMOUTH ARGYLE	1-1	Cascarino	3490		11	7		3	8	1	6				4	9	2		10			5	
34	8	BLACKPOOL	2-2	Cascarino, Robinson	4537		11	7		3	10	1	6				4	9	2	12	8			5	
35	15	Cardiff City	1-1	Cascarino	2579	12	11	7		3		1	6		10			9	2	4	8			5	
36	18	BRENTFORD	1-2	Robinson	3558	12	11	7	8	3		1	6		10			9	2	4				5	
37	22	Swansea City	2-2	Sage, Weatherly	3364			7	8	3		1	6		10		12	11	2	4	9			5	
38	29	READING	3-0	Tempest 2, Horrix (og)	5710			7	12	3		1			10		4	11	2	6		9	8	5	
39	31	Brentford	2-1	Robinson, Elsey	4702			7		10	12	1	3				4	11	2	6		9	8	5	
40	Apr 4	ROTHERHAM UNITED	3-0	Hales, Weatherly, Robinson	4525			7		3	10	1	6				4	11	2			9	8	5	
41	7	Derby County	0-2		11351			7		3	12	1	6				4	11	2	10		9	8	5	
42	12	Walsall	1-4	Tempest	3889				12	3		1	6		10		4	11	2	7		9	8	5	
43	19	WOLVERHAMPTON W.	2-0	Hales, Mehmet (p)	3681	11		7		3	8	1	6		10		4	12	2			9		5	
44	25	Doncaster Rovers	3-2	Robinson, Tempest, Hales	1659	7				3	8	1	6		10		4	11	2			9		5	
45	29	NEWPORT COUNTY	0-1		2566	7		12		3	8	1	6		10		4	11	2			9		5	
46	May 3	BRISTOL ROVERS	2-0	Robinson, Mehmet (p)	2050	7				3		1		12	10		4	11	2	6		9		5	8

	Byrne DS	Cascarino AG	Cochrane GT	Collins P	Elsey KW	Hales DD	Hillyard RW	Hinnigan JP	Macowat IS	Mehmet DN	Musker R	Oakes KB	Robinson MJ	Sage M	Shaw PK	Shearer DJ	Tempest DM	Tong DJ	Weatherly CM	Westley GN
Apps	23	34	38	23	46	29	46	39	3	31	9	40	33	46	24	23	9	5	38	1
Goals	3	14	5	1	5	8		2		7	1	2	10	2		9	4		7	

One own goal

F.A. Cup

						Byrne DS	Cascarino AG	Cochrane GT	Collins P	Elsey KW	Hales DD	Hillyard RW	Hinnigan JP	Macowat IS	Mehmet DN	Musker R	Oakes KB	Robinson MJ	Sage M	Shaw PK	Shearer DJ	Tempest DM	Tong DJ	Weatherly CM	Westley GN
R1	Nov 16	NORTHAMPTON T	3-0	Cascarino, Mehmet, Cochrane	3991	12	11	7		3	9	1			10		4	6	2		8			5	
R2	Dec 7	BOGNOR REGIS TOWN	6-1	* see below	4228		11	7	10	3	9	1					4	6	2		8			5	
R3	Jan 4	DERBY COUNTY	1-1	Robinson	8983	12	11	7		3		1	6		10		4	9	2		8			5	
rep	13	Derby County	1-3	(aet) Robinson	10959	12	11	7		3		1	6		10	5		9	2	4	8				

Scorers in R2: Cascarino 2, Robinson, Shearer, Cochrane, Hales

F.L. Cup (Milk Cup)

						Byrne DS	Cascarino AG	Cochrane GT	Collins P	Elsey KW	Hales DD	Hillyard RW	Hinnigan JP	Macowat IS	Mehmet DN	Musker R	Oakes KB	Robinson MJ	Sage M	Shaw PK	Shearer DJ	Tempest DM	Tong DJ	Weatherly CM	Westley GN
R1/1	Aug 20	Southend United	1-1	Shearer	2008		11	7	12	3		1			10	9	4		2	6	8			5	
R1/2	Sep 3	SOUTHEND UNITED	2-0	Cascarino 2	3106	7	11	8	10	9		1	3		12		4		2	6				5	
R2/1	24	PORTSMOUTH	1-3	Cascarino	4617		11	7	5	9		1	3	12	10		4		2	6				8	
R2/2	Oct 8	Portsmouth	1-2	Dillon (og)	7629	8	11	7	10	3	9	1					4		2	6				5	

A.M. Cup (Freight Rover Trophy)

						Byrne DS	Cascarino AG	Cochrane GT	Collins P	Elsey KW	Hales DD	Hillyard RW	Hinnigan JP	Macowat IS	Mehmet DN	Musker R	Oakes KB	Robinson MJ	Sage M	Shaw PK	Shearer DJ	Tempest DM	Tong DJ	Weatherly CM	Westley GN
Gp	Jan 22	Derby County	2-0	Robinson, Cascarino	3721		11	7	10	3	8	1	6					9	2	4				5	
Gp	29	BRENTFORD	1-1	Hales	1464	12	11	7	10	3	8	1	6			14	4	9	2					5	
QF	Feb 24	CAMBRIDGE UNITED	2-0	Collins, Hinnigan	1812		11	7	10	3	8	1	6		14		4	9	2		12			5	
SF	Apr 16	Bristol City	0-3		5707	7		14	8	3		1	6		10		4	11	2	12		9		5	

1986/87

5th in Division Three

#	Month	Day	Opponent	Score	Scorers	Att	Beeney MR	Berry LD	Cascarino AG	Collins P	Elsey KW	Eves MJ	Gernon FAJ	Gordon CK	Greenall CA	Haylock P	Hillyard RW	Hinnigan JP	Jacobs SD	Kite PD	Lovell SJ	Oakes KB	Pearce GC	Pritchard HK	Quow TS	Robinson MJ	Shearer DJ	Smith DA	Weatherly CM	Westley GN
1	Aug	23	Newport County	2-1	Weatherly, Shearer	2533			11	10	3					2	1					12	4	7	6	9	8		5	
2		30	BRISTOL CITY	1-1	Shearer	4185			11	10	3	12				2	1	6					4	7		9	8		5	
3	Sep	6	Rotherham United	1-0	Shearer	3243			11		3	12				2	1	6					4	7	10	9	8		5	
4		13	MIDDLESBROUGH	0-0		4888			11			10			6	2	1	4					3	7		9	8	12	5	
5		16	YORK CITY	2-0	Weatherly, Eves	4115			11			10			6	2	1	4					3	7		9	8		5	
6		27	BRENTFORD	2-0	Eves, Robinson	4710			11		3	10			6	2	1						4	7		9	8		5	
7		30	Mansfield Town	0-1		3046			11	12	3	10			6	2	1						4	7		9	8		5	
8	Oct	4	BURY	1-0	Cascarino	4326			11		3	10			6	2	1						4	7	12	9	8		5	
9		15	Chester City	1-1	Greenall	2198			11		10				6	2	1	4					3	7		9	8		5	
10		18	CARLISLE UNITED	1-0	Pritchard	4204			11		10	8			6	2	1	4					3	7		9	8		5	
11		21	Darlington	1-1	Shearer	1512			11		10				6	2	1	4					3	7		9	8		5	
12		25	Port Vale	2-1	Shearer (p), Pritchard	3055			11		10				6	2	1	4					3	7		9	8	12	5	
13	Nov	1	CHESTERFIELD	3-0	Greenall, Shearer, Pritchard	4373			11		10				6	2	1	4					3	7		9	8	12	5	
14		4	BLACKPOOL	2-1	Shearer, Weatherly	5951			11		10				6	2	1	4					3	7		9	8		5	
15		7	Doncaster Rovers	0-2		2691			11		10				6	2	1	4					3	7		9	8	12	5	
16		22	NOTTS COUNTY	3-1	Shearer 2, Cascarino	5514			11		10				6	2	1	4					3	7		9	8		5	
17		29	Wigan Athletic	1-3	Shearer	2492			11		10				6	2	1	4					3	7		9	8	12	5	
18	Dec	2	Bournemouth	2-0	Robinson, Pritchard	7756			11	7	10				6	2	1	4					3	12		9	8		5	
19		13	Bolton Wanderers	0-3		4867			11	7	10				6	2	1	4					3	8	12			9	5	
20		19	BRISTOL ROVERS	4-1	Pritchard, Robinson, Cascarino 2	4473			11		10				6	2	1	4					3	7		9		8	5	
21		26	Fulham	2-2	Parker (og), Collins	5894				12	10				6	2	1	4					3	7		9	8	11	5	
22		27	SWINDON TOWN	1-3	Greenall	9982				9	10				6	2	1	4					3	7		11	12	8	5	
23	Jan	1	WALSALL	4-0	Pritchard 3, Elsey	6003	1			12	10				6	2		4					3	7	8		9	11	5	
24		3	Notts County	1-3	Cascarino	5832	1		11		10				6	2		4					3	7	8	9		12	5	
25	Feb	3	ROTHERHAM UNITED	1-0	Pritchard	3862			11		3				6	2	1						4	7	8	10	12	9	5	
26		7	York City	1-2	Smith	2845			11		3	10			6	2	1		12				4	7	8			9	5	
27		14	CHESTER CITY	1-2	Quow	4438			11		3	8			6	2	1		10					7	4	12		9	5	
28		17	NEWPORT COUNTY	1-1	Gordon	3643			11		3			8	6	2	1		10					7	4			9	5	
29		21	Brentford	2-3	Cascariono, Gordon	4015			11		3			8	6	2	1		10					7	4			9	5	
30		28	MANSFIELD TOWN	2-0	Cascarino, Pritchard	4251			11		3			8	6	2			10	1				7	4			9	5	
31	Mar	3	Chesterfield	0-1		2026			11		3			8	6	2		12	10	1				7	4			9	5	
32		7	PORT VALE	0-0		3929			11		3	8			6	2		4		1				7	10		12	9	5	
33		14	Carlisle United	4-2	Pritchard, Shearer 2, Cascarino	2117			11		10		3		6	2		4		1				7		9	8		5	
34		17	DARLINGTON	4-1	Cascarino 3, Shearer	3558			11		10	9	3		6	2		4		1				7	12		8		5	
35		21	BOURNEMOUTH	2-1	Weatherly, Shearer	7577			11		10		3		6	2		4		1				7		9	8	12	5	
36		28	Bury	0-1		2197		6	11				3			2		4		1				7	10		9	8	5	12
37	Apr	4	DONCASTER ROVERS	2-1	Elsey, Cascarino	3501		4	11		10		3		6	2				1				7	12	9	8		5	
38		11	Blackpool	1-0	Shearer	2558		4	11		10		9		6	2				1			3	7			8	12	5	
39		18	Walsall	0-1		5109		4	11		10		9			2			6	1	12		3	7			8		5	
40		20	FULHAM	4-1	Shearer (p), Lovell, Cascarino 2	6123		4	11		10		6			2				1	9		3	7			8		5	
41		22	Bristol City	0-2		10260		4	11		10		6			2				1	9		3	12		7	8		5	
42		25	Bristol Rovers	1-0	Cascarino	3174		4	11		10		6			2				1			3	11		9	8	12	5	
43		28	Middlesbrough	0-3		11937		2	11		10		4		6					1			3	7		9	8	12	5	
44	May	2	WIGAN ATHLETIC	0-0		5408		4	11		10		3			2		6		1	8			7			12	9	5	
45		4	Swindon Town	1-1	Pritchard	10287		4	11		10		6		5	2				1	9		3	7	8			12		
46		9	BOLTON WANDERERS	1-0	Cascarino	5319		4	11		10		3		6	2				1	8			7	5		12	9		
						Apps	2	11	43	8	43	12	14	4	37	45	27	27	7	17	6	1	33	46	19	30	36	27	44	1
						Goals			16	1	2	2		2	3						1			12	1	3	16	1	4	

One own goal

Play Offs

Rd	Month	Day	Opponent	Score	Scorers	Att	Beeney MR	Berry LD	Cascarino AG	Collins P	Elsey KW	Eves MJ	Gernon FAJ	Gordon CK	Greenall CA	Haylock P	Hillyard RW	Hinnigan JP	Jacobs SD	Kite PD	Lovell SJ	Oakes KB	Pearce GC	Pritchard HK	Quow TS	Robinson MJ	Shearer DJ	Smith DA	Weatherly CM	Westley GN
SF1	May	14	SUNDERLAND	3-2	Cascarino 3	13804		4	11		10		3		6	2				1	12			7	5		8	9		
SF2		17	Sunderland	3-4	Cascarino 2, Pritchard	25470		4	11		10				6	2				1			3	7	5		12	9	8	
F1		22	SWINDON TOWN	1-0	Smith	16775		4	11		10				6	2				1			3	7	5		8	9		
F2		25	Swindon Town	1-2	Elsey	14382		4	11		10				6	2				1	9		3	7	5		8	12		
rep		29	Swindon Town	0-2		18491		4	11		10				6	2				1			3	7	5	9	8	12		

SF won on the away goals rule. Final replay at Selhurst Park.

F.A. Cup

Rd	Month	Day	Opponent	Score	Scorers	Att	Beeney MR	Berry LD	Cascarino AG	Collins P	Elsey KW	Eves MJ	Gernon FAJ	Gordon CK	Greenall CA	Haylock P	Hillyard RW	Hinnigan JP	Jacobs SD	Kite PD	Lovell SJ	Oakes KB	Pearce GC	Pritchard HK	Quow TS	Robinson MJ	Shearer DJ	Smith DA	Weatherly CM	Westley GN
R1	Nov	15	Kettering Town	3-0	Robinson, Hinnigan, Kellock (og)	2845			11	12	10				6	2	1	4					3	7		9	8	14	5	
R2	Dec	6	CHELMSFORD CITY	2-0	Cascarino 2	5843			11	7	10				6	2	1	4					3			9	8		5	
R3	Jan	19	Wigan Athletic	1-2	Greenall (p)	3459			11	12	10				6	2	1		4				3	7	8	14		9	5	

F.L. Cup (Littlewoods Challenge Cup)

Rd	Month	Day	Opponent	Score	Scorers	Att	Beeney MR	Berry LD	Cascarino AG	Collins P	Elsey KW	Eves MJ	Gernon FAJ	Gordon CK	Greenall CA	Haylock P	Hillyard RW	Hinnigan JP	Jacobs SD	Kite PD	Lovell SJ	Oakes KB	Pearce GC	Pritchard HK	Quow TS	Robinson MJ	Shearer DJ	Smith DA	Weatherly CM	Westley GN
R1/1	Aug	25	NORTHAMPTON T	1-0	Weatherly	2948			11	14	3	12				2	1					6	4	7	10	9	8		5	
R1/2	Sep	3	Northampton Town	2-2	Cascarino 2	2724			11	10	3					2	1	6					4	7	12	9	8		5	
R2/1		24	Oxford United	0-6		5246			11	6		10				2	1	4					3	7	14	9	8		5	
R2/2	Oct	7	OXFORD UNITED	1-1	Cascarino	3033	1		11		5	10				2		6					4	7	8			9		

J Gorman played at 12 in R2/1 and 3 in R2/2

A.M. Cup (Freight Rover Trophy)

Rd	Month	Day	Opponent	Score	Scorers	Att	Beeney MR	Berry LD	Cascarino AG	Collins P	Elsey KW	Eves MJ	Gernon FAJ	Gordon CK	Greenall CA	Haylock P	Hillyard RW	Hinnigan JP	Jacobs SD	Kite PD	Lovell SJ	Oakes KB	Pearce GC	Pritchard HK	Quow TS	Robinson MJ	Shearer DJ	Smith DA	Weatherly CM	Westley GN
PR	Nov	25	Notts County	5-0	Cascarino 2, Shearer 2, Robinson	1668			11	6	10					2	1	4					3	7	12	9	8	14	5	
PR	Dec	16	NORTHAMPTON T	1-0	Pritchard	2047			11	12	10					2	1	4	5				3	7	6	9		8		14
R1	Jan	26	COLCHESTER UNITED	2-0	Smith, Cascarino	1984			11		3				6	2	1		12				4	7	8	10		9	5	
QF	Feb	10	Port Vale	3-3	Elsey, Cascarino, Smith	2768			11		10	8			6	2	1		12				3	7	4	14		9	5	
SF	Mar	10	Bristol City	0-2		10540			11		3	14			6	2		4	10	1				7		9	8	12	5	

1987/88

13th in Division Three

	Date	Opponent	Score	Scorers	Att	Berry LD	Cooper MD	Docker I	Elsey KW	Eves MJ	Gernon FAJ	Greenall CA	Haines IG	Haylock P	Hillyard RW	Kite PD	Lillis JW	Lovell SJ	Luff NJ	Palmer LJ	Parks A	Peacock GK	Pearce GC	Pritchard HK	Quow TS	Shearer DJ	Shipley GM	Smith DA	Smith MA	Walker A	Weatherly CM	West G
1	Aug 15	BLACKPOOL	0-0		4336				10		3	6		2		1		9						7	12	8	4	11				5
2	22	Grimsby Town	0-2		2901				10	12	3	6		2		1		9						7	11	8	4					5
3	29	SOUTHEND UNITED	8-1	* see below	4171				10			6		2		1	12	9					3	7	14	8	4	11				5
4	31	Wigan Athletic	1-1	Shearer	3412				10			6		2		1		9					3	7		8	4	11				5
5	Sep 5	CHESTERFIELD	10-0	* see below	4100				10			6		2		1	12	9					3	7	14	8	4	11				5
6	12	Fulham	2-0	Lovell, Shearer	4704				10			6		2	1			9					3	7		8	4	11				5
7	15	SUNDERLAND	0-0		9098				10			6		2				9			1		3	7		8	4	11				5
8	19	YORK CITY	3-1	Elsey 2, West	5501				10			6		2				9			1		3	7	12	8	4	11				5
9	26	Bristol City	3-3	Lovell, D Smith, Elsey	10080	14			10	12		6		2		1		9					3	7	4	8		11				5
10	29	CHESTER CITY	0-1		5199	12			10			6		2		1		9					3	7	4	8		11				5
11	Oct 3	Doncaster Rovers	2-4	Lovell, Eves	1747	6			10	14				2		1	12	9					3	7	4	8		11				5
12	10	BRISTOL ROVERS	3-0	D Smith, Lovell, Pritchard	4399	6	8							2		1		9				10	3	7	4			11				5
13	17	Mansfield Town	2-2	Lovell, Quow (p)	2957	6			8					2		1		9				10	3	7	4			11				5
14	20	Preston North End	1-1	Cooper	5666	11	8		6					2		1		9				10	3	7	4			12				5
15	24	NOTTS COUNTY	3-1	Lovell 2, Cooper	5551		8		4			6		2		1		9				10	3	7				11				5
16	31	Port Vale	0-0		3495		8		10			6		2		1		9				11	3	7	4							5
17	Nov 3	BRENTFORD	0-1		4513		8		10			6		2		1	12	9				11	3	7	4						14	5
18	7	BRIGHTON & HOVE ALB	1-1	Greenall (p)	6439		8		10			6		2		1	11	9	12				3	7	4						14	5
19	21	Northampton Town	1-2	Lovell	5151		8		3			6	14	2		1	11	9						7	4				10		12	5
20	28	BURY	3-3	West, Eves 2	3974		8		10	12		6		2		1		9					3	7	4						11	5
21	Dec 12	Rotherham United	2-1	Pritchard, Eves	2557		14		10	8	12	6		2		1		9				11	3	7	4						5	
22	18	WALSALL	0-1		4144		12		10	8		6		2		1		9				11	3	7	4							5
23	26	BRISTOL CITY	1-1	D Smith	6261		12		10	8		6		2		1		9				4	3	7				11			14	5
24	28	Aldershot	0-6		4734		8		2		3	6				1		9				10		7	12			11			4	5
25	Jan 1	Southend United	3-1	Peacock, Cooper, Lovell	5581		8		10		6			2	1			9				4	3	7	12			11				5
26	2	FULHAM	2-2	Cooper 2	5918		8		10		6			2	1			9				4	3	7				11				5
27	16	York City	2-0	Lovell, Pritchard	2129		8		10		3	6		2	1			9				4		7	12			11			14	5
28	23	WIGAN ATHLETIC	0-1		4256		12		10		3	6		2	1			9				4		7	8			11			14	5
29	30	Sunderland	1-2	Cooper	16195		10		2			6			1			9				4	3	7	8			11				5
30	Feb 2	GRIMSBY TOWN	1-1	Cooper	2990	12	10		2			6			1			9				4	3	7	8			11				5
31	6	Chesterfield	4-1	Hunter (og), Lovell 3	2141		10		2			6			1			9				4	3	7	8			11			12	5
32	13	ALDERSHOT	2-1	Lovell (p), Gernon	3909		10		4		12			2	1			9					3	7	8			11			6	5
33	20	Blackpool	3-3	Lovell 2, Elsey	3405		10		4		6			2	1			9					3	7	8			11			5	
34	27	DONCASTER ROVERS	3-1	Lovell 2 (1p), Cooper	4049	12	10		4		6			2		1		9					3	7	8			11			5	
35	Mar 2	Chester City	1-3	Pritchard	1646	14	10		4	12	6			2		1		9					3	7	8		11					5
36	5	MANSFIELD TOWN	0-0		3627	5	10		4	12	6			2		1		9					3	7	8		11					
37	12	Bristol Rovers	0-2		3856	2	10				6					1		9					3	7	8		4	11			12	5
38	19	PORT VALE	0-0		3367	2			14		6				1			9				4	3	7	8		10	11			12	5
39	26	Notts County	1-0	Lovell	6478	2	10				3				1			9				4			8		7	11		6		5
40	Apr 2	Brighton & Hove Albion	0-2		9262	2	10				3				1			9				4		12	8		7	11		6		5
41	4	NORTHAMPTON T	1-2	Lovell	4131	2	12		14	10	3				1			9				4			8		7	11		6		5
42	9	Brentford	2-2	Peacock, Eves	3875	2			7	10	3				1			9				4		12	8			11		6		5
43	23	PRESTON NORTH END	4-0	Lovell, Eves 2, D Smith	2823	2		12		10	3				1		7	9				4			8			11	14		6	5
44	30	Bury	1-2	Pritchard	1433	2	12			10	3				1			9				4		7	8			11		6		5
45	May 2	ROTHERHAM UNITED	0-2		2943	2	12			10					1			9		3		4		7	8			11		6		5
46	7	Walsall	0-0		8850	2	11		3	10						1		9				4			8					6	7	5
					Apps	20	31	1	39	15	21	25	1	32	18	26	7	46	1	1	2	26	32	42	40	11	15	35	2	7	17	42
					Goals		8		6	7	1	2						25				2		8	1	5	2	7				2

Scorers in game 5: Pritchard 2, Shearer 2, Shipley 2, Elsey 2, D Smith, Greenall

Scorers in game 3: Lovell 4, Shearer, D Smith 2, Pritchard

One own goal

F.A. Cup

	Date	Opponent	Score	Scorers	Att	Berry LD	Cooper MD	Docker I	Elsey KW	Eves MJ	Gernon FAJ	Greenall CA	Haines IG	Haylock P	Hillyard RW	Kite PD	Lillis JW	Lovell SJ	Luff NJ	Palmer LJ	Parks A	Peacock GK	Pearce GC	Pritchard HK	Quow TS	Shearer DJ	Shipley GM	Smith DA	Smith MA	Walker A	Weatherly CM	West G
R1	Nov 14	FULHAM	2-1	Lillis, Pritchard	6444		8		3			6		2		1	11	9						7	4				10		12	5
R2	Dec 5	WALSALL	2-1	Lovell, Elsey	4916				10	8	12	6		2		1		9					3	7	4						11	5
R3	Jan 9	BIRMINGHAM CITY	0-3		9267		8		10	12		6		2		1		9				4	3	7				11				5

F.L. Cup (Littlewoods Challenge Cup)

	Date	Opponent	Score	Scorers	Att	Berry LD	Cooper MD	Docker I	Elsey KW	Eves MJ	Gernon FAJ	Greenall CA	Haines IG	Haylock P	Hillyard RW	Kite PD	Lillis JW	Lovell SJ	Luff NJ	Palmer LJ	Parks A	Peacock GK	Pearce GC	Pritchard HK	Quow TS	Shearer DJ	Shipley GM	Smith DA	Smith MA	Walker A	Weatherly CM	West G
R1/1	Aug 18	BRIGHTON & HOVE ALB.	1-0	Greenall	4162				10		3	6		2		1		9						7		8	4	11				5
R1/2	26	Brighton & Hove Albion	0-1	(aet)	5479				10	14	3	6		2		1		9						7	12	8	4	11				5
R2/1	Sep 22	Stoke City	0-2		7198				10	12		6		2		1		9					3	7	4	8		11				5
R2/2	Oct 6	STOKE CITY	0-1		5039	6			10	12				2		1	14	9					3	7	4	8		11				5

R1/2 won 5-4 on penalties

A.M. Cup (Sherpa Van Trophy)

	Date	Opponent	Score	Scorers	Att	Berry LD	Cooper MD	Docker I	Elsey KW	Eves MJ	Gernon FAJ	Greenall CA	Haines IG	Haylock P	Hillyard RW	Kite PD	Lillis JW	Lovell SJ	Luff NJ	Palmer LJ	Parks A	Peacock GK	Pearce GC	Pritchard HK	Quow TS	Shearer DJ	Shipley GM	Smith DA	Smith MA	Walker A	Weatherly CM	West G
PR	Oct 13	Aldershot	1-3	Lovell	1810	6	8							2		1		9				10	3	7	4			11				5
PR	27	LEYTON ORIENT	2-2	Greenall 2 (1p)	2558	14	8		4			6		2		1	12	9				10	3	7				11				5

1988/89

23rd in Division Three: Relegated

	Date		Opponents	Score	Scorers	Att	Burley GE	Clarke BR	Cooper MD	Docker I	Eeles AG	Gavin PJ	Haines IG	Haylock P	Hillyard RW	Joseph F	Kite PD	Lillis JW	Lovell SJ	Manuel WAJ	O'Shea TJ	Peacock GK	Pearson R	Perry A	Quow TS	Reeves A	Shipley GM	Smith DA	Stimson MN	Walford SJ	Walker A	Weatherly CM	West G	Williams JS
1	Aug	27	SWANSEA CITY	2-3	Peacock, Lovell	4309	2	5	10					3	1			12	9			4			8		7	11			6			
2	Sep	3	Aldershot	2-0	Shipley, Lovell	2477	2	5	13					3	1			10	9			4			8		7	11			6	12		
3		10	SHEFFIELD UNITED	2-1	Lovell, Lillis	4912	2							3	1			10	9			4			8		7	11			6	13	5	12
4		17	Huddersfield Town	1-1	Lovell	4688	2	6						3	1			10	9			4		12	8			11				7	5	
5		20	Mansfield Town	1-2	Lovell	3153	2	6						3	1			10	9			4		12	8			11				7	5	
6		24	READING	0-1		4446	2			12				3	1			10	9			4		7	8			11			6		5	
7	Oct	1	Brentford	0-1		4839	2	5	10					3			1		9			4		7	8			12			6	11		
8		4	BRISTOL CITY	0-1		2966	2	5	12					3			1		9			4		7	8			11			6	10		
9		8	CHESTERFIELD	0-1		2877	2	5		13				3			1	12	9			4		7	8			11			6	10		
10		15	Southend United	1-2	Lovell	3200	2	5	11					3			1	12	9			4		7	8						6	10		
11		22	BURY	3-4	Lillis, Lovell (p), Cooper	2702	2	5	11					3			1	7	9			4			8						6	10		12
12		25	Preston North End	0-5		6390	2		7					3			1	12	9			4			8			11			6	10	5	13
13		29	WOLVERHAMPTON W.	1-3	Lovell	5185	2	5		11				3			1	8	9			4			12			13			6	10		7
14	Nov	5	Cardiff City	0-1		3640	2			10			12	3			1	7	9			4		13	8			11			6	5		
15		8	BLACKPOOL	1-0	Burley	3432	2		12	10			5	3			1	7	9			4		8				11			6			
16		12	Bristol Rovers	0-2		4826	2		12	10			5	3			1	8	9			4					7	11			6			
17		26	Notts County	2-1	Quow, Smith	4611	2		7	10			5	3			1	12	9			4			8			11			6			
18	Dec	3	CHESTER CITY	0-2		3212	2		7	5				3			1	12	9			4			8		10	11			6			
19		18	Northampton Town	2-1	Lovell 2 (1p)	3829	2		8	10			5	3			1		9			4					7	11		6				
20		26	FULHAM	0-1		5773	2		8	10			5	3			1		9			4			12		7	11		6				
21		30	PORT VALE	1-0	Cooper	4593	2		8	10			5	3			1		9			4			12		7	11		6				
22	Jan	2	Wigan Athletic	0-3		3090	2		7	11			5	3			1		9			4			8		10			6		13		12
23		6	Bolton Wanderers	1-2	Peacock	4187	2		7	10			5	3			1		9			4			13		8	11				6	12	
24		14	ALDERSHOT	1-1	Peacock	3780	2			10				3			1		9			4					8	11				6	5	7
25		21	Sheffield United	2-4	West, Cooper	9336	2		8	10			13	7			1		9			4		12				11	3		6		5	
26		28	HUDDERSFIELD T	1-2	Peacock (p)	3531	2		9		8		6	10			1					4		7			12	11	3				5	
27	Feb	4	BRENTFORD	0-0		4002	2			10				13			1	12	9		8	4					7	11	3		6		5	
28		11	Bristol City	0-1		7319	2			8							1	10	9	6	7					4	12	11	3		5			
29		18	Chesterfield	1-3	Lovell	3432	2			8				10			1	13	9	12	7	4				6		11	3		5			
30		25	SOUTHEND UNITED	1-1	Walker	3579	2			10							1		9		7	4		8		6		11	3		5			
31		28	PRESTON NORTH END	1-3	Burley	3038	2			10						7	1	12	9		8	4				6		11	3		5			
32	Mar	4	Bury	0-1		4313	2			10						7	1	8	9	5		4		12		6		11	3					
33		11	CARDIFF CITY	1-2	Boyle (og)	2934	2			10	7					8	1		9	5		4				6		11	3					
34		14	Wolverhampton Wan.	1-6	Gavin	12574	2			10	7	9			1	8				5		4				6			3					12
35		19	Swansea City	2-3	Gavin, Lillis	4252	2			10		9			1	8		12		5	4					6		11	3					7
36		24	WIGAN ATHLETIC	2-1	Gavin, Peacock	3446	2			10		9			1	8				5	4	12				6		11	3					7
37		27	Fulham	2-1	Peacock 2	6476	2			10		9			1	8				13	5	4				6		11	3					7
38	Apr	1	NORTHAMPTON T	1-0	Gavin	3447	2			10		9			1	8				12	5	4				6		11	3					7
39		4	BOLTON WANDERERS	0-1		3081	2			10		9			1	8				13	5	4	12			6		11	3					7
40		8	Port Vale	1-2	Lovell	5358	2			10		9			1	8			13	7	5	4				6		11	3					12
41		15	MANSFIELD TOWN	3-0	Gavin, Peacock, Joseph	2414	2			10		9			1	12			8	7	5	4				6		11	3					
42		22	Reading	2-1	Lovell, Gavin	3511	2			10		9		12	1	13			8	7	5	4				6		11	3					
43		28	BRISTOL ROVERS	2-3	Lovell (p), Smith	3998	2			3		9			1	12			10	8	6	7				5		11				4		
44	May	1	Blackpool	1-4	Peacock	2152	2			13		9		3	1	12			8	7	5	4				6		11				10		
45		6	Chester City	0-2		2156	2			3		9		12	1	13			8	7	5	4	10			6		11						
46		13	NOTTS COUNTY	2-1	Gavin, Manuel	2871	2			3		9	6		1				8	7	10	4	5					11						

LA Guscott played at 13 in game 34 and 12 (subbed) in game 37

PCWJ Beadle played at 12 in game 33 and 11 in game 34

	Burley GE	Clarke BR	Cooper MD	Docker I	Eeles AG	Gavin PJ	Haines IG	Haylock P	Hillyard RW	Joseph F	Kite PD	Lillis JW	Lovell SJ	Manuel WAJ	O'Shea TJ	Peacock GK	Pearson R	Perry A	Quow TS	Reeves A	Shipley GM	Smith DA	Stimson MN	Walford SJ	Walker A	Weatherly CM	West G	Williams JS
Apps	46	10	18	35	3	13	12	31	19	15	27	22	39	17	17	44	3	13	20	18	14	42	18	4	22	17	10	13
Goals	2		3			7				1		3	14	1		9			1		1	2			1		1	

One own goal

F.A. Cup

	Date		Opponents	Score	Scorers	Att	Burley GE	Clarke BR	Cooper MD	Docker I	Eeles AG	Gavin PJ	Haines IG	Haylock P	Hillyard RW	Joseph F	Kite PD	Lillis JW	Lovell SJ	Manuel WAJ	O'Shea TJ	Peacock GK	Pearson R	Perry A	Quow TS	Reeves A	Shipley GM	Smith DA	Stimson MN	Walford SJ	Walker A	Weatherly CM	West G	Williams JS
R1	Nov	19	PETERBOROUGH UTD.	3-3	Lovell, Quow, Smith	4509	2		13	10			5	3			1	8	9			4			12			11			6			7
rep		23	Peterborough United	0-1		4494	2		7	10			5	3			1		9						8		4	11			6			

F.L. Cup (Littlewoods Challenge Cup)

	Date		Opponents	Score	Scorers	Att	Burley GE	Clarke BR	Cooper MD	Docker I	Eeles AG	Gavin PJ	Haines IG	Haylock P	Hillyard RW	Joseph F	Kite PD	Lillis JW	Lovell SJ	Manuel WAJ	O'Shea TJ	Peacock GK	Pearson R	Perry A	Quow TS	Reeves A	Shipley GM	Smith DA	Stimson MN	Walford SJ	Walker A	Weatherly CM	West G	Williams JS
R1/1	Aug	30	Cambridge United	2-1	Walker, Lovell	2296	2	5	12					3	1			10	9			4			8		7	11			6			
R1/2	Sep	6	CAMBRIDGE UNITED	3-1	Lovell, Lillis 2	3066								2	1			10	9			4			8		7	11			6	5	12	
R2/1		27	Millwall	0-3		6518	2		10	12				3	1				9			4		7	8						6	11	5	
R2/2	Oct	11	MILLWALL	1-3	Quow (p)	5729	2	5	9	11			13	3			1	12				4		7	8						6	10		

FAJ Gernon played at 3 in R1/2

A.M. Cup (Sherpa Van Trophy)

	Date		Opponents	Score	Scorers	Att	Burley GE	Clarke BR	Cooper MD	Docker I	Eeles AG	Gavin PJ	Haines IG	Haylock P	Hillyard RW	Joseph F	Kite PD	Lillis JW	Lovell SJ	Manuel WAJ	O'Shea TJ	Peacock GK	Pearson R	Perry A	Quow TS	Reeves A	Shipley GM	Smith DA	Stimson MN	Walford SJ	Walker A	Weatherly CM	West G	Williams JS
PR	Nov	29	Brentford	0-2		3713	2		6				5	3	1			10	9			4			8			11						13
PR	Dec	10	FULHAM	2-1	Lillis, Peacock	1970	2		7	10			5	3			1	8				4					9	11		6				12
R1	Jan	17	Torquay United	0-3		1844	2			10			3	7			1		9			4					8	11			6		5	

EA Collins played at 7 on Nov 29

1989/90

14th in Division Four

	Date	Opponent	Score	Scorers	Att	Beadle PCWJ	Clarke BR	Docker I	Eeles AG	Gavin PJ	Haines IG	Haylock P	Heritage PM	Hillyard RW	Johnson PE	Joseph F	Kimble GL	Lim HC	Lovell SJ	Manuel WAJ	Norris R	O'Connor MA	O'Shea TJ	Palmer LJ	Pearson R	Place BA	Pulis AR	Smith G	Thompson SA	Trusson MS	Walker A
1	Aug 19	ALDERSHOT	0-0		3665	9			8		4	7		1	3	12			10	11	2				5				6		
2	26	Doncaster Rovers	0-0		1840	9			8		4	7		1	3	11			10		2			6	5			13	12		
3	Sep 2	SCUNTHORPE UNITED	0-3		3462				8	9	4	2	12	1	3	11			10		13			6	5					7	
4	9	Hartlepool United	2-1	Palmer, Heritage	1379				8	9	4	2	12	1	3				10	11				6						7	5
5	16	BURNLEY	0-0		3853				8	9	4	2	12	1	3				10	11				6						7	5
6	23	Carlisle United	0-3		3185				8	13	4	2	9	1	3				10	11				6	12					7	5
7	26	SOUTHEND UNITED	5-0	Trusson, Lovell 2 (1p), Eeles, Manuel	3840			12	8	13	4	2	9	1	3				10	11				6						7	5
8	30	Peterborough United	1-1	Lovell	4199				8	12	4	2	9	1	3				10	11				6						7	5
9	Oct 6	Halifax Town	1-0	Lovell	1776				8	12	4	2	10	1	3				9	11				6						7	5
10	14	STOCKPORT COUNTY	0-3		3950				8	13	4	2	10	1	3				9	11	12		7	6	5						
11	17	Grimsby Town	0-2		3447				8	12	4	2	10	1	3				9	11			7	6	5						
12	21	CHESTERFIELD	3-0	Palmer, Lovell 2 (2p)	2791				8	10	4	2	13	1	3				9	11			7	6		12					5
13	31	ROCHDALE	1-0	Lovell	3127				8	10	4	2	12	1	3				9	11				6						7	5
14	Nov 4	SCARBOROUGH	2-0	Haylock, Manuel	3436				8	10	4	2	13	1	3				9	11			12	6						7	5
15	11	Lincoln City	3-1	Trusson, Heritage, Lovell	3612				8	13		2	10	1	3				9	11			12	6		4				7	5
16	14	Torquay United	2-0	Heritage, Palmer	2318				8	13	12	2	10	1	3				9	11			4	6		5				7	
17	24	COLCHESTER UNITED	3-3	Heritage, Lovell (p), O'Shea	3806			12		13		2	10	1	3				9	11			8	6		5				7	4
18	Dec 9	York City	0-1		2134					12	4	2	10	1	3				9	11			8	6						7	5
19	16	Exeter City	1-3	Lovell (p)	3818					13	4	2	10	1	3				9	12		11	8	6						7	5
20	26	MAIDSTONE UNITED	1-2	Walker	11605					13	4	2	8	1	3				9	10		11	12	6						7	5
21	30	WREXHAM	1-0	Johnson	3727					9		2	10	1	3							11	8	6			4			7	5
22	Jan 1	Hereford United	2-1	Heritage, Johnon	2759					9		2	10	1	3							11	8	6			4			7	5
23	13	DONCASTER ROVERS	3-1	Heritage, Brevett (og), O'Connor	3817					9		2	10	1	3				12	7		11	8	6			4				5
24	20	Aldershot	0-1		2592			7	12	9		2	10	1					13	3		11	8	6			4				5
25	27	HARTLEPOOL UNITED	0-0		3690			7	12	13		2	10	1	3				9	4		11	8	6							5
26	Feb 10	Burnley	2-1	Eeles, Lovell (p)	7274			7	12	13	6	2	10	1	3				9			11	8				4				5
27	13	Scunthorpe United	0-0		2226			7	6		4	2	10	1	3				9			11	8	12							5
28	17	YORK CITY	0-0		3665			7			6	2	10	1	3		12		9	4		11	8								5
29	23	Colchester United	0-2		4456			7	13	9	6	2	10	1	3					4		11	8							12	5
30	27	CARLISLE UNITED	2-1	Manuel, Heritage	2981			7		9		2	10	1	3				12	4			8	6						11	5
31	Mar 3	CAMBRIDGE UNITED	1-0	Gavin	4183					9		2	10	1	3				12	4			8	6			7			11	5
32	6	PETERBOROUGH UTD.	0-0		4415		5	7		9	12	2	10	1	3				13	4			8	6						11	
33	9	Southend United	0-2		4515		5		13	9	12	2	10	1	3				7	4			8	6						11	
34	16	HALIFAX TOWN	3-1	Lovell (p), O'Shea, Heritage	3846					12		2	10	1	3		4		7	13		9	8	6						11	5
35	19	Stockport County	0-1		3378			13	12	9	10	2			3		11	1	7	4			8	6							5
36	24	GRIMSBY TOWN	1-2	Lovell	4138					13		2	10	1	3		12		7			9	8	6			4			11	5
37	31	Chesterfield	0-2		4282			2	13	9				1	3		10		7			12	8	6			4			11	5
38	Apr 7	TORQUAY UNITED	0-2		2873	13			12			2	10	1	3		11		7			9	8	6			4				5
39	10	Rochdale	0-1		1334	13	6	12	7			2	10	1	3		11			9			8				4				5
40	14	HEREFORD UNITED	0-1		2382	13		12	7	6		2	10	1	3		11			9			8				4				5
41	16	Maidstone United	1-0	Heritage	5003			10	7			2	8	1	3		11		9	6			12				4				5
42	21	EXETER CITY	1-1	Beadle	3469	13		10	7			2	8	1	3		11		9				12	6			4				5
43	24	Wrexham	1-2	Walker	3498	13		10	7			2	8	1	3		11		9				12	6			4				5
44	28	LINCOLN CITY	1-1	Lovell (p)	2684	12		10	7			2	8		3		11	1	9				13	6			4				5
45	May 1	Cambridge United	1-2	Lovell	4963	8		10	13			2	12		3		11	1	9				7	6			4				5
46	5	Scarborough	1-0	Lovell	1809	8		10	7		4		13		3		11	1	9		12		2	6							5
					Apps	10	3	20	33	34	26	44	42	42	45	3	14	4	41	32	5	15	36	39	6	4	16	1	2	25	38
					Goals	1			2	1		1	9		2				16	3		1	2	3						2	2

One own goal

F.A. Cup

	Date	Opponent	Score	Scorers	Att	Beadle PCWJ	Clarke BR	Docker I	Eeles AG	Gavin PJ	Haines IG	Haylock P	Heritage PM	Hillyard RW	Johnson PE	Joseph F	Kimble GL	Lim HC	Lovell SJ	Manuel WAJ	Norris R	O'Connor MA	O'Shea TJ	Palmer LJ	Pearson R	Place BA	Pulis AR	Smith G	Thompson SA	Trusson MS	Walker A
R1	Nov 18	WELLING UNITED	0-0		5598				8	12	4	2	10	1	3				9	11				6		5				7	
rep	22	Welling United	0-1		4020			12		13	4	2	10	1	3				9	11			8	6		5				7	

F.L. Cup (Littlewoods Challenge Cup)

	Date	Opponent	Score	Scorers	Att	Beadle PCWJ	Clarke BR	Docker I	Eeles AG	Gavin PJ	Haines IG	Haylock P	Heritage PM	Hillyard RW	Johnson PE	Joseph F	Kimble GL	Lim HC	Lovell SJ	Manuel WAJ	Norris R	O'Connor MA	O'Shea TJ	Palmer LJ	Pearson R	Place BA	Pulis AR	Smith G	Thompson SA	Trusson MS	Walker A
R1/1	Aug 22	LEYTON ORIENT	1-4	Lovell	3258	9			8		4	7		1	3	12			10	11	2			13	5				6		
R1/2	29	Leyton Orient	0-3		2818	9			8		4	7		1	3	11			10		2			6	5			12	13		

A.M. Cup (Leyland DAF Cup)

	Date	Opponent	Score	Scorers	Att	Beadle PCWJ	Clarke BR	Docker I	Eeles AG	Gavin PJ	Haines IG	Haylock P	Heritage PM	Hillyard RW	Johnson PE	Joseph F	Kimble GL	Lim HC	Lovell SJ	Manuel WAJ	Norris R	O'Connor MA	O'Shea TJ	Palmer LJ	Pearson R	Place BA	Pulis AR	Smith G	Thompson SA	Trusson MS	Walker A
PR	Nov 7	Southend United	0-1		1650				8	12		2	10	1	3				9	11			4	6		5				7	
PR	28	CAMBRIDGE UNITED	2-0	Lovell, Walker	1044			13		7	12	2	10		3			1	9	11			8	6		5					4
R1	Jan 24	Bristol Rovers	0-1		2724			7	12	9		2	10					1	13	3		11	8	6			4				5

1990/91

15th in Division Four

						Beadle PCWJ	Butler PA (Tony)	Carpenter R	Clarke BR	Crown DI	Dempsey MAP	Docker I	Dunne JJ	Eeles AG	Gleasure PF	Hague P	Haines IG	Harle MJL	Heritage PM	Hillyard RW	Johnson PE	Kimble GL	Lim HC	Lovell SJ	Manuel WAJ	McDonald DH	O'Connor MA	O'Shea TJ	Owers AR	Palmer LJ	Trusson MS	Walker A	West G
1	Aug 25	DARLINGTON	1-0	Lovell (p)	3718	13			4				2						10	1	11	12		9	3		7	6			8	5	
2	31	Torquay United	1-3	Lovell (p)	3047	10							2				4			1	11	13		9	3		7	12		6	8	5	
3	Sep 8	HARTLEPOOL UNITED	3-0	Lovell 2, Heritage	3180							12	2						10	1	11	4		9			7	6		3	8	5	
4	15	Scarborough	1-2	Lovell	1499	12							2						10	1	11	4		9			7	6		3	8	5	
5	19	Hereford United	1-1	Heritage	2632	12							2						10		11	4	1	9			7	6		3	8	5	
6	22	MAIDSTONE UNITED	0-2		8004					13		12	2						10		11	4	1	9			7	6		3	8	5	
7	29	York City	1-1	Docker	2264							12							10		11	4	1	9	6	2	7			3	8	5	
8	Oct 2	CARLISLE UNITED	2-1	Lovell 2 (1p)	3052	12						8							10		11	4	1	9	6	2	7			3		5	
9	6	ROCHDALE	2-2	Lovell 2	3340	10						8		12					13		11	4	1	9	6	2				3	7	5	
10	13	Scunthorpe United	0-1		2357				3		12	8							10		11	4	1	9	6	2				13	7	5	
11	20	Blackpool	0-2		3041				4	10		8							12		11	13	1	9	3	2	7				6	5	
12	23	ALDERSHOT	1-1	Walker	3149					10		8							12		11	4	1	9	3	2	7			13	6	5	
13	27	WREXHAM	2-3	Docker, Carpenter	3092			13		10		8							12		11	4	1	9	3	2	7			6		5	
14	Nov 3	Doncaster Rovers	1-1	Lovell	2500				4	10		8							12		11		1	9	3	2	7				6	5	
15	9	Halifax Town	2-1	Crown, Trusson	1708					10		8	4								11		1	9	3	2	7				6	5	
16	24	CARDIFF CITY	4-0	* See below	2821				4	10		8	11										1	9	3	2	7				6	5	
17	Dec 1	Chesterfield	1-1	Lovell	3468				4	10		8	11										1	9	3		7	2			6	5	
18	15	BURNLEY	3-2	Crown 3	3743	11			4	10		8	12						13				1	9	3		7	2			6	5	
19	22	Lincoln City	1-1	Lovell	2685	13			4	10		8	11						12				1	9	3		7	2			6		5
20	26	WALSALL	1-0	Lovell	3755				4	10		8	11										1	9	3		7	2			6	5	
21	29	NORTHAMPTON T	0-0		4969	12			4	10		8	11										1	9	3		7	2			6	5	
22	Jan 1	Stockport County	1-1	Beadle	2859	12			4	10		8	11										1	9	3		7	2			6	5	
23	11	TORQUAY UNITED	2-2	Crown, Uzzell (og)	4352	7			4	10		8	11	13				3				12	1	9				2			6	5	
24	25	SCARBOROUGH	1-1	Beadle	3776	6			4	10		8	11	12								13	1	9	3		7	2				5	
25	29	Darlington	1-1	Crown	2882				4	10		8	11	12								6	1	9	3		7	2				5	
26	Feb 2	HEREFORD UNITED	2-1	Walker, O'Connor	3252	12			4	10		8	11								13	6	1	9	3		7	2				5	
27	15	Cardiff City	0-2		2170	13			4	10		8									12	11	1	9	3		7	2			6	5	
28	22	HALIFAX TOWN	1-0	Crown	2829	8			4	10											11	12	1	9	3		7	2			6	5	
29	26	PETERBOROUGH UTD.	2-3	Trusson, Beadle	3154	13			4	10		12									11	8	1	9	3		7	2			6	5	
30	Mar 2	CHESTERFIELD	0-1		3113	7				10					1		4				11	8		9	3		12	2		13	6	5	
31	9	Burnley	2-2	Lovell, Crown	6459	9				10			2		1		4				11			8	3		7	12			6	5	
32	12	Carlisle United	4-0	Beadle 2, Lovell, Crown	2633	9				10			2		1	12	4				11			8	3		7	13			6	5	
33	16	YORK CITY	0-0		3047	9				10			2			5	4				11	12	1	8	3		7				6		
34	19	SCUNTHORPE UNITED	1-1	Trusson (p)	2319					10			2				4				11	12	1	8	3		7	9			6	5	
35	23	Rochdale	3-1	Beadle 2, Crown	1654	9				10			2				4					12	1	8	3		7	11			6	5	
36	30	Walsall	0-0		3074	9				10			7				4					12	1	8			11	2		3	6	5	
37	Apr 1	LINCOLN CITY	2-2	Crown, Walker	3770					10		9	2				4					12	1	8			7	11	13	3	6	5	
38	6	Northampton Town	1-2	Tusson (p)	2993							9	2	13			4					7	1	8	12			11	10	3	6	5	
39	13	STOCKPORT COUNTY	1-3	Lovell	2927			2	4			9		7									1	8	13		11		10	3	6	5	
40	16	Peterborough United	0-2		5831			2	4								9					11	1	8	12		7		10	3	6	5	
41	20	BLACKPOOL	2-2	Palmer, Lovell	3016		9	2								4						11	1	8	13		7		10	3	6	5	
42	24	Maidstone United	1-3	Lovell	2935		9	2								4						11	1	8	12		7		10	3	6	5	
43	27	Aldershot	0-1		2083		9	2				13				4						11	1	8	12		7		10	3	6	5	
44	30	Hartlepool United	0-1		3782		9	2				7				4						11	1	8	12		13		10	3	6	5	
45	May 4	Wrexham	0-3		1231		9	12		10		7				4		13				11	1	8	3			2	6			5	
46	11	DONCASTER ROVERS	2-0	O'Connor, Lovell	2656		9	13		10	12	7					4					11	1	8			3	2	6			5	
					Apps	22	6	9	20	30	2	31	26	6	3	7	12	2	15	4	24	34	39	46	38	10	41	29	10	21	39	44	1
					Goals	7		1		12		3							2					19			3			1	4	4	

Scorers in game 16: O'Connor, Crown, Walker, Docker

DC Jordan played at 12 in games 39 and 41

One own goal

F.A. Cup

						Beadle PCWJ	Butler PA (Tony)	Carpenter R	Clarke BR	Crown DI	Dempsey MAP	Docker I	Dunne JJ	Eeles AG	Gleasure PF	Hague P	Haines IG	Harle MJL	Heritage PM	Hillyard RW	Johnson PE	Kimble GL	Lim HC	Lovell SJ	Manuel WAJ	McDonald DH	O'Connor MA	O'Shea TJ	Owers AR	Palmer LJ	Trusson MS	Walker A	West G
R1	Nov 17	Bournemouth	1-2	Crown	6113				2	10		8	4						12			11	1	9	3		7				6	5	

F.L. Cup (Rumbelows Cup)

						Beadle PCWJ	Butler PA (Tony)	Carpenter R	Clarke BR	Crown DI	Dempsey MAP	Docker I	Dunne JJ	Eeles AG	Gleasure PF	Hague P	Haines IG	Harle MJL	Heritage PM	Hillyard RW	Johnson PE	Kimble GL	Lim HC	Lovell SJ	Manuel WAJ	McDonald DH	O'Connor MA	O'Shea TJ	Owers AR	Palmer LJ	Trusson MS	Walker A	West G
R1/1	Aug 28	SHREWSBURY TOWN	1-0	Lovell	2613	13							2				4		10	1	11	12		9	3		7			6	8	5	
R1/2	Sep 4	Shrewsbury Town	0-2		2193	13						12	2				4		10	1	11			9			7	6		3	8	5	

A.M. Cup (Leyland DAF Cup)

						Beadle PCWJ	Butler PA (Tony)	Carpenter R	Clarke BR	Crown DI	Dempsey MAP	Docker I	Dunne JJ	Eeles AG	Gleasure PF	Hague P	Haines IG	Harle MJL	Heritage PM	Hillyard RW	Johnson PE	Kimble GL	Lim HC	Lovell SJ	Manuel WAJ	McDonald DH	O'Connor MA	O'Shea TJ	Owers AR	Palmer LJ	Trusson MS	Walker A	West G
PR	Nov 6	Bournemouth	0-0		2784				4	10		8	12						13		11		1	9	3	2	7				6		5
PR	27	MAIDSTONE UNITED	4-1	Walker 2, Crown, Lovell	3582				4	10		8	11										1	9	3	2	7	12			6	5	
R1	Jan 8	HEREFORD UNITED	0-1		1455	7			4	10		8	11	13				3				12	1	9				2			6	5	

1991/92

11th in Division Four

						Arnott AJ	Beadle PCWJ	Berkley AJ	Butler PA (Tony)	Carpenter R	Clark PP	Clarke BR	Crown DI	Dempsey MAP	Dunne JJ	Eeles AG	Elsey KW	Green RE	Harrison LD	Lim HC	Lovell SJ	Martin EJ	O'Connor MA	O'Shea TJ	Osborne LW	Palmer LJ	Polston AA	Smith NJ	Thomas RC	Trusson MS	Walker A
1	Aug 17	SCUNTHORPE UNITED	4-0	Elsey, Crown, O'Connor, Beadle	3463		13		6		7		9			11	4			1	8		10	2		3				12	5
2	24	York City	1-1	Crown	2328		12		6		7		9			11	4			1	8	3	10	2						13	5
3	Sep 4	Hereford United	0-2		2544		13		6		7		9			11	4			1	8		10	2		3				12	5
4	7	SCARBOROUGH	2-0	Arnott, Lovell	3269	13	9				7	6				11	4			1	8		10	2		3				12	5
5	14	Wrexham	1-2	Elsey	1637	12	9				7	6		13		11	4			1	8		10	2						3	5
6	17	Blackpool	0-2		3035		9				7	6	13	12		11	4			1	8		10	2						3	5
7	21	BARNET	3-3	Eeles, Crown 2	4858		9			3	7	6	8	12		11	4			1	13		10	2							5
8	28	Crewe Alexandra	1-2	Trusson (p)	3126		9				7	6	8	12		11	3			1	13		10	2						4	5
9	Oct 5	CHESTERFIELD	0-1		2829	9					7	6	8	13		11	3			1	10		12	2						4	5
10	12	Halifax Town	3-0	Crown 2, Beadle	1435	12	9				7		8			4	3				10		11	2						6	5
11	19	Doncaster Rovers	1-1	Lovell	1468		9			12	7		8			4	3			1	10		11	2						6	5
12	26	NORTHAMPTON T	3-1	Crown 3	2543		9				7		10	12		6	3			1	8		11	2				4			5
13	Nov 2	Carlisle United	0-0		1672		9				7		8	12		6	3			1	10		11	2				4			5
14	5	CARDIFF CITY	0-0		2467	13	9				7		8	12		6	3			1	10		11	2				4			5
15	9	MAIDSTONE UNITED	1-1	O'Connor	6717	9	12				7		8	6			3			1	10		11	2				4			5
16	23	Mansfield Town	3-4	Lovell, Crown, Arnott	3287	9			5		7		8	6		12	3			1	10		11	2			13	4			
17	Dec 14	Rotherham United	1-1	Crown	3137	9	12				7		8							1	10		11	2	6		3	4			5
18	21	YORK CITY	1-1	Crown	2700	9	13				7		8			12	3			1	10		11	2	6			4			5
19	26	Scunthorpe United	0-2		3883	12	9				7		8	6		13	3			1	10		11	2				4			5
20	Jan 1	HEREFORD UNITED	2-1	Lovell, Smith	3203	13	9	12			7	5	8	6						1	10	3	11	2				4			
21	4	Lincoln City	0-1		2169	9				4	7	5	8	6			13			1	10	3	11	2							12
22	11	WALSALL	4-0	Crown 3, Elsey	2726			13			7	12	10	6			9			1	8	3	11	2				4			5
23	18	Burnley	1-4	Walker	8908			13			7	12	8	6			9			1	10	3	11	2				4			5
24	Feb 1	DONCASTER ROVERS	2-1	Smith, O'Connor	2366	13	9				7			6			8			1	10	3	11	2		12		4			5
25	8	Northampton Town	0-0		3183	12	9				7			6			8			1	10	3	11	2				4			5
26	15	ROTHERHAM UNITED	5-1	Lovell 3, Dempsey, Crown	2488	13					7		9	6			8			1	10	3	11	2		12		4			5
27	22	Walsall	1-0	Dempsey	2987		12				7		9	6	4		8			1	10	3	11	2		13					5
28	29	LINCOLN CITY	1-3	Lovell	3156		13				7		9	6			8			1	10	3	11	2		12		4			5
29	Mar 3	BURNLEY	3-0	Crown, Beadle, Lovell	3738		8				7		9	6						1	10	3	11	2		12		4			5
30	7	Rochdale	1-2	Crown	1941		8				7		9	6						1	10	3	11	2		12		4			5
31	10	Cardiff City	3-2	Green 2, Crown	8521		8				7		9	6	12			2		1	10		11			3		4			5
32	14	CARLISLE UNITED	1-2	Crown	2864	12					7		9	6	13			2		1	10		11		8	3		4			5
33	17	ROCHDALE	0-0		2322	12					7		9	6	11			2		1	10	3			8			4			5
34	21	Maidstone United	1-1	Lovell	3264	8					7		9	6	11		12	2		1	10	3						4			5
35	28	MANSFIELD TOWN	2-0	Lovell, Beadle	2583		8				7		9	12	6			2		1	10	3						4	11		5
36	31	WREXHAM	2-1	Lovell (p), Green	2982		8				7		9		6			2		1	10	3	4						11		5
37	Apr 4	Scarborough	1-2	Crown	1174		8				7		9	12	6			2		1	10	3	4						11		5
38	11	BLACKPOOL	3-2	Lovell, Crown, Beadle	3677		8				7		9		6			2		1	10	3	4						11		5
39	18	Barnet	0-2		4049		8				7		9	12				2		1	10	3	4					6	11		5
40	20	CREWE ALEXANDRA	0-1		2930		8				7		9	13	12			2		1	10	3	4					6	11		5
41	25	Chesterfield	3-3	Thomas, Lovell, Green	2109		9				7	6			12			2	1		10	3	4					8	11		5
42	May 2	HALIFAX TOWN	2-0	Lovell 2 (1p)	2404	13	8		9		7							2	1		10	3	4		12			6	11		5
					Apps	19	33	3	5	3	42	11	36	30	11	17	27	12	2	39	42	22	39	30	5	11	2	26	8	10	40
					Goals	2	5						22	2		1	3	4			16		3					2	1	1	1

KG Branaghan played at 1 in game 10

F.A. Cup

						Arnott AJ	Beadle PCWJ	Berkley AJ	Butler PA (Tony)	Carpenter R	Clark PP	Clarke BR	Crown DI	Dempsey MAP	Dunne JJ	Eeles AG	Elsey KW	Green RE	Harrison LD	Lim HC	Lovell SJ	Martin EJ	O'Connor MA	O'Shea TJ	Osborne LW	Palmer LJ	Polston AA	Smith NJ	Thomas RC	Trusson MS	Walker A
R1	Nov 18	Brentford	3-3	Walker 2, Smith	5838	13	9				7		8	6		12	3			1	10		11	2				4			5
rep	26	BRENTFORD	1-3	Walker	7328	9	13				7		8	6		12	3			1	10		11	2				4			5

F.L. Cup (Rumbelows Cup)

						Arnott AJ	Beadle PCWJ	Berkley AJ	Butler PA (Tony)	Carpenter R	Clark PP	Clarke BR	Crown DI	Dempsey MAP	Dunne JJ	Eeles AG	Elsey KW	Green RE	Harrison LD	Lim HC	Lovell SJ	Martin EJ	O'Connor MA	O'Shea TJ	Osborne LW	Palmer LJ	Polston AA	Smith NJ	Thomas RC	Trusson MS	Walker A
R1/1	Aug 20	Portsmouth	1-2	Beadle	4801		12		6		7		9			11	4			1	8	3	10	2						13	5
R1/2	27	PORTSMOUTH	3-4	Crown, Walker, Beadle	5114		13		6		7		9			11	4			1	8		10	2		3				12	5

A.M. Cup (Autoglass Trophy)

						Arnott AJ	Beadle PCWJ	Berkley AJ	Butler PA (Tony)	Carpenter R	Clark PP	Clarke BR	Crown DI	Dempsey MAP	Dunne JJ	Eeles AG	Elsey KW	Green RE	Harrison LD	Lim HC	Lovell SJ	Martin EJ	O'Connor MA	O'Shea TJ	Osborne LW	Palmer LJ	Polston AA	Smith NJ	Thomas RC	Trusson MS	Walker A
PR	Nov 20	Fulham	0-2		1108	9		12	13	8	7	5		6		11				1	10	3					2	4			
PR	Dec 10	MAIDSTONE UNITED	4-2	Smith 2, Crown, Haylock (og)	2300			12			7		8	6		9					10		11	2			3	4			5
R1	Jan 14	Fulham	0-2		1483	12		13			7	5	10	6			9			1	8	3	11	2				4			

RT Dalton played at 1 on Dec 10.

Expunged League Games

					Arnott AJ	Beadle PCWJ	Berkley AJ	Butler PA (Tony)	Carpenter R	Clark PP	Clarke BR	Crown DI	Dempsey MAP	Dunne JJ	Eeles AG	Elsey KW	Green RE	Harrison LD	Lim HC	Lovell SJ	Martin EJ	O'Connor MA	O'Shea TJ	Osborne LW	Palmer LJ	Polston AA	Smith NJ	Thomas RC	Trusson MS	Walker A
Nov 30	ALDERSHOT	3-1	Crown, Arnott, Smith	2566	9	13				7		8	6		12				1	10		11	2			3	4			5
Feb 11	Aldershot	0-0		2986	13	9				7			6			8			1	10	3	11	2		12		4			5

Aldershot resigned from the Football League and their record was expunged. Appearances and goals not included in a player's record.

1992/93

21st in the new Football League Division Three

No	Date	Opponent	Score	Scorers	Att	Arnott AJ	Aylott TKC	Baker DP	Barrett S	Breen GP	Butler PA (Tony)	Carpenter R	Clark PP	Crane SJ	Crown DI	Dempsey MAP	Dunne JJ	Eeles AG	Forster NM	Green RE	Hague P	Henry LA	Lim HC	Lovell SJ	Martin EJ	O'Connor MA	Palmer LJ	Ritchie PM	Roeder GV	Smith NJ	Stephenson P	Watson PD
1	Aug 15	NORTHAMPTON T	2-3	Osborne, O'Connor	3869		9		1	5	4		7			12				2		11		13		10	3			6		
2	22	Bury	0-1		1936	12			1	5	4		7		8	13				2		11		9		10	3			6		
3	29	BARNET	1-1	Crown	3896		9		1	5	4		7		8	12				2		11		13		10	3			6		
4	Sep 1	WREXHAM	4-1	Aylott, Lovell 3 (1p)	2499		9		1	5	4		7		8				12	2		13		11		10	3			6		
5	5	Scarborough	1-1	Aylott	1412		9			5	4		7		8				13	2		12	1	11		10	3			6		
6	12	CHESTERFIELD	0-0		2976	12	9			5	4		7						8	2		3	1	11		10				6		
7	15	Rochdale	1-1	Henry	1879	9				5	4	10	7			12			8	2		3	1	11						6		
8	19	Cardiff City	1-3	Forster	6356		9			5	4	12	7						8	2		3	1	11		10				6		
9	26	WALSALL	0-1		2714		9		1	5	4	12	7			13			8	2		3		11		10				6		
10	Oct 3	CREWE ALEXANDRA	1-2	Clark	2443		9		1	5	4	2	7			8			13			3		11		10	12			6		
11	10	Doncaster Rovers	0-1		2477	9			1	5	4	2	7					8	12			3		11	10					6		
12	24	Halifax Town	0-2		1343					5	4		7		9			8	12	2		3	1	10		11				6		
13	31	TORQUAY UNITED	0-2		3005						4	12	7		9			8	13	2		11	1	10	3	5				6		
14	Nov 3	HEREFORD UNITED	3-1	Forster 2, Arnott	2043	9			1	5	4	10				11			8	2		7			3					6		
15	7	Carlisle United	0-1		3213	9			1		4	10				11			8	2	5	7			3	12				6		
16	21	DARLINGTON	3-1	Crown, Parkin (og), Forster	2567	9			1	5	4		7		8				10	2					3					6	11	
17	28	Lincoln City	1-1	Arnott	3175	9			1	5	4		7		8				10	2					3					6	11	
18	Dec 12	Shrewsbury Town	1-2	Arnott	2442	9			1	5	4		7		8	13			10	2					3	12				6	11	
19	18	COLCHESTER UNITED	0-1		2366	9	12		1	5	4		7									2			3	10				6	11	
20	26	BURY	1-4	Smith	3728	9				5	4		7							2		10	1		3					6	11	
21	28	Scunthorpe United	2-2	Arnott, Stephenson	2835	9				12	4		7							2		10	1			13	3		5	6	11	
22	Jan 8	ROCHDALE	4-2	Arnott 2, Green, Baker	3050	9		10	1	5	4	6	7							2						8	3				11	
23	16	Walsall	1-1	Smith	3253	9		10	1	5	4	8	7							2						12	3			6	11	
24	23	CARDIFF CITY	0-1		4066	9		10	1	5	4	8	7						12	2							3			6	11	
25	Feb 6	Northampton Town	2-2	Baker, Ritchie	3812			10	1		4	8	7							2					3			9	5	6	11	
26	13	SCARBOROUGH	3-1	Richie 2, Stephenson	2923			10	1		4	8								2		7			3			9	5	6	11	
27	16	Chesterfield	1-1	Green	2721			10	1		4	8								2		7			3			9	5	6	11	
28	20	Wrexham	0-2		4415		12	10	1	13	4	8								2		7			3	11		9	5	6		
29	27	DONCASTER ROVERS	1-1	Crown	2995			10	1	5	4	8			13		12			2		7			3	11		9		6		
30	Mar 2	Barnet	0-2		3446			9	1	5	4	10			8		7			2					3			11		6		
31	6	Crewe Alexandra	1-3	Martin	3216			9	1	5	4	10	13		8			7		2					3	12			11	6		
32	9	York City	1-1	Eeles	3327			9	1	5	4		7		8			11		2		12			3	10				6		
33	13	CARLISLE UNITED	1-0	Smith	3422			9	1		4	2	7		8			10	11	5		3								6		
34	20	Hereford United	1-3	Crown	2138			9	1	13	4	6	7		8	12		10	11	5		2										3
35	23	LINCOLN CITY	3-1	Green, Forster 2	2934			9	1		4	5	7	12	8	11		6	10	2		3										
36	27	Darlington	1-1	Crane	2404			9	1	13	4	5	7	8		11		6	10	2		3								12		
37	Apr 2	YORK CITY	1-4	Baker	3946			9	1		4	5	7	8		11		6	10	2		3								12		
38	6	SHREWSBURY TOWN	1-0	Crown	3129			9	1		4	5	7	12	8	11			10	2					3					6		
39	12	SCUNTHORPE UNITED	1-1	Baker	3763			9	1		4	5	7		8	11		12	10	2					3					6		
40	16	Colchester United	0-3		4695			9	1		4	5	7	13	8	11		12	10	2					3					6		
41	May 1	HALIFAX TOWN	2-0	Eeles, Baker	6985			9	1			5	7	12	8		2	10	11	4					3					6		
42	8	Torquay United	1-2	Baker	4645			9	1		6	5	7	12			2	10	11	4					3					8		
					Apps	15	10	21	34	29	41	28	35	7	20	16	4	14	26	39	1	28	8	13	22	21	10	6	6	39	12	1
					Goals	6	2	6					1	1	5			2	6	3		1		3	1	1		3		3	2	

SA Houghton played in games 19 to 21 incusive at 8 (subbed in game 21)
LW Osborne played at 8 (subbed) in game 1, scoring 1 goal

One own goal

F.A. Cup

Rd	Date	Opponent	Score	Scorers	Att	Arnott AJ	Aylott TKC	Baker DP	Barrett S	Breen GP	Butler PA (Tony)	Carpenter R	Clark PP	Crane SJ	Crown DI	Dempsey MAP	Dunne JJ	Eeles AG	Forster NM	Green RE	Hague P	Henry LA	Lim HC	Lovell SJ	Martin EJ	O'Connor MA	Palmer LJ	Ritchie PM	Roeder GV	Smith NJ	Stephenson P	Watson PD
R1	Nov 14	KETTERING TOWN	3-2	Clark, Crown, Forster	3962	9			1		4	5	7		8	11			10	2					3	12				6		
R2	Dec 5	COLCHESTER UNITED	1-1	Crown	5319	9			1	5	4		7		8	11			10	2		13			3	12				6		
rep	16	Colchester United	3-2	Forster, Arnott, Henry (p)	4440	9	12		1	5	4		7			11			8			2			3	10	13			6		
R3	Jan 2	HUDDERSFIELD TOWN	0-0		5413	9				5	4	6	7					11		2		10	1			8	3					
rep	13	Huddersfield Town	1-2	Green (p)	5144	9			1	5	4	10	7					11		2						8	3			6		

F.L. Cup (Coca Cola Cup)

Rd	Date	Opponent	Score	Scorers	Att	Arnott AJ	Aylott TKC	Baker DP	Barrett S	Breen GP	Butler PA (Tony)	Carpenter R	Clark PP	Crane SJ	Crown DI	Dempsey MAP	Dunne JJ	Eeles AG	Forster NM	Green RE	Hague P	Henry LA	Lim HC	Lovell SJ	Martin EJ	O'Connor MA	Palmer LJ	Ritchie PM	Roeder GV	Smith NJ	Stephenson P	Watson PD
R1/1	Aug 18	NORTHAMPTON T	2-1	Crown, Lovell	2245	12			1	5	4		7		9					2		11		8		10	3			6		
R1/2	Sep 9	Northampton Town	2-0	Crown, Aylott	2390		9			5	4	13	7		8				12	2		3	1	11		10				6		
R2/1	23	SOUTHAMPTON	0-0		7488		9		1	5	4		7			12			8	2		3		11		10				6		
R2/2	Oct 7	Southampton	0-3		6764	9			1	5	4	2	7				8	13	12			3		11		10				6		

A.M. Cup (Autoglass Trophy)

Rd	Date	Opponent	Score	Scorers	Att	Arnott AJ	Aylott TKC	Baker DP	Barrett S	Breen GP	Butler PA (Tony)	Carpenter R	Clark PP	Crane SJ	Crown DI	Dempsey MAP	Dunne JJ	Eeles AG	Forster NM	Green RE	Hague P	Henry LA	Lim HC	Lovell SJ	Martin EJ	O'Connor MA	Palmer LJ	Ritchie PM	Roeder GV	Smith NJ	Stephenson P	Watson PD
R1	Dec 1	Leyton Orient	1-4	Aylott	1667		9									11				2	5	10	1			8	3		4	6	7	13
R1	8	FULHAM	3-3	Henry 2, O'Connor	1085		9		1							11				2	4	10				8	3			6	7	12

K Hunt played at 12 on Dec 1. MN Joseph played at 5 on Dec 8.

1993/94

16th in Division Three

							Arnott AJ	Baker DP	Banks S	Barrett S	Breen GP	Butler PA (Tony)	Carpenter R	Clark PP	Crane SJ	Dunne JJ	Eeles AG	Forster NM	Green RE	Hague P	Henry LA	Martin EJ	Micklewhite G	Palmer LJ	Reinelt RS	Smillie N	Smith NJ	Trott RF	Watson PD
1	Aug	14	CHESTERFIELD	0-2		3485	9			1		5	8	4	13			10	12			2	7			11	6		3
2		21	Rochdale	0-3		2092				1		5	4	12	13			10	6			2	7		9	11	8		3
3		28	SCARBOROUGH	2-2	Baker, Forster	2526	10	9		1			6	4		2		13	5				7	3	12	11	8		
4		31	DONCASTER ROVERS	0-0		2923		9	1				6	4	8	2			5				7	3	12	11	10		
5	Sep	4	Wycombe Wanderers	1-1	Forster	6226		9	1				6	4	12	2		8	5				7	3		11	10		
6		11	TORQUAY UNITED	2-2	Forster, Green (p)	2927		9	1				6	4		2		8	5				7	3		11	10		
7		18	Shrewsbury Town	2-2	Baker, Green (p)	2811		9	1			4	6			2		8	5				7	3	12	11	10		
8		25	SCUNTHORPE UNITED	1-0	Smillie	2872		9	1			4				2		8	5			6		3	7	11	10		
9	Oct	2	Carlisle United	2-1	Forster 2	6449		9	1			4	6	12		2		8	5					3	7	11	10		
10		9	Walsall	0-1		4639	12	9	1			4	6			2		8	5					3	7	11	10		
11		16	DARLINGTON	2-1	Arnott, Smith	3063	9			1		4	6		12	2		10	5					3	7	11	8		
12		23	Crewe Alexandra	0-1		3611	9			1	12	4	6		13	2		10	5				7	3		11	8		
13		30	COLCHESTER UNITED	3-0	Green, Forster, Reinelt	3964	9			1		4	6			2		10	5				7	3	12	11	8		
14	Nov	2	HEREFORD UNITED	2-0	Arnott, Forster	3168	9	13		1	12	4	6			2		10	5				7	3		11	8		
15		6	Mansfield Town	1-2	Forster	2421		9		1		4	7			2		10	5			6		3	12	11	8		
16		20	WIGAN ATHLETIC	2-2	Forster, Baker	2751		9	1		5	4	7			6		10				2	11	3			8		
17		27	Lincoln City	1-3	Baker	2979		9	1		5	4	7			6		10				2	11	3			8		
18	Dec	11	ROCHDALE	1-2	Forster	2493		9	1			5	6	4		2		10					7	3	8	11			
19		18	Chesterfield	2-3	Micklewhite, Forster	2348		9	1				6			2		10	5	4			7	3	8	11			
20		27	NORTHAMPTON T	1-0	Terry (og)	4573			1				6	4		2		10	5		9	12	7	3	8	11			
21	Jan	1	BURY	1-0	Smillie	3576			1				6	4		2		10	5		9		7	3	12	11	8		
22		3	Doncaster Rovers	0-0		1830			1		2		6	4				10	5		9		7	3	12	11	8		
23		15	Darlington	1-2	Henry	2111			1		2		6	4				8	5		9		7	3		11	10		
24		22	WALSALL	1-1	Baker	3211		8	1			4	6			2		12	5		9		7	3		11	10		
25		29	Colchester United	2-1	Smith, Forster	3273		8	1			4				2		12	5		9		7	3	6	11	10		
26	Feb	5	CREWE ALEXANDRA	1-3	Forster	3713		8	1			4	6			2		12	5		9		7	3		11	10		
27		12	Preston North End	0-0		6167		12	1		2	4	6					8	5		9		7	3		11	10		
28		19	Scarborough	1-1	Baker	1527		12	1		4		6			2		8	5		9		7	3		11	10		
29		26	WYCOMBE WANDERERS	0-1		4302		9	1		4		6			2		8	5		13		7	3	12	11	10		
30	Mar	1	Chester City	0-1		3128		9	1		4		6			2		12	5		8				11	7	10		3
31		5	Torquay United	1-0	Green	3353		9	1		4	12	6			2		13	5		8				11	7	10		3
32		12	SHREWSBURY TOWN	0-2		3095		9	1		4	12	6			2		8	5						11	7	10		3
33		19	Scunthorpe United	1-1	Baker	2386		9	1		4		6			2		10	5		11				12	7	8		3
34		26	CARLISLE UNITED	2-0	Carpenter (p), Forster	2627		9	1		4	10	6			2		8	5						11	7			3
35	Apr	2	Northampton Town	2-1	Carpenter, Forster	4628		9	1		4	10	6			2		8	5			11				7			3
36		4	CHESTER CITY	2-2	Baker, Butler	3165		9	1		4	10	6			2		8	5		12	11			7				3
37		12	PRESTON NORTH END	2-2	Forster 2	2453		9	1		4	10	6			2		8	5						11	7			3
38		16	Hereford United	0-2		1964	13	9		1	4	10	6			2		8	5				11			7	12		3
39		19	Bury	0-0		1687		9		1	4	10	6			2		8	5				11			7	12		3
40		23	MANSFIELD TOWN	1-0	Forster	2464		9		1	4	10	6			2		8	5				12		7		11		3
41		30	Wigan Athletic	0-2		1346	13	9		1	4		6			2		8	5				11			7	12	10	3
42	May	7	LINCOLN CITY	1-1	Carpenter (p)	2759	13	9		1	4		6	10		2		8	5				7	3		11	12		
						Apps	10	33	29	13	22	27	40	13	6	37	0	41	39	1	14	9	29	28	25	38	35	1	14
						Goals	2	8				1	3					18	4		1		1		1	2	2		

One own goal

F.A. Cup

							Arnott AJ	Baker DP	Banks S	Barrett S	Breen GP	Butler PA (Tony)	Carpenter R	Clark PP	Crane SJ	Dunne JJ	Eeles AG	Forster NM	Green RE	Hague P	Henry LA	Martin EJ	Micklewhite G	Palmer LJ	Reinelt RS	Smillie N	Smith NJ	Trott RF	Watson PD
R1	Nov	13	Yeading	0-0		2285	12	9	1			4	7			6		10	5			2		3	11		8		
rep		30	YEADING	3-1	Smith, Micklewhite, Butler	3231		9	1			4	7	5		2		10					11	3	12	6	8		
R2	Dec	4	Plymouth Argyle	0-2		6051		9	1		6	4		5		2		10	12				11	3	7		8		

R1 played at Hayes

F.L. Cup (Coca Cola Cup)

							Arnott AJ	Baker DP	Banks S	Barrett S	Breen GP	Butler PA (Tony)	Carpenter R	Clark PP	Crane SJ	Dunne JJ	Eeles AG	Forster NM	Green RE	Hague P	Henry LA	Martin EJ	Micklewhite G	Palmer LJ	Reinelt RS	Smillie N	Smith NJ	Trott RF	Watson PD
R1/1	Aug	17	BRIGHTON & HOVE ALB.	1-0	Reinelt	3330				1		5			12		4	10	6			2	7		9	11	8		3
R1/2		25	Brighton & Hove Albion	0-2		4410	10			1		5	8	12	13	2	4	9	6				7			11			3

A.M. Cup (Autoglass Trophy)

							Arnott AJ	Baker DP	Banks S	Barrett S	Breen GP	Butler PA (Tony)	Carpenter R	Clark PP	Crane SJ	Dunne JJ	Eeles AG	Forster NM	Green RE	Hague P	Henry LA	Martin EJ	Micklewhite G	Palmer LJ	Reinelt RS	Smillie N	Smith NJ	Trott RF	Watson PD
R1	Sep	28	COLCHESTER UNITED	0-0		1091		9		1	6			4	10		7			5		2			8			12	3
R1	Nov	9	Cambridge United	0-2		1463		9	1			4	7	13	8				5	6		2		3	11		10		12

MAP Dempsey played at 11 on Sep 28.

1994/95

19th in Division Three

No	Date	Opponent	Score	Scorers	Att	Arnott AJ	Baker DP	Banks S	Barrett S	Bodley MJ	Brown SR	Butler PA (Tony)	Carpenter R	Dunne JJ	Foster AM	Freeman DBA	Green RE	Hutchinson IN	Knott GR	Lindsey S	Martin EJ	Micklewhite G	Palmer LJ	Pike C	Ramage AW	Reinelt RS	Ritchie PM	Smillie N	Smith NJ	Trott RF	Watson PD	Watts GS
1	Aug 13	HARTLEPOOL UNITED	0-0		2959	10	13		1			6		2	9		5					4	3		12			7	8		11	
2	20	Wigan Athletic	3-0	Foster, Reinelt, Watson	1514		10		1			6		2	9		5					4	3			7			8		11	
3	27	ROCHDALE	1-1	Butler	3009	13	10		1			6	12	2	9		5					4	3			7			8		11	
4	30	Scunthorpe United	0-3		2098	9	10		1			6	12	2			5					4	3			7			8		11	
5	Sep 3	Exeter City	0-3		2241	9		1				6	12	2			5					4				7		11	8		3	10
6	10	SCARBOROUGH	3-1	Palmer, Ritchie, Baker	2438		9	1				6	4	2			5						3			7	10		8		11	
7	13	PRESTON NORTH END	2-3	Smith, Baker	2653		9	1				6	4	2			5					12	3			7	10		8		11	
8	17	Hartlepool United	0-2		1756		9	1				6	4	2			5									7	10		8	3	11	
9	24	Walsall	1-2	Micklewhite	3654		9	1				6	4	2			5					7				12	10	11	8		3	
10	Oct 1	MANSFIELD TOWN	0-2		2569			1				6	4	2			5					7	3	9		12	10		8		11	
11	8	TORQUAY UNITED	1-0	Pike	2450	13		1				6	4	2			5					7	3	9		10			8		11	12
12	15	Hereford United	1-2	Arnott	2470	13		1				6	4	2			5	12				7	3			10			8		11	9
13	22	Bury	2-3	Pike 2 (1p)	2976	13		1				6	4	2			5					7	3	9	12	10			8		11	
14	29	DARLINGTON	2-1	Pike, Smillie	2841			1				6	4	2			5					7		9		10		11	8		3	
15	Nov 5	Colchester United	2-2	Reinelt, Pike	3817	8		1				6	4	2			5	12				7		9		10		11			3	
16	19	CHESTERFIELD	1-1	Reinelt	2730	5		1				6	4	2	8							7		9		10		11	12	13	3	
17	26	Lincoln City	1-1	Arnott	2919	5		1		6			4		8			12				7		9		10		11	2		3	
18	Dec 10	WIGAN ATHLETIC	0-1		2257	2		1		6		5	4		9							12		10		8		11	7		3	
19	17	Rochdale	1-2	Foster	1665	2		1		12		5	4		9		6					8		10		13		11	7		3	
20	26	FULHAM	4-1	Reinelt, Micklewhite, Foster 2	4737	2		1		3		5	4		9		6					7		10		11			8			
21	27	Barnet	0-1		2074	2		1		3		5	4		9		6	10				8				11			7			
22	31	CARLISLE UNITED	0-1		3709	2		1		3		5	4		9		6	12		13		7		10		11			8			
23	Jan 14	Northampton Town	0-2		5529	2		1		3		5	4		9		6					7		10		12			8		11	
24	Feb 4	LINCOLN CITY	0-0		4191			1						2	10		5			8		7		9	4	12		11		6	3	
25	7	Doncaster Rovers	2-1	Pike 2	1740			1						2	9		5			8		7		10	4			11		6	3	
26	11	Chesterfield	0-2		3070			1						2	9		5			8		7		10	4	12		11		6	3	
27	18	NORTHAMPTON T	3-1	Ramage, Green, Foster	4072			1				11		2	10		5		7			8		9	4					6	3	
28	21	Darlington	0-2		1548			1				11		2	9		5		7			8		10	4	12				6	3	
29	25	Mansfield Town	0-4		3182	8		1				6		2	9		5					7		10	4	12				3	11	
30	Mar 4	WALSALL	1-3	Foster	3757	2		1				6		7	10	12	5		11			8		9		13			4		3	
31	11	Scarborough	0-0		1949	2		1				6		7	10		5		11			8		9					4		3	
32	18	SCUNTHORPE UNITED	2-2	Foster, Pike	2501			1				6	7	2	10	12	5		11			8		9					4		3	
33	25	EXETER CITY	3-0	Foster, Pike (p), Butler	3364			1				6	7	2	10		5				3	8		9					4		11	
34	Apr 1	Preston North End	1-1	Dunne	9095	6		1					7	4	10		5			2	3			9	8						11	
35	4	BURY	1-1	Brown	2957	6		1			9		4	7	10		5			2	3	8									11	
36	8	Carlisle United	0-2		6786	6		1			9	12	8	7	10		5			2	3			13					4		11	
37	11	COLCHESTER UNITED	1-3	Watson	3404	6		1			9		8	2	10		5				3	7							4		11	
38	15	BARNET	2-1	Brown, Pike	3457	6		1			9		8	7			5			2				10	12			11	4		3	
39	17	Fulham	0-1		3612	6		1			9		8	7	10		5			2					13			11	4	12	3	
40	22	DONCASTER ROVERS	4-2	Kirby (og), Pike 3	3069	6		1			10	12		7	13		5			2	3	8		9					4		11	
41	29	HEREFORD UNITED	0-0		4200	6		1			9	5		7	10					2	3	8							4		11	
42	May 6	Torquay United	1-3	Stamps (og)	2638	6		1			9	5		7	12					2				10	8			11	4		3	
					Apps	28	8	38	4	7	8	33	29	35	29	2	37	5	5	12	7	35	10	27	12	27	5	15	33	9	39	3
					Goals	2	2				2	2		1	8		1					2	1	13	1	4	1	1	1		2	

AJ Kennedy played in games 7 at 13 and 8 at 12

PAF Wilson played at 13 in games 4 and 5

Two own goals

F.A. Cup

Rd	Date	Opponent	Score	Scorers	Att	Arnott AJ	Baker DP	Banks S	Barrett S	Bodley MJ	Brown SR	Butler PA (Tony)	Carpenter R	Dunne JJ	Foster AM	Freeman DBA	Green RE	Hutchinson IN	Knott GR	Lindsey S	Martin EJ	Micklewhite G	Palmer LJ	Pike C	Ramage AW	Reinelt RS	Ritchie PM	Smillie N	Smith NJ	Trott RF	Watson PD	Watts GS
R1	Nov 11	Heybridge Swifts	2-0	Reinelt, Pike	4614	8		1				6	4	2			5					7		9		10		11			3	
R2	Dec 3	FULHAM	1-1	Pike	6253	5		1					2		9		6					7		10		8		11	4		3	
rep	13	Fulham	2-1	(aet) Pike, Reinelt	6536	5		1				8	2		9		6					7		10		12		11	4		3	
R3	Jan 7	SHEFFIELD WEDNESDAY	1-2	Pike (p)	10425	2		1				5	4		9		6					7		10		11			8		3	

R1 played at Colchester

F.L. Cup (Coca Cola Cup)

Rd	Date	Opponent	Score	Scorers	Att	Arnott AJ	Baker DP	Banks S	Barrett S	Bodley MJ	Brown SR	Butler PA (Tony)	Carpenter R	Dunne JJ	Foster AM	Freeman DBA	Green RE	Hutchinson IN	Knott GR	Lindsey S	Martin EJ	Micklewhite G	Palmer LJ	Pike C	Ramage AW	Reinelt RS	Ritchie PM	Smillie N	Smith NJ	Trott RF	Watson PD	Watts GS
R1/1	Aug 16	READING	0-1		2556	12	10		1			6		2	9		5					4	3			7			8		11	
R1/2	23	Reading	0-3		3436	12	10		1			6		2	9		5					4	3			7			8		11	

A.M. Cup (Auto Windscreens Shield)

Rd	Date	Opponent	Score	Scorers	Att	Arnott AJ	Baker DP	Banks S	Barrett S	Bodley MJ	Brown SR	Butler PA (Tony)	Carpenter R	Dunne JJ	Foster AM	Freeman DBA	Green RE	Hutchinson IN	Knott GR	Lindsey S	Martin EJ	Micklewhite G	Palmer LJ	Pike C	Ramage AW	Reinelt RS	Ritchie PM	Smillie N	Smith NJ	Trott RF	Watson PD	Watts GS
R1	Sep 27	BRIGHTON & HOVE ALB.	1-1	Carpenter	963			1				6	4	2			5					7				9	10	11	8		3	12
R1	Nov 8	Brentford	1-3	Pike	1795	2			1			6	4					7				13	3	9	12	10				5		

Played on Nov 8: Kamara (at 8, subbed) and Hooker (11)

1995/96

Second in Division Three: Promoted

No.	Date	Opponent	Score	Scorers	Att	Arnott AJ	Bailey DL	Brown SR	Butler PA (Tony)	Butler S	Carpenter R	Castle SC	Dunne JJ	Fortune-West LPO	Foster AM	Freeman DBA	Gayle J	Green RE	Harris MA	Manuel WAJ	Martin D	Micklewhite G	Naylor DJ	O'Connor MA	Puttnam DP	Ratcliffe S	Rattray KW	Smith NJ	Stannard JD	Thomas GA	Watson AF	Watson PD
1	Aug 12	WIGAN ATHLETIC	2-1	Foster, F-West	4099	13		14	4				2	9	10			6	5		7		3	11		8			1			12
2	19	Lincoln City	3-0	F-West, Bailey, Brightwell (og)	2822		10		4					9	14			6	5		7		3	11		8	13	2	1			12
3	26	CAMBRIDGE UNITED	3-0	F-West, Bailey, Rattray	5093		10		4					9				6	5				3	11		8	7	2	1			
4	29	Barnet	2-0	Rattray, Taylor	3077		10		4					9	12			6	5				3	11		8	7	2	1			
5	Sep 2	COLCHESTER UNITED	0-1		7667		10		4					9	12			6	5		13		3	11		8	7	2	1			
6	9	Scunthorpe United	1-1	Bailey	2423		10		4		12			9	13			6	5				3	11		8	7	2	1			
7	12	Hereford United	0-0		1740		10							9	12			6	5				3	11		8	7	2	1		4	
8	16	CARDIFF CITY	1-0	F-West	5314		10							9	12			6	5				3	11		8	7	2	1		4	
9	23	Chester City	1-1	Martin	3886		10							9	12			6	5		13		3	11		8	7	2	1		4	
10	30	BURY	3-0	Bailey, F-West 2	6018		10							9	14			6	5		13	12	3	11		8	7	2	1		4	
11	Oct 7	ROCHDALE	1-0	A Watson	7782		10							9				6	5		7		3	11	12	8		2	1		4	
12	14	Darlington	0-1		2043		10		14					9				6	5		7		3	11	12	8	13	2	1		4	
13	21	DONCASTER ROVERS	4-0	O'Connor, Ratcliffe, Bailey, Harris	6302		10							9					5		7	6	3	11		8		2	1		4	
14	28	Hartlepool United	1-1	Bailey (p)	2355		10		6					9		14			5		7	12	3	11	13	8		2	1		4	
15	31	Exeter City	0-0		3024		10		7					9		12			5			6	3	11		8		2	1		4	13
16	Nov 4	NORTHAMPTON T	0-0		7206		10								13	9		6	5		7	12	3	11		8		2	1		4	
17	18	Scarborough	2-0	Green, F-West	1546		10							9				6	5		7	2		11	12	8	13	4	1			3
18	25	FULHAM	1-0	F-West	7608		10		13					9				6	5		7	2		11	12	8		4	1			3
19	Dec 16	Bury	0-1		3045		10		4	11				9				2	5		7	13	3		12	8	6		1			
20	23	Preston North End	0-0		10682		10		4	9				12				6	5		7	2	3		11	8			1			
21	26	PLYMOUTH ARGYLE	1-0	S Butler (p)	9651		10		4	9				13				6	5		7	2	3		11	8		12	1			
22	Jan 1	Leyton Orient	1-0	F-West	7090		10		6	9				11				2	5		7	12	3			8		4	1			
23	9	CHESTER CITY	3-1	S Butler 3	9186		10		6	11				9				2	5		7	12	3		13	8		4	1			
24	13	LINCOLN CITY	2-0	F-West, Ratcliffe	8040		10		6	11				9				2	5		7	12	3		13	8	14	4	1			
25	20	Wigan Athletic	1-2	Green	2773		10		6	11	12			9				5				2			7	8	4		1	3		13
26	30	MANSFIELD TOWN	2-0	Rattray, T Butler	6111		10		6	11	13			9				2		14		7			12	8	4		1	5		3
27	Feb 3	Cambridge United	0-0		4114		10		6		14		13	9				2	5			4			11	8	7		1	3		12
28	10	TORQUAY UNITED	2-0	Smith, Ratcliffe	7116		10		6	11				9				2	5			12				8	7	4	1	3		
29	13	BARNET	1-0	S Butler	6428		10		6	11				9				2	5		13	12			14	8	7	4	1	3		
30	17	HEREFORD UNITED	1-1	Castle	6987		10		6	9		8				14		2	5		7	11	12		13			4	1	3		
31	24	Cardiff City	0-2		3028		10		6			8				9		2	5		7	11	3		12			4	1			
32	27	SCUNTHORPE UNITED	0-0		5547		10		6			8			12	9		2	5		7	11	3		13			4	1			
33	Mar 2	Plymouth Argyle	0-1		8540		13		6		11	8		9		10		2	5		7		3				12	4	1			
34	9	PRESTON NORTH END	1-1	Harris	10595		10		6		11	8		9		13		2	5		7		3		12		14	4	1			
35	12	Torquay United	0-0		2406		10		6		11	12		9					5		7	13	3			8		4	1	2		
36	16	Mansfield Town	1-0	Gayle	2698		13		6		11			10			9		5		7	12	3		14	8		4	1	2		
37	23	LEYTON ORIENT	1-1	Gayle	8004		10		6	12							9	2	5	13	7				11	8		4	1	3		
38	30	Rochdale	0-2		2098		14		6	9	7							2	5	10		4	3		11	8	12		1			
39	Apr 2	DARLINGTON	0-0		6419		14			10	7			9				2	5	12		4			11	8	6		1	3		
40	6	HARTLEPOOL UNITED	2-0	T Butler, Bailey	6263		14		6	10				13			9	2	5	3		12			11	8	7	4	1			
41	8	Doncaster Rovers	1-0	Bailey	1783		11		6		7			10		13	9		5	12			3			8		4	1	2		
42	13	EXETER CITY	1-0	Puttnam	7692		10		6	12				13			9		5	3		2			11	8	7	4	1			
43	16	Colchester United	1-1	Gayle	4953		11		6	13				10			9		5	3	7	12				8		4	1	2		
44	20	Northampton Town	1-1	F-West	7427		11		6	14	12			10			9		5	3	7	13				8		4	1	2		
45	27	Fulham	0-0		10320		11			12				10			9		5		7	3			13	8	6	4	1	2		
46	May 4	SCARBOROUGH	1-0	F-West	10420		4		6	14				10			9		5	3	7	2			11	8	13		1	12		
					Apps	1	45	1	36	20	12	6	2	40	11	9	9	35	44	10	31	31	31	18	26	41	26	37	46	15	10	8
					Goals		8		2	5		1		12	1		3	2	2		1		1	1	1	3	3	1			1	

A Ansah played at 13 (subbed) in game 38 and 13 in game 39

One own goal

F.A. Cup

Rd	Date	Opponent	Score	Scorers	Att	Arnott AJ	Bailey DL	Brown SR	Butler PA (Tony)	Butler S	Carpenter R	Castle SC	Dunne JJ	Fortune-West LPO	Foster AM	Freeman DBA	Gayle J	Green RE	Harris MA	Manuel WAJ	Martin D	Micklewhite G	Naylor DJ	O'Connor MA	Puttnam DP	Ratcliffe S	Rattray KW	Smith NJ	Stannard JD	Thomas GA	Watson AF	Watson PD
R1	Nov 13	Wycombe Wanderers	1-1	Bailey	5064		10									13		6	5		7	2	3	11	12	8	9	4	1			
rep	21	WYCOMBE WANDERERS	1-0	Howard (og)	8585		10							9				6	5		7	2		11	12		8	4	1			3
R2	Dec 2	HITCHIN TOWN	3-0	F-West 2, Ratcliffe	7142		10		12					9				6	5		7	2	3			8		4	1			11
R3	Jan 6	Reading	1-3	Martin	10324		10		6		12		13	9				2	5		7	11	3		14	8		4	1			

F.L. Cup (Coca Cola Cup)

Rd	Date	Opponent	Score	Scorers	Att	Arnott AJ	Bailey DL	Brown SR	Butler PA (Tony)	Butler S	Carpenter R	Castle SC	Dunne JJ	Fortune-West LPO	Foster AM	Freeman DBA	Gayle J	Green RE	Harris MA	Manuel WAJ	Martin D	Micklewhite G	Naylor DJ	O'Connor MA	Puttnam DP	Ratcliffe S	Rattray KW	Smith NJ	Stannard JD	Thomas GA	Watson AF	Watson PD
R1/1	Aug 15	BRISTOL ROVERS	1-1	Naylor	3827		10		4				2	9	12			6	5		7		3	11		8			1			
R1/2	23	Bristol Rovers	2-4	Bailey, F-West	3601		10		4					9	12			6	5				3	11		8	7	2	1			

A.M. Cup (Auto Windscreens Shield)

Rd	Date	Opponent	Score	Scorers	Att	Arnott AJ	Bailey DL	Brown SR	Butler PA (Tony)	Butler S	Carpenter R	Castle SC	Dunne JJ	Fortune-West LPO	Foster AM	Freeman DBA	Gayle J	Green RE	Harris MA	Manuel WAJ	Martin D	Micklewhite G	Naylor DJ	O'Connor MA	Puttnam DP	Ratcliffe S	Rattray KW	Smith NJ	Stannard JD	Thomas GA	Watson AF	Watson PD
R1	Oct 17	Cardiff City	2-3	Freeman, Foster (p)	1034	13			5		2		12		10	9		6			7	8			11		4	14	1			3
R1	Nov 7	HEREFORD UNITED	2-2	T Butler, Foster	1866				4		5		2		9	10		6				8	3				7					11

Played at Nov 7 at 1, A Nicholls, and at 12, KJ Bremner

1996/97

11th in Division Two

						Akinbiyi AP	Armstrong SC	Bailey DL	Bryant M	Butler S	Butters G	Chapman IR	Ford JS	Fortune-West LPO	Galloway MA	Green RE	Harris MA	Hessenthaler A	Humphrey J	Manuel WAJ	Marshall AJ	Morris MJ	O'Connor MA	Onuora I	Pennock AB	Pinnock JE	Piper LH	Puttnam DP	Ratcliffe S	Smith NJ	Stannard JD	Thomas GA
1	Aug 17	BRISTOL CITY	3-2	F-West, Harris, Piper	7212			14	6	10		7	3	9			5	4	2					11			13	12	8		1	
2	24	Wycombe Wanderers	1-1	Ratcliffe	4582			10	6	14		3	12	9			5	4	2					11			13		8	7	1	
3	27	Brentford	0-2		5384			12	6	10		3		9			5	4	2					11			13		8	7	1	
4	31	CHESTERFIELD	0-1		5984				6	10		3		9			5	4	2					11			13	12	8	7	1	
5	Sep 7	BURNLEY	1-0	F-West	6114			12	6	10		3		9			5	4	2										8	7	1	
6	10	Luton Town	1-2	Chapman	5171			13	6	10		3		9			5	4	2					12			11		8	7	1	
7	14	Walsall	0-1		3419			11	6	13		3		9			5	4	2					10			12		8	7	1	
8	21	ROTHERHAM UNITED	3-1	Onuora 3	4852			13	6	10		3	12				5	4	2					9			14	11	8	7	1	
9	28	Stockport County	1-2	Onuora	6049			14	6			11	3				5	4	2			10		9			12	13	8	7	1	
10	Oct 1	NOTTS COUNTY	1-0	Onuora	5583			12	6			11					5	4				3		9			10	7	8	2	1	
11	5	BOURNEMOUTH	1-1	Onuora	5966			10	6			11					5	4				3	7	9			14	12	8	2	1	13
12	12	Blackpool	0-2		4320			13	6			11					5					3	7	9			10	12	8	2	1	4
13	15	Shrewsbury Town	2-1	Onuora, Bailey	2042			10	6								5			4		3	7	9				11	8	2	1	12
14	19	MILLWALL	2-3	Butler 2 (2p)	9305		11	10	6	7							5			4		3		9				12	8	2	1	
15	26	PRESTON NORTH END	1-1	Onuora	6264		11	10	6	7	3					5		4						9					8	2	1	
16	29	Plymouth Argyle	0-2		4787		11	10		12	3					5		4		13			7	9					8	2		6
17	Nov 2	Bristol Rovers	0-0		5530		11	10	6	7	3					5		4						9					8	2		
18	9	WREXHAM	1-2	Ratcliffe	5093		11	10	6	7	3					5		4					13	9			12		8	2		
19	19	Peterborough United	1-0	Onuora	4136		7	10	6	11	3					5	12	4		13				9					8	2	1	
20	23	YORK CITY	0-1		5005		11	10	6	9	3					5				12	1		4				13	7	8	2		
21	30	Preston North End	0-1		9616		11	10		9	3	14				5	6			12	1				4		13	7	8	2		
22	Dec 3	CREWE ALEXANDRA	2-1	Pennock, Smith	3572		11	13		10	3	12				5	6			7	1		4	9	8					2		
23	14	BURY	2-2	Butler, Ratcliffe	5542		11			10	3					5		7		12	1		2	9	4				8			6
24	21	Watford	0-0		7809				6	10	3					5		7		12	1		11	9	4		13		8	2		
25	26	LUTON TOWN	1-2	Onuora	8491				6	10	3					5		7		12			11	9	4		13		8	2	1	
26	28	Burnley	1-5	Bailey	9824			10	5	12	3	4				2				13			11	9	7					8	1	6
27	Jan 18	Notts County	1-1	Puttnam	5008	9			6	10	3					5		7					11		4			12	8	2	1	
28	25	PLYMOUTH ARGYLE	4-1	Curran (og), Green, Ratcliffe, Akinbiyi	5465	9			6	10	3	12				5		7					11		4				8	2	1	
29	Feb 1	Wrexham	1-1	Akinbiyi	3153	9		11	6	10	5							7					3		4				8	2	1	
30	8	BRISTOL ROVERS	1-0	Hessemthaler	6933	10		11	6								5	7					3	9	4				8	2	1	12
31	15	York City	3-2	Onuora, Ratcliffe, Akinbiyi	2748	10		11	6							5	3	7						9	4			13	8	2	1	12
32	22	PETERBOROUGH UTD.	2-1	Onuora 2	6550	10			6		3	11				5		7					12	9	4				8	2	1	
33	Mar 1	Crewe Alexandra	2-3	Green, Akinbiyi	3555	10		12		14	3					5	6	7					11	9	4				8	2	1	13
34	8	WATFORD	3-1	Hessenthaler, Onuora(p), Butler	7385	8		13		10	3					5		7					11	9	4			12	6	2	1	14
35	15	Bury	0-3		3492	10		12	2	8	3					5		7						9	4				6	11	1	
36	22	WYCOMBE WANDERERS	1-0	Onuora	5925	10		12		8	3	11				5		7						9	4				6	2	1	
37	25	Rotherham United	2-1	Onuora, Ratcliffe	2664	10			6	12	3	11				5		7					13	9	4				8	2	1	
38	29	Bristol City	1-0	Onuora (p)	11276	10		12	6	13	3	11			4	5		7						9	2				8		1	
39	31	BRENTFORD	1-2	Onuora	7359	10			6	13	3	11			4	5	14	7					12	9	2				8		1	
40	Apr 5	Chesterfield	2-2	Butler, Onuora	3926	10			6	12	3	11			8	5		7						9	4					2	1	
41	12	Bournemouth	2-2	Butler, Pennock	5008	10			6	8	3				12	13		7					11	9	5				4	2	1	
42	16	STOCKPORT COUNTY	1-0	Butler	4482	10			14	9	3	11			6	5		7						12	4		13		8	2	1	
43	19	BLACKPOOL	2-3	Galloway, Butler	5146	10			5	9	3				6			7					11	12	4				8	2	1	
44	26	Millwall	2-0	Akinbiyi, Onuora	8946	10			5	11	3				6	4								9	7				8	2	1	
45	29	WALSALL	2-0	Onuora, Butler	4090				5	11	3				13	6		7						9	4	14	10		8	2	1	
46	May 3	SHREWSBURY TOWN	2-0	Akinbiyi 2	6176	10			6	11	3				12	5		7						9	4	14	13		8	2	1	
					Apps	19	10	30	39	38	30	23	4	7	9	29	21	38	9	11	5	6	22	40	26	2	19	14	43	42	38	10
					Goals	7		2		9		1		2	1	2	1	2						21	2		1	1	6	1		

Played in one game: R Carpenter (5, at 11), AJ Sambrook (45, 12)

JA Gould played at 1 in games 16, 17 and 18

One own goal

F.A. Cup

						Akinbiyi AP	Armstrong SC	Bailey DL	Bryant M	Butler S	Butters G	Chapman IR	Ford JS	Fortune-West LPO	Galloway MA	Green RE	Harris MA	Hessenthaler A	Humphrey J	Manuel WAJ	Marshall AJ	Morris MJ	O'Connor MA	Onuora I	Pennock AB	Pinnock JE	Piper LH	Puttnam DP	Ratcliffe S	Smith NJ	Stannard JD	Thomas GA
R1	Nov 16	HEREFORD UNITED	1-0	Butler	5280				6	10	3	13				5	12	4					11	9			7	14	8	2	1	
R2	Dec 7	Cardiff City	2-0	Onuora, Hessenthaler	3474			13		10	3	11	12			5	6	7		4			2	9	8						1	
R3	Jan 21	DERBY COUNTY	0-2		9508				6	10	3	12				5		7					11		4			13	8	9	1	2

F.L. Cup (Coca Cola Cup)

						Akinbiyi AP	Armstrong SC	Bailey DL	Bryant M	Butler S	Butters G	Chapman IR	Ford JS	Fortune-West LPO	Galloway MA	Green RE	Harris MA	Hessenthaler A	Humphrey J	Manuel WAJ	Marshall AJ	Morris MJ	O'Connor MA	Onuora I	Pennock AB	Pinnock JE	Piper LH	Puttnam DP	Ratcliffe S	Smith NJ	Stannard JD	Thomas GA
R1/1	Aug 20	Swansea City	1-0	Torpey (og)	2711			9	6			7	3				5	4	2					11				12	8	10	1	
R1/2	Sep 3	SWANSEA CITY	2-0	F-West, Butler	3633			13	6	10		3		9			5	4	2					11			14	7	8	12	1	
R2/1	17	Barnsley	1-1	Ratcliffe	4491			11	6	12		3	2				5	4						9			10	13	8	7	1	
R2/2	24	BARNSLEY	1-0	Puttnam	5666			12	6			11	3					4	2			5		9			10	13	8	7	1	
R3	Oct 22	Coventry City	2-2	Onuora, Ratcliffe	10603			10	6	7		11					5	4				3		9				12	8	2	1	
rep	Nov 13	COVENTRY CITY	1-0	Smith	12639		11	10	6	7						5	3	4						9					8	2	1	
R4	26	Ipswich Town	0-1		13537		11	10		9						5	3	4			1		7		6		12	13	8	2		

A.M. Cup (Auto Windscreens Shield)

						Akinbiyi AP	Armstrong SC	Bailey DL	Bryant M	Butler S	Butters G	Chapman IR	Ford JS	Fortune-West LPO	Galloway MA	Green RE	Harris MA	Hessenthaler A	Humphrey J	Manuel WAJ	Marshall AJ	Morris MJ	O'Connor MA	Onuora I	Pennock AB	Pinnock JE	Piper LH	Puttnam DP	Ratcliffe S	Smith NJ	Stannard JD	Thomas GA
R1	Dec 10	CARDIFF CITY	1-2	Piper	1193		11	10				4	3				12		2	6	1				8	13	9	7				5

Lost in sudden death extra time

1997/98

8th in Division Two

No	Date	Opponent	Score	Scorers	Att	Akinbiyi AP	Ashby BI	Bailey DL	Bartram VL	Bryant M	Butler S	Butters G	Corbett JJ	Fortune-West LPO	Galloway MA	Green RE	Hessenthaler A	Masters NB	Moss NG	Ndah GE	Onuora I	Patterson M	Pennock AB	Pinnock JE	Piper LH	Pollitt MF	Ratcliffe S	Smith PW	Southall LN	Stannard JD	Statham B	Thomas GA	Walton MA
1	Aug 9	PRESTON NORTH END	0-0		6573	10	5	13		6	9	3		14	8	12	7	11	1								2	4					
2	16	Burnley	0-0		11805	10	5			6	9	3	13	12	8	14	7	11	1								2	4					
3	23	WALSALL	2-1	Smith, Akinbiyi	5081	10	5			6	9	3		12	8	13	7		1						14		2	4			11		
4	30	York City	1-2	Bailey	2853	10	5	12		6	9	3					7		1	11							2	4			8		
5	Sep 2	Brentford	0-2		4903	10	5	9		6	12	3			8		7		1								2	4			11		
6	5	BOURNEMOUTH	2-1	Butters (p), Butler	5167	10	5	9			11	3			6	12	7		1								2	4			8		
7	13	Bristol Rovers	2-1	Butler, Akinbiyi	6572	10	5	12		6	9	3		13			7		1	11							2	4			8		
8	20	WATFORD	2-2	Butters, Butler	7834	10	5	13		6	9	3		12	14	2	7		1	11							8	4					
9	27	Carlisle United	1-2	Butters (p)	5063	10	5			6	9	3			8	2	7		1	11								4					
10	Oct 4	BRISTOL CITY	2-0	Akinbiyi 2	6201	10	5			6	9	3	11	14	12	2	7		1		13						8	4					
11	11	WYCOMBE WANDERERS	1-0	Akinbiyi	5479	10	5	12			9	3			13	6	7	11									8	4		1	2		
12	18	Northampton Town	1-2	Akinbiyi	7191	10	5	11			9				3	6	7										8	4		1	2		
13	21	Wigan Athletic	4-1	* see below	3214	10	5	11			9			12	3	6	7										8	4		1	2		
14	25	PLYMOUTH ARGYLE	2-1	Akinbiyi, F-West	6797	10	5	11			9			13	3	6	7				12						8	4		1	2		
15	Nov 1	MILLWALL	1-3	F-West	8378	10	5				12	3		8		6	7				9	11					13	4		1	2		
16	4	Chesterfield	1-1	Akinbiyi	3420	10	5				13	3		8		12	7				9	11	6				14	4		1	2		
17	7	Oldham Athletic	1-3	Butters	5338	10	5	12		13	8	3				6	7				9	11						4		1	2		
18	18	BLACKPOOL	1-1	Butters (p)	5040	10	5			13	9	3			11	6	7				12	2					8	4		1			
19	21	Fulham	0-3		8280	10	5	11		6	13	3			9		7				8	2					12	4		1			
20	29	GRIMSBY TOWN	0-2		4902	10	5	9		12	13	6			11		7	3			8							4		1	2		
21	Dec 2	Luton Town	2-2	Akinbiyi 2	5255	10	5			6					11	12	7	3			9						8	4		1	2		
22	13	SOUTHEND UNITED	1-2	Southall	4774	10	5			6	14				11	12	7	3			9	2				1		4	8		13		
23	20	Wrexham	0-0		2827	10						6			11	2	7	3			9					1	12	4	8			5	
24	26	Bournemouth	0-4		5672	10				14	13	6			12	5	7	3			9		2			1	11	4	8				
25	29	BRENTFORD	3-1	Aspinall (og), Akinbiyi 2	5786	10	5			12	9	6					7	3					8			1		4	11		2		
26	Jan 3	BURNLEY	2-0	Butler, Smith	5746	10	5			2	9	6			11							3	8			1		4	7		12		
27	10	Preston North End	3-1	Butters, Galloway, Onoura	7776		5			2	9	6			8	3					10					1		4	7		11		
28	17	YORK CITY	0-0		5785		5			2	9	6		12	11	3	7				10							4	8	1			
29	31	BRISTOL ROVERS	1-1	Onoura	5681	10	5			13	9	6	12	14	11	3	7				8							4	2	1			
30	Feb 8	Watford	2-0	Akinbiyi 2	10498	10	5			14	9	6	12		11		7				13	2	3					4	8				1
31	14	Bristol City	2-0	Corbett, Southall	11781	10	5			13	9	6	2		11		7				12		3				14	4	8	1			
32	21	CARLISLE UNITED	1-0	Butler	6250	10	5				13	6	11		12		7				9	2	3					4	8	1			
33	24	NORTHAMPTON T	1-0	Butters (p)	6405	10	5				9	6					7				11	2	3					4	8	1			
34	28	Wycombe Wanderers	0-1		5583	10	5				9	6			11		7				12	2	3					4	8	1			
35	Mar 3	OLDHAM ATHLETIC	2-1	Kelly (og), Akinbiyi	5247	10	5			13	9	6			12		7				11	2	3					4	8	1			
36	7	Millwall	0-1		8241	10	5			12	9	6	14		13		7				11	2	3					4	8	1			
37	14	CHESTERFIELD	1-0	Corbett	5672	10	5			6	9		13	14	8	12	7	11				2	3					4		1			
38	21	Blackpool	1-2	F-West	4344	10	5		1	6	9		11	12	8							2	3					4	7				
39	28	FULHAM	2-0	Akinbiyi 2	10507	10	5		1	6	12		11	9	8							2	3					4	7				
40	31	Walsall	0-1		3117	10	5		1	6	12		13	9	8		7					2	3					4	11				
41	Apr 4	Grimsby Town	0-0		5500	10	5		1	6	12				8		7					2	3					9	11			4	
42	11	LUTON TOWN	2-1	Akinbiyi 2	6846	10	5		1	6	9		14	13	8		7					2	3					4	11			12	
43	13	Southend United	0-0		6151	10	5		1	6			11	12	8		7					2	3					4	9				
44	18	WREXHAM	1-1	Akinbiyi	7869	10	5		1	6	9		13	12	8		7					2	3					4	11				
45	25	Plymouth Argyle	1-0	Smith	7941	10	5		1	6	13		9		11	3	7					2	8	14				4			12		
46	May 2	WIGAN ATHLETIC	0-0		10339	10			1	6	14		11	9	8	5	7	3				2						4	13		12		

Scorers in game 13: Akinbiyi, Ratcliffe, Butler (p), Fortune-West

	Akinbiyi AP	Ashby BI	Bailey DL	Bartram VL	Bryant M	Butler S	Butters G	Corbett JJ	Fortune-West LPO	Galloway MA	Green RE	Hessenthaler A	Masters NB	Moss NG	Ndah GE	Onuora I	Patterson M	Pennock AB	Pinnock JE	Piper LH	Pollitt MF	Ratcliffe S	Smith PW	Southall LN	Stannard JD	Statham B	Thomas GA	Walton MA
Apps	44	43	13	9	35	43	31	16	20	39	25	42	11	10	4	22	23	20	1	1	6	21	46	23	20	20	3	1
Goals	21		1			6	7	2	4	1						2						1	3	2				

Two own goals

F.A. Cup

Round	Date	Opponent	Score	Scorers	Att	Akinbiyi AP	Ashby BI	Bailey DL	Bartram VL	Bryant M	Butler S	Butters G	Corbett JJ	Fortune-West LPO	Galloway MA	Green RE	Hessenthaler A	Masters NB	Moss NG	Ndah GE	Onuora I	Patterson M	Pennock AB	Pinnock JE	Piper LH	Pollitt MF	Ratcliffe S	Smith PW	Southall LN	Stannard JD	Statham B	Thomas GA	Walton MA
R1	Nov 14	Bristol Rovers	2-2	Onoura, Akinbiyi	4825	10	5				8	3			6		7				9	11					12	4		1	2		
rep	25	BRISTOL ROVERS	0-2		4459	10	5			3	9	6		12	13		7				8	11					14	4		1	2		

F.L. Cup (Coca Cola Cup)

Round	Date	Opponent	Score	Scorers	Att	Akinbiyi AP	Ashby BI	Bailey DL	Bartram VL	Bryant M	Butler S	Butters G	Corbett JJ	Fortune-West LPO	Galloway MA	Green RE	Hessenthaler A	Masters NB	Moss NG	Ndah GE	Onuora I	Patterson M	Pennock AB	Pinnock JE	Piper LH	Pollitt MF	Ratcliffe S	Smith PW	Southall LN	Stannard JD	Statham B	Thomas GA	Walton MA
R1/1	Aug 12	BIRMINGHAM CITY	0-1		5246	10				6	9	3		12	8	5	7		1								2	4					
R1/2	26	Birmingham City	0-3		7921	10	5			6	9	3	14		8	12	7		1						13		2	4					

MA O'Connor played at 11 (subbed) in R1/1. IR Chapman played at 11 (subbed) in R1/2

A.M. Cup (Auto Windscreens Shield)

Round	Date	Opponent	Score	Scorers	Att	Akinbiyi AP	Ashby BI	Bailey DL	Bartram VL	Bryant M	Butler S	Butters G	Corbett JJ	Fortune-West LPO	Galloway MA	Green RE	Hessenthaler A	Masters NB	Moss NG	Ndah GE	Onuora I	Patterson M	Pennock AB	Pinnock JE	Piper LH	Pollitt MF	Ratcliffe S	Smith PW	Southall LN	Stannard JD	Statham B	Thomas GA	Walton MA
R1	Dec 9	PETERBOROUGH UTD.	0-1		905	13	5			6	10		12			14	7	3			9						8	4	11	1	2		

1998/99

4th in Division Two

	Date	Opponent	Score	Scorers	Att	Asaba CE	Ashby BJ	Bartram VL	Brown KJ	Browning MT	Bryant M	Butler S	Butters G	Carr DJ	Dobson AJ	Edge R	Elliott ST	Galloway MA	Hessenthaler A	Hodge J	Lisbie KA	Nosworthy NPH	Patterson M	Pennock AB	Pinnock JE	Rolling FJ	Saunders MP	Smith PW	Southall LN	Stannard JD	Taylor RA	Williams PRC
1	Aug 8	WALSALL	0-1		5712		5	1			12	9		6				13	7	8			2	3				4	14		10	11
2	15	York City	1-1	Saunders	2634		5	1			12			6					7	8			2	3			9	4	13		11	10
3	22	BRISTOL ROVERS	0-0		4896		5	1			12	9		6					8	7			2	3	14			4	13		11	10
4	29	Blackpool	2-2	Saunders, Carr	3994	9	5	1			12			6					8	14			2	3			7	4	13		11	10
5	Sep 1	WREXHAM	4-0	Smith, Hessenthaler 2, Asaba	5349	9	5	1			14			6				13	8	10			2	3			7	4			11	12
6	5	Chesterfield	0-1		3766	9		1			5				3	13		7	8						12	6	10	4	2			11
7	8	NORTHAMPTON T	2-3	Smith 2 (1p)	4917	9		1			5	7		6	3				8				2		12		10	4	13			11
8	12	Colchester United	1-1	Asaba	4612	9		1			5	13		6		12		3	8				2				7	4	10		11	
9	19	BURNLEY	2-1	Galloway, Taylor	5702	9	2	1			5			6				10	8	12			7	3				4	13		11	
10	26	Preston North End	1-1	Asaba	10506	9	2	1			5			6		12		10		13			7	3			8	4	14		11	
11	Oct 3	MACCLESFIELD TOWN	2-2	Carr, Hodge	6093	9	2	1			5	13		6				10		12			7	3			8	4			11	
12	10	WYCOMBE WANDERERS	3-0	Saunders, Taylor 2	4575	9	5	1			12	14		6				10		7			2				8	4	13		11	3
13	17	Reading	0-0		11467		3	1				9		5		12		6		13			4	2				8	7		11	10
14	20	Bournemouth	3-3	Asaba 2, Southall	5183	9	5	1			13			6		12				14			2	3			8	4	10		11	7
15	24	LUTON TOWN	1-0	Asaba	5602	9	5	1			6						8			7			3	2			12	4	10		11	
16	31	Lincoln City	2-1	Asaba 2	4366	9	5	1			6			3		13	8		12				7	2			10	4			11	
17	Nov 7	WIGAN ATHLETIC	2-0	Asaba, Balmer (og)	5869	9	5	1			6			3			8		12				7				10	4	2		11	
18	10	OLDHAM ATHLETIC	2-1	Asaba, Patterson	5188	9	5				6			3			8		13	12			7				10	4	2	1	11	
19	21	Manchester City	0-0		26529	9	5			8	6			3			14	12	10				7	13				4	2	1	11	
20	28	FULHAM	1-0	Taylor	7614	9	5	1						3		7		10	8	13		12		6				4	2		11	
21	Dec 12	Stoke City	0-0		17233	9		1			5		3					10	8	12			7	6				4	2		11	
22	19	NOTTS COUNTY	4-0	Asaba 3, Taylor	6072	9	3	1			5							10	8	12			7	6				4	2		11	
23	29	MILLWALL	1-1	Galloway	9221	9	3	1			5							10	8	12			7	6			13	4	2		11	
24	Jan 2	BLACKPOOL	1-0	Southall	7022	9	3	1			5							10	8	13			7	6			12	4	2		11	
25	9	Walsall	1-2	Patterson	5495	9	3	1					5					10	8	12			7	6			13	4	2		11	
26	16	YORK CITY	3-1	Asaba, Taylor, Butters	6242	9	3	1					5			14		8		10		12	7	6	13		4		2		11	
27	30	Millwall	3-3	Southall, Taylor, Saunders	10442	9	3	1					5						8	12			7	6			10	4	2		11	
28	Feb 6	CHESTERFIELD	3-1	Asaba, Hessenthaler, Southall	6582	9		1					5	3					8				7	6			10	4	2		11	
29	13	Northampton Town	1-0	Smith	5981	9	3	1					5						8				7	6			10	4	2		11	
30	20	COLCHESTER UNITED	1-1	Asaba	7119	9		1					5	3				10	8	12			7	6				4	2		11	
31	23	Bristol Rovers	1-0	Hessenthaler	5735	9	3	1					5					12	8				7	6			10	4	2		11	
32	27	Burnley	5-0	Taylor 5 (1p)	8981	9	3	1					5	12				13	8	14			7	6			10	4	2		11	
33	Mar 6	PRESTON NORTH END	1-1	Taylor	9581	9	3	1					5						8	12	13		7	6			10	4	2		11	
34	9	Macclesfield Town	0-1		1868	9	3	1			7		5	13					8	12	11			6			10	4	2			
35	13	Wigan Athletic	1-4	Lisbie	4248	9	3	1					5						8	12	10		7	6				4	2		11	
36	20	LINCOLN CITY	4-0	Hessenthaler 2, Lisbie 2	7023		3	1					5	12					8		9		7	6			10	4	2		11	
37	27	Luton Town	0-1		6705	9		1		13			5	3				12	8	14			7	6			10	4	2		11	
38	Apr 1	READING	2-1	Saunders, Asaba	8195	9	3	1		13			5						8	12			7	6			10	4	2		11	
39	5	Wycombe Wanderers	2-0	Ashby, Asaba	6688	9	3	1		13			5						8	12	14		7	6			10	4	2		11	
40	9	BOURNEMOUTH	2-1	Hessenthaler, Lisbie	7813	9	3	1					5	14					8	13	12		7	6			10	4	2		11	
41	13	Fulham	0-3		13119	13	3	1					5	12				10	8	14	9		7	6				4	2		11	
42	17	MANCHESTER CITY	0-2		10400	9	3	1	2				5	13					8	12			7	6			10	4			11	
43	20	Wrexham	1-2	Butters	1871	9	3	1					5	12					8				7	6			10	4	2		11	
44	24	Oldham Athletic	4-1	Asaba, Smith, Galloway, Taylor	5331	9	3	1	7				5	12				10	8			13		6				4	2		11	
45	May 1	STOKE CITY	4-0	Taylor 2, Butters, Smith	8367	9	3	1	12				5					10	8	14			7	6			13	4	2		11	
46	8	Notts County	1-0	Asaba	7815	9		1	14				5	3				10	8	12			7	6			13	4	2		11	
					Apps	41	38	44	4	4	23	7	23	30	2	8	5	25	39	34	7	3	42	40	4	1	34	45	42	2	43	10
					Goals	20	1						3	2				3	7	1	4		2				5	6	4		16	

One own goal

Play Offs

	Date	Opponent	Score	Scorers	Att	Asaba CE	Ashby BJ	Bartram VL	Brown KJ	Browning MT	Bryant M	Butler S	Butters G	Carr DJ	Dobson AJ	Edge R	Elliott ST	Galloway MA	Hessenthaler A	Hodge J	Lisbie KA	Nosworthy NPH	Patterson M	Pennock AB	Pinnock JE	Rolling FJ	Saunders MP	Smith PW	Southall LN	Stannard JD	Taylor RA	Williams PRC
SF1	May 16	Preston North End	1-1	Taylor	18584	9	3	1	12				5					10	8	14			7	6			13	4	2		11	
SF2	19	PRESTON NORTH END	1-0	Hessenthaler	10505	9	3	1					5					10	8	12			7	6			13	4	2		11	
F	30	Manchester City	2-2	Asaba, Taylor	76935	9	3	1					5	13				10	8	12			7	6			14	4	2		11	

Final at Wembley Stadium. Lost on 1-3 on penalties a.e.t.

F.A. Cup

	Date	Opponent	Score	Scorers	Att	Asaba CE	Ashby BJ	Bartram VL	Brown KJ	Browning MT	Bryant M	Butler S	Butters G	Carr DJ	Dobson AJ	Edge R	Elliott ST	Galloway MA	Hessenthaler A	Hodge J	Lisbie KA	Nosworthy NPH	Patterson M	Pennock AB	Pinnock JE	Rolling FJ	Saunders MP	Smith PW	Southall LN	Stannard JD	Taylor RA	Williams PRC
R1	Nov 14	Oldham Athletic	0-2		3173	9	5				12			3		2		14	8	13			7	6				4	10	1	11	

F.L. Cup (Worthington Cup)

	Date	Opponent	Score	Scorers	Att	Asaba CE	Ashby BJ	Bartram VL	Brown KJ	Browning MT	Bryant M	Butler S	Butters G	Carr DJ	Dobson AJ	Edge R	Elliott ST	Galloway MA	Hessenthaler A	Hodge J	Lisbie KA	Nosworthy NPH	Patterson M	Pennock AB	Pinnock JE	Rolling FJ	Saunders MP	Smith PW	Southall LN	Stannard JD	Taylor RA	Williams PRC
R1/1	Aug 11	Southend United	0-1		2509		5	1			12			6				9	7	8			2	3	14			4	13		10	11
R1/2	18	SOUTHEND UNITED	0-1		3417		5	1			3	11		6					8	7			2		9			4				10

A.M. Cup (Auto Windscreens Shield)

	Date	Opponent	Score	Scorers	Att	Asaba CE	Ashby BJ	Bartram VL	Brown KJ	Browning MT	Bryant M	Butler S	Butters G	Carr DJ	Dobson AJ	Edge R	Elliott ST	Galloway MA	Hessenthaler A	Hodge J	Lisbie KA	Nosworthy NPH	Patterson M	Pennock AB	Pinnock JE	Rolling FJ	Saunders MP	Smith PW	Southall LN	Stannard JD	Taylor RA	Williams PRC
R1	Dec 5	Colchester United	5-1	Asaba, Pennock, Taylor 2, Smith	1742	9	5	1			2		3					10		7		12		6	13			4	8		11	
R2	Jan 5	Swansea City	1-0	Hessenthaler	5126	9		1			5		4	6		3		10	8	7					12		11		2			
R3	23	Torquay United	1-0	Taylor	3171	9	3	1					5			8							7	6			10	4	2		11	
SFS	Feb 16	Millwall	0-1		11555		9	1			3		5	7					8	12				6			10	4	2		11	

SF (South) lost in sudden death extra time

Played in R2: B Statham (at 13)

1999/2000

Third in Division Two: Promoted after play off

No	Date	Opponent	Score	Scorers	Att	Asaba CE	Ashby BI	Bartram VL	Bass JDM	Bryant M	Butler S	Butters G	Edge R	Gooden TM	Hessenthaler A	Hodge J	Lee CE	Lewis KJ	Matthews LJ	McGlinchey BK	Miller BS	Nosworthy NPH	Omoyimni E	Onoura I	Patterson M	Pennock AB	Rowe RC	Saunders MP	Smith PW	Southall LN	Taylor RA	Thomson A
1	Aug 7	Bury	1-2	Thomson	4014		3	1		7		5			8		13					11			2	6			4	10	12	9
2	14	BRISTOL ROVERS	0-1		6234		3	1		12		5			8	14				7		13				6			4	10	11	9
3	21	Blackpool	1-1	Ashby	4203		5	1							8			7				12			2	6		3	4	10	11	9
4	28	WYCOMBE WANDERERS	2-2	Taylor (p), McGlinchey	6180		5	1							8	12		7		14	6	13			2			3	4	10	11	9
5	30	Stoke City	1-1	Taylor	8369		5								8	12	9	7			13				2	6		3	4	10	11	14
6	Sep 4	OLDHAM ATHLETIC	2-1	Taylor, Omoyimni	5884		5	1							8	14		7			12	13	11		2	6		3	4	10	9	
7	11	Oxford United	2-1	Southall (p), Omoyimni	5418		5	1							8			7				9	11		2	6		3	4	10		12
8	18	PRESTON NORTH END	0-2		6610		5								8			7			13	12	11		2	6		3	4	10	9	
9	25	Cambridge United	2-2	Taylor, Butters	4708		5	1				13			8		12	7							2	6		3	4	10	11	9
10	Oct 2	MILLWALL	2-0	Lewis, Taylor	6616		5	1				12			8			7					13		2	6		3	4	10	11	9
11	9	WREXHAM	5-1	Thomson, Southall, Taylor 3	5997		3	1				5	12		8	13		7				10				6			4	2	11	9
12	16	Luton Town	1-3	Lewis	6394		2	1				5			8	12		7		10		13	11			6		3	4			9
13	19	Brentford	2-1	Omoyimni, Saunders	6264		6	1				5	8			12		7		10			13					3	4	2	11	9
14	23	CAMBRIDGE UNITED	2-1	Thomson 2	6417		2	1				5			8	13		7		11		12	9			6		3	4	10		14
15	Nov 2	BRISTOL CITY	3-0	Taylor 3	6728		2	1				5	7		8	12		13					11			6		3	4	10	14	9
16	6	Notts County	1-1	Taylor	6023		2	1				5	7		8	13		12					11			6		3	4	10	9	
17	12	BOURNEMOUTH	4-1	Hessenthaler, Thomson, Taylor 2	6336		3	1				5	7		8			10		12		14				6		13	4	2	11	9
18	23	Scunthorpe United	4-1	Taylor,Thomson,Lewis,Nosworthy	3444		3	1			14	5	7		8			10				13				6		12	4	2	11	9
19	27	Cardiff City	2-1	Hessenthaler, Thomson	7608		3	1				5	7		8			11				10				6	12		4	2		9
20	Dec 4	BURY	1-0	Edge	7036		3	1				5	7		8	13		11		14		10				6	12		4	2		9
21	26	COLCHESTER UNITED	2-1	Rowe, Southall	7338		3	1				5	7		8	12						10				6	9	11	4	2		13
22	28	Wigan Athletic	0-2		8054		3	1				5	7		8	12		11				10				6	9	13	4	2		14
23	Jan 3	READING	2-2	Southall, Thomson	7443		6	1				5	7		8			11						9			10	3	4	2		12
24	15	Bristol Rovers	1-2	Onoura	8331		3	1		6		5	7	13	8	12		11						9			10		4	2		
25	22	BLACKPOOL	1-3	Southall	6805		6	1		12		5	3	11	8	7								9			10		4	2		
26	Feb 1	Chesterfield	0-0		2898		2	1		6		5	3	11	12			7						9			13	8		4		10
27	5	STOKE CITY	3-0	Onoura, Gooden, Rowe	7801		6	1				5	3	11	8			7						9			13	12	4	2		10
28	12	Oldham Athletic	3-1	Gooden, Ashby, Rowe	5144		6	1				5	3	11	8			7				13		9			10	12	4	2		
29	26	Preston North End	2-0	Asaba 2	13246	12		1				5		3	8			7				13		9		6		11	4	2		10
30	Mar 4	OXFORD UNITED	1-0	Lewis	6966	13	3	1				5		11	8			7						9		6	14	12	4	2		10
31	7	NOTTS COUNTY	0-1		6915	13		1				5			8			7		11		12		9		6	14	3	4	2		10
32	11	Bristol City	1-0	Hessenthaler	9332	10		1			13	5			8			7				11		9		6	12	3	4	2		
33	14	BURNLEY	2-2	Butters, Asaba	7347	10		1		13		5			8			7		12		11		9		6	14	3	4	2		
34	18	SCUNTHORPE UNITED	3-1	Lewis, Thomson, Southall (p)	6822	10		1				5	3		8			7				11		9		6	12		4	2		13
35	21	Bournemouth	1-0	Onoura	4443		2	1				5	3					7		12		11		9		6	13		4	8		10
36	25	Colchester United	1-2	Rowe	4337		6	1	2		14	5	3					7		12		11		9			10		4	8		
37	28	Wycombe Wanderers	0-1		4183		6	1	2		12	5	3					7	13	8		11		9			10			4		
38	Apr 1	CHESTERFIELD	1-0	Butler	6772		6	1	2		9	5		3	8			7	10			11					13		12	4		
39	7	Reading	2-2	Southall, Onoura	11064		6	1	2			5	3	11	8			7	9					13			12		4	10		
40	15	WIGAN ATHLETIC	2-1	Onoura, Lewis	7746		2				13	5	3	11	8			7						9		6	12		4	10		
41	18	Burnley	3-0	Gooden, Ashby, Smith	17026		2	1	14			5		3	8			7	13	12		11		9		6			4	10		
42	22	LUTON TOWN	2-0	Hessenthaler, Southall	8667	9	2	1			11	5		3	8			7	13			12				6			4	10		
43	24	Millwall	2-2	Gooden, Hessenthaler	17929	14	2	1				5	3	11	8			7				12		9		6	13		4	10		
44	29	BRENTFORD	2-0	Onoura, Butler	9001	10	2	1	12		13	5	3	11	8			14						9		6			4	7		
45	May 2	CARDIFF CITY	4-1	Asaba 3, Southall	9176	10	2	1	12		14	5	3	11	8			13						9		6			4	7		
46	6	Wrexham	0-1		8811	10	2	1			14	5	3	11	8			12						9		6			4	7		13
					Apps	11	41	43	7	6	10	40	26	16	42	15	3	42	5	13	4	29	9	22	9	34	22	26	44	45	15	28
					Goals	6	3				2	2	1	4	5			6		1		1	3	6			4	1	1	9	15	9

S Mautone played in game 40 at 1. MT Browning played in game 25 at 13
MA Galloway played at 14 in game 1 and 2 in game 2
JE Pinnock played at 14 in game 11 and 13 in game 36
AS Williams played at 1 in games 5 and 8

Play Offs

Rd	Date	Opponent	Score	Scorers	Att	Asaba CE	Ashby BI	Bartram VL	Bass JDM	Bryant M	Butler S	Butters G	Edge R	Gooden TM	Hessenthaler A	Hodge J	Lee CE	Lewis KJ	Matthews LJ	McGlinchey BK	Miller BS	Nosworthy NPH	Omoyimni E	Onoura I	Patterson M	Pennock AB	Rowe RC	Saunders MP	Smith PW	Southall LN	Taylor RA	Thomson A
SF1	May 13	Stoke City	2-3	Gooden, Hessenthaler	22124		2	1				5	3	11	8			7						9		6			4	10		
SF2	17	STOKE CITY	3-0	Ashby, Onoura, Smith	10386	10	2	1			12	5	3	11	8			7				13		9		6			14	4		
F	28	Wigan Athletic	3-2	McGibbon (og), Butler, Thomson	53764	10	2	1			12	5	3	11	8			7						9		6			13	4		14

Final at Wembley Stadium, a.e.t.

MT Browning played at 12 in SF1

F.A. Cup

Rd	Date	Opponent	Score	Scorers	Att	Asaba CE	Ashby BI	Bartram VL	Bass JDM	Bryant M	Butler S	Butters G	Edge R	Gooden TM	Hessenthaler A	Hodge J	Lee CE	Lewis KJ	Matthews LJ	McGlinchey BK	Miller BS	Nosworthy NPH	Omoyimni E	Onoura I	Patterson M	Pennock AB	Rowe RC	Saunders MP	Smith PW	Southall LN	Taylor RA	Thomson A
R1	Oct 30	Cheltenham Town	1-1	Southall	3188		2	1			9	5	13		8			7		11		12				6		3	4	10		
rep	Nov 9	CHELTENHAM TOWN	3-2	Thomson, Pennock, McGlinchey	4352		2	1				5	7		13	8		14		10		12				6		3	4		11	9
R2	20	DARLINGTON	3-1	Butters, Taylor 2	5168		2	1			9	5	7					10		8		12				6		3		4	11	
R3	Dec 11	Walsall	1-1	Southall	4314		3	1				5	7		8			12		11		10				6		9	4	2		
rep	Jan 8	WALSALL	2-1	(aet) Barras (og), Thomson	6538		6	1			12	5	7		8	13		11				10						3	4	2		9
R4	11	BRADFORD CITY	3-1	Thomson, Ashby, Hodge	7091		3	1		6		5	7		8	10		11				12							4	2		9
R5	29	SHEFFIELD WEDNESDAY	3-1	Saunders, Thomson, Southall	10130		2	1				5	3		8	7						12				6		13	4	10		9
R6	Feb 20	Chelsea	0-5		34205	12	2	1				5	3		8			7				13				6		11	4	10		9

MT Browning played at 11 (subbed) in R5 and 14 in R6

F.L. Cup (Worthington Cup)

Rd	Date	Opponent	Score	Scorers	Att	Asaba CE	Ashby BI	Bartram VL	Bass JDM	Bryant M	Butler S	Butters G	Edge R	Gooden TM	Hessenthaler A	Hodge J	Lee CE	Lewis KJ	Matthews LJ	McGlinchey BK	Miller BS	Nosworthy NPH	Omoyimni E	Onoura I	Patterson M	Pennock AB	Rowe RC	Saunders MP	Smith PW	Southall LN	Taylor RA	Thomson A
R1/1	Aug 11	Brighton & Hove Albion	2-0	Ormerod (og), Hessenthaler	5613		3	1		13		5			8	14	2			7		11				6		9	4	10	12	
R1/2	24	BRIGHTON & HOVE ALB.	2-0	Taylor, Southall	4592		5	1							8	4	14	7		12	13				2	6		3		10	11	9
R2/1	Sep 14	BOLTON WANDERERS	1-4	Hessenthaler	4996		5								8	7				10	12	13	11			6		3	4	2		9
R2/2	21	Bolton Wanderers	0-2		3673		3					5			8			7		10	2	13	11			6			4			9

JE Pinnock played at 14 in R2/1. MA Galloway played at 12 in R2/2
AS Williams played at 1 in R2/1 and R2/2

A.M. Cup (Auto Windscreens Shield)

Rd	Date	Opponent	Score	Scorers	Att	Asaba CE	Ashby BI	Bartram VL	Bass JDM	Bryant M	Butler S	Butters G	Edge R	Gooden TM	Hessenthaler A	Hodge J	Lee CE	Lewis KJ	Matthews LJ	McGlinchey BK	Miller BS	Nosworthy NPH	Omoyimni E	Onoura I	Patterson M	Pennock AB	Rowe RC	Saunders MP	Smith PW	Southall LN	Taylor RA	Thomson A
R1	Dec 7	TORQUAY UNITED	0-3		2718		5				14	6			12			7		3		8				2	9	13	4	11		

Played at 1: CH Mitten

2000/01

13th in Division One

No.	Month	Day	Opponents	Score	Scorers	Att.	Asaba CE	Ashby BJ	Bartram VL	Browning MT	Butters G	Crofts AL	Edge R	Gooden TM	Hessenthaler A	Hope CJ	Ipoua G	James KE	King MF	Lewis KJ	Lovell M	McGlinchey BK	Nosworthy NPH	Onoura I	Patterson M	Pennock AB	Phillips ME	Rose RA	Saunders MP	Shaw P	Smith PW	Southall LN	Thomson A
1	Aug	12	STOCKPORT COUNTY	1-3	Butters	9429	9	2	1		5		3	11	8	6			12										14	10	4	7	13
2		19	Tranmere Rovers	2-3	Asaba, Southall p)	8355	9	2	1		5		3	11	8	6			12	7												4	10
3		25	PORTSMOUTH	1-1	Thomson	8749	9	4	1	7	5		3	11	8	6		13		14					2							12	10
4		28	Burnley	1-1	Asaba	14450	9	4	1		5		3	11	8	6			13	7			12		2							10	
5	Sep	2	WOLVERHAMPTON W.	1-0	Lewis	10017	9		1	13	5		3	11	8	6			10	7					2				12			4	
6		9	Grimsby Town	0-1		4512	9		1	7	5		3		8	6		12				11							10		4	2	13
7		13	Queen's Park Rangers	2-2	Asaba, Hessenthaler	10655	9	2	1	11	5		3		8	6			10	12											4	7	13
8		16	HUDDERSFIELD T	2-1	Butters, Smith	8503	9	2	1	11	5		3		8	6			10	14									13		4	7	12
9		23	Fulham	0-3		13032	9	2	1	11	5		3		8	6		12	10	13											4	7	14
10		30	SHEFFIELD WEDNESDAY	2-0	Butters, Thomson	9099		3	1	11	5				8	6			10	14					2				12	13	4	7	9
11	Oct	6	BOLTON WANDERERS	2-2	Smith, Onoura	9327	9	3	1		5				8	6				11				13	2				12	14	4	7	10
12		14	Wimbledon	4-4	Thomson 2, Saunders, Asaba	9030	9	3	1		5				8	6				14					2	12			11	13	4	7	10
13		17	Watford	0-0		12356		3	1				12		8	6			14					13	2	5			11	10	4	7	9
14		21	BARNSLEY	0-0		9030	9	3	1					12	8	6								13	2	5			11	14	4	7	10
15		25	Birmingham City	0-1		26044		3	1					11	14	6				13				9	2	5			7	8	4	12	10
16		28	CREWE ALEXANDRA	0-1		8347		3	1					11	8	6			14					9	2	5			7	10	4	13	12
17	Nov	4	Sheffield United	2-1	Smith, Thomson	14028		3	1	14				11	8	6			13					9	2	5			12	7	4		10
18		12	NOTTM. FOREST	1-3	Onoura	9866		3	1					11	8	6			13					9	2	5				7	4	12	10
19		18	West Bromwich Albion	1-3	King	16410		3	1	13				11	8	6			14					9	2	5			12	7	4		10
20		25	Blackburn Rovers	2-1	Hessenthaler, Curtis (og)	18061		3	1	12					8	6			10					13	2	5			11	9	4	7	
21	Dec	2	BIRMINGHAM CITY	1-2	King	9247		3	1	8						6		12	10					14	2	5			11	9	4	7	13
22		9	Norwich City	0-1		16725	13	3	1	8					12	6			10					14	2	5			11		4	7	9
23		16	PRESTON NORTH END	4-0	Asaba 2, Ashby, King	8198	9	2	1				3			6			13	7			12			5			11	10	4	8	14
24		22	Stockport County	2-2	Lewis, King	6095	9	2	1				3			6			12	7				13		5			11	10	4	8	
25		26	CRYSTAL PALACE	4-1	Asaba 3, Onoura	10334	9	2	1				3		12	6			14	7				13		5			11	10	4	8	
26	Jan	1	Portsmouth	0-0		14446	9	2	1				3		14	6			12	7				13		5			11	10	4	8	
27		13	BURNLEY	0-0		9331	9	2	1				3			6				7				12		5			11	10	4	8	
28		20	Crystal Palace	2-2	Saunders 2	18823	9	2	1	12			3			6				7						5			11	10	4	8	
29	Feb	3	Wolverhampton Wan.	1-1	King	26627	13	2	1	14			3	11		6			10					12		5			7	9	4	8	
30		10	GRIMSBY TOWN	1-0	King	8633	14	2	1	12			3	11		6			10							5			7	9	4	8	13
31		17	Huddersfield Town	3-2	Saunders 2, King	10576	14	2	1	12			3	11		6			10					13		5			7	9	4	8	
32		20	QUEEN'S PARK RANGERS	0-1		10430	13	2	1	14			3	11		6			10						12	5			7	9	4	8	
33		24	FULHAM	0-2		9931	12	3	1	8				11		6			10					13	2	5				9	4	7	
34	Mar	3	Sheffield Wednesday	1-2	Asaba	18702	13	3	1	8				11		6			10					12		5			7	9	4	2	
35		6	WIMBLEDON	0-0		8625		3	1	8				11		6			10					9	12	5			7	13	4	2	14
36		10	Bolton Wanderers	3-3	King 2, Southall	13161			1	8						6		7	10				11	9	2	5					4	3	12
37		20	TRANMERE ROVERS	2-1	King (p), Onoura	8233		3	1	8						6			10				11	9	2	5				12	4	7	13
38		25	Barnsley	1-3	King	13609		3	1	8						6	13	12	10				11	9		5				7	4	2	
39		31	Preston North End	0-0		13550			1	8						6	13		10				11	9	2	5			12	7	4	3	
40	Apr	7	NORWICH CITY	4-3	Hope, Onoura 3	9631			1	8						6	13	14	10				11	9	2	5			12	7	4	3	
41		14	SHEFFIELD UNITED	4-1	Onoura, King 2, Shaw	9429			1	8						6	12		10				11	9	2	5				7	4	3	
42		16	Crewe Alexandra	1-2	Hope	7051		13	1	8						6	14		10					9	2	5		12	11	7	4	3	
43		21	WEST BROMWICH ALB.	1-2	Onoura	9920		13	1	8						6	14		10				11	9	2	5			12	7	4	3	
44		28	Nottingham Forest	1-0	King	20617		3	1	8						6	13		10				11	9	2	5		12	14		4	7	
45	May	1	WATFORD	0-3		9068		3	1	8		13				6	12		10		14			9		5		7	11		4	2	
46		6	BLACKBURN ROVERS	1-1	King (p)	10277		3	1	8						6	13		10					9	2	5	14	12	11		4	7	
						Apps	25	40	46	31	12	1	20	18	23	46	9	7	38	17	1	1	10	31	28	35	1	4	35	33	42	44	24
						Goals	10	1			3				2	2			15	2				9					5	1	3	2	5

One own goal

F.A. Cup

Round	Month	Day	Opponents	Score	Scorers	Att.	Asaba CE	Ashby BJ	Bartram VL	Browning MT	Butters G	Crofts AL	Edge R	Gooden TM	Hessenthaler A	Hope CJ	Ipoua G	James KE	King MF	Lewis KJ	Lovell M	McGlinchey BK	Nosworthy NPH	Onoura I	Patterson M	Pennock AB	Phillips ME	Rose RA	Saunders MP	Shaw P	Smith PW	Southall LN	Thomson A
R3	Jan	6	Bournemouth	3-2	Hope, Hessenthaler, Shaw	7403			1	12	2		3		8	6			14	11				9	13	5				10	4	7	
R4		28	CHELSEA	2-4	Shaw, Onoura	10419		2	1				3			6			10	7				13	12	5			11	9	4	8	14

F.L. Cup (Worthington Cup)

Round	Month	Day	Opponents	Score	Scorers	Att.	Asaba CE	Ashby BJ	Bartram VL	Browning MT	Butters G	Crofts AL	Edge R	Gooden TM	Hessenthaler A	Hope CJ	Ipoua G	James KE	King MF	Lewis KJ	Lovell M	McGlinchey BK	Nosworthy NPH	Onoura I	Patterson M	Pennock AB	Phillips ME	Rose RA	Saunders MP	Shaw P	Smith PW	Southall LN	Thomson A
R1/1	Aug	22	TORQUAY UNITED	2-0	Asaba, Thomson	2743	9	3	1	4	5			11	8	6		12		7					2								10
R1/2	Sep	5	Torquay United	2-3	Asaba, Aggrey (og)	1351	9		1	4	5		3	11		6			10	7					2				12			8	
R2/1		20	Manchester City	1-1	Smith	17408	9	2	1	11	5		3		8	6			10	13									14		4	7	12
R2/2		26	MANCHESTER CITY	2-4	(aet) Thomson 2	6520		2	1	11	5		3		8	6			10	13					12						4	7	9

RC Rowe played at 13 in R1/2

2001/02

12th in Division One

							Ashby BJ	Bartram VL	Brown JR	Browning MT	Butters G	Edge R	Gooden TM	Hessenthaler A	Hope CJ	Ipoua G	James KE	King MF	Nosworthy NPH	Onuora I	Osborn SE	Patterson M	Pennock AB	Perpetuini DP	Rose RA	Samuel JL	Saunders MP	Shaw P	Smith PW	Spiller D	Taylor RA
1	Aug	11	PRESTON NORTH END	5-0	Browning 2, Ashby, Onuora, Gooden	9412	4	1		8		3	11		6	10				9		2	5	12			13	14	7		
2		18	Sheffield United	0-0		16998	4	1		8		3	11		6	10				9		2	5					12	7		
3		25	BARNSLEY	3-0	Onuora, King 2	8292	4	1		8		3	11	14	6			10		9		2	5				12	13	7		
4		27	West Bromwich Albion	0-1		18180	4	1		8		3	11	12	6	13		10		9		2	5						7		
5	Sep	8	Portsmouth	1-2	Onuora	17224	4	1		8		3	11	12	6			10		9		2	5					13	7		
6		14	Bradford City	1-5	King	14101	4	1		8				11	6	12		10				2	5	3			14	9	7	13	
7		18	WOLVERHAMPTON W.	2-3	Ipoua, King (p)	8966	5	1		8	14		11	4	6	13	12	10						3			2	9	7		
8		22	ROTHERHAM UNITED	2-1	King, Hope	7688	5	1		8		3	11	4	6			10		9		2		13				12	7		
9		25	Grimsby Town	2-1	Hope, King	4859	5	1		8		3	11	4	6			10		9		2		13			12		7		
10		29	COVENTRY CITY	1-2	Shaw	9435	5	1		8		3	11	4	6	13		10	2	9				14				12	7		
11	Oct	13	NORWICH CITY	0-2		9166		1		8	4	3			6	9		10			12	2	5				11		7		13
12		20	Wimbledon	1-3	Butters	8042		1		8	4	3			6	9		10			14	2	5				11	13	7		12
13		23	Birmingham City	1-2	Ipoua	27101		1			4				6	9	13	12	8		11	2	5	3				10	7		14
14		27	WALSALL	2-0	Perpetuini, Ipoua	7548		1			4				6	10		12	8	9	11	2		3		5			7		13
15		30	BURNLEY	2-2	Osborn, Ipoua	8067		1		12	4				6	10		13	8	9	11	2		3		5			7		
16	Nov	3	Manchester City	1-4	King	33067		1		12	4			8	6	10		13	2	9	11			3		5			7		14
17		10	Crewe Alexandra	0-0		5419	3	1		4					6	8		10	2	9	11			12		5			7		13
18		18	WATFORD	0-0		8733	3	1		4					6	8		10	2	9	11			12		5			7		
19		21	CRYSTAL PALACE	3-0	Ipoua 2, Onuora	9396	5	1		4					6	8		10	2	9	11			3			12	13	7		
20		24	Millwall	2-1	Ipoua, King	15214	5	1		4	13				6	8		10	2	9	11			3		12		14	7		
21		27	Stockport County	2-0	Onuora, King	4854		1		7	4				6	8		10	3	9	11			12		5			2		
22		30	BIRMINGHAM CITY	1-1	Purse (og)	8575		1		7	4				6	8		10	3	9	11			12		5		13	2		
23	Dec	8	Nottingham Forest	2-2	Shaw 2	18303		1			5				6	8	12	10	2		11			3			7	9	4		13
24		15	SHEFFIELD WEDNESDAY	2-1	Shaw, Osborn	8586		1		4	5				6	8		10	2		11			3				9	7		12
25		22	Barnsley	1-4	Morgan (og)	11965		1		4	5				6	8	12		2		11			3				10	7		9
26		26	PORTSMOUTH	2-0	King, Shaw	10447	5	1		4			12		6	13		10	2		11			3				8	7		9
27		29	WEST BROMWICH ALB.	2-1	Hope, Smith	9912	5	1		4					6			10	2	13	11	12		3				8	7		9
28	Jan	12	SHEFFIELD UNITED	0-1		8814	5	1		4					6	12		10	2	9	11			3				8	7		
29		16	Crystal Palace	1-3	Onuora	17646	5	1		4			13		6	14		10	2	9	11	12		3				8	7		
30		19	Preston North End	2-0	Osborn, Smith	13289	5	1		4			3		6	14	12	10	8		11	2					13	9	7		
31		29	STOCKPORT COUNTY	3-3	Woodthorpe (og), Osborn, King (p)	7217	5	1		4			13		6	14		10	2	9	11	12		3				8	7		
32	Feb	2	Coventry City	2-1	Onuora, King	14337	5	1		4			11	12	6			10		9		2		3				8	7		
33		9	WIMBLEDON	0-0		8494	5	1		4			11	14	6	13		10		9	12	2		3				8	7		
34		23	BRADFORD CITY	0-4		7789	5	1		4				12	6	13		10		9	11	2		3			14	8	7		
35		26	Rotherham United	2-3	Onuora, King	6005	5	1		4				11	6	12		10	2	9				3				8	7		
36	Mar	2	Wolverhampton Wan.	0-2		25908	5	1		4		3	14	8	6	12		10	2		11						13	9	7		
37		5	GRIMSBY TOWN	2-1	Shaw, Ipoua	7025			1	12	5	3	11	4	6	9	14	10	2								13	8	7		
38		9	Sheffield Wednesday	0-0		20361			1		5	3	11	4	6	12		10	2	9								8	7		
39		16	NOTTM. FOREST	3-1	King 2, Browning	8928			1	4	5	3	11		6	13		10	2	9				12			14	8	7		
40		19	Norwich City	1-2	Onuora	16479			1	4	5		11		6	13	12	10	2	9				3			14	8	7		
41		24	MILLWALL	1-0	King	8082			1	4	5		11		6	9	13	10	2					3			12	8	7		
42		30	Walsall	1-1	Saunders	6190			1	4	5		11		6	9		10	2	13	12			3			14	8	7		
43	Apr	1	CREWE ALEXANDRA	1-0	King (p)	7748			1	12	5		14		6	13		10	2	9	11			3			7	8	4		
44		6	Burnley	0-2		16236	2		1	4	5		11		6	14	13			9				3	12		8	10	7		
45		13	MANCHESTER CITY	1-3	Onuora	9494	2		1	4	5		11		6	13	12	10		9	14				3			8	7		
46		21	Watford	3-2	Hope, Shaw, Onuora	15674	2		1	4	5			14	6	13		10		9	11		12		3			8	7		
						Apps	28	36	10	42	23	14	25	17	46	40	10	42	29	33	28	20	10	34	3	8	19	37	46	1	11
						Goals	1			3	1		1		4	8		17		11	4			1			1	7	2		

Three own goals

F.A. Cup

R3	Jan	6	Wolverhampton Wanderers	1-0	Shaw	15271	5	1		4			12		6	13		10	2	9	11			3				8	7		
R4	Feb	5	BRISTOL ROVERS	1-0	Mauge (og)	9772	5	1		4			11		6	14		10	12	9	13	2		3				8	7		
R5		16	Arsenal	2-5	King, Gooden	38003	5	1		14			11	12	6	13		10		9	7	2		3				8	4		

F.L. Cup (Worthington Cup)

R1	Aug	21	Oxford United	2-1	(aet) King (p), Onuora	5886	4	1		8		3	11		6	10		13		9		2	5	14				12	7		
R2	Sep	11	MILLWALL	2-1	King, Nethercott (og)	7511	4	1		8			11	14	6	13		10		9		2	5	3				12	7		
R3	Oct	9	SOUTHAMPTON	0-2		7948		1		13	4	3		8	6	12		10		9		2	5				11	14	7		

2002/03

11th in Division One

	Date	Opponent	Score	Scorers	Att	Ashby BJ	Awuah J	Bartram VL	Brown JR	Edge R	Edusei A	Hessenthaler A	Hope CJ	Ipoua G	James KE	Johnson L	Johnson T	King MF	Nosworthy NPH	Osborn SE	Patterson M	Pennock AB	Perpetuini DP	Rose RA	Saunders MP	Shaw P	Sidebe M	Smith PW	Southall LN	Spiller D	Wallace R
1	Aug 10	Wimbledon	1-0	Ipoua	2476	3			1	5		6	4	10			12		2	8					13	9	11	7			
2	13	DERBY COUNTY	1-0	Shaw	8775	3			1	5		6	4	10			13		2	8					12	9	11	7			
3	17	MILLWALL	1-0	Ipoua	7543	3			1	5		6	4	10	14		13		2	8					12	9	11	7			
4	24	Norwich City	0-1		20588	3			1	5		6	4	10	14		13		2	8					12	9	11	7			
5	26	PRESTON NORTH END	1-1	Saunders	7785	3			1	5		6	4	10			12		2				13		8	9	11	7			
6	31	Leicester City	0-2		30067	3			1	5		6	4	10			11		2		12				8	9		7			13
7	Sep 7	PORTSMOUTH	1-3	James	8717	3		1		5		6	4	10	12		11				2		13		8	9		7			
8	14	Brighton & Hove Albion	4-2	Shaw 2, Perpetuini, James	6733	3			1	5		6	4	10	11	13						12	8		2	9		7			
9	18	Nottingham Forest	1-4	Hessenthaler	16073	3	12		1	5		6	4	10	11								8		2	9		7			
10	21	SHEFFIELD UNITED	1-1	Shaw	7497	3	12		1	5			4	10	11	13						6	8		2	9		7			
11	29	Crystal Palace	2-2	Perpetuini, Mullins (og)	15699	3		12	1				4	10		5	13		2			6	8			9		7			11
12	Oct 5	COVENTRY CITY	0-2		7722	3			1			6	4	10	13	5	12		2				8	14		9		7			11
13	12	Rotherham United	1-1	Wallace	6094	3			1			6	4	10	12				2				8		5	9		7			11
14	19	WATFORD	3-0	Sidibe, Ipoua, James	8728	3			1			6	4	10	14	13	12		2				8		5	9	11	7			
15	26	Ipswich Town	1-0	Sidibe	24176	3			1			6	4		14	13	10	12	2				8		5	9	11	7			
16	29	WOLVERHAMPTON W.	0-4		10036	3			1			6	4	10	14		12		2				8		5	9	11	7		12	
17	Nov 2	Grimsby Town	1-1	Saunders	5715	3			1			6	4	10	12		13		2				8		5	9	11	7			
18	9	READING	0-1		8511	3			1			6	4	13	9		12	10	2				8		5		11	7			
19	16	SHEFFIELD WEDNESDAY	1-1	T Johnson	8028	3			1	2		6	4				11	10					8		5	9	12	7		13	
20	23	Walsall	0-1		6630	3			1	2		6	4	14			11	10	12				8		5	9	13	7			
21	30	STOKE CITY	1-1	Shaw	8150				1	6			4		12	3	8	10	2						5	9	11	7			13
22	Dec 7	Bradford City	3-1	King 2 (1p), Wallace	10711				1	8		6	4	14		3		10	2						5	9	11	7	12		13
23	14	Sheffield Wednesday	2-0	Wallace, Smith	17715	3			1			6	4	12		8		10	2				13		5	9		7	14		11
24	21	BURNLEY	4-2	Wallace, Shaw, Smith, King	7905	3			1			6	4	13				10	2				12		5	9		7	8		11
25	26	Millwall	2-2	Saunders, King (p)	10947	3			1			6	4	13				10	2				12		5	9		7	8		11
26	Jan 11	Derby County	1-1	Ipoua	22769	3			1			6	4	11				10	2						5	9	12	7	8		
27	18	LEICESTER CITY	3-2	Shaw, Elliott (og), Sidibe	8609	3			1	2		6	4	10		14									5	9	11	7	8	13	12
28	Feb 1	Preston North End	0-3		12121	3			1	2		6	4	10					13				14		5	9	11	7	8		12
29	10	Reading	1-2	Wallace	11030				1	5		6	4	12	9	3			2				13				11	7	8		10
30	15	GRIMSBY TOWN	3-0	Wallace 2, Hope	7158	3			1	5		6	4	10					2				12			9	13	7	8	14	11
31	22	Portsmouth	0-1		19521	3			1	5		6	4	10					2							9	12	7	8		11
32	25	NORWICH CITY	1-0	Wallace	7935	3			1	5		6	4						2				13		12	9	11	7	8		10
33	Mar 1	BRIGHTON & HOVE ALB	3-0	Shaw, T Johnson (p), Southall	9178	3			1	5			4				12		2	14			13		6	9	11	7	8		10
34	4	NOTTM. FOREST	1-4	Wallace	7277	3			1	5			4			13	11		2	12			14		6	9		7	8		10
35	11	WIMBLEDON	3-3	Shaw 2, Wallace	7884	3			1	5		6	4	13		12				9					8	10		7	2		11
36	15	ROTHERHAM UNITED	1-1	Wallace	7284				1	5		6	4	10			13		3	12					8	9		7	2		11
37	18	Watford	1-0	Shaw	10492				1	5		6	4	13			10		3	8						9	12	7	2		11
38	22	Wolverhampton Wan.	0-6		25171			1		5			4	12			10		3	6					8	9	11	7	2		
39	25	Sheffield United	2-2	Osborn, Shaw	15799			1		5			4			2	10		3	9			13		12	8	11	7	6		
40	29	IPSWICH TOWN	1-3	Smith	8508			1		5			4	13		2	10		3	8			12		6	9		7			11
41	Apr 5	Stoke City	0-0		12746	3		1		5			4			14	13		2	8						9	11	7	6	12	10
42	12	WALSALL	0-1		6972	3		1		5	12		4			13	10		2	8						9	11		6	7	
43	19	Burnley	0-2		14031	3	13	1		5	14		4						2	8			12			9	11	7	6	10	
44	21	BRADFORD CITY	1-0	Shaw	6281	3			1	5			4						2	10						9	11	7	8	6	
45	26	Coventry City	0-0		14795	3	11		1	5			4			13			10	8			12			9		7	2	6	
46	May 4	CRYSTAL PALACE	2-1	Nosworthy 2	9315	3			1	5		12	4						10	8			13	14		9	11	7	2	6	
					Apps	38	4	8	39	34	2	33	46	33	15	18	26	10	39	18	2	3	29	2	34	44	30	45	24	10	22
					Goals							1	1	4	3		2	4	2	1			2		3	13	3	3	1		11

Two own goals

F.A. Cup

	Date	Opponent	Score	Scorers	Att	Ashby BJ	Awuah J	Bartram VL	Brown JR	Edge R	Edusei A	Hessenthaler A	Hope CJ	Ipoua G	James KE	Johnson L	Johnson T	King MF	Nosworthy NPH	Osborn SE	Patterson M	Pennock AB	Perpetuini DP	Rose RA	Saunders MP	Shaw P	Sidebe M	Smith PW	Southall LN	Spiller D	Wallace R
R3	Jan 7	SHEFFIELD WEDNESDAY	4-1	King 2 (1p), Ipoua, Hope	6434	3			1			6	4	11				10	2						5	9	12	7	8	13	
R4	25	LEEDS UNITED	1-1	Sidibe	11093	3			1	2		6	4	10											5	9	11	7	8		12
rep	Feb 4	Leeds United	1-2	Ipoua	29355				1	2		6	4	12	7	3	13		5				9				11		8		10

F.L. Cup (Worthington Cup)

	Date	Opponent	Score	Scorers	Att	Ashby BJ	Awuah J	Bartram VL	Brown JR	Edge R	Edusei A	Hessenthaler A	Hope CJ	Ipoua G	James KE	Johnson L	Johnson T	King MF	Nosworthy NPH	Osborn SE	Patterson M	Pennock AB	Perpetuini DP	Rose RA	Saunders MP	Shaw P	Sidebe M	Smith PW	Southall LN	Spiller D	Wallace R
R1	Sep 10	Torquay United	1-0	Hessenthaler	1981	3			1	5		6	4	10	11						2		12		8	9		7			
R2	Oct 1	Stockport County	2-1	Ipoua, T Johnson	2396	3		1					4	10		5	13		2				8	14		9		7		6	11
R3	Nov 6	Chelsea	1-2	King	28033	3			1			6	4	10			13	12	2				8		5	9	11	7		14	

R2 a.e.t.

A Crofts played at 12 on Oct 1

GILLINGHAM AGAINST OTHER CLUBS (IN THE FOOTBALL LEAGUE)

		Home:					*Away:*					*Totals:*		
	p	*w*	*d*	*l*	*f*	*a*	*w*	*d*	*l*	*f*	*a*	*f*	*a*	*% won*
Aberdare Athletic	12	5	0	1	14	4	1	1	4	5	13	19	17	50.00
Accrington Stanley	2	1	0	0	2	1	0	0	1	0	3	2	4	50.00
Aldershot	56	13	8	7	52	31	9	4	15	29	49	81	80	39.29
Aston Villa	2	0	1	0	0	0	0	0	1	1	2	1	2	0.00
Barnet	8	2	2	0	7	5	1	0	3	2	5	9	10	37.50
Barnsley	20	4	5	1	16	9	1	2	7	10	25	26	34	25.00
Barrow	20	6	2	2	21	12	4	3	3	11	14	32	26	50.00
Birmingham City	4	0	1	1	2	3	0	0	2	1	3	3	6	0.00
Blackburn Rovers	6	0	2	1	3	4	1	0	2	4	8	7	12	16.67
Blackpool	26	6	5	2	21	16	1	4	8	12	28	33	44	26.92
Bolton Wanderers	12	3	1	2	9	7	3	1	2	8	9	17	16	50.00
Bournemouth	78	19	11	9	55	44	11	7	21	45	74	100	118	38.46
Bradford City	26	8	4	1	24	13	3	4	6	16	23	40	36	42.31
Bradford PA	8	2	1	1	8	5	0	1	3	0	6	8	11	25.00
Brentford	72	16	6	14	50	43	13	8	15	51	56	101	99	40.28
Brighton & Hove Alb.	76	16	14	8	49	27	5	8	25	34	90	83	117	27.63
Bristol City	50	11	9	5	42	27	6	4	15	30	52	72	79	34.00
Bristol Rovers	80	23	7	10	60	40	8	4	28	40	82	100	122	38.75
Burnley	28	7	6	1	23	12	5	3	6	21	23	44	35	42.86
Bury	44	13	5	4	38	26	4	3	15	23	40	61	66	38.64
Cambridge United	14	6	0	1	15	4	2	2	3	10	12	25	16	57.14
Cardiff City	32	8	5	3	29	13	4	1	11	13	30	42	43	37.50
Carlisle United	38	10	6	3	24	12	8	2	9	23	25	47	37	47.37
Charlton Athletic	24	3	5	4	13	14	0	4	8	6	19	19	33	12.50
Chester City	42	13	4	4	31	18	4	8	9	24	33	55	51	40.48
Chesterfield	54	16	5	6	52	20	7	8	12	34	39	86	59	42.59
Colchester Uunited	56	13	6	9	42	34	3	14	11	33	53	75	87	28.57
Coventry City	38	7	4	8	28	32	4	3	12	21	51	49	83	28.95
Crewe Alexandra	30	8	2	5	22	13	3	3	9	18	27	40	40	36.67
Crystal Palace	62	15	8	8	54	39	7	8	16	38	70	92	109	35.48
Darlington	34	10	4	3	29	14	3	8	6	20	24	49	38	38.24
Derby County	6	2	0	1	5	4	0	1	2	1	4	6	8	33.33
Doncaster Rovers	48	18	5	1	54	17	10	7	7	29	29	83	46	58.33
Exeter City	94	24	13	10	84	61	7	15	25	52	91	136	152	32.98
Fulham	32	10	2	4	27	16	3	4	9	15	26	42	42	40.62
Gateshead	4	2	0	0	8	4	0	1	1	2	4	10	8	50.00
Grimsby Town	32	9	3	4	22	12	1	5	10	10	26	32	38	31.25
Halifax Town	18	8	1	0	19	4	3	4	2	10	8	29	12	61.11
Hartlepool United	28	11	3	0	36	6	2	4	8	12	22	48	28	46.43
Hereford United	22	6	2	3	21	12	1	5	5	7	15	28	27	31.82
Huddersfield Town	12	3	1	2	10	10	2	1	3	8	9	18	19	41.67
Hull City	14	5	0	2	8	5	1	4	2	4	6	12	11	42.86
Ipswich Town	14	0	5	2	5	8	1	4	2	7	15	12	23	7.14
Leicester City	2	1	0	0	3	2	0	0	1	0	2	3	4	50.00
Leyton Orient	46	9	7	7	31	22	7	5	11	27	38	58	60	34.78
Lincoln City	42	11	7	3	36	19	7	4	10	27	33	63	52	42.86
Luton Town	48	11	6	7	31	22	3	5	16	25	68	56	90	29.17
Macclesfield Town	2	0	1	0	2	2	0	0	1	0	1	2	3	0.00
Maidstone United	6	0	1	2	2	5	1	1	1	3	4	5	9	16.67
Manchester City	4	0	0	2	1	5	0	1	1	1	4	2	9	0.00
Mansfield Town	50	13	10	2	41	19	2	7	16	20	47	61	66	30.00
Merthyr Town	20	7	2	1	22	5	2	3	5	8	17	30	22	45.00
Middlesbrough	4	1	1	0	5	1	0	1	1	1	4	6	5	25.00

	Home:						Away:					Totals:		
	p	*w*	*d*	*l*	*f*	*a*	*w*	*d*	*l*	*f*	*a*	*f*	*a*	*% won*
Millwall	76	16	8	14	53	51	4	9	25	38	94	91	145	26.32
Newport County	74	18	9	10	67	41	8	8	21	40	74	107	115	35.14
Northampton Town	90	23	7	15	83	63	8	7	30	38	84	121	147	34.44
Norwich City	50	15	4	6	51	30	3	6	16	15	44	66	74	36.00
Nottingham Forest	8	1	0	3	6	12	1	1	2	6	15	12	27	25.00
Notts County	24	8	1	3	22	11	3	4	5	13	18	35	29	45.83
Oldham Athletic	26	10	1	2	26	16	3	2	8	18	25	44	41	50.00
Oxford United	28	9	2	3	25	14	4	7	3	19	19	44	33	46.43
Peterborough Utd	32	6	9	1	25	18	3	5	8	10	21	35	39	28.12
Plymouth Argyle	60	16	5	9	45	32	3	8	19	24	59	69	91	31.67
Port Vale	28	4	8	2	14	12	4	4	6	19	20	33	32	28.57
Portsmouth	24	5	3	4	17	15	0	4	8	8	24	25	39	20.83
Preston North End	42	10	7	4	38	21	3	10	8	13	25	51	46	30.95
Queen's Park Rangers	56	9	10	9	38	35	4	10	14	26	56	64	91	23.21
Reading	84	24	10	8	75	41	12	7	23	45	78	120	119	42.86
Rochdale	28	6	7	1	20	12	2	3	9	10	21	30	33	28.57
Rotherham United	38	10	6	3	30	16	4	6	9	14	24	44	40	36.84
Scarborough	14	5	2	0	14	5	2	3	2	7	6	21	11	50.00
Scunthorpe United	30	5	6	4	23	15	4	6	5	19	22	42	37	30.00
Sheffield United	16	4	2	2	16	10	3	2	3	9	15	25	25	43.75
Sheffield Wednesday	16	4	4	0	9	4	1	2	5	4	8	13	12	31.25
Shrewsbury Town	44	12	5	5	38	23	3	8	11	25	38	63	61	34.09
Southampton	14	4	2	1	9	4	1	1	5	4	15	13	19	35.71
Southend United	80	26	8	6	72	32	6	12	22	41	79	113	111	40.00
Southport	22	8	1	2	27	12	1	6	4	10	16	37	28	40.91
Stockport County	32	6	5	5	20	22	2	5	9	13	27	33	49	25.00
Stoke City	6	2	1	0	8	1	0	3	0	1	1	9	2	33.33
Sunderland	2	0	1	0	0	0	0	0	1	1	2	1	2	0.00
Swansea City	26	4	7	2	17	10	3	2	8	14	20	31	30	26.92
Swindon Town	78	20	15	4	65	34	5	10	24	29	76	94	110	32.05
Thames	4	2	0	0	5	1	0	1	1	2	5	7	6	50.00
Torquay United	72	16	12	8	55	44	8	8	20	42	65	97	109	33.33
Tranmere Rovers	24	3	7	2	15	12	0	5	7	9	19	24	31	12.50
Walsall	92	30	4	12	94	46	11	11	24	45	79	139	125	44.57
Watford	80	14	14	12	59	55	8	10	22	38	81	97	136	27.50
West Bromwich Alb.	4	1	0	1	3	3	0	0	2	1	4	4	7	25.00
Wigan Athletic	26	7	3	3	20	10	4	3	6	19	24	39	34	42.31
Wimbledon	12	2	3	1	10	5	3	1	2	11	9	21	14	41.67
Wolverhampton W.	10	2	0	3	6	10	1	1	3	5	16	11	26	30.00
Workington	24	7	4	1	31	14	2	5	5	14	22	45	36	37.50
Wrexham	32	7	4	5	29	20	2	4	10	13	27	42	47	28.12
Wycombe Wan.	10	3	1	1	7	3	1	2	2	4	4	11	7	40.00
York City	36	7	7	4	21	16	5	6	7	21	30	42	46	33.33

TOTALS TO END 2002/03:

	Home:						Away:					Totals:		
	p	*w*	*d*	*l*	*f*	*a*	*w*	*d*	*l*	*f*	*a*	*f*	*a*	*Points*
	3176	806	424	358	2616	1654	319	418	851	1609	2872	4225	4526	3473
Comprising:														
New 1st/Old 2nd	138	31	17	21	103	85	16	23	30	78	113	181	198	181
New 2nd/Old 3rd	1196	311	163	124	973	573	147	169	282	643	941	1616	1514	1485
New 3rd/Old 4th	718	196	94	69	634	354	75	109	175	356	565	990	919	842
Div 3 (South)	1124	268	150	144	906	642	81	117	364	532	1253	1438	1895	965

1981/82 Division 3

1	Burnley	46	13	7	3	37	20	8	10	5	29	25	80
2	Carlisle United	46	17	4	2	44	21	6	7	10	21	29	80
3	Fulham	46	12	9	2	44	22	9	6	8	33	29	78
4	Lincoln City	46	13	7	3	40	16	8	7	8	26	24	77
5	Oxford United	46	10	8	5	28	18	9	6	8	35	31	71
6	GILLINGHAM	46	14	5	4	44	26	6	6	11	20	30	71
7	Southend United	46	11	7	5	35	23	7	8	8	28	28	69
8	Brentford	46	8	6	9	28	22	11	5	7	28	25	68
9	Millwall	46	12	4	7	36	28	6	9	8	26	34	67
10	Plymouth Argyle	46	12	5	6	37	24	6	6	11	27	32	65
11	Chesterfield	46	12	4	7	33	27	6	6	11	24	31	64
12	Reading	46	11	6	6	43	35	6	5	12	24	40	62
13	Portsmouth	46	11	10	2	33	14	3	9	11	23	37	61
14	Preston North End	46	10	7	6	25	22	6	6	11	25	34	61
15	Bristol Rovers	46	12	4	7	35	28	6	5	12	23	37	61
16	Newport County	46	9	10	4	28	21	5	6	12	26	33	58
17	Huddersfield Town	46	10	5	8	38	25	5	7	11	26	34	57
18	Exeter City	46	14	4	5	46	33	2	5	16	25	51	57
19	Doncaster Rovers	46	9	9	5	31	24	4	8	11	24	44	56
20	Walsall	46	10	7	6	32	23	3	7	13	19	32	53
21	Wimbledon	46	10	6	7	33	27	4	5	14	28	48	53
22	Swindon Town	46	9	5	9	37	36	4	8	11	18	35	52
23	Bristol City	46	7	6	10	24	29	4	7	12	16	36	46
24	Chester	46	2	10	11	16	30	5	1	17	20	48	32

1982/83 Division 3

1	Portsmouth	46	16	4	3	43	19	11	6	6	31	22	91
2	Cardiff City	46	17	5	1	45	14	8	6	9	31	36	86
3	Huddersfield Town	46	15	8	0	56	18	8	5	10	28	31	82
4	Newport County	46	13	7	3	40	20	10	2	11	36	34	78
5	Oxford United	46	12	9	2	41	23	10	3	10	30	30	78
6	Lincoln City	46	17	1	5	55	22	6	6	11	22	29	76
7	Bristol Rovers	46	16	4	3	55	21	6	5	12	29	37	75
8	Plymouth Argyle	46	15	2	6	37	23	4	6	13	24	43	65
9	Brentford	46	14	4	5	50	28	4	6	13	38	49	64
10	Walsall	46	14	5	4	38	19	3	8	12	26	44	64
11	Sheffield United	46	16	3	4	44	20	3	4	16	18	44	64
12	Bradford City	46	11	7	5	41	27	5	6	12	27	42	61
13	GILLINGHAM	46	12	4	7	37	29	4	9	10	21	30	61
14	Bournemouth	46	11	7	5	35	20	5	6	12	24	48	61
15	Southend United	46	10	8	5	41	28	5	6	12	25	37	59
16	Preston North End	46	11	10	2	35	17	4	3	16	25	52	58
17	Millwall	46	12	7	4	41	24	2	6	15	23	53	55
18	Wigan Athletic	46	10	4	9	35	33	5	5	13	25	39	54
19	Exeter City	46	12	4	7	49	43	2	8	13	32	61	54
20	Orient	46	10	6	7	44	38	5	3	15	20	50	54
21	Reading	46	10	8	5	37	28	2	9	12	27	51	53
22	Wrexham	46	11	6	6	40	26	1	9	13	16	50	51
23	Doncaster Rovers	46	6	8	9	38	44	3	3	17	19	53	38
24	Chesterfield	46	6	6	11	28	28	2	7	14	15	40	37

1983/84 Division 3

1	Oxford United	46	17	5	1	58	22	11	6	6	33	28	95
2	Wimbledon	46	15	5	3	58	35	11	4	8	39	41	87
3	Sheffield United	46	14	7	2	56	18	10	4	9	30	35	83
4	Hull City	46	16	5	2	42	11	7	9	7	29	27	83
5	Bristol Rovers	46	16	5	2	47	21	6	8	9	21	33	79
6	Walsall	46	14	4	5	44	22	8	5	10	24	39	75
7	Bradford City	46	11	9	3	46	30	9	2	12	27	35	71
8	GILLINGHAM	46	13	4	6	50	29	7	6	10	24	40	70
9	Millwall	46	16	4	3	42	18	2	9	12	29	47	67
10	Bolton Wanderers	46	13	4	6	36	17	5	6	12	20	43	64
11	Orient	46	13	5	5	40	27	5	4	14	31	54	63
12	Burnley	46	12	5	6	52	25	4	9	10	24	36	62
13	Newport County	46	11	9	3	35	27	5	5	13	23	48	62
14	Lincoln City	46	11	4	8	42	29	6	6	11	17	33	61
15	Wigan Athletic	46	11	5	7	26	18	5	8	10	20	38	61
16	Preston North End	46	12	5	6	42	27	3	6	14	24	39	56
17	Bournemouth	46	11	5	7	38	27	5	2	16	25	46	55
18	Rotherham United	46	10	5	8	29	17	5	4	14	28	47	54
19	Plymouth Argyle	46	11	8	4	38	17	2	4	17	18	45	51
20	Brentford	46	8	9	6	41	30	3	7	13	28	49	49
21	Scunthorpe United	46	9	9	5	40	31	0	10	13	14	42	46
22	Southend United	46	8	9	6	34	24	2	5	16	21	52	44
23	Port Vale	46	10	4	9	33	29	1	6	16	18	54	43
24	Exeter City	46	4	8	11	27	39	2	7	14	23	45	33

1984/85 Division 3

1	Bradford City	46	15	6	2	44	23	13	4	6	33	22	94
2	Millwall	46	18	5	0	44	12	8	7	8	29	30	90
3	Hull City	46	16	4	3	46	20	9	8	6	32	29	87
4	GILLINGHAM	46	15	5	3	54	29	10	3	10	26	33	83
5	Bristol City	46	17	2	4	46	19	7	7	9	28	28	81
6	Bristol Rovers	46	15	6	2	37	13	6	6	11	29	35	75
7	Derby County	46	14	7	2	40	20	5	6	12	25	34	70
8	York City	46	13	5	5	42	22	7	4	12	28	35	69
9	Reading	46	8	7	8	31	29	11	5	7	37	33	69
10	Bournemouth	46	16	3	4	42	16	3	8	12	15	30	68
11	Walsall	46	9	7	7	33	22	9	6	8	25	30	67
12	Rotherham United	46	11	6	6	36	24	7	5	11	19	31	65
13	Brentford	46	13	5	5	42	27	3	9	11	20	37	62
14	Doncaster Rovers	46	11	5	7	42	33	6	3	14	30	41	59
15	Plymouth Argyle	46	11	7	5	33	23	4	7	12	29	42	59
16	Wigan Athletic	46	12	6	5	36	22	3	8	12	24	42	59
17	Bolton Wanderers	46	12	5	6	38	22	4	1	18	31	53	54
18	Newport County	46	9	6	8	30	30	4	7	12	25	37	52
19	Lincoln City	46	8	11	4	32	20	3	7	13	18	31	51
20	Swansea City	46	7	5	11	31	39	5	6	12	22	41	47
21	Burnley	46	6	8	9	30	24	5	5	13	30	49	46
22	Orient	46	7	7	9	30	36	4	6	13	21	40	46
23	Preston North End	46	9	5	9	33	41	4	2	17	18	59	46
24	Cambridge United	46	2	3	18	17	48	2	6	15	20	47	21

1985/86 Division 3

1	Reading	46	16	3	4	39	22	13	4	6	28	29	94
2	Plymouth Argyle	46	17	3	3	56	20	9	6	8	32	33	87
3	Derby County	46	13	7	3	45	20	10	8	5	35	21	84
4	Wigan Athletic	46	17	4	2	54	17	6	10	7	28	31	83
5	GILLINGHAM	46	14	5	4	48	17	8	8	7	33	37	79
6	Walsall	46	15	7	1	59	23	7	2	14	31	41	75
7	York City	46	16	4	3	49	17	4	7	12	28	41	71
8	Notts County	46	12	6	5	42	26	7	8	8	29	34	71
9	Bristol City	46	14	5	4	43	19	4	9	10	26	41	68
10	Brentford	46	8	8	7	29	29	10	4	9	29	32	66
11	Doncaster Rovers	46	7	10	6	20	21	9	6	8	25	31	64
12	Blackpool	46	11	6	6	38	19	6	6	11	28	36	63
13	Darlington	46	10	7	6	39	33	5	6	12	22	45	58
14	Rotherham United	46	13	5	5	44	18	2	7	14	17	41	57
15	Bournemouth	46	9	6	8	41	31	6	3	14	24	41	54
16	Bristol Rovers	46	9	8	6	27	21	5	4	14	24	54	54
17	Chesterfield	46	10	6	7	41	30	3	8	12	20	34	53
18	Bolton Wanderers	46	10	4	9	35	30	5	4	14	19	38	53
19	Newport County	46	7	8	8	35	33	4	10	9	17	32	51
20	Bury	46	11	7	5	46	26	1	6	16	17	41	49
21	Lincoln City	46	7	9	7	33	34	3	7	13	22	43	46
22	Cardiff City	46	7	5	11	22	29	5	4	14	31	54	45
23	Wolverhampton W.	46	6	6	11	29	47	5	4	14	28	51	43
24	Swansea City	46	9	6	8	27	27	2	4	17	16	60	43

1986/87 Division 3

1	Bournemouth	46	19	3	1	44	14	10	7	6	32	26	97
2	Middlesbrough	46	16	5	2	38	11	12	5	6	29	19	94
3	Swindon Town	46	14	5	4	37	19	11	7	5	40	28	87
4	Wigan Athletic	46	15	5	3	47	26	10	5	8	36	34	85
5	GILLINGHAM	46	16	5	2	42	14	7	4	12	23	34	78
6	Bristol City	46	14	6	3	42	15	7	8	8	21	21	77
7	Notts County	46	14	6	3	52	24	7	7	9	25	32	76
8	Walsall	46	16	4	3	50	27	6	5	12	30	40	75
9	Blackpool	46	11	7	5	35	20	5	9	9	39	39	64
10	Mansfield Town	46	9	9	5	30	23	6	7	10	22	32	61
11	Brentford	46	9	7	7	39	32	6	8	9	25	34	60
12	Port Vale	46	8	6	9	43	36	7	6	10	33	34	57
13	Doncaster Rovers	46	11	8	4	32	19	3	7	13	24	43	57
14	Rotherham United	46	10	6	7	29	23	5	6	12	19	34	57
15	Chester City	46	7	9	7	32	28	6	8	9	29	31	56
16	Bury	46	9	7	7	30	26	5	6	12	24	34	55
17	Chesterfield	46	11	5	7	36	33	2	10	11	20	36	54
18	Fulham	46	8	8	7	35	41	4	9	10	24	36	53
19	Bristol Rovers	46	7	8	8	26	29	6	4	13	23	46	51
20	York City	46	11	8	4	34	29	1	5	17	21	50	49
21	Bolton Wanderers	46	8	5	10	29	26	2	10	11	17	32	45
22	Carlisle United	46	7	5	11	26	35	3	3	17	13	43	38
23	Darlington	46	6	10	7	25	28	1	6	16	20	49	37
24	Newport County	46	4	9	10	26	34	4	4	15	23	52	37

1987/88 Division 3

1	Sunderland	46	14	7	2	51	22	13	5	5	41	26	93
2	Brighton & Hove Albion	46	15	7	1	37	16	8	8	7	32	31	84
3	Walsall	46	15	6	2	39	22	8	7	8	29	28	82
4	Notts County	46	14	4	5	53	24	9	8	6	29	25	81
5	Bristol City	46	14	6	3	51	30	7	6	10	26	32	75
6	Northampton Town	46	12	8	3	36	18	6	11	6	34	33	73
7	Wigan Athletic	46	11	8	4	36	23	9	4	10	34	38	72
8	Bristol Rovers	46	14	5	4	43	19	4	7	12	25	37	66
9	Fulham	46	10	5	8	36	24	9	4	10	33	36	66
10	Blackpool	46	13	4	6	45	27	4	10	9	26	35	65
11	Port Vale	46	12	8	3	36	19	6	3	14	22	37	65
12	Brentford	46	9	8	6	27	23	7	6	10	26	36	62
13	GILLINGHAM	46	8	9	6	45	21	6	8	9	32	40	59
14	Bury	46	9	7	7	33	26	6	7	10	25	31	59
15	Chester City	46	9	8	6	29	30	5	8	10	22	32	58
16	Preston North End	46	10	6	7	30	23	5	7	11	18	36	58
17	Southend United	46	10	6	7	42	33	4	7	12	23	50	55
18	Chesterfield	46	10	5	8	25	28	5	5	13	16	42	55
19	Mansfield Town	46	10	6	7	25	21	4	6	13	23	38	54
20	Aldershot	46	12	3	8	45	32	3	5	15	19	42	53
21	Rotherham United	46	8	8	7	28	25	4	8	11	22	41	52
22	Grimsby Town	46	6	7	10	25	29	6	7	10	23	29	50
23	York City	46	4	7	12	27	45	4	2	17	21	46	33
24	Doncaster Rovers	46	6	5	12	25	36	2	4	17	15	48	33

1988/89 Division 3

1	Wolverhampton Wan.	46	18	4	1	61	19	8	10	5	35	30	92
2	Sheffield United	46	16	3	4	57	21	9	6	8	36	33	84
3	Port Vale	46	15	3	5	46	21	9	9	5	32	27	84
4	Fulham	46	12	7	4	42	28	10	2	11	27	39	75
5	Bristol Rovers	46	9	11	3	34	21	10	6	7	33	30	74
6	Preston North End	46	14	7	2	56	31	5	8	10	23	29	72
7	Brentford	46	14	5	4	36	21	4	9	10	30	40	68
8	Chester City	46	12	6	5	38	18	7	5	11	26	43	68
9	Notts County	46	11	7	5	37	22	7	6	10	27	32	67
10	Bolton Wanderers	46	12	8	3	42	23	4	8	11	16	31	64
11	Bristol City	46	10	3	10	32	25	8	6	9	21	30	63
12	Swansea City	46	11	8	4	33	22	4	8	11	18	31	61
13	Bury	46	11	7	5	27	22	5	6	12	28	45	61
14	Huddersfield Town	46	10	8	5	35	25	7	1	15	28	48	60
15	Mansfield Town	46	10	8	5	32	22	4	9	10	16	30	59
16	Cardiff City	46	10	9	4	30	16	4	6	13	14	40	57
17	Wigan Athletic	46	9	5	9	28	22	5	9	9	27	31	56
18	Reading	46	10	6	7	37	29	5	5	13	31	43	56
19	Blackpool	46	10	6	7	36	29	4	7	12	20	30	55
20	Northampton Town	46	11	2	10	41	34	5	4	14	25	42	54
21	Southend United	46	10	9	4	33	26	3	6	14	23	49	54
22	Chesterfield	46	9	5	9	35	35	5	2	16	16	51	49
23	GILLINGHAM	46	7	3	13	25	32	5	1	17	22	49	40
24	Aldershot	46	7	6	10	29	29	1	7	15	19	49	37

1989/90 Division 4

1 Exeter City	46	20	3	0	50	14	8	2	13	33	34	89
2 Grimsby Town	46	14	4	5	41	20	8	9	6	29	27	79
3 Southend United	46	15	3	5	35	14	7	6	10	26	34	75
4 Stockport County	46	13	6	4	45	27	8	5	10	23	35	74
5 Maidstone United	46	14	4	5	49	21	8	3	12	28	40	73
6 Cambridge United	46	14	3	6	45	30	7	7	9	31	36	73
7 Chesterfield	46	12	9	2	41	19	7	5	11	22	31	71
8 Carlisle United	46	15	4	4	38	20	6	4	13	23	40	71
9 Peterborough United	46	10	8	5	35	23	7	9	7	24	23	68
10 Lincoln City	46	11	6	6	30	27	7	8	8	18	21	68
11 Scunthorpe United	46	9	9	5	42	25	8	6	9	27	29	66
12 Rochdale	46	11	4	8	28	23	9	2	12	24	32	66
13 York City	46	10	5	8	29	24	6	11	6	26	29	64
14 GILLINGHAM	46	9	8	6	28	21	8	3	12	18	27	62
15 Torquay United	46	12	2	9	33	29	3	10	10	20	37	57
16 Burnley	46	6	10	7	19	18	8	4	11	26	37	56
17 Hereford United	46	7	4	12	31	32	8	6	9	25	30	55
18 Scarborough	46	10	5	8	35	28	5	5	13	25	45	55
19 Hartlepool United	46	12	4	7	45	33	3	6	14	21	55	55
20 Doncaster Rovers	46	7	7	9	29	29	7	2	14	24	31	51
21 Wrexham	46	8	8	7	28	28	5	4	14	23	39	51
22 Aldershot	46	8	7	8	28	26	4	7	12	21	43	50
23 Halifax Town	46	5	9	9	31	29	7	4	12	26	36	49
24 Colchester United	46	9	3	11	26	25	2	7	14	22	50	43

1990/91 Division 4

1 Darlington	46	13	8	2	36	14	9	9	5	32	24	83
2 Stockport County	46	16	6	1	54	19	7	7	9	30	28	82
3 Hartlepool United	46	15	5	3	35	15	9	5	9	32	33	82
4 Peterborough United	46	13	9	1	38	15	8	8	7	29	30	80
5 Blackpool	46	17	3	3	55	17	6	7	10	23	30	79
6 Burnley	46	17	5	1	46	16	6	5	12	24	35	79
7 Torquay United	46	14	7	2	37	13	4	11	8	27	34	72
8 Scunthorpe United	46	17	4	2	51	20	3	7	13	20	42	71
9 Scarborough	46	13	5	5	36	21	6	7	10	23	35	69
10 Northampton Town	46	14	5	4	34	21	4	8	11	23	37	67
11 Doncaster Rovers	46	12	5	6	36	22	5	9	9	20	24	65
12 Rochdale	46	10	9	4	29	22	5	8	10	21	31	62
13 Cardiff City	46	10	6	7	26	23	5	9	9	17	31	60
14 Lincoln City	46	10	7	6	32	27	4	10	9	18	34	59
15 GILLINGHAM	46	9	9	5	35	27	3	9	11	22	33	54
16 Walsall	46	7	12	4	25	17	5	5	13	23	34	53
17 Hereford United	46	9	10	4	32	19	4	4	15	21	39	53
18 Chesterfield	46	8	12	3	33	26	5	2	16	14	36	53
19 Maidstone United	46	9	5	9	42	34	4	7	12	24	37	51
20 Carlisle United	46	12	3	8	30	30	1	6	16	17	59	48
21 York City	46	8	6	9	21	23	3	7	13	24	34	46
22 Halifax Town	46	9	6	8	34	29	3	4	16	25	50	46
23 Aldershot	46	8	7	8	38	43	2	4	17	23	58	41
24 Wrexham	46	8	7	8	33	34	2	3	18	15	40	40

1991/92 Division 4

1 Burnley	42	14	4	3	42	16	11	4	6	37	27	83
2 Rotherham United	42	12	6	3	38	16	10	5	6	32	21	77
3 Mansfield Town	42	13	4	4	43	26	10	4	7	32	27	77
4 Blackpool	42	17	3	1	48	13	5	7	9	23	32	76
5 Scunthorpe United	42	14	5	2	39	18	7	4	10	25	41	72
6 Crewe Alexandra	42	12	6	3	33	20	8	4	9	33	31	70
7 Barnet	42	16	1	4	48	23	5	5	11	33	38	69
8 Rochdale	42	12	6	3	34	22	6	7	8	23	31	67
9 Cardiff City	42	13	3	5	42	26	4	12	5	24	27	66
10 Lincoln City	42	9	5	7	21	24	8	6	7	29	20	62
11 GILLINGHAM	42	12	5	4	41	19	3	7	11	22	34	57
12 Scarborough	42	12	5	4	39	28	3	7	11	25	40	57
13 Chesterfield	42	6	7	8	26	28	8	4	9	23	33	53
14 Wrexham	42	11	4	6	31	26	3	5	13	21	47	51
15 Walsall	42	5	10	6	28	26	7	3	11	20	32	49
16 Northampton Town	42	5	9	7	25	23	6	4	11	21	34	46
17 Hereford United	42	9	4	8	31	24	3	4	14	13	33	44
18 Maidstone United	42	6	9	6	24	22	2	9	10	21	34	42
19 York City	42	6	9	6	26	23	2	7	12	16	35	40
20 Halifax Town	42	7	5	9	23	35	3	3	15	11	40	38
21 Doncaster Rovers	42	6	2	13	21	35	3	6	12	19	30	35
22 Carlisle United	42	5	9	7	24	27	2	4	15	17	40	34

1992/93 New Football League Division 3

1 Cardiff City	42	13	7	1	42	20	12	1	8	35	27	83
2 Wrexham	42	14	3	4	48	26	9	8	4	27	26	80
3 Barnet	42	16	4	1	45	19	7	6	8	21	29	79
4 York City	42	13	6	2	41	15	8	6	7	31	30	75
5 Walsall	42	11	6	4	42	31	11	1	9	34	30	73
6 Crewe Alexandra	42	13	3	5	47	23	8	4	9	28	33	70
7 Bury	42	10	7	4	36	19	8	2	11	27	36	63
8 Lincoln City	42	10	6	5	31	20	8	3	10	26	33	63
9 Shrewsbury Town	42	11	3	7	36	30	6	8	7	21	22	62
10 Colchester United	42	13	3	5	38	26	5	2	14	29	50	59
11 Rochdale	42	10	3	8	38	29	6	7	8	32	41	58
12 Chesterfield	42	11	3	7	32	28	4	8	9	27	35	56
13 Scarborough	42	7	7	7	32	30	8	2	11	34	41	54
14 Scunthorpe United	42	8	7	6	38	25	6	5	10	19	29	54
15 Darlington	42	5	6	10	23	31	7	8	6	25	22	50
16 Doncaster Rovers	42	6	5	10	22	28	5	9	7	20	29	47
17 Hereford United	42	7	9	5	31	27	3	6	12	16	33	45
18 Carlisle United	42	7	5	9	29	27	4	6	11	22	38	44
19 Torquay United	42	6	4	11	18	26	6	3	12	27	41	43
20 Northampton Town	42	6	5	10	19	28	5	3	13	29	46	41
21 GILLINGHAM	42	9	4	8	32	28	0	9	12	16	36	40
22 Halifax Town	42	3	5	13	20	35	6	4	11	25	33	36

1993/94 Division 3

1 Shrewsbury Town	42	10	8	3	28	17	12	5	4	35	22	79
2 Chester City	42	13	5	3	35	18	8	6	7	34	28	74
3 Crewe Alexandra	42	12	4	5	45	30	9	6	6	35	31	73
4 Wycombe Wanderers	42	11	6	4	34	21	8	7	6	33	32	70
5 Preston North End	42	13	5	3	46	23	5	8	8	33	37	67
6 Torquay United	42	8	10	3	30	24	9	6	6	34	32	67
7 Carlisle United	42	10	4	7	35	23	8	6	7	22	19	64
8 Chesterfield	42	8	8	5	32	22	8	6	7	23	26	62
9 Rochdale	42	10	5	6	38	22	6	7	8	25	29	60
10 Walsall	42	7	5	9	28	26	10	4	7	20	27	60
11 Scunthorpe United	42	9	7	5	40	26	6	7	8	24	30	59
12 Mansfield Town	42	9	3	9	28	30	6	7	8	25	32	55
13 Bury	42	9	6	6	33	22	5	5	11	22	34	53
14 Scarborough	42	8	4	9	29	28	7	4	10	26	33	53
15 Doncaster Rovers	42	8	6	7	24	26	6	4	11	20	31	52
16 GILLINGHAM	42	8	8	5	27	23	4	7	10	17	28	51
17 Colchester United	42	8	4	9	31	33	5	6	10	25	38	49
18 Lincoln City	42	7	4	10	26	29	5	7	9	26	34	47
19 Wigan Athletic	42	6	7	8	33	33	5	5	11	18	37	45
20 Hereford United	42	6	4	11	34	33	6	2	13	26	46	42
21 Darlington	42	7	5	9	24	28	3	6	12	18	36	41
22 Northampton Town	42	6	7	8	25	23	3	4	14	19	43	38

1994/95 Division 3

1 Carlisle United	42	14	5	2	34	14	13	5	3	33	17	91
2 Walsall	42	15	3	3	42	18	9	8	4	33	22	83
3 Chesterfield	42	11	7	3	26	10	12	5	4	36	27	81
4 Bury	42	13	7	1	39	13	10	4	7	34	23	80
5 Preston North End	42	13	3	5	37	17	6	7	8	21	24	67
6 Mansfield Town	42	10	5	6	45	27	8	6	7	39	32	65
7 Scunthorpe United	42	12	2	7	40	30	6	6	9	28	33	62
8 Fulham	42	11	5	5	39	22	5	9	7	21	32	62
9 Doncaster Rovers	42	9	5	7	28	20	8	5	8	30	23	61
10 Colchester United	42	8	5	8	29	30	8	5	8	27	34	58
11 Barnet	42	8	7	6	37	27	7	4	10	19	36	56
12 Lincoln City	42	10	7	4	34	22	5	4	12	20	33	56
13 Torquay United	42	10	8	3	35	25	4	5	12	19	32	55
14 Wigan Athletic	42	7	6	8	28	30	7	4	10	25	30	52
15 Rochdale	42	8	6	7	25	23	4	8	9	19	44	50
16 Hereford United	42	9	6	6	22	19	3	7	11	23	43	49
17 Northampton Town	42	8	5	8	25	29	2	9	10	20	38	44
18 Hartlepool United	42	9	5	7	33	32	2	5	14	10	37	43
19 GILLINGHAM	42	8	7	6	31	25	2	4	15	15	39	41
20 Darlington	42	7	5	9	25	24	4	3	14	18	33	41
21 Scarborough	42	4	7	10	26	31	4	3	14	23	39	34
22 Exeter City	42	5	5	11	25	36	3	5	13	11	34	34

1995/96 Division 3

1 Preston North End	46	11	8	4	44	22	12	9	2	34	16	86
2 GILLINGHAM	46	16	6	1	33	6	6	11	6	16	14	83
3 Bury	46	11	6	6	33	21	11	7	5	33	27	79
4 Plymouth Argyle	46	14	5	4	41	20	8	7	8	27	29	78
5 Darlington	46	10	6	7	30	21	10	12	1	30	21	78
6 Hereford United	46	13	5	5	40	22	7	9	7	25	25	74
7 Colchester United	46	13	7	3	37	22	5	11	7	24	29	72
8 Chester City	46	11	9	3	45	22	7	7	9	27	31	70
9 Barnet	46	13	6	4	40	19	5	10	8	25	26	70
10 Wigan Athletic	46	15	3	5	36	21	5	7	11	26	35	70
11 Northampton Town	46	9	10	4	32	22	9	3	11	19	22	67
12 Scunthorpe United	46	8	8	7	36	30	7	7	9	31	31	60
13 Doncaster Rovers	46	11	6	6	25	19	5	5	13	24	41	59
14 Exeter City	46	9	9	5	25	22	4	9	10	21	31	57
15 Rochdale	46	7	8	8	32	33	7	5	11	25	28	55
16 Cambridge United	46	8	8	7	34	30	6	4	13	27	41	54
17 Fulham	46	10	9	4	39	26	2	8	13	18	37	53
18 Lincoln City	46	8	7	8	32	26	5	7	11	25	47	53
19 Mansfield Town	46	6	10	7	25	29	5	10	8	29	35	53
20 Hartlepool United	46	8	9	6	30	24	4	4	15	17	43	49
21 Leyton Orient	46	11	4	8	29	22	1	7	15	15	41	47
22 Cardiff City	46	8	6	9	24	22	3	6	14	17	42	45
23 Scarborough	46	5	11	7	22	28	3	5	15	17	41	40
24 Torquay United	46	4	9	10	17	36	1	5	17	13	48	29

1996/97 Division 2

1 Bury	46	18	5	0	39	7	6	7	10	23	31	84
2 Stockport County	46	15	5	3	31	14	8	8	7	28	27	82
3 Luton Town	46	13	7	3	38	14	8	8	7	33	31	78
4 Brentford	46	8	11	4	26	22	12	3	8	30	21	74
5 Bristol City	46	14	4	5	43	18	7	6	10	26	33	73
6 Crewe Alexandra	46	15	4	4	38	15	7	3	13	18	32	73
7 Blackpool	46	13	7	3	41	21	5	8	10	19	26	69
8 Wrexham	46	11	9	3	37	28	6	9	8	17	22	69
9 Burnley	46	14	3	6	48	27	5	8	10	23	28	68
10 Chesterfield	46	10	9	4	25	18	8	5	10	17	21	68
11 GILLINGHAM	46	13	3	7	37	25	6	7	10	23	34	67
12 Walsall	46	12	8	3	35	21	7	2	14	19	32	67
13 Watford	46	10	8	5	24	14	6	11	6	21	24	67
14 Millwall	46	12	4	7	27	22	4	9	10	23	33	61
15 Preston North End	46	14	5	4	33	19	4	2	17	16	36	61
16 Bournemouth	46	8	9	6	24	20	7	6	10	19	25	60
17 Bristol Rovers	46	13	4	6	34	22	2	7	14	13	28	56
18 Wycombe Wanderers	46	13	4	6	31	14	2	6	15	20	42	55
19 Plymouth Argyle	46	7	11	5	19	18	5	7	11	28	40	54
20 York City	46	8	6	9	27	31	5	7	11	20	37	52
21 Peterborough United	46	7	7	9	38	34	4	7	12	17	39	47
22 Shrewsbury Town	46	8	6	9	27	32	3	7	13	22	42	46
23 Rotherham United	46	4	7	12	17	29	3	7	13	22	41	35
24 Notts County	46	4	9	10	20	25	3	5	15	13	34	35

1997/98 Division 2

1	Watford	46	13	7	3	36	22	11	9	3	31	19	88
2	Bristol City	46	16	5	2	41	17	9	5	9	28	22	85
3	Grimsby Town	46	11	7	5	30	14	8	8	7	25	23	72
4	Northampton Town	46	14	5	4	33	17	4	12	7	19	20	71
5	Bristol Rovers	46	13	2	8	43	33	7	8	8	27	31	70
6	Fulham	46	12	7	4	31	14	8	3	12	29	29	70
7	Wrexham	46	10	10	3	31	23	8	6	9	24	28	70
8	GILLINGHAM	46	13	7	3	30	18	6	6	11	22	29	70
9	Bournemouth	46	11	8	4	28	15	7	4	12	29	37	66
10	Chesterfield	46	13	7	3	31	19	3	10	10	15	25	65
11	Wigan Athletic	46	12	5	6	41	31	5	6	12	23	35	62
12	Blackpool	46	13	6	4	35	24	4	5	14	24	43	62
13	Oldham Athletic	46	13	7	3	43	23	2	9	12	19	31	61
14	Wycombe Wanderers	46	10	10	3	32	20	4	8	11	19	33	60
15	Preston North End	46	10	6	7	29	26	5	8	10	27	30	59
16	York City	46	9	7	7	26	21	5	10	8	26	37	59
17	Luton Town	46	7	7	9	35	38	7	8	8	25	26	57
18	Millwall	46	7	8	8	23	23	7	5	11	20	31	55
19	Walsall	46	10	8	5	26	16	4	4	15	17	36	54
20	Burnley	46	10	9	4	34	23	3	4	16	21	42	52
21	Brentford	46	9	7	7	33	29	2	10	11	17	42	50
22	Plymouth Argyle	46	10	5	8	36	30	2	8	13	19	40	49
23	Carlisle United	46	8	5	10	27	28	4	3	16	30	45	44
24	Southend United	46	8	7	8	29	30	3	3	17	18	49	43

1998/99 Division 2

1	Fulham	46	19	3	1	50	12	12	5	6	29	20	101
2	Walsall	46	13	7	3	37	23	13	2	8	26	24	87
3	Manchester City	46	13	6	4	38	14	9	10	4	31	19	82
4	GILLINGHAM	46	15	5	3	45	17	7	9	7	30	27	80
5	Preston North End	46	12	6	5	46	23	10	7	6	32	27	79
6	Wigan Athletic	46	14	5	4	44	17	8	5	10	31	31	76
7	Bournemouth	46	14	7	2	37	11	7	6	10	26	30	76
8	Stoke City	46	10	4	9	32	32	11	2	10	27	31	69
9	Chesterfield	46	14	5	4	34	16	3	8	12	12	28	64
10	Millwall	46	9	8	6	33	24	8	3	12	19	35	62
11	Reading	46	10	6	7	29	26	6	7	10	25	37	61
12	Luton Town	46	10	4	9	25	26	6	6	11	26	34	58
13	Bristol Rovers	46	8	9	6	35	28	5	8	10	30	28	56
14	Blackpool	46	7	8	8	24	24	7	6	10	20	30	56
15	Burnley	46	8	7	8	23	33	5	9	9	31	40	55
16	Notts County	46	8	6	9	29	27	6	6	11	23	34	54
17	Wrexham	46	8	6	9	21	28	5	8	10	22	34	53
18	Colchester United	46	9	7	7	25	30	3	9	11	27	40	52
19	Wycombe Wanderers	46	8	5	10	31	26	5	7	11	21	32	51
20	Oldham Athletic	46	8	4	11	26	31	6	5	12	22	35	51
21	York City	46	6	8	9	28	33	7	3	13	28	47	50
22	Northampton Town	46	4	12	7	26	31	6	6	11	17	26	48
23	Lincoln City	46	9	4	10	27	27	4	3	16	15	47	46
24	Macclesfield Town	46	7	4	12	24	30	4	6	13	19	33	43

1999/2000 Division 2

1	Preston North End	46	15	4	4	37	23	13	7	3	37	14	95
2	Burnley	46	16	3	4	42	23	9	10	4	27	24	88
3	GILLINGHAM	46	16	3	4	46	21	9	7	7	33	27	85
4	Wigan Athletic	46	15	3	5	37	14	7	14	2	35	24	83
5	Millwall	46	14	7	2	41	18	9	6	8	35	32	82
6	Stoke City	46	13	7	3	37	18	10	6	7	31	24	82
7	Bristol Rovers	46	13	7	3	34	19	10	4	9	35	26	80
8	Notts County	46	9	6	8	32	27	9	5	9	29	28	65
9	Bristol City	46	7	14	2	31	18	8	5	10	28	39	64
10	Reading	46	10	9	4	28	18	6	5	12	29	45	62
11	Wrexham	46	9	6	8	23	24	8	5	10	29	37	62
12	Wycombe Wanderers	46	11	4	8	32	24	5	9	9	24	29	61
13	Luton Town	46	10	7	6	41	35	7	3	13	20	30	61
14	Oldham Athletic	46	8	5	10	27	28	8	7	8	23	27	60
15	Bury	46	8	10	5	38	33	5	8	10	23	31	57
16	Bournemouth	46	11	6	6	37	19	5	3	15	22	43	57
17	Brentford	46	8	6	9	27	31	5	7	11	20	30	52
18	Colchester United	46	9	4	10	36	40	5	6	12	23	42	52
19	Cambridge United	46	8	6	9	38	33	4	6	13	26	32	48
20	Oxford United	46	6	5	12	24	38	6	4	13	19	35	45
21	Cardiff City	46	5	10	8	23	34	4	7	12	22	33	44
22	Blackpool	46	4	10	9	26	37	4	7	12	23	40	41
23	Scunthorpe United	46	4	6	13	16	34	5	6	12	24	40	39
24	Chesterfield	46	5	7	11	17	25	2	8	13	17	38	36

2000/01 Division 1

1	Fulham	46	16	5	2	49	14	14	6	3	41	18	101
2	Blackburn Rovers	46	15	5	3	43	20	11	8	4	33	19	91
3	Bolton Wanderers	46	10	10	3	40	28	14	5	4	36	17	87
4	Preston North End	46	12	6	5	32	18	11	3	9	32	34	78
5	Birmingham City	46	14	3	6	34	22	9	6	8	25	26	78
6	West Bromwich Albion	46	13	5	5	37	23	8	6	9	23	29	74
7	Burnley	46	14	5	4	30	17	7	4	12	20	37	72
8	Wimbledon	46	7	11	5	33	26	10	7	6	38	24	69
9	Watford	46	11	6	6	46	29	9	3	11	30	38	69
10	Sheffield United	46	14	4	5	34	18	5	7	11	18	31	68
11	Nottingham Forest	46	11	3	9	28	24	9	5	9	27	29	68
12	Wolverhampton Wan.	46	7	9	7	25	20	7	4	12	20	28	55
13	GILLINGHAM	46	9	6	8	32	28	4	10	9	29	38	55
14	Crewe Alexandra	46	12	5	6	30	24	3	5	15	17	38	55
15	Norwich City	46	10	7	6	25	18	4	5	14	21	40	54
16	Barnsley	46	11	3	9	32	26	4	6	13	17	36	54
17	Sheffield Wednesday	46	9	4	10	34	38	6	4	13	18	33	53
18	Grimsby Town	46	10	4	9	26	27	4	6	13	17	35	52
19	Stockport County	46	6	11	6	29	26	5	7	11	29	39	51
20	Portsmouth	46	9	8	6	31	25	1	11	11	16	34	49
21	Crystal Palace	46	6	6	11	28	34	6	7	10	29	36	49
22	Huddersfield Town	46	7	6	10	29	26	4	9	10	19	31	48
23	Queen's Park Rangers	46	6	9	8	24	28	1	10	12	21	47	40
24	Tranmere Rovers	46	8	7	8	30	33	1	4	18	16	44	38

2001/02 Division 1

1	Manchester City	46	19	3	1	63	19	12	3	8	45	33	99
2	West Bromwich Albion	46	15	4	4	36	11	12	4	7	25	18	89
3	Wolverhampton Wan.	46	13	4	6	33	18	12	7	4	43	25	86
4	Millwall	46	15	3	5	43	22	7	8	8	26	26	77
5	Birmingham City	46	14	4	5	44	20	7	9	7	26	29	76
6	Norwich City	46	15	6	2	36	16	7	3	13	24	35	75
7	Burnley	46	11	7	5	39	29	10	5	8	31	33	75
8	Preston North End	46	13	7	3	45	21	7	5	11	26	38	72
9	Wimbledon	46	9	8	6	30	22	9	5	9	33	35	67
10	Crystal Palace	46	13	3	7	42	22	7	3	13	28	40	66
11	Coventry City	46	12	4	7	33	19	8	2	13	26	34	66
12	GILLINGHAM	46	12	5	6	38	26	6	5	12	26	41	64
13	Sheffield United	46	8	8	7	34	30	7	7	9	19	24	60
14	Watford	46	10	5	8	38	30	6	6	11	24	26	59
15	Bradford City	46	10	1	12	41	39	5	9	9	28	37	55
16	Nottingham Forest	46	7	11	5	26	21	5	7	11	24	30	54
17	Portsmouth	46	9	6	8	36	31	4	8	11	24	41	53
18	Walsall	46	10	6	7	29	27	3	6	14	22	44	51
19	Grimsby Town	46	9	7	7	34	28	3	7	13	16	44	50
20	Sheffield Wednesday	46	6	7	10	28	37	6	7	10	21	34	50
21	Rotherham United	46	7	13	3	32	29	3	6	14	20	37	49
22	Crewe Alexandra	46	8	8	7	23	32	4	5	14	24	44	49
23	Barnsley	46	9	9	5	37	33	2	6	15	22	53	48
24	Stockport County	46	5	1	17	19	44	1	7	15	23	58	26

2002/03 Division 1

1	Portsmouth	46	17	3	3	52	22	12	8	3	45	23	98
2	Leicester City	46	16	5	2	40	12	10	9	4	33	28	92
3	Sheffield United	46	13	7	3	38	23	10	4	9	34	29	80
4	Reading	46	13	3	7	33	21	12	1	10	28	25	79
5	Wolverhampton Wan.	46	9	10	4	40	19	11	6	6	41	25	76
6	Nottingham Forest	46	14	7	2	57	23	6	7	10	25	27	74
7	Ipswich Town	46	10	5	8	49	39	9	8	6	31	25	70
8	Norwich City	46	14	4	5	36	17	5	8	10	24	32	69
9	Millwall	46	11	6	6	34	32	8	3	12	25	37	66
10	Wimbledon	46	12	5	6	39	28	6	6	11	37	45	65
11	GILLINGHAM	46	10	6	7	33	31	6	8	9	23	34	62
12	Preston North End	46	11	7	5	44	29	5	6	12	24	41	61
13	Watford	46	11	5	7	33	26	6	4	13	21	44	60
14	Crystal Palace	46	8	10	5	29	17	6	7	10	30	35	59
15	Rotherham United	46	8	9	6	27	25	7	5	11	35	37	59
16	Burnley	46	10	4	9	35	44	5	6	12	30	45	55
17	Walsall	46	10	3	10	34	34	5	6	12	23	35	54
18	Derby County	46	9	5	9	33	32	6	2	15	22	42	52
19	Bradford City	46	7	8	8	27	35	7	2	14	24	38	52
20	Coventry City	46	6	6	11	23	31	6	8	9	23	31	50
21	Stoke City	46	9	6	8	25	25	3	8	12	20	44	50
22	Sheffield Wednesday	46	7	7	9	29	32	3	9	11	27	41	46
23	Brighton & Hove Albion	46	7	6	10	29	31	4	6	13	20	36	45
24	Grimsby Town	46	5	6	12	26	39	4	6	13	22	46	39

Name		D.O.B	Place of Birth	Died	First Season	Last Season	Previous Club	Next Club	Appearances				Goals			
									Lge	FAC	FLC	Oth.	Lge	FAC	FLC	Oth.
Ackland ME	Mike	04/06/35	Sidcup		1956		Local	Bromley	2	0	0	0	0	0	0	0
Adams MR	Micky	08/11/61	Sheffield		1979	1982	App.	Coventry City	92	6	5	1	4	0	0	0
Adey AL	Arthur	01/03/30	Glasgow		1954		Doncaster Rovers	Bradford Park Ave	7	0	0	0	1	0	0	0
Aitken GL	Glenn	30/09/52	Woolwich		1972	1974	Chelsea	Wimbledon	23	1	1	0	0	0	0	0
Akinbiyi AP	Ade	10/10/74	Hackney		1996	1997	Norwich City	Bristol City	63	2	2	1	28	0	1	0
Albury WF	Bill	10/08/33	Portsmouth		1959		Portsmouth	Yeovil Town	38	4	0	0	12	0	3	0
Allen HA	Henry	1896	Hackney		1923		Southend Utd.	Charlton Ath.	6	2	0	0	0	0	0	0
Ames LEG	Les	03/12/05	Elham	1990	1931		Clapton Orient		5	0	0	0	1	0	0	0
Amos ST	Stanley	1907	Cradley Heath		1926	1927	Cradley Hth St Lukes	Cradley Hth St Lukes	31	4	0	0	12	0	0	0
Ansah A	Andy	19/03/69	Lewisham		1995		Peterborough U (loan)		2	0	0	0	0	0	0	0
Anstiss HA	Harry	22/08/1899	Chiswick	1964	1934		Crewe Alexandra	Tunbridge Wells	33	1	0	0	6	0	0	0
Arblaster WJ	Bill	1900	Darlaston		1926	1927	Merthyr Town		54	5	0	0	23	0	1	0
Armfield WC	Billy	07/07/04	Handsworth		1932		Exeter City	Droitwich	30	0	0	0	7	0	0	0
Armstrong GS	Gary	02/01/58	West Ham		1975	1979	App.	Wimbledon	94	4	4	0	2	0	0	0
					1983		Barnet	Crewe Alexandra								
Armstrong SC	Craig	23/05/75	South Shields		1996		Nottm. Forest (loan)		10	0	2	1	0	0	0	0
Armstrong W	Bill	03/07/12	Throckley	1995	1936	1937	Swindon Town	Shorts Sports	61	4	0	4	0	0	0	0
Arnold WJ	William	01/03/00	Bromley	1977	1922				2	0	0	0	1	0	0	0
Arnott AJ	Andy	18/10/73	Chatham		1991	1995	Trainee	Leyton Orient	73	12	5	4	12	0	1	0
Arnott JH	John	06/09/32	Sydenham		1962	1967	Bournemouth	Dover	186	8	12	0	2	0	1	0
Asaba CE	Carl	28/01/73	Westminster		1998	2000	Reading	Sheffield Utd.	77	2	3	8	36	2	0	2
Ashby BJ	Barry	20/11/70	Park Royal		1997	2002	Brentford		228	17	16	11	6	0	1	1
Awuah J	Jones	07/10/83	Ghana		2002		Trainee		4	0	0	0	0	0	0	0
Aylott TKC	Trevor	26/11/57	Bermondsey		1992		Oxford United	Wycombe Wan.	10	2	2	2	2	1	0	1
Ayres H	Harry	10/03/20	Redcar	2003	1950	1954	Fulham	Sittingbourne	136	7	0	0	2	0	0	0
Bacon RAS	Ron	04/03/35	Fakenham		1958	1960	Norwich City	King's Lynn	128	9	2	0	15	0	0	0
Bailey DL	Dennis	13/11/65	Lambeth		1995	1997	QPR	Lincoln City	88	5	9	1	11	1	1	0
Bailey RR	Ray	16/05/44	St Neots		1966	1970	Bedford Town	Romford	160	10	10	0	7	0	3	0
Baird RA	Ronald	1908	Gillingham		1929		RN Depot Chatham	Redhill	1	0	0	0	0	0	0	0
Baker DP	Paul	05/01/63	Newcastle		1992	1994	Hartlepool Utd.	York City	62	3	2	2	16	0	0	0
Balcombe SL	Leslie	1904	Lambeth	1938	1934	1935	Tunbridge Wells	Ashford Town	14	0	0	0	1	0	0	0
Baldwin JG	George	26/07/21	Islington	1976	1951		Gravesend & N'fleet		1	0	0	0	0	0	0	0
Baldwin W	Bill	31/01/07	Leigh	1982	1934	1935	Southport	Crewe Alexandra	60	3	0	3	23	0	4	1
Ballagher J	John	21/03/36	Ashton-under-Lyne		1962	1963	Doncaster Rovers	Margate	41	2	2	0	10	2	0	0
Ballsom WG	George	30/10/12	Trealaw	1983	1935	1937	Tunbridge Wells Rgs	Cardiff City	45	1	0	3	0	0	0	0
Banks S	Steve	09/02/72	Hillingdon		1993	1994	West Ham Utd.	Blackpool	67	7	0	2	0	0	0	0
Barker AM	Mickey	23/02/56	Bishop Auckland		1978	1979	Newcastle United	Ferryhill	64	2	4	0	2	1	0	0
Barnard WE	Wally	1898	Tottenham		1923		Tottenham Hotspur	Brentford	3	0	0	0	0	0	0	0
Barrett S	Scott	02/04/63	Alvaston		1992	1994	Colchester Utd.	Cambridge Utd.	51	4	7	3	0	0	0	0
Barrie G	George	17/07/04	Balgonie		1933	1936	Crystal Palace		87	2	0	3	1	0	0	0
Bartley JWE	Jim		Bilston		1926	1929	Bilston U	Canterbury Waverley	25	0	0	0	0	0	0	0
Bartram VL	Vince	07/08/68	Birmingham		1997	2002	Arsenal		186	13	12	10	0	0	0	0
Bass JDM	Jon	01/07/76	Weston-super-Mare		1999		Birmingham C (loan)		7	0	0	0	0	0	0	0
Batchelor JWF	James	26/07/1895	Strood		1922		Chatham Town	Brentford	3	0	0	0	0	0	0	0
Battiste W	Wally	11/06/1892	Worksop	1965	1920	1924	Grimsby Town	Millwall	152	13	0	0	8	0	0	0
					1930		Millwall									
Baxter LR	Larry	24/11/31	Leicester		1955	1957	Norwich City	Torquay United	64	4	0	0	7	0	0	0
Baxter TJC	Tom	Oct 1893	Wandsworth		1920		Chelsea		21	2	0	0	0	0	0	0
Beacham AJ	Jack	15/08/02	Birmingham	1982	1929	1931	Brentford	Worcester C	109	4	0	0	0	0	1	0
Beadle PCWJ	Peter	13/05/72	Lambeth		1988	1991	Trainee	Tottenham Hotspur	67	2	6	1	13	2	0	0
Bean RE	Ron	10/04/26	Crayford	1992	1951		Gravesend & N'fleet	Released	3	0	0	0	0	0	0	0
Beby JV	Jack	23/08/07	Gillingham	1976	1929		Grenadier Guards	Leicester City	20	0	0	0	0	0	0	0
Beeney MR	Mark	30/12/67	Pembury		1986		App.	Maidstone Utd.	2	0	1	0	0	0	0	0
Bellotti DC	Derek	25/12/46	East Ham		1966	1969	Bedford Town	Charlton Ath.	35	3	5	0	0	0	0	0
Bentley A	Alf	28/10/31	Aylesham	1996	1958	1961	Margate	Tunbridge Wells	13	0	0	0	0	0	0	0
Berkley AJ	Austin	28/01/73	Gravesend		1991		Trainee	Swindon Town	3	0	0	3	0	0	0	0
Berry LD	Les	04/03/56	Plumstead		1986	1987	Brighton & Hove A.	Maidstone Utd.	31	0	1	7	0	0	0	0
Berry WG	Bill	10/08/04	Hackney	1972	1923	1925	Charlton Ath.	Brentford	79	8	0	0	10	0	2	0
Bethell R	Roy	09/08/06	Watford	1976	1929	1934	Charlton Ath.		165	7	0	1	32	0	2	0
Bettridge W	Walter	Oct 1886	Oakthorpe	1931	1922		Chelsea	Peterboro & Fletton	19	0	0	0	0	0	0	0
Bickle MJ	Mike	25/01/44	Plymouth		1971	1972	Plymouth Argyle	Retired	32	4	2	0	7	0	0	0
Bishop GA	George	1901	Tredegar		1929	1931	Merthyr Town	Southampton	94	4	0	0	0	0	0	0
Blake AJ	Tony	26/02/27	Cofton Hackett		1952		Birmingham City	Retired	10	0	0	0	1	0	0	0
Bodley MJ	Mick	14/09/67	Hayes		1994		Southend Utd. (loan)		7	0	0	0	0	0	0	0
Bond GA	George	11/02/10	Ilford	1982	1935		Northfleet	Malta	9	0	0	0	2	0	0	0
Boswell J	Jimmy	13/03/22	Chester		1950	1957	Chester	Gravesend & N'fleet	342	36	0	0	6	0	0	0
Boswell W	Bill	05/08/02	Cradley Heath	1977	1927		Wolves	Worcester City	17	3	0	0	4	0	1	0
Bottiglieri A	Tony	29/05/62	Chatham		1979	1981	App.	(Finland)	9	2	0	0	0	0	0	0
Bowman RD	Richie	25/09/54	Lewisham		1981	1983	Reading	Retired	26	3	3	0	6	0	1	0
Boylen RH	Robert	05/01/07	Newcastle	1992	1930		Luton Town	Gateshead	3	0	0	0	0	0	0	0
Bradley PJ	Patrick	1901	Coatbridge		1926	1927	Wolves	Walsall Wood	33	5	0	0	3	0	0	0
Brallisford A	Albert	09/10/11	Belle Vue, Hartlepool	1991	1937		Darlington	Glentoran	14	2	0	0	3	0	0	0
Branagan KG	Keith	10/07/66	Fulham		1991		Millwall (loan)		1	0	0	0	0	0	0	0
Branfield J	Jack	25/10/1891	Gillingham		1920	1921		Sheppey United	57	7	0	0	0	0	0	0
Brasted GA	Gordon	30/06/33	Burnham-on-Crouch	2000	1956		Arsenal	Retired	5	0	0	0	4	0	0	0
Breen GP	Gary	12/12/73	Hendon		1992	1993	Maidstone Utd.	Peterborough Utd.	51	5	4	1	0	0	0	0
Brennan TJ	Thomas	07/02/11	Calderbank		1929	1930	Brentford	Crystal Palace	16	0	0	0	2	0	0	0
Brickenden NR	Norman	20/07/14	Isle of Sheppey	1972	1937		Sheppey United	Sittingbourne	3	0	0	0	0	0	0	0
Briggs J	Jackie	27/10/24	Barnsley	1992	1950	1952	Army	Folkestone Town	52	14	0	0	14	4	0	0
Brindley JC	Bill	29/01/47	Nottingham		1976		Notts County	Grantham	20	1	3	0	1	0	0	0
Brodie CTG	Chic	22/02/37	Duntocher	2000	1957		Manchester City	Aldershot	18	4	0	0	0	0	0	0

Name		D.O.B	Place of Birth	Died	First Season	Last Season	Previous Club	Next Club	Appearances				Goals			
									Lge	FAC	FLC	Oth.	Lge	FAC	FLC	Oth.
Bromage E	Enos	22/10/1898	Mickleover	1978	1927		Derby County	West Bromwich A.	21	1	0	0	6	0	0	0
Brown F	Fred	28/06/1895	Gainsborough	1960	1924	1926	Brighton & Hove A.	Gainsborough Trin.	95	13	0	0	25	0	5	0
Brown G	Gordon	04/02/32	Dunfermline		1959	1960	Newport County	Ashford Town	67	5	1	0	13	0	0	0
Brown JR	Jason	18/05/82	Southwark		2001	2002	Charlton Ath.		49	3	2	0	0	0	0	0
Brown JT	John		Sheffield		1927		Shrewsbury T (loan)		2	0	0	0	0	0	0	0
Brown KJ	Kenny	11/07/67	Upminster		1998		Millwall	Kingstonian	4	0	0	1	0	0	0	0
Brown S	Sidney		Brierley Hill		1927		Port Vale	West Bromwich A.	8	0	0	0	0	0	0	0
Brown SRMcN	Steve	06/12/73	Southend-on-Sea		1994	1995	Colchester Utd.	Lincoln City	9	0	0	0	2	0	0	0
Brown WFT	Billy	07/02/43	Croydon		1965	1967	Bedford Town	Portsmouth	105	3	8	0	33	1	0	0
Browning MT	Marcus	22/04/71	Bristol		1998	2001	Huddersfield T	Bournemouth	78	6	7	1	3	0	0	0
Bruce H	Harry	May 1905	Coundon		1928		Birmingham	Torquay United	30	2	0	0	0	0	0	0
Bruce SR	Steve	31/12/60	Corbridge		1979	1983	App.	Norwich City	205	14	15	3	29	6	2	0
Bryant M	Matt	21/09/70	Bristol		1996	1999	Bristol City	Released	103	5	10	4	0	0	0	0
Buckle GF	George	1907	Lewisham		1931		Army	Aldershot	29	1	0	0	0	0	0	0
Burgess MR	Mike	17/04/32	Montreal, Canada		1962	1965	Halifax Town	Aldershot	110	4	6	0	2	0	0	0
Burke JJ	Johnny	28/06/11	Dublin	1987	1950		Millwall	Retired	5	9	0	0	0	0	0	0
Burley GE	George	03/06/56	Cumnock		1988		Sunderland	Motherwell	46	2	3	3	2	0	0	0
Burnett N	Norman		Dundee	1982	1931		Sunderland		7	0	0	0	0	0	0	0
Burrows PA	Phil	08/04/46	Stockport		1977		Hereford Utd. (loan)		5	0	0	0	0	0	0	0
Burtenshaw CE	Charlie	16/10/22	Portslade		1950	1951	Luton Town	Snowdown CW	28	7	0	0	4	2	1	0
Burtenshaw WF	Bill	13/12/25	Portslade		1950	1951	Luton Town	Snowdown CW	39	9	0	0	8	0	1	0
Butler CJW	Charlie	1897	Watford		1923	1926	Manchester Utd.	Grays Thurrock	76	6	0	0	0	0	0	0
Butler PA (Tony)	Tony	28/09/72	Stockport		1990	1995	Trainee	Blackpool	148	13	12	6	5	0	1	1
Butler S	Steve	27/01/62	Birmingham		1995	1999	Cambridge Utd.	Peterborough Utd.	118	8	8	4	22	1	1	1
Butters G	Guy	30/10/69	Hillingdon		1996	2001	Portsmouth	Brighton & Hove A.	159	14	9	11	16	0	1	0
Buttress MD	Mike	23/03/58	Peterborough		1977	1978	Aston Villa	Telford United	7	0	0	0	0	0	0	0
Byrne DS	David	05/03/61	Hammersmith		1985		Kingstonian	Millwall	23	3	2	2	3	0	0	0
Campbell CWG	Charlie	27/03/17	Chatham	2002	1937		Gillingham Nomads		7	0	0	1	0	0	0	0
Campbell D	Don	19/10/32	Bootle		1962	1963	Crewe Alexandra	Folkestone Town	29	3	1	0	0	0	0	0
Campbell J	Joe	28/03/25	Glasgow		1950		Leyton Orient	Bedford Town	12	0	0	0	2	0	0	0
Carberry R	Bert	16/01/31	Glasgow		1956		Bedford Town	Port Vale	1	0	0	0	0	0	0	0
Carpenter R	Richard	30/09/72	Sheerness		1990	1996	Trainee	Fulham	122	10	3	6	4	0	0	1
Carr DJ	Darren	04/09/68	Bristol		1998		Chesterfield	Brighton & Hove A.	30	1	2	3	2	0	0	0
Carr J	Jackie	12/01/24	Bishopbriggs		1950		Alloa Athletic	Chelmsford City	11	3	0	0	2	0	2	0
Carter AJ	Albert	1898	Milton		1920		Zion		2	0	0	0	0	0	0	0
Cartmell JR	John	28/08/1890	Blackpool	1979	1923		Bournemouth	Brentford	4	1	0	0	0	0	0	0
Cascarino AG	Tony	01/09/62	St Pauls Cray		1981	1986	Crockenhill	Millwall	219	17	18	15	78	11	9	12
Cassell L	Leo		Ramsgate		1921				5	0	0	0	1	0	0	0
Castle FR	Fred	10/04/02	Pen-y-graig	1982	1929		Chesterfield	Derry City	16	0	0	0	4	0	0	0
Castle SC	Steve	17/05/66	Barkingside		1995		Birmingham City (loan)		6	0	0	0	1	0	0	0
Cavener P	Phil	02/06/61	Tynemouth		1983		Burnley	Northampton Town	10	0	0	1	1	0	0	0
Cawston MW	Mervyn	04/02/52	Diss		1976		Norwich City	Southend Utd.	19	1	1	0	0	0	0	0
Chadwick DE	Dave	19/08/43	Ootacamund, India		1974		Bournemouth	Dallas Tornado	35	1	0	0	3	0	0	0
Challis RLA	Roger	03/08/43	Rochester		1960	1962	Trainee	Crewe Alexandra	10	0	2	0	0	0	0	0
Chance GH	George	25/12/1896	Stourbridge	1952	1924		Bristol Rovers	Millwall	40	7	0	0	4	0	0	0
Chapman IR	Ian	31/05/70	Brighton		1996	1997	Brighton & Hove A.	Retired	23	3	6	1	1	0	0	0
Cheesmur FH	Fred	16/01/08	Wandsworth	1987	1929	1930	Charlton Ath.	Sheffield Utd.	55	2	0	0	19	0	1	0
Cherry RA	Rex	11/11/33	Penistone		1952	1953	Army	Hastings United	10	0	0	0	4	0	0	0
Chiswick PJH	Peter	19/09/29	Plaistow	1962	1956		West Ham Utd.	Margate	14	0	0	0	0	0	0	0
Clark JF	John		Dumbarton		1933		Wolves		5	0	0	1	0	0	0	0
Clark PP	Paul	14/09/58	Benfleet		1991	1993	Southend Utd.	Chelmsford City	90	9	7	5	1	0	1	0
Clark R	Ron	21/05/32	Clarkston		1956	1957	Kilmarnock	Oldham Athletic	33	1	0	0	6	0	2	0
Clarke BR	Brian	10/10/68	Eastbourne		1988	1991	Trainee	Sittingbourne	44	1	2	5	0	0	0	0
Clarke CJ	Colin	30/10/62	Newry		1983		Peterborough U (loan)		8	0	0	0	1	0	0	0
Cochrane GT	Terry	23/01/53	Killyleagh		1983	1985	Middlesbrough	Millwall	107	13	7	4	18	0	3	0
Cockburn WR	Bill	03/05/37	Shotton	1995	1960	1961	Burnley	Hastings United	62	1	1	0	1	0	0	0
Collins AJ	Albert	16/01/1899	Rainham	1969	1929	1933	Millwall	Canterbury Waverley	170	8	0	0	4	0	0	0
Collins P	Paul	11/08/66	West Ham		1983	1986	App.	Wycombe Wan.	37	4	7	9	3	0	0	1
Collins WH	Bill	15/02/20	Belfast		1950		Luton Town	Snowdown CW	13	3	0	0	0	1	0	0
Cook G	George	20/11/04	Shankhouse		1924		Bedlington U	Preston NE	7	1	0	0	0	0	0	0
Cooper MD	Mark	05/04/67	Watford		1987	1988	Tottenham Hotspur	Leyton Orient	49	4	3	4	11	0	0	0
Corbett JJ	Jimmy	06/07/80	Hackney		1997		Trainee	Blackburn Rovers	16	0	0	1	2	0	0	0
Cosgrove WH	William	1898	London		1923		Custom House		15	2	0	0	3	0	0	0
Cousans WE	Eric	10/09/29	Doncaster		1955		Walsall	Dover	2	0	0	0	0	0	0	0
Coxhill D	David	10/04/52	Northfields		1973	1974	Millwall	Dover	34	1	3	0	1	0	0	0
Crabbe SAJ	John'Buster'	20/10/54	Weymouth		1976	1980	Southampton	Carlisle Utd.	181	12	10	0	13	1	0	0
Craddock CW	Joe	02/08/02	Grimsby	1976	1924	1925	Chatham Centrals	Brentford	16	0	0	0	3	0	0	0
Crane SJ	Steve	03/06/72	Orsett		1992	1993	USA	Hornchurch	13	0	2	2	1	0	0	0
Crawford GW	George	10/12/05	Sunderland	1975	1927	1928	Sunderland	Bournemouth	40	3	0	0	1	0	0	0
Crickmore CA	Charlie	11/02/42	Hull		1966	1967	Bournemouth	Rotherham Utd.	53	2	8	0	13	4	0	0
Crockford H	Harold	25/09/1893	Derby	1983	1924		Chesterfield	Accrington Stanley	7	0	0	0	1	0	0	0
Crofts AL	Andrew	29/05/84	Gillingham		2000		Trainee		1	0	0	0	0	0	0	0
Crombie TR	Tom	03/06/30	Kirkcaldy		1955	1956	Blackpool	Folkestone	17	3	0	0	0	0	0	0
Crompton W	Wilf	01/04/08	Blackburn	1971	1934		Burnley	Luton Town	14	0	0	1	6	0	0	0
Cronin WJ	William	10/10/12	(Scotland)	1986	1931				2	0	0	0	0	0	0	0
Cropper A	Arthur	02/01/06	Brimington	1949	1932		Clapton Orient	Yarmouth Town	16	3	0	0	2	0	1	0
Crossan EG	Errol	06/10/30	Montreal, Canada		1955	1956	Manchester City	Southend Utd.	76	4	0	0	16	0	1	0
Crown DI	David	16/02/58	Enfield		1990	1992	Southend Utd.	Dagenham & Red.	86	5	4	5	39	3	3	2
Dalton BL	Bryan	09/01/17	Arundel		1937		Reading		6	0	0	1	0	0	0	0
Daniel RC	Ray	10/12/64	Luton		1983		Luton Town (loan)		5	0	0	0	0	0	0	0

Name		D.O.B	Place of Birth	Died	First Season	Last Season	Previous Club	Next Club	Appearances Lge	FAC	FLC	Oth.	Goals Lge	FAC	FLC	Oth.
Dann RW	Reg	06/06/17	Maidstone	1948	1935		Aylesford PM	Tottenham Hotspur	8	0	0	0	0	0	0	0
Darling HL	Len	09/08/11	Gillingham	1958	1932		Chatham Town	Brighton & Hove A.	14	1	0	0	0	0	0	0
Darrell MA	Mike	14/01/47	Bilston		1970		Birmingham City (loan)		22	0	0	0	1	0	0	0
Darvell RD	Roger	10/02/31	High Wycombe		1957		Charlton Ath.	Southport	3	0	0	0	0	0	0	0
Davis CH	Charles	22/09/02	Tynemouth	1987	1924		Liverpool	West Stanley	5	2	0	0	0	0	0	0
Davis JL	John	31/03/57	Hackney		1975		Crystal Palace	Sheffield Wed.	3	1	0	0	0	0	0	0
Day JN	Jack	21/01/24	Northfleet		1950		Brighton & Hove A.		1	1	0	0	0	0	0	0
Death WG	Billy	13/11/00	Rotherham	1984	1930		Exeter City	Mansfield Town	27	2	0	0	6	0	3	0
Dee A	Amos		Merthyr Tydfil		1927		Wolves	Bradford City	4	0	0	0	0	0	0	0
Dempsey MAP	Mark	10/12/72	Dublin		1990	1993	Trainee	Leyton Orient	48	5	1	6	2	0	0	0
Dibden WK	Keith	17/12/33	Totton		1957		Southampton	Hastings United	1	1	0	0	0	0	0	0
Dobson AJ	Tony	05/02/69	Coventry		1998		Portsmouth (loan)		2	0	0	0	0	0	0	0
Docker I	Ian	12/09/69	Gravesend		1987	1990	Trainee	Redbridge Forest	87	4	3	7	3	0	0	0
Dodds JA	Jim	07/09/14	Belfast		1936		Fulham	Glentoran	25	0	0	1	6	0	0	1
Dominy AA	Arthur	11/02/1893	South Stoneham	1974	1927	1928	Everton	Clapton Orient	55	2	0	0	17	0	0	0
Donaghy E	Edward	08/01/00	Grangetown		1927		Derby County	(France)	4	0	0	0	0	0	0	0
Doncaster AR	Dick	13/05/08	Barry Dock		1934	1935	Reading	Yeovil & Petters	68	2	0	2	18	0	0	0
Donn AN	Nigel	02/03/62	Maidstone		1980	1981	App.	Leyton Orient	3	0	2	0	0	0	0	0
Donoghue F	Frank	1916	Openshaw		1937		Portsmouth	Yeovil & Petters	1	0	0	0	0	0	0	0
Dorling GJ	George	27/07/18	Edmonton	1987	1950		Tottenham Hotspur	Snowdown CW	10	14	0	0	0	0	0	0
Dowell L	Leonard	13/06/02	Edinburgh		1927	1930	Sittingbourne	Ashford Town	55	2	0	0	7	0	0	0
Duncan CJ	Colin	05/08/57	Plymstock		1979	1983	Oxford United	Reading	85	7	6	3	5	0	0	0
Duncan WMcK	William	20/07/13	Dundee		1935	1937	Carlisle Utd.		51	2	0	3	8	0	0	0
Dunne JJ	Joe	25/05/73	Dublin		1990	1995	Trainee	Colchester Utd.	115	6	7	6	1	0	0	0
Durkin J	John	18/04/30	Hill o' Beath		1953	1954	Hearts	Ramsgate Ath.	30	4	0	0	5	0	1	0
Durnion AJ	Andy	18/02/07	Bellshill	1988	1929		Brentford	Thames	19	1	0	0	9	0	0	0
Durrell JT	Joe	15/03/53	Stepney		1975	1976	Bristol City	Tonbridge	49	2	3	0	9	0	0	0
Edgar J	Johnny 'Tich'	09/04/36	Worsborough Dale		1958		Barnsley	York City	45	2	0	0	23	0	1	0
Edge R	Roland	25/11/78	Gillingham		1998	2002	Trainee	Hibernian	102	13	6	5	1	0	0	0
Edmed RA	Dick	14/02/04	Gillingham	1983	1923	1925	Rochester Sports	Liverpool	24	3	0	0	7	0	0	0
Edusei A	Akwasi	12/9/86	Camberwell		2002		App.		2	0	0	0	0	0	0	0
Eeles AG	Tony	15/11/70	Chatham		1988	1993	Trainee	Dover Athletic	73	5	7	6	5	0	0	0
Elliott ST	Stuart	27/08/77	Hendon		1998		Newcastle U (loan)		5	0	0	0	0	0	0	0
Ellis FC	Fred	07/10/00	Sheerness	1970	1925	1930	Sheppey United	Watford	108	5	0	0	1	0	0	0
Elsey KW	Karl	20/11/58	Swansea		1985	1987	Cardiff City	Reading	155	12	13	16	16	0	1	2
					1991		Maidstone Utd.	Sittingbourne								
Emanuel WJM	John 'Ivor'	19/04/48	Swansea		1975		Bristol City	Newport County	4	0	0	0	0	0	0	0
Emmerson GAH	George	15/05/06	Bishop Auckland	1966	1937		Tunbridge Wells		10	0	0	0	0	0	0	0
Evans A	Arthur	13/05/33	Urmston		1953	1954	Stockport Co.	Released	14	0	0	0	0	0	0	0
Evans JL	John	04/10/37	Wattstown		1957		Lovell's Athletic	Llanelli	7	0	0	0	0	0	0	0
Evans WE	Billy	05/09/21	Birmingham	1960	1953	1954	Notts County	Grimsby Town	89	3	0	0	12	0	0	0
Eves MJ	Mel	10/09/58	Wednesbury		1986	1987	Sheffield Utd.	West Bromwich A.	27	2	6	2	9	0	0	0
Fairclough A	Albert	04/10/1891	St Helens	1958	1926		Derby County		11	0	0	0	3	0	0	0
Farrall A	Alec	03/03/36	West Kirby		1960	1964	Preston NE	Lincoln City	202	9	9	0	19	0	2	0
Feely PJ	Peter	03/01/50	City of London		1974	1975	Fulham	Sheffield Wed.	41	1	1	0	22	0	0	0
Ferguson ASB	Alex	05/08/03	Lochore	1974	1925	1926	Wigan Borough	Swansea Town	67	6	0	0	0	0	0	0
Fisher F	Fred	11/04/10	Hucknall		1935		Swindon Town	Clapton Orient	17	0	0	1	6	0	0	0
Fishlock LB	Laurie	02/01/07	Battersea	1986	1937		Fulham		20	0	0	0	2	0	0	0
Fletcher JA	Jimmy	10/11/31	Wouldham		1957		Maidstone United	Southend Utd.	23	4	0	0	8	0	5	0
Fogarty WF	Bill	27/06/57	Dulwich		1974	1976	App.	Charlton Ath.	29	1	1	0	0	0	0	0
Folds RJ	Bobby	18/04/49	Bedford		1968	1970	App.	Northampton Town	44	3	2	0	1	1	0	0
Foley PJ	Peter	10/09/56	Bicester		1982		Oxford United	Bulova (Hong Kong)	5	0	0	0	0	0	0	0
Forbes AS	Alex		Bo'ness		1932	1934	Bournemouth	Retired	69	6	0	1	1	0	0	0
Ford AC	Andy	04/05/54	Minehead		1980	1981	Swindon Town	Dartford	62	7	6	3	3	1	1	0
Ford C	Colin	18/09/60	Lewisham		1979		App.	Welling United	1	0	0	0	0	0	0	0
Ford JS	Jon	12/04/68	Birmingham		1996		Bradford City	Barnet	4	1	3	1	0	0	0	0
Forrester GL	George	08/06/27	Cannock	1981	1950	1954	West Bromwich A.	Reading	100	14	0	0	3	1	2	0
Forster NM	Nicky	08/09/73	Oxted		1992	1993	Horley Town	Brentford	67	6	5	0	24	0	2	0
Forsyth J	Jim	18/10/04	Armadale	1982	1928		Portsmouth	Millwall	34	2	0	0	0	0	0	0
Fortune-West LPO	Leo	09/04/71	Stratford		1995	1997	Stevenage Borough	Lincoln City	67	4	4	0	18	2	2	0
Foster AM	Adrian	19/03/71	Kidderminster		1994	1995	Torquay United	Hereford Utd.	40	3	4	2	9	0	0	2
Foster J	Jabez	15/09/02	Darlaston		1926		Bristol Rovers	Wellington	21	1	0	0	4	0	0	0
Fowler AJ	Arthur	20/11/11	Rothwell		1935	1937	Swindon Town	Dartford	28	2	0	1	2	0	1	0
Fox FS	Fred	22/11/1898	Highworth	1968	1922	1924	Preston NE	Millwall	106	13	0	0	0	0	0	0
Francis GE	George	04/02/34	Acton		1962	1963	Brentford	Hastings United	51	3	4	0	19	1	1	0
Freeman CR	Charlie	22/08/1887	Overseal	1956	1921	1922	Chelsea	Maidstone Utd.	82	6	0	0	21	0	3	0
Freeman DBA	Darren	22/08/73	Brighton		1994	1995	Horsham Town	Fulham	11	1	0	2	0	0	0	1
French JB	Jim		Tannochside		1930		Airdrieonians	Tunbridge Wells	18	2	0	0	1	0	0	0
Friday TJ	Terry	01/05/36	Sittingbourne		1960		Sheppey United	Sheppey United	2	0	0	0	0	0	0	0
Fry DP	David	05/01/60	Bournemouth		1983	1984	Crystal Palace	Millwall	49	7	0	2	0	0	0	0
Funnell A	Tony	20/08/57	Eastbourne		1978	1979	Southampton	Brentford	33	2	3	0	10	0	0	0
Furie JPC	John	13/05/48	Hammersmith		1967		Watford	Chelmsford City	17	1	0	0	0	0	0	0
Gage LA	Larry	10/09/22	Walthamstow	1996	1950		Fulham	Bedford Town	40	4	0	0	0	0	0	0
Galloway MA	Mick	13/10/74	Nottingham		1996	1999	Notts County	Chesterfield	75	3	4	5	5	0	0	0
Galvin D	David	05/10/46	Denaby		1969	1976	Wolves	Wimbledon	246	15	15	0	17	2	1	0
Garner P	Paul	01/12/55	Edlington		1983		Sheffield Utd. (loan)		5	0	0	0	0	0	0	0
Gauden A	Allan	20/11/44	Ashington		1974	1975	Hartlepool Utd.	Gateshead	41	1	3	0	3	0	0	0
Gavin PJ	Pat	05/06/67	Hammersmith		1988	1989	Hanwell Town	Leicester City	47	2	0	3	8	0	0	0
Gayle J	John	30/07/64	Bromsgrove		1995		Birmingham City (loan)		9	0	0	0	3	0	0	0
Gear FJ	Francis	1897	Tottenham	1958	1925		Millwall	Ashford Rail Works	3	0	0	0	0	0	0	0

Name		D.O.B	Place of Birth	Died	First Season	Last Season	Previous Club	Next Club	Appearances				Goals			
									Lge	FAC	FLC	Oth.	Lge	FAC	FLC	Oth.
Geddes J	John	11/04/08	Lochgelly	1937	1929		Glasgow Celtic	Rhyl Athletic	11	1	0	0	1	0	0	0
Gellatly CT	Charlie	18/04/1910	Brodsworth	1973	1931	1933	Leicester City		56	4	0	1	0	0	0	0
Gernon FAJ	Irvin	30/12/62	Birmingham		1986	1988	Ipswich Town	Reading	35	1	3	1	1	0	0	0
Gibbs BR	Brian	06/10/36	Gillingham, Dorset		1962	1968	Bournemouth	Colchester Utd.	259	9	16	0	101	3	6	0
Gibson MJ	Mike	15/07/39	Derby		1972	1973	Bristol City	Retired	80	2	4	0	0	0	0	0
Gilbert CG	Carl	20/03/48	Folkestone		1967	1969	Army	Bristol Rovers	30	0	0	0	11	0	0	0
Gilbey TE	Tom	20/01/1898	Bishop Auckland	1962	1920		Darlington		11	3	0	0	6	0	2	0
Gleasure PF	Peter	08/10/60	Luton		1990		Northampton T (loan)		3	0	0	0	0	0	0	0
Godfrey PR	Peter	15/03/38	Woolwich		1961	1964	Charlton Ath.	Chesterfield	66	4	1	0	9	0	1	0
Gooden TM	Ty	23/10/72	Canvey Island		1999	2001	Swindon Town	Canvey Island	59	3	4	3	5	0	1	1
Goodman AA	Bert	03/09/1890	Dalston	1959	1925		Charlton Ath.	Clapton Orient	6	0	0	0	0	0	0	0
Gordon CK	Colin	17/01/63	Stourbridge		1986		Wimbledon (loan)		4	0	0	0	2	0	0	0
Gore SP	Syd	23/09/00	Faversham		1920	1929	Faversham Rgs	Chatham Town	40	1	0	0	0	0	0	0
Gould JA	Jonathan	18/07/68	Paddington		1996		Coventry City (loan)		3	0	0	0	0	0	0	0
Grace DG	Derek	29/12/44	Chiswick		1965		Exeter City	Margate	4	0	1	0	0	0	0	0
Graham CJ	John		Newcastle		1931		Newcastle United	Shelbourne	2	0	0	0	0	0	0	0
Grant WF	William	07/10/33	Spittalfield		1956		Brechin City	(Canada)	1	0	0	0	0	0	0	0
Gray IW	Irvine	27/02/33	Hoyland		1956		Barnsley	Sittingbourne	9	0	0	0	0	0	0	0
Green HR	Rodney	24/06/39	Halifax		1964		Bradford City	Grimsby Town	33	3	1	0	17	0	0	0
Green MC	Mike	08/09/46	Carlisle		1968	1970	Carlisle Utd.	Bristol Rovers	132	10	5	0	24	0	4	0
Green RE	Richard	22/11/67	Wolverhampton		1991	1997	Swindon Town	Walsall	216	17	11	7	16	0	1	0
Greenall CA	Colin	30/12/63	Billinge		1986	1987	Blackpool	Oxford United	62	6	3	9	5	1	1	2
Greenhalgh JR	Jimmy	25/08/23	Manchester		1956		Wigan Athletic	Lincoln City	16	1	0	0	1	0	0	0
Gregory BC	Brian	11/01/55	Belfast		1974		Amateur	Margate	2	0	0	0	0	0	0	0
Grewcock N	Neil	26/04/62	Leicester		1981	1982	Leicester City	Kettering Town	34	2	4	0	4	0	0	0
Griffiths EG	Evan	19/04/43	Aylesham		1960	1961	Juniors	Tunbridge Wells	1	0	1	0	0	0	0	0
Griffiths JA	Joseph				1920			Sheppey United	5	0	0	0	0	0	0	0
Griffiths S	Stan	08/02/11	Pentre	2003	1933		Chester	Cardiff City	4	0	0	0	0	0	0	0
Guscott LA	Lindon	29/03/72	Lambeth		1988		Trainee	Tonbridge	2	0	0	0	0	0	0	0
Hague P	Paul	16/09/72	Shotley Bridge		1990	1993	Trainee	Leyton Orient	9	0	0	4	0	0	0	0
Haines IG	Ivan	14/09/68	Chatham		1987	1990	Juniors	Sittingbourne	51	4	5	4	0	0	0	0
Hales DD	Derek	15/12/51	Lower Halstow		1984	1985	Charlton Ath.	Retired	40	2	1	3	9	0	1	1
Hales RJ	Richard	24/08/24	Gillingham		1951		Sittingbourne	Faversham Town	5	0	0	0	0	0	0	0
Hales WH	Bill	06/01/20	Gillingham	1984	1950	1951	Sittingbourne	Snowdown CW	15	0	0	0	9	0	0	0
Hall P	Peter	29/09/39	Stoke-on-Trent		1967		Bedford Town	Retired	9	0	0	0	1	0	0	0
Hall T	Tom	1895	Newburn		1920	1925	Newcastle United	(trainer)	190	17	0	0	47	0	8	0
Hall W	Billy	24/07/30	Gosport		1952		Gosport Borough		9	0	0	0	0	0	0	0
Handford PM	Phil	18/07/64	Chatham		1982	1983	App.	Wimbledon	32	1	2	1	1	0	1	0
Hannaway J	Jack	22/10/27	Bootle		1957	1959	Manchester City	Southport	126	9	0	0	4	0	1	0
Hanney WPE	William	07/05/04	Wigston	1990	1928		Derby County	Birmingham	11	0	0	0	4	0	0	0
Harbot JW	Jimmy	16/08/07	Bolton	1992	1930		Royal Marines	Charlton Ath.	2	0	0	0	1	0	0	0
Harle MJL	Mike	31/10/72	Lewisham		1990		Trainee	Sittingbourne	2	0	0	1	0	0	0	0
Harris MA	Mark	15/07/63	Reading		1995	1996	Swansea City	Cardiff City	65	6	8	1	3	0	0	0
Harrison LD	Lee	12/09/71	Billericay		1991		Charlton Ath. (loan)		2	0	0	0	0	0	0	0
Harrison R	Robert	25/12/47	Chatham		1966		Amateur	Margate	1	0	0	0	0	0	0	0
Hartley S	Syd	22/01/14	Gomersal	1987	1936	1937	Clapton Orient	Bristol Rovers	77	2	0	4	2	0	0	0
Harvey JD	James	07/08/11	York		1934		Frickley Col.	Frickley Col.	15	1	0	1	0	0	0	0
Hawkins DJ	David	11/08/31	Kingston		1955		Sheppey United	Margate	14	0	0	0	8	0	0	0
Haylock P	Paul	24/03/63	Lowestoft		1986	1989	Norwich City	Maidstone Utd.	152	10	14	18	1	0	0	0
Hazel C	Cliff	14/09/37	Woolwich		1957		Hastings U	Millwall	2	0	0	0	0	0	0	0
Hebden GHR	George	02/06/00	West Ham	1973	1927	1928	QPR	QPR	70	5	0	0	0	0	0	0
Henderson J	Jock	1895	Kelty		1922	1923	Mid Rhondda	Dunfermline	76	6	0	0	9	0	0	0
Henderson P	Peter	29/09/52	Berwick-on-Tweed		1980	1981	Chester	Chester	7	0	4	1	3	0	0	0
Hendrie R	Dick	1898	Airdrie	1964	1923	1925	Maidstone Utd.	Brentford	71	7	0	0	0	0	0	0
Henry LA	Liburd	29/08/67	Dominica		1992	1993	Maidstone Utd.	Peterborough Utd.	42	3	4	2	2	0	1	2
Henson L	Len	06/08/21	Hull		1950	1951		Whitstable Town	8	0	0	0	0	0	0	0
Herbert FW	Fred	06/01/20	Cliffe		1937		Kent Alloys		17	0	0	1	7	0	0	0
Heritage PM	Peter	08/11/60	Bexhill		1989	1990	Hythe Town	Hereford Utd.	57	3	2	4	11	0	0	0
Hessenthaler A	Andy	17/08/65	Gravesend		1996	2002	Watford		234	18	22	10	17	3	2	3
High SC	Stan	18/02/08	Hetton-le-Hole	1982	1932		Accrington Stanley	Dartford	11	2	0	0	0	0	0	0
Hill HA	Henry	19/09/47	Lambeth		1971		Ipswich Town	Margate	2	0	2	0	0	0	0	0
Hill KG	Kenny	07/03/53	Canterbury		1971	1976	App.	Maidstone Utd.	125	1	12	0	7	1	0	0
Hillier S	Stan	1904	London		1926	1927	Bradford City		26	0	0	0	4	0	0	0
Hillman DV	Dennis	27/11/18	Southend-on-Sea	1994	1951		Colchester Utd.	Hastings United	21	0	0	0	0	0	0	0
Hillyard RW	Ron	31/03/52	Brinsworth		1974	1990	York City	Retired	563	34	44	14	0	0	0	0
Hilton PJ	Pat	01/05/54	Aylesham		1975	1976	Blackburn Rovers	Aldershot	26	2	0	0	1	0	0	0
Hinnigan JP	Joe	03/12/55	Liverpool		1984	1986	Preston NE	Wrexham	103	8	8	8	7	0	1	1
Hodge J	John	01/04/69	Ormskirk		1998	1999	Walsall	Northampton Town	49	5	5	6	1	0	1	0
Hodge MJ	Martin	04/02/59	Southport		1982		Everton (loan)		4	0	0	0	0	0	0	0
Hodnett JE	Joe	18/07/1896	Bilston	1943	1927		Brentford	Stafford Rangers	16	1	0	0	1	0	0	0
Holland GA	George	11/12/17	Wolverhampton	1997	1937		Bradford PA	Shrewsbury Town	10	1	0	0	0	0	0	0
Holland T	Tom	16/07/02	Sheffield	1987	1932	1935	Watford	Aylesford Paper Mills	119	6	0	1	0	0	0	0
Holt A	Andy		Sheffield		1920		Chesterfield	Mansfield Town	6	0	0	0	0	0	0	0
Hook AE	Albert		Sittingbourne		1924		Maidstone Utd.	Sittingbourne	20	7	0	0	1	0	0	0
Hope CJ	Chris	14/11/72	Sheffield		2000	2002	Scunthorpe Utd.		138	8	10	0	7	0	2	0
Hopkins TE	Tom	1911	Broad Lanes		1933	1936	Bilston	London Paper Mills	87	4	0	3	1	0	0	1
Horrix DV	Dean	21/11/61	Taplow	1990	1982		Millwall	Reading	14	0	0	0	0	0	0	0
Houghton SA	Scott	22/10/71	Hitchin		1992		Tottenham H. (loan)		3	0	0	0	0	0	0	0
Housden D	Denis	15/03/53	City of London		1971	1972	App.	Canterbury City	16	0	1	0	1	0	0	0
Howard JF	Fred		Long Eaton		1920	1921	Derby County	Ayr United	18	2	0	0	3	0	2	0

Name		D.O.B	Place of Birth	Died	First Season	Last Season	Previous Club	Next Club	Appearances Lge	FAC	FLC	Oth.	Goals Lge	FAC	FLC	Oth.
Huddart DJ	Dave	18/11/37	Maryport		1962	1964	Aldershot	Ramsgate Ath.	10	1	1	0	0	0	0	0
Hudson GA	Geoff	14/10/31	Leeds		1963	1964	Crewe Alexandra	Lincoln City	81	3	5	0	0	0	0	0
Hughes A	Arthur	23/11/27	Linlithgow		1955		Grimsby Town	Dover Athletic	5	0	0	0	1	0	0	0
Hughes HJ	Harry	08/10/29	Nuneaton		1958	1962	Bournemouth	Guildford City	204	13	4	0	14	0	2	0
Hughes SJ	Billy	29/07/60	Folkestone		1975	1980	App.	Crystal Palace	126	5	6	0	8	0	0	0
Humphrey J	John	31/01/61	Paddington		1996		Charlton Ath.	Brighton & Hove A.	9	0	3	1	0	0	0	0
Hunt DP	Dennis	08/09/37	Portsmouth		1958	1967	Army	Brentford	321	17	17	0	6	0	0	0
Hunt PJ	Peter	02/07/52	Stepney		1977	1978	Charlton Ath.	Gravesend & N'fleet	23	4	1	0	0	0	0	0
Hutchinson IN	Ian	07/11/72	Stockton		1994		Cork City	Halifax Town	5	0	0	0	0	0	0	0
Hutton J	Joe	18/11/27	Dundee		1957		Stoke City	Millwall	36	2	0	0	6	0	1	0
Ipoua G	Guy	14/01/76	Douala, Cameroon		2000	2002	Scunthorpe Utd.	Livingston	82	6	6	0	12	1	2	0
Jacks GC	George	14/03/46	Stepney		1972	1975	Millwall	Gravesend & N'fleet	159	5	10	0	20	1	0	0
Jackson R	Richard	04/07/00	Spennymoor		1932	1933	Rotherham Town	Canterbury Waverley	63	6	0	1	0	0	0	0
Jacobs SD	Steve	05/07/61	West Ham		1986		Charlton Ath.	Retired	7	1	0	4	0	0	0	0
Jacques J	Joe	12/09/44	Consett	1981	1972	1974	Southend Utd.	Dartford	73	1	2	0	1	0	0	0
James KE	Kevin	03/01/80	Southwark		2000	2002	Charlton Ath.		32	1	2	0	3	0	0	0
Jamieson HJ	Harold	09/12/08	Wallsend		1930	1931	Crawcrook Alb.	Kilwinning Rgs	17	1	0	0	1	0	0	0
Jenkins RJ	Randolph	05/09/23	Sligo		1950		Fulham	Fulham	2	3	0	0	0	0	1	0
Jervis WJ	William	22/01/42	Liverpool		1961		Blackburn Rovers	Stalybridge Celtic	1	0	0	0	0	0	0	0
Johnson JD	Jeff	26/11/53	Cardiff		1982	1984	Newport County	Port Vale	88	9	8	2	4	1	1	0
Johnson KP	Kevin	29/08/52	Doncaster		1973		Southend Utd. (loan)		1	0	0	0	0	0	0	0
Johnson LD	Leon	10/05/81	Shoreditch		2002		Southend Utd.		18	1	1	0	0	0	0	0
Johnson PE	Peter	05/10/58	Harrogate		1989	1990	Southend Utd.	Airdrieonians	69	2	4	3	2	0	0	0
Johnson T	Tommy	15/01/71	Newcastle		2002		Glasgow Celtic		26	1	2	0	2	1	0	0
Johnston TB	Tommy	18/08/27	Loanhead		1961		Leyton Orient	Folkestone	35	1	0	0	10	0	0	0
Jolley TA	Terry	13/04/59	Greenhithe		1976	1979	App.	Dover	21	1	0	0	5	0	0	0
Jones EJ	John				1937				5	0	0	0	0	0	0	0
Jones NE	Norman		Liverpool		1923	1926	Derby County		98	13	0	0	2	0	1	0
Jones WG	William		Chatham		1929	1931	Chatham Town	Sittingbourne	46	1	0	0	2	0	0	0
Jordan DC	David	26/10/71	Gillingham		1990		Trainee	Ashford Town	2	0	0	0	0	0	0	0
Joseph F	Francis	06/03/60	Kilburn		1988	1989	Sheffield Utd.	Crewe Alexandra	18	0	2	0	1	0	0	0
Judges BJ	Barry	23/09/40	Rainham, Kent		1957	1958	Trainee	Gravesend & N'fleet	3	0	0	0	0	0	0	0
Keegan JE	Jimmy	23/10/1898	Barrow	1973	1924		Barrow	Peterboro & Fletton	4	0	0	0	0	0	0	0
Kelly J	John	04/05/02	Wishaw		1926		Brighton & Hove A.	Crystal Palace	16	0	0	0	0	0	0	0
Kelly JL	Jim	14/07/26	Holborn	1996	1951		Watford	Folkestone Town	3	0	0	0	0	0	0	0
Kemp DM	David	20/02/53	Harrow		1981		Plymouth Argyle (loan)		9	2	0	0	2	0	0	0
Kennedy AJ	Andy	08/10/64	Stirling		1994		Brighton & Hove A.	Hong Kong	2	0	0	0	0	0	0	0
Kent MJ	Mike	12/01/51	North Anston		1970		Wolves (loan)		11	0	0	0	0	0	0	0
Kidd GI	George	20/05/09	Dundee	1988	1931	1934	Charlton Ath.	Luton Town	119	3	0	2	2	0	0	0
Kimble GL	Garry	06/08/66	Poole		1989	1990	Maidstone Utd.	Peterborough Utd.	48	1	1	1	0	0	0	0
King G	George	05/01/23	Warkworth		1952		Bradford City	King's Lynn	19	2	0	0	5	0	0	0
King MF	Marlon	26/04/80	Dulwich		2000	2002	Barnet		90	6	7	0	36	4	3	0
Kingshott FJ	Freddie	20/06/29	St Pancras		1955	1956	Doncaster Rovers	Dartford	45	5	0	0	0	0	0	0
Kingsnorth TH	Tom	16/04/17	Sittingbourne		1950		Lloyds Paper Mills	Sittingbourne	28	14	0	0	0	0	0	0
Kirman H	Harold	03/12/30	Hull		1953		Hull City	Hull City	8	0	0	0	0	0	0	0
Kite PD	Phil	26/10/62	Bristol		1986	1988	Southampton	Bournemouth	70	5	5	10	0	0	0	0
Knight GJ	Graham	05/01/52	Rochester		1970	1978	App.	Maidstone Utd.	246	13	15	0	10	0	0	0
Knott GR	Gareth	19/01/76	Blackwood		1994		Tottenham Hotspur (loan)		5	0	0	0	0	0	0	0
Laing D	Davie	20/02/25	Strathmiglo		1957	1958	Hibernian	Margate	82	6	0	0	5	0	0	0
Lambert K	Ken	07/06/28	Sheffield		1952		Barnsley	Swindon Town	37	0	0	0	10	0	0	0
Lansdowne W	Billy	28/04/59	Epping		1982		Charlton Ath.	Kalmar FF (Swe)	6	0	0	0	2	0	0	0
Lee CE	Christian	08/10/76	Aylesbury		1999		Northampton Town	Bristol Rovers	3	0	2	0	0	0	0	0
Lee TC	Trevor	03/07/54	Lewisham		1980	1982	Colchester Utd.	Bournemouth	47	2	2	3	14	0	0	0
Legge AE	Albert	19/01/01	Hednesford	1998	1928		Wolves	Charlton Ath.	31	1	0	0	5	0	0	0
Leslie JA	John	25/10/55	Plumstead		1983	1984	Wimbledon	Millwall	65	8	6	2	12	1	4	0
Lester FC	Fred	20/02/11	Rochester	1974	1930	1937	Chatham Town	Sheffield Wed.	201	7	0	3	0	0	0	0
Lewin DR	Ron	21/06/20	Edmonton	1985	1950	1954	Fulham	Chatham	191	13	0	0	1	0	0	0
Lewis D	Dan	04/12/02	Mardy	1965	1931		Arsenal	Retired	6	0	0	0	0	0	0	0
Lewis DIE	Derek	10/06/29	Edmonton	1953	1950	1951	Bury Town	Preston NE	48	3	0	0	31	0	1	0
Lewis KJ	Junior	09/10/73	Wembley		1999	2000	Hendon	Leicester City	59	9	6	4	8	0	0	0
Lewis T	Trevor	06/01/21	Blackwood		1952	1954	Coventry City	Kidderminster Harr.	26	0	0	0	2	0	0	0
Ley OAG	George	07/04/46	Exminster		1974	1975	Dallas Tornado	Dallas Tornado	87	3	3	0	3	0	0	0
Liddle JF	Fred	18/09/04	Dunston-on-Tyne		1932	1933	Newcastle United	Coventry City	81	6	0	1	18	0	1	0
Lillis JW	Jason	01/10/69	Chatham		1987	1988	Trainee	Jaro (Finland)	29	2	4	3	3	2	1	1
Lim HC	Harvey	30/08/67	Halesworth		1989	1992	Ornskoldsvik (Swe)	Kettering Town	90	4	3	8	0	0	0	0
Lindsey K	Keith	25/11/46	Scunthorpe	2003	1972	1974	Port Vale	Dartford	73	0	2	0	5	0	0	0
Lindsey S	Scott	04/05/72	Walsall		1994		Bridlington Town	Dover Athletic	12	0	0	0	0	0	0	0
Lisbie KA	Kevin	17/10/78	Hackney		1998		Charlton Ath. (loan)		7	0	0	0	4	0	0	0
Livesey CE	Charlie	06/02/38	West Ham		1961	1962	Chelsea	Watford	47	1	0	0	17	0	0	0
Lloyd KJJ	Kevin	12/06/58	Wolverhampton		1980		Cardiff City	Worcester City	1	1	0	0	0	0	0	0
Loasby H	Harry	1910	Kettering		1930		Northampton Town	Luton Town	35	2	0	0	19	0	3	0
Loftus JL	Leo	24/01/06	Ferryhill	1992	1935		Brighton & Hove A	Barrow	2	0	0	0	0	0	0	0
Long TG	Trevor	01/07/31	Smethwick		1952	1954	Wolves	Reading	67	3	0	0	15	0	1	0
Lovell M	Mark	16/07/83	Beckenham		2000		Trainee	Leyton Orient	1	0	0	0	0	0	0	0
Lovell SJ	Steve	16/07/60	Swansea		1986	1992	Millwall	Sittingbourne	233	10	17	15	94	5	2	3
Lucas P	Paul	27/04/36	Coseley	1992	1956	1957	Aston Villa	Released	44	3	0	0	7	0	0	0
Luff NJ	Neil	09/04/69	Bletchley		1987		Trainee	Thanet United	1	0	0	0	0	0	0	0
McAleer J	Joe	08/03/10	Blythswood		1936		Clapton Orient	Brideville	9	0	0	1	3	0	0	0
McAlpine JW	Jim	05/02/1887	Ravenscraig		1921	1922	Millwall	Retired	47	4	0	0	0	0	0	0
McCafferty J	Jim		Stevenston		1929		Shieldmuir Celtic		14	1	0	0	0	0	0	0

Name		D.O.B	Place of Birth	Died	First Season	Last Season	Previous Club	Next Club	Appearances Lge	Appearances FAC	Appearances FLC	Appearances Oth.	Goals Lge	Goals FAC	Goals FLC	Goals Oth.
McCorkindale J	John	10/08/34	Campbeltown		1957		Tonbridge	Hastings United	8	0	0	0	0	0	0	0
McCormick D	Donald				1920			Sheppey United	1	0	0	0	0	0	0	0
McDonagh JM	Jim 'Seamus'	06/10/52	Rotherham		1984		Notts County (loan)		10	0	0	0	0	0	0	0
McDonald DH	David	02/01/71	Dublin		1990		Tottenham H. (loan)		10	0	0	2	0	0	0	0
McDonald J	James	18/04/32	Greenock		1956		Dumbarton	Released	1	0	0	0	0	0	0	0
McGlinchey BK	Brian	26/10/77	Derry		1999	2000	Port Vale	Plymouth Argyle	14	4	4	1	1	0	1	0
McGregor J	John	02/08/00	Darlington	1993	1930	1931	Royal Navy	Crystal Palace	68	2	0	0	2	0	0	0
Machin M	Mel	16/04/45	Newcastle-under-Lyme		1966	1970	Port Vale	Bournemouth	157	12	8	0	11	0	1	0
McIntyre PF	Patrick	14/03/43	Aylesham		1960	1962	Juniors	Dover	10	0	1	0	0	0	0	0
McKee F	Frank	25/01/23	Cowdenbeath	1988	1952	1954	Birmingham City	Gloucester City	53	4	0	0	0	0	0	0
McKee R	Reg	1900	Erith		1925	1926	Erith & Belvedere	Charlton Ath.	38	2	0	0	14	0	1	0
McManus EJ	Eddie	08/08/37	Ramsgate		1960		Bournemouth	Gravesend & N'fleet	3	0	0	0	0	0	0	0
McMillan ST	Stuart	17/09/1896	Leicester	1963	1920	1921	Chelsea	Wolves	30	4	0	0	2	0	0	0
Macowat IS	Ian	19/11/65	Oxford		1984	1985	Everton	Crewe Alexandra	5	0	1	2	0	0	0	0
McVeigh J	Jim	02/07/49	Bamford		1970	1971	Wolves	Maidstone Utd.	48	1	2	0	1	0	0	0
McWhirr J	James	13/01/05	Partick	1976	1925		Ashfield (Glasgow)	Norwich City	6	0	0	0	0	0	0	0
Maguire LGR	Les	31/01/29	Bethnal Green		1950	1951		Tonbridge	6	0	0	0	2	0	0	0
Maher J	Johnny	06/11/33	Manchester		1955		Walsall	Guildford City	2	0	0	0	1	0	0	0
Manuel WAJ	Billy	28/06/69	Hackney		1988	1996	Tottenham Hotspur	Brentford	108	4	2	6	4	0	0	0
Marks CWA	Charlie	21/12/19	Eccles, Kent		1950	1956	Tooting & Mitcham	Tonbridge	265	20	0	0	8	0	1	0
Marsden H	Harry	1902	Bentley		1934		Brighton & Hove A.	York City	31	1	0	1	0	0	0	0
Marshall AJ	Andy	14/04/75	Bury St Edmunds		1996		Norwich City (loan)		5	0	1	1	0	0	0	0
Marshall F	Frank	1904	Shettleston	1928	1924	1926	Shettleston	Brentford	101	13	0	0	16	0	4	0
Marshall OT	Owen	17/09/1892	Nottingham	1963	1921	1922	Chelsea	Maidstone Utd.	39	3	0	0	0	0	0	0
Martin D	Dave	25/04/63	East Ham		1995		Bristol City	Leyton Orient	31	4	1	1	1	0	1	0
Martin EJ	Eliot	27/09/72	Plumstead		1991	1993	Trainee	Chelmsford City	60	4	2	4	1	0	0	0
					1994		Chelmsford City	Margate								
Martin HJ	Henry		Chatham		1921	1922	Chatham Town		7	0	0	0	2	0	0	0
Martin SH	Sydney		Durban, South Africa		1929		Grimsby Town		2	1	0	0	0	0	0	0
Mason SM	Sam	04/07/06	Fauldhouse	1974	1926		Partick Thistle	Exeter City	19	0	0	0	1	0	0	0
Masters NB	Neil	25/05/72	Lisburn		1997		Wolves		11	0	0	1	0	0	0	0
Matthews GT	Terry	25/02/36	Leyton		1962		Aldershot	Ashford Town	10	1	1	0	1	0	0	0
Matthews LJ	Lee	16/01/79	Middlesbrough		1999		Leeds United (loan)		5	0	0	0	0	0	0	0
Mautone S	Steve	10/08/70	Myrtleford, Australia		1999		Crystal Palace	Slough Town	1	0	0	0	0	0	0	0
Mehmet DN	David	02/12/60	Camberwell		1982	1985	Charlton Ath.	Millwall	132	11	9	3	39	1	3	0
Meredith JF	John	23/09/40	Hatfield, South Yorks		1963	1968	Chesterfield	Bournemouth	228	11	12	0	7	0	0	0
Meston SW	Sammy	30/05/02	Southampton	1953	1926	1927	Southampton	Everton	61	7	0	0	8	0	1	0
Micallef C	Tarki	24/01/61	Cardiff		1984		Newport County	Cardiff City	2	0	0	0	0	0	0	0
Micklewhite G	Gary	21/03/61	Southwark		1993	1995	Derby County	Slough Town	95	10	4	4	3	0	1	0
Millar W	Willie	24/07/24	Irvine	1995	1953	1955	Swindon Town	Accrington Stanley	91	6	0	0	35	0	3	0
Miller BS	Barry	29/03/76	Greenford		1999		Farnborough Town	Doncaster Rovers	4	0	3	0	0	0	0	0
Miller MJ	Mark	22/09/62	Tynemouth		1981	1982	Whitley Bay	Whitley Bay	9	1	0	0	1	0	0	0
Miller RE	Ralph	22/06/41	Slough		1965	1967	Charlton Ath.	Bournemouth	103	2	8	0	4	0	0	0
Millington T	Tommy	12/01/06	Wrexham	1968	1927	1928	Everton	Oswestry Town	38	2	0	0	2	0	0	0
Mills AS	Arthur	1906	Karachi, India		1933		Luton Town	Burton Town	33	2	0	1	12	0	1	0
Milton A	Alfred	1896	Masborough		1920		Coventry City		1	0	0	0	0	0	0	0
Moffatt RW	Bob	07/10/45	Portsmouth		1965	1967	Portsmouth	Margate	24	0	0	0	1	0	0	0
Mooney H	Hugh	23/05/07	Belfast	1975	1933		Aberdeen		4	0	0	0	0	0	0	0
Moorcroft M	Maurice	04/11/29	Chesterfield		1952		Sheffield Utd.	Released	8	0	0	0	0	0	0	0
Moore H	Howard	05/03/47	Canterbury		1967		Coventry City	Southend Utd.	17	0	2	0	0	0	0	0
Moore SC	Sammy	06/09/34	Birmingham	1994	1958	1959	Walsall	Dover	33	0	0	0	9	0	0	0
Morgan E	Ernie	13/01/27	Barnsley		1953	1956	Lincoln City	Chatham T (coach)	155	8	0	0	73	0	4	0
Morgan W	Wendell	22/04/35	Gorseinon		1957		Brentford	Swansea Town	34	4	0	0	3	0	1	0
Morris FW	Fred	15/06/29	Oswestry	1997	1960		Crewe Alexandra	Chester	11	0	0	0	1	0	0	0
Morris MJ	Mark	26/09/62	Morden		1996		Bournemouth (loan)		6	0	2	0	0	0	0	0
Moss NG	Neil	10/05/75	New Milton		1997		Southampton (loan)		10	0	0	0	0	0	0	0
Moss RG	Roy	05/09/41	Maldon		1962	1963	Tottenham Hotspur	Johannsburg Bros (SA)	14	2	0	0	3	0	0	0
Murray JG	John	15/07/27	Lambeth		1951		Sittingbourne	Betteshanger CW	4	0	0	0	0	0	0	0
Musker R	Russell	10/07/62	Liverpool		1983	1985	Bristol City	Torquay United	64	10	3	2	7	0	1	0
Naylor DJ	Dominic	12/08/70	Watford		1995		Plymouth Argyle	Leyton Orient	31	3	2	1	1	1	0	0
Ndah GE	George	23/12/74	Dulwich		1997		Crystal Palace (loan)		4	0	0	0	0	0	0	0
Neal RG	Reginald	1914	Blackpool		1937		Southport		14	0	0	0	2	0	0	0
Needham GW	George	28/04/1894	Staveley	1967	1920	1923	Derby County	Northampton Town	122	9	0	0	13	0	2	0
Nekrews TJ	Tommy	20/03/33	Chatham		1953	1957	Chelsea	Watford	42	0	0	0	0	0	0	0
Newman RV	Ron	19/01/34	Fareham		1963	1965	Crystal Palace	Atlanta Chiefs	93	3	5	0	20	2	0	0
Niblett V	Vic	09/12/24	Frimley		1951	1955	West Ham Utd.	(trainer)	154	10	0	0	0	0	0	0
Nichol JB	Jimmy	07/04/03	Tollcross	1954	1925	1937	Glasgow Perthshire	Portsmouth	91	6	0	1	2	0	0	0
Nicholl TJ	Terry	16/09/52	Wilmslow		1976	1980	Southend Utd.	Wichita Wings (US)	184	13	7	0	11	0	1	0
Nicol G	George	14/02/03	Saltcoats	1968	1932	1934	Brighton & Hove A.		66	5	0	1	38	0	4	0
Norris R	Russell	01/02/71	Hoo		1989		Trainee	Dartford	5	0	2	0	0	0	0	0
North EJ	Joe	23/09/1895	Burton-on-Trent	1955	1923		Reading	Norwich City	39	4	0	0	11	0	6	0
Nosworthy NPH	Nyron	11/10/80	Brixton		1998	2002	Trainee		110	12	5	3	3	0	0	0
Oakes KB	Keith	03/07/56	Bedworth		1984	1986	Newport County	Fulham	86	7	9	4	7	0	0	1
O'Connor MA	Mark	10/03/63	Rochford		1989	1992	Bournemouth	Bournemouth	156	13	12	7	9	0	0	1
					1995	1997	Bournemouth	(coaching staff)								
O'Donnell N	Neil	21/12/49	Glasgow		1974	1975	Norwich City	Sheffield Wed.	24	0	4	0	0	0	0	0
Ollerenshaw E	Ernest	11/04/1893	Hollingworth	1965	1920		Manchester City		1	0	0	0	0	0	0	0
Omoyimni E	Manny	28/12/77	Nigeria		1999		West Ham Utd. (loan)		9	0	2	0	3	0	0	0
O'Neill J	James	26/08/14	Dumfries		1937		Gateshead	Notts County	8	0	0	0	0	0	0	0
Onuora I	Iffy	28/07/67	Glasgow		1996	1997	Mansfield Town	Swindon Town	148	9	11	4	49	2	3	1
					1999	2001	Swindon Town	Sheffield United								

Name		D.O.B	Place of Birth	Died	First Season	Last Season	Previous Club	Next Club	Appearances				Goals			
									Lge	FAC	FLC	Oth.	Lge	FAC	FLC	Oth.
Orford CH	Charles	12/01/1899	Hackney	1977	1924				1	0	0	0	0	0	0	0
Orr A	Albert	05/09/04	Eccles	1974	1934		Torquay United	Stalybridge Celtic	12	0	0	0	0	0	0	0
Osborn KG	Ken	23/11/48	Hampstead		1968	1969	QPR	Dartford	2	0	0	0	0	0	0	0
Osborn SE	Simon	19/01/72	New Addington		2001	2002	Port Vale	Walsall	46	3	0	0	5	0	0	0
Osborne LW	Lawrie	20/10/67	Stratford		1991	1992	Maidstone Utd.		6	0	0	0	1	0	0	0
O'Shea TJ	Tim	12/11/66	Pimlico		1988	1991	Leyton Orient	Eastern (HK)	112	3	3	7	2	0	0	0
Oswald W	Willie	03/08/00	Dundee		1922		Dundee Celtic	St Johnstone	13	0	0	0	3	0	0	0
Ovard FC	Frank	16/12/55	Evesham		1981		Maidstone Utd.	Maidstone Utd.	6	3	0	0	0	0	0	0
Overton J	John	02/05/56	Rotherham		1976	1980	Aston Villa	Frickley Ath.	178	12	15	0	10	1	0	0
Owers AR	Adrian	26/02/65	Danbury		1990		Brighton & Hove A. (loan)		10	0	0	0	0	0	0	0
Owers P	Phil	28/04/55	Bishop Auckland		1975		Darlington	Darlington	2	0	0	0	0	0	0	0
Palmer LJ	Lee	19/09/70	Gillingham		1987	1994	Trainee	Cambridge Utd.	120	8	8	7	5	0	0	0
Palmer W	Bill	1888	Barnsley		1922		Bristol Rovers	Doncaster Rovers	36	2	0	0	5	0	0	0
Parker WS	William				1931				1	0	0	0	0	0	0	0
Parks A	Tony	26/01/63	Hackney		1987		Tottenham Hotspur (loan)		2	0	0	0	0	0	0	0
Parmenter TL	Terry	21/10/47	Romford		1971	1972	Orient	Romford	49	4	1	0	0	0	0	0
Parry W	Bill	18/02/33	Blaenau Ffestiniog		1955	1960	Tottenham Hotspur	Margate	200	18	2	0	4	0	0	0
Pateman GE	George	08/05/10	Chatham	1973	1929	1930	Canterbury Waverley	Portsmouth	17	0	0	0	5	0	0	0
Patrick WCG	Bill	12/03/32	Lochgelly	2003	1958	1959	Coventry City	Folkestone Town	47	3	0	0	14	0	1	0
Patterson M	Mark	13/09/68	Leeds		1997	2002	Plymouth Argyle	Dover Athletic	124	7	12	4	2	0	0	0
Payne B	Brian	04/11/37	Altrincham		1957	1959	Huddersfield T	Gravesend & N'fleet	36	4	0	0	3	0	2	0
Payton CC	Cliff	16/10/35	Brighton		1958	1959	Tonbridge	Dartford	24	1	0	0	5	0	0	0
Peach DS	David	21/01/51	Bedford		1969	1973	Bedford Town	Southampton	187	9	9	0	30	1	0	0
Peacock GK	Gavin	18/11/67	Eltham		1987	1988	QPR	Bournemouth	70	2	4	5	11	0	0	1
Pearce GC	Graham	08/07/59	Hammersmith		1986	1987	Brighton & Hove A.	Brentford	65	6	6	10	0	0	0	0
Pearce H	Harold		Oakengates		1928		Oakengates Town	Charlton Ath.	9	0	0	0	2	0	0	0
Pearson R	Ricky	18/10/70	Ulcombe		1988		Trainee	Wycombe Wan.	9	0	1	0	0	0	0	0
					1989		Wycombe Wan.	Ashford Town								
Pennock AB	Adrian	27/03/71	Ipswich		1996	2002	Bournemouth	Gravesend & N'fleet	168	11	9	11	2	0	1	1
Perpetuini DP	David	26/09/79	Hitchin		2001	2002	Watford		63	4	5	0	3	0	0	0
Perry A	Andy	28/12/62	Dulwich		1988		Portsmouth	Woking	13	0	2	0	0	0	0	0
Phillips ME	Michael	22/01/83	Dulwich		2000		Trainee		1	0	0	0	0	0	0	0
Phoenix WE	Eric	20/01/32	Manchester		1954	1955	Hastings United	Exeter City	17	0	0	0	2	0	0	0
Picken AH	Albert	04/08/04	Wellington	1989	1928		Derby County	Wellington T	8	1	0	0	1	0	0	0
Pickering WH	Bill	01/11/01	Birmingham	1971	1926	1927	Merthyr Town	Huddersfield T	45	4	0	0	0	0	0	0
Pike C	Chris	19/10/61	Cardiff		1994		Hereford Utd.	Barry Town	27	4	0	1	13	0	4	1
Pinnock JE	James	01/08/78	Dartford		1996	1999	Trainee	Kingstonian	9	0	3	4	0	0	0	0
Piper GH	Gilbert	21/06/21	Northfleet	1987	1950		Tottenham Hotspur	Dartford	4	11	0	0	0	0	0	0
Piper LH	Lenny	08/08/77	Camberwell		1996	1997	Wimbledon	Welling United	20	1	4	1	1	0	0	1
Place BA	Brendan	13/12/65	Dublin		1989		Athlone Town	Longford Town	4	2	0	2	0	0	0	0
Pollitt MF	Mike	29/02/72	Bolton		1997		Notts County (loan)		6	0	0	0	0	0	0	0
Pollock S	Stewart	25/09/33	Bellshill		1956		Motherwell	Ramsgate Ath.	10	1	0	0	0	0	1	0
Polston AA	Andy	26/07/70	Walthamstow		1991		Tottenham H. (loan)		2	0	0	2	0	0	0	0
Poulton GH	George	23/04/29	Holborn		1951		Army	Leyton Orient	5	0	0	0	1	0	0	0
Pound JHK	Ken	24/08/44	Portsmouth		1969	1970	Bournemouth	Weymouth	73	7	3	0	11	0	1	0
Powell CD	Colin	07/07/48	Hendon		1981	1982	Charlton Ath.	Dartford	55	8	7	3	1	0	1	0
Poxton JH	Jimmy	02/02/03	Staveley	1971	1927	1928	West Bromwich A.	Millwall	43	1	0	0	8	0	1	0
Price KG	Ken	26/02/55	Dudley		1976	1982	Southend Utd.	Reading	255	21	18	0	78	7	4	0
Pritchard HK	Howard	18/10/58	Cardiff		1986	1987	Bristol City	Walsall	88	5	8	12	20	0	1	2
Proverbs RJ	Roy	08/07/32	Wednesbury		1957	1961	Bournemouth	Canterbury City	143	7	3	0	2	0	0	0
Pulis AR	Tony	16/01/58	Newport		1989		Bournemouth	Bournemouth(p/coach)	16	0	0	1	0	0	0	0
Pulley GA	Gordon	18/09/36	Stourbridge		1958	1965	Millwall	Peterborough Utd.	203	10	9	0	46	4	1	0
Purcell GW	George	18/02/05	Barnsley		1932	1933	Exeter City	Gainsborough Trin.	47	6	0	0	18	0	2	0
Puttnam DP	David	03/02/67	Leicester		1995	1996	Lincoln City	Swansea City	40	5	6	2	2	1	0	0
Pybus G	George	22/07/11	Brandon		1935		Chelsea	Folkestone Town	6	0	0	1	1	0	0	0
Quirke DJ	David	11/01/47	Ballina		1967	1973	Bedford Town	Durban U (SA)	230	11	13	0	0	3	0	0
Quow TS	Trevor	28/09/60	Peterborough		1986	1988	Peterborough Utd.	Northampton Town	79	5	11	11	3	1	1	0
Rackstraw C	Charlie	23/04/38	Sheffield		1964	1966	Chesterfield	Bradford City	94	5	5	0	25	1	1	0
Raleigh S	Simeon	24/03/09	Rotherham	1934	1932	1934	Hull City		83	5	0	1	34	0	0	0
Ramage AW	Andy	03/10/74	Barking		1994		Dagenham & Red.	Sligo Rovers	12	0	0	1	1	0	0	0
Ramsay R	Raymond				1922		Walsall		3	0	0	0	0	0	0	0
Ramsell LT	Leonard	20/08/1897	Gillingham	1975	1924		Chatham Town	Chatham Town	10	1	0	0	2	0	0	0
Randle HC	Harry	31/07/06	Stonebroom	1976	1934	1936	Southend Utd.	Accrington Stanley	110	5	0	4	2	0	0	0
Ratcliffe S	Simon	08/02/67	Davyhulme		1995	1997	Brentford	Retired	105	7	11	1	10	2	1	0
Rattray KW	Kevin	06/10/68	Tottenham		1995		Woking	Barnet	26	2	1	2	3	0	0	0
Read AH	Arthur	1894	Saxilby		1922	1923	Aberdare Ath.	Lincoln City	61	6	0	0	3	0	0	0
Read TW	Trevett				1923		Royal Navy		1	0	0	0	0	0	0	0
Reay AF	Archie	15/09/01	West Derby	1962	1922		Brentford	Norwich City	15	2	0	0	0	0	0	0
Record CR	Charles	26/07/02	Gillingham		1925				3	0	0	0	1	0	0	0
Reddock C	Charlie	1902	Rutherglen		1925		Shettleston	Brentford	29	1	0	0	0	0	0	0
Reeves A	Alan	19/11/67	Birkenhead		1988		Norwich City (loan)		18	0	0	0	0	0	0	0
Reinelt RS	Robbie	11/03/74	Loughton		1993	1994	Wivenhoe Town	Colchester Utd.	52	7	3	4	5	1	2	0
Renwick J	James	1910	Larkhill		1931		East Stirling	East Stirling	5	0	0	0	3	0	0	0
Richards AC	Albert	18/07/03	Chatham	1973	1925		Luton Town	Chatham Town	25	0	0	0	4	0	0	0
Richardson DJ	Damien	02/08/47	Dublin		1972	1980	Shamrock Rovers	Gravesend & N'fleet	323	14	20	0	94	5	3	0
Riddick GG	Gordon	06/11/43	Langleybury		1966	1969	Luton Town	Charlton Ath.	114	4	7	0	24	1	2	0
Ridley RM	Bob	30/05/42	Reading		1961	1966	Portsmouth	Westfield Appollon (SA)	73	2	4	0	8	1	0	0
Rigg T	Tommy	20/02/20	Bedlington	1995	1951	1955	Consett	Gateshead (trainer)	192	9	0	0	0	0	0	0
Riggs LJ	Les	30/05/35	Portsmouth		1953	1965	Crewe Alexandra	Ramsgate Ath (p/m)	170	12	0	0	4	0	2	0
Ritchie PM	Paul	25/01/69	St Andrews		1992	1994	Dundee (loan)		11	0	0	1	4	0	0	0
Rivers W	Wally	08/01/09	Throckley		1928		Throckley Welfare	Crystal Palace	5	0	0	0	1	0	0	0

Name		D.O.B	Place of Birth	Died	First Season	Last Season	Previous Club	Next Club	Appearances				Goals			
									Lge	FAC	FLC	Oth.	Lge	FAC	FLC	Oth.
Robertson JW	Jim 'Jock'	21/02/1898	Chatham	1970	1920	1932	Chatham Centrals	Canterbury Waverley	358	30	0	0	1	0	0	0
Robinson CA	Charlie	1906	Pegswood		1933	1934	Exeter City	Accrington Stanley	34	1	0	0	0	0	0	0
Robinson MJ	Martin	17/07/57	Ilford		1984	1986	Charlton Ath.	Southend Utd.	96	11	3	11	23	0	6	2
Robinson RJC	Robert	09/11/06	Borden	1990	1929		RAF		2	0	0	0	0	0	0	0
Robinson TE	Tommy	11/02/09	Coalville	1982	1936		Northampton Town	Walsall	35	2	0	2	12	0	0	1
Robinson TJD	Thomas	14/09/1893	Liverpool	1951	1920		Everton		2	1	0	0	1	0	0	0
Roe A	Archie	09/12/1893	Hull	1947	1920		Birmingham	Castleford Town	16	1	0	0	2	0	0	0
Roeder GV	Glenn	13/12/55	Woodford		1992		Purfleet	Watford (manager)	6	0	0	1	0	0	0	0
Rogers D	David	1892	Stockport		1926	1927	Swindon Town		58	3	0	0	0	0	0	0
Rogers KJ	Kenny	21/11/54	Chatham		1972	1973	App.	Canterbury City	13	0	0	0	1	0	0	0
Rolling FJ	Franck	23/08/68	Colmar, France		1998		Bournemouth	Wycombe Wan.	1	0	0	0	0	0	0	0
Ronaldson K	Ken	27/09/45	Leith		1969	1970	Bristol Rovers	Released	6	1	1	0	0	0	1	0
Rose RA	Richard	08/09/82	Pembury		2000	2002	Trainee		9	0	1	0	0	0	0	0
Rossiter A	Bud	24/11/07	Ashford, Kent	1993	1935		Crystal Palace	Clapton Orient	19	2	0	1	0	0	0	0
Rossiter DP	Don	08/06/35	Strood		1957		Dartford	Dover	1	0	0	0	0	0	0	0
Rotherham AE	Albert	Nov 1903	Wednesbury		1931		Bath City		4	0	0	0	0	0	0	0
Rowden HL	Horace	04/03/00	Gillingham		1921	1923	Chatham Centrals		9	0	0	0	0	0	0	0
Rowe RC	Rodney	30/07/75	Huddersfield		1999	2000	York City	Hull City	22	0	1	1	4	0	0	0
Rushbury DG	David	20/02/56	Wolverhampton		1984		Carlisle Utd.	Doncaster Rovers	12	0	0	0	0	0	0	0
Russell GT	George	07/07/1893	Chatham		1920				3	0	0	0	0	0	0	0
Russell HW	Hughie	10/03/21	Redcar	1991	1950	1951	Army	Retired	61	16	0	0	8	12	0	0
Rutherford J	Jack	1892	Bedlington	1930	1924	1926	York City		84	5	0	0	1	0	1	0
Rutherford J(2)	Jack	06/11/08	Nenthead		1928	1930	Crawcrook Celtic	Watford	44	2	0	0	0	0	0	0
Ryder R	Bob	11/07/43	Bolton		1964	1967	Nantwich	Bedford Town	8	0	0	0	0	0	0	0
Sage M	Mel	24/03/64	Gillingham		1981	1985	App.	Derby County	132	12	10	5	5	0	2	0
Sambrook AJ	Andy	13/07/79	Chatham		1996		Trainee	Released	1	0	0	0	0	0	0	0
Samuel JL	JLloyd	29/03/81	Trinidad		2001		Aston Villa (loan)		8	0	0	0	0	0	0	0
Sanders PCW	Peter	07/09/42	Newport		1961		Newport County	Prescot Cables	2	0	0	0	0	0	0	0
Saunders MP	Mark	23/07/71	Reading		1998	2002	Plymouth Argyle		148	10	8	7	15	0	1	0
Saunders R	Ron	06/11/32	Birkenhead		1957	1958	Tonbridge	Portsmouth	49	4	0	0	20	0	6	0
Savage WHM	William	Mar 1886	Chatham	1975	1923				4	0	0	0	0	0	0	0
Scarth JW	Jimmy	26/08/26	North Shields	2000	1951	1954	Tottenham Hotspur	Gravesend & N'fleet	138	7	0	0	24	0	1	0
Scott A	Allan	1910	Birkenhead		1933		Swindon Town	London Paper Mills	25	2	0	1	11	0	1	0
Scott EJ	Edwin	21/05/17	Portsmouth		1935	1937			50	4	0	1	3	0	1	0
Scott G	George	14/08/04	Blackhill		1930	1931	Newcastle United	North Shields	39	0	0	0	7	0	0	0
Scotting A	Alen	02/04/66	Dartford		1983		Charlton Ath.	Bromley	2	0	0	1	0	0	0	0
Sharpe JWH	John	09/10/57	Portsmouth		1978	1984	Southampton	Southampton	194	16	16	6	2	0	0	0
Shaw GE	George	13/10/00	Swinton	1973	1920		Rossington Main	Doncaster Rovers	3	0	0	0	0	0	0	0
Shaw J	James	08/08/04	Goldenhill		1931		Brentford		9	1	0	0	0	0	0	0
Shaw P	Paul	04/09/73	Burnham		2000	2002	Millwall		114	7	6	0	21	0	3	0
Shaw PK	Peter	09/01/56	Northolt		1981	1985	Charlton Ath.	Bromley	143	11	15	2	2	2	1	0
Shearer DJ	David	16/10/58	Caol		1984	1987	Grimsby Town	Bournemouth	93	8	10	8	42	2	4	2
Shearing PF	Peter	26/08/38	Uxbridge		1971	1972	Bristol Rovers	Charlton Ath (ass.mgr)	39	3	3	0	0	0	0	0
Shepherd JHE	John	29/05/32	Kensington		1959	1960	Brighton & Hove A.	Ashford Town	54	3	2	0	23	0	3	0
Shinners P	Paul	08/01/59	Westminster		1984		Fisher Athletic	Leyton Orient	4	2	0	2	0	0	0	1
Shipley GM	George	07/03/59	Newcastle		1987	1988	Charlton Ath.	Lincoln City	29	1	4	2	3	0	0	0
Shipley T	Thomas		Durham		1931	1932	Portsmouth		16	2	0	0	1	0	0	0
Shipperley DJ	Dave	12/04/52	Uxbridge		1974	1977	Charlton Ath.	Charlton Ath.	144	8	8	0	10	0	1	0
Sidebe M	Mamady	18/12/79	Timbuktu, Mali		2002		Swansea City		30	3	1	0	3	0	1	0
Simms S	Sammy	1888	Atherton	1952	1921		Swindon Town		7	1	0	0	1	0	0	0
Simpson C	Cyril	18/08/42	Aylesham		1959	1961	Local	Tunbridge Wells	18	0	1	0	0	0	0	0
Simpson GL	George	03/12/33	Shirebrook		1956		Hereford Utd.	Headington Utd.	8	0	0	0	1	0	0	0
Simpson JL	John	05/10/33	Appleby	1993	1957	1971	Lincoln City	Maidstone Utd.	571	26	19	0	0	0	0	0
Simpson TJN	Terry	08/10/38	Southampton		1968		Walsall	Swaythling Ath.	36	3	2	0	4	0	0	0
Sinning AE	Arthur	1902	Tottenham		1923		Tottenham Hotspur		12	1	0	0	2	0	0	0
Sisson T	Tom	19/10/1894	Basford	1976	1920	1922	Hucknall Byron	Lincoln City	73	6	0	0	0	0	0	0
Sitton JE	John	21/10/59	Hackney		1981	1984	Millwall	Leyton Orient	107	10	5	3	5	0	0	0
Skivington MN	Mike	24/12/21	Glasgow		1950		Leyton Orient	Brentford	8	4	0	0	0	0	0	0
Sly H	Harold	26/02/04	Appley Bridge		1927	1928	Tamworth Castle	Brighton & Hove A.	15	1	0	0	1	0	0	0
Smeaton AR	Arthur	27/09/00	South Shields	1956	1930		Luton Town		3	0	0	0	0	0	0	0
Smethurst CFV	Charles	1911	Bolsover		1936		Halifax Town		3	0	0	1	0	0	0	0
Smillie AT	Andy	15/03/41	Minster, Sheppey		1968	1970	Southend Utd.	Folkestone	94	5	2	0	7	0	2	0
Smillie N	Neil	19/07/58	Barnsley		1993	1994	Brentford	Wycombe W(yth coach)	53	4	2	1	3	0	0	0
Smith AA	Albert	1911	Bolsover		1931		Sheffield Wed.		2	0	0	0	1	0	0	0
Smith DA	David	25/06/61	Sidcup		1986	1988	Welling United	Bristol City	104	5	7	15	10	0	1	3
Smith DL	Dave	1905	Coatbridge		1929	1930	Hamilton Acad.	Brentford	26	1	0	0	0	0	0	0
Smith F	Fred		Oldham		1937		Exeter City		15	1	0	0	2	0	0	0
Smith G (1)	George	1903	Liverpool		1923		Liverpool	Tranmere Rovers	11	2	0	0	1	0	0	0
Smith G	Gary	30/12/68	Chasetown		1989		Chasetown	Hythe Town	1	0	1	0	0	0	0	0
Smith J	John				1937		Exeter City		14	0	0	1	0	0	0	0
Smith MA	Malcolm	03/08/70	Maidstone		1987		Trainee	Hythe Town	2	1	0	0	0	0	0	0
Smith NJ	Neil	30/09/71	Lambeth		1991	1996	Tottenham Hotspur	Fulham	212	18	15	8	10	1	2	2
Smith PJ(1)	Peter	06/05/32	Gosport		1954	1956	Fleetland	Snowdown CW	6	0	0	0	0	0	0	0
Smith PJ	Peter	27/05/35	Balham		1958	1959	Tunbridge Wells	Bedford Town	39	4	0	0	2	0	0	0
Smith PW	Paul	18/09/71	East Ham		1997	2002	Brentford		268	17	15	11	18	1	0	2
Smith RGJ	Bobby	15/12/41	Bournemouth		1962		Portsmouth		7	0	1	0	0	0	0	0
Smith SJ	Syd	11/07/1895	Aston		1924		Norwich City		4	3	0	0	0	0	1	0
Southall LN	Nicky	28/01/72	Stockton		1997	2002	Grimsby Town	Bolton Wanderers	178	13	7	12	18	1	3	0
Sowden PT	Paddy	01/05/29	Bradford		1952	1955	Hull City	Accrington Stanley	134	6	0	0	27	0	1	0
Sparrow BE	Brian	24/06/62	Bethnal Green		1983		Arsenal (loan)		5	2	0	1	1	0	0	1

Name		D.O.B	Place of Birth	Died	First Season	Last Season	Previous Club	Next Club	Appearances Lge	FAC	FLC	Oth.	Goals Lge	FAC	FLC	Oth.
Spearritt EA	Eddie	31/01/47	Lowestoft		1976		Carlisle Utd.	Brisbane Lions (Aus)	19	1	2	0	1	0	0	0
Speed JG	John				1929		Royal Navy		6	0	0	0	1	0	0	0
Sperring GB	George	30/04/35	Epsom		1955		Local		1	0	0	0	0	0	0	0
Spiller D	Daniel	10/10/81	Maidstone		2001	2002	Trainee		11	1	2	0	0	0	0	0
Stacey TJ	Terry	28/09/36	Mitcham		1963	1964	Watford	Ramsgate Ath.	17	1	0	0	0	0	0	0
Stanbury GH	George	24/10/05	Plymouth		1933		Plymouth Argyle	Crystal Palace	1	0	0	0	0	0	0	0
Stannard JD	Jim	06/10/62	Harold Hill		1995	1998	Fulham	Retired	106	10	10	2	0	0	0	0
Statham B	Brian	21/05/69	Zimbabwe		1997	1998	Brentford	Chesham United	20	2	2	2	0	0	0	0
Stephenson P	Paul	02/01/68	Wallsend		1992		Millwall (loan)		12	0	0	2	2	0	0	0
Stimson MN	Mark	27/12/67	Plaistow		1988		Tottenham H. (loan)		18	0	0	0	0	0	0	0
Stinson HMJ	Hugh	18/05/37	Waterfoot		1959		Accrington Stanley	Hastings United	1	0	0	0	0	0	0	0
Stocks DH	David	20/04/43	Dulwich		1965		Charlton Ath.	Bournemouth	45	1	1	0	0	0	0	0
Stokes WD	Wayne	16/02/65	Wolverhampton		1982	1983	Coventry City	Aylesbury Utd.	3	0	0	0	0	0	0	0
Stringfellow P	Peter	21/02/39	Walkden		1962	1963	Sankey's	Chesterfield	35	0	3	0	2	2	0	0
Sutton G	Gary	02/02/62	Folkestone		1980	1982	App.		11	2	3	1	0	0	0	0
Swaine MA	Mark	13/02/58	Hammersmith		1974		App.	Fulham	1	0	0	0	0	0	0	0
Sykes AV	Arthur	1902	Swindon		1924	1925	Maidstone Utd.	Folkestone	7	0	0	0	0	0	0	0
Syred TG	Thomas		Gillingham		1933	1934		Burnley	9	0	0	1	1	0	0	0
Tadman GH	George	05/11/14	Rainham, Kent	1994	1935		Bristol Rovers	Charlton Ath.	40	2	0	2	18	0	1	0
Taylor A	Albert	1910	Ashington		1937		Lincoln City	Bexleyheath	9	0	0	1	3	0	0	0
Taylor DG	Dave	17/09/40	Rochester		1957	1958	Juniors	Portsmouth	21	0	0	0	3	0	0	0
Taylor FE	Frank	16/07/01	Wolverhampton	1973	1928		Bournemouth		29	2	0	0	8	0	0	0
Taylor J	Jim	13/05/34	Strood		1956	1957	Charlton Ath.	Watford	30	3	0	0	16	0	0	0
Taylor RA	Robert	30/04/71	Norwich		1998	2001	Brentford	Manchester City	69	3	3	6	31	1	2	5
Taylor RJ	Bob	16/03/36	Croydon		1956	1958	Crystal Palace	Millwall	31	0	0	0	5	0	0	0
Taylor RV	Rod	09/09/43	Corfe Castle		1963	1965	Portsmouth	Bournemouth	11	1	1	0	0	0	1	0
Taylor TC	Thomas		Gillingham		1925			New Brighton	1	0	0	0	0	0	0	0
Taylor TWJ	Tommy	10/09/46	Wandsworth		1965		Portsmouth	Bournemouth	20	0	0	0	0	0	0	0
Tempest DM	Dale	30/12/63	Leeds		1985		Huddersfield T (loan)		9	0	0	1	4	0	0	0
Terry PA	Pat	02/10/33	Lambeth		1958	1960	Swansea Town	Northampton Town	108	9	2	0	60	0	6	0
Thear AC	Tony	04/02/48	Edmonton		1966	1968	Luton Town	Bedford Town	7	0	2	0	1	0	0	0
Thomas DWJ	Dave	06/07/17	Stepney	1991	1950	1952	Watford	Sittingbourne	80	7	0	0	42	0	4	0
Thomas GA	Glen	06/10/67	Hackney		1995	1997	Barnet	Brighton & Hove A.	28	1	0	1	0	0	0	0
Thomas RC	Rod	10/10/70	Harlesden		1991		Watford (loan)		8	0	0	0	1	0	0	0
Thompson SA	Steve	17/02/72	Manchester		1989		Trainee	Tonbridge	2	0	2	0	0	0	0	0
Thompson TN	Tom	1894	Seaham Harbour		1920	1923	Sunderland	Guildford United	73	3	0	0	2	0	0	0
Thomson A	Andy	01/04/71	Motherwell		1999	2000	Oxford United	QPR	52	6	6	1	14	3	4	1
Thomson J	Jim		Dundee		1921	1922	Dundee	Barrow	39	0	0	0	0	0	0	0
Thorpe IR	Ian	03/09/53	Blackheath		1973		Charlton Ath.	Folkestone	5	0	0	0	0	0	0	0
Tong DJ	David	21/09/55	Blackpool		1985		Bristol City	Cambridge Utd.	5	0	0	0	0	0	0	0
Tooze RW	Bob	19/12/46	Bristol		1971		Shrewsbury T (loan)		7	0	0	0	0	0	0	0
Torr F	Frank	04/12/09	Chesterfield	1981	1932		Bradford PA	Aldershot	1	0	0	0	0	0	0	0
Towers EJ	Jim	15/04/33	Shepherds Bush		1962		Millwall	Aldershot	8	0	0	0	6	0	0	0
Travers JEG	George	04/11/1888	Birmingham	1946	1921		Norwich City	Nuneaton Town	10	0	0	0	1	0	0	0
Tredwell JW	Joseph	08/09/1896	West Ham	1967	1923				2	0	0	0	0	0	0	0
Trott RF	Robin	17/08/74	Orpington		1993	1994	Trainee	Mansion (HK)	10	0	0	2	0	0	0	0
Trusson MS	Mike	26/05/59	Northolt		1989	1991	Brighton & Hove A.	Hong Kong	74	3	4	4	7	0	0	0
Tudor TE	Ed	15/03/35	Neston		1958		Bolton Wanderers		1	0	0	0	0	0	0	0
Turton GF	Geoffrey	1914	Sheffield		1935		West Bromwich A.	Crystal Palace	11	0	0	1	0	0	0	0
Tweed GE	George	04/12/10	Newmarket	1971	1937		Bristol Rovers	Bath City	31	2	0	1	0	0	0	0
Tydeman R	Dick	26/05/51	Chatham		1969	1976	App.	Charlton Ath.	371	22	23	3	15	1	2	0
					1981	1983	Charlton Ath.	Peterborough Utd.								
Tyler S	Syd	07/12/04	Wolverhampton	1971	1927	1928	Wolves	Millwall	76	5	0	0	0	0	0	0
Vaessen LH	Leon	08/11/40	Market Bosworth		1961	1962	Millwall	Dover	29	1	0	0	0	0	0	0
Vallance HB	Hugh	14/06/05	Wolverhampton	1973	1931	1934	Tunbridge WR	Kidderminster Harr.	18	0	0	0	10	0	0	0
Vango AJ	Alf	23/12/00	Walthamstow	1977	1924		Gnome Ath.	Walthamstow Ave.	5	0	0	0	0	0	0	0
Varty WC	William	25/06/06	Throckley	1965	1934		Blackpool	Gateshead	10	1	0	0	2	0	0	0
Veck R	Bobby	01/04/20	Titchfield	1999	1950		Southampton	Chelmsford City	36	1	0	0	12	0	0	0
Wakefield GE	George		Bradford		1921		Bradford City		10	1	0	0	0	0	0	0
Waldock R	Ronnie	06/12/32	Heanor		1961	1963	Middlesbrough	Margate	66	4	1	0	14	1	0	0
Walford SJ	Steve	05/01/58	Highgate		1988		West Ham Utd. (loan)		4	0	0	1	0	0	0	0
Walker A	Alan	17/12/59	Mossley		1987	1991	Millwall	Plymouth Argyle	151	5	8	6	8	2	3	3
Walker CJ	Cyril	24/02/14	Newport Pagnell		1937		Watford	Sheffield Wed.	10	0	0	1	3	0	0	1
Walker PJA	Pat	20/12/59	Carlow		1977	1980	App.	Frolunda (Swe)	51	1	0	0	3	0	0	0
Walker PL	Phil	29/08/54	Fulham		1982		Charlton Ath. (loan)		2	0	0	0	0	0	0	0
Wallace R	Rod	02/10/69	Greenwich		2002		Bolton Wanderers		22	2	1	0	11	1	0	0
Walton MA	Mark	01/06/69	Merthyr Tydfil		1997		Norwich City (loan)		1	0	0	0	0	0	0	0
Ward J	John		Birtley		1925		Darlington	Fatfield Albion	2	0	0	0	0	0	0	0
Warsap WJB	Johnny	18/05/21	Leytonstone	1992	1950	1952	Army		9	9	0	0	1	2	0	0
Waterall TW	Tommy	24/10/1884	Radford	1951	1921		Watford	Sheppey United	18	1	0	0	1	0	0	0
Watkins ET	Ernie	03/04/1898	Finchley	1976	1931		Fulham	Charlton Ath.	4	0	0	0	0	0	0	0
Watson AF	Alex	05/04/68	Liverpool		1995		Bournemouth (loan)		10	0	0	0	1	0	0	0
Watson PD	Paul	04/01/75	Hastings		1992	1995	Trainee	Fulham	62	6	4	7	2	0	0	0
Watson T	Tommy	23/08/43	Lesmahagow		1970	1971	Walsall	Maidstone Utd.	49	1	5	0	7	2	0	0
Watson WJB	Jimmy	01/01/14	Durham	1979	1935	1937	Northampton Town	Notts County	110	5	0	5	38	0	5	2
Watts GS	Grant	05/11/73	Croydon		1994		Crystal Palace	Sheffield Utd.	3	0	0	1	0	0	0	0
Watts JA	James	25/10/33	Cowes		1956		Local	Maidstone Utd.	12	0	0	0	1	0	0	0
Waugh J	John		Chopwell		1920	1921	Dundee Hibs	Darlington	60	4	0	0	4	0	0	0
Weatherly CM	Mark	18/01/58	Ramsgate		1974	1988	App.	Hythe Town	458	33	38	14	46	5	4	0
West E	Ted	04/11/30	Parbold		1954	1956	Doncaster Rovers	Oldham Athletic	98	2	0	0	0	0	0	0

Name		D.O.B	Place of Birth	Died	First Season	Last Season	Previous Club	Next Club	Appearances				Goals			
									Lge	FAC	FLC	Oth.	Lge	FAC	FLC	Oth.
West G	Gary	25/08/64	Scunthorpe		1987	1988	Lincoln City	Port Vale	53	3	6	4	3	0	0	0
					1990		Port Vale (loan)									
Westley GN	Graham	04/03/68	Hounslow		1985	1986	QPR	Barnet	2	0	0	1	0	0	0	0
Weston AD	Tony	03/04/45	Yalding		1964	1969	Bromley	Ashford Town	162	7	10	0	3	0	0	0
Westwood DR	Danny	25/07/53	Dagenham		1975	1981	QPR	Barnet	211	12	12	3	74	1	2	0
Wheatley SJ	Steve	12/04/59	Bishop Auckland		1976	1977	App.	Dover	4	0	0	0	0	0	0	0
Wheeler AJ	Alf	1910	Bilston		1936		Norwich City	Northampton Town	8	0	0	2	3	0	0	2
White D	Dean	04/12/58	Hastings		1978	1982	Chelsea	Millwall	116	14	2	3	26	0	2	0
White J	Jimmy	13/06/42	Poole		1963	1965	Portsmouth	Bournemouth	65	2	3	0	1	0	0	0
White WW	Willie	26/07/07	Altrincham		1930	1931	Charlton Ath.	Aldershot	64	1	0	0	18	0	0	0
Whitelaw DL	Dave	09/08/09	Glasgow	1989	1935	1937	Southend Utd.	Wrexham	114	6	0	6	0	0	0	0
Whyte C	Campbell		Lochgelly		1929		Third Lanark	Northampton Town	24	0	0	0	3	0	0	0
Wiggins JA	Joe	01/04/09	Wembley	1982	1934		Leicester City (loan)		12	0	0	0	0	0	0	0
Wigmore C	Clive	1892	Worksop	1969	1920		Aston Villa		9	0	0	0	0	0	0	0
Wilcox JC	Joe	19/01/1894	Coleford	1956	1927	1928	QPR	Kidderminster Harr.	56	4	0	0	27	0	3	0
Wilkinson T	Thomas		Glasgow		1924		Mary Hull YC		5	0	0	0	0	0	0	0
Wilks A	Alan	05/10/46	Slough		1971	1975	QPR	Folkestone	151	7	13	0	29	3	2	0
Williams AL	Bert	18/05/13	Newtown	1971	1931	1934	Wrexham	York City	50	1	0	1	6	0	0	1
Williams AS	Anthony	20/09/77	Bridgend		1999		Blackburn Rov. (loan)		2	0	22	0	0	0	0	0
Williams HF	Horace				1922		Dundee Hibernians		26	2	0	0	10	0	1	0
Williams JS	Jerry	24/03/60	Didcot		1988		Reading	Aldershot	13	1	0	2	0	0	0	0
Williams LT	Leslie	1916	Medway		1937		Chatham Town		1	0	0	0	0	0	0	0
Williams NJ	Nigel	29/07/54	Canterbury		1976	1978	Wolves	Dartford	53	4	3	0	1	0	0	0
Williams PRC	Paul	11/09/69	Leicester		1998		Plymouth Argyle	Bury	10	0	2	0	0	0	0	0
Williams TH	Tommy	23/05/1899	Easington	1960	1923		Charlton Ath.	Ashington	16	0	0	0	6	0	0	0
Williams WJ	Jack	18/07/06	Wolverhampton	1982	1928		Wolves	Brighton & Hove A.	9	0	0	0	0	0	0	0
Williams WL	Bill	1914	Swansea		1937		Watford		1	0	0	0	0	0	0	0
Williams WT	Bill	23/08/42	Esher		1967	1971	Mansfield Town	Maidstone Utd.	171	9	8	0	8	0	0	0
Williamson M	Micky	30/05/42	Ashbourne		1965		Derby County	Ramsgate Ath.	1	1	0	0	0	0	0	0
Wilson J	Joe		Spennymoor		1928	1929		Walsall	31	1	0	0	0	0	0	0
Wilson K	Keith	14/12/35	Beverley		1961		Southampton	Retired	5	0	0	0	2	0	0	0
Wilson PAF	Paul	22/02/77	Maidstone		1994		Trainee	Gravesend & N'fleet	2	0	0	0	0	0	0	0
Wilson RSW	Bobby	29/06/34	Musselburgh		1960		Norwich City	Accrington Stanley	35	3	2	0	0	0	0	0
Wilson TH	Tom	23/11/17	Lewisham	1959	1936	1937	Sheppey United	Gravesend & N'fleet	66	16	0	1	4	4	1	0
Wilson WR	William	.Nov 1915	Rotherham		1936		Bristol Rovers	Aldershot	5	0	0	1	0	0	0	0
Wiltshire DJ	Dave	08/07/54	Folkestone		1973	1975	Canterbury City	Aldershot	62	3	4	0	2	0	0	0
Wood AB	Arthur	08/05/1890	Southampton	1977	1920	1921	Fulham	Newport County	49	4	0	0	11	0	0	0
Woodhead A	Andrew	12/07/66	Wallsend		1983		App.	Berwick Rangers	2	0	1	1	0	0	0	0
Woodley DG	Derek	02/03/42	Isleworth	2002	1967	1970	Southend Utd.	Folkestone	100	9	5	0	9	0	0	0
Woods A	Albert	24/07/07	Faversham	1982	1930			Brentford	2	0	0	0	0	0	0	0
Woolcott RA	Roy	29/07/46	Leyton		1971		Tottenham H. (loan)		13	0	0	0	5	0	0	0
Woolven LE	Lewis	08/12/07	Chatham	1978	1929	1931	Whitstable Town	Maidstone Utd.	6	0	0	0	0	0	0	0
Wright GW	George	19/03/30	Ramsgate	2000	1962		Leyton Orient	Ramsgate Ath.	4	0	0	0	0	0	0	0
Wright H	Harry	05/04/00	Staveley		1920	1921	Welbeck Col.	Welbeck Col.	33	3	0	0	0	0	0	0
Yeo BG	Brian	12/04/44	Worthing		1963	1974	Portsmouth	Folkestone (Mgr)	356	16	15	0	136	4	9	0
Young A	Alf	27/11/00	Wingate	1975	1928		Hartlepools Utd.	Workington	18	1	0	0	0	0	0	0
Young AW	Archie	10/12/06	Twechar		1937		Exeter City	Rochdale	21	1	0	1	0	0	0	0
Young CF	Charlie	14/02/58	Nicosia, Cyprus		1977	1981	Aston Villa	Retired	28	3	3	0	1	1	0	0

Played in FA Cup Only

Name		D.O.B	Place of Birth	Died	First Season	Last Season	Previous Club	Next Club	Lge	FAC	FLC	Oth.	Lge	FAC	FLC	Oth.
Jones D	David		Manchester		1955				0	1	0	0	0	0	0	0

Played in League Cup Only

Name		D.O.B	Place of Birth	Died	First Season	Last Season	Previous Club	Next Club	Lge	FAC	FLC	Oth.	Lge	FAC	FLC	Oth.
Gorman J	John				1986		(youth coach)		0	0	2	0	0	0	0	0

Played in Miscellaneous Games Only

Name		D.O.B	Place of Birth	Died	First Season	Last Season	Previous Club	Next Club	Lge	FAC	FLC	Oth.	Lge	FAC	FLC	Oth.
Bremner KJ	Kevin	07/10/57	Banff		1995		Deveronvale	(youth coach)	0	0	0	1	0	0	0	0
Collins EA	Eamonn	22/10/65	Dublin		1988		Portsmouth (loan)		0	0	0	1	0	0	0	0
Dalton RT	Richard	14/10//65	Waterford		1991		Airdrie	Farnborough T	0	0	0	1	0	0	0	0
Edwards P					1984				0	0	0	2	0	0	0	0
Hooker JW	Jon	31/05/73	London		1994		(On trial)		0	0	0	1	0	0	0	0
Hunt K	Kevin	04/07/75	Chatham		1992		Trainee	Gravesend & N'fleet	0	0	0	1	0	0	0	0
Joseph MNA	Matt	30/09/72	Bethnal Green		1992		Arsenal	Cambridge U	0	0	0	1	0	0	0	0
Kamara AS	Abdul	10/02/74	Southampton		1994		(On trial)		0	0	0	1	0	0	0	0
Maudsley R	Richard				1937				0	0	0	1	0	0	0	0
Mitten CH	Charlie	09/10/74	Plumstead		1999		Dover Athletic	Margate	0	0	0	1	0	0	0	0
Nicholls A	Alan	28/08/73	Birmingham	1995	1995		Plymouth Argyle	Stalybridge Celtic	0	0	0	1	0	0	0	0
Young I	Ian				1984		Trainee		0	0	0	1	0	0	0	0

SOUTHERN LEAGUE APPEARANCES AND GOALS
1894/95 to 1919/20

1900		Ambler CJ	14	0
1902		Archer A	25	0
1908	1910	Arthurs CH	48	5
1894	1895	Ashdown AH	15	0
1898	1903	Atherton J	119	2
1894		Auld H	10	0
1897		Bailey	3	0
1909	1914	Bailey AV	136	0
1900		Bailey T	1	0
1907		Barker	4	0
1904	1905	Barnfather P	39	4
1908	1909	Bateup E	78	0
1905		Beadsworth A	21	3
1909		Beale PE	3	0
1919		Beale RH	12	0
1911		Bell A	2	0
1912		Bell MD	28	0
1901		Blair J	28	1
1919		Bluer AW	3	0
1912		Boden J	16	5
1903	1904	Boucher T	39	7
1919		Bower W	3	0
1908		Boyle P	39	0
1902	1903	Bradbury JJL	49	2
1914	1919	Branfield J *	23	0
1906		Brisley J	1	0
1908		Brown J	1	0
1895	1896	Bruce D	15	0
1895		Bryan T	5	1
1919		Buchanan R	19	0
1894	1897	Buckland H	30	9
1904	1905	Bull A	33	0
1898		Bunyan C	24	0
1914		Burgess GF	4	0
1905		Burns AJ	11	3
1912	1913	Caldwell T	51	5
1905		Campbell J	15	3
1898		Campbell L	20	4
1910		Cannon F	23	1
1899		Carter J	24	0
1919		Cartwright W	21	0
1919		Cavanna R	5	0
1919		Chalmers D	12	1
1911	1912	Church AG	15	1
1903		Clutterbuck HJ	33	0
1895		Cochrane P	5	0
1895	1896	Cockrill J	22	1
1903		Connor MJ	4	0
1898		Cooper	4	0
1911		Corbett F	22	6
1908	1913	Court AC	104	33
1900	1901	Crane AE	16	0
1912		Crane HE	12	0
1906		Cunliffe D	36	15
1903		Davidson A	3	0
1902		Daw EC	25	0
1906		Daws	2	1
1919		Dawson H	2	0
1919		Denny C	1	0
1894		Dickenson J	2	0
1903		Dickenson J	11	5
1911	1913	Diddams E	8	0
1897		Docherty	1	0
1895		Drew WH	2	0
1901	1902	Dunkley AE	37	6
1908		Eames W	18	5
1919		Elliott CJ	4	0
1902	1906	Elliott J	134	2
1901		Evans	10	0
1903	1905	Evans C	23	0
1897		Fairclough WO	3	0
1904		Felton FJ	2	0
1897		Ferguson	3	1
1905	1907	Floyd WB	88	0
1897		Ford GF	22	8
1913	1914	Fotheringham CD	4	1
1901		French J	14	0
1896	1902	Frettingham JA	153	64
1911	1913	Frost CJ	12	2
1913	1919	Frost WG	13	0
1908	1909	Fullarton D	26	0
1907		Fullerton J	35	0
1897	1898	Gallacher H	27	2
1895	1896	Garside E	2	0
1895	1896	Gascoigne JW	33	0
1896	1897	Gentle A	27	0
1913	1914	Gilligan SA	65	15
1894	1900	Gladwell AP	42	12
1912	1914	Glen P	56	16
1899		Glover J	24	0
1906		Godley J	5	1
1911	1913	Goffin RFA	77	12
1902	1903	Goldie H	41	2
1919		Gore SP	1	0
1901		Gosnell AA	4	1
1897	1900	Graham J	72	1
1899		Gray E	3	0
1914		Gray GR	16	0
1899		Gray T	16	2
1898		Grieve T	17	6
1904	1905	Griffiths FJ	52	0
1919		Griffiths JA *	3	1
1911		Gudgeon CW	1	0
1895		Guthrie J	3	0
1912	1913	Hafekost CH	51	15
1908		Hales WH	16	1
1914		Hall FJ	1	0
1919		Harris AR	2	0
1901	1902	Harris W	32	0
1896		Harrison	3	0
1906	1907	Hartley F	33	14
1900		Harvey	2	0
1906	1907	Harvey EA	64	1
1909	1911	Hawkes JM	27	0
1900		Haywood A	23	1
1908		Henderson W	8	0
1908		Henderson WP	27	0
1919		Hibden WJ	15	0
1909	1910	Higgins M	73	1
1909		Hobson J	18	2
1897		Hodgkinson J	3	0
1910		Holmes T	37	0
1914		Hooper W	25	1
1907		Hopkins J	11	2
1900		Hulmes T	20	1
1913		Hulses S	1	0
1900	1901	Humphrey W	28	0
1919		Hunter W	1	0
1894	1899	Hutcheson DS	83	36
1898	1900	Innes RA	77	7
1894		James A	4	0
1897		Janes JT	15	0
1894	1896	Jenner A	5	3
1910	1919	Johns CW	47	6
1909	1914	Johnson AJ	132	5
1899		Jones	1	0
1897		Jones S	10	0
1919		Joyce JW	2	0
1894	1895	Keefe D	5	0
1919		Kelly H	21	1
1911		Kelly T	16	0
1919		Kennedy JJ	9	0
1901	1902	Killean E	29	0
1897	1898	King ES	38	0
1901		Knowlden	1	0
1912		Lagan TH	14	0
1903	1904	Lagar F	18	0
1896		Lawrie	1	0
1911	1919	Lee A	150	15
1919		Lee H	22	4
1906		Lee W	22	4
1901	1904	Leigh W	94	27
1898		Lennox M	16	4
1898		Leonard P	1	0
1912	1919	Leslie TH	142	7
1900	1903	Lissenden AJ	31	2
1906		Lissenden G	5	0
1895		Lister A	4	3
1903	1907	Lloyd GH	136	0
1899	1901	Lockie J	31	0
1914		Lovett M	2	0
1909		Luff JT	2	0
1906		Lunn	23	0
1899	1900	MacDonald J	31	10
1909	1919	Mahon J	254	5
1894	1895	Manning F	24	5
1905	1907	Marriott W	77	15
1905	1907	Martin J	92	1
1909	1911	Massey GH	29	2
1905	1908	Maven FJ	114	3
1900		May G	3	0
1909		McArthur J	3	0
1919		McCormick D *	4	1
1902	1903	McCurdy W	52	0
1898		McDonald J	23	6
1907		McGibbon CE	32	14
1904	1905	McKie J	46	7
1906	1907	McKinnell	3	0
1907		McLachlan	1	0
1895		McNamee	10	1
1894	1897	Meager AE	57	1
1919		Meath JH	2	0
1903	1907	Metherell HS	8	0
1899		Miller	1	0
1901	1902	Milward A	52	13
1906		Morgan W	16	0
1904		Morris JJ	33	7
1910	1914	Mosley A	167	0
1919		Nash HE	13	0
1900	1902	Neame SR	34	0
1919		Neill J	9	0
1900		Neyland M	8	4
1899		Nobbs	6	0
1908	1911	Nobbs AH	111	0
1905		Orr J	8	0
1901		Otty WJ	6	0
1905		Page	1	0
1899		Pangbourne T	21	6
1907		Pass JE	8	1
1894	1896	Pellatt D	44	3
1913		Pepper W	1	0
1896		Peters J	19	4
1905		Phillips H	14	1
1907		Pickering J	22	7
1908	1910	Pickett AE	88	15
1913	1914	Pinkney E	63	13
1899		Pinnell A	2	0
1908		Powell H	23	3
1902	1903	Raisbeck W	56	2
1919		Ramsell LT	9	0
1919		Read B	17	4
1894		Read R	1	0
1919		Read TW	2	0
1919		Redpath A	12	1
1908	1909	Reid J	41	15
1897		Remnant	3	1
1908	1910	Reynolds J	97	15
1896	1897	Roadley T	18	0
1903		Roberson J	18	4
1898	1900	Robertson JS	63	0
1919		Robertson JW *	7	0
1898		Robertson W	2	0
1907		Robotham H	30	0
1894		Rule R	9	18
1894		Russell AE	11	0
1907		Salter HJ	30	7
1902		Satterthwaite CO	30	12
1909	1910	Satterthwaite JN	53	18
1919		Savage W	18	3
1901		Scott F	15	2
1895		Scott P	1	0
1903		Sears AE	1	0
1899	1900	Seeley G	47	7
1896		Shaves W	3	0
1908		Shepherd HC	10	0
1905		Sheridan J	8	1
1899		Shinner J	1	0

SOUTHERN LEAGUE APPEARANCES AND GOALS

1894/95 to 1919/20 (cont)

1903		Singleton HB	31	1
1896	1897	Skea DF	25	9
1902		Smith G	30	10
1903		Smith L	2	0
1906	1907	Smith S	71	5
1905		Snelgrove GW	4	0
1895		Spooner J	2	0
1907		Spriggs F	8	2
1919		Steel A	23	1
1919		Steel RL	19	2
1903		Stevenson J	28	6
1895		Strachan J	10	7
1909	1911	Strang T	81	1
1897		Stuart J	3	1
1909	1910	Sutherland A	46	0
1899		Swan A	27	6
1913	1914	Tatton JH	49	2
1909	1912	Taylor J	123	37
1904		Taylorson	1	0
1894	1896	Thomas WE	25	2
1914		Thomas WSL	18	3
1904	1905	Travers P	38	3
1904		Turner J	29	9
1919		Turner TF	1	0
1906		Walker G	28	0
1895	1896	Walker J	17	3
1907		Walker RH	8	0
1904	1905	Walton J	62	0
1906		Warrington J	15	1
1896	1898	Watson J	55	2
1894	1895	Watson JT	8	0
1904		Watts EA	30	0
1911	1914	Weavers SD	17	2
1894	1906	Webb A	3	3
1914		Weightman D	22	7
1895		Welch C	1	0
1910	1911	Westwood E	13	1
1903	1904	White JW	66	2
1898		White W	3	0
1911		Whiteside E	19	4
1913		Whiteside T	1	0
1897		Whittingham	1	0
1908		Whyman A	40	8
1895		Wilson J	9	0
1914		Wimsett WJ	6	0
1912		Wolstenholme A	24	4
1919		Wood AB *	31	12
1908		Wood H	11	2
1901	1902	Wright R	5	0
1896		Wynn	1	0
1901		Youngs WW	2	0

1938/39 to 1949/50

1946	1947	Akers W	40	20
1949		Armstrong G	9	0
1938		Armstrong W *	39	0
1949		Bates WH	7	0
1946		Berwick C	2	0
1946	1949	Boswell J *	126	5
1938		Bradbury T	33	0
1938		Brallisford A *	5	1
1946	1949	Briggs J *	106	39
1938		Bryant HA	5	0
1947		Burgess C	3	0
1947	1949	Burke JJ *	92	0
1949		Burtenshaw CE *	26	3
1949		Burtenshaw WF *	18	12
1938		Campbell CWG *	8	0
1948	1949	Carr J *	62	24
1946	1947	Chapman H	13	0
1949		Collier F	0	0
1946	1947	Collins L	35	0
1949		Collins WH *	36	0
1949		Cook V	2	0
1938		Costello R	36	0
1947	1949	Day JN *	17	0
1938		Day R	12	3
1947		Diggins B	2	1
1947		Dimmock E	1	0
1938		Donoghue F *	6	0
1946	1949	Dorling GC *	106	3
1946		Edwards F	1	0
1938		Foreman E	6	0
1947	1949	Forrester GL *	97	27
1948		Gore LF	15	2
1948		Granville NY	6	0
1949		Hales WH *	10	6
1946	1948	Henson L *	15	0
1938		Herbert FW *	4	1
1946		Hole V	11	7
1946		Hopper T	4	2
1938		Johnson W	36	14
1938		Jones EJ *	2	0
1946	1949	Kingsnorth TH	135	10
1948		Lambourne JC *	1	0
1938		Langmaid A	7	0
1946	1949	Marks CWA *	112	0
1938		McAdams TE	2	0
1938		McGee T	30	11
1949		McGuire LGR *	4	1
1949		Millbank JH	3	0
1947		Milton G	1	0
1947		Morris R	1	0
1938		Neal RG *	37	2
1946	1948	Nobbs J	8	2
1948		O'Sullivan CJ	1	0
1946	1949	Piper GH *	116	4
1946	1948	Poole CJ	77	12
1949		Poulton GH	1	0
1946		Price R	6	0
1938		Ross J	9	3
1938		Rowley HB	40	38
1946	1949	Russell HW *	125	98
1938		Scott EJ *	32	6
1947		Skinner GEH	2	0
1938		Smith A	2	0
1938		Smith J *	42	0
1938		Strong GJ	19	0
1946		Sylvester D	2	0
1946	1949	Trumper S	14	5
1938		Tweed GE *	6	0
1948		Vigor DRJ	9	0
1947		Walker D	5	2
1946	1949	Warsap WJB *	89	28
1938		Whitelaw DL *	25	0
1949		Williams HS	18	18
1938		Williams LT *	1	0
1938	1948	Wilson TH *	129	69

Note:

1938/39 to 1949/50 totals exclude the three games played in 1939/40 and all wartime appearances.

Appearances and goals are for League games only; all cup ties are excluded.

* Players with an asterisk also played in the Football League and their personal details will be found in the previous section.
If they played in the F.A. Cup, their appearances and goals in non-FL seasons are included in their career totals.

Hughie Russell; scored 9 goals against Gloucester City in November 1946

GILLINGHAM'S MANAGERS

	From:	To:	
W Ironside Groombridge	1896	1906	(Secretary/Manager)
Steve Smith	1906	1908	
W Ironside Groombridge	1908	1919	(Secretary/Manager)
George Collins	1919	1920	
Robert Brown	1920		
John McMillan	1920	1923	
Harry Curtis	1923	1926	
Albert Hoskins	1926	1929	
Dick Hendrie	1929	1931	
Fred Maven	1932	1937	
Allan Ure	1937	1938	
Bill Harvey	1938	1939	
Archie Clark	1939	1958	
Harry Barratt	1958	1962	
Freddie Cox	1962	1965	
Basil Hayward	1966	1971	
Andy Nelson	1971	1974	
Len Ashurst	1974	1975	
Gerry Summers	1975	1981	
Keith Peacock	1981	1987	
Paul Taylor	1988		
Keith Burkinshaw	1988	1989	
Damien Richardson	1989	1992	
Glen Roeder	1992	1993	
Mike Flanagan	1993	1995	
Neil Smillie	1995		
Tony Pulis	1995	1999	
Peter Taylor	1999	2000	
Andy Hessenthaler	2000		(Player/manager)

Archie Clark, Gill's manager for 18 years

1947/48, runners-up in the Southern League. Clockwise from top left; Forrester, Briggs, Russell, Wilson, Warsap, Akers, Boswell, Poole, Collins, Burke, Marks, Dorling, Kingsnorth, Piper.